T0191634

Communications in Computer and Information Science 1046

Commenced Publication in 2007
Founding and Former Series Editors:
Phoebe Chen, Alfredo Cuzzocrea, Xiaoyong Du, Orhun Kara, Ting Liu,
Krishna M. Sivalingam, Dominik Ślęzak, Takashi Washio, and Xiaokang Yang

More information about this series at http://www.springer.com/series/7899

Mayank Singh · P. K. Gupta ·
Vipin Tyagi · Jan Flusser ·
Tuncer Ören · Rekha Kashyap (Eds.)

Advances in Computing and Data Sciences

Third International Conference, ICACDS 2019
Ghaziabad, India, April 12–13, 2019
Revised Selected Papers, Part II

 Springer

Editors
Mayank Singh
University of KwaZulu-Natal
Durban, South Africa

Vipin Tyagi
Department of Computer Science
and Engineering
Jaypee University of Engineering
and Technology
Guna, Madhya Pradesh, India

Tuncer Ören
School of Electrical Engineering
and Computer Science
University of Ottawa
Ottawa, ON, Canada

P. K. Gupta
Computer Science and Engineering
Jaypee Institute of Information
Technology
Waknaghat, Himachal Pradesh, India

Jan Flusser
ÚTIA AV ČR
Institute of Information Theory
and Automation
Prague 8, Praha, Czech Republic

Rekha Kashyap
CSE Department
Inderprastha Engineering College
Ghaziabad, Uttar Pradesh, India

ISSN 1865-0929   ISSN 1865-0937 (electronic)
Communications in Computer and Information Science
ISBN 978-981-13-9941-1   ISBN 978-981-13-9942-8 (eBook)
https://doi.org/10.1007/978-981-13-9942-8

This Springer imprint is published by the registered company Springer Nature Singapore Pte Ltd.
The registered company address is: 152 Beach Road, #21-01/04 Gateway East, Singapore 189721, Singapore

Preface

Computing techniques like big data, cloud computing, machine learning, the Internet of Things etc. are playing the key role in processing of data and retrieval of advanced information. Several state-of-art techniques and computing paradigms have been proposed based on these techniques. This volume contains papers presented at the Third International Conference on Advances in Computing and Data Sciences (ICACDS 2019) held during April 12–13, 2019, at Inderprastha Engineering College, Ghaziabad, UP, India. The conference was organized specifically to help researchers, academics, scientists, and industry come together and to derive benefits from the advances of next-generation computing technologies in the areas of advanced computing and data sciences.

The Program Committee of ICACDS 2019 is extremely grateful to the authors who showed an overwhelming response to the call for papers submitting over 621 papers in two tracks in advanced computing and data sciences. All submitted papers went through a peer review process and finally 112 papers were accepted for publication in Springer's CCIS series. We are very thankful to our reviewers for their efforts in finalizing the high-quality papers.

The conference featured many distinguished personalities including Prof. K. K. Agarwal, Chairman-NAAC, Prof. J. S. P. Rai, Vice Chancellor Jaypee University of Engineering and Technology, Raghogarh, Guna; Prof. Rajkumar Buyya, University of Melbourne, Australia; Prof. Viranjay M. Srivastava, University of KwaZulu-Natal, Durban, South Africa; Prof. Baisakhi Chakraborty, National Institute of Technology, Durgapur; Prof. Parteek Bhatia, Thapar Institute of Engineering and Technology, Patiala, India; Prof. S. K. Mishra, Majmaah University, Saudi Arabia; Prof. Arun Sharma, Indira Gandhi Delhi Technical University for Women, India; Prof. Prathmesh Churi, NMIMS University, Mumbai; Dr. Anup Girdhar, CEO and Founder, Sedulity Solutions & Technology, India, among many others. We are very grateful for the participation of all speakers in making this conference a memorable event.

The Organizing Committee of ICACDS 2019 is indebted to Prof. B. C. Sharma, Director Inderprastha Engineering College, for the confidence that he invested in us in organizing this international conference, and all the faculty and staff of the CSE Department, IPEC, Ghaziabad for their support in organizing the conference and for making it a grand success.

We would also like to thank Dr. Divya Jain, JUET Guna; Dr. Neelesh Jain, JUET Guna; Dr. Prateek Pandey, JUET Guna; Dr Nilesh Patel, JUET Guna; Dr. Ratnesh Litoriya, JUET Guna; Mr. Kunj Bihari Meena, JUET Guna; Dr. Deepshikha Tiwary, Thapar University Patiala; Dr. Ghanshyam Raghuwanshi, Manipal University, Jaipur; Dr. Vibhash Yadav, REC Banda; Dr. Sandhya Tarar, GBU Noida; Mr. Nishant Gupta, MGM CoET, Noida; Mr. Rohit Kapoor, SK Info Techies; Mr. Akshay Chaudhary and

Ms. Akansha Singh from GISR Foundation; Mr. Deepak Singh, Mr. Atul Kumar, and Ms. Shivani Gupta from Consilio Intelligence Research Lab for their support. Our sincere thanks to Consilio Intelligence Research Lab, GISR Foundation, Print Canvas, IP Moment, Aptron, VGeekers and Tricky Plants for sponsoring the event.

June 2019

Mayank Singh
P. K. Gupta
Vipin Tyagi
Jan Flusser
Tuncer Ören
Rekha Kashyap

Organization

Steering Committee

Chief Patron

Vinay Kumar Pathak (Vice-chancellor)	APJAKTU, Lucknow, India
S. S. Jain (Chairman)	Inderprastha Engineering College, Ghaziabad, India

Patron

B. C. Sharma (Director)	Inderprastha Engineering College, Ghaziabad, India

Steering Committee

Alexandre Carlos Brandão Ramos	UNIFEI, Brazil
Mohit Singh	Georgia Institute of Technology, USA
H. M. Pandey	Edge Hill University, UK
M. N. Hooda	BVICAM, Delhi, India
S. K. Singh	IIT BHU, Varanasi, India
Jyotsna Kumar Mandal	University of Kalyani, West Bengal, India

Honorary Chairs

Viranjay M. Srivastava	University of KwaZulu-Natal, Durban, South Africa
V. K. Singh	Inderprastha Engineering College, Ghaziabad, India

General Chairs

Mayank Singh	University of KwaZulu Natal, Durban, South Africa
Rekha Kashyap	Inderprastha Engineering College, Ghaziabad, India

Advisory Board Chairs

Tuncer Ören	University of Ottawa, Canada
Jan Flusser	Institute of Information Theory and Automation, Czech Republic

Technical Program Committee Chairs

P. K. Gupta	Jaypee University of Information Technology, Solan, India
Vipin Tyagi	Jaypee University of Engineering & Technology, Guna, India

Program Chairs

Ulrick Klauck	Aalen University, Germany
Shailendra Mishra	Majmaah University, Saudi Arabia

Conveners

Gaurav Agrawal	Inderprastha Engineering College, India
Sandhya Tarar	Gautam Buddha University, India

Co-conveners

Prathamesh Churi	NMIMS University, India
Shikha Badhani	DU, India

Conference Chairs

Ravi Tomar	University of Petroleum and Energy Studies, India
Jagendra Singh	Inderprastha Engineering College, India

Conference Co-chairs

Lavanya Sharma	Amity University, India
Vibhash Yadav	Rajkiya Engineering College Banda, India
Rakesh Saini	DIT University, India
Abhishek Dixit	Tallinn University of Technology, Estonia
Vipin Deval	Tallinn University of Technology, Estonia

Organizing Chairs

Pooja Tripathi	Inderprastha Engineering College, India
Mandeep Katre	Inderprastha Engineering College, India

Organizing Secretariat

Chahat Sharma	Inderprastha Engineering College, India
Krista Chaudhary	Krishna Engineering College, Ghaziabad, India
Umang Kant	Krishna Engineering College, Ghaziabad, India

Creative Head

Deepak Singh	Consilio Intelligence Research Lab, India

Marketing Head

Akshay Chaudhary	GISR Foundation, India

Organizing Committee

Registration

Tripti Sharma	Inderprastha Engineering College, India
Amrita Bhatnagar	Inderprastha Engineering College, India
Kirti Jain	Inderprastha Engineering College, India
Harshita	Inderprastha Engineering College, India

Publication

Jagendra Singh	Inderprastha Engineering College, India

Cultural

Diksha Dani	Inderprastha Engineering College, India
Anjali Singhal	Inderprastha Engineering College, India
Nidhi Agrawal	Inderprastha Engineering College, India
Prachi	Inderprastha Engineering College, India

Transportation

Mandeep Katre	Inderprastha Engineering College, India
Pushendra Singh	Inderprastha Engineering College, India
Shailendra Singh	Inderprastha Engineering College, India
Alok Katiyar	Inderprastha Engineering College, India
Sandeep Agrawal	Inderprastha Engineering College, India

Hospitality

Neeta Verma	Inderprastha Engineering College, India
Gaurav Srivastava	Inderprastha Engineering College, India
Vanshika Gupta	Inderprastha Engineering College, India
Udit Bansal	Inderprastha Engineering College, India

Stage Management

Sweeta Bansal	Inderprastha Engineering College, India
Chahat Sharma	Inderprastha Engineering College, India
Anchal Jain	Inderprastha Engineering College, India

Technical Session

Pranshu Saxena	Inderprastha Engineering College, India
Anjali Singhal	Inderprastha Engineering College, India
Diksha Dani	Inderprastha Engineering College, India
Alka Singhal	Inderprastha Engineering College, India
Jagendra Singh	Inderprastha Engineering College, India
Sneh Prabha	Inderprastha Engineering College, India
Pooja Singhal	Inderprastha Engineering College, India

Shweta Chaku	Inderprastha Engineering College, India
Naman Sharma	Inderprastha Engineering College, India
Preeti	Inderprastha Engineering College, India
Kumud Alok	Inderprastha Engineering College, India

Finance

Gaurav Agrawal	Inderprastha Engineering College, India
Mandeep Katre	Inderprastha Engineering College, India
Amit Sharma	Inderprastha Engineering College, India
Vipin Kumar Singhal	Inderprastha Engineering College, India

Food

Archana Agrawal	Inderprastha Engineering College, India
Harendra Singh	Inderprastha Engineering College, India
Swapna Singh	Inderprastha Engineering College, India
Shraddha Srivastava	Inderprastha Engineering College, India
Shiva Soni	Inderprastha Engineering College, India

Advertising

Monika Bansal	Inderprastha Engineering College, India
Shelly Gupta	Inderprastha Engineering College, India
Kamna Singh	Inderprastha Engineering College, India

Press and Media

Monika Bansal	Inderprastha Engineering College, India
Chahat Sharma	Inderprastha Engineering College, India
Bharti	Inderprastha Engineering College, India

Editorial

| Pranshu Saxena | Inderprastha Engineering College, India |

Sponsored by

Consilio Intelligence Research Lab

Co-sponsored by

GISR Foundation
IP Moment
Print Canvas
VGeekers
Tricky Plants

Contents – Part II

Contents – Part I

Advanced Computing

A Face Detection Using Support Vector Machine: Challenging Issues, Recent Trend, Solutions and Proposed Framework

Suraj Makkar[1] and Lavanya Sharma[2(✉)]

[1] Department of Computer Science, Manav Rachna University, Faridabad, India
Surajmakkar1@gmail.com
[2] Amity Institute of Information Technology,
Amity University, Noida, Uttar Pradesh, India
lsharma6@amity.edu

Abstract. Face detection comes under the domain of object detection and tracking. Face detection is an integral part of the motion based object detection which combines digital image processing and computer vision for the detection of instances and faces as well. This paper provides a brief overview of the recent trends; current open challenging issues and their solutions available for efficient detection of faces form video stream or still images. This paper also discusses various approaches which are widely used to detect the faces in the dynamic background, illumination and other current challenges. In the last section, a framework for face detection is also proposed using SVM classifier.

Keywords: Deep Convolution Neural Networks · RBF · PCA · FLD · SVM · MEDA · Object detection and tracking · Morphological operators

1 Introduction

In the last few decades, the development in the biometrics technology including fingerprints, face recognition, iris detection and the voice print are among the major real-time applications. But in the last decade, the focus has been shifted to the face recognition as developments have been made both in the stationary or static face detection as well as moving or motion based faces. Face detection is the first step for any machine learning applications and all the remaining steps are based on this initial step such as face recognition, automated focusing of cameras, criminal detection and many more face processing software's or systems [1]. The features of human face are complex and vary from individual to individual which makes it more difficult to automatically detect the human face and it becomes a significant problem during sweating, complex backgrounds, illumination and ageing comes in play as it makes it more difficult to store all those things in the database to face detection system [2, 3, 20, 24, 26].

© Springer Nature Singapore Pte Ltd. 2019
M. Singh et al. (Eds.): ICACDS 2019, CCIS 1046, pp. 3–12, 2019.
https://doi.org/10.1007/978-981-13-9942-8_1

There are mainly three steps for face detection in video streaming. Firstly, the face is detected from the static image. Secondly, segment that particular into smaller segments using some tools. Then extract the important features from each face and divided them into no. of frames. Lastly, the extracted features are matched with all the features already stored in the database also known as the verification phase. The two most important factors that play the most important role in face detection is face modelling and face segmentation as without them no further steps can be performed accurately. The various other aspects that are taken into consideration are posing of the face, resolution focus, and distortion in the voice colour, shadow, backgrounds, light and change in features [3–5]. There is development in face detection on still images but due to the continuous development in this field now the technology has become much capable of detecting the faces by a moving camera and automated face detection systems have been developed and more developments are being made continuously. To develop an automated face recognition system one must be aware of all the factors that come in play like the image patterns and image segmentation. Firstly, selecting a face as a subject from a dynamic background for accurate verification of the face. Secondly, verification and classification of the images using appropriate algorithms for the proper detection of the faces [1, 6]. Face detection is used for a real-time application such as commercial, personal and law enforcement departments for various security aspects. The system that is developed should be accurate to the utmost level but not considering only the accuracy part, Time factor should be taken in consideration [7, 8, 10, 21, 26] (Fig. 1).

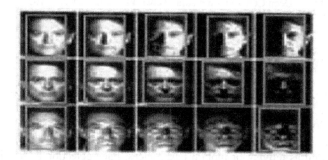

Fig. 1. Face detection: using Support Vector Machine classifier [1, 2]

This paper is categorized into 6 sections. Firstly, Sect. 1 deals with the basic background of the face detection technique. In the next Sect. 2, current existing work is discussed with their open challenges. Section 3 deals with the various face detection approach. Section 4 provides details about various challenging issues presents in this area. Then, in the next Sect. 5, real-time applications are discussed of this domain. Section 6, a proposed framework is provided to handle some of the challenging issues. In the last Sect. 7, conclusion and future work are discussed.

2   Literature Review

This section deals with the work done by various researchers in this specific domain to date. Sharifara et al. [10] presents a detailed overview of updated face detection techniques such as feature and appearance based. Tayyab et al. [11] Focused on detection on datasets of coloured images. In this paper, Skin Color Segmentation and 2D DCT were used for Feature Extraction but false detection rate decreases with the increase in the number of images. El-Bakry [12] proposed a new approach to identify frontal views. By Combining a Neural Network and Image Decomposition to get low computation time because of sub-images set with same no. of fast neural networks by applying parallel processing techniques. Huang et al. [14] proposed a real-time face detection system using the three steps. (1) Detection of face Candidates. (2) Verification by HOG and second class SVM. (3) Face Tracking. But this proposed system is restricted by the search space and feature extraction includes face color, size, face area and edge for higher accuracy in the crowd for real-time analysis. Dang [15] Provides an overview of various Face Detection Algorithms and features such as viola- Jones, SMQT, SNOW classifiers, SVM. Authors also compared results in terms of Precision and Recall using Deval Software. In this approach, SVM have least values in terms of accuracy in Face Detection. Only a few performance metrics are discussed by the authors for experimental analysis. Fernandez et al. [16] developed a system using Viola Jones and Neural Networks for recognizing faces including 3 factors: Distance, illumination and angle from the camera. Lang [18] proposed a technique for face detection with the AdaBoost classifier to increase the efficiency, speed and accuracy of the Conventional AdaBoost classifier. Tsai et al. [9] developed an efficient face detection system by using the Eigenface algorithm with a neural network. in order to get less false alarm edges are detected using geometric distribution.

3   Face Detection Approaches

In literature, various architecture and models are used for face detection. The neural network is widely used for face detection and recognition because these models can simulate in the same manner as biological neurons work in the human brain [11, 15, 17]. Some of the approaches which are widely used are:

Principal Component Analysis (PCA): This is a statistical approach is widely for representation and recognition of faces, pattern recognition, and image compression. In this approach, Eigenvectors are calculated which are also referred to as Yoo [5] presents a hybrid approach namely optimized face recognition algorithm using information extracted from detected face region. PCA is basically a procedure that involves the orthogonal transformations to convert the set of organisations of the correlated values to a completely uncorrelated linear variables mainly called as principal components. This approach is closely related to factor analysis which involves more domain specific assumptions about the structure whuch further helps it in solving the eigenvectors of little different matrix.

Deep Convolution Neural Networks: This network is a class of deep and a feedforward ANN applied to analyze visual images. Wang [1] proposed a method by combining local binary patterns (LBP) with this approach for the detection of faces in case of small and medium databases. Triantafyllidou [2] proposed two methods which efficiently detect the faces under unimpeded pose variants and occlusion. This scheme also meets the issues and the huge dissimilarities of real-time face detection. This approach uses less preprocessing than other image processing approaches. It is designed in such a way that it has one input and output layer and multiple hidden layers that comprises of Convolutional layers which further have activation layers, pooling layers, fully connected layers and normalization layers.

Fisher Linear Discriminant (FLD): Huilin [6] proposed a new method of feature extraction, namely, 2- DFLD. Experiments on two datasets: ORL and UMIST which outperform very well as compared to the others, in terms of efficiency and performance both. LDA (Linear Discriminant Analysis), Normal discriminant Analysis (NDA) and Discriminant Function Analysis are the generalization of the Fisher Linear Discriminant which is involved in statics and machine learning to achieve the linear combination of features that expands or divide two or more classes of various objects as well as events.

Radial Basis Function Neural Networks (RBF): This network uses RBF as activation functions and results of this network is a linear combination of RBF of input and neuron parameters. This network is used as function approximation, time series prediction and classification. Er [3] presents an efficient where an RBF neural classifier is used with less no. of high dimension training sets on ORL database. This method performs well in terms of error rates and learning efficiency. Aziz [4] also proposed a face detection system using RBF networks with variance spread value.

Support Vector Machine Classifier (SVM): This network is based on supervised learning rule which analyzes the data used for classification of objects. Due to supervised learning classifier the data is to be labelled. It doesn't work on the unlabeled data In the case of unlabeled supervision first Support Vector Clustering algorithm is being applied. It constructs a hyper plane or set of hyper planes in high dimensional hyperspace which can be used for classification or regression. Kwang [6] proposed a method for face recognition using SVM as a face recognizer where grey scale images are input directly to the recognizer.

Multiple Exemplar Discriminant Analysis (MEDA): LDA is a single-exemplar technique where each class during cataloguing is represented as a single pattern such as sample mean of a class. MEDA provides the better result as compared to the LDA or PCA in this approach each class is represented using several exemplars or a complete set of sample's [7].

4   Challenging Issues

There are many challenges in the face recognition systems as well which includes both some of the internal as well as the external factors which may result in the accuracy or efficiency of a face recognition system. Intrinsic factors are can further be categorized into two categories i.e. the change in facial expressions, age and second, the change in the ethnicity of an individual and further extrinsic factors mainly involves the illumination factor. Some further factors are discussed that becomes a challenge for the developer [10, 11, 14, 18, 20, 24, 26]:

Motion and Shadowing: Due to the motion and shadowing in the video it becomes a challenge for the algorithm to automatically detect the face. Illumination also plays a vital role in the detection of the face as a difference in the light variations it results in a decrease in the efficiency of the system [1, 4, 20–27]. As shown in Fig. 2.

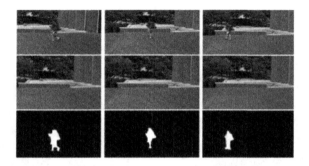

Fig. 2. Shadowing and illumination variation in motion detection. [27]

Posture: Pose or the angle of the face to the camera sometimes also becomes a challenge for the detection of the face by the system as a change in angle results in a change of the pose [5].

Expressions: Expressions or emotions vary from time to time which results in a change in the size of the human face which sometimes leads to a decrease in the efficiency of the developed system [6].

Ageing: As human face is somewhere unique but they are not rigid as they change with time like scars on a face increases due to ageing which may lead to reduced efficiency [12].

Occlusion: Occlusion is blockage of some parts. It means when the whole image is not available as in case of beard, glasses or hairs the whole image is not available it becomes a very important challenge in front of the developers to make a system which can detect image with missing features taken from EURECOM KinectFace dataset as shown in Fig. 3 [15, 21, 22, 27, 28].

Quality of Image: Low-resolution images also plays the role of a challenge in front. Sometimes similarity in the faces of some individuals even makes it difficult for

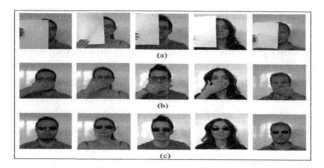

Fig. 3. RGB Occluded images: (a) by paper, (b) by hand, and (c) by glasses

humans to differentiate so it almost becomes impossible in case of similar faces for the system to detect the faces. Other challenges can be noise distortion and illumination variations in the image or camera distortion [11, 22] as shown in Fig. 4.

Fig. 4. Effect of Illumination on Face Detection [22]

Light Intensity: Many times the light intensity also plays a major role in the face detection. Light intensity plays a major role in this filed.

Change in Feature of Individual: Most of the people nowadays change their style on frequent basis. So it also rises as a challenge in front of the face detection system.

Illumination: When we present two faces with different illumination as the image processed might be during different illumination scale and when detected it might be in different illumination factor.

Transformation: The same face can be viewed as different to the system as when processed at different scales. This rises as a challenge before the system.

5   Recent Trends

There are many applications of face recognition and face detection and some of the latest applications as shown in Fig. 5 and discussed below.

Fig. 5. Video Surveillance: Row-Wise (a) Airport (b) Indoor Home (c) Airport (d) Shopping Complex [1, 10, 12]

Payments: From last decade cards are being used for payments but when a system is developed that logins into your account just by detecting the face behind the payment will lead to a more secure and faster system of payments. Recently, one such system is also launched by master card [12–14, 20, 26].

Access and Security: After the fingerprint locks in mobile phones, facial recognition is the new trend in the field of mobile phones. But it can further be used for more secure ways like entering into the home, cars, bank lockers etc. [10, 17, 18, 20, 21].

Law Enforcement and Criminal Identification: It is also helping in detecting the criminals and verifying it from the database of the system. Currently, some countries like UK and USA are also applying it for criminal identification [2, 9, 22, 23].

Advertising: The technology is bringing the tremendous growth in the field of advertising or product endorsing as the screen will detect the face of the person and will show them the ads which will more likely be useful or productive for them. For example: If a male between age 18–21 comes in front of screens, It will more likely popup the ad of some games [16, 19, 24, 25].

Healthcare: The work in this field is also started by facial recognition so for basic illness patient can be treated by this technology but obviously, when it comes to major illness you have to visit but this will reduce the lines in hospital and make the healthcare system more fast and efficient. This can also be used for saving the record of the patient and keeping his records [10, 15, 26].

6 Proposed Framework

Face detection system with the most important area of research nowadays with its various applications in different fields either for the personal use or for the commercial use Various possible developments with more accuracy can be done in the field where large masses of people are involved and activities have to be tracked as in keep track that no criminal activities take place where large masses are involved. As of now, technology is developed to a high extent but still, it needs more training to detect the image of how the human brain does it. The proposed framework comprises of four major steps including Image acquisition, preprocessing, search space reduction, detection and classification using Support Vector Machine classifier (SVM). At every stage, various methods are applied and the result of each stage is considered as input to the next step. Some of the important steps involve in this proposed work are:

1. In the first stage few initial frames form PET 2000 datasets are used. After the first step, the second step is Acquisition step, Generally, this step involves pre-processing of input frames, such as scaling etc.
2. In the next step preprocessing of image is done which includes various noise mean filter, block-based equalization technique.
3. In order to enhance the quality of detected output, several morphological operations such as dilation, erosion, infill and regionprop a preprocessing unit were applied. Morphological operators mainly deal with tools which are used for extraction of Image components that are expedient in the representation and description of shape.
4. In the last step, after search reduction process the classification of detected object is done using SVM classifier to get the resultant image with less no. of false alarm. The proposed framework is depicted in Fig. 6.

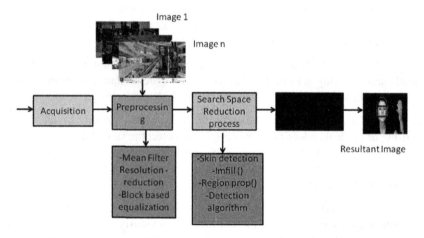

Fig. 6. Framework: improved face detection using Support Vector Machine Classifier

7 Conclusion and Future Work

This paper focuses on the most promising approaches used for the detection of faces in complex background and other challenging conditions. This paper deals with recent trends, current open challenging issues in case of both outdoor and indoor video sequences and their solutions available for efficient detection of faces. In the last section, a framework for face detection is also proposed using SVM classifier with lesser no. of false alarm. In future, we will implement the proposed framework and also compare the outcomes of proposed work with various state-of-art methods.

References

1. Wang, M., Wang, Z., Li, J.: Deep convolutional neural network applies to face recognition in small and medium databases. In: 2017 4th International Conference on Systems and Informatics (ICSAI), pp. 1368–1372 (2018)
2. Triantafyllidou, D., Tefas, A.: Face detection based on deep convolutional neural networks exploiting incremental facial part learning. In: 23rd International Conference on Pattern Recognition (ICPR), pp. 3560–3565 (2017)
3. Er, M.J., Wu, S., Lu, J., Toh, H.L.: Face recognition with radial basis function (RBF) neural networks. IEEE Trans. Neural Netw. **13**, 697–710 (2002)
4. Aziz, K.A.A., Ramlee, R.A., Abdullah, S.S., Jahari, A.N.: Face detection using radial basis function neural networks with variance spread value. In: 2009 International Conference of Soft Computing and Pattern Recognition, pp. 399–403 (2009)
5. Yoo, S.H., Oh, S.K., Pedrycz, W.: Optimized face recognition algorithm using radial basis function neural networks and its practical applications. Neural Netw. **69**, 111–125 (2015)
6. Kim, K., et al.: Face recognition using support vector machines with local correlation kernels. Int. J. Pattern Recogn. Artif. Intell. **16**, 97–111 (2002)
7. Zhou, S.K., Chellappa, R.: Multiple-exemplar discriminant analysis for face recognition. In: Proceedings of the 17th International Conference on Pattern Recognition, ICPR 2004, vol. 4, pp. 191–194 (2004)
8. Ohlyam, S., Sangwan, S., Ahuja, T.: A survey on various problem & challenges in face recognition. Int. J. Eng. Res. Technol. **2**(6), 2533–2538 (2013)
9. Tsai, C.C., et al.: Face detection using eigenface and neural network. In: 2006 IEEE International Conference on Systems, Man and Cybernetics, pp. 4343–4347 (2007)
10. Sharifara, A., et al.: A general review of human face detection including a study of neural networks and haar feature–based cascade classifier in face detection. In: 2014 International Symposium on Biometric and Security Technologies (ISBAST 2015) (2015)
11. Tayyab, M., Zafar, M.F.: Face detection using 2D-discrete cosine transform and back propagation neural network. In: 2009 International Conference of Emerging Technologies (2009)
12. El-Bakry, H.M.: Face detection using neural networks and image decomposition. In: Proceedings of International Joint Conference on Neural Networks, IJCNN 2002 (2002)
13. Jamil, N., Iqbal, S., Iqbal, N.: Face recognition using Neural Networks. In: Proceedings of IEEE International Multi Topic Conference, Technology for the 21st Century, pp. 416–419 (2001)
14. Huang, D.Y., Chen, C.H., Chen, T.Y.: Real-time face detection using a moving camera. In: 2018 32nd International Conference on Advanced Information Networking and Applications Workshops (2018)
15. Dang, K., Sharma, S.: Review and comparison on face detection algorithms. In: 2017 7th International Conference on Cloud Computing, Data Science & Engineering – Conference (2017)
16. Fernandez, M.C.D., et al.: Simultaneous face detection and recognition using Viola-Jones algorithm and artificial neural networks for identity verification. In: 2014 IEEE Region 10 Symposium (2014)

17. Hilado, S.D.F., Dadios, E.P.: Face detection using neural networks with skin segmentation. In: 2011 IEEE 5th International Conference on Cybernetics and Intelligent Systems (CIS), pp. 261–265 (2011)
18. Lang, L., Gu, W.: Study on face detection algorithm for real-time face detection system. In: 2009 Second International Symposium on Electronic Commerce and Security (2009)
19. Face Detection Technologies. https://disruptionhub.com/5-applications-facial-recognition-technology/. Accessed 15 Oct 2018
20. Sharma, L., Lohan, N.: Performance analysis of moving object detection using BGS techniques in visual surveillance. Int. J. Spatio-Temporal Data Sci. Indersci. 1(1), 22–53 (2019)
21. Sharma, L., Yadav, D.K.: Histogram based adaptive learning rate for background modelling and moving object detection in video surveillance. Int. J. Telemed. Clin. Pract. Indersci. 2(1), 74–92 (2017)
22. Sharma, L., Lohan, N., Yadav, D.K.: A study of challenging issues on video surveillance system for object detection. J. Basic Appl. Eng. Res. 4(4), 313–318 (2017)
23. Sharma, L., Singh, S., Yadav, D.K.: Fisher's linear discriminant ratio based threshold for moving human detection in thermal video. Infrared Phys. Technol. 78, 118–128 (2016)
24. Sharma, L., Yadav, D.K., Bharti, S.: An improved method for visual surveillance using background subtraction technique. In: IEEE 2nd International Conference on Signal Processing and Integrated Networks (SPIN 2015), pp. 421–426. Amity University Noida, India (2015)
25. Yadav, D.K., Sharma, L., Bharti, S.: Fuzzy-rule based threshold for moving human detection in video. In: International Conference on Advanced and Agile Manufacturing (ICAM 2015) (2015)
26. Yadav, D.K., Sharma, L., Bharti, S.: Moving object detection in real-time visual surveillance using background subtraction technique. In: IEEE 14th International Conference in Hybrid Intelligent Computing (HIS 2014), pp. 79–84. Gulf University for Science and Technology, Kuwait (2014)
27. Min, R., Kose, N., Dugelay, J.L.: KinectFaceDB: a kinectdatabase for face recognition. IEEE Trans. Syst. Man Cybern.: Syst. 44(11), 1534–1548 (2014)
28. Zohra, F.T., et al.: Occlusion detection and localization from kinect depth images. In: 2016 International Conference on Cyberworlds, pp. 189–196 (2016)

Empirical Study of Test Driven Development with Scrum

Vikas Aggarwal[1] and Anjali Singhal[2(✉)]

[1] Central Research Lab, BEL, Ghaziabad, India
vikasaggarwal@bel.co.in
[2] Inderprastha Engineering College, Ghaziabad, India
anjali.singhal@ipec.org.in

Abstract. Now days, Agile development methodologies are becoming popular in various IT industries. This methodology is combination of different stages in repetitive and incremental manner. Its main focus is to increase the adaptability in process, which in turn increases customer satisfaction. There are various development frameworks in agile methodology like Scrum and Kanban. There is also another programming practice known as Test Driven Development. It starts with developing test for a feature, before its implementation. It is also known as test first programming. The main objective of this paper is to adopt an approach in which TDD can be merged with Scrum to add benefits of TDD in Scrum and also to provide a comprehensive review of this approach.

Keywords: Sprint · Sprint backlog · Product backlog

Nomenclature: Test Driven Development (TDD) ·
Software Development Life Cycle (SDLC)

1 Introduction

Developing software is a critical process, in which well structured guidelines are required. A development approach followed to develop software plays a vital role in terms of quality and reliability of final Software product. There are various development methodologies starting from traditional development models like waterfall model to agile development methodologies. Though traditional methods are structured in nature and are stable, but they are less flexible and adaptable. They involve heavy weight development methods with complex designs and heavy documentation. So software engineers felt a requirement of methodologies which are more flexible. From past two decades, new methodologies have been introduced, which are flexible and easily adaptable [4–6, 19–21, 33]. Agile methodologies are among them. They basically involve methods, which are able to maintain the software quality, simpler designs along with continuous customer interaction [1]. These methodologies have short-short development cycles, which make it more flexible. If any change is required, it can be easily implemented. These methods are mainly used, where the requirements are not fixed or not clear. At regular intervals, there is interaction between all stakeholders. This helps in filling the gaps between requirements and designs to make effective

© Springer Nature Singapore Pte Ltd. 2019
M. Singh et al. (Eds.): ICACDS 2019, CCIS 1046, pp. 13–21, 2019.
https://doi.org/10.1007/978-981-13-9942-8_2

software. Customer has a vital role in overall success of project, as their decision is foremost in deciding the requirements to implement in the next development cycle. Output of every stage is a working product delivered to the customer for feedback. It enables the ability to incorporate rapid development and change (if required). This also reduces the communication cost and time among stakeholders, which in turn reduces the elapsed time between decision making and its consequences. Basic idea in this methodology involves frequent communications among stakeholders, short delivery of working software and assessment of progress in terms of working software. Among various frameworks available in Agile, scrum is widely used. Its main focus is on frequent delivery of software with time boxed effort (Sprint). Sometimes sprints are too short that they lack in proper testing and documentation. This may result in increase in defect rate [2]. TDD is a methodology, that focuses on testing. If Scrum and TDD can be combined, it can merged the good practices of Scrum (i.e. good team management and sprints) and of TDD (i.e. rigorous testing). This can improve the quality of process as well as the quality of product.

2 Related Work

There are various frameworks in agile methodology like Scrum and Kanban. Each has their advantages and disadvantages. Scrum framework is generally used for developing complex software. It is consist of Scrum teams, every one having specific roles and rules [7]. Every component of this framework has a specific purpose. Rules are there to govern the events, their relationships and their interactions. The scrum team is consisting of scrum master, a set of developers and Product owner. Each has their own roles and responsibilities. Product owner manages the product backlog; i.e. they ensure that, what items will be included in product backlog, to achieve the desired goal. Development team is consisting of professional programmers. They are responsible for implementing the product backlog into desired functionality. The Scrum master has a role of assisting scrum team in adhering to scrum practices and rules. Tasks of developing software are divided in various sprints. Sprint is a time-box, in which the defined tasks are to be completed and delivered. So basically, this framework is a pack of team, which work together in incremental and iterative manner. This framework ensures effective use of time and money [7]. Emphasis is on leadership and its collaboration among the team, rather than commanding and controlling the team [8, 9].

Testing has significant role in quality of software. If testing is good, the quality of the software will be definitely very good. Test Driven Development is of the technique, which rigorously supports testing [10, 11, 16]. In this case the developer first designs the test-cases from the requirements, before developing the application software. This process facilitates the developer to think about the code design and use of different functionalities before actually implementing them. TDD is based on basic three steps. In first step, the developer tries to extract functionalities/features from the requirements before developing the actual application. This enables the developers to think about the code design and use of different functionalities before actually implementing them. As this technique focuses on small functionalities with large number of test cases, the rework time of developer is lessened and better quality of product is created. Code designed in this technique is more maintainable, flexible and secure.

3 Interaction Model

The Developing software is a critical task. It requires well structured guidelines. This paper is basically focused on finding the outcome of merging TDD with Scrum. TDD used to manage programming of code and scrum used to manage the project team and their activities. The main aim is to combine positive aspects of TDD and scrum, to provide benefit to the development of software. Different studies done by different researchers show that there are various factors, which affect the development of the software [12, 15, 17, 18]. TDD and Scrum have their own pros and cons. They have common goals of improving productivity and increase in customer satisfaction. So they are largely adopted by the software industries, first for their rapid development and secondly for emphasis on software quality with rigorous testing.

Scrum is time boxed iterative and evolutionary approach of development, in which a project is broken into series of sprint [14, 25]. In this requirements are evolved as the project progresses over the time. The response of feedbacks from prior sprints decides the future of the development process of software. It includes some of the management's best practices like daily scrum meeting, planning cycle of every sprint, managing sprint backlog and product backlog. This is created by Product owner. The project starts with building the product backlog, having the list of features to be included in new product sprint backlog, having to-do list of team members. After that it is prioritized by the stakeholders. Once the features are prioritized, the Sprint planning is done. In this meeting is done to decide the list of features to be developed in the first Sprint. In this a rough idea of sprint budget is also decided. Once the development stars, Scrum daily meeting is held every day. In this the progress in the project done after the previous meeting is discussed. During Scrum Cycle, the estimates are updated as per the progress and requirements. For this a burn down-chart chart is prepared. This helps in getting accurate estimates and scheduling the work. These estimates help in making charts for next sprints, so that the team can meet the Sprint goals and finish the work by desired date [26–28].

TDD requires a developer to design test cases that originates from a set of requirements and process continues with the implementation in a small chunk of tasks in incremental manner [22–24] (Fig. 1).

TDD is based on three basic steps:

- Developer first tries to extract functionalities/features from the requirements and write a code just enough to be compiled. As the actual functionality is not yet developed, the test fails. This failed test is called as Red Test.
- After Red Test, the developer writes a production code (Actual Code) of one unit. It is just enough to pass Unit Test case. This failed test is called as Green Test.
- After Green test, the developer restructures the production code. They modify the working code and try to clean it, by removing duplication without changing the functionality. This step is called as Re-factor. The developers re-test the code to

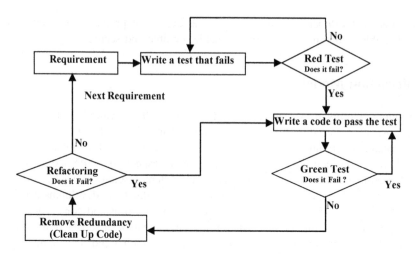

Fig. 1. TDD methodology

ensure that the behavior of the code is not broken. The process is continued with the implementation of small- small functionalities.

Software is written in smaller units that are highly tested. It increases the abstractness in the code, which in turn increase coupling in the code. This makes the software more flexible [3, 29]. Series of experiments have been done to compare TDD with other methods. TDD produces better quality and productivity. This is due to the way the test cases were designed as the software was being developed [30–32, 34–36].

4 Implementation

This paper focuses on merging TDD with Scrum. We took two cases, first case using only Scrum methodology and second case using Scrum and TDD both. In first case project was to design code for e-commerce site. As in this case Scrum framework was used, a product backlog was prepared and the work was divided into sprints. Product backlog contains the list of features to be build in software product and sprint backlog consists of teams to-do list (Fig. 2).
Item in product backlog were:

- Following work to be done in Sprint1
  - Create plan, schedule to setup project base
  - Database Creation
  - Coding for Login Page
  - Test Functionalities for Login page
- Following work to be done in Sprint2
  - Coding for Category Page
  - Coding for payment page
  - Test Functionalities for Category page and Payment page

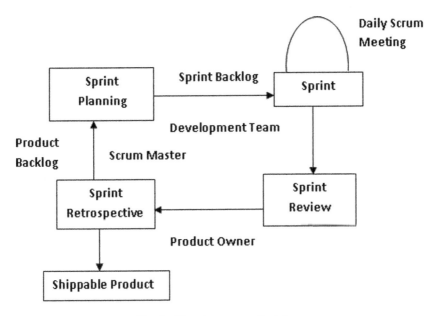

Fig. 2. Case 1 scrum methodology

- Following work to be done in Sprint3
  - Coding for Contact page
  - Test Functionalities of Contact page
  - Final Testing for full software product

In this after developing the code the testing was done. More time was spent on development as compared to the testing. Along with this testing was done manually, so testing was not thorough.

In second case, we design the same application with features of TDD merged with features of Scrum (Fig. 3).

In this case also the tasks were divided in Sprints and a product backlog was prepared.

Item in product backlog were:

- Following work to be done in Sprint1
  - Create plan, schedule to setup project base
  - Setup of Database and testing framework
- As in this case TDD is merged with Scrum, so before starting with any coding a test case will be written and tested in Sprint2
  - Test case and Coding for Login Page
    Initially it will be 'Red' i.e. failed.
    The next step is to develop to develop the function which is just enough for Login Screen.
    Once the login screen passes the test, then refactoring i.e. formatting of that screen is done.

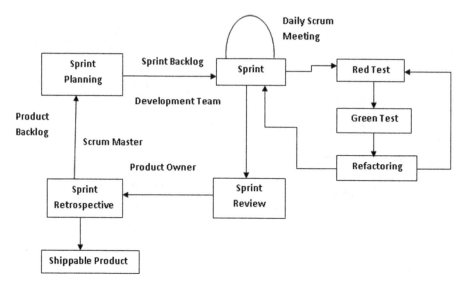

Fig. 3. Case 2 TDD merged with Scrum

- – Similarly Test case and Coding for payment page
- • Same development workflow was applied to contact page in Sprint3
  - – Test case and Coding for Contact page
  - – Refactoring is done to make the full software fully functional as a whole.

At the end application was developed with the features of Scrum and TDD.

5 Comparison in Terms of Quality and Duration

In first case, testing was done after the coding. The testing of all the cases could not be done thoroughly. So there were chances that some of the cases of functionality may have some bug. Whereas in second case as the focus was only on the desired result, i.e. code was as per test case, the testing was thorough. Along with that, the adding of functionality was done increment order (as per Scrum framework), and the functionalities which were coded prior were tested again (as per TDD framework). So if any problem occurred, it was fixed before proceeding to writing code for next functionality. As a result quality of the software was improved.

Scrum is focused on overall development process and group of developers instead of code, whereas TDD focuses on code and aims on work cycles of developers. So when they are combined the quality of code as well as the quality of software development process is improved.

Due to refactoring part of TDD, the design of code was much improved. It was also much cleaner than that of software designed in the first case. This version is more flexible, maintainable and extensible. In terms of time, the time pent in final output of second case was lesser as compared to first case. As in first case testing was done after the coding, lots of time was spent on finding the problems, testing them and fixing the same. In second version, as TDD was implemented along with Scrum, problems were identified and fixed side by side.

In second case there is better ability to implement changes in code on continuous basis. In Scrum it is the duty of scrum owner to produce working code at the end of every sprint so that technical debt for going forward can be minimized. Side by side the code should be flexible to adopt changes based on stakeholder feedback. In TDD, the work on coding is preceded by the test cases, so that there should not be any after-thought after code implementation. For any new implementation, test are written first, they are failed and then code is written to make the test work. For a Scrum owner, it becomes beneficial that a developer creates unit tests for every code and has the proper mechanism to continuously validate the code. So when TDD is merged with Scrum, it provides a powerful combination to assure that code is stable all the time and all the parts of code are being properly tested. This combination provides greater code coverage, which in turn increases the confidence to do changes in to implemented code. Adopting TDD ensures that the quality of code is maintained and changes can be done to the implemented code without affecting the working of software. This facilitates the Scrum owner to address the customer need and managing the code in a better way.

6   Conclusion

The features of Scrum i.e. collective ownership and programmer courage and the features of TDD i.e. refactoring and continuous integration are successfully combined together and applied on a software development process. In first case software is developed using only Scrum framework and another software development process, features of TDD were implemented with Scrum. The outcome obtained is that using TDD with Scrum improves the process of development in terms of quality and time. TDD helps the scrum team to make rapid changes whilst ensuring high quality. It also reduces total cost of ownership and makes application more modular. The designed code in second case is cleaner, which make it more maintainable and flexible. Time is used more efficiently in second case. As testing is done side by side and changes done to fix the bugs were also done side by side, so response time in second case is better. In future, it is intended to apply this integration for large projects too, so that Agile methodology can be more enhanced.

References

1. Anwer, F., Aftab, S., Waheed, U., Muhammad, S.S.: Agile software development models TDD, FDD, DSDM, and crystal methods: a survey. Int. J. Multidiscip. Sci. Eng. **8**, 2 (2017)
2. Ghafoor, F., Shah, I.A., Rashid, N.: Issues in adopting agile methodologies in global and local software development: a systematic literature review protocol with preliminary results. Int. J. Comput. Appl. **160**, 7 (2017)
3. Ashraf, S., Aftab, S.: IScrum: an improved scrum process model. Int. J. Modern Educ. Comput. Sci. **8**, 16–24 (2017)

4. Fucci, D., Erdogmus, H., Turhan, B., Oivo, M., Juristo, N.: A dissection of the test-driven development process: does it really matter to test-first or to test-last? IEEE Trans. Softw. Eng. **43**(7), 597–614 (2017)
5. Anand, R.V., Dinakaran, M.: Popular agile methods in software development: review and analysis. Int. J. Appl. Eng. Res. **11**, 3433–3437 (2016)
6. Ashmore, S., Runyan, K.: Introduction to Agile Methods. Pearson Education Inc, Fort Worth (2015)
7. Andrade, C., Lopes, J., Barbosa, W., Costa, M.: Identifying difficulties in the implementation and contract management in agile projects in Belo Horizonte. Abakós **3**, 18–37 (2014)
8. Matharu, G.S., Mishra, A., Singh, H., Upadhyay, P.: Empirical study of agile software development methodologies: a comparative analysis. ACM SIGSOFT Softw. Eng. Notes **40**, 1–6 (2015)
9. Pham, A., Pham, P.V.: Scrum in Action: Agile Software Project Management and Development. Course Technology, Boston (2012)
10. Janzen, D., Saiedian, H.: Test-driven development concepts, taxonomy, and future direction. IEEE Softw. **38**, 43–50 (2005)
11. Romano, B.L., Da Silva, A.D.: Project management using the scrum agile method. In: 12th International Conference on Informational Technology - New Generations (ITNG), pp. 774–776 (2015)
12. Cao, L., Ramesh, B.: Agile requirements engineering practices: an empirical study. IEEE Softw. **25**, 60–67 (2008)
13. Schwaber, K.: Agile Project Management witch Scrum. Microsoft Press, Reedmond (2013)
14. Punch, K.F.: Introduction to Social Research: Quantitative and Qualitative Approaches, 3rd edn. Sage publications, London (2013)
15. Waldmann, B.: There's never enough time: Doing requirements under resource constraints and what requirements engineering can learn from agile development. In: 19th IEEE International Requirements Engineering Conference (RE), pp. 301–305 (2011)
16. Bender, J., McWherter, J.: Professional Test-Driven Development with C#: Developing Real World Applications with TDD. Wiley Publishing, Inc., Canada (2011)
17. Käpyaho, M.: Agile requirements engineering with interactive prototyping: a case study (2013)
18. Campanelli, A.S., Parreiras, F.S.: Agile methods tailoring – a systematic literature review. J. Syst. Softw. **110**, 85–100 (2015)
19. Stettina, C.J., Hörzb, J.: Agile portfolio management: an empirical perspective on the practice in use. Int. J. Project Manag. **33**, 140–152 (2015)
20. Diebold, P., Ostberg, J.-P., Wagner, S., Zendler, U.: What do practitioners vary in using scrum? In: Lassenius, C., Dingsøyr, T., Paasivaara, M. (eds.) XP 2015. LNBIP, vol. 212, pp. 40–51. Springer, Cham (2015). https://doi.org/10.1007/978-3-319-18612-2_4
21. Tomanek, M., Klima, T.: Penetration testing in agile software development projects. Int. J. Cryptogr. Inf. Secur. **5**, 1–7 (2015)
22. George, B., Williams, L.: A structured experiment of test-driven development. Inf. Softw. Technol. **46**, 337–342 (2004)
23. Janzen, D.S., Saiedian, H.: Does test-driven development really improve software design quality? IEEE Softw. **25**, 77–84 (2008)
24. Siniaalto, M., Abrahamsson, P.: A comparative case study on the impact of test-driven development on program design and test coverage. In: IEEE Software (2007)
25. Sharma, S., Hasteer, N.: A comprehensive study on state of Scrum development. In: IEEE Software Computing, Communication and Automation (ICCCA), pp. 867–872 (2016)
26. Darwish, N.R., Megahed, S.: Requirements engineering in scrum framework, requirements engineering. Int. J. Comput. Appl. **149**, 24–29 (2016)

27. Khalane, T., Tanner, M.: Software quality assurance in Scrum: the need for concrete guidance on SQA strategies in meeting user expectations. In: International Conference on Adaptive Science and Technology (ICAST), pp. 1–6 (2013)

28. Kroizer, S.: Acceptance tests driving development in scrum. In: Proceedings of the 28th Pacific Northwest Software Quality Conference (PNSQC 2010), pp. 263–276 (2010)

29. Schwaber, K., Sutherland, J.: The Scrum Guide. http://www.scrumguides.org/docs/scrumguide/v2016/2016-Scrum-Guide-US.pdf

30. Nagappan, N., Maximilien, E.M., Bhat, T., Williams, L.: Realizing quality improvement through test driven development: results and experiences of four industrial teams. Empirical Softw. Eng. **13**(3), 289–302 (2008)

31. Huang, L., Holcombe, M.: Empirical investigation towards the effectiveness of Test First programming. Inf. Softw. Technol. **51**, 182–194 (2009)

32. Rafique, Y., Misic, V.B.: The effects of test-driven development on external quality and productivity: a meta-analysis. IEEE Trans. Software Eng. **39**, 835–856 (2013)

33. Lenberg, P., Feldt, R., Wallgren, L.G.: Behavioral software engineering: a definition and systematic literature review. J. Syst. Softw. **107**, 15–37 (2015). https://doi.org/10.1016/j.jss.2015.04.084

34. Bogart, C., Kästner, C., Herbsleb, J., Thung, F.: How to break an API: cost negotiation and community values in three software ecosystems. In: Proceedings of the 2016 24th ACM SIGSOFT International Symposium on Foundations of Software Engineering, ser. FSE 2016, pp. 109–120 (2016)

35. Madeyski, L.: Test-Driven Development: An Empirical Evaluation of Agile Practice, 1st edn. Springer, Heidelberg (2010). https://doi.org/10.1007/978-3-642-04288-1

36. Kropp, M., Meier, A., Anslow, C., Biddle, R.: Satisfaction, practices, and influences in agile software development. In: Proceedings of the 22nd International Conference on Evaluation and Assessment in Software Engineering, EASE 2018, pp. 112–121 (2018)

37. Rahman, F., Devanbu, P.: How, and why, process metrics are better. In: Proceedings of the 2013 International Conference on Software Engineering, ser. ICSE 2013, pp. 432–441 (2013)

Microprocessor Based Edge Computing for an Internet of Things (IoT) Enabled Distributed Motion Control

Wasim Ghder Soliman$^{(\boxtimes)}$ and D. V. Rama Koti Reddy

Instrument Technology, College of Engineering, Andhra University,
Visakhapatnam 530003, India
wasimsoliman1987@gmail.com, rkreddy_67@yahoo.co.in

Abstract. Edge computing reduces latency, energy overhead and communication bandwidth bottlenecks. In this paper, a designed Proportional-Integrator (PI) motion controller for a Permanent Magnetic DC (PMDC) motor is integrated with IoT technology. This controller receives the preferred speed from the cloud, performs all necessary computation at Edge Level, derives actions and sends both output (real) speed and Integral Absolute Error (IAE) performance index (as an indication of controller performance) to the cloud. Firstly, both system identification and PI controller tuning are performed with the help of MATLAB Simulink and MATLAB support package for ARDUINO. ARDUINO Mega development board is used to implement the controller. An inbuilt PYTHON program in Raspberry Pi 3 is used as a software Gateway to enable receiving/sending data between the controller and the cloud (ThingS-peak.com IoT platform in our case). However, all necessary computations are intended to take place at Edge level only and this is for the tasks of improving latency, power consumption and bandwidth. Gateway level is used to gather the data coming from Edge level and send it to Cloud level; it is also used to send the data coming from Cloud level to the Edge level. Cloud level is the user interface to the system and enables him to control the speed and receive the controller working performance. An integrated work is the main contribution of current paper in which an attempt to construct a link between research works in both control systems and industrial IoT fields.

Keywords: Edge computing · Internet of Things (IoT) ·
Python programming · Permanent magnet direct current (PMDC) motor ·
Proportional Integral (PI) speed controller ·
Integral of absolute error (IAE) performance index

1 Introduction

Integrating the controllers in the industry with the state of the art Internet of Things (IoT) technology results in Industrial IoT (IIoT). Ubiquitous connection and observation, is one of its specifications. Global economy, business and life are expected to be transformed by IoT [1]. Controlling and monitoring things through mobiles and laptops is one of IoT main aspects [3]. For the purpose of global management of the industry

© Springer Nature Singapore Pte Ltd. 2019
M. Singh et al. (Eds.): ICACDS 2019, CCIS 1046, pp. 22–31, 2019.
https://doi.org/10.1007/978-981-13-9942-8_3

and to lessen expansive systems with keeping improved quality, industrial monitoring is used [4]. Several communication protocols should be supported by the IoT Gateway and several middleware are developed to support that [5, 6]. IoT is a notable concept that has evolved in a significant way over the past few years [7, 8] and has several existing definitions, also. Due to a development of the past technologies and the emanations of recent ones, many of those definitions have improved. In order to develop IoT architecture, main IoT methodologies should be clear. Ashton presented the Internet of Things (IoT) terminology in 1998, as objects were connected by Radio-Frequency Identification (RFID) and the information of the objects was used on the internet in supply chains. In 2003–2004, Internet 0 concept [9] appears. This concept includes that internet connectivity can be provided to everyday devices. Here the devices are constrained devices. In 2009, CASAGRAS definition [10] is introduced. This definition extends the object physical meaning to virtual one. A lot of questions rise due to the large number consideration of both virtual and physical meaning such as: how to connect a lot of things to the internet? What technology types can be used to connect this large number to the internet? How much the data size that will be received and stored or transmitted? How a specific object can be called by the user? In order to answer the previous questions the technology of identifying the object is required. Different objects lead to different services, data and interoperability of devices. An event should be sent as an indication of any change in the situation of an object and an appropriate action is to be decided accordingly. However, security and privacy issues are missed. The main focus of the definition of SAP [11] is on smart objects, active objects and physical objects. Objects are treated as sharers of the IoT information network. With this information, different kinds of services can be available. The possibility of device to device communication is presented. Definition of Future Internet Assembly/Real Word Internet [12] includes that: devices with both computing and communication abilities and objects which do not have RFIDs communication or computing power (ex: virtual things) can be connected according to this definition. The main focuses on the definition of EPoSS [13] are on things with intelligence, unique IP address based on protocols standardizations.

1.1   Related Work

By tacking the advantages of previous mentioned definitions and shifting the concepts in the industrial domain, several developments can be resulted in the industry. Variety set of microprocessor architectures and the diversity of IoT applications make determining the appropriate microprocessor architectures very challenging [1]. Edge computing reduces latency, energy overhead and communication bandwidth bottlenecks. The IoT devices at Edge level should be provided with all necessary algorithms required for desired computations. The recent state-of-the-art of Internet of Things (IoT) in industries has been summarized systematically in [2]. An attempt to apply the controller from the cloud was included in [14] along with mitigation mechanisms to overcome the delay problems. Many industrial applications are expected from PMDCs due to their big thrust force, high speed and high precision [15–18]. Research work includes a variety of methods for parameters estimation of PMDC motors. The most recent research was carried on by the authors of [18]. To design appropriate controller of a given motor, precise parameters estimation is required. They have used both standard and dynamic particle swarm optimization (PSO), ant colony optimization (ACO), and artificial bee colony (ABC) in order to estimate PMDC motor parameters, they have not attempted any controller design of that motor. Direct measurements of armature current and voltage and rotor speed to identify the parameters have been done in [19] without going through any controller design after the estimation. A Multi-Objective Optimization (EMOO) algorithm to tune the Proportional Integral (PI) speed regulator in the Permanent Magnet DC (PMDC) motor drive system is used [20], the work has not included hardware validation, they have shown simulation results but they have not performed hardware implantation. This paper intends to make an integrated work. This work includes system identification, PI controller design, simulation validation and hardware implementation with IoT integration. In any controller design, reducing error area between the desired and real output is one of the important aspects. This reduction can be gained by making it as objective function of the optimization algorithm and this is what this work includes. After performing system identification of the PMDC motor, the controller design intended to get the PI controller parameters i.e. the proportional gain k_C and the integral time constant t_i so that they are providing the best IAE performance index, which indicates an efficient reduced error area, then the attempt to integrate the PI controller with IoT technology, as it is depicted in Fig. 1, is performed.

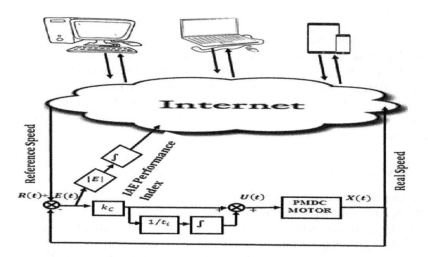

Fig. 1. Block diagram of the integrated system.

The controller will receive the desired speed from the cloud, performs all necessary computation at Edge Level, derives actions and publish both its performance index and output (real) speed to the cloud. The user has the facility to use desktop, laptop, tablet or mobile device to send and receive the data. This proposed system can be extended to any number of actuators in the industry and any value of interest can also be published. In this block diagram we have: R(t) is the Reference speed, X(t) is the Output speed, E

(t) is the Error between reference and output speed, k_C is the Proportional gain of the PI controller, t_i is the Integral time constant of the PI controller, and U(t) is the controller output.

2 Work Procedure

The work includes two parts, the first part is the Software part and includes MATLAB SIMULINK with support package for ARDUINO that used to interface the PMDC motor with MATLAB program to perform both system identification and PI controller tuning, and the Python program acts as a software Gateway for receiving/ sending data from/to cloud. Second part is the Hardware part and includes a developed PMDC motor prototype kit which includes inbuilt driving circuit, ARDUINO MEGA Board and Raspberry Pi 3 development board. Figure 2 illustrates the experimental setup

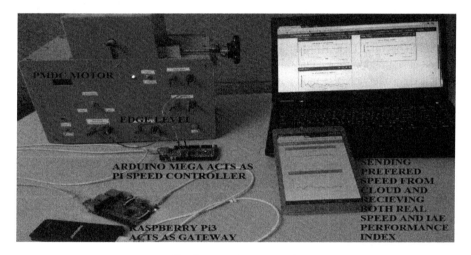

Fig. 2. Experimental work.

2.1 PMDC Motor Prototype

It includes: (1) PMDC motor: with the specification of: maximum speed is 1500 RPM, maximum input Voltage is 12 V_{dc}, and maximum input current is 1.5 A. (2) Feedback sensor: It is an IR sensor along with a slotted disk mounted on front of the motor axis so that this arrangement gives 12 pulses per full rotation. (3) PIC 16F876 SP microcontroller: it is the brain of the developed prototype. A Frequency to Voltage converter is programmed inside the microcontroller to be used for speed measurement. Pulses from the IR sensor are fed to the microcontroller circuit with the programmed frequency to voltage (F_ to _V) converter for measurement of speed in terms of DC voltage values. This microcontroller enables the possibility of interfacing other microcontrollers or programmable logic controllers (PLCs) with the developed PMDC prototype for the purpose of speed control.

2.2   System Identification and PI Controller Design for the PMDC Motor

A PRBS (Pseudo Random Binary Sequence) test [21, 23] is performed during the system identification procedure, this insures that: the obtained transfer function is a result of random sets of pulse width modulation (PWM) applied to the motor armature. Both input and output data are given to the motor with the help of ARDUINO support package from MATLAB and imported to the system identification tool, then the following transfer function is obtained by sampling time equal to 0.001 s:

$$G_s = \frac{92.46\,s + 4.893}{s^2 + 124.2\,s + 4.173} \tag{1}$$

Then Integral Absolute Error performance index [22, 23] is used as an objective function of an optimization tuning algorithm for the PI controller using MATLAB Optimization Tools. The results are $k_C = \mathbf{0.1587}$, $t_i = \mathbf{0.0037}$, where: k_C and t_i are the proportional gain and the integral time constant, respectively. Both disturbance rejection and set point tracking of a designed PI controller are shown in Fig. 3. The PMDC motor is given a set point of 900 RPM, then at simulation time 5 s the set point is changed to become 1100 RPM and the PMDC motor follows this new trajectory after that and at simulation time equal to 10 s. the set point is changed to become 1300 RPM and the controller lets the motor to run at this speed. A positive load is applied at simulation time equal to 21 s. and the controller rejects this disturbance and comes back to the required speed, then at simulation time equal to 24 s. a negative load is applied and the controller makes the motor to return back to the required speed.

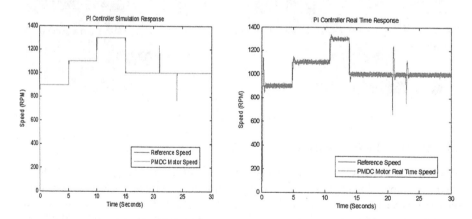

Fig. 3. Simulation and real time responses: disturbance rejection and set point tracking

Same mentioned test sequence is applied practically to verify the ability of the designed PI controller to track the preferred speed and to reject any disturbance on the motor shaft, This is depicted in Fig. 3 (right side) which shows the real time response for the designed speed controller. Controller response characteristics are illustrated in Table 1. The unit of both rise and settling times is milliseconds. It is the normal situation to get the difference between simulation and real time results as the simulation test tends to give ideal values. However, the real time response is near to simulated one and from figure number 4, we can observe that: the controller behavior is acceptable.

Table 1. Characteristics of controller response.

Response characteristics	Simulation response	Real time response
Rise time (ms)	12.09	13.05
Settling time (ms)	2427	2994
Overshoot (%)	30.06	35.12
IAE index	0.4	1.39

3 Proposed Method for PI Controller Integration with IoT Technology

The process of IoT integration consists of three levels as shown in Fig. 4. Those levels are: Edge Level, Gateway Level and Cloud Level. This section includes the detailed explanation for the mentioned levels along with required graphic curves. However, all necessary computations are intended to take place at Edge level only and this is for the tasks of improving latency, power consumption and bandwidth. Here a reference speed of 1000 RPM is sent from cloud i.e. from ThingSpeak.com website by the user.

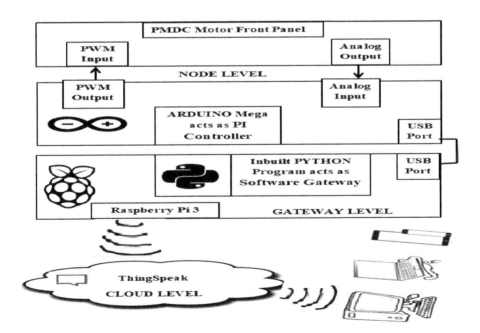

Fig. 4. Block diagram for integration with IoT

3.1   Edge Level

For the aim of improved latency, bandwidth and energy consumption the focus here is on edge computing. Edge computing in this proposed method is divided into two parts. The first part is done with the help of an inbuilt circuit inside the PMDC motor prototype, and this circuit includes the PIC 16F876 SP microcontroller performing the task of F/V converter and providing an analog output voltage. Second part is the PI controller computation with help of ARDUINO Mega 2560, whereas the PI controller code is written after obtaining its parameters values i.e. k_C and t_i as mentioned in the previous section. As depicted in Fig. 1, this controller will receive its reference speed from the cloud, so once the controller receives the preferable speed, its computations start for sending both output speed and IAE performance index. IAE performance index computations are done at the edge level also in which the written code for PI controller intends to have a portion for such computation by integrated the absolute value of the resulted error in each controller loop. Figure 5 depicts IAE performance index value, reference speed and output (Real) speed at edge level i.e. through ARDUINO Mega serial monitor.

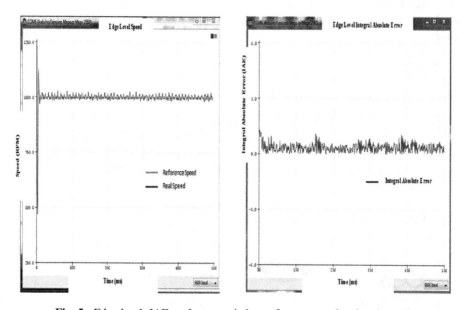

Fig. 5.   Edge level: IAE performance index, reference speed and real speed

3.2   Gateway Level

There are no computations to be done in the Gateway level, the task here is to aggregate the data coming from Edge level, i.e. ARDUINO Mega and sending them to the cloud, at the same time receiving the preferred speed from cloud and sending it to the Edge level. This task is accomplished by using Raspberry Pi 3 that has inbuilt

PYTHON program. The code is written in PYTHON in order to perform the previous mentioned task after connecting ARDUINO Mega to one serial port of Raspberry Pi 3, where ARDUINO IDE has been installed. In addition, the code is intended to give the user the possibility to show all three values of interest, i.e. reference speed, real speed and IAE performance index. Figure 6 illustrates both reference speed and real speed in the gateway level, where left axis is considered for real speed values and right axis is considered for reference speed values.

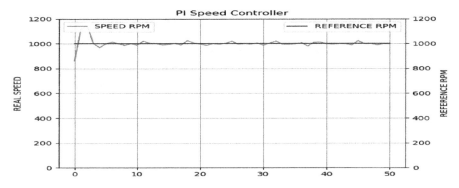

Fig. 6. Gateway level: reference and real speed

Real speed and IAE performance index are shown in Fig. 7, where left axis is considered for real speed values and right axis is considered for IAE performance index values.

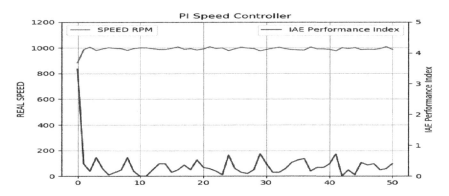

Fig. 7. Gateway level: both performance index and real speed

3.3 Cloud Level

From Cloud level the user will be able to specify the preferred speed through ThingSpeak.com website and after sending this value the user will receive both real speed and IAE values. The methodology here is to update the field titled Reference Speed by using the following command:

https://api.thingspeak.com/update?api_key="Writing Key" &field1="Reference Speed"

Where, Writing Key can be obtained after creating the channel and Reference Speed is the user preferable speed of rotation per minute (RPM). As shown in Fig. 8, the created channel includes three fields: field 1 titled reference speed, field 2 titled Real Speed and field 3 titled IAE performance index. The user has the ability to use a mobile device or tablet also.

Fig. 8. Cloud level: reference speed, real speed and IAE performance index

4   Conclusion

In current work, the main focus is on edge computing to avoid delay problems, reduce the amount of data to be sent, enhance controller performance and reduce power consumption, so all the necessary computations are done in Edge level letting both Gateway and Cloud levels for the task of data of interest transmission. In addition, this work can be extended to include more values of interest, i.e. there is a possibility to send and receive other values, for example armature voltage can be introduced and any other performance indexed values can be included also. For the task of having more values of interest, the only thing to do is to add their related codes at Edge level, then the microprocessor will do the computation function. The work included in this paper is a step toward shifting Internet of Things concept to industry domain using cheap, easy and widely available platforms and it can be extended to any number of working actuators in the industry.

References

1. Tosiron, A., Anita, R., et al.: Microprocessor optimizations for the internet of things: a survey. IEEE Trans. Comput. Aided Des. Integr. Circ. Syst. **37**(1), 7–20 (2018)
2. Xu, L.D., He, W., Shancang, L.: Internet of things in industries. IEEE Trans. Ind. Inform. **10**, 1–11 (2014)
3. John, A.: Research directions for the internet of things. IEEE J. Internet of Things **1**(1), 3–9 (2014)
4. Shanzhi, C., Dake, L., et al.: A vision of IoT: applications, challenges, and opportunities with china perspective. IEEE Internet of Things J. **1**(4), 349–359 (2014)
5. Liu, T., Martonosi, M.: A middleware system for managing autonomic, parallel sensor systems. ACM SIGPLAN Not. **38**(10), 107–118 (2003)
6. Heinzelman, W.B., Murphy, A.L., Carvalho, H.S., Perillo, M.A.: Middleware to support sensor network applications. IEEE Netw. **18**(1), 6–14 (2004)
7. Ashton, K.: That 'internet of things' thing, in the real world things matter more than ideas. RFID J. (2009). Atmel Corporation.www.atmel.com
8. IEEE: Internet of Things. http://iot.ieee.org/about.html. Accessed Jan 2017
9. Gershenfeld, N., Krikorian, R., Cohen, D.: The internet of things. Sci. Am. **291**(4), 76–81 (2004)
10. http://cordis.europa.eu/search/index.cfm?fuseaction=news.document&N_RCN=30283
11. http://services.future-internet.eu/images/1/16/A4_Things_Haller.pdf
12. Deploying RFID - Challenges, Solutions, and Open Issues. Book edited by C. Turcu, under CC BY-NC-SA 3.0 license, 17 August 2011. ISBN 978-953-307-380-4
13. EPOSS, E. ETP EPOSS IOT Definition (2011). http://old.smartsystemsintegration.org/internet-of-things/Internet-of-Thingsin2020EC-EPoSSWorkshopReport-2008v3.pdf/download
14. Saad, M., Pavlos, N., et al.: Delay mitigation in offloaded cloud controllers in industrial IoT. IEEE Access **5**, 4418–4430 (2017)
15. Zhang, D., Chen, Y.K., Tom, C., et al.: Compensation scheme of position angle errors of permanent-magnet linear motors. IEEE Trans. Magn. **43**(10), 3868–3871 (2007)
16. Tan, K.K., Lee, T.H., Dou, H.F., Chin, S.J., Zhao, S.: Precision motion control with disturbance observer for pulse width-modulated driven permanent-magnet linear motors. IEEE Trans. Magn. **3**, 1813–1818 (2003)
17. Otten, G., Vries, T.J.A., Amerongen, J., Rankers, A.M., Gaal, E.W.: Linear motor motion control using a learning feedforward controller. IEEE/ASME Trans. Mechatron. **2**(3), 179–187 (1997)
18. Sankardoss, V., Geethanjali, P.: PMDC motor parameters estimation using bio-inspired optimization algorithms. IEEE Access **5**, 11244–11254 (2017)
19. Salah, M., Abdelatif, M.: Parameters identification of a permanent magnet DC Motor. Conference Paper, pp. 675–685 (2010). 10.2316/P
20. Kumar, C.A.: Multi-objective PI controller design with an application to speed control of permanent magnet DC motor drives. In: ICSCCN, pp. 424–429. IEEE (2011)
21. Vermeulen, H.J., Strauss, J.M.: Off-line identification of an open-loop automatic voltage regulator using pseudo-random binary sequence perturbations. IEEE, 0-7803-5546-6/99/, pp. 799–802 (1999)
22. Martins, F.G.: Tuning PID controllers using the ITAE criterion. Tempus Publ. **21**(5), 867–873 (2005)
23. Wasim, S., et al.: Microprocessor based permanent magnetic DC motor system identification and optimal PI controller design. In: Proceedings of the 12th INDIACom, IEEE Conference ID: 42835, pp. 1020–1026 (2018)

Cyber Threat Analysis of Consumer Devices

Hemant Gupta[1]($\boxtimes$) and Mayank Singh[2]($\boxtimes$)

[1] School of Computer Science, Carleton University, Ottawa, Canada
hemantgupta@cmail.carleton.ca
[2] Department of Computer Science and Engineering,
University of KwaZulu-Natal, Durban 4041, South Africa
mayank.singh@ieee.org

Abstract. Security is a crucial aspect of our lives. The concept of smart home infrastructure drives the idea of providing flexibility to the end-user, to control their home devices from the remote location. It contains the upgrade of home-devices from traditional mode to the internet. Manufactures of smart home devices focusing on the usability part and do not develop the smart home devices from scratch they use the solutions already provided by big IT companies. Due to the lack of the standard for IoT devices communication, these devices are incompatible with each other. Different types of attacks done on many smart home devices using malicious firmware, insecure communication channel, physical uploading the malicious software and many more. In this paper, we represent the analysis of the survey on different smart home solutions and devices done by many researchers in the past few years and solutions provided by them. Analyzing different authors work and recent incidents, we found that we are still far behind the smart home security. It is not only the responsibility of manufactures but also the duty of the end-user to take the security of these devices seriously by using proper preventive measures.

Keywords: Smart home · Internet of Things · Security · Smart bulb · Vulnerabilities

1 Introduction

Internet of Things (IoT) is one the rising topic in the economic world. The rapid growth of IoT devices promotes the usage of the smart home, a home system in which all the appliances, sensors, and services can be connected through the communication network and can be remotely monitored and controlled [1].

Smart home involves home automation with different high-level functionality like voice-controlled lights and door openers, automatic water flow sensors and smart meters used for energy efficiency, IP-enabled cameras, and many more [4]. Even though these devices are secure, attackers can manipulate these smart devices to cause physical, financial and psychological harm to the user. The old smart home system had a steep learning curve, hard device setup procedures, and mostly the user had to do the changes by himself manually. Nowadays, companies have implemented advanced systems that are easier for the user to set up because they are cloud-based and provide a programming framework for third-party developers to build apps [11].

© Springer Nature Singapore Pte Ltd. 2019
M. Singh et al. (Eds.): ICACDS 2019, CCIS 1046, pp. 32–45, 2019.
https://doi.org/10.1007/978-981-13-9942-8_4

The high diffusion of connected devices in the IoT has created a massive demand for robust security in response to the rising demand of millions of connected devices and services all over the world. The number of threats has been rising rapidly, and the amount of attacks has also been increased concerning impact and complexity. Attackers are becoming more sophisticated, efficient and effective. Therefore, to make the smart device which we use in our houses more secure, we need protection against threats and vulnerabilities. One example of a severe attack used by attackers is Mirai which self-propagating botnet virus [20].

Security is characterized as a procedure of ensuring an object against physical harm, unapproved access, robbery, or misfortune, by keeping up high confidentiality and integrity of data about the object and making the data about that object accessible when required [13]. An object is known as secure if the procedure can keep up its most extreme intrinsic values under various conditions. Security prerequisites in the smart home are not quite the same as some other frameworks. Subsequently, smart home security requires keeping up the most intrinsic value of both tangible objects (gadgets) and intangible ones (administrations, data, and information).

In this paper, we discuss different security issues related to smart home solution and devices. In Sect. 2, we are going to discuss the survey of different papers about smart home and its devices. In Sect. 3, we discuss the recent attacks on consumer devices. In Sect. 4, we discuss the summary of all vulnerabilities in smart home discussed in the previous section. In Sect. 5, we provide some preventive measures can be used by end-users and manufactures to avoid attacks. In Sect. 6, we provide a conclusion about the security related to smart homes.

2 Smart Home Threat Analysis

The smart home merely means building automation for home. It involves the automation of lights (smart bulbs), air conditioning (HVAC), security (smart locks). Smart home gives flexibility to users to control their home devices remotely through WIFI or internet. Smart home devices are consisting of sensors and switches connected to a central hub called gateway from which the system is controlled through as user interfaces like smart apps or mobile software or web interface. The smart home is heavily fragmented. Different manufacturers only focus on making devices, and there are no fixed standards that every industry has to follow, and due to which devices manufactured by different manufacturers are incompatible with each other [4].

Figure 1 taken from [5] shows the diagram of how the smart home system communicates. Any device that uses electric power can be connected to the home network. When the user gives the command by voice, remote control, tablet or smartphone, the home devices react. Most applications relate to lighting, home security, home theatre and entertainment, and thermostat regulation. Users manage their local network; smart devices associated with the local network and install SmartApps from an application store using smartphone application. Cloud backend runs Smart Devices, which are software wrappers for physical devices in the user's home. All communication between device, hub and the cloud are done over SSL-protected protocol. Apps and devices are communicating in two ways: the first one is when apps can invoke operations on devices via method calls. The second way is the app can send SMS and make network calls using smart devices APIs, i.e., software development kit (SDK) [1].

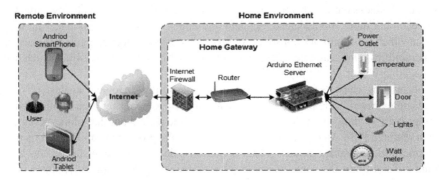

Fig. 1. Smart home communication system

Liu et al. [1] discussed the main problem with smart home devices are the smart solution but poor protection. The first problem that Liu and his team [1] find concerning is Wi-Fi provisioning, i.e., the Joylink app encodes the Wi-Fi credentials into a sequence of IP address which makes the credentials available to anyone in the vicinity. Wi-Fi credentials which broadcast by Joylink have no relationship with the user account. Therefore, the device does not send any acknowledgement about the Wi-Fi it connects. Thus, the whole configuration seems normal except when the device goes offline due to shut down the Wi-Fi by the attacker. Single party generates all the keys. A local adversary can launch the man in the middle (MITM) attack and can easily expose all those keys by eavesdropping the communication as there is no end to end encryption of data, throughout the whole process of communication, all commands and device uploaded data are visible to the cloud. An attacker can use those keys for traffic decryption, device hijacking. Another problem is related to the firmware modification [2]. The verification of the integrity of the update file is still missing, which allows attackers to modify the firmware and inject malicious code [1]. After analysis from this paper, we can say that design flaws in SDK and relevant network communication protocols, devices are inevitably vulnerable and can violate user's security and privacy [1].

Jang et al. [3] addressed the problem related to multi-user controls in smart home devices. Currently, most of the IoT devices implement a coarse-grained access model where a person in the house has complete access to the device or no access.

Avizheh et al. [12] propose a secure logging system for smart homes. Smart home devices generate notifications and communicate with each other and to the outside world. With the help of a proper logging system with fault detection, forensics and accounting we can detect any intrusion and attacks. Now we discuss the security issues in the few consumer IoT devices used in the smart home system.

2.1 Smart Lock

Smart locks are one of the common IoT consumer device used by many people. It follows the trend used in newer car models where the device automatically unlocks the door if it infers that a legitimate user intends to enter [14]. Many attacks took place on smart locks due to its weakness in system design. There are many issues related to the smart locks. An attacker can monitor the physical interactions of the owner with the smart lock and can also interact with the smart lock at any time. A guest user holds the legitimate access because he avoids the revocation of his access by putting the smartphone in flight mode. The attacker can also steal the authorizing device like user's smartphone. And common of all is relay attack.

Many authors have suggested different solutions for increasing the security for this. Ho et al. [9] indicate one novel defence based on the body area networks. Danalock is one of the locks studied by researchers [9] which allows users of any access level to interact with the lock, even when no internet connection. It helps the user to access lock even when the server is unreachable, but it also helps the guest user to avoid revocation by putting the phone in flight mode. Another one is Lockitron which has the embedded Wi-Fi modem connect directly to Lockitron servers. Lockitron servers send the request directly to lock through TCP connection. The side-effect of this design is if the server is down then authorized user is unable to unlock the house. However, it prevents the guest user with revoked keys to access the house. Geo-fencing (geofencing) is a feature that uses the global positioning system (GPS) or radio frequency identification (RFID) to define geographical boundaries, and Danalock uses it to makes relay attack more difficult but does not entirely prevent them.

Ho and his team [9] also suggested a solution for smart lock security issues by using vibrato protocol which is a touch-based intent communication (TBIC) through bone conduction. But this protocol requires the new hardware and not every person wears the smart device. Another problem with this protocol relies on sensing vibration in the human body, so using a relay attack with surface vibration, an attacker can generate the same frequency of vibration and able to unlock the door. Another weakness of this approach is the user cannot open a lock with a not correctly tied watch or a wristband/bracelet.

2.2 Smart Thermostat

The smart thermostat is the device that lets us remotely control the house temperature through the smartphone for controlling the heating. NEST [15] is one of the companies which develop smart thermostat. NEST thermostat learns from the user's input and starts making changes accordingly from the learning it has done. It connects to the internet, and with the Zip Code it checks the outside temperature and learns from the user behavior such as what temperature user set if colder outside and so on. It also shows some signal when the device is in energy saving mode. NEST also indicates that how is using heating and cooling system and how much energy user is consuming. It is also one of the expensive devices.

Security is also one of the most significant challenges for these thermostats. In August 2016 two researchers have developed first-ever ransomware for the thermostat

[16]. After many security issues reported, NEST starts sending the signed firmware updates to the device, but due to the lack of hardware protection, attackers can install malicious software on the thermostat by just accessing the device physically. An attacker can trigger a complete reset by inserting a USB (i.e. Universal Serial Bus) flash drive to enter developer mode, and then it takes 5 s to load a custom firmware. The compromised NEST thermostat then behaves as a point of source to attack other nodes within the local network. Any information stored within the NEST device is available to the attacker, who is now accessing the device remotely. With the help of compromised NEST device, an attacker could also manipulate ARP packets by pretending as the router, allowing the seizing of targeted network traffic. Beyond the NEST Thermostat, we believe that most of the current IoT and wearable devices suffer from similar issues, due to improper hardware protection to avoid similar attacks.

2.3 Smart Bulb

Smart Bulbs are another type of common IoT devices used in smart homes. They communicate through a wireless network allowing the user to control the intensity and sometimes color from his portable devices like laptop and smartphone. Many people use Philips Hue Smart Lamps which communicate using ZigBee wireless connectivity.

Ronen et al. [7] suggest, there are many modes of attack on IoT devices, like denial of service (DoS), limiting the functionality of the device, spoofing, man in the middle. However, researchers found a new type of attack on the functionality of smart bulbs by misusing the LED's API to switch between different level of light intensities which are not recognizable through human eye but detect through the detector, i.e., light sensor. The method can be used to send the information from one point to another. Philips has 256 levels of light intensities. Another hardware is the controller that acts as a gateway between the internet or LAN and the lights. The controller can control several different lights. The researchers used the undocumented API command to form a pulse width modulation (PWM) signal tailored to specific covert channel requirement to change the duty cycle of the smart bulb. Authors were able to differentiate between 253 out of 255 brightness levels. Researchers believe that with the help of highly sensitive light sensors and a higher sampling rate, this method is used to send data secretly. Using the available API's attacker were able to create the strobe of lights at frequency ranges that are known to induce seizures in photosensitive epilepsy. In this paper, researchers had used the network to develop unintended effects in the physical world by finding new ways to exploit the smart bulbs.

Ronen et al. [10], researchers use the smart bulbs communication to cause distributed denial of service (DDoS) attack. They created a worm, and it spreads from one bulb to its neighbor using the ZigBee wireless connectivity and their physical proximity. DDoS can easily achieve by plugging in a single infected bulb or over-the-air firmware updates. Communication between the lamp and their controller is carried out using ZigBee protocol [8] which is used by many IoT devices due to simplicity, wide availability, low cost, and low power consumption and robustness. Philips Hue bulb contains Zigbee chip which ignores any request for reset or change affiliation until it sent from a ZigBee transmitter within proximity. First significant bug in the Atmel microcontroller used by the smart bulbs is in proximity test, which enables any Zigbee transmitter to start the factory reset procedure which dissociates lamp from the current configuration. After that with a few command transmitters can take full control of the bulb. With reverse engineering and side channels attack, the authors were able to deduce all the secret cryptographic elements used by Philips for the firmware update. After this, researchers create a malicious firmware and upload it into any Philips smart bulb which spreads like a worm in the whole network like a chain reaction. The author believes that the same manner of the leaked Zigbee master, many other devices key might also get leaked. The use of global symmetric encryption for light bulbs is a significant security risk, and it enables attackers to form a chain reaction of corrupt software. Security by uncertainty has failed time after time.

3   Other Cyber-Attacks on IoT Devices

Many cyber-attacks took place every month. Few attackers became successful in exploiting the system. In January 2018, many critical cyber-attacks were reported in different domain like healthcare, finance, business and identity theft. We are going to discuss these attacks and how an attacker can exploit the weakness in the system.

3.1   Healthcare

Recently using local access attacks two recent security incidents took place. Philips is one of the big companies developing many products. However, the question here arises are they giving the same attention to the security of their product? Philips is currently working on developing IoT (i.e., Internet of things) devices to make human life easier and more comfortable. One of its devices is Philips Smart Bulb, which has been used by many researchers to prove that it can be used in large-scale denial of service attacks [10]. Now, another vulnerability of insufficient session expiration came into the picture from one of its healthcare devices, i.e., Philips IntelliSpace Cardiovascular (ISCV) which is cardiac image and information management systems [21]. ISCV helps the clinicians to get web-based echo reporting, delivering diagnostic quality viewing of echo images of the patient anytime and anywhere [22]. According to Philips, ISCV is deployed across the healthcare and public health sector and is used all over the world. With the help of this attack, an attacker can gain access to the sensitive health information of individuals and may even be able to modify the information. Let's take a simple example of the insufficient session expiration attack. Alice logs in on to her laptop and leaves it unattended without locking the system. In this case, Alice did not close her session, i.e., now Bob can go to her laptop and steal the information he wanted.

Insufficient session expiration means when a system allows an attacker to use old credentials for authorization. In a website where the session timeout parameter is explicitly defined, this can be done by setting the value of session timeout tag to −1, which means the session is never going to expire. Figure 2 is an example.

With the help of this vulnerability, an attacker might get hold of session id using network sniffer or cross-site scripting attack. Furthermore, a user accessing a website

```
<web-app>
[...snipped...]

<session-config>
<session-timeout>-1</session-timeout>

</session-config>
```

Fig. 2. Example of insufficient session expiration [23]

on the shared computer with no session expiration can result in the access to browser history and web pages used by the victim.

Wearable devices are currently facing many challenges regarding security. There are many types of attacks like Replay attack, Man in the middle attack, data modification and masquerading attack. Wearable devices are meant to make human life more manageable and allow smooth data exchange between user end to the remote server. Wearable devices are used in many areas like health, sports, entertainment and security. Size limitation and memory capacity is the biggest concern in the case of wearable devices. Security breaches in healthcare devices may have life-threatening consequences. Alkeem et al. [24] suggested that due to the increase in healthcare wearable devices healthcare system facing issues related to security concerning access sensitive data about the patients. They proposed the security framework based on authentication using biometrics and role-based access control (RBAC) method.

According to the McAfee Labs Threats Report [25] for March 2018, 2017 saw a 211% increase in security incidents as compared with 2016. Main vulnerabilities in healthcare organization contain hardcoded, embedded passwords, remote code execution, unsigned firmware, default passwords, password sharing. A recent example of failure in the healthcare industry is last year's WannaCry ransomware outbreak [26]. Hospitals across the UK hit by this ransomware and sue to which systems have been taken offline. Researchers have suggested the ransomware attacks are exploiting a known software flaw dubbed EternalBlue.

3.2   AADHAR Card - Database Breach

Software security is an essential concern for people in the case where crucial information is considered. In the below incident, there is no technical fault in the system, or of any hackers exploiting a bug in the software. Unfortunately, in today's world security is given the least priority in the complete development cycle of the product. Everyone is focused on the development of the new products, but there are quite a few who still take security as an integral part of the product design. Aadhar Card [27] is a digital identity which contains a QR-code which can be verified online from anywhere. Currently, the Aadhar card is used as an identity proof in almost every field like banking, private and government sector, passport development. This amount of detailed information collected is of critical importance for the individual. Such data leaks are very beneficial for the hackers, and such an incident came into the site on Jan9, 2018 [28]. According to the article, UIDAI (Unique Identification Authority of India) restricted about 5000 officials from accessing the Aadhar portal. There are two issues that we came across in this incident. First, giving high-level authorization to the officials (might be government or private), and the second problem is keeping a centralized database system for the whole information. In the next section, we are going to discuss these two issues in more technical details and how it helps attackers.

In case of this incident, the problem was related to the software security, it means they can view an individual's information without their permission, and they also have the rights to add any individual as an admin official with same rights and permission. This problem is related to providing wrong authorization permissions. Due to this authorization problem hackers got access to the whole database of the residents.

Another is the attacker has the authorization to easily access the whole database because it required only single credentials to access the complete centralized database. Due to these two big design issues, we are facing very severe implications. An attacker might download the whole database and sell it to anyone. An attacker might use an individual's details to perform any financial truncations. Terrorists update their information in the database, and it will cause a national level threat. This problem exists in the software of UIDAI from the beginning. An attacker can clean the whole database, and due to the centralized database, it will be very hard to recover any data.

3.3 ATM Hijacking

Using malware to infect a device is typically considered a critical attack. We have heard much news in the past about jackpotting the Automatic Teller Machine (ATM) by infecting it with malware in many countries. However, it was only reported to have been done in the USA just recently [29]. According to the reports, ATM's that were targeted belong to two companies Diebold Nixdorf and NCR Corp. These companies have alerted the banks. Hijackers are putting a malware named as Ploutus.D into the ATM to dispense cash out of ATM. The Attack is significant because since 2013 attackers are using the same malware to infect ATM in other countries but ATM development companies in the USA did not pay attention, or we can say that ignore it. In case of previous attacks, attackers dressed as an ATM technician and broke the lock of the ATM. The malware was contained in a boot disk which was inserted into the disk section of the ATM, that installed the malware into ATM. Criminals have created an interacting interface to communicate with ATM software on the infected ATM and can withdraw all the money [30]. Attackers who have designed Ploutus malware are updating it and using to attack the number of ATMs from different companies. Thus, hackers are well versed in ATM software architecture.

4 Summary of Vulnerabilities

We have studied different types of vulnerabilities by which an attacker can successfully attack the smart home. Let's discuss this one by one.

Insecure Web Interface - Insecure web interfaces [1, 11] are prevalent as the intent is to have the interfaces exposed only on the internal networks. However, threats from the internal users are as significant as threats from external users. There are many ways of in which an insecure web interface might occur.

a. Account Enumeration – It is a process in which in response to a failed authentication attempt, SmartApp or IoT device web server returns mentioning either the account identifier is incorrect, or the account password is wrong. It allows an attacker to determine the valid account identifiers recognized by the application iteratively and after many tries, he/she can guess both correct account identifier and account password. It is one of vulnerability.

b. Account Lockout – Many application websites do not have an account lockout in case of invalid identifiers by which an attacker can efficiently use a brute force attack to and tries to access the smart home application apps until he/she is successful. Therefore, it is necessary to lockout account after having 5 to 10 failed attempts.

c. Weak Default Credentials- One of the most significant problems with smart devices is people do not change the default password. They do not consider the severity of not changing the default password. Some people use the same password for all devices and easy to remember password from their personal information like date of birth. People also used to write the password on their device. If an adversary can get hold of that password, he/she can access the communication of the devices in the house and also able to attack.

d. SQL Injection- SQL injection is a code injection technique that might destroy databases by placement of malicious code in SQL statements, via web page input. SQL injection occurs when the user wants to search details of a particular entity, and instead of it, the attacker will give a SQL statement that user unknowingly run on the database. Using SQL injection vulnerability attacker can get the logs of the smart home devices. Using these logs attacker will be able to monitor the movements and access the data of different people in the house.

e. Session Management- Suppose we are accessing out smart home devices from the unregistered computer and after our work is done, we did not log out, just close the window. Now if there is no idle session timeout then any adversary who can access that computer and can easily control the devices or change password or modify their functionality

These all vulnerabilities are used by the attacker to attack the smart home devices. All smart home devices are connected to the internet for updating device and their functionality. If the interface is not secure (i.e., web communication using HTTP over TLS, implementing proper lockout and session expiration policy), then communication with that interface is also not trusted.

Authentication and Authorization - Many researchers have used these two terms as one, but there is a difference. Authentication means checking the identity of the person or device using their unique id or password or any other means. Authorization suggests different levels of permissions that a person holds. It might be possible two people are authentic to use a device, but only one person is authorized to perform any modification. In the smart home, we had multiple users and did not want to give everyone admin level permissions [1, 9, 14]. There are many reasons for poor authentication and authorization-

a. Poor Password Complexity and Protection- End-user, keeps the default password for the devices which is terrible from the security perspective and as we discussed in previous points sometime user placed the password such that it is easily in reach of the attacker. Mirai Botnet attack [20] on all IoT devices is the example in which an attacker tries to take control of the device remotely by a testing device with default passwords.
b. Lack of Two Factor Authentication - This one of the most severe vulnerability in this section. Two-factor authentication is the process in which user has two different keys required, i.e., something that the user knows (first factor) and something that the user has (second factor) before successfully authenticating the user's identity. Therefore, if a hacker only gains access to one factor, it will not be enough to gain authentication, making the system more secure.
c. Insecure Password Recovery – In case of authentication, the user sometimes forgot his password and wanted a method to recover the password, the process of recovery must be secure and encrypted, but many manufacturers send the plaintext password to the user through register electronic mail. If an attacker is monitoring the communication of emails, he/she can easily get the hold of the password.
d. Lack of Role Based Access Control (RBAC) - Many smart home apps do not have different levels of authorities. Therefore, every user in the house has admin level access. Also, if an attacker can get hold of any one of these devices, he can easily manipulate them for his purposes. With the help of RBAC, we can design an authorization matrix between roles and different authorization levels.

Due to these unfortunate choices of security used by manufacturers and users, its a paradise for an attacker. An attacker can monitor whole communication and can access any personal data and can cause even life-threatening attacks by accessing and modifying settings of different medical IoT devices like insulin monitor, heart rate monitor [17].

Insecure Software/Firmware - Devices should have the capability to be updated by itself when a manufacturer releases new software updates. Software/firmware updates can be insecure when the updated files themselves and the communication medium is not protected [7] [10].

a. Encryption not Used to fetch Updates- Channel used or communication with the software server for querying and getting the software/firmware from that server are not secure.
b. Update Not verified before Upload- Many smart home devices do not check the firmware/software integrity. The manufacturer does not use any digital signature to authenticate the firmware.

Software/Firmware can also be insecure if they contain hardcoded sensitive data such as credentials. Attackers use multiple ways such as capturing update files through unencrypted connections, the integrity of the update file cannot be verified, or they can perform their malicious update through DNS hijacking [18].

Other security issues for the smart home includes insecure mobile interfaces and insecure cloud interface with weak credentials allowing attackers to exploit. The main problem with the smart home consumer IoT devices is data privacy which is the collection of personal data, and health-related information can be used against user to control over one's life.

5 Proposed Preventive Measures

Basic security functions of the components of the smart home system are classified as confidentiality, integrity and availability. Many researchers have suggested different methods to protect the smart home network and devices against different attacks and vulnerabilities. Few of them can easily be implemented by manufacturers and used by end-users to protect themselves against any attacks. Please find few measures suggested by researchers and us to protect end-users against these attacks and vulnerabilities:

Password Security: Default password and default username should be changed during the initial setup phase. Ensure that the password recovery mechanism is robust, i.e., the manufacturer will not send plaintext password in case of recovery and do not provide an attacker with the information indicating valid account. The manufacturer should send the link for resetting the password on registered contact details. Ensuring valuable information like passwords are not hardcoded in the firmware directly [10]. Not using the same cryptographic key for all the devices of the same type, this will protect against the denial of service attack which sometimes used as a chain reaction [10].

Secure Communication Channel: All Cryptographic keys used should be generated by negotiating through a secure channel [1]. Data communication should always be through the secure channel encrypted over SSL/TLS or Wi-Fi Protected Access 2 (WPA2).

Access Control: Using granular access control methods like role-based access control [3] and two-factor authentication [10] where ever it is possible to improve the security measures.

Logging System: Enable logging of all type of security events in the home. Ensure notifying end user in case of any unauthorized or malicious entry or event.

Secure Update: Firmware or software file should be digitally signed using acceptable methods to verify the integrity of the software/firmware [10]. Ensuring the device can update itself through legitimate manufacturers website [19].

Physical Security: Data storage mediums such as USB ports should not be easily accessible and cannot be used to access the device maliciously.

Network Access: We can reduce the network accessibility of all medical devices and systems which helps the patient to avoid any remote attacks. We can also make sure that these medical devices are not accessible through the internet, they can only be used with the help of a short-range connection like low power Bluetooth. It will prevent the patient reports from getting stolen and used for any adverse purposes.

Firewall: We can also implement a security firewall for all medical and remote devices. With the help of the firewall, we can increase the level of protection for the devices. We do not allow our devices to get connected to the business networks to avoid many open sessions.

Expiration Time: We can set the expiration time as an absolute value as suggested above. With the help of this after this value, the user will authenticate again. It will reduce the attack surface and will avoid the loss of patient information.

Token: We can also use the token system, i.e., one-time password with a predefined timer which allows only people to access the device which has the token and once it is used, cannot be used again. Using this method combined with predefined time we can forcefully expire the session after the time is finished.

Logout: Logout option should be easily visible to the user, and once the user ends with the session, the logout function explicitly invalidates a user's session and disallow reuse of the session.

Other researchers like Nausheen et al. [31] and Hossinzadeh et al. [32] suggested two techniques for security in the IoT environment. They suggested that by applying to obfuscate and diversifying the software and code, i.e., operating systems and APIs on IoT devices. It mitigates the risk of large-scale attacks and also targeted attacks.

6 Conclusion and Future Work

In this paper, we have studied the security and privacy threats present in smart home solutions, apps, and devices and recent attacks taking place in other fields of IoT. Manufacturers are focusing on the user authentication, not the device and its communication network. Most of the vulnerabilities and attacks are caused due to the design flaws in the devices. Security is not considered as part of the design phase of the software, and when it was implemented at the end of the development cycle, there was always some vulnerabilities and gap left in the security of the device. Main security challenges are confidentiality, privacy and entity trust. Many IoT devices use the symmetric cryptographic algorithms for encryption; if an attacker gets hold of the key either from the manufacturer or by reverse engineering device, he can easily able to create attacks like DoS. IoT devices are small therefore cannot perform massive calculations. We could use a low-cost asymmetric public key cryptography for IoT devices [6].

Manufacturers primary goal is to ease the usability for end-users, due to which there is a trade-off between the usability and security. We must make this trade-off better regarding increased security with easily usable device for which both the security community and academia must take part in this process. We also must increase the awareness about the security to the ordinary people who are not academically inclined.

In the future, we will analyze all the vulnerabilities or attacks on IoT device based on user negligence or software vulnerabilities. We will also like to develop an automatic secure software development platform for IoT device where user interaction is minimal. There is lot of scope for improvement in IoT device mainly for low-level (8-bit or 16-bit) devices as due to their low computational power manufacturers uses minimal or very low security.

We can conclude that a lot of work remains to be done in the field of security for the Smart home and its devices, by both manufacturers and end-users. As future actions, the aim is to gain better in-depth knowledge of the threats facing Smart home infrastructure, as well as its consequences and look for better solutions.

Acknowledgement. We are thankful to Dr. Paul Van Oorschot for his guidance and constant supervision as well as for providing necessary information and support.

References

1. Liu, H., Li, C., Jin, X., Li, J., Zhang, Y., Gu, D.: Smart solution, poor protection: an empirical study of security and privacy issues in developing and deploying smart home devices. In: Proceeding of Internet of Things on Security and Privacy, IoTS&P@CCS in Dallas, TX, USA, 3 November 2017
2. Kanuparthi, A., Karri, R., Addepalli, S.: Hardware and embedded security in the context of internet of things. In: Proceedings of the 2013 ACM Workshop on Security, Privacy & Dependability for Cyber Vehicles (CyCAR 2013), pp. 61–64. ACM, New York (2013)
3. Jang, W., Chhabra, A., Prasad, A.: Enabling multi-user controls in smart home devices. In: Proceeding of Internet of Things on Security and Privacy, IoTS&P@CCS in Dallas, TX, USA, 3 November 2017
4. ABIresearch. Smart, April 2017. https://www.abiresearch.com/market-research/service/smart-home/
5. Oblick, D.: Just what is a 'smart-home' anyway?, May 2016. https://www.cnbc.com/2016/05/09/just-what-is-a-smart-home-anyway.html
6. Ozmen, M.O., Yavuz, A.A.: Low-cost standard public key cryptography services for wireless IoT systems. In: Proceeding of Internet of Things on Security and Privacy, IoTS&P@CCS in Dallas, TX, USA, 3 November 2017
7. Ronen, E., Shamir, A.: Extended functionality attacks on IoT devices: the case of smart lights. In: Proceedings of IEEE European Symposium on Security and Privacy (2016)
8. https://www.zigbee.org/zigbee-for-developers/applicationstandards/zigbee-light-link/
9. Ho, G., Leung, D., Mishra, P., Hosseini, A., Song, D., Wagner, D.: Smart locks: lessons for securing commodity internet of things devices. In: Proceedings of the 11th ACM on Asia Conference on Computer and Communications Security (ASIA CCS 2016), pp. 461–472. ACM, New York (2016)
10. Ronen, E., Shamir, A., Weingarten, A.O., O'Flynn, C.: IoT goes nuclear: creating a Zigbee chain reaction. IEEE Secur. Priv. **16**(1), 54–62 (2018)
11. Fernandes, E., Jung, J., Prakash, A.: Security analysis of emerging smart home applications. In: Proceeding of 37th IEEE Symposium on Security and Privacy (2016)
12. Avizheh, S., Doan, T.T., Liu, X., Safavi-Naini, R.: A secure event logging system for smart homes. In: Proceeding of Internet of Things on Security and Privacy, IoTS&P@CCS in Dallas, TX, USA, 3 November 2017

13. Nawir, M., Amir, A., Yaakob, N., Lynn, O.B.: Internet of Things (IoT): taxonomy of security attacks. In: The Proceedings of 3rd International Conference on Electronic Design (ICED), 11–12 August 2016
14. Bauer, L., Garriss, S., Reiter, M.K.: Detecting and resolving policy misconfigurations in access-control systems. ACM Trans. Inf. Syst. Secure. **14**(1), 28 (2011). Article id 2
15. Hernandez, G., Arias, O., Buentello, D., Jin, Y.: Smart Nest Thermostat: A Smart Spy in Your Home. http://www.cisco.com/web/about/ac79/docs/innov/IoT_IBSG_0411FINAL.pdf
16. King, R.: Nest is Turning Up the Security on Its Thermostats, 7 March 2017. http://fortune.com/2017/03/07/nest-thermostat-security/
17. Twentyman, J.: Hacking medical devices is the next big security concern | Financial Times (2018). https://www.ft.com/content/75912040-98ad-11e7-8c5c-c8d8fa6961bb
18. Qadir, M.: What is DNS hijacking and How It Works? PureVPN Blog (2018). https://www.purevpn.com/blog/dns-hijacking/
19. Gilburg, J.: Rsaconference.com (2018). https://www.rsaconference.com/writable/presentations/file_upload/spo2-r10_zero-touch-device-onboarding-to-iot-control-platforms.pdf
20. Shoemaker, A.: Incapsula.com (2018). https://www.incapsula.com/blog/how-to-identify-a-mirai-style-ddos-attack.html. Accessed 10 July 2018
21. Ics-cert.us-cert.gov: Philips IntelliSpace Cardiovascular System Vulnerability | ICS-CERT, 25 January 2018. https://ics-cert.us-cert.gov/advisories/ICSMA-18-025-01
22. Pennic, J.: Philips Unveils IntelliSpace Cardiovascular 2.1: 5 Things to Know, 29 August 2018. Hitconsultant.net. http://hitconsultant.net/2016/08/29/philips-unveils-intellispace-cardiovascular-2-1-10-things-know/
23. Cwe.mitre.org: CWE - CWE-613: Insufficient Session Expiration (3.0) (2018). http://cwe.mitre.org/data/definitions/613.html
24. Al Alkeem, E., Yeun, C.Y., Zemerly, M.J.: Security and privacy framework for ubiquitous healthcare IoT devices. In: 2015 10th International Conference for Internet Technology and Secured Transactions (ICITST), London, pp. 70–75 (2015)
25. Mcafee.com: McAfee Labs Threats Report, June 2018. https://www.mcafee.com/enterprise/en-us/assets/reports/rp-quarterly-threats-jun-2018.pdf
26. Palmer, D.: After WannaCry ransomware attack, the NHS is toughening its cyber defences | ZDNet (2018). ZDNet: https://www.zdnet.com/article/after-wannacry-ransomware-attack-the-nhs-is-toughening-its-cyber-defences/
27. Singh, K.: What is Aadhaar card and where is it mandatory?, 27 March 2017. The Indian Express. http://indianexpress.com/article/what-is/what-is-aadhaar-card-and-where-is-it-mandatory-4587547/
28. Agarwal, S.: UIDAI firewalls 5,000 officials post 'breach', 9 January 2018. The Economic Times. https://economictimes.indiatimes.com/news/politics-and-nation/uidai-firewalls-5000-officials-postbreach/articleshow/62423133.cms
29. Kerk, J.: First ATM 'Jackpotting' Attacks Hit US, 29 January 2018. https://www.bankinfosecurity.com/first-cases-atm-jackpotting-hit-us-a-10610
30. Regalado, D.: Criminals Hit the ATM Jackpot, 11 October 2013. https://www.symantec.com/connect/blogs/criminals-hit-atm-jackpot
31. Nausheen, F., Begum, S.H.: Healthcare IoT: benefits, vulnerabilities and solutions. In: 2018 2nd International Conference on Inventive Systems and Control (ICISC), Coimbatore, pp. 517–522 (2018)
32. Hosseinzadeh, S., Rauti, S., Hyrynsalmi, S., Leppänen, V.: Security in the Internet of Things through obfuscation and diversification. In: 2015 International Conference on Computing, Communication and Security (ICCCS), Pamplemousses, pp. 1–5 (2015)

Recognition of Hand Gestures and Conversion of Voice for Betterment of Deaf and Mute People

Shubham Kr. Mishra, Sheona Sinha, Sourabh Sinha,
and Saurabh Bilgaiyan$^{(\boxtimes)}$

School of Computer Engineering, KIIT Deemed to be University,
Bhubaneswar, India
{1606511,1606508,saurabh.bilgaiyanfcs}@kiit.ac.in,
sourabhsinha693@gmail.com

Abstract. Around 5% of people across the globe have difficulty in speaking or are unable to speak. So, to overcome this difficulty, sign language came into the picture. It is a method of non-verbal communication which is usually used by deaf and mute people. Another problem that arises with sign language is that people without hearing or speaking problems do not learn this language. This problem is severe as it creates a barrier between them. To resolve this issue, this paper makes use of computer vision and machine learning along with Convolutional Neural Network. The objective of this paper is to facilitate communication among deaf and mute and other people. For achieving this objective, a system is built to convert hand gestures to voice with gesture understanding and motion capture. This system will be helpful for deaf and mute people as it will increase their communication with other people.

Keywords: Sign language · Gesture recognition · Computer vision ·
Image processing · Convolutional Neural Network

1 Introduction

The language for deaf and mute people is sign language. This language is composed of conventional gestures, hand signs, finger spellings and hand gestures that represent the letters of alphabets. Sign language dates back to the 17th century where it was known as visual language. Sign languages are different in different countries, like in America, its American Sign Language, in India its Indian Sign Language and likewise in other countries [1]. Sign language as defined earlier is primarily composed of gestures.

The gesture is a form of nonverbal communication in visible actions of hand, face and other body parts convey a particular message. Manual gestures led to the evolution of language and this theory is known as Gestural Theory. This theory came in the 18th century and was the work of Abbé de Condillac [2]. Broca's and Wernicke's areas of the brain are used for gesture processing [3].

With technology, gestures can be recognized by the computer and are termed as gesture recognition. It is a well-known topic in computer science as well as language

© Springer Nature Singapore Pte Ltd. 2019
M. Singh et al. (Eds.): ICACDS 2019, CCIS 1046, pp. 46–57, 2019.
https://doi.org/10.1007/978-981-13-9942-8_5

technology. Interpretation of human gestures by the use of mathematical algorithms is the goal of gesture recognition. Use of camera and computer vision algorithms for interpretation of sign language is one of the many advances made in this field. Techniques from computer vision and image processing can also be used for gesture recognition.

Utilization of computer algorithms for managing and extracting useful information from digital images is called Image Processing. Image processing is modeled in the form of multi-dimensional systems [4]. The use of computer algorithms gives image processing advantage over analog means as it avails the implementation of those methods that provide sophisticated performance at various tasks [5]. Image processing is used for projection, multiscale signal analysis, feature extraction, and classification. Various techniques are used by image processing, few of which are Principal Component Analysis (PCA), Pixelation, Independent Component Analysis (ICA), Linear Filtering, Partial Differential Equations (PDE), Neural Networks, Image editing, Image restoration, and Hidden Markov Models [5].

To make computers gain understanding from videos and digital images is altogether a separate field, and the ways to do this job is dealt with by Computer Vision (CV). Computer vision is an interdisciplinary field that automates the tasks that humans do visually. Computer vision provides decisions by producing symbolic and numeric information from the real world. This generation of information is made possible by extraction of high dimensional features which is further made possible by acquiring the digital images, then processing those images that further led to an understanding of those images [6]. Using models constructed by aids of physics, geometry, statistics and learning theory, the understanding of images is seen as the disentangled form of symbolic information that can be extracted from digital images [7].

This paper is divided into 6 sections. The second section is all about the related works in this field. The third section is about other hand gesture recognition techniques that can be used. The fourth section is some basic concepts that are to be known before moving to the proposed system architecture. The fifth section is about how the system that is been proposed by this paper works along with results of recognition of various words and the last section is about the conclusion and future work that would be accomplished with help of the proposed paper.

2   Related Works

Some recent reviews explained various application on gesture recognition and the increasing importance of these applications in everyday life. For example:- Robot Control and Surveillance, Human-Computer Interaction, etc. These applications make use of different algorithms and tools. This section displays a few of these many research papers that demonstrate different types of gesture recognizing systems that make use of different algorithms:-

Shinde, et al. proposed in their paper a real-time, two-way talking approach based on image processing for hearing impaired and dumb people. In their proposed work, they created a system that recognized hand gestures with an accuracy of 82% and converted the speech into gestures/text with an accuracy of 84%. The authors suggested for more research in feature extraction to get more accurate results. Sood, et al.

proposed "AAWAAZ" which is a communication system for deaf and dumb. They proposed through their paper a system for recognition of gestures. Their future works include recognition of both hands as well creating an application for easy handle by deaf and mute people. Ahire, et al. proposed a paper that gave approach about two-way communication between deaf and dumb people. In their paper, they made use of Eigen Object Recognizer which states that more the practice datasets, more the efficiency. They further wish to build a system for blind people using the same technique. Prajapati, et al. proposed a conversion of hand gesture to voice using hand gesture recognition technique. They proposed a system for deaf and mute people that make use of image processing. Their system gave responses with an accuracy of 90% and was correct for most test cases. Raheja, et al. proposed an android based application for portable hand sign recognition. Their proposed system is an application that can be deployed on Android devices. Their system gives overall accuracy of 90% when android devices and computer with webcams are tested. Exclusively, their system's Android version provides 77% accuracy. Their future works include the use of a custom camera instead of webcams. Rajaganapathy, et al. proposed a paper for conversion of sign language to speech using gesture recognition technique. Authors have proposed a system that makes use of Kinect sensors. In their future works they will try to use another feature of Kinect sensors, that is, face recognition.

3   Gesture Recognition Techniques

3.1   Glove Based Methods

Multi-parameterized data is formed by making use of sensor devices that are attached to hand for creating a digitized image of a hand and to get the motion of fingers is termed as glove- based method. For more ease in the collection of data, i.e., hand movement and configuration, extra sensors are used [8]. Sentences are produced by combining computer analysis sensor data, finger flexures, and static data that are directly obtained from the sensors. Nowadays, the neural network is also being used to improve the system's performance [9]. Less computational time along with fast response are the two main advantages of glove-based method. One of the approaches in this method is the use of Accelerometer (ACC) and Surface Electromyography (sEMG) [10] sensors which are both used for measurement of gestures. Information of movement of hands and fingers are captured by ACA. Generation of different sign gestures is the work of sEMG. Speech/Text are produced by recognizing gestures that are obtained by processing the output signals of the sensors which are done by computers. The crucial disadvantage of this method is that it lacks in providing natural interaction to its users. The system that this paper proposes will not make use of gloves; instead it will be based on vision-based method.

3.2   Vision-Based Method

It requires a camera for its application [11]. The main advantage of vision based method is that it realizes natural interaction that was not provided by usage of extra devices. By describing the artificial vision, these systems try to complement biological vision by implementing hardware and/or software. To meet accuracy, robustness and other requirements, these systems need to be optimized, when there are a lot of challenges. These challenges are the requirements, few of which are: background invariance, lighting insensitivity, person and camera independence for achieving real-time performance. Analysis followed by recognition of static images are carried by using algorithms that produce sentences.

The algorithms that are followed are:-

Hidden Markov Model (HMM). Markov model is a branch of Probability Theory which is based on Markov Property. The property states it the current state on which future states depends and not on the past events. This assumption is helpful in computation that is otherwise intractable. In the Hidden Markov Model, states are partially observable. Observations are typically insufficient for determination of state but they are related to the state. This model finds its use in speech recognition. In speech recognition, the hidden state is text and data for observation is audio waveform [12]. For non- stationary data and more complex data structures, triplet Markov models and pairwise Markov models are generalized.

Artificial Neural Network (ANN). Taking inspiration from neural networks of animal brains, artificial neural network is established [13]. Artificial neurons at the connecting part have signals passing by. These signals, on the implementation of ANN, are represented as real numbers. By making use of non-linear functions of the sum of inputs, these real numbers are computed to get the output. These artificial neurons are collected into layers. Different types of transformation on inputs takes place in different layers. After traveling through multiple layers the signal traverses from the first layer/input layer to the last layer/output layer [13]. ANN find its use in various fields some of which are a medical diagnosis, machine translation, speech recognition, computer vision, playing board games and social network filtering.

Convolutional Neural Network (CNN). CNN is an extension of an artificial neural network with a deep, feed forward asset added to it. CNN is applied to analyzing visual imagery. Convolutional Neural Network is part of deep learning. It makes use of multilayer perceptrons that gives an advantage of minimal preprocessing. Space Invariant or Shift Invariant ANN are some of the names of Convolutional Neural Networks. These names are based on the translation invariant characteristics and shared weights [14]. Like Artificial Neural Networks, it also finds its inspiration in biological processes in which the pattern between neurons resembles animal visual cortex. It finds its uses in image and video recognition, recommender system, natural language processing, and medical image analysis. This paper makes use of 3D Convolutional Neural Network. Earlier, the value of a unit at a position (x, y, z) in the ith layer in the jth feature map is denoted as V_{ij}^{xy}, is given by,

$$V_{ij}^{xyz} = \tanh\left(b_{ij} + \sum_{m}\sum_{p=0}^{P_i-1}\sum_{q=0}^{Q_i-1}\sum_{r=0}^{R_i-1} w_{ijm}^{pqr} v_{(i-1)m}^{(x+p)(y+p)(z+r)}\right) \tag{1}$$

where tanh(.) is the hyperbolic tangent function, b_{ij} is the bias for this feature map, w_{ijm}^{pqr} is the value at position (p, q, r) of the kernel linked to the kth feature map, m indexes over the set of feature maps in the $(i-1)^{th}$ layer linked to the current feature map, and P_i, Q_i and R_i are the height, width and size of the kernel, respectively. The parameters of CNN are usually learned using either supervised or unsupervised approaches [15].

4 Basic Concepts

4.1 Grayscaling

Conversion to the image that can be manipulated by computer from a continuous- tone image is the work of Grayscaling. A weighted combination of frequencies is used for measuring the light intensity of each pixel. When the captured frequency is only a single frequency, then in these cases there are monochromatic images. The frequencies can be from anywhere in the electromagnetic spectrum be its visible light, ultraviolet, infrared, etc. Grayscale as its name suggest consists of images that contains only shades of gray unlike one- bit bitonal white and black images [16].

4.2 Canny Edge Detection

The technique of extracting structured data from captured image which further results in a reduction of the amount of data that is to be processed is called Canny Edge Detection [17].

Criteria for edge detection includes:

- Accurate detection of almost all edges shown in image with less error rate.
- Accurate localization of the edge detected on the center of the edge.
- Detected edges must be marked one time only and false edges should not be created by image noises.

The Canny edge detection algorithm is broken into 5 steps. These are:

Smoothing. Removal of noise from the image by blurring it as noises in images is inevitable no matter which camera is used. Removing noises is necessary as noises can be mistaken for edges. Smoothing is done by Gaussian filtering. For Gaussian filter kernel of size $(2m+1) \times (2m+1)$, the equation is given by,

$$H_{pq} = \frac{1}{2\pi\sigma^2} \exp\left(-\frac{(a-(m+1))^2 + (b-(m+1))^2}{2\sigma^2}\right) \tag{2}$$

$$1 \le a, b \le (m+1)$$

Finding Gradients. Edges of images with a large magnitude of gradients should be selected. Gradients of each pixel in a smoothed image are determined by using Sobel-operator. Before using Sobel-operator, gradients are approximated in x- and y-direction by using kernels. G_x and G_y are the gradients in x- and y- directions respectively,

$$|G| = \sqrt{G_x^2 + G_y^2}$$
$$|G| = |G_x| + |G_y| \tag{3}$$

Non-maximum Suppression. Only those edges are marked which have local maxima. This step is basically used for conversion of "blurred" edges into "sharp" edges. In this step, we follow the following steps:

- Relating to 8-connected neighborhood, change the gradient direction to possible nearest 45°.
- Do a comparison of edge strength between the current pixel and that of a pixel in negative and positive gradient direction.
- Conserve edge strength of those current pixels that has larger value otherwise suppress it.

Double Thresholding. Thresholds are used for determining potential edges. The edges are termed as strong when their edge pixels are more than the high threshold. Those edges are suppressed that have value less than the low threshold. The third category is of weak edges where edge pixels are between two thresholds.

Edge Tracking by Hysteresis. Final edges are drawn by suppressing those edges that are not linked to strong edges. In the final image, strong edges are included and only those weak edges are included that are connected to strong edges.

4.3   Gaussian Blur

Gaussian smoothing or also termed as Gaussian blur is a field of Image processing in which by making use of Gaussian function, images are blurred. It finds its uses in the reduction of image noise and reduction of details [18]. The act of combining Gaussian function and image is done mathematically by using Gaussian blur.

One dimensional formula of Gaussian function:

$$G(a) = \frac{1}{\sqrt{2\pi\sigma^2}} e^{-\frac{a^2}{2\sigma^2}} \tag{4}$$

The product of Gaussian functions in each direction results in two-dimensional formula:

$$G(a,b) = \frac{1}{\sqrt{2\pi\sigma^2}} e^{-\frac{a^2+b^2}{2\sigma^2}} \tag{5}$$

Where a is the distance from the origin in the x-axis, b is the distance from the origin in the y-axis, and σ is the standard deviation of the Gaussian distribution. The formula is given above results in a surface whose contours are concentric circles with a Gaussian distribution from the center point, when applied in two dimensions.

5   Proposed System Architecture and Results

Sign language is used as a medium of communication between deaf and dumb people. It becomes difficult for them to communicate with other people as other people do not learn sign language and thus to overcome this problem. Figure 1 shows the block diagram of the proposed system architecture. Each step will be explained in detail.

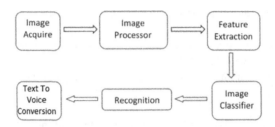

Fig. 1. System architecture block diagram.

5.1   Image Acquirer

The first stage of any vision system is the image acquisition stage [19]. Retrieving image from some source is defined as image acquirer for which a number of input devices are available these are hand images, data gloves, markers, and drawings. The image is acquired by using the normal camera used by different mobile devices with their own specifications. It is the first step in the workflow sequence because, without an image, no processing is possible. This paper proposes use of the OpenCV library for the image acquiring part. OpenCV simplifies the task through its inbuilt function

```
variable_name=cv2.video capture(0);
```

By default, images are continuously captured by the webcam at a frame rate of 30–40 frames per second [20]. And we can read the image by using OpenCV in-built 'read' function (Fig. 2 gives an example).

```
ret,frame=variable_name.read()
```

Fig. 2. Image acquired by using code snippet given above.

5.2   Image Processor

Image Processing is for image enhancement and for getting good results. The RGB image is acquired using the camera. By use of OpenCV, the input sequence of RGB images gets converted to gray images [21].

Separation of hand objects in an image from its background is the work Background Segmentation [21]. Removal of connected components or insignificant smudges in the image that has pixels less than P pixels, where p is variable value is the work of Noise elimination. Images are captured in RGB color space but they need to be converted to a grayscale image for two primary reasons:

1. Many OpenCV functions are optimized to work only on Grayscale images.
2. An RGB image would have thrice the number of features, which would increase the cost of Convolutional Neural Networks multifold [22] (Fig. 3 shows an example).

```
img_gray=cv2.cvtColor(frame_passed,cv2.COLOR_BGR2GRAY)
```

Fig. 3. Image converted to grayscale after using the above code snippet.

One more practical problem is the quality of frames being captured. Most of the webcams and video camera provide low-quality images and that could have been a major hurdle in edge-detection. Thus, this paper makes use of the blurring algorithms like Gaussian blur, bilateral blur to remove noise and strengthen the edges in images. So, we have used Gaussian blur algorithm to sharpen the images [18] (Fig. 4 shows the blurring effect).

Gaussian blurring effect is achieved by multiplying parts of images with the Gaussian kernel [18] (Table 1 shows an example of a Gaussian Kernel matrix).

Table 1. Gaussian kernel.

1	4	6	4	1
4	16	24	16	4
6	24	36	24	6
4	16	24	16	4
1	4	6	4	1

This matrix is divided by 256 i.e. the sum of all individual elements of matrix.
```
img_grey_blur=cv2.GaussianBlur(img_gray,threshold_value1
(e.g. 20),threshold_value2(e.g. 80))
```

Fig. 4. Image obtained on the right is after applying Gaussian Blurring.

5.3 Feature Extractor

For feature extraction different features like binary area, centroid, peak calculation, angle calculation, thumb detection, finger region or edge detection of the hand region is calculated. From the initial set, data is processed and hence builds derived values for the work of Feature extraction [23]. Feature extraction is intended to be non- redundant and informative. It facilitates sequential learning with generalization and in some cases leads to better human interpretations. The raw and initial set of variables are reduced to groups (features) for processing that precisely and totally describe the original set. Because of following steps, it is also known as the dimensionality reduction process [24]. There are many data analysis software packages for dimension reduction and feature extraction. Some of the numerical programming environments are SciLab, NumPy, R Language and the MATLAB [25]. These provide some of the feature extraction techniques by use of built-in commands. This paper makes use of NumPy environment for feature extraction. Feature Extraction is done by using edge detection. Edges can be defined as a sudden change and discontinuities in the picture [26]. OpenCV provides many edge detection algorithms like Sobel, Laplacian, Canny Algorithms. This paper makes use of the Canny algorithm as it was giving the best results (Figs. 5 and 6 shows two examples).
```
canny_edges=cv2.Canny(img_gray_blur,threshold1,threshold2)
```

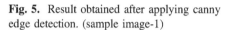

Fig. 5. Result obtained after applying canny edge detection. (sample image-1)

Fig. 6. Result obtained after applying canny edge detection. (sample image-2)

5.4   Image Classifier

Classification system database is very important that contains predefined sample patterns of the object under consideration that compare with the test object to classify its appropriate class. In a typical classification, system image is captured by a camera and consequently processed [27]. The neural network is one of the classification algorithms. Feeding the output to units in the next layer is called feed-forward. When signals are traversing from a unit to another unit, then it is termed as Weightings. To adapt the neural network to the particular problem at hand, these weightings are tuned in the training phase. For each hand gesture, a binary code sequence is generated which arranges the different hand gestures in different categories by making use of 2D Convolutional Neural Networks. By making use of customised datasets of words, the proposed system was trained.

5.5   Recognition

By making use of mathematical algorithms, with the aim of interpreting human gestures is topic of Gesture Recognition in the field of language technology and computer science. Mobile and computers are input devices that read input of gestures of the hand. Gestures are taken as input when the computer reads the movements of the body and sends it to the computer. The input is then interpreted by making use of artificial intelligence [28] (Fig. 7 shows recognition of digit 0). 10 Testing datasets were built for this purpose of which two are shown in Fig. 7 (i.e., digit 0) and in Fig. 8 (i.e., word "victory"). The recognizied word are the converted to voice by making use of Google audio built-in function "gTTS" in the following code:

```
tts = gTTS(text="victory", lang='en')
```

Fig. 7. Recognition of "0".   **Fig. 8.** Recognition of "Victory".

6 Conclusion

This paper proposes a research area in Computer Vision by creating a system that can recognize hand gestures without using sensors. The system proposed through this paper efficiently recognizes some of the keywords that are to be used in day to day life. This system is built for the betterment of deaf and mute people. In this paper, the research has been done in the field of Computer Vision and Machine Learning along with Convolutional Neural Networking. The proposed system is checked on 10 testing sets and worked with the accuracy of 86%. The proposed system works on recognition of words along with alphabets unlike other already proposed systems which recognises only alphabets. The system requires proper background light along with steady hands for correct recognition. Further extension of this system in an application format that could be easily installed in mobile phones which will definitely make it a lot easier for deaf and mute people to communicate. Extension of this paper includes recognition of Indian Sign Language (ISL) and other sign languages.

References

1. Bhat, S., Amruthesh, M., Ashik, Das, C., Sujith: Translating Indian sign language to text and voice messages using flex sensors. Int. J. Adv. Res. Comput. Commun. Eng. (4), 430–434 (2015)
2. Corballis, M.C.: The gestural origins of language. WIREs Cogn. Sci. **1**, 2–7 (2010)
3. Xu, J., Gannon, P., Emmorey, K., Smith, J., Braun, A.: Symbolic gestures and spoken language are processed by a common neural system. Proc. Natl. Acad. Sci. U.S.A. **106**(49), 20664–20669 (2009)
4. Chakravorty, P.: What is a signal. IEEE Signal Process. Mag. **35**(5), 175–177 (2018)
5. Tang, J., Rangayyan, R., Yao, J., Yang, Y.: Digital image processing and pattern recognition techniques for detection of cancer. Pattern Recogn. **42**(6), 1015–1016 (2009)
6. Klette, R.: Concise Computer Vision, pp. 1–429. Springer, Heidelberg (2014). https://doi.org/10.1007/978-1-4471-6320-6
7. Morris, T.: Computer Vision and Image Processing, pp. 1–320. Palgrave Macmillan. Springer (2014)
8. Garg, P., Aggarwal, N., Sofat, S.: Vision based hand gesture recognition. World Acad. Sci. Eng. Technol. Int. J. Comput. Electr. Autom. Control Inf. Eng. **3**(1), 186–191 (2009)

9. Li, Y., Chen, X.: Sign-component-based framework for chinese sign language recognition using accelerometer and sEMG data. IEEE Trans. Biomed. Eng. **59**(10), 2695–2704 (2012)
10. Chen, F., Fu, C., Huang, C.: Hand gesture recognition using a real-time tracking method and hidden Markov models. Image Vis. Comput. **21**, 745–758 (2003)
11. Quek, F.: Towards a vision based hand gesture interface. In: Proceedings of Virtual Reality Software and Technology, pp. 17–31. ACM (1994)
12. Wikipedia: Markov model (2018). https://en.wikipedia.org/w/index.php?
13. Cranenburgh, S.V., Alwoshee, A.: An artificial neural network based approach to investigate travellers' decision rules. Transp. Res. Part C: Emerg. Technol. **98**(1), 152–166 (2019)
14. Jeanguillaume, C., Colliex, C.: Spectrum image: the next step in EELS digital acquisition and processing. Ultramicroscopy **28**(1), 252–257 (1989)
15. Zhang, W., Itoh, K., et al.: Parallel distributed processing model with local space-invariant and its optical architecture. Appl. Opt. **29**(32), 4790–4797 (1990)
16. Jimenez-Fernandez, V.M., et al.: Exploring the use of two-dimensional piecewise-linear functions as an alternative model for representing and processing grayscale-images. J. Appl. Res. Technol. **14**(5), 311–318 (2016)
17. Ding, L., Goshtasby, A.: On the canny edge detector. Pattern Recogn. **34**(3), 721–725 (2001)
18. Coa, Z., Wei, Z., Zhang, G.: A no-reference sharpness metric based on the notion of relative blur for Gaussian blurred images. J. Vis. Commun. Image Represent. **25**(7), 1763–1773 (2014)
19. Ji, S., Xu, W., Yang, M., Yu, K.: 3D convolutional neural networks for human action recognition. IEEE Trans. Pattern Anal. Mach. Intell. **35**(1), 221–231 (2013)
20. Johnston, L.: What are webcam frame rates? (2018). https://www.lifewire.com/webcam-framerates
21. Shinde, S.S., Autee, R.M., Bhosale, V.K.: Real time two way communication approach for hearing impaired and dumb person based on image processing. In: IEEE International Conference on Computational Intelligence and Computing Research (ICCIC), pp. 1–5. IEEE (2016)
22. Seo, Y., Shin, K.S.: Hierarchical convolutional neural networks for fashion image classification. Expert Syst. Appl. **116**, 328–339 (2018)
23. Shi, D., Zhu, L., Cheng, Z., Li, Z., Zhang, H.: Unsupervised multi-view feature extraction with dynamic graph learning. J. Vis. Commun. Image Represent. **56**, 256–264 (2018)
24. Cai, J., Luo, J., Wang, S., Yang, S.: Feature selection in machine learning: a new perspective. NeuroComputing **300**, 70–79 (2018)
25. Xue, Y., Wang, Q., Yin, X.: A unified approach to sufficient dimension reduction. J. Stat. Plan. Infer. **197**, 168–179 (2018)
26. Di, H., Gao, D.: Gray-level transformation and Canny edge detection for 3D seismic discontinuity enhancement. Comput. Geo Sci. **72**, 192–200 (2014)
27. Gaur, R., Chouhan, V.S.: Classifiers in Image processing. Int. J. Future Revolut. Comput. Sci. Commun. Eng. **3**(6), 22–24 (2017)
28. Rehm, M., Bee, N., André, E.: Wave like an egyptian – accelerometer based gesture recognition for culture specific interactions. Br. Comput. Soc. **1**, 13–22 (2008)

General Outlook of Wireless Body Area Sensor Networks

Sharmila[✉], Dhananjay Kumar, KumKum Som, Pramod Kumar,
and Krista Chaudhary

Department of CSE, Krishna Engineering College, Mohan Nagar, Ghaziabad,
Uttar Pradesh, India
Sharmilalece@gmail.com

Abstract. One of the most promising fields is Wireless Body Area Sensor network (WBASN) which consists of a large number of wearable or implantable sensor nodes for collecting physiological data from the patients. The healthcare data is most sensitive digital data which contains high, delicate private data, and it needs to be shared among the peoples such as health specialists, pharmacist, family members, insurance companies, hospitals, etc. Due to the openness of wireless network, WBASN is vulnerable to a different variety of attacks; it needs high-security mechanisms to secure the data. The breach of healthcare information is one of the most crucial concern nowadays. In this paper, we mainly emphasise the general outlook of wireless body area sensor networks, which includes the architecture of healthcare system, various research domain, need of security and privacy of WBASNs. Further, the pro and cons of different security mechanism for WBASNs are discussed.

Keywords: Security · Privacy · Wireless body area sensor networks · Healthcare system · Attack

1 Introduction

Internet of Things (IoT) offers facilities without the intervention of human being for a various range of applications such as healthcare system, remote monitor the patient, etc. Remote Patient Monitoring integrates the physiological data collected from the human body and also other data such as health record, and geographical data of patients. Data privacy ensures that the person keeps control over the access of data. Due to the privacy breaches, the patient and healthcare providers can erode the trust in the system. Most of the healthcare providers break up the privacy of patient's data by providing it to the third party. Internet of Things [1] plays a significant role in the healthcare system without any human involvement.

Modern healthcare system architecture consists of Body Sensor Network (BSN) [2] which continuously monitor the patient and transmit the information to the remote healthcare professionals or remote cloud-based server. The challenges of designing an efficient healthcare architecture are based on how to transfer the sensitive data secure and efficiently, the process of aggregation and indexing a large stream of continuous data while preserving privacy.

M. Singh et al. (Eds.): ICACDS 2019, CCIS 1046, pp. 58–67, 2019.
https://doi.org/10.1007/978-981-13-9942-8_6

The security challenges of healthcare system [3] defined in two ways: (1) how to secure the communication between wearable sensor nodes to the gateway (2) how to secure the sensitive data in the data storage.

The primary key features and its challenges of WBASN's is as follows,

1. Fast Storage and Access: The body area sensor networks generate a huge volume of data which needs to be processed rapidly to provide quick response for some diseases. Generally, sensor nodes are limited in energy, processing, communication range, storage, and computation. The sensor nodes have a great challenge to perform computation processing and storage resources. The data which generated from the patient's body sensors are not necessary to be a sensitive data or store [4].

2. Authentication of Users: To prevent the attacker from intercepting the flow of data, the authentication of the user is a must [5]. An authenticated node only can participate in the data transfer. Even though the symmetric and asymmetric algorithms are used to provide confidentiality of the data which cannot be decrypted without using the key. In asymmetric cryptography algorithm uses a trusted third party to serve the public and private key pairs. The dependencies of a trusted third party lead to security pitfall, stop monitoring the real-time patient's data, fault tolerance, and create bottleneck problems in the Internet of Things settings. The basic asymmetric cryptography algorithms have more complex computation as compared to the symmetric key algorithm. Most of the healthcare architecture system uses a symmetric key algorithm to generate a key between the BSN and patient-centric agent; asymmetric algorithm and Blockchain are used to secure sensor data provider and database.

3. Role-Based Access: Role-based access control discusses the delimited rights of healthcare experts on patient's data according to the proficiency. The healthcare information contains the sensitive information about patient's health; patients can allow restricting the access based on role.

The main contribution of this paper is to address the challenges and issues of WBASNs. The rest of the paper organized as follows. Section 2 presents the architecture of the healthcare system. Section 3 offers a brief introduction to WBASN architecture. Section 4 discusses the need for security and privacy as well as a literature review of WBASN.

2 The General Architecture of the Healthcare System

The general architecture of a healthcare system consists of three tiers. The tier 1 and tier 2 is the architecture of WBASN [8]. Tier 3 is the data storage. Once the data collected from the gateway node, the data is either stored in a distributed/local access database or centralized remote access database. Figure 1 shows the architecture of a healthcare system which consists of wireless body area sensor networks and health blockchain. The body area sensor nodes are deployed on the body of the user and which consists of wearable nodes or implantable nodes to measure the physiological signs and sends the signals to the gateway node. The gateway nodes perform the aggregation operation and transmit the physiological data to the hospitals or healthcare professionals.

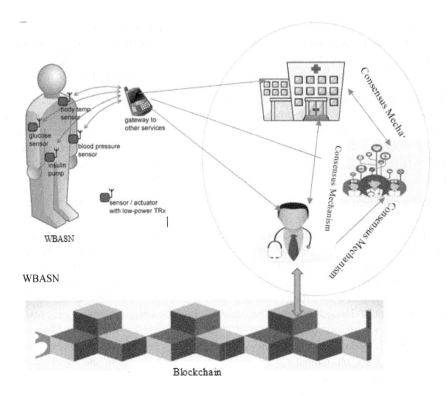

Fig. 1. Healthcare system with a body sensor network and blockchain

In case of distributed data storage and access, the nodes form a group and provide a blockchain node. The healthcare blockchain is maintained employing a consensus mechanism, digital signature, and hash function. Once the node receives physiological data from the gateway node, it checks the validity of the message by using a consensus mechanism. If the message is valid, the digitally signed message is put it on blockchain otherwise it will reject the message. The distributed storage healthcare system provides the solution for integrity and vulnerability problems of healthcare data storage by make use of multi-node backup and digital signature [9].

The privacy problem can be solved by using a key management scheme in WBAN to secure the broadcast message from the sensor nodes to the gateway as well as a gateway to the health blockchain. Firstly, the biosensor nodes placed on the user's body generates a key using physiological signals or lightweight key management scheme to encrypt the signals. Secondly, the gateway node sends the encrypted message to the healthcare blockchain. The healthcare professional/hospital or blockchain node does not have any knowledge about the decryption key; they could not be able to perform decryption.

Figure 2 shows the various research domains [8] in the healthcare system. In the past, the various research methodologies are used to analyses the information security of healthcare system such as design, qualitative and quantitative research. The design methodology focusses on algorithms, prototypes ad framework to solve a particular problem on the information system. The qualitative research on healthcare examines the influence of HIPAA regulation on practices [11]. The quantitative methods include statistical modeling, review based research, fraud control, medical errors, and public policy.

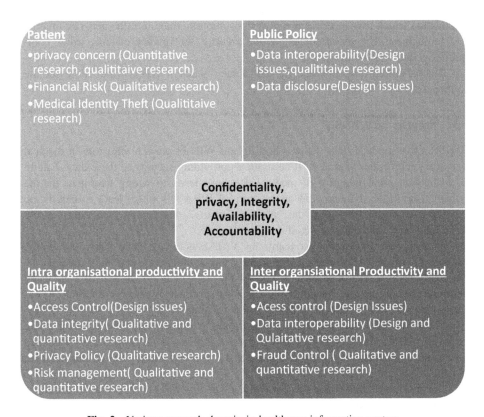

Patient

- privacy concern (Quantitative research, qualititaive research)
- Financial Risk(Qualitative research)
- Medical Identity Theft (Qualititaive research)

Public Policy

- Data interoperability(Design issues,qualititaive research)
- Data disclosure(Design issues)

Confidentiality, privacy, Integrity, Availability, Accountability

Intra organisational productivity and Quality

- Access Control(Design issues)
- Data integrity(Qualitative and quantitative research)
- Privacy Policy (Qualitative research)
- Risk management(Qualitative and quantitative research)

Inter organsiational Productivity and Quality

- Acess control (Design Issues)
- Data interoperability (Design and Qulaitative research)
- Fraud Control (Qualitative and quantitative research)

Fig. 2. Various research domain in healthcare information system

3   Wireless Body Area Sensor Networks (WBASNs)

Due to the recent advancement in wearable sensors, a miniature of sensor nodes and low power microelectronic devices which enabled the design and increases rapidly the use of wireless sensor networks to monitor and control the environment uninterruptedly. One of the most critical applications of WSNs is health monitoring. The wireless body area network consists of enormous number of tiny sensor nodes which placed on the human body to monitor the different signs of a body part and provide the real-time feedback to the healthcare professional and user. Wireless Body Area Sensor Networks perform the following operation such as monitoring, sampling, processing, and communication. WBASNs were emerging as well as essential techniques which revolutionize the way of looking for healthcare which is termed as E-Healthcare [13]. It provides an opportunities to monitor the patient on real-time remotely and continuously and then processed data and communicate to the medical database. The medical data stored in the database shared among various users such as healthcare professionals, researchers, insurance companies, and government agencies. WBSNs have technical as well as social challenges to adopt it for practical applications. The main objectives of technical challenges are in system design and implementation such as minimizes the delay, needless communication which associated with energy consumption, maximize the network lifetime and throughput. The social challenges are security, the privacy of data, value, compatibility, and without difficulty.

This paper addresses the security and privacy issues of WBANS not addressed the routing issues of WBSNs.

3.1 Security of WBASN

The sensitive medical data which stored in the WBAN plays a vital role in medical diagnosis and further treatment. It necessitates providing security to these data. Failure of authenticity and integrity of medical data will leads to wrong treatment for the patient. Due to the dynamic and open nature of WBASNs which leads to data being lost. It is essential to protect the patient's sensitive data against malicious attack, modification of data and ensures the fault tolerance.

The privacy is essential concerns in WBASNs which hold back the public acceptance of WBASNs technology. Only the authorized users must access the patient's sensitive data otherwise the patient's privacy could be ill-treated. The Health Insurance Portability and Accountability Act (Government Agencies) of 1996 [14] has mentioned the set of necessary privacy rules to protect the patient's sensitive information. In WBASNs, the private data's are stored in a distributed manner which could be easily seeped due to physical compromise of the node. The data encryption and authenticated accesses control must be desired to protect the privacy of the sensitive patient's data.

The design of security and privacy mechanisms for WBANs have more challenges to balance security, resource constraints, and real-time application. Due to the resource constraint nature of sensor nodes, it needs lightweight cryptographic techniques to secure the data. The real-time application issues need to be considered such as conflicts between safety, security, usability, and accessibility in case of emergency. Researchers have been proposed several prototypes implemented for WBASNs; still the security and privacy issues are addressed few. Table 1 shows the different security mechanisms for WBASNs.

Security in Wireless Body Area Networks. WBASNs consists of considerable number of tiny sensor nodes. Each sensor nodes are resource constraints regarding limited power, storage (memory), communication range, limited processing, computational competency, and security vulnerabilities, etc. The traditional security algorithm proposed for other networks are not suitable for WBASNs due to resource constraint like sensor nodes.

The security standard for WBASNs was defined by IEEE 802.15.6 which defines three levels of security as follows,

Table 1. Pros and Cons of different security mechanism for WBASNs.

Category	Survey	Area of Interest	Pros	Cons
WBASN	Lamport et al. [7]	Password authentication with insecure communication	• The mobile user can authenticate with the remote server • Generate session key	• Not addressed the privacy issues
	Li et al. [1]	• Public key and identity cryptography protocol	• The user generates own public and private key pair	• High computational cost and certification required • Not suitable for WBASN
	Liu et al. [2]	• Certificate less signature scheme	• Without certificate, the user can anonymously access healthcare service	• Public key replacement attack • Not support forward security and scalability
	Xiong et al. [3]	• Anonymous Certificate less remote authentication protocol	• Scalability • Revocation	• Expensive bilinear pairing operations
	Shen et al. [4]	• Certificate multilayer authentication protocol	• No certificate • Reduce client storage	• Privacy of client not addressed
	Omala et al. [5]	• The efficient remote authentication scheme	• Overcome the limitation of application provider impersonate the client	Conditional privacy of client not addressed in case of emergency

Level-0 Unsecured Communication. In this level, the data transmitted in an unsecured manner. It does not provide any measure of security such as authenticity, integrity, privacy, confidentiality, and validation.

Level 1 Authentication Without Encryption. In this module, the data is authenticated but not encrypted frames. It provides the measure of integrity, authenticity, and defense of the replay attack. This level does not provide privacy of data and confidentiality.

Level 2 Authentication and Encryption. In this level, the message is encrypted, and authenticated frames are transmitted which is considered as the highest level. It provides authentication, confidentiality of the message, integrity, validation of the message, and defense against a replay attack, privacy, and confidentiality. It addresses the problems of level 0 and level 1. Security in Wireless Body Area Networks.

4   Need for Security and Privacy of WBASNs

The security and privacy are crucial components for patient's related system. Concerning security, the data is stored securely and transferred. The privacy means a data can be view and use by the authorized person. Some of the security requirements of WBASs are as follows.

4.1   Data Storage Threats for WBANs

Generally, the wireless body sensor network works in an open environment can be easily accessed by the various staff at hospital Microsoft virtual academy which causes the threat to the data. In WBANs, the communication is carried out in an open/wireless channel which makes data prone to modified, snooped, and injected. Two types of threats considered such as node compromised and network dynamics. Node compromise Threats: WBAN consists of more number of sensor nodes which are not-tamper proof. Before sensor nodes placed in the human body, the secret information such as encrypted data, and encryption key. If the attacker compromises the sensor nodes, the secret key information can be retrieved quickly. The gateway/server may not be trustworthy; the attacker was trying to access the patient's private data from the node. The attack can be carried out by either internet or merely capture the node in person.

Network Dynamic Threats. Generally, WBASN is highly dynamic. Due to the network connectivity or accidental failure node may join or leave from the network often.

Needs for the Security of Distributed Data Storage. The main requirements for distributed data storage are confidentiality, the integrity of dynamic data, and dependability.

Confidentiality. The patient's data need to be kept confidential to prevent the data storage from leakage. The confidentiality of the data resists against the node capture attacks. From the compromised node, the attacker gains nothing or little bit information from the data stored at the captured data.

Dynamic Integrity. In wireless body area sensor networks, the patient-related data is sensitive data and significant. If the sensitive data is modified which leads to catastrophic consequences.

Dependability. Dependability of patient's related data is an essential concern in WBASNs because retrieve correct data from the failed node become a life-threatening issue. The Fault tolerance is needed to tackle the threats caused by network dynamics.

4.2   Data Access Security Requirements

Access Control. Access control is one of the vital parameters needs to be enforced in WBASNs to prevent the privacy of the data which cannot be accessed by unauthorized persons.

Scalability. The access control should be scalable because of various patient-related data of users.

Flexibility: The patients should have the flexibility to access the data.

Accountability: The user of WBASNs misuses the privilege of data to carry out unauthorized actions on patient's related data which should be identified and accountable.

Revocability. The rights of users should be underprivileged in time if they are identified as compromised or behave act as a malicious node.

Non-repudiation. The source of a patient's related data cannot be denied by the sender that generated it.

4.3   Other Requirements

The other requirements of data security and privacy for WBAN are authentication and availability.

Authentication. It is a necessary security service to prevent inject false data, DoS attacks, and to verify the authenticity of user identity before access the data.

Availability. The patient's data should be available even under the DoS attacks.

4.4   Open Areas for Research

The need and security issues of WBASNs proves the need for further research in this area of WBASNs. Most of the works have been only focused on security issues which failed to address the privacy and Quality of Service (QoS) along with security. For the healthcare system, the data security along with the privacy acts as a better platform. Most of the research works are carried out on static wearable or implanted sensor networks. It needs further research in the direction of mobility of WBASNs (M-healthcare system). Healthcare information contains high, delicate private data, and it needs to be shared among peoples such as health specialists, pharmacist, family members, insurance companies, hospitals etc. Healthcare organization have not only their patient's medical details which include insurance and financial account information. The healthcare system needs a high level of reliable policy sets to protect the privacy of patient's. Some challenging issues need to be addressed are summarized below:

Communication and Services. Due to the rapid development of technologies and communications which provides low power data broadcastings. A distinctive example is the Bluetooth, GPS, RFID, wireless sensor networks, video surveillance, wireless fidelity and Frequency modulation radio reception and transmission, for embedding applications. Incorporating these new technologies can improve the performance of Wireless body area sensor networks.

Sensor Devices. The main characteristics for sensor nodes are comfortable to wear, do not need skillful features, and not required precise patients positioning. Researchers need to address signal processing, sensor materials, signal acquisition, conditioning etc. The sensor nodes are implanted or worn by the people. It is necessary to addresses the physical compatibility of sensor nodes with human tissues and the size of body area sensor node.

Media Access Control. Some of the critical issues need to be address in MAC protocols for body area sensor node are as follows:

Capacity of Network. The size of packet generated by the body area sensor nodes is relatively small and very limited performance capacity due to inefficient MAC operation. WBASN needs reduced overhead MAC protocols.

Heterogeneity of Sensor Nodes. The characteristics of sensor nodes have diverse memory capacity, limited power consumption, and QoS requirements. Due to the heterogeneity nature of senor devices leads to a significant challenges.

Quality of Support (QoS). The following issues need to be addressed on the QoS.

Delay and Energy Consumption. The less duty cycle leads to lesser throughput and higher packet delay. The dynamic change of duty cycle is needed for better performance.

Synchronization. The critical problem of distributed data collection need to be addressed. Many scheme have been studied for WSNs, limited scheme has been done for WBASNs. It needs tight synchronization to measure a delay between two nodes which comprise clocks. Synchronization between the two clocks plays very important role in the accuracy of delay measurement.

Other Issues. Some of the other open research issues as follows:

- Power supply
- Standardization
- Security and privacy

5 Summary

In recent days, the wearable sensor devices are an integral part of human being which improves the quality of life. The wireless body area sensor networks take along out many challenges such as energy consumption, QoS, security, and privacy which are highlighted in this paper. The security of data and privacy in wireless body area senor networks and e-healthcare system is an important research area and still have a more number of challenges to overcome. In this paper, the needs and current measure of security and privacy of WBASN have been discussed along with the open area of research in the area of WBASNs have been outlined.

References

1. Li, M., Yu, S., Guttman, J.D., Lou, W., Ren, K.: Secure ad hoc trust initialization and key management in wireless body area networks. ACM Trans. Sens. Netw. **9**(2), 1–35 (2013)
2. Liu, J., Zhang, Z., Chen, X., Kwak, K.S.: Certificateless remote anonymous authentication schemes for wireless body area networks. IEEE Trans. Parallel Distrib. Syst. **25**(2), 332–342 (2014)
3. Xiong, H., Qin, Z.: Revocable and scalable certificateless remote authentication protocol with anonymity for wireless body area networks. IEEE Trans. Inf. Forensics Secur. **10**(7), 1442–1455 (2015)
4. Shen, J., Chang, S., Shen, J., Liu, Q., Sun, X.: A lightweight multi-layer authentication protocol for wireless body area networks. Future Gener. Comput. Syst. **78**, 956–963 (2018)
5. Wang, C., Zhang, Y.: New authentication scheme for wireless body area networks using the bilinear pairing. J. Med. Syst. **39**(11), 136 (2015)
6. Alemdar, H., Ersoy, C.: Wireless sensor networks for healthcare: a survey. Comput. Netw. **54**(15), 2688–2710 (2010)
7. Lamport, L.: Password authentication with insecure communication. Commun. ACM **24**(11), 770–772 (1981)
8. Alam, M.M., Hamida, E.B.: Strategies for optimal mac parameters tuning in IEEE 802.15.6 wearable wireless sensor networks. J. Med. Syst. **39**(9), 1–16 (2015)
9. Ren, Y., Wang, G., Yu, L., Shi, B., Hu, W., Wang, Z.: Rigorous or tolerant. Future Gener. Comput. Syst. **83**(C), 476–484 (2018)
10. Omala, A.A., Mbandu, A.S., Mutiria, K.D., Jin, C., Li, F.: Provably secure heterogeneous access control scheme for wireless body area network. J. Med. Syst. **42**(6), 1–14 (2018)
11. Liu, X., Jin, C., Li, F.: An improved two-layer authentication scheme for wireless body area networks. J. Med. Syst. **42**(8), 1–14 (2018)
12. Shen, J., Chang, S., Liu, Q., Shen, J., Ren, Y.: Implicit authentication protocol and self-healing key management for WBANs. Multimed. Tools Appl. **77**(9), 11381–11401 (2018)
13. Jian, L., Yang, X., Zhou, Z., Zhou, K., Liu, K.: Multi-scale image fusion through rolling guidance filter. Future Gener. Comput. Syst. **83**(C), 310–325 (2018)
14. Lei, M., Yang, Y., Ma, N., Sun, H., Zhou, C., Ma, M.: Dynamically enabled defense effectiveness evaluation of a home Internet based on vulnerability analysis and attack layer measurement. Pers. Ubiquit. Comput. **22**(1), 153–162 (2018)
15. Body sensor Networks. http://ubimon.doc.ic.ac.uk/bsn/m621.html

Hybrid Fuzzy C-Means Using Bat Optimization and Maxi-Min Distance Classifier

Rahul Kumar[1], Rajesh Dwivedi[1($\boxtimes$)], and Ebenezer Jangam[2]

[1] Indian Institute of Technology (ISM), Dhanbad, India
Rahulkumar7275@gmail.com, anubhav.dwivedi8@gmail.com
[2] Vignan Foundation for Science Technology and Research, Vadlamudi, India
ebenezer.jangam@gmail.com

Abstract. Fuzzy c-means (FCM) is a frequently used clustering method because of its efficiency, simplicity and easy implementation. Major drawbacks of FCM are sensitivity to initialization and local convergence problem. To overcome the drawbacks, the proposed method describes a hybrid FCM using Bat optimization and Maxi-min classifier. Maxi-min classifier is used to decide the count of clusters and then pass that count to randomized fuzzy c-means algorithm, which improves the performance. Bat optimization is a global optimization method used for solving many optimization problems due to its high convergence rate. Two popular datasets from kaggle are used to show the comparison between proposed technique and the fuzzy c means algorithm in terms of performance. Experiment results showing that the proposed technique is efficient and the results are encouraging.

Keywords: Fuzzy clustering · Maxi-min Distance classifier ·
Bat optimization · Randomize fuzzy clustering · Big data processing

1 Introduction

Clustering is a procedure of dividing a set of n objects into K disjoint groups based on a similarity index. The objects in a group or cluster are alike and the objects of different groups are not alike when similarity index is considered. During 1955–67, different versions of K-means algorithm were proposed by researchers working in different fields. K means algorithm brought a revolution in the field of data clustering as it is efficiency, simplicity and easy implementation. Although K-means is a popular clustering algorithm, it is not suitable for datasets without well defined boundaries among the clusters.

In 1983, Fuzzy c-means Clustering [1] was developed by Bezdek to perform the clustering on those dataset which do not have well defined boundaries among the clusters. Fuzzy c-means clusters the data points such that a data point can be a member of more than one cluster with a determined degree. This determined

M. Singh et al. (Eds.): ICACDS 2019, CCIS 1046, pp. 68–79, 2019.
https://doi.org/10.1007/978-981-13-9942-8_7

degree is called the membership value of data points and membership value remains in range between 0 to 1.

Even though fuzzy c-means is one of the most commonly used techniques, there are some problems. The main problems associated with fuzzy c-means are (i) randomly generated cluster centers are used for initialization and (ii) probability of getting trapped in local minima is high.

In spite of the popularity of fuzzy c-means, the drawback of the algorithm is that it can be trapped at the local optimum rather than global optimum [2]. In this paper, we propose Randomized Fuzzy c-means clustering with Maximin Distance Classifier [3] based on Bat optimization. Bat optimization [4] has a property of achieving a high rate of converging at global optimum. Bat optimization is swarm based optimization technique. There are many other swarm based optimization techniques like [5], ACO [6], GA [7], Simulate annealing [8] etc. But due to good convergence rate, we use Bat Optimization. For achieving good performance result in the average case, we first randomize the data and then de-randomize the data.

Another problem with fuzzy c-means is uncertainty about the count of clusters at the time of initialization. Fuzzy c-means expects that number of clusters to be chosen randomly. This results in uncertainty if prior knowledge is not available about the number of clusters. To resolve this problem, Maxi-min Distance Classifier algorithm is used. in proposed method. First, the Maxi-min Distance Classifier is applied to know the count of clusters and then pass count to the Fuzzy c-means algorithm.

The organization of paper is in following manner. Section 2 outlines the existing techniques to optimize the fuzzy c-means clustering. Section 3 gives details about Min-max distance classifier. Section 4 contains the fuzzy c-means algorithm. Section 5 describes the bat based fuzzy c-means and Sect. 6 contains details about the proposed algorithm using bat optimization and min-max classifier. Section 7 contains the details about the datasets, experimental results and comparisons. Section 8 concludes the paper.

2   Related Works

Shen and Shi [9] proposed a solution to the convergence problem of Fuzzy c-means using fuzzy decision theory. In Fuzzy c-means clustering, convergence depends on initial weighting parameters, but the solution proposed was based on Fuzzy Decision theory which adaptively and automatically chooses the weighting parameters.

Izakian and Abraham [10] used Particle Swarm Optimization (PSO) for stochastic global optimization. They proposed a Hybrid technique for Fuzzy clustering which is based on Fuzzy PSO and FCM.

Li and Liu [11] proposed a fuzzy clustering algorithm based on PSO to remove the shortcoming of FCM like low convergence rate, local optimum and sensitivity to initialization.

Wang and Fang [12] developed and evaluated an algorithm based on data density pattern to solve initialization problem of PSO based FCM because PSO based FCM incurs more computation cost and random initialization in processing big data.

Wang [13] compared the similarities and differences between the three type of fuzzy c-means techniques, they are None Euclidean Relational fuzzy c-means (NERFCM), fuzzy c-means (FCM) and Traditional Relational fuzzy c-means (RFCM).

Kwok and Smith [14] introduced Parallel FCM for a large data set. An algorithm is designed to perform better on parallel computers of the (SPMD) single program multiple data with MPI.

Congli and Dawei [15] introduced a different and new velocity equation of PSO algorithm based on FCM for analysis of current particle's position. PSO with constriction factor (CPSO), the proposed algorithm gives a better result as compare to standard PSO (SPSO) in tests with a set of six benchmark functions with different dimensions.

Researchers have applied different metaheuristic optimization algorithms such as Particle Swarm Optimization (PSO), ant colony optimization (ACO) and Artificial bee colony (ABC) for the various applications. The benefit of using these optimization techniques that they can give the global optimization results without trapping into local optimum.

Due to the simplicity and versatility of PSO, it is widely used in many applications. On the other hand, clustering methods based on PSO take more time for execution when compared with partitional clustering techniques. Moreover, for current PSO algorithms, it is required to tune multiple parameters in order to obtain good solutions. Hence, a solution is proposed in the paper for the local convergence problem of fuzzy c-means using bat optimization and minmax classifier.

3   Maximin Distance Classifier

Maxi-min distance classifier clusters the data based on euclidean norm concept. Initially, a cluster center is chosen randomly and new cluster centers are added using the following algorithm.

3.1   Maximin Distance Classifier Algorithm

Let cluster centers are represented using $c_1, c_2, c_3, \ldots, c_n$. Let the arithmetic mean of distances between the centers be m. Let c be the data point which is the candidate for the new cluster center. Let t be the threshold.

In Fuzzy c-means, the number of clusters is to be chosen randomly without any prior knowledge about cluster numbers. By using the Maxi-min Distance Classifier, the possible counts of clusters can be estimated and can be passed to the Fuzzy c-means. The maximin distance classifier algorithm is described in Algorithm 1.

Algorithm 1. Maximin Distance Classifier Algorithm

Input: Data set having Integer type data points

Output: Number of clusters

1: Randomly select a data point x_1 and designate as cluster center with a name c_1.

2: Determine the farthest data point (max) from x_1 and call that cluster center c_2.

3: Compute the distance s from each data point x in the remaining sample to c_1 and c_2 where distance $s = min||x - c_i||$ and $1 \le i \le n$.

4: For every pair of these computations, (min step), save the minimum distance.

5: Select the maximum of these (max step) minimum distances.

6: If this distance is an appreciable fraction of the distance between cluster centers c_1 and c_2 the corresponding data point for which the distance is maximum is identified as a new cluster center c_3. Continue the process with the existing cluster centers.

7: Otherwise, terminate the algorithm.

---

4   Fuzzy C-Means Clustering

The count of clusters calculated by Maxi min Distance classifier is passed to Fuzzy c-means Algorithm. In fuzzy clustering, a data point or object may belong to more than one class or group with a determined degree called fuzzy membership value which lies between 0 and 1. The goal of Fuzzy c-means is to minimize the objective function in Eq. (1).

In Fuzzy c-means n (data points) objects are grouped into c clusters; U is fuzzy membership matrix.

The distance between each data point (object) and cluster center is called Euclidean distance $d_{ij} = ||x_i - v_j||$.

Where d_{ij} is Euclidean distance between data point x_i to the cluster center v_j.

$N = n_1, n_2, n_3, \ldots \ldots, n_n$ are objects (data points) and $V = v_1, v_2, v_3, v_4, \ldots \ldots, v_c$ are cluster centers where c is the total number of Clusters. Fuzzy c-means is a repetitive algorithm which optimizes the cost function in 1.

$$J(U,V) = \sum_{k=1}^{n} \sum_{j=1}^{c} u_{ik}^{m} ||x_k - v_i||^2 \tag{1}$$

Where U is fuzzy membership Matrix and $u_{ik} \in [0,1]$ $\sum_{j=1}^{c} u_{jk} = 1$
value of i is between $[1, c]$
value of k is between $[1, n]$

value of j is between $[1, c]$

Here, $m \in (1, \infty)$ where m is weighting constant called fuzzifier. An Initial guess of each cluster centers is given in 2.

$$V_j = \frac{\sum_{i=1}^n u_{ij}^m x_i}{\sum_{i=1}^n u_{ij}^m} where \; i = 1, 2, 3, \ldots \ldots, c. \tag{2}$$

Fuzzy C- Means clustering algorithm is defined in Algorithm 2.

Algorithm 2. Fuzzy C-Means algorithm

Input: Data set and output from maximin distance classifier

Output: Clusters

1: Initialize the fuzzy membership matrix randomly i.e. $U = [u_{ij}]$ matrix and $U^{(0)}$

2: In this step calculate the centers of vectors $V^{(s)} = [V_j]$ with $U^{(k)}$ and $V_j = \frac{\sum_{i=1}^n u_{ij}^m x_i}{\sum_{i=1}^n u_{ij}^m}$

3: Update the membership matrix $U^{(s)}$, $U^{(s+1)}$ and $u_{ij} = \frac{1}{\sum_{k=1}^c (\frac{||x_i - v_j||}{||x_i - v_k||})^{\frac{2}{m-1}}}$

4: Normalize U

5: If $||U^{(s+1)} - U^{(s)}|| < \epsilon$ then end; else return to step 2.

6: Randomise data.

7: Derandomise data.

---

5   Bat Based Fuzzy C-Means

Bat based clustering was firstly introduced by Xin-She Yang in 2010. Researchers found that Bat based methods are efficient and effective in many cases. When compared to other optimization techniques, Bat optimization had reported good convergence rate.

The randomize fuzzy c-means with Maximin classifier are considered as input to Bat based improvement in clustering. In our proposed work, Maximin classifier is applied on data items then the resulting number of clusters is passed to fuzzy c-means. The fuzzy c-means is then randomized and Bat optimization is used for converging at the global optimal solution.

These Bats pick data items one by one sequentially and drop it one by one in clusters. The quality of the clusters is compared; if the quality is improved the drop is permanent otherwise Bat drop the data item in another cluster and check for quality and it is repeated. The quality of clusters are measured by two parameters named divided constant (d_c) and divided energy (d_e). (d_c) and (d_e) are defined in 3 and 4.

$$d_c = \frac{\sum_{j=1}^n \sum_{i=1}^c (u_{ij})^2}{n} \tag{3}$$

$$d_e = \frac{\sum_{j=1}^n \sum_{i=1}^c u_{ij} \log_a u_{ij}}{n} \tag{4}$$

two parameters d_c and d_e are used to measure that how compact the clusters are, this abstraction known as is fuzziness of the fuzzy membership matrix. As the value of fuzzy partition or fuzzy membership value decrease, the d_e value increase in that ratio. From these parameters and with divided constant (d_c) and divided energy (d_e), the probability of drop the data in point at any cluster is calculated as $d_d = d_e/d_c$.

If $d_d - d_{d-1} > 0.000001$ (value of epsilon) then we put that data item in that cluster permanently and we update the value of to next value which is minimum and further iteration is continued with the updated cluster indexes ($d_d = d_{d-1}$) Otherwise further iteration is continued with old value of cluster indexes for n number of times where n is equal to data items. We further improve the performance of clustering by calculating intra-cluster distance and inter-cluster distance and minimizing intra-clustering distance and maximizing inter-cluster distance. This is also an iterative process and we iterate until intra-clustering and inter clustering distance does not improve.

Intra cluster and Inter cluster distance can be calculated by using 5 and 6.

$$Intraclusterdistance = \sum_{j=1}^{c}\sum_{i=1}^{n}(\|x_i - v_j\|)^2 \tag{5}$$

$$Interclusterdistance = \sum_{j=1}^{c}\sum_{i=1}^{c}(\|v_i - v_j\|)^2 \tag{6}$$

6 Proposed Work

6.1 Hybrid Clustering Algorithm Using Bat Based Randomized Fuzzy C-Means Algorithm and Maximin Distance Classifier Algorithm

We propose a hybrid clustering technique which combines Maximin classifier, fuzzy c-means, and bat optimization. First, we calculate the possible number of clusters by Maximin distance classifier algorithm. The number of clusters is passed to fuzzy c-means and the fuzzy c-means is randomized to improve the cluster initialization problem. Bat Optimization is applied to solve local convergence and global optimum of fuzzy c-means. The Bat Algorithm (BA), based on the echolocation behaviour of bats. The capability of echolocation of microbats is fascinating as these bats can find their prey and discriminate different types of insects even in complete darkness. The proposed algorithm is defined in Algorithm 3.

7 Results and Comparisons

The proposed method is compared with the basic fuzzy c-means algorithm by considering two machine learning dataset named as Iris and 2-D dataset.

Algorithm 3. Proposed Algorithm

Input: Dataset having Integer type data points.

Output: clusters

1: Calculate the maximum number of cluster possible using MAXIMIN distance classifier algorithm.

2: Give previously calculated cluster centers as input to fuzzy-c-means and initialize fuzzy membership matrix with random values.

3: Calculate fuzzy membership U_{ij} for every data point and calculate fuzzy membership matrix U.

4: Compute fuzzy centers V_j again.

5: Repeat step 2 to step 3 until a minimum value of cost function $u_{ij} = \dfrac{1}{\sum_{k=1}^{c}(\frac{||x_i - v_j||}{||x_i - v_k||})^{\frac{2}{m-1}}}$ is accomplished.

6: Randomise and derandomize the data.

7: Do de Fuzzification for assigning data points to the specific clusters.

8: Bat Based Refinement

      a. The output of Randomize fuzzy c-means with maximin distance classifier is input to bat based refinement.

      b. for i=1 to n do

      b-1. Let the bat pick an item sequentially

      b-2. the item into some other cluster.

      b-3. Check the quality of clustering by using some parameters given in 7,8,9 and 10.

$$\frac{\sum_{j=1}^{n}\sum_{i=1}^{c}(u_{ij})^2}{n} \tag{7}$$

$$\frac{\sum_{j=1}^{n}\sum_{i=1}^{c}u_{ij}\log_a u_{ij}}{n} \tag{8}$$

$$Interclusterdistance = \sum_{j=1}^{c}\sum_{i=1}^{c}(||v_i - v_j||)^2 \tag{9}$$

$$Intraclusterdistance = \sum_{j=1}^{c}\sum_{i=1}^{n}(||x_i - v_j||)^2 \tag{10}$$

      c. If the quality of clustering is improved then drop that item permanently.

      d.Repeat form point a.

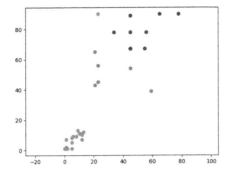

Fig. 1. Fuzzy c-means for the simple 2-D data set with 3-cluster centers

Initially, fuzzy c-means is applied for the simple 2-D data set with 3-cluster centers. It is observed that one point is misclassified if fuzzy c-means is used as shown in Fig. 1.

Fuzzy c-means with Bat optimization is applied on the same data set. Performance of Fuzzy c-means with Bat optimization is plotted in Fig. 2. It is observed that all the points are classified correctly.

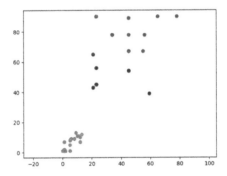

Fig. 2. Fuzzy c-means with bat optimization is for the simple 2-D data set with 3-cluster centers

Table 1 compares the Elapsed time, Intra-cluster distance, Inter-cluster distance, and Accuracy of both Fuzzy c-means and Fuzzy c-means with Bat optimization.

Figures 3 and 4 are plotted based on the performance of Fuzzy c-means and Bat based fuzzy c-means for Iris data set for 3 clusters. It can be observed that some points in Fuzzy c-means is not clustered correctly and performance is improved if Fuzzy c-means with Bat optimization is used.

Table 1. Comparison of various parameters of Fuzzy C-Means and Bat based Fuzzy c-means for 2d dataset with 3-cluster center

Clustering algorithm	Data set	Inter cluster distance	Intra cluster distance	Elapsed time	Accuracy (%)
Fuzzy c-means	2-D data	7.018	259.236	0.050	86.111
Fuzzy c-means with Bat optimization	2-D data	7.1038	128.5	0.0499	88.889

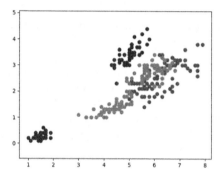

Fig. 3. Performance of fuzzy c-means for iris dataset

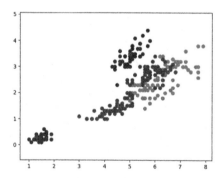

Fig. 4. Fuzzy c-means using Bat Optimization for the Iris data set

Table 2 compares the Intra-cluster distance, Inter-cluster distance, Elapsed time and Accuracy of both Fuzzy c-means and Fuzzy c-means with Bat optimization when Iris dataset is used. The parameters Intra-cluster distance, Inter-cluster distance, Elapsed time and Accuracy have improved for fuzzy c-means with Bat optimization in comparison to the fuzzy c-means algorithm.

Table 2. Comparison of various parameters of Fuzzy C-Means and Bat based Fuzzy c-means optimization for Iris Dataset

Clustering algorithm	Data set	Inter cluster distance	Intra cluster distance	Elapsed time	Accuracy (%)
Fuzzy c-means	Iris data	1.929	33.96	0.22	89.33
Fuzzy c-means with Bat optimization	Iris data	2.16	33.69	0.237	93.44

Fuzzy c-means and Bat based fuzzy c-means are evaluated with 6 clusters using 2-D dataset. In Fig. 5(a), the performance of Fuzzy c-means clustering with 6 clusters for 2D dataset is shown. In Fig. 5(b), the performance of Fuzzy c-means with Bat optimization with 6 clusters is shown. It is observed that the performance of Fuzzy c-means with Bat optimization is higher than that of the fuzzy c-means algorithm.

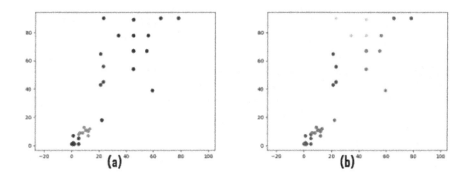

Fig. 5. (a) The performance of Fuzzy c-means clustering for 2D dataset with 6-clusters (b) the performance of Fuzzy c-means with Bat optimization with 6 clusters is shown

Table 3 contains the comparison of Intra-cluster distance, inter-cluster distance, Elapsed time and Accuracy of Fuzzy c-means and bat optimization based fuzzy c-means with 6 clusters on the 2-d data set. Figure 6(a) is the graphical representation of Accuracy of Fuzzy c-means and Fuzzy c-means with 3 clusters for both the data sets. Figure 6(b) is the graphical representation of intra-cluster distance of Fuzzy c-means and Fuzzy c-means with 3 clusters for both the data sets. It can be observed that fuzzy C- means using bat optimization is giving better results in comparison to fuzzy c-means.

Table 3. Comparison of various parameters of Fuzzy C-Means and Bat based Fuzzy c-means for 2d dataset with 6-cluster

Clustering algorithm	Data set	Inter cluster distance	Intra cluster distance	Elapsed time	Accuracy (%)
Fuzzy c-means	Iris data	10.1038	90.5	0.5499	83.889
Fuzzy c-means with Bat optimization	Iris data	10.164	83.69	0.237	88.44

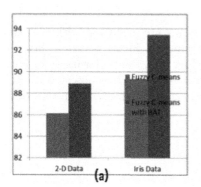
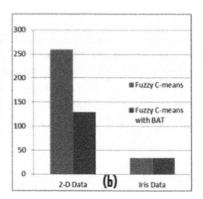

Fig. 6. (a) Graphical representation of Accuracy of Fuzzy c-means and Fuzzy c-means with 3 clusters for both the data sets (b) Graphical representation of intra-cluster distance of Fuzzy c-means and Fuzzy c-means with 3 clusters for both the data sets

8   Conclusion

We proposed a hybrid technique using minmax classifier, fuzzy c-means, and bat optimization to solve the problem of unknown cluster numbers, initialization of cluster centers and local convergence of the fuzzy c-means algorithm. It is observed that the proposed hybrid technique performs better than the original fuzzy c-means algorithm. For one data set (2-D data set) performance is increased from 86.111 to 88.889 and for another data set (iris dataset) performance is increased from 89.33 to 93.44. Moreover, the intra-cluster distance decreased when Bat based Fuzzy c-means is used.

References

1. Bezdek, J.C., Ehrlich, R., Full, W.: FCM: the fuzzy c-means clustering algorithm. Comput. Geosci. **10**(2–3), 191–203 (1984)
2. Silva Filho, T.M., et al.: Hybrid methods for fuzzy clustering based on fuzzy c-means and improved particle swarm optimization. Expert Syst. Appl. **42**(17–18), 6315–6328 (2015)

3. Hathaway, R.J., Bezdek, J.C.: Local convergence of the fuzzy c-means algorithms. Pattern Recogn. **19**(6), 477–480 (1986)
4. Jayabarathi, T., Raghunathan, T., Gandomi, A.H.: The bat algorithm, variants and some practical engineering applications: a review. In: Yang, X.-S. (ed.) Nature-Inspired Algorithms and Applied Optimization. SCI, vol. 744, pp. 313–330. Springer, Cham (2018). https://doi.org/10.1007/978-3-319-67669-2_14
5. Chawla, A., et al.: Landslide susceptibility mapping in Darjeeling Himalayas, India. Adv. Civil Eng. **2018** (2018)
6. Chawla, A., et al.: Landslide susceptibility Zonation mapping: a case study from Darjeeling District, Eastern Himalayas. India. J. Indian Soc. Remote Sens. **47**, 1–15 (2019)
7. Whitley, D.: A genetic algorithm tutorial. Stat. Comput. **4**(2), 65–85 (1994)
8. Kirkpatrick, S., Daniel Gelatt, C., Vecchi, M.P.: Optimization by simulated annealing. Science **220**(4598), 671–680 (1983)
9. Shen, Y., Shi, H., Zhang, J.Q.: Improvement and optimization of a fuzzy c-means clustering algorithm. In: Proceedings of the 18th IEEE Instrumentation and Measurement Technology Conference, IMTC 2001. Rediscovering Measurement in the Age of Informatics (Cat. No. 01CH 37188), vol. 3. IEEE (2001)
10. Izakian, H., Abraham, A., Snášel, V.: Fuzzy clustering using hybrid fuzzy c-means and fuzzy particle swarm optimization. In: 2009 World Congress on Nature and Biologically Inspired Computing (NaBIC). IEEE (2009)
11. Wang, J., et al.: Evaluate clustering performance and computational efficiency for PSO based fuzzy clustering methods in processing big imbalanced data. In: 2017 IEEE International Conference on Communications (ICC). IEEE (2017)
12. Li, L., Liu, X., Xu, M.: A novel fuzzy clustering based on particle swarm optimization. In: 2007 First IEEE International Symposium on Information Technologies and Applications in Education. IEEE (2007)
13. Wang, Z.: Comparison of four kinds of fuzzy c-means clustering methods. In: 2010 Third International Symposium on Information Processing. IEEE (2010)
14. Kwok, T., Smith, K., Lozano, S., Taniar, D.: Parallel fuzzy c- means clustering for large data sets. In: Monien, B., Feldmann, R. (eds.) Euro-Par 2002. LNCS, vol. 2400, pp. 365–374. Springer, Heidelberg (2002). https://doi.org/10.1007/3-540-45706-2_48
15. Zhou, D., et al.: Randomization in particle swarm optimization for global search ability. Expert Syst. Appl. **38**(12), 15356–15364 (2011)

Network Motifs: A Survey

Deepali Jain and Ripon Patgiri[(⊠)]

National Institute of Technology Silchar, Silchar, India
jaindeepali010@gmail.com, ripon@cse.nits.ac.in

Abstract. Network motifs are the building blocks of complex networks. Studying these frequently occurring patterns disclose a lot of information about these networks. The applications of Network motifs are very much evident now-a-days, in almost every field including biological networks, World Wide Web (WWW), etc. Some of the important motifs are feed forward loops, bi-fan, bi-parallel, fully connected triads. But, discovering these motifs is a computationally challenging task. In this paper, various techniques that are used to discover motifs are presented, along with detailed discussions on several issues and challenges in this area.

Keywords: Complex networks · Motifs · Network motifs · Big graph ·
Biological networks

1 Introduction

Complex Networks have been studied in a wide area of science like Biochemistry, Biology, Computer Science and many more. They have many patterns hidden inside, that need to be discovered. Analyzing their internal properties become important, in order to understand the evolution of these networks and exploiting their local structures reveal many important insights that help in a better understanding of the overall network. Milo et al. [26] defines network motifs as the building block of complex networks. There are numerous networks consisting of recurring patterns, for example, protein-protein interaction (PPI), food webs, electronic circuits, gene regulatory network, World Wide Web (WWW), neuronal networks, etc. Researchers have recursively found network motifs, like feed for- ward loop (FFL) and bi-fan, in different biological networks [17, 39]. Therefore, discovering these network motifs can lead us to identify the key control mechanisms of the complex networks under consideration. Thus, this sort of important motif discovery could improve the accuracy and efficiency of many important tasks like studying the effects of medications in biological networks, understanding the interactive social behavior of consumers, analysis of DNA sequences in gene regulatory networks, etc.

Motifs can be simply defined as recurring patterns, found in complex net- works. Discovering them consist of two main steps: (a) calculating the number of subgraphs in the network, and (b) evaluating the significance of these subgraphs. If two networks share similar significance profiles, they are considered to have same structural and functional properties. Significance profile is a metric which measures the significance of subgraphs' frequencies [39]. Network-motif detection techniques can be classified

© Springer Nature Singapore Pte Ltd. 2019
M. Singh et al. (Eds.): ICACDS 2019, CCIS 1046, pp. 80–91, 2019.
https://doi.org/10.1007/978-981-13-9942-8_8

into exact counting methods and approximate methods [17]. The major limitation of exact methods is that it takes a lot of computation time, for providing the capability to detect motifs upto a maximum of six nodes. Whereas, in-exact methods are developed to overcome the limitation of exact methods and hence can find motifs upto larger size [9, 13]. The computationally challenging nature of this problem of motif discovery is also due to the fact that, it involves dealing with the sub-graph isomorphism problem, which is a *NP*-complete problem whose polynomial time solution does not exist yet.

2 Preliminaries

Finding Network motifs in a large graph (target network/original network) is known as a Network Motif Detection problem. All the target networks and motifs are represented as Graphs which is defined in Definition 1.

Definition 1. *A Graph G = {V, E} consists of vertices V = {v} and edges E = {u, v} is said to be a Graph, where there is an edge connecting two nodes.*

Isomorphic Graphs
Two graphs $G = \{V, E\}$ and $H = \{V', E'\}$ are said to be isomorphic if bijective function f exists between V and V' such that for each edge $\{u, v\} \in E$ there is an edge $\{f(u), f(v)\} \in E'$ (Fig. 1).

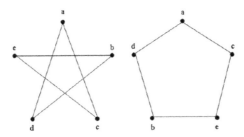

Fig. 1. Isomorphic graphs

Induced Subgraph
A graph H is an induced subgraph of G if it is completely depicted by vertices and edges of G. Network motifs are found in the target network. They are the subsets of target graphs. But there are also the motifs whose shapes are different, but possess the identical mathematical properties. So, isomorphic induced subgraphs can be counted to calculate the frequency of motifs.

Frequency
The frequency of a pattern is the number of times it is occurring within the target network. It can also be called as *subgraph frequency*. In other words, the frequency also defines the way by which motifs are present in the target network.

Thresholds

This is used to check whether subgraphs can be called as motifs or not. It can be done by its statistically over-representation in the target network.

- **Z-score:** It measures the number of motifs in the target network as compared to random networks. It can be calculated as follows

$$z(m) = \frac{f_{in} - f_{rand}}{\sqrt{\sigma_{rand}^2}} \tag{1}$$

Where in Eq. (1), m represents the motifs, f_{in} represents number of motifs in target networks, f_{rand} is the mean and σ_{rand} is the standard deviation of motif appearance in the target network.

- **P-value:** It is a probability value that lies between 0 and 1. It can be de- fined as the number of occurrences the motifs are present in target network as compared to the number of occurrences it is present in random network divided by the total number of random networks. A statistically significant motif has a P-value < 0.01 [39].

- **Significance Profile:** It is a vector of Z-scores of a set of motifs, which is nor- malized to 1 [26]. Significance profile can be calculated as

$$SP_i = \frac{z_i}{\sqrt{\sum_{i=1}^{n} z_i^2}} \tag{2}$$

Where in Eq. (2), z_i is the Z-score of motif i and n represents the number of motifs.

Different Types of Motifs:

There are generally five types of motifs [2, 11, 24, 33, 40]:

Single Node with Self-edge: The motif of this type is Autoregulation [33]. There are two types of Autoregulation motifs, namely, negative Autoregulation (NAR) and positive Autoregulation (PAR) [2, 33].

Pair-Wise: It can be identified with interaction between the two proteins [2].

Cascade: It is the sequence of activation of genes. Downstream gets activated when upstream reaches the threshold value [33].

Hub: A pattern of the regulator is identified with this type of motif that regulates a group of target genes [2, 11]. One of the examples of this type is Single- input module (SIM).

Bipartite: This type of motif includes a set of regulators in which a set of genes is jointly controlled [2, 33]. Examples include dense overlapping regulons (DOR) or multi-input motifs (MIMs) and bi-fan [2].

Clique: This includes protein complex in which three or more proteins interact to form a clique [2] (Fig. 2).

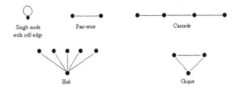

Fig. 2. Different types of motifs

3 Application Areas

There are many domains in which motifs can be discovered. One of the major application areas is Biological Networks, from where the term 'Network Motif' has originated. Brief descriptions of some of these networks are given below:

Biological Networks
Biological network is the representation of biological functions which are described by the network. It includes networks like Protein-Protein Interaction networks, Gene Regulatory networks, Metabolic networks, Signaling Networks, Food Webs, Neuronal Networks, etc.

Social Networks
Social network consists of nodes and edges where nodes represent individual or group of people or organization, and the edges represent the interaction between them. This type of network is useful to study the relationships among various groups or people. The term itself defines the social structure that is depicted by the interactions among individuals, groups or even organizations. Studying the social network has always been a topic of great interest. Several methods have been proposed to study social networks. Sub-graph pattern in these large social networks can help us understand the relationships between two groups or individuals or organizations. Thus, motifs help in disclosing the hidden properties inside the large social networks.

Electronic Circuits
It is a collection of interconnected components. Milo et al. [26] expresses that one of the possible functions of these circuits is that the output is activated only when the input signal is constant and it goes off when the input signal is deactivated. According to [26], similar motifs can be found in electronic circuits as well as in gene regulatory networks.

Temporal Networks
These networks [10] are also known as time varying networks whose links are activated only at a certain point of time. It means that edges are not activated all the time. The links have the information on its activation along with characteristics, such as weight. Since many complex networks like biological networks, social networks, etc. can actually have time varying components, temporal networks can also be thought of as specific instances of these complex network.

4 Applications

4.1 Motifs in Vehicular Technology [41]

Placement of Cache plays an important role in Vehicle-to-Vehicle (V2V) communication. But the existing technology on V2V communication does not account for spatio temporal communication patterns. It has been shown that by identifying V2V motifs for cache placement strategies, one can easily spread popular contents in the entire network. However, for this to work, the network should be chosen wisely, such that it can dynamically select the well-efficient set of cars that will cache popular contents.

4.2 Temporal Motifs in Communication Network [18]

It has been observed that communication patterns that involve a lot of individuals, get affected by the attributes such as sex and age. Temporal motifs found in communication networks help in studying the call sequence patterns, which cannot be analyzed through static networks. In [18], communication records are represented as colored temporal network. In this way, sex-related differences can be found, which are usually present in communication networks. Hence, temporal motifs also help in revealing the presence of temporal homophily.

4.3 Spatio Temporal Network Motif Reveals the Biological Traits [16]

Spatio temporal Network motifs help in revealing how the developmental process in Drosophila melanogaster takes place. These kinds of motifs are the spatio temporal sequences that are active only at specific time points and body parts. It shows that gene network regulates developmental processes, which are temporal and spatial in nature. In this way, network motifs can be considered as 'conceptual tools', which give important insights for understanding the functions and principles of biological networks.

4.4 Network Motifs Predict Protein-Protein Interaction (PPI) [6]

In [6], three-node and four-node motifs are observed, which helps in predicting the interaction between protein-protein partners. Sometimes network motifs also help to predict the functions of unknown protein in PPI network [35].

4.5 Motifs Predict Breast Cancer [7]

Network motifs in the human signaling networks help in identifying breast cancer patients. There are some cancer-associated motifs in breast cancer that are found with the help of three node motifs in human signaling networks [7]. In this way, network motifs help in diagnosing breast cancer and provide therapy for the disease.

5   Techniques Used for Network Motif Detection

5.1   MTMO

MTMO is a network-centric algorithm which was developed in 2017. It counts non induced occurrences of sub trees. This technique involves two subtasks, namely enumeration and classification. MTMO uses a rooted tree, which is labeled in order to avoid the number of isomorphism tests. It also uses an array-based indexing scheme, as this leads to the simplification of the subtree counting method. The algorithm is applied on yeast with Protein-Protein interaction (PPI) data, and also on two other networks which are electronic circuits and dolphin social networks. The algorithm is compared with its basic algorithm known as NTMO and it is found that the speedup of MTMO [19] is faster than NTMO while counting k-subtrees. The value of k varies from 3 to 12. It is also found that MTMO is 70 times faster when the subtrees of size 7 are counted in yeast net- work, whereas only 34 times faster in electronic network. Higher speedup was observed using MTMO, when compared to MODA [29]. In addition to it, the space complexity of MTMO is also shown to be comparatively lesser. The algorithm has also been compared with FASCIA [34] and again it is found that the execution time for generating subtrees of size 7 is less than 1 s in case of MTMO as compared to FASCIA, which takes 22 s for the same. As the MODA algorithm is based on pattern growth approach, which takes huge time in enumerating k-size subtrees, MTMO is used for improving the time complexity. Although, MTMO is applied for undirected network in [19], it can also be applied on directed graphs. MTMO is similar, in terms of performance, to Kavosh [12] in enumerating non induced subtrees, which is one of the best algorithms for this task. When compared to Ferreiras algorithm [8], MTMO is shown to be much easier to implement.

5.2   Network Motif Discovery: A GPU Approach

Mining network motifs are computationally challenging task, since, it requires a lot of time for enumeration and for counting the frequency of these subgraphs. So, to overcome this, there is another approach known as Graphical Processing Unit (GPU) [20]. In this approach, GPUs are exploited in order to run more than one individual isomorphism tests. In this way, it takes less computational time. The fact that the CPU-based approaches for isomorphism tests are not well suited for GPU since it is difficult to inherit the various procedures of CPU- based approaches to GPU algorithms. Therefore, GPU-based approach uses filter-refinement paradigm which is designed by considering three factors, namely, load balancing, branch divergences and memory access patterns on the GPU. This algorithm is tested on seven biological networks, namely, Yeast (YE), H. sapiens (HS), Yeast PPI (YP), M. musculus (MM), D. melanogaster (DM), A. Salina (AT), C. elegans (CE). In comparison with CPU based approach, GPU-based technique is efficient and also cost-effective.

5.3 Efficient Motif Discovery for Large-Scale Time Series in Healthcare

Since existing methods are not well suited for discovering temporal motifs. So, [21] represents a new technique known as Motif Discovery Method for Large-scale time series (MDLats). This technique is implemented on Hadoop. It uses benefits of both exact and inexact algorithms to reduce the computation time and therefore maintains the balance between accuracy and efficiency. It does this by computing standard motifs and then final motifs are discovered along with similar subsequences. There are two most popular exact algorithms known as Brute Force (BF) [22] and Mueen Keogh (MK) [27]. Since these algorithms are inefficient, they are not suitable for large time-series. On comparing this technique [21] with the existing methods, MDLats has the following advantages which are as follows: (1) It improves efficiency while preserving accuracy. (2) It generates all the motifs, not only the similar one, but also provides additional information for time series analysis. (3) It can discover different motif length. (4) This technique is extremely useful when time series are regular and fluctuations in them are sparse. (5) It is scalable. In this technique, firstly, 'Standard Motifs' are to be found whose calculation leads to Final Motif Discovery Module which results in 'final motif'. The proposed algorithm has compared with two exact methods, Brute Force (BF) [22] and Mueen-Keogh (MK) [27] and one inexact method which is Random Projection (RP) [5]. The results show that the execution time of MDLats is faster than BF and MK. In addition to, MDLats discover all similar sequences for all motif types. It is accurate as compared to RP and better balances the number of motifs discovered (Table 1).

Table 1. Various datasets used in [20]

Dataset name	Vertices	Edges	AVG deg.	MAX out-deg.	MIN in-deg.
Yeast (YE)	688	1079	3.14	71	13
H.sapiens (HS)	1509	5598	7.42	71	45
YeastPPI (YP)	2361	6646	5.63	64	47
M.musculus (MM)	4293	7987	3.72	91	111
D.melanogaster (DM)	6303	18,224	5.78	88	122
A.thaliana (AT)	9,216	50,669	11.00	58	89
C.elegans (CE)	17,179	124,599	14.51	67	107

5.4 Finding Network Motifs Using MCMC Sampling

This technique uses a novel sampling based method. There are three critical performance metrics, namely, accuracy, convergence and execution time on which the quality of sampling depends. [31] presents two random walk based methods that are MHRW (Metropolis-Hastings random walk) and SRW-RW (Simple Random Walk with Reweighting). Both these methods are based on Monte Carlo Markov Chain (MCMC) sampling method. It used five graphs as their datasets in which ca-AstroPh is the largest with 17,903 vertex and 196,972 edges. This method is faster than FANMOD [38] for all the datasets given in [31] based on the error percentage metrics. Moreover, it does not require the complete access over the network (Tables 2, 3, and 4).

Table 2. Various datasets used in [19]

Dataset name	Vertices	Edges	AVG deg.	MAX deg.
YeastPPI	2361	6646	5.630	64
Electronic	252	399	3.167	14
Dolphins	62	159	5.129	12

Table 3. Various datasets used in [15]

Dataset name	Directionality	Vertices	Edges	Description
Yeast	Directed	688	1079	Yeast Transcription Network
E.coli	Directed	672	1275	Metabolic pathway of bacteria E.coli
Social	Directed	67	182	A real social network
Electronic	Directed/ Undirected	252	399 (both dir and undir)	Electronic circuit
YeastPPI	Undirected	2361	6646	Protein-protein interaction net- work in budding yeast
Dolphins	Undirected	62	159	Frequent associations between a group of dolphins

Table 4. Dataset statistics in [31]

Dataset name	Vertices	Edges	AVG deg.
Yeast	222,4	6,609	5.94
Jazz	198	2,742	27.49
ca-GrQc	4,158	13,422	6.43
ca-HepTh	8,638	24,806	5.74
ca-AstroPh	17,903	196,972	22.0

5.5 QuateXelero: An Accelerated Exact Network Motif Detection Algorithm

One of the methods for fast motif detection known as QuateXelero [15] which uses Quaternary tree data structure. This algorithm is based upon ESU (FANMOD) [37] motif detection algorithm. The main aim of this algorithm is to reduce the number of calls to NAUTY algorithm [25]. The approach is applied on six different networks. There are three biological networks, namely, the metabolic pathway of bacteria E. coli [14], the transcription network of Yeast S. cerevisiae [1], and the protein-protein interaction network of the budding Yeast [3, 4] and three non-biological networks, namely, a real social network [12], a dolphin social network [23] [28] and an electronic network [26]. The algorithm has compared with Kavosh [12] and G-tries [30]. The algorithm is 86 times faster when 8-size motif is to be found in Yeast network and 21 times faster in case of E.coli network in identifying 9- size motifs. On comparing with G-Tries, it has been found that QuateXelero is always much faster than ESU of G-trees. But it is slower when motif size increases.

6 Issues and Challenges

These structures are highly complex for the discovery of exact motifs. There are many issues and challenges while discovering motifs:

Representation of Motifs in Complex Networks: One of the major issues is the way by which motifs are represented in the large complex network. When the motif size gets increased, it takes large computation time.

Huge Memory Consumption: Sometimes discovering network motifs also become difficult as it consumes a lot of memory when the network size is large, for example, a considerable amount of memory is consumed while constructing the quaternary tree [15].

Unnecessary Time Consumption: There are some tools which are designed specifically for discovery of motifs in particular network, for example MAVisto [32]. Motif-centric algorithm takes unnecessary time for counting the subgraphs that may even not found in target network.

Subgraph Isomorphism Problem: Finding the frequency of motifs in a network is a computationally challenging task as it involves a sub-graph isomorphism problem which is a *NP* - complete problem.

Cost Issue: There are also cost challenges in finding the motifs as the size of motifs increases.

Scalability Issue: There is also a scalability problem with increasing size of the motifs. In RAND-ESU [36], there is a poor accuracy and convergence behavior as the motif size increases.

Open Exploration of Motifs Is Not Always Possible: There are some of the existing sampling methods that require random access to vertices and edges which is a limitation of the network as open access is not always possible.

7 Future Direction

Motifs are very crucial to disclose the internal properties of complex networks. Studying their internal properties leads to the formation of networks. Although there are many algorithms to find network motifs, but when the motif size increases, even existing algorithms are not very much suitable. Therefore, it is still required to develop advanced algorithms that can discover motifs in a computationally less time, when the motif size increases. There are also many factors that need to be considered while designing an algorithm for motif detection such as scalability factor, accuracy, convergence. Therefore, it is an open area for research for motif detection techniques.

8 Conclusion

Network Motifs are recurrent patterns that are statistically significant. Since finding frequency of motifs is a *NP* - complete problem, therefore, their detection is a computationally challenging task. There are many exact as well as in-exact algorithms that discover network motifs in large complex networks but these algorithms fails when motif size increases. Since network motifs play a very important role in determining the functional properties of large complex networks, therefore, study of motifs become important. This survey gives a brief description of network motif detection techniques. Several issues and challenges associated with motif discovery are also discussed. Since computation problem associated with motifs is a big challenge that needs to be worked upon, hence, there is a scope for research in this area.

Acknowledgement. Authors would like to acknowledge TEQIP-III, NIT Silchar for supporting this research work.

References

1. Alon: The S.cerevisiae database. https://www.weizmann.ac.il/mcb/UriAlon/
2. Alon, U.: Network motifs: theory and experimental approaches. Nat. Rev. Genet. **8**(6), 450 (2007)
3. Batagelj, V., Mrvar, A.: Pajek datasets. https://www.kegg.jp/
4. Bu, D., et al.: Topological structure analysis of the protein–protein interaction network in budding yeast. Nucleic Acids Res. **31**(9), 2443–2450 (2003)
5. Buhler, J., Tompa, M.: Finding motifs using random projections. J. Comput. Biol. **9**(2), 225–242 (2002)
6. Chen, J., Hsu, W., Lee, M.L., Ng, S.-K.: Labeling network motifs in protein interactomes for protein function prediction. In: IEEE 23rd International Conference on Data Engineering, ICDE 2007, pp. 546–555. IEEE (2007)
7. Chen, L., et al.: Identification of breast cancer patients based on human signaling network motifs. Sci. Rep. **3**, 3368 (2013)
8. Ferreira, R., Grossi, R., Rizzi, R.: Output-sensitive listing of bounded-size trees in undirected graphs. In: Demetrescu, C., Halldórsson, M.M. (eds.) ESA 2011. LNCS, vol. 6942, pp. 275–286. Springer, Heidelberg (2011). https://doi.org/10.1007/978-3-642-23719-5_24
9. Grochow, J.A., Kellis, M.: Network Motif discovery using subgraph enumeration and symmetry-breaking. In: Speed, T., Huang, H. (eds.) RECOMB 2007. LNCS, vol. 4453, pp. 92–106. Springer, Heidelberg (2007). https://doi.org/10.1007/978-3-540-71681-5_7
10. Holme, P., Saramäki, J.: Temporal networks. Phys. Rep. **519**(3), 97–125 (2012)
11. Jin, G., Zhang, S., Zhang, X.-S., Chen, L.: Hubs with network motifs organize modularity dynamically in the protein-protein interaction network of yeast. PLoS ONE **2**(11), e1207 (2007)

12. Kashani, Z.R.M., et al.: Kavosh: a new algorithm for finding network motifs. BMC Bioinform. **10**(1), 318 (2009)
13. Kashtan, N., Itzkovitz, S., Milo, R., Alon, U.: Efficient sampling algorithm for estimating subgraph concentrations and detecting network motifs. Bioinformatics **20**(11), 1746–1758 (2004)
14. KEGG: KEGG: Kyoto encyclopedia of genes and genomes. https://www.kegg.jp/
15. Khakabimamaghani, S., Sharafuddin, I., Dichter, N., Koch, I., Masoudi-Nejad, A.: QuateXelero: an accelerated exact network motif detection algorithm. PLoS ONE **8**(7), e68073 (2013)
16. Kim, M.-S., Kim, J.-R., Kim, D., Lander, A.D., Cho, K.-H.: Spatiotemporal network motif reveals the biological traits of developmental gene regulatory networks in drosophila melanogaster. BMC Syst. Biol. **6**(1), 31 (2012)
17. Kim, W., Li, M., Wang, J., Pan, Y.: Biological network motif detection and evaluation. BMC Syst. Biol. **5**(3), S5 (2011)
18. Kovanen, L., Kaski, K., Kertész, J., Saramäki, J.: Temporal motifs reveal homophily, gender-specific patterns, and group talk in call sequences. Proc. Natl. Acad. Sci. **110**, 18070–18075 (2013)
19. Li, G., Luo, J., Xiao, Z., Liang, C.: MTMO: an efficient network-centric algorithm for subtree counting and enumeration. Quant. Biol. **6**(2), 142–154 (2018)
20. Lin, W., Xiao, X., Xie, X., Li, X.-L.: Network motif discovery: A GPU approach. IEEE Trans. Knowl. Data Eng. **29**(3), 513–528 (2017)
21. Liu, B., Li, J., Chen, C., Tan, W., Chen, Q., Zhou, M.: Efficient motif discovery for large-scale time series in healthcare. IEEE Trans. Industr. Inf. **11**(3), 583–590 (2015)
22. Lonardi, J., Patel, P.: Finding motifs in time series. In: Proceedings of the 2nd Workshop on Temporal Data Mining, pp. 53–68 (2002)
23. Lusseau, D., Schneider, K., Boisseau, O.J., Haase, P., Slooten, E., Dawson, S.M.: The bottlenose dolphin community of doubtful sound features a large proportion of long-lasting associations. Behav. Ecol. Sociobiol. **54**(4), 396–405 (2003)
24. Madar, D., Dekel, E., Bren, A., Alon, U.: Negative auto-regulation increases the input dynamic-range of the arabinose system of escherichia coli. BMC Syst. Biol. **5**(1), 111 (2011)
25. McKay, B.D., et al.: Practical graph isomorphism. Vanderbilt University, Nashville (1981)
26. Milo, R., Shen-Orr, S., Itzkovitz, S., Kashtan, N., Chklovskii, D., Alon, U.: Net-work motifs: simple building blocks of complex networks. Science **298**(5594), 824–827 (2002)
27. Mueen, A., Keogh, E., Zhu, Q., Cash, S., Westover, B.: Exact discovery of time series motifs. In: Proceedings of the 2009 SIAM International Conference on Data Mining, pp. 473–484. SIAM (2009)
28. Newman: Newman Mark network data (2009). http://www-personal.umich.edu/
29. Omidi, S., Schreiber, F., Masoudi-Nejad, A.: MODA: an efficient algorithm for net-work motif discovery in biological networks. Genes Genet. Syst. **84**(5), 385–395 (2009)
30. Ribeiro, P., Silva, F.: G-tries: an efficient data structure for discovering network motifs. In: Proceedings of the 2010 ACM Symposium on Applied Computing, pp. 1559–1566. ACM (2010)
31. Saha, T.K., Hasan, M.A.: Finding network motifs using MCMC sampling. In: Mangioni, G., Simini, F., Uzzo, S.M., Wang, D. (eds.) Complex Networks VI. SCI, vol. 597, pp. 13–24. Springer, Cham (2015). https://doi.org/10.1007/978-3-319-16112-9_2
32. Schreiber, F., Schwobbermeyer, H.: MAVisto: a tool for the exploration of network motifs. Bioinformatics **21**(17), 3572–3574 (2005)
33. Shoval, O., Alon, U.: SnapShot: network motifs. Cell **143**(2), 326 (2010)
34. Slota, G.M., Madduri, K.: Fast approximate subgraph counting and enumeration. In: 2013 42nd International Conference on Parallel Processing (ICPP), pp. 210–219. IEEE (2013)

35. Turkett, W., Fulp, E., Lever, C., Allan, J.E.: Graph mining of motif profiles for computer network activity inference. In: Ninth Workshop on Mining and Learning with Graphs (2011)
36. Wernicke, S.: A faster algorithm for detecting network motifs. In: Casadio, R., Myers, G. (eds.) WABI 2005. LNCS, vol. 3692, pp. 165–177. Springer, Heidelberg (2005). https://doi.org/10.1007/11557067_14
37. Wernicke, S.: Efficient detection of network motifs. IEEE/ACM Trans. Comput. Biol. Bioinform. (TCBB) **3**(4), 347–359 (2006)
38. Wernicke, S., Rasche, F.: FANMOD: a tool for fast network motif detection. Bioinformatics **22**(9), 1152–1153 (2006)
39. Wong, E., Baur, B., Quader, S., Huang, C.-H.: Biological network motif detection: principles and practice. Brief. Bioinform. **13**(2), 202–215 (2011)
40. Yeger-Lotem, E., et al.: Network motifs in integrated cellular networks of transcription–regulation and protein–protein interaction. Proc. Natl. Acad. Sci. **101**(16), 5934–5939 (2004)
41. Zeng, T., Semiari, O., Saad, W.: Spatio-temporal motifs for optimized vehicle-to-vehicle (v2v) communications. In: 2018 International Conference on Computing, Networking and Communications (ICNC), pp. 789–794, March 2018

Multiple Image Watermarking for Efficient Storage and Transmission of Medical Images

Rakhshan Anjum[1], Priyanka Verma[1]($\boxtimes$), and Sunanda Verma[2]

[1] EXTC, MPSTME, NMIMS University, Mumbai, India
priyanka.verma@nmims.edu
[2] Noida International University, Greater Noida, India

Abstract. In today's digital era, managing patient's records can be one of the most challenging task for hospitals and health care centers. In hospitals, patient's medical data like medical reports and images (like x-ray, CT and MRI) etc. are stored at different locations at server side that results in more memory utilization. Also, Medical applications like telemedicine require exchange of medical data between two health care centers that needs huge transmission bandwidth. As a result, the use of watermarking in medical applications would prove to be advantageous as multiple images can be hidden into a single image. Multiple image watermarking system is proposed in this paper which thereby can result in efficient memory and bandwidth utilization. The algorithm simultaneously embeds three different medical images as multiple watermarks into all the three color planes (Red, Green and Blue planes) of cover image there by reducing the memory for compact storage and bandwidth requirement during transmission thereby retaining the quality of images. For maintaining the confidentiality as well as security, Arnold's scrambling method is used for encrypting the watermarks. The Performance indicators used for measuring the quality of watermarked image are peak signal to noise ratio (PSNR) and correlation coefficient.

Keywords: Medical image watermarking · Discrete wavelet transform · Image scrambling

1 Introduction

High resolution CT images may be as large as 1000 images of 512×512 pixels of each, which requires more than 500 MB of storage capacity per study. Even 2D radiography already requires 8 MB per image. It is clear that the storage and visualization of large data sets require large disk capacity and computer memory.

The two problems are highlighted in this paper. Firstly, storage of medical data on the database and secondly transmitting medical data as an application to tele-medicine. Recent advancements in information and communication technologies have contributed in improving the quality of telemedicine. The proliferation of digital media has opened up new challenges of transmitting medical data across the globe via internet, computer network and telecommunication & other electronics communication medium. Telemedicine is a method of transmitting and receiving medical records and images

M. Singh et al. (Eds.): ICACDS 2019, CCIS 1046, pp. 92–102, 2019.
https://doi.org/10.1007/978-981-13-9942-8_9

among the doctors and hospitals all over the world [1]. Transmitting medical data over a communication medium open up ways to different possible threats that can affect the security of medical information. Medical information requires special attention as the patient health is based on diagnosis made by the medical information [2, 3].

Medical information should be

1. Confidential: Only doctors and the medical staff could access the patient's medical information.
2. Should be robust to the tampering as well as basic attacks.

Medical image watermarking involves the embedding of patient's electronic record (EPR) into cover medical image. A general medical image watermarking system is shown in Fig. 1. The Patient's EPR, hospital's logo or related medical diagnosis is taken as watermark and embedded into the cover medical image to form the water-marked image.

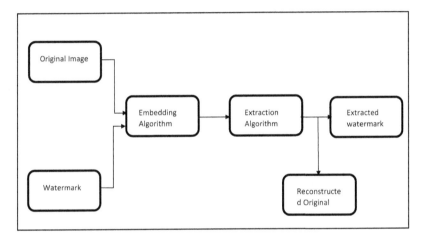

Fig. 1. Digital watermarking system

In medical image watermarking, watermark must be embedded in such a way that the quality of the cover image should not get degraded. Data storage and Bandwidth are the two major concerns in telemedicine scenario, since exchange of medical data requires higher transmission bandwidth and more memory to store them, especially in teleradiology applications. For efficient use of transmission bandwidth and storage, we propose to send multiple watermarks together in cover images, using a simplified approach. In this paper we have proposed a frame work of embedding three different watermarks in a single medical image using 2-level discrete wavelet transform. The three watermarks will be encrypted using Arnold's method for maintaining the robustness and integrity of the hidden data.

2 Literature Survey

In recent years, digital watermarking emerged as a technique for medical information management especially in telemedicine applications. This section presents a detailed review of the techniques and the methodology used in medical image watermarking.

Giakoumaki et al. [11] proposed robust 3-level wavelet based multiple watermarking to embed watermarks into the detailed coefficients of cover image. Quantization function is used for extraction of watermarks. However the computational complexity is high. Navas et al. [3] proposed Integer wavelet transform (IWT) based medical watermarking that embeds and recovers 3400 characters without any noise. The computational cost of this method is also very high.

Singh et al. [12] proposed wavelet based spread spectrum multiple watermarking scheme for embedding both text and image as watermarks of different size with peak signal the noise ratio (PSNR) 32.48 dB which can be improved further. Nanmaran et al. [13] proposed IWT based robust multiple image watermarking which embeds watermarks into Y components of YCbCr providing PSNR of 47 dB and correlation factor of 0.96.

Anand et al. [4] proposed a method in which the patient's medical text data was encrypted using logarithmic technique and ECG signal was encrypted by using two techniques DPCM and ADM and after that it was interleaved with medical images.

Wakatani et al. [5] proposes a technique to embed the medical information into non ROI to improve the quality of medical image. Chao et al. [6] in 2012 proposed medical image watermarking system based on discrete cosine transform (DCT) to hide the medical data into the quantized coefficients of cover image but the quality of medical image degrades after the extraction of watermark.

Mostafa et al. [7] have proposed a system wherein the patient's EPR was encoded by BCH code and then embedded into the cover image using 2nd level discrete wavelet packet transform. The proposed technique has the limitation that the computation time higher for decoding the BCH code.

Giakoumaki et al. [8] proposed a technique for embedding multiple watermarks into a medical image using 4-level wavelet transform. In this technique four multiple watermarks were taken and each watermark was embedded at each decomposition level and the sub bands of DWT coefficients of the cover image. Robustness of the watermark was enhanced by BCH error correcting codes.

Singh et al. [9] proposes a multiple hybrid watermarking technique that makes use of combination of DWT, DCT and SVD. In this method medical image was taken as image watermark, patient record was taken as text watermark. Only text watermark was encrypted before embedding to increase the security and the robustness.

3   Proposed Watermarking Scheme

The proposed medical image watermarking method is algorithm composed of two stages: embedding stage and extracting stage.

3.1   Embedding Stage

The watermark embedding process is shown in Fig. 2. A grayscale MRI medical image of size 1024 × 1024 × 3 is taken as the host cover image to hide the three watermarks. The cover image is decomposed into three color planes (R, G and B). MRI image is taken as watermark 1, CT scan image is taken as watermark 2 and patient's EPR is taken as watermark 3. All three watermarks are scrambled by Arnold's scrambling method [10] to provide security of the watermark so that it cannot be tampered or modified.

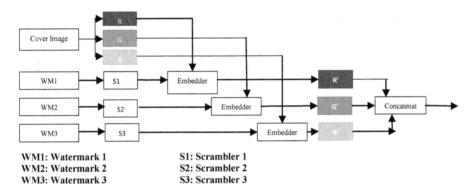

WM1: Watermark 1   **S1: Scrambler 1**
WM2: Watermark 2   **S2: Scrambler 2**
WM3: Watermark 3   **S3: Scrambler 3**

Fig. 2. Watermarking embedding process

In embedding algorithm, two level wavelet decomposition is done. The coefficients of LL planes are selected for embedding the watermarks in the color planes. The following equations explain embedding process in watermark embedder

$$LL_{Red} = LL1 + \alpha \, * \, WM1 \tag{1}$$

$$LL_{Green} = LL2 + \alpha \, * \, WM2 \tag{2}$$

$$LL_{Blue} = LL3 + \alpha \, * \, WM3 \tag{3}$$

Where LL1 is 2nd level approximation coefficient of red plane, LL2 is 2nd level approximation coefficient of green plane and LL3 is 2nd level approximation coefficient of blue plane whereas LL_{Red}, LL_{Green} and LL_{Blue} are the watermarked approximation coefficients and α is the scaling factor, ranging from 0.009 to 0.9 which gives weight to the watermark. The relation between the scaling factor α, PSNR and CC is explained in the result section.

The cover medical image and the patient's data in which two are medical images for diagnosis and one is patient's EPR is taken as three watermarks and are shown below in Fig. 3.

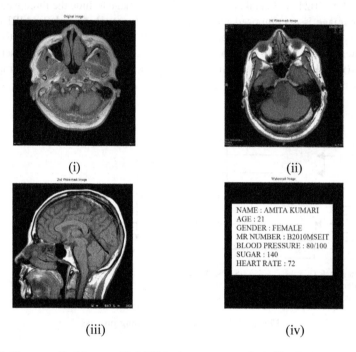

(i)   (ii)

(iii)   (iv)

Fig. 3. (i) Cover medical image, (ii) MRI brain as watermark 1 (iii) CT brain watermark 2 (iv) Patient's EPR as watermark 3

The Watermarked Planes and the final watermarked cover medical image are shown below in Fig. 4.

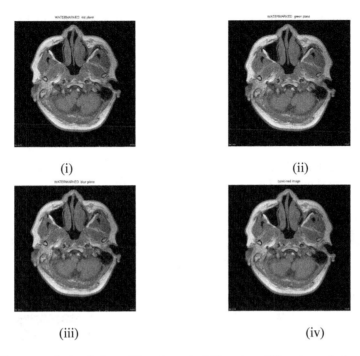

Fig. 4. (i) watermarked red plane, (ii) watermarked blue plane (iii) watermarked green plane (iv) Final watermarked image

3.2 Extraction Stage

The watermark extraction process is shown in Fig. 5. The watermarked cover medical image is separated into three color planes R', G' and B. 2nd level wavelet decomposition is done on the all the three watermarked color planes (R', G', B') to get the sub bands LL, LH, HL and HH.

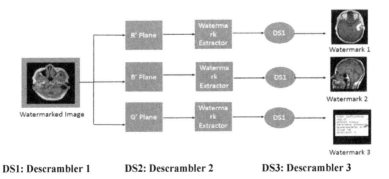

DS1: Descrambler 1   DS2: Descrambler 2   DS3: Descrambler 3

Fig. 5. Watermarking extraction process

The following equations explains the extraction process in watermark extractor, where WM1, WM2 and WM3 are the extracted watermarks which will be further decoded by Arnold's descrambler [10].

$$WM1 = (LL_{Red} - LL1)/\alpha \qquad (4)$$

$$WM2 = (LL_{Green} - LL2)/\alpha \qquad (5)$$

$$WM3 = (LL_{Blue} - LL3)/\alpha \qquad (6)$$

The extracted images will be descrambled using Arnold's transform. The extracted watermarks are shown in Fig. 6 with scaling factor α of 0.9.

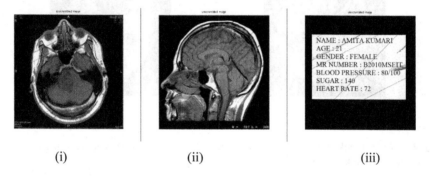

(i)   (ii)   (iii)

Fig. 6. (i) Extracted watermarked 1, (ii) Extracted watermarked 2 (iii) Extracted watermarked 3 with $\alpha = 0.9$

4   Performance Evaluation Parameters

The performance of the proposed method is measured by evaluating quality of the watermarked cover image and the robustness of the hidden watermark. The quality of the watermarked image is evaluated by different parameters like peak signal to noise ratio (PSNR), mean square error (MSE), structural similarity index (SSIM), and image Fidelity (IF). On the other hand, robustness of watermark is evaluated using Correlation Coefficient (CC) and similarity measure (SIM). Since the watermarks are also medical images which further needs to be diagnosed with cover image, quality of watermarks needs to be evaluated too after extraction.

- Mean Square Error (MSE): Mean square error is the sum of square of error between the cover image and the watermarked image. Mathematically it is given by Eq. 7

$$MSE = \frac{1}{MN} \sum_{m=0}^{N-1} \sum_{n=0}^{M-1} (I_o(m,n) - I_{WM}(m,n))^2 \qquad (7)$$

Where I_o the original is cover image and I_{WM} is the watermarked image and m and n are rows and columns of an image.

- Peak Signal to Noise ratio (PSNR): It is the performance indicator to evaluate the quality of watermarked image.

$$PSNR(I_o, I_{WM}) = 10 * \log_{10} \frac{(MAX_i^2)}{MSE} \tag{8}$$

Where MAX_i is the maximum gray level value of cover image.

- Structural Similarity (SSIM) Index: This parameter is used to evaluate the similarity between two images. It is the statistical measure to evaluate the quality of water-marked image.
- Image Fidelity (IF): Image fidelity is defined as the amount of imperceptibility of the watermark. The higher value of the IF signifies more imperceptible in the watermarked image

$$IF = 1 - \frac{\sum\limits_{m,n} \sum_{m,n} (I_o(m,n) - I_{WM}(m,n))^2}{\sum_{m,n} (I_o(m,n))^2} \tag{9}$$

- Correlation Coefficient: Correlation coefficient gives compatibility between original and decoded watermark.

$$CC = \frac{\sum\limits_{m=0}^{M-1} \sum\limits_{n=0}^{N-1} (W_o(m,n) \times W_d(m,n))^2}{\sum\limits_{m=0}^{M-1} \sum\limits_{n=0}^{N-1} (W_o(m,n))^2} \tag{10}$$

Where W_o is the original watermark and W_d is the decoded watermark.

5   Results and Discussion

The experimentation of the proposed method is done on various type of medical images such as MRI, CT etc. taken from the MedPix™ Medical Image Database [14]. The sizes of these images are 1024×1024 pixels. Total number of images taken for analysis is 35. The quality of watermarked images evaluated in terms of PSNR (Peak Signal to Noise Ratio), SSIM and IFM. If the value of PSNR is less, the watermark is more perceptible.

It is found out that even after embedding three watermarks into the cover image, PSNR value of 55.49 dB achieved which clearly justifies high quality retained while reconstructing the watermarked image even after embedding three watermarks. SSIM obtained is 0.999 which is as close to 1 indicates both the original cover image and watermarked image are similar. IF is also 1 which is on higher side, signifies that imperceptibility of the watermark is more in main (cover) image. CC is the correlation coefficient between original image and watermarked image.

From the comparison Table 1 of performance parameters with different scaling factor, it can be observed that by increasing the value of scaling factor α, the correlation between the transmitted and received data reduces negligibly but at the same time IFM and SSIM is also reducing. Also with the increasing value of scaling factor α, the value of PSNR decreases and MSE increases. The variation of PSNR and MSE with varying scaling factor is shown in Fig. 7.

Table 1. Performance parameters comparison table for different scaling factor

Scaling factor (α)	PSNR	MSE	CC	IFM	SSIM
0.009	55.49	0.19	1	1	0.9999
0.03	44.47	2.32	1	0.9999	0.9826
0.05	41.18	4.96	0.9999	0.9998	0.9706
0.09	36.26	15.42	0.9998	0.9994	0.9331
0.3	26.00	163.26	0.9979	0.9931	0.7885
0.5	21.55	455.75	0.9940	0.9806	0.7185
0.9	16.50	1455	0.9806	0.9382	0.6420

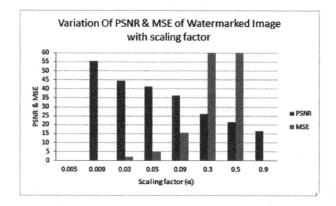

Fig. 7. Variation of PSNR & MSE of watermarked image with scaling factor

Table 2 indicates the robustness of watermark which is evaluated by correlation coefficient parameter since watermark images carrying the medical data of patient its quality should also be retained after extraction. The value of CC should be as close to 1. It should be noticed that CC1 is the correlation coefficient between first original and extracted watermark, CC2 is the correlation coefficient between second original and extracted watermark and CC3 is the correlation coefficient between third original and extracted watermark.

Table 2. Performance parameters for extracted watermarks

Scaling factor	CC1	CC2	CC3
0.005	0.171	0.0871	0.1387
0.009	0.0603	0.1263	0.1562
0.03	0.2099	0.2624	0.2901
0.05	0.3294	0.3617	0.4103
0.09	0.5843	0.5912	0.6234
0.3	0.9368	0.93	0.9324
0.5	0.974	0.9716	0.9703
0.9	0.9869	0.9873	0.988
1	0.9872	0.9884	0.9894

The value of scaling factor (0.009) is taken to achieve high PSNR for watermarked images and value of scaling factor (0.9) is taken to achieve high CC for extracted watermarks. The variation of correlation coefficients for extracted watermark is shown in Fig. 8 which indicates the value of correlation coefficient increased as the scaling factor increased. Basically scaling factor is inversely proportional to PSNR whereas directly proportional to correlation coefficient (CC).

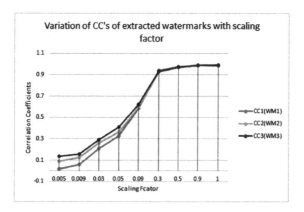

Fig. 8. Variation of CC's of extracted watermarks with scaling factor

Table 3 gives comparative analysis of proposed method with related research works in terms of PSNR and CC. It is observed that proposed method gives higher value of PSNR and CC as compared to other related multiple watermarking techniques.

Table 3. Comparative analysis of proposed method with related works

Reference no.	Methodology used	PSNR (in dB)	CC
Proposed method	2-level DWT with Arnold scrambling	55.49 dB	0.98
[3]	IWT	44 dB	Not tested
[12]	Spread spectrum based DWT	37.75 dB	0.7544
[13]	IWT	47 dB	0.96

6 Conclusions

In proposed multiple image watermarking technique, since three different images of patients data is being embedded in single image the requirement of storage space is reduced as it is evident that, the memory required to store four different images would be more than that required to store one watermarked image. Also, we require less bandwidth since four images are being sent on link in bandwidth of just a single image. The robustness and quality of extracted information is quantified by observing the results. Imperceptibility of the received data is increased when scaling factor of discrete wavelet transform is low, whereas for higher values of scaling factor correlation between images reduces.

References

1. David, B., Florence, V., Friede, A., Sheehan, J., Sisk, J.: Bringing health care applications to the internet. IEEE Internet Comput. 5(3), 42–46 (2001)
2. Chao, H.M., Hsu, C.M., Miaou, A.-G.: A data hiding technique with authentication, integration and confidentiality for electronic patient records. IEEE Trans. Inf. Technol. Biomed. 6(1), 46–53 (2002)
3. Navas, K.A., Thampy, S.A., Sasikumar, M.: ERP hiding in medical images for telemedicine. In: Proceedings of World Academy of Science and Technology, vol. 28, pp. 266–269 (2008)
4. Acharya, R.U., Anand, D., Bhat, S.P.: Niranjan compact storage of medical images with patient information. IEEE Trans. Inf. Technol. Biomed. 5, 320–323 (2001)
5. Wakatani, A.: Digital watermarking for ROI medical images by using compressed signature image. In: Proceedings of the 35th Annual Hawaii International Conference on System Sciences, Big Island, Hawaii (2002)
6. Chao, H.M., Hsu, C.M., Miaou, S.G.: A data-hiding technique with authentication, integration, and confidentiality for electronic patient records. IEEE Trans. Inf. Technol. Biomed. 6, 46–53 (2002)
7. Mostafa, S.A.K., El-sheimy, N., Tolba, A.S., Abdelkader, F.M., Elhindy, H.M.: Wavelet packets based blind watermarking for medical image management. Open Biomed. Eng. J. 4, 93–98 (2010)
8. Giakoumaki, A., Pavlopoulos, S., Koutsouris, D.: Secure and efficient health data management through multiple watermarking on medical images. Med. Biol. Eng. Comput. 44, 619–631 (2006)
9. Singh, A.K., Dave, M., Mohan, A.: Hybrid technique for robust and imperceptible multiple watermarking using medical images. Multimed. Tools Appl. 75(14), 8381–8401 (2016)
10. Lulu, W., Chong, Z.: Arnold scrambling based on digital image encryption technique. J. Natl. Defense Technol. Base 10, 27–31 (2010)
11. Giakoumaki, A., Pavlopoulos, S., Koutouris, D.: A medical image watermarking scheme based on wavelet transform. In: Proceedings 25th Annual International Conferences of IEEE-EMBS, San Francisco, pp. 1541–1544 (2004)
12. Singh, A.K., Kumar, B., Dave, M., Mohan, A.: Multiple watermarking on medical images using selective DWT coefficients. J. Med. Imaging Health Inf. 5(3), 607–614 (2015)
13. Nanmaran, R., Thirugnanam, G., Mangaiyarkarasi, P.: Medical image multiple watermarking scheme based on integer wavelet transform and extraction using ICA. In: Singh, M., Gupta, P., Tyagi, V., Flusser, J., Ören, T. (eds.) ICACDS 2018. CCIS, vol. 905, pp. 44–53. Springer, Singapore (2018). https://doi.org/10.1007/978-981-13-1810-8_5
14. MedPix™ Medical Image Database. http://rad.usuhs.mil/medpix/medpix.html

Empirical Analysis of Defects in Handheld Device Applications

Mamta Pandey, Ratnesh Litoriya[(✉)], and Prateek Pandey

Jaypee University of Engineering and Technology,
Raghogarh, Guna, M.P., India
mamta.pandey07@gmail.com, litoriya.ratnesh@gmail.com,
pandeyprat@yahoo.com

Abstract. A lot of effort and literature has been developed for conventional software. Defect prediction models can be helpful for project managers to improve the quality of software. However, there is insufficient literature concerning the defect proneness of handheld device (mobile) applications, (henceforth HHDA) instead of conventional applications. Still, no efforts were accomplished to figure out the distinct characteristics of handheld device app bugs and their dispersion among the layered architecture of applications. This paper aims to investigate bug proneness of handheld device applications in contrast with the conventional application. In this work, the authors analyzed the bug distribution of HHDA and conventional apps in the different layer of the architecture. There are 15591 bugs of 28 distinct applications have considered. Two-way ANOVA and Bootstrapping approach have used. This empirical analysis firmly administers that mobile application is more defect prone as compared to conventional applications in the presentation layer.

Keywords: HHDA · Conventional applications · Defect prone ·
Bug distribution · Two way ANOVA

1 Introduction

Testing practices can ensure software quality of mobile applications. A variety of literature on testing have been introduced and various attempts also been established to validate those techniques [1, 2]. There is very insufficient literature available to understand the distinct characteristics of mobile applications defect and distribution of bugs in the various layer of the architecture. The specific technology used to built mobile applications (HTML, JavaScript, and CSS) which will introduce to precise bugs (bug related OS incompatibility, interface issues, security issues, etc.) and deal with these bugs ad-hoc based testing required. The characteristics of the mobile-based apps are different from conventional applications. Likewise, the bugs/defects may also be different for both applications. In the rest part of this paper, we will use the term "Conventional" to recognize the entire applications employing non – mobile graphical user interface (GUI).

Previously a minor study presented nature of mobile app defect and classification of defects [3]. There are various phases of analysis of bugs; in the first step generic

© Springer Nature Singapore Pte Ltd. 2019
M. Singh et al. (Eds.): ICACDS 2019, CCIS 1046, pp. 103–113, 2019.
https://doi.org/10.1007/978-981-13-9942-8_10

software bugs have discarded, and initial classification was prepared according to the characteristics of mobile systems. Further, software testers and researchers can use analysis for the structure of fault seeders [4].

In this article, we have analyzed the distribution of bugs of mobile and conventional applications according to the layered architecture of applications. On the bases of analysis, some research questions have formulated –

RQ: Are mobile applications

(i)   More defected
(ii) Less defected
(iii) Equally defected.

In their different layers such as presentation, business, and data layer than conventional applications?

To justification of the above question, we organized observational analysis based on manual classification bugs by using manual bug tracking systems comprehended in various open Github and Sourceforge applications.

The conception of this article has taken from [4]; in explanatory way (1) we have analyzed the distribution of bugs of applications in the various layer of architecture, (2) 15591 bug have retrieved from 28 applications in this empirical investigation, (3) We have analyzed larger experimental observation of the bugs.

The formulation of this article has given the following:
Related work has explained in Sect. 2. Design of experimental observation has detailed in Sect. 3. Analysis of data has discussed in Sect. 4. Discussion of paper has presented in Sect. 5. Threads of validity discussed in Sect. 6. At last in Sect. 7, the paper has concluded and the scope of future work drawn.

2   Related Works

This work is the affiliate to (1) mobile app testing; (2) bug classifications and models and (3) model forecasting and bug proneness. The outline of available literature for the individual point has given one by one.

2.1   Mobile Application Testing

The pervasiveness of mobile devices is continuously growing and taking over to conventional (desktop) computers. Various tools and techniques have been presented by the researchers for testing of mobile applications. The testing of mobile applications performed by developers or testers in a different way instead of conventional applications such as unit testing and GUI testing [5], security and compatibility testing [6]. Existing literature shows that available tools and techniques are mainly based on abduction effectiveness (e.g. Appium, Robotium, and MonkeyRunner). They save whole access of user's interactions with GUI of the application and replay at the time of specific testing. To analyze, the correct behavior of HHDA, apps tested by test patterns,

Morgado & Paiva have proposed an automatic testing method combining reverse engineering with testing [7]. Model-based testing techniques have described the functional test case generation based on the performance of an application under test and the starting model-based technique (MBT) was proposed by [8].

The objective of proposing refined HHDA testing technique is making HHDA impressive and adequate even the nature of HHDA is very complex and dynamic. Dynamic techniques are used by these testing approaches, test cases generated and on the bases of advanced analysis techniques such as model checking for boosting the testing of mobile applications. Mobile applications have difficult to handle exceptions with compatibility, middleware, memory constraints and restrictions the battery. There are various bugs hazards occur in mobile applications that developers have to face [9]. The objective of these investigations is exploring deficiencies that are manifested by means of failure of the mobile applications and java exception that generally appeared in mobile software.

After reviewing various literature one thing could monitor that maximum of the analyzed mobile application testing techniques have mostly concentrated on user interface and functional testing. Customized models are designed for unconventional development scenario like web and Agile practices [10, 11]. The outcomes achieved in the observational analysis contribute a durable indication that the presentation layer in the mobile application is more bug prone than other layers. Testing techniques of HHDA are major concentrating on the presentation layer.

2.2 Bugs Classification in HHDA

Various types of effort have been applied by researchers to analyze and classify bug in HHDA. Different types of bugs appear in the individual type of software and this is very important to understand the reason behind it.

Bugs classification and models are used to organize software errors for individual kind of software systems. Analysis of bug taxonomy methods and application of fault (bug) injection for accomplishing inject fault in each analogous application to the initial one [12]. Jiang et al. [11] detected bugs related to HHDA by using static analysis. They used 64 Android apps and found that resource leak and layout energy defect are 87.5% and 78.1% respectively. Banerjee et al. considered 30 Android apps and presented an automated test generation framework that detects bugs related to battery consumption and hotspot [13].

This paper extends the work of Zhou et al. [4], which analyzed bugs and bug fixing in open source projects: Desktop vs. Android vs. iOS. They considered few bug reports in some open source projects on the desktop, Android, and iOS and irrespective of bug classification, they found that smartphone platforms are still maturing.

After analyzing adequate literature we found that very few researchers have performed analysis on bugs of HHDA, but no any researcher have paid attention to the classification of bugs particularly in the context of HHDA. In this paper, we have made a classification of bugs in HHDA and then compared the result with the conventional apps.

3   Empirical Method of Analysis and Implementation

The empirical method of analysis has deliberated in this section. We have come up with simplified examples of the bug taxonomy.

3.1   Method

We determined bug taxonomy by using bug tracking systems from Github and Sourceforge applications. A transparent and clear-cut procedure has followed to – (1) different applications database, (2) selection of respective bug and (3) bug classification strategy.

Detail process for selection of applications and classification of bugs in this empirical method has shown in Fig. 1 by means of BPMN [14]. In this paper, BPMN has been decided for exemplification of the workflow of the process because it is a slandered modeling language. Various activities have represented by using different symbols such as - rounded corner rectangle represents activities, diamond denotes gateways. Diamonds consists of a circle are comprehensive decision nodes represents whole outgoing activities which are executed in lateral to recognize the global activity. At last, circles denote first and final activities.

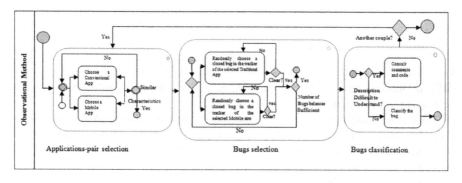

Fig. 1. The procedure of applications selection and bug classification

There are three prime sections in figure -

1. *Selection of applications* - In this section we select such pair of applications those have identical feature. Some adjustable benchmark has built for choosing the pair of applications. There are some criteria have decided for the selection of applications – (1) Category of application and domain, (2) similar characteristic but different user interface (3) same age gap of applications and (4) proportional amount of code. Initially, two criteria would obligatorily while remaining criteria are flexible. Count and dissemination of bugs vary according to the life of the applications.
2. *Selection of bugs* - This section comes under the bug explanation of particular selected applications. Selection of bugs has been done on the arbitrary bases. We choose such bugs from bug archive those earlier fixed by the application developer;

such bug also called closed bugs. These bugs considered from two categories of applications, mobile and conventional. We have discarded unambiguous bug for increasing the efficiency of the taxonomy of bugs. Bugs assumed as unambiguous those easily tracked by bug tracker system with clear explanation.

3. *Taxonomy of bugs* - This section analyzed all bugs those collected in the above steps and classified to them. Each bug of both applications has analyzed properly so that bug can understand. After analysis there are five types of taxonomy conceivable - user face the problem during use of applications in layout this types of bugs classified under the graphical user interface (GUI), and this comes under the presentation layer. Bugs related to the computational issue, i.e. cost didn't take from the user by the proper process; this class of bug comes under business logic. Bugs related to SQL or while copying some data from one place to another bug occurred categorized under the data logic.

3.2 Defect Analysis

We have manually categorized in various sections such as defect id, explanation, and class. We took the pair of applications on the base of the domain, technology, LOCs, and a number of downloads and mentioned the detail of applications in Table 1. Here category of bugs considered as the dependent variable. At the presentation level, three classifications of bugs have selected Logic, Unknown, and Presentation. Proportions of both types of applications considered as derived dependent variable.

Table 1. Analysis of various test applied in each app domain

	Domain	Raw data		Bootstrapping	
		OR	p-value	OR	p-value
Content-based	Books & references	2.70	0.171	2.780	0.014
	Business	3.57	0.020	3.611	**<0.001**
	Documenter	2.15	0.036	2.211	0.010
	Productivity	2.27	0.027	2.312	0.011
	Tool	2.19	0.018	2.253	0.010
	Editor	2.18	0.018	2.230	0.109
	Finance	2.11	0.019	2.190	0.100
Theme based	Conferencing	3.79	0.011	3.950	**<0.001**
	Video players & Editors	2.32	0.017	2.381	0.110
	Entertainment	2.20	0.013	2.294	0.013
	plotting	4.78	0.002	4.810	**<0.001**
	Communication	2.37	0.021	2.412	0.011
	Lifestyle	2.35	0.036	2.396	0.012
	Game	3.15	0.024	3.194	**0.005**

3.3 Formulation of Hypothesis

We performed a broad scale observational analysis to justify our hypotheses. Some hypothesis has generated here -

RQ1: Are HHDA are more bug prone than conventional apps in the presentation layer?

To explore and justify hypothesis we can develop two null hypotheses to be examined in the observation -

$H1_0$: Mean proportion of bug of mobile and conventional apps is the same.
$H2_0$: There is no dependency on the distribution of bugs in presentation, logic, business, and unknown in mobile and conventional apps.

Above hypotheses are addressing the bug-prone of the presentation layer of both categories of apps. Final hypotheses are more comprehensive to recognize the classification of bugs. Hypothesis $H1_0$ concentrates on the bug-prone of the presentation layer whether the second part hypothesis indicates the distribution of bugs on the different layer. In order above hypotheses, we have derived some alternate hypotheses which are given following -

$H1_a$: Mean proportion of bug in both categories apps is not the same.
$H2_a$: Both categories of apps affected by the distribution of bugs in the different layer.

Corresponding we will analyze the influence of bug distribution in different layers of both categories of apps. Hence we formulate another research question i.e. RQ2.

RQ2: Does domain of apps affect the bug-prone of the presentation layer of both categories of apps?

To analyze the RQ2, we can generate some null hypotheses and related alternate hypotheses.

$H3_0$: Bug distributed in both categories of apps is independent in types of apps.
$H3_1$: Bug distribution in both categories of apps is dependent on types of apps.

3.3.1 Analysis of Process

To analyze the number of bugs in each app, we have plotted bar chart after that performed different hypotheses accordingly.

The standard significant level α is 5% adopted, and null hypothesis has rejected [15]. In our observation data point is not so large, and there are non - normal distributions in our dataset that's why we used a non-parametric test. $H1_0$ have no directionality; we select two-tailed test.

To figure out and the better understanding of the distribution of bugs among all classified layers, i.e. business, logic, and presentation, we used the strategy which mentioned below-

$$Business \rightarrow 0, \ Logic \rightarrow 1, \ presentation \rightarrow 2$$

The median value of each pair of apps has compared by using Mann - Whitney test. To analyze hypothesis $H3_0$, we observed possible cooperation of app type and domain and analyzed the defectiveness of apps in the presentation layer. To get more confirmation about the defect, we compare each app of each domain according to their combination. One tail Mann Whitney test performed in each domain of apps. We have applied Bootstrapping technique in each combination of app and again took sample S_n, and iteration cycle was R_n times and mean of sample statistics have calculated. The value of $S_n = 260$ and resample size $R_n = 990$ is chosen. We obtain various errors during the Mann-Whitney test, after that we applied correlation [16, 17]. Above analysis do not present any particular figure of difference but it provides the significance of the difference. The sensible importance of analysis has shown. There are two types of measure used to confirm this analysis - $H_0 1$ analyzed by using Cohen d and $H_0 2$, $H_0 3$ analyzed by using odds ratio. Cohen d (Cohen d = 3.9) analyze the effect size for the comparison of two mean

$$Cohen's \ d = (M2 - M1)/SDpooled \tag{1}$$

$$SDpooled = \sqrt{((SD12 + SD22)/2)} \tag{2}$$

By using formula (1) and (2), we can measure the strength of the relationship between mobile and conventional apps. In our study mean of the proportion of bugs treated as a dependent variable. The range of interval of d is considered $d \in (0.3, 0.7)$, and medium for $d \in (0.7, 0.8)$ and large for $d \geq 0.9$.

4   Analysis of Data

There is a total of 28 apps (14 conventional and 14 HHDA) from different domain have considered, and 15591 various bugs were categorized.

Figure 2 is presenting the result, defect percentage of HHDA on business, presentation and logic layer are 35%, 47%, and 26% respectively. Similarly, the defect percentage of conventional apps in different layer, i.e. business, logic and presentation layer are 30%, 38%, and 22% respectively. It concluded that HHDA are more defect prone in presentation layer than conventional apps.

i. The quantity of proportion of bugs presentation layer in the HHDA (median = 53%) is more than conventional apps (35%). We considered a few numbers of apps (14 mobile and 14 conventional apps). The first null hypothesis was rejected because p-value = 0.003 (from two-tailed Mann-Whitney test) it is too small. We calculated p-value = 0.003 from the Mann-Whitney test which is too small and $H1_0$ has rejected.

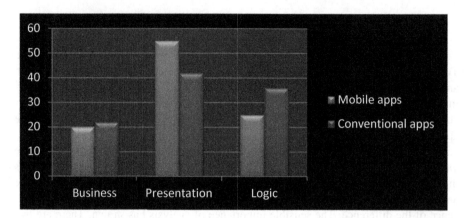

Fig. 2. Bug percentages in a different layer of mobile and conventional apps

ii. We used the Mann Whitney test to analyze $H2_0$. In outcome p-value is less than 0.01, So $H2_0$ can be rejected. We have ignored 'unknown' categories of bugs to the calculation of odds ratio during comparison of bugs of HHDA and conventional apps in the presentation layer. The value of the odds ratio is 1.98. It represents, the defect in the mobile app is approx double than popular apps in presentation versus logic layer.

iii. To check the dependency of distribution of bugs across the all considered layer (business, presentation, and logic) two-way ANOVA and result is analyzed. We analyzed and recognized the effect of app type $p < 0.03$ and from the previous test, we found $p = 0.037$(app domain), there is no any interaction between 0.03 and 0.037.

We compared the combination of apps with the help of the Mann Whitney test and result analyzed by Bonferroni correlation analysis. The variable for Bonferroni correlation analysis $\alpha_b = 0.005$.

Bootstrapping technique has used for justification of sample size (as we have discussed previously) and various test have performed to analyze the sample size. Highlighted values represent that they are implicitly significant the Bonferroni correction. The application of Bootstrapping improves the outcome according to expectation. We analyzed, one domain of content base presents a symbolic diversity whereas in another case no such kind of diversity occur (ratio is 1:7). The statistical difference of bug proneness between mobile and conventional apps has observed by (ratio is 5:1); means there is no any difference in the visually based domain group. Another thing we have observed during analysis maximum ratio is near about 2 except a few domains with ratio 3:3. It is determined from ANOVA there is no any interaction between two variables. The distribution of bugs is little affected by app domain, and hypothesis $H3_0$ is rejected. Figure 2 will compare the bugs of HHDA and conventional apps on the presentation layer. We have considered one app for a domain.

5   Result and Discussions

An observational analysis of data was performed, and it is concluded that HHDA are more bug prone than conventional apps in the presentation layer. Initially, $H1_0$ and $H2_0$ have rejected with immense confidence value $p < 0.001$ and $H2_a$ can be treated as valid. It is very clear from the hypothesis that – (a) the significant difference between the mobile app and conventional apps in the presentation layer and (b) bug in the different layer of mobile and conventional apps varies on apps type. We have observed the value of effect size i.e. Cohen $d = 3.9$ is very high for the first hypothesis, and the value of the odds ratio is 1.98 for the anther hypothesis. The outcome also affirms the effect of the domain of apps on the distribution of bugs between mobile and conventional apps. In the case of apps, those belong from the game domain (visual-based) have to defect varies significantly. Visual-based apps require complicated and large user interface (UI) which is the main reason of elaboration of the difference of bugs. There are two domains of apps Business and Lifestyle lie outside of this assumption. The framework of Business is very complicated that is the reason for increase bugs of the presentation layer in the HHDA, and major analysis is required for more confirmation. The Lifestyle domain comes under the visual based. There are the various user interface and pictures included, so the complexity of such apps is also higher than other apps and bugs at the presentation layer in HHDA are more. We have left the reason for increasing bugs in the mobile app at the presentation layer for the future study. There are some facts about HHDA - (a) the development method of HHDA and conventional apps are almost the same, but the number of LOC may be the reason for producing bugs and another (b) After being similar functionality in a pair of apps is distinct even with identical quantity of codes, the reason of more bug-prone of HHDA. The determination of these facts we would be required some real data related presentation layer size after that comparison of defect density of apps. In this paper, we have not analyzed defect density of apps, but we are in support of the calculation of defect density (Fig. 3).

6   Threats of Validity

There is some validity described in this section such as – (1) internal validity, (2) construct validity and (3) conclusion validity and (4) external validity.

When dependent variables affected by extraneous factors i.e. known as internal validity, the outcome of this validity will influence overall factors. Such kind of factor is identified in our research during the selection of applications and bugs. The distinct selection of applications and distribution of bugs accordingly retrieved consequences. For more confirmation of this threat, we have selected pair of applications (mobile and conventional) with similar nature.

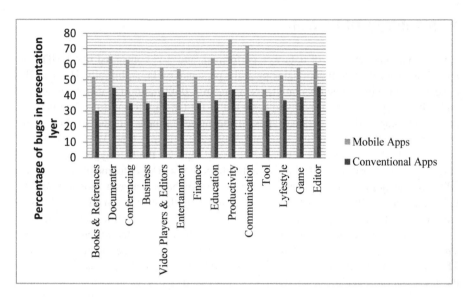

Fig. 3. Bugs of the presentation layer in mobile and conventional apps

7 Conclusion and Future Work

Distribution of defects in the presentation layer of different applications (mobile and conventional) has observed by analysis and correlation of defects. Our analysis presents various types of bugs of the present level of the mobile and conventional applications. The presence of bugs in the mobile applications is on business, presentation and logic layer are 35%, 47%, and 26% respectively. In contrast, conventional applications the number of errors is in a different layer, i.e. business, logic, and presentation layer are 30%, 38%, and 22% respectively. It has been observed many defects in the mobile applications are more than conventional applications.

A different observation in our empirical analysis is the domain factor of each application affects the distribution of bugs. The portion of a graphical user of every application is more bug-prone than the textual portion. The achieved outcomes show that it is prime experimental analysis for mobile application has done to the best of our knowledge. We have considered the limited number of bugs and domain name, but in future, more bugs with other domain names can be considered. We will also focus on defect density of various apps in our future work.

References

1. Vasquez, M.L., Moran, K., Poshyvanyk, D.: Continuous, evolutionary and large-scale: a new perspective for automated mobile app testing. In: International Conference on Software Maintenance and Evolution, pp. 399–410 (2017)
2. Hess, S., Kiefer, F., Carbon, R.: Quality by construction through mConcAppt. In: 8th International Conference on the Quality of Information and Communications Technology, pp. 313–318 (2012)
3. Harrold, M.J., Offutt, A.J., Tewary, K.: An approach to fault modeling and fault seeding using the program dependence graph. J. Syst. Softw. **36**, 273–295 (1997)
4. Zhou, B., Neamtiu, I., Gupta, R.: A cross-platform analysis of bugs and bug-fixing in open source projects: desktop vs. Android vs. iOS. In: Proceedings of the 19th International Conference on Evaluation and Assessment in Software Engineering (2015)
5. Kim, H., Choi, B., Wong, W.E.: Performance testing of mobile applications at the unit test level. In: 3rd International Conference on Secure Software Integration and Reliability Improvement, pp. 171–180 (2009)
6. Liu, Z., Hu, Y., Cai, L.: Research on software security and compatibility test for mobile application. In: 4th Edition of the International Conference on the Innovative Computing Technology, pp. 140–145 (2014)
7. Morgado, I.C., Paiva, A.C.: Testing approach for mobile applications through reverse engineering of UI patterns. In: 30th International Conference on Automated Software Engineering Workshop, pp. 42–49 (2015)
8. Shabaan, M.M., Hamza, H.S., Omar, Y.K.: Effects of FSM minimization techniques on number of test paths in mobile applications MBT. In: 15th International Conference on Software Engineering Research, Management and Applications, pp. 297–302 (2017)
9. Coelho, R., Almeida, L., Gousios, G., Deursen, A.V., Treude, C.: Exception handling bug hazards in Android results from a mining study and an exploratory survey. Technical Report Series, pp. 1–44. Delft University of Technology Software Engineering Research Group (2016)
10. Gatou, C., Politis, A., Zevgolis, D.: The importance of mobile interface icons on user interaction. Int. J. Comput. Sci. Appl. **9**, 92–107 (2012)
11. Jiang, H., Yang, H., Qin, S., Su, Z., Zhang, J., Yan, J.: Detecting energy bugs in Android apps using static analysis. In: Duan, Z., Ong, L. (eds.) ICFEM 2017. LNCS, vol. 10610, pp. 192–208. Springer, Cham (2017). https://doi.org/10.1007/978-3-319-68690-5_12
12. Lo, D., Cheng, H., Han, J., Khoo, S.C., Sun, C.: Classification of software behaviours for failure detection: a discriminative pattern mining approach. In: Proceedings of the 15th ACM SIGKDD International Conference on Knowledge Discovery and Data Mining, pp. 557–566 (2009)
13. Banerjee, A., Chong, L.K., Chattopadhyay, S., Roychoudhury, A.: Detecting energy bugs and hotspots in mobile apps. In: Proceedings of the 22nd ACM SIGSOFT International Symposium on Foundations of Software Engineering, pp. 588–598 (2014)
14. Bhattacharya, P., Ulanova, L., Neamtiu, L., Koduru, S.C.: An empirical analysis of bug reports and bug fixing in open source. In: Proceedings of 17th European Conference on Software Maintenance and Reengineering, pp. 133–143 (2013)
15. Wohlin, C., Runeson, P., Höst, M., Ohlsson, M., Regnell, B., Wesslén, A.: Experimentation in Software Engineering. An Introduction. Kluwer Academic Publishers, Dordrecht (2000)
16. Shaffer, J.P.: Multiple hypothesis testing. Ann. Rev. Psychol. **46**, 561–584 (1995)
17. Litoriya, R., Kothari, A.: Cost Estimation of web projects in context with Agile paradigm: improvements and validation. Int. J. Softw. Eng. **6**(2), 91–114 (2013)

Lexical Text Simplification Using WordNet

Debabrata Swain[(⊠)], Mrunmayee Tambe, Preeti Ballal,
Vishal Dolase, Kajol Agrawal, and Yogesh Rajmane

Department of IT-MCA, Vishwakarma Institute of Technology, Pune, India
debabrata.swain@vit.edu

Abstract. Internet is distributed environment and hence, huge amount of information is available on it. People use internet to access the information on the web. While referring to any information people face difficulty to understand the complex sentences and words used related to technology and science. Technical and scientific words are mostly found in research papers, medical reports, newspapers and other reading material. Text simplification is a technique used to automatically transform complicated text into simpler form. In the proposed system an efficient text simplification technique has been developed using word net model available in the Natural Language toolkit (NLTK). The dataset used for experimentation is collected through a random survey from web sources. Here, the proposed system is divided into 3 phases. In the first phase data collection and pre-processing has been performed. In second phase complex words are identified and in the 3rd phase replacement of complex words with their simple synonyms is being done. The performance of the system has been analyzed by user review to accuracy of 87%.

Keywords: Text simplification ·
Lexical simplification and syntactic simplification · Tokenization

1 Introduction

Text simplification is a procedure of simplifying grammatically complex text into simple text retaining its semantic meaning. Information of various domains is available on internet like medical reports, research papers, e-learning websites, agriculture and sports. Complex sentences and words related to information are difficult to understand by technically illiterate person. Its application to the medical field is important as the majority of health information, needs understanding skills that an ordinary adult doesn't have [1]. This restricts on improving the health conditions in spite of available health information. Adult literacy is a concern in developed and developing countries, one in six adults in the United Kingdom have limited educational skills [2] and only a quarter of Brazilians who have studied for 8 years can be considered fully educated [21]. Aphasia readers have problem in understanding long and complex sentences and Dyslexia readers face trouble in reading difficult words [3]. Text Simplification is a technique that helps in solving these problems. Text simplification targets mainly to make information available to the target people in simpler and understandable format.

Simplification approaches such as substituting or removing words, splitting, dropping, or merging sentences are used to create simpler text. Different simplification

© Springer Nature Singapore Pte Ltd. 2019
M. Singh et al. (Eds.): ICACDS 2019, CCIS 1046, pp. 114–122, 2019.
https://doi.org/10.1007/978-981-13-9942-8_11

techniques are applied based on context, length, and syntactic structure of the source words and sentences [18]. Lexical simplification technique is used to simplify text which replaces difficult words with frequently used and easy words. Lexical simplification incorporates: identification of the complex words; locating synonyms by various similarity measures; ranking and selecting the best suitable word based on criteria such as language model; and preserving the grammar and syntax of a sentence correct [4].

Rule-based systems use handwritten rules for syntactic simplification, and replace difficult words using predefined vocabulary [20]. By determining the difficult sentences, a sentence with a particular structure can be converted into a simple structure. For example, if a long sentence contains "not only" and "but also", it could be split into two sentences [4]. System needs to define the rules which needs a significant human involvement and is not preferable.

Text simplification relates to many Natural language Processing tasks like parsing, machine translation and summarization [19]. Most of the work on text simplification uses natural language processing approach to simplify text. Lexical simplification technique along with the natural language toolkit has been used in this paper. There are mainly 3 steps in lexical simplification. Firstly, data is collected which includes the complex words and their associated synonyms and collected data is preprocessed. Secondly complex words form the documents are to be identified which contains list of substitutions for those words. Finally, the complex words identified are replaced by the proper substitutions without affecting the meaning of the text. Tokenization used transforms text into pieces called tokens, removing away certain special characters such as punctuations. NLTK contains the word tokenize package which helps to tokenize the sentence into tokens and store in a list form along with its tags.

2   Literature

Sasikiran Kandula et al. has proposed an efficient text simplification system for the semantic and syntactic understanding of various health related terms.

In semantic simplification the system has analyzed 150 diabetes related records and recognized key relations used to describe usual semantic groups [5] of health concepts. The relationship between the difficult and easy terms is dependent on the semantic type of difficult terms. Syntactic simplification is applied at the sentence level. Sentences having more than 10 words are processed. Part of speech (POS) tagger a sentence with more than 10 words is tokenized and each token (word) is labeled with a Part of Speech tagger. Open source software open-NLP has been used to perform this task developed by (Morton, Bierner, Baldridge, Kottmann). Grammar [9] simplifier-module breaks longer sentences into two or more smaller sentences based on work of Siddharthan [7]. Identifies POS pattern and applies rules to generate shorter sentences. Output validator checks the output produced against sentence too short i.e. sentence should contain less than seven words. Tokens are represented as null links. Open NLP score is also checked and if score is less than −6 then the sentence is improbable to be English sentence. Validation is performed by considering two sets and results are verified based on it. User testing of this tool shows considerable improvement in the score of about 50% to 60% is considered to represent reasonable readability.

Joachim Bingel, Gustavo H. Paetzold, Anders Søgaard et al. developed a framework for adaptive lexical simplification, showing how the user's feedback can be used to enhance the text. Lexi, an open-source tool for adaptive text simplification that has been used to test the text [10]. Replacing single words with simpler synonyms using pipeline approach. Pipeline consist of four steps first Complex words identification. Second substitution generation to generate a simpler word for replacement. Third is the substitution selection and finally these words are ranked in order of simplicity known as substitution ranking. Adaptive complex words identification is done. Lexi stores user information and simplification histories in a PostgreSQL database.

Seid Muhie Yimam Chris Biemann et al. Par4sim is a Text simplification system with integrated adaptive paraphrase ranking model tool [11]. This tool is integrated with the Amazon Mechanical Turk crowdsourcing platform to collect data for text simplification. In the tool text can be reloaded, undo redo can be done, we can highlight difficult words and shows instructions for the users and animations. Dataset used is Word Net and distributional thesaurus [12] to produce results for complex words. Phrase2Vec model using English Wikipedia and the AQUAINT corpus of English news text has been trained and used. Learning to rank model contains ranking model based on training data ranking list. Ranklib [12], a well-known learning-to-rank library in Java from the Lemur Project is used to build the Ranking models. To train the learning to rank model LambdaMART algorithm has been used. The performance of the adaptive system on the collected data, has been evaluated in iterative way. In every iteration, the usage data exclusively from the previous iterations to train the learning-to-rank model. The result shows that, in every iteration, there is a large increase in performance based on the NDCG@10 evaluation metric.

David Kauchak et al. argued that the Patient Protection and Affordable Care Act (ACA, a law that came into action in the United States in 2010) to be fruitful, more effort is required to improve the health education of millions of Americans [17]. This paper examines sixteen features forecasting the difficulty of health text using six machine learning algorithms. Sixteen features used are character count, word count, nouns, adjective, adverb, verbs, average frequency, median frequency, frequency rank, specificity and ambiguity. The 6 different algorithms used to determine the accuracy of the features are Random forest – 84.14%, Decision tree – 76.75%, Linear regression – 74.62%, SVM – 74.48%, KNN – 63.82%, Naive Bayes – 59.41%.

Tong Wang and John Rochford and Jipeng Qiang and Ping Chen et al. Neural Machine Translation (NMT) is a newly recommended machine translation approach is used. It achieves very magnificent results on Machine Translation (MT) tasks. A large neural network was attempt to build such that every component is linked based upon training sentence pairs. NMT introduces RNN encoder and decoder model to explain difference between text simplification and machine translation tasks [4]. Recurrent Neural Network Encoder-Decoder (Cho et al. 2014; Vinyals, Sutskever and Le 2014) is a Neural Machine Translation model (NMT model) that can be unitedly trained to increase the Conditional probability of a target sequence given a source sequence p $(Y|X)$.

The deep neural network can learn all simplification rules by itself.

Xing Xing Zhang and Mirella Lapata. Authors have developed a reinforcement learning-based model which simplify the text, the model can incorporate simpleness, grammar, and accuracy to the input. Author proposed a lexical simplification feature that improves the performance of the previous system. Overall, author finds that reinforcement learning shows great effect to add basic knowledge to the simplification task hence, achieving good results across multiple datasets. Author obtained results for randomly sampled hundered sentences. Besides comparing system outputs of PBMT-R, Hybrid, EncDecA, DRESS, and DRESS-LS, author set an upper bound by extracting the ratings of the gold standard reference. Results are obtained individually and in combination. Results are for fluency, simplicity and adequacy.

3 Modules

3.1 NLTK (Natural Language Tool Kit)

Natural Language Tool Kit is a platform to work with spoken language data. It provides an interface for multiple corpora like Word Net with a collection of processing libraries for classification, tokenization, stemming, tagging, parsing and many more. NLTK is adaptive for linguists, students, educators and researchers. It is free to use and is publicly accessible. It is a suitable collection to manipulate natural language.

It aims at helping with Natural Language Processing methodology by providing a large set of sub-modules providing facilities for multiple techniques. NLTK helps from dividing data into sentences from a large corpus, decomposing the sentences into words, identifying the part of speech of the words.

NLTK is used in this system for the following main reasons:

- Simplicity:
  It provides an intelligent framework with big building blocks, providing a practical knowledge of NLP without delay which happens with processing annotated language data.
- Consistency:
  Provides stable interfaces and data structures and methods which can be easily understood.
- Extensibility:
  Provides a structure for new software modules with alternative executions and competing approaches to the task.
- Modularity:
  Provides elements with independent use.

3.2 Word Net

Word Net is a large lexical dataset of English words. Verbs, Nouns, Adjectives, and Adverbs are collected together into sets of synonyms called Synsets. Synsets are linked by means of idea-based and word-based relations. Word Net's structure makes it a useful device for computer-based study of language and natural language processing.

It is a NLTK corpus reader, available open source under NLTK module. The Word Net is being evolved because of multiple users accessing it for text related problem statements. The NLTK corpus reader gives access to the Open Multilingual Word Net.

3.3   POS Tagger

A Part-Of-Speech tagger (POS-tagger), deals with a sequence of words, and links a part of speech tag to each word. It is a software application that accepts text in some language and allocates a part of speech (POS) to each word like Noun, Verb etc. Part of Speech Tagging is also called as grammatical tagging or word category disambiguation. It works with the help of the provided word's definition and its context i.e. the relationship of the word with its neighboring words in the sentence. Part of Speech Tagging is done in the context of computational linguistics using algorithms and hidden parts of speech. Research on parts of speech tagging has been nearly tied to corpus linguistics.

A single word may show more than one part of speech at different times. In natural languages a large percentage of word-forms are ambiguous. For example,

(1)   The heavens are above. (Here, above is an adverb.)
(2)   Our blessings come from above. (Here, above is a Noun.)

Grammatical context is a way to determine this ambiguity. Semantic analysis can also be used to infer that above is used as an adverb in the first sentence whereas it is used as a noun in the second sentence (Fig. 1).

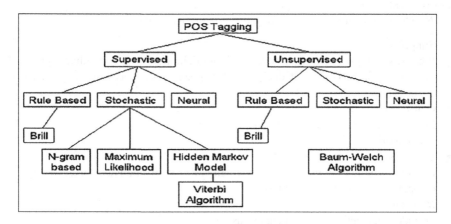

Fig. 1. POS tagging modules

4   Proposed Architecture

A system which fully focuses on Lexical Simplification in which complex words are identified and replaced. Lexical simplification focuses on replacement of complex words with easy-to-read (or understand) expressions while keeping the meaning of the actual text components (Fig. 2).

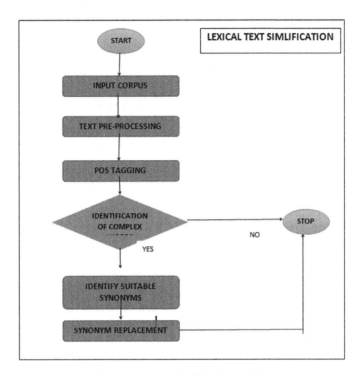

Fig. 2. Lexical text simplification architecture

Lexical Text simplification provides the solution for at least two tasks: (i) Finding the set of synonymic applicants for a given word, normally depending on a dictionary and (ii) Substituting the target word by a synonym which is easy to read and understand in the given context. For the first task, lexical resources such like Word Net could be used. For the second task a simple approach of replacing words is used.

Lexical POS Tagging is Based on Following Formula. Our framework divides Part-Of-Speech tagging into two parts: (i) First, allocating tags and probabilities $p(Y|M)$ to each word Y in a sentence and each of its possible analyses M and (ii) Second, re-scoring the different analyses of the complete sentence using parallel weighted models for word and tag sequences. In the first part, the tag profile for a word Y and the probabilities $p(y|m)$ for each of its tags is calculated from a training collection. The probabilities are independent of neighboring words and tags.

$$P(Y|M) = P(y_1, y_2, \ldots \ldots y_n | m_1, m_2, \ldots \ldots m_n)$$

From the chain rule:

$$= \prod_{j=1}^{v} P(y_j | y_1 m_1 \ldots \ldots y_{j-1} m_{j-1} m_j)$$

Simplifying assumption: Probability of word depends only on its own tag $P(y_j|m_j)$
So,

$$\approx \prod_{j=1}^{v} P(y_j|m_j)$$

$$M' = \mathrm{argmax}_{M \in m} \prod_{j=1}^{v} P(m_j|m_{j-1}) \prod_{j=1}^{v} P(y_j|m_j)$$

Proposed Algorithm. Following steps are used for Lexical Text Simplification using the proposed system.

1. Input corpus:
   In this step, the input text is accepted from the user for simplification.
2. Perform text preprocessing:
   After accepting input, the pre-processing of the input text is being performed. In this phase, main purpose is to perform tokenization of the sentence. In tokenization sentence is parsed into separate words
3. Perform POS Tagging:
   In this step, the parts-of-speech of the tokenized words is identified. Each word is been assigned with a tag containing abbreviation of parts-of-speech. Depending on parts-of-speech the list is separated into list of Adverbs, Adjectives, Nouns.
4. Complex words identification:
   In this step, the lists created in previous step are merged. The words in merged list are compared in sentence to find position of each word. A complete set of complex words and their position in sentence is created.
5. Suitable Synonym identification:
   This step focuses on finding the suitable simple synonym for complex words. Here, synset is used for synonym identification. Alternatives are then stored and kept ready to perform replacement according to their position.
6. Perform synonym replacement:
   After finding synonyms of complex words, the replacement of words in sentence takes place depending upon the relative position of the complex word.

5   Performance Analysis

The performance is being analyzed by random survey. Multiple reviews from users have been collected on the basis of simplified text. In order to evaluate the performance of the system, a random survey has been conducted. In the survey input is collected from 100 people of different domain. Users provided complicated sentences to the system and a simplified version of the sentence were provided to them in return. After taking the input the data is fed to system.

The results of the performance are as follows:

Out of 100 records 35 records belong to engineering domain, 35 records are from medical domain and 30 records are from financial domain. Out of 100 records, user provided positive feedback for 87 records (Table 1).

Table 1. Performance analysis

Domain	Number of records	Positive reviews	Percentage
Engineering	35	32	91%
Medical	35	29	82.85%
Finance	30	26	86.66%
	100	87	87%

6   Conclusions

The system is performing satisfactory, using Word Net repository. Texts from multiple domains are simplified up to a certain level but there are some cases where synonyms cannot be found for certain words. Using POS tagging is a fast approach. Data can be easily analyzed and divided into tokens using Tokenization with high performance. Simplification of words does not depend on the content of the sentence. In future scope of the system, simplification can be based on the context and subject of the sentence provide by the user.

References

1. Panzer, A.M., Kindig, D.A., Nielsen-Bohlman, L.: Health Literacy: A Prescription to End Confusion. National Academy Press, Washington, D.C. (2004)
2. Skeppstedt, M., Kvist, M., Abrahamsson, E., Forni, T.: Medical text simplification using synonym replacement: adapting assessment of word difficulty to a compounding language (2014)
3. Tyagi, S., Chopra, D., Mathur, I., Joshi, N.: Classifier based text simplification for improved machine translation (2015)
4. Wang, T., Qiang, J., Rochford, J., Chen, P.: Text simplification using neural machine translation (2016)
5. McCray, A.T., Bodenreider, O.: Exploring semantic groups through visual approaches. J. Biomed. Inform. **36**(6), 414–432 (2003)
6. Baldridge, J., Bierner, G., Morton, T., Kottmann, J.: OpenNLP. A Java-based NLP Toolkit (2005)
7. Siddharthan, A.: Syntactic simplification and text cohesion. Res. Lang. Comput. **4**, 77–109 (2006)

8. Curtis, D., Leroy, G., Zeng-Treitler, Q., Smith, C.A., Keselman, A., Logan, R.: Developing informatics tools and strategies for consumer-centered health communication. J. Am. Med. Inform. Assoc. **15**(4), 473–483 (2008)
9. Sleator, D., Grinberg, D., Lafferty, J.: A robust parsing algorithm for link grammars (1995)
10. Bingel, J., Paetzold, G.H., Søgaard, A.: Lexi: a tool for adaptive, personalized text simplification (2018)
11. Yimam, S.M., Biemann, C.: Par4Sim – adaptive paraphrasing for text simplification
12. Biemann, C., Riedl, M.: Text: now in 2D! A framework for lexical expansion with contextual similarity. J. Lang. Model. **1**(1), 55–95 (2013)
13. Siddharthan, A.: An architecture for a text simplification system. In: Proceedings of the IEEE Language Engineering Conference (2002)
14. Dymetman, M., Cancedda, N., Specia, L., Turchi, M., Cristianini, N.: Estimating the sentence-level quality of machine translation systems. In: 13th Conference of the European Association for Machine Translation (2009)
15. Aluisio, S., Scarton, C., Specia, L., Gasperin, C.: Readability assessment for text simplification. In: Proceedings of the NAACL HLT 2010 Fifth Workshop on Innovative Use of NLP for Building Educational Applications. Association for Computational Linguistics (2010)
16. Etayo, E., Martínez, E.G., Saggion, H., Bourg, L., Anula, A.: Text simplification in simplext: making text more accessible. Procesamiento del lenguaje natural **47**, 341–342 (2011)
17. Kauchak, D., Pentoney, C., Leroy, G., Mouradi, O.: Text simplification tools: using machine learning to discover features that identify difficult text (2014)
18. Petersen, E., Ostendorf, M.: Text simplification for language learners: a corpus analysis. In: Speech and Language Technology for Education (2007)
19. Chandrasekar, R., Doran, C., Srinivas, B.: Motivations and methods for text simplification. In: Proceedings of the International Conference on Computational Linguistics, pp. 1041–1044 (1996)
20. Mandya, A.A., Siddharthan, A.: Text simplification using synchronous dependency grammars: generalising automatically harvested rules. In: 8th International Natural Language Generation Conference, pp. 16–25 (2014). Research Output: Chapter in Book/Report/Conference Proceeding, Conference Contribution
21. Margarido, P.R.A., Pardo, T.A.S., Antonio, G.M., Fuentes, V.B., Aires, R., Aluísio, S.M., Fortes, R.P.M.: Automatic summarization for text simplification: evaluating text understanding by poor readers. In: Proceedings of the XIV Brazilian Symposium on Multimedia and the Web (2008). https://doi.org/10.1145/1809980.1810057

Analysis and Impact of Trust and Recommendation in Social Network Based Algorithm for Delay Tolerant Network

Abhilasha Rangra, Vivek Kumar Sehgal$^{(\boxtimes)}$, and Shailendra Shukla

Jaypee University of Information Technology, Wakhnaghat, India
vivekseh@ieee.org

Abstract. In delay tolerant network data, routing is a field of concern in late years and a lot of researchers suggested many techniques for routing. Number of nodes is very less in delay tolerant sparse network, even criteria of losing data is huge. Many approaches been proposed in recent past but most of them failed to perform significantly. An opinion dynamic based approach proposed in this work, which calculates the trust value of a node due to which source node decide whether to send the data to the next node or not because of security issues as in network malicious nodes can be present, and it also calculate an opinion with other nodes too in a network. An opinion calculated based on parameters like packet delivery delay, number of packets lost and residual energy. The result also shows the improvement in various performance parameters in the network.

Keywords: Delay tolerant network (DTN) · Data routing

1 Introduction

Mobile Ad Hoc Network (MANET) is sum of all the moving nodes that interchange data with one another without any established defined communication links & infrastructure. It is self-configuring mobile nodes network, which linked by wireless connections with arbitrary topology [1]. It also provides connectivity of a network between mobile nodes over capacity to develop multi-hop [2]. In MANETs, critical network-layer operations are data packet forwarding & ad hoc routing, which linked with each node and gets functionality of shifting data from source to final destination. Ad hoc routing protocols exchange routing information in nodes & routing states is maintained, accordingly a teach node [3]. In previous years, MANETs got a lot of recognition because of self-configuration, self-maintenance capabilities. DTNs grabbed many recognitions in past years [4]. In DTN, many a times for exchanging data there no end-to-end route in sources to destinations, as nodes not in a particular position in nature, sparse node density, wireless propagation results & other unfavorable fact. Due to this, end-to-end paths fail to work in traditional ad hoc routing protocols, DTN architecture created to use as in between layer, called bundle layer, in between of application with transport layers of networks is linked. Services provided as in network message storage with retransmission, validate forwarding, interoperable naming & coarse-grained classes of

© Springer Nature Singapore Pte Ltd. 2019
M. Singh et al. (Eds.): ICACDS 2019, CCIS 1046, pp. 123–133, 2019.
https://doi.org/10.1007/978-981-13-9942-8_12

service [5, 6]. Bundle protocol also specified by DTN architecture, even it manages exchange of bundles, which is, application layer data. Atop transfer protocols (TCP, UDP), and atop bottom layer protocols (Bluetooth, Ethernet) manage with help of bundle protocol. The "bundle" expression chosen to apply self-notable of data: messages expected to store huge metadata to authorize processing by recipient without flexible in application layer, if applicable metadata query & response messages anticipated by source with "bundled" into one application data unit. Bundle protocol gets data from application when operating atop transport layer.

2   Background and Related Work

Many papers illustrated how data transferred from one node to another without any wired connection where connectivity is not proper [7, 8]. DATA MULE specifies for mobile nodes, which take information from other nodes around it, and then send to the first source station. Even storage is effective in this until it reaches its source station from where it started. In this paper, it illustrated that nodes influenced to move for transferring the data in an efficient way for message transferring [9]. The "active" scheme movement in which nodes send the information and command on nodes movements. On the other hand, there is proactively which used in message ferrying project shows the different movement of nodes for "message ferry" for transferring the data [10]. They two are similar in influence over nodes but in message ferries, information regarding route given by message ferry nodes only. Then after this, there is an invention of Epidemic Routing in disjoint network where data transferring takes place and in this, there is no influence on nodes travelling or nothing clue about future topology of a network [11]. Every node who generate data organizes space. After crossing from one side to another two nodes, interchange its summary vectors to check whether the data presented in other node not repeated. After this new information only transferred. This way data with nodes in disconnect network transfers. Transferring data surely done if path exists but costly for operations as network is full. To overcome this problem easy technique used for decreasing traffic with transferring duplicate with probability $p < 1$, for randomized traffic [12]. Another method proposed in which it assigns duplicate copies of data, separate them, and stop until transferring source meets final node [13]. Many solutions proposed with "probability to send" for decreasing the traffic with Epidemic Routing with respect for sending data. The criteria is on either location information, utility metrics, contact history. In this paper author proposed for send data to meet nodes in order of probability for sending, which is on contact information. If connectivity stays, enough all information is sent, basic Epidemic Routing [14]. It is also depending upon probability based, from previous meets with the nodes to check the probability of node meeting again, nodes mainly used increased the probability but early encounters are losing their chance. In order to evaluate the cost, we describe the probability based on nodes meets [15, 16]. Another area used "previous encounter since time elapsed" to send data to destinations. Information send to neighbor who meets final node more frequently than source and other nodes for sending data to a final node [17, 18]. Author illustrated an algorithm for routing given which is depends on detached delay-tolerant MANETs in social network. The process uses real trace data, which SimBet Routing attain delivery performance with respect to Epidemic routing, without additional overhead [18]. Author introduced adaptive fault-tolerant quality of service (QoS) control algorithms apply on hop-to-hop data transferring utilizing source & path dismissal. Main idea is assuring application QoS needs. Numerical data presented with proved with ample simulation, accomplished by physical interpretations given, to show flexibility of our design algorithm [19]. We proposed in our work that Sim-Bets Routing metric combination with centrality of nodes, own social similarity. If destination not familiar with its contacts, data travelled to central node where finding of potential increased. With respect to encounter-based strategies, SimBets Routing improves as encountered not reliable. We will use human behavior as a trust parameter as there are many malicious nodes present in the network to we will check the reliable node and done sending the information from source to destination. The rest of the paper is organized as follows: Sect. 3 there is a discussion about the proposed work and algorithm, in Sect. 4 there is a discussion about the experiments and result, and at last there is a summary of the conclusion of the whole paper, and the work which is to be done in the future given in Sect. 5.

3 Proposed Technique

The problem of data transfer in sparse delay tolerant network can evaluated using the values of Similarity, between ness and trust value of the node based on the social influence factor. The values of these functions can give as:

3.1 Similarity Calculation

Similarity is the numerical count value of the common neighbors between the source node & destination one. Similarity utility value of source node according to destination one is by ratio of no of same neighbors to all number of neighbors of destination one.

$$SimU_i = \frac{Sim_i}{Sim_i + Sim_j} \tag{1}$$

3.2 Betweenness Calculation

Betweenness between the two nodes calculated using the ego network of the node. Ego network of a node simply formed by the number of neighbors of the node considered. Calculating betweenness of 2 nodes ego network is having critical role to play and evaluated using adjacency matrix. An adjacency matrix 'A' can be maintained by updating '1' if there is a direct link between the two nodes else '0'. Betweenness value of the source node is simply the reciprocal of the value calculated using $A^2[1 - A]$. The product of A^2 and $[1 - A]$ is taken as the scalar product and the value is simply the reciprocal of the numerical value. Then the betweenness utility function evaluated with the following formula:

$$BetU_i = \frac{Bet_i}{Bet_i + Bet_j} \tag{2}$$

Therefore, the objective SimBeT utility function is a multi-objective constraint optimization function, which given by the equation:

$$SimBeTU_i = \alpha SimU_i + \beta BetU_i \tag{3}$$

Where α, β and γ weights given to the equation and their value is:

$$\alpha + \beta = 1 \tag{4}$$

3.3   Opinion Dynamics Based Optimization

The thesis proposes a novel Human Opinion Dynamics (HOD) based optimization technique to solve the problem of sparse delay tolerant network. The problem at hand is a multi-objective constraint optimization problem and it attempted to solve by the proposed algorithm. The Human Opinion Dynamics based optimization technique is a novel meta-heuristic algorithm based on the group discussion behavior of humans. As the humans interact with each other, their opinion about any particular topic starts varying. This utilized in this thesis and opinions formed about the optimal sizing and the allocation of the new routing technique. These opinions are updated using the below mentioned algorithm.

3.4   Opinion Dynamics Model

For a long duration of time, modelling human behavior is fascinating field of research & lot methods given to follow real life dynamics into mathematical model. It is one of the latest research areas, which claimed to solve very difficult optimization problem. This methodology support in Social Impact Theory Optimization (SITO), they found restricted problem in utility in high dimensionality & focused on discrete opinion formation. For making an optimizer, HOD model utilized which indicates as a Continuous Opinion Dynamics Optimizer (CODO). Opinion formation mechanism, brunch of individuals during a discussion method is applicable and four primitive fundamentals point view area, social arrangements, restore order, social impact. Platform for dissimilar individuals to communicate with everyone in which every single individual put on nodes of social graph which is created by Social structure. Updated version is Moore's neighborhood of cellular automata model employed in which every individual present as neighbors of everyone preferably immediate orthogonal members in Van

Neuman topology & immediate eight neighbors in simplistic Moore's topology. Social space is dissimilar from opinion space & mention to hyperspace, in which opinions of every individual cause impact on everyone & updated under condition of update rule. From PSO there is main dissimilarities of HOD based optimization, which is, in opinion space, traffic can occur too, which is 2 individuals have same opinion during same time period whereas 2 insects not have same position in swarm during same time. Opinions should be continuous which is good for our problem of optimization in which optimizing parameters of any value within certain finite range. Opinions effect by opinions of their neighbors according to their social influence, which describe as ratio of social rank of any individual to distance between them and given by:

$$w_{ij} = \frac{SR_j(t)}{d_{ij}(t)}. \tag{5}$$

Here, SR described by fitness value of individual, in which fitness value is error, which has to optimize. In this i stands for node concerned & j for the neighbor of concerned node. Every single opinion modified by rule given as:

$$\Delta o_i = \frac{\sum\limits_{j=1}^{N} (o_j(t) - o_i(t))w_{ij}(t)}{\sum\limits_{j=1}^{N} w_{ij}(t)} + \eta_i(t), j \neq i, \tag{6}$$

In this $o_j(t)$ is opinion of neighbors of single i, w_{ij} is social influence factor, & η is adaptive noise produced to justify individualization in society in some criteria consensus limit reached.

3.5   Trust of a Node

Trust of a node calculated using the opinion of the neighboring nodes whose value depends on number of previous interactions of the source node with the destination node. It simply given as the ratio of the numerical count value of number of previous interactions in the middle of the nodes & total interactions I of the destination node.

$$TrstU_i = \frac{I_{i,j}}{I_j} \tag{7}$$

The above-discussed algorithm applied to our problem for optimizing the objective function described in Eq. 3. The complete process of our methodology described below.

4 Algorithm: HOD Based Routing in Sparse Delay Tolerate Network

Begin

Initialize opinions for nodes

Allocate current node and neighbor node to opinion1 and opinion2

a: in network number of nodes present

l: total neighbor nodes present

lp: loops present

tp: total opinions   d: space of domain

f(s): function as an objective function of similarity & betweenness

Explain objective function of f(s), where
s=(s1,........,sd)

Create initial population opinions or si (b=1,2 ,...., a)

While (b<lp)

        For c=1 to tp (all opinions)

            Assign current node & neighbor nodes

    End for

    Keep best individual to bfn

        For c=1 to tp (all opinions)

For d=1 to tp (for all opinions)

  If d not equal to c

        Compute social influence w_{jk}

End if

End for

Compute η standard deviation

If c not equal to bfn

Taking discussed equation change opinions

End if

End while

End procedure

4.1 Flowchart

The algorithmic flow chart is shown in Fig. 1.

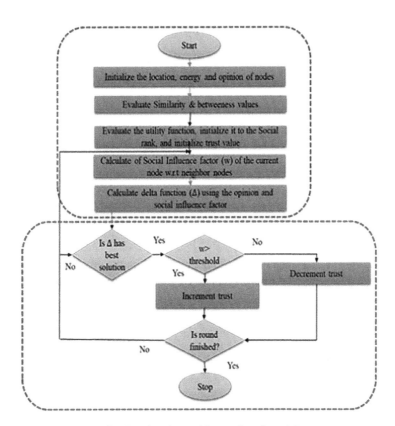

Fig. 1. Flowchart with trust-based model

5 Results and Discussions

The following method executed using the Network Simulator ns-2.35. The network designed using the 20 nodes, which placed in the network. Their performance evaluated based on various performance parameters, which are:

5.1 Energy Consumption

In network, total energy consumed while transmitting or receiving the data in network from source to destination. Figure 2 shows comparison of SimBet approach and our proposed trust-based approach. It is clear from the graph that the energy consumed in the proposed approach is less as compared to the basic approach.

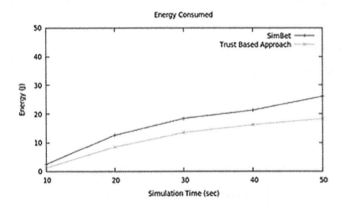

Fig. 2. Energy consumed in the network

5.2 Packet Delivery Ratio

It defined as follows:

$$\text{Packet delivery ratio} = \frac{\text{total packets received}}{\text{total packets generated}} \tag{8}$$

Figure 3 display the difference of Simbet method with the proposed approach. The packet delivery ratio for the proposed approach better compared to the basic approach because the packet lost in the network reduces.

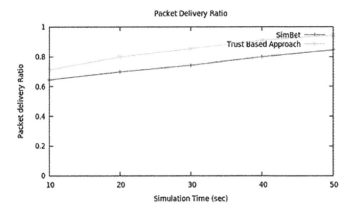

Fig. 3. Packet delivery ratio

5.3 End to End Delay

It defines as follows:

$$\text{Delay} = (\text{Packet received by receiver time} - \text{generated time}) \tag{9}$$

Figure 4 shows the comparison between the SimBet function and the proposed trust approach with respect to time. The delay in the proposed method decrease due to the reduction in number of retransmissions.

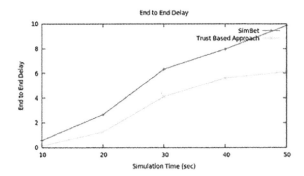

Fig. 4. Packet delivery delay

5.4 Malicious Nodes

In network if there is any malicious nodes lies then the probability of packet delivery ratio with respect to simulation time increase as we can see from the Fig. 5 given below.

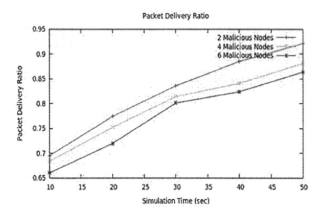

Fig. 5. Malicious node

6 Conclusion

Delay tolerant sparse network is a network having very fewer nodes available for communication. There are many approaches proposed in the recent past but still routing is a major concern in these types of networks. A novel opinion-based approach is proposed and the trust of each node computed opinion based on different nodes. In network the routing and route selection decisions of the node based on trust value. Result also verifies the proposed technique. In future, other machine learning algorithms be implemented and their results must be compared with the present work.

References

1. Gao, W., Li, Q., Zhao, B., Cao, G.: Multicasting in delay tolerant networks: a social network perspective. In: Proceedings of the Tenth ACM International Symposium on Mobile Ad Hoc Networking and Computing, pp. 299–308. ACM (2009)
2. Liu, Y., et al.: Performance and energy consumption analysis of a delay-tolerant network for censorship-resistant communication. In: Proceedings of the 16th ACM International Symposium on Mobile Ad Hoc Networking and Computing, pp. 257–266. ACM (2015)
3. Costa, P., Mascolo, C., Musolesi, M., Picco, G.P.: Socially-aware routing for publish-subscribe in delay-tolerant mobile ad hoc networks. IEEE J. Sel. Areas Commun. **26**(5), 748–760 (2008)
4. Dang, H., Wu, H.: Clustering and cluster-based routing protocol for delay-tolerant mobile networks. IEEE Trans. Wirel. Commun. **9**(6), 1874–1881 (2010)
5. Lo, S.-C., Tsai, C.-C., Lai, Y.-H.: Quota-control routing in delay-tolerant networks. Ad Hoc Netw. **25**, 393–405 (2015)
6. Frenkiel, R.H., Badrinath, B.R., Borres, J., Yates, R.D.: The infostations challenge: balancing cost and ubiquity in delivering wireless data. IEEE Pers. Commun. **7**(2), 66–71 (2000)

7. Shah, R.C., Roy, S., Jain, S., Brunette, W.: Data MULEs: modeling a three-tier architecture for sparse sensor networks. In: Proceedings of First IEEE International Workshop Sensor Network Protocols and Applications (SNPA 2003), pp. 30–41, May 2003
8. Li, Q., Rus, D.: Sending messages to mobile users in disconnected ad-hoc wireless networks. In: Proceedings of ACM MobiCom, pp. 44–55, August 2000
9. Zhao, W., Ammar, M., Zegura, E.: A message ferrying approach for data delivery in sparse mobile ad hoc networks. In: Proceedings of ACM MobiHoc, pp. 187–198, May 2004
10. Vahdat, A., Becker, D.: Epidemic routing for partially connected ad hoc networks. Technical report, April 2000
11. Spyropoulos, T., Psounis, K., Raghavendra, C.S.: Spray and wait: an efficient routing scheme for intermittently connected mobile networks. In: Proceedings of ACM SIGCOMM Workshop Delay-Tolerant Networking (WDTN 2005), pp. 252–259, August 2005
12. Burgess, J, Gallagher, B., Jensen, D., Levine, B.N.: MaxProp: routing for vehicle-based disruption-tolerant networking. In: Proceedings of IEEE INFOCOM, March 2006
13. Lindgren, A., Doria, A., Schelén, O.: Probabilistic routing in intermittently connected networks. In: Proceedings of First International Workshop Service Assurance with Partial and Intermittent Resources (SAPIR 2004), pp. 239–254, August 2004
14. Khelil, A., Marron, P.J., Rothermel, K.: Contact-based mobility metrics for delay-tolerant ad hoc networking. In: Proceedings of 13th IEEE International Symposium Modeling, Analysis, and Simulation of Computer and Telecommunication Systems (MASCOTS 2005) pp. 435–444 (2005)
15. Tan, K., Zhang, Q., Zhu, W.: Shortest path routing in partially connected ad hoc networks. In: Proceedings of IEEE Global Telecommunication Conference (GLOBECOM 2003), vol. 2, pp. 1038–1042, December 2003
16. Dubois-Ferriere, H., Grossglauser, M., Vetterli, M.: Age matters: efficient route discovery in mobile ad hoc networks using encounter ages. In: Proceedings of ACM MobiHoc, pp. 257–266 (2003)
17. Grossglauser, M., Vetterli, M.: Locating nodes with ease: last encounter routing in ad hoc networks through mobility diffusion. In: Proceedings of IEEE INFOCOM, vol. 3, pp. 1954–1964 (2003)
18. Daly, E.M., Haahr, M.: Social network analysis for routing in disconnected delay-tolerant manets. In: Proceedings of the 8th ACM International Symposium on Mobile Ad Hoc Networking and Computing, pp. 32–40. ACM (2007)
19. Chen, H., Lou, W.: Contact expectation based routing for delay tolerant networks. Ad Hoc Netw. **36**, 244–257 (2016)

Formation of Hierarchies in the System of Organization of State Construction Supervision in Case of Reorientation of Urban Areas

Dmitriy Topchiy$^{(\boxtimes)}$ ⑩ and Andrey Tokarskiy

Moscow State University of Civil Engineering, Yaroslavskoe shosse, 26,
Moscow 129337, Russia
{89161122142, 89253221611}@mail.ru

Abstract. The article describes the principles of creating a unified system of modules interacting with each other in the implementation of projects for the conversion of industrial facilities. The main criteria of forming a complex organizational system, which includes a large number of functional subsystems and modules related to investment, design, production and information components of the structure of the project, are described. For decades, the principles of urban planning of various cities and megacities in the Soviet Union and later in Russia were formed on the same basic principles. Clearly distinguished contours of residential buildings, industrial areas, as well as forest areas and urban infrastructure. Over time, the urban environment absorbed new territories, developing not only geographically, but also forming new modern social requirements. So were formed new principles of design of space-planning solutions of residential premises of apartment buildings, requirements for the formation of "green" urban areas, otherwise began to form the structure of educational institutions. In addition, the approach to the preservation and development of urban Geoecology has changed significantly. Basically, this factor served as the basis for the formation of municipal programs of renovation of industrial areas that have an impact on the environment of the city.

By creating qualitative and quantitative characteristics of the individual elements of the system under consideration, it is possible to formulate the basic requirements for the source data necessary to create a structured model of organizational design and project management. At the same time, the system should function reliably in the interaction of all integrated structures of the project under the influence of the external environment. For decades, the principles of urban planning of various cities and megacities in the Soviet Union and later in Russia were formed on the same basic principles. Clearly distinguished contours of residential buildings, industrial areas, as well as forest areas and urban infrastructure. Over time, the urban environment absorbed new territories, developing not only geographically, but also forming new modern social requirements. So were formed new principles of design of space-planning solutions of residential premises of apartment buildings, requirements for the formation of "green" urban areas, otherwise began to form the structure of educational institutions. In addition, the approach to the preservation and development of urban Geoecology has changed significantly. Basically, this

© Springer Nature Singapore Pte Ltd. 2019
M. Singh et al. (Eds.): ICACDS 2019, CCIS 1046, pp. 134–143, 2019.
https://doi.org/10.1007/978-981-13-9942-8_13

factor served as the basis for the formation of municipal programs of renovation of industrial areas that have an impact on the environment of the city. The principles and nature of urban clusters are described in detail, their separate types and types, as well as the relationship and the main criteria for their functioning are highlighted.

Keywords: Organization of production operations · Efficiency assessment · Area retrofitting · Construction inspection · State construction supervision

1 Introduction

Hierarchy is the organizational form of the management of complex structural elements of different nature, oriented toward ensuring joint and purposeful functioning. The hierarchical organization is designed to optimize the processes of interaction and decision-making, both in the existing management structure and in the complex system itself, in the possibilities for adapting its structure and functions to the changes in external and internal conditions of functioning [1].

The structure of the hierarchy is determined by the scale of the complex system, the functional diversity of its elements, the features of the environmental impact and the opportunities (technical and human) to make decisions in a dynamic environment.

2 Materials and Methods

The hierarchical organization of a complex system is a multi-level structure, consisting of interconnected subsystems, the elements of which are functionally capable of making decisions. The hierarchy of the organization determines the order of subordination and interaction of subsystems and elements in the management system, the distribution of managerial functions and responsibilities. The superior elements of the hierarchy of management have the priority in decisions and the right to intervene in the actions and decisions of subordinate and certain subordinated elements.

When organizing interaction between structural elements, both vertical and horizontal structured ordering of these subsystems are possible:

- with horizontal structuring, the subsystems exert significant influence on each other due to the presence of complex direct and reverse links between them, which does not allow to determine the vertical hierarchy of subordination of goals;
- with vertical structuring, the subsystems are structured according to the level of complexity and responsibility of decision making. The behavior of each of the subsystems, regardless of the type of structuring, is described by the corresponding model with variables and parameters corresponding to a particular level of the hierarchy [2].

The main mechanism for synthesizing the hierarchical structure of the system of construction production is the procedure for the separation of functions for the direct management of a complex polyergic system and functions for the coordination of the activities of the main structural elements of the studied organization (subjects of investment activity in construction):

– Investors are the individuals and legal entities that make capital investments in the formation of construction projects using their own or borrowed funds and form the conditions for financial (material) provision of construction production;
– Builders are physical and legal entities that provide the conditions for the production of construction processes (organization and formation of the construction system of capital construction projects) in accordance with the accepted design and organizational and technological solutions;
– Customers (technical customers, government customers) are the individuals and legal entities that provide a substantive application of investments in construction and are the main consumers of construction products. Depending on the practical situation, the customers get possibility and availability to act as developers and investors;
– Designers (general designers) are the individuals and legal entities that form (develop, establish) indicators of the functional efficiency and quality of construction products (in the format of the relevant sections of the design estimates) [3];
– Contractors (general contractors) are physical and legal entities that directly carry out construction processes (form actual quality indicators of construction products);
– State construction supervision consists of federal or regional executive authorities, which are authorized to conduct state construction supervision for the established procedure for the formation of construction products.

Figure 1 presents an enlarged scheme of interaction between the main construction industry participants (except the state construction supervision agencies).

Until the moment that the developer (customer) submit the notification of the commencement of construction, there is required mandatory assessment of the conformity of the construction project and related research processes, design, expertise of design solutions (project documentation) which is carried out by persons (organizations) that have carried out the relevant survey, design and expert activities. The results of conformity assessment are formalized in the form of relevant conclusions on compliance, state expertise and are used as a ground for obtaining a building permit [5].

The interaction of the builder (customer) with the executive agencies of state construction supervision in the construction of capital construction projects is carried out according to the following formalized procedures (with the exception of specially protected areas and objects of cultural heritage) [6]:

– issuance (extension) of the building permit the state construction supervision agency develops and issues the relevant document (permit) to the representatives of the developer (customer) in case of positive result;
– notice of the beginning of construction. The state construction supervision agency develops and issues the program of inspections to the representatives of the developer (customer) and the contractor (general contractor) and assignment of the risk category to the construction project, taking into account the risk-oriented approach: "… in accordance with the criteria for referring the under construction,

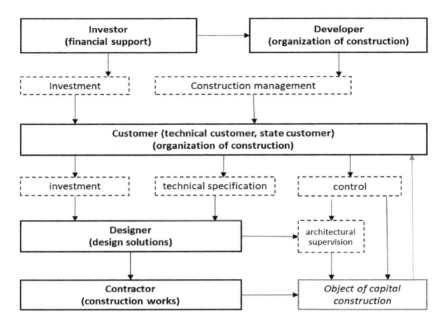

Fig. 1. Scheme of interaction between the main construction industry participants [4].

reconstructed capital construction objects to risk categories …", in case of positive result [5];

- issuance of a document confirming the main works on the construction (reconstruction) of the object of individual housing construction, carried out with the involvement of the funds of the parent (family) capital. The state construction supervision agency develops and issues the relevant document to the representatives of the builder (customer) in case of positive result;
- notification of the completion of construction. |The state construction supervision agency develops and issues the relevant document (notification) to the representatives of the builder (customer) in case of positive result;
- issuing a conclusion on the compliance of the constructed (reconstructed, repaired) capital construction object with the requirements of technical regulations and project documentation. The state construction supervision agency develops and issues the relevant document (conclusion) to the representatives of the developer (customer) in case of positive result;
- issuance of a permit for commissioning an object. The state construction supervision agency develops and issues the relevant document (permit) to the representatives of the developer (customer) in case of positive result.

The implementation of compliance checks: "… the conformity of execution of works and building materials used in the construction process… and the conformity of the results of such work and the requirements of technical regulations, other regulatory enactments and project documentation …" is the main format for interaction between the state construction supervision agencies and the contractor to perform tasks like "… warning, detection and suppression of violations of the law on urban development, including technical regulations, and project documentation committed by the developer, the customer, the contractor …" [7].

The results of the compliance checks are fixed by a special act (which indicates the detected violations and instructions for their elimination), which is sent to: the developer, the customer, the contractor (depending on which construction participant is responsible for the violations committed) for acquaintance and execution of the requirements specified in the act [8].

Refusal to eliminate the detected violations (as well as incomplete, substandard or untimely fulfillment of prescriptions) may serve as the basis for refusal to issue a conclusion on the conformity of the constructed (reconstructed, repaired) capital construction object with the requirements of technical regulations and project documentation and/or permission to commission the facility [9].

Maintenance of the established quality of building products (by the contractor) is provided by the following construction industry participants:

- by developer (customer, technical customer) through relevant activities within the framework of building control (technical supervision) of the volumes and quality of construction works and processes (carried out by the contractor) for all the phases and cycles of construction. The representatives of the developer services (customer), participating in surveying and controlling activities (input, operational, acceptance control) are subject to mandatory registration in the state construction supervision agencies and bear personal responsibility for the quality of construction products (similar to the contractor representatives) [10];
- by designer through relevant activities under the supervision of the quality of the practical implementation of appropriate design solutions. The representatives of the design organizations (designers, appointed and/or involved by the developer or the customer to the author supervision) carry out oversight activities in the format of random checks of conformity (input, operational, acceptance control) design solutions, but suppress the noticed violations only with the participation of the representatives of the state construction supervision agencies. The representatives of supervision are responsible for quality of construction, conducting oversight activities and correcting violations and deviations [11];
- by contractor through relevant activities within the framework of the practical implementation of the established organizational and technological construction sequence (especially during the input and operational control of parameters of building processes) [12]. The representatives of the contractor are directly responsible for the quality of the finished construction projects [13].

Figure 2 provides an illustration of the hierarchical interaction between the main construction industry participants to ensure the quality of construction products [14].

Virtually any complex system can be represented by a structure in which dynamic interaction occurs between the elements of the artificial environment (material objects and objects), the human factor and the influence of the natural environment.

Such a complex system is a building production system designed to form building products of various functional purposes. The end result of the functioning of the building production system is a completed construction object—a building or a

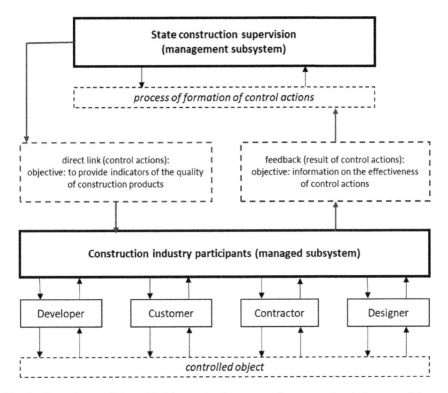

Fig. 2. The scheme of hierarchical interaction between main construction industry participants to ensure the quality of construction products [15].

construction of a specific purpose and of established quality, which becomes the main indicator of its functional efficiency. The concept of the construction production system involves the use (for evaluation, organization and management of production and non-production processes of interaction between the structural elements of the system) of methods and techniques of system analysis, characterized by the following features:

- system approach is used for analysis of systems only;
- mandatory hierarchical approach and multilevel (iterative) nature of the analysis of the subject of research;
- analysis of the mechanism of integration and influence of structural elements in the complex of structural elements and complexes on the end result of the functioning of the system;
- orientation of research to obtain quantitative characteristics that determine the behavior or state of the system.

In the accepted formulation of the analysis, the system of construction production is considered as a complex polyergic and hierarchical system consisting of a set of less complex subsystems (systems, elements). Each of these subsystems can be considered as an independent object of study (Table 1).

Table 1. Presents the main features of the concept of a building production system as a complex polyergic system.

Types of system features	Quality characteristic features of the system
Functional	- The presence of a common task and a single goal of work for all elements of the system - Random random nature of external influences that affect the operation of the system - The presence of direct and inverse relationships between structural elements, the complex nature of their interaction, especially under the influence of external factors. Possibility of reaction of elements to external factors, adaptation to changing conditions - Reliability and stability of a system consisting of various elements with a non-uniform degree of reliability - The ability of the system to develop (move to a higher level) and decline (move to a lower level)
Structural	- A significant number of structural elements that make up the system - The possibility of combining elements into groups (subsystems) according to some established features - Availability of hierarchical structure and functioning criteria - Dynamic States and relations
Ergonomic	- The subjective nature of the decisions - The possibility of accidental and deliberate errors - The unpredictability of performance, behavior, mood, inability to predict the results of decisions to implement

However, the main feature of the functioning of a building production system (like the Palaearctic system) is the growing discrepancy between technical characteristics and technological capabilities (construction machines and means of mechanization for building capital construction systems) and indicators of organizational and technological reliability aimed at maintaining the established quality level of building products stage of construction.

The system-technical approach to the analysis of the functioning of a unified and integrated system of construction production involves the analysis of the conditions of interaction of technical, organizational, administrative structural elements aimed at ensuring the established level of quality of construction products.

The system of "state construction supervision" is (in most cases) an obligatory and necessary structural element (subsystem) of a unified and integral system of construction production.

This structural element is designed to perform the supervisory functions necessary to ensure; an established level of quality, safety and timeliness of building systems for capital construction facilities.

The system (subsystem) of "state construction supervision" is interconnected with the systems (subsystems) of "Construction Management" and "construction organization" of a single and integral system of construction production. The control actions of the system (subsystem) of the "state construction supervision" are implemented by the actions of construction personnel (including operators of construction machinery and mechanisms).

The effectiveness of the system (subsystem) of the "state construction supervision" is determined by: professional training and production discipline of personnel; rational organization of the internal structure of the service; the quality of interaction with external (organizational, managerial, expert) structures.

Using the system analysis methodology is a rational way of determining the features of the essential mechanism of functioning of the system (subsystem) of the "state construction supervision" as an integrated, developing (taking into account the life cycle of the respective capital construction object) and multi-level hierarchical organization.

From the point of view of system analysis, the tasks assigned to the structure (system, subsystem) of state supervision to ensure the established quality of construction products must be considered and solved in a holistic context (the effectiveness of a modern building production system) as a result of the interaction of various investment subjects in construction.

The analysis of the functioning of the system (subsystem) of the "state structural supervision" allows the use of any number of considered systems engineering principles (or their combinations), in combination with more specific (inherent in organizational systems) forms and methods of system analysis based on the conceptual provisions of the general system theory.

The need for a system-technical approach to the analysis of the functioning of the organizational-technical (integrated) structure arose after the occurrence of situations in which separate, even well-functioning elements (subsystems), United by a certain interaction format, did not constitute a well-functioning system. In a complex system (subsystem) it often turns out that the adjustment of the solution (or adaptation to the actual conditions of the construction site) is much more expensive than the maintenance of specialists and technical units of the system (subsystem) "state construction supervision". It is for this reason that it is advisable to start the process of "monitoring" a capital construction project from the earliest periods of the life cycle.

The inevitable consequence of this approach is the complexity of the functional load on the structure of the system (subsystem) "state construction supervision", which involves the use of tools and results of simulation and experimental modeling, system analysis methods (concept systems, use of modern scientific and technical developments) to achieve the established quality of construction products.

In the overwhelming common of cases, decision-making should be carried out in conditions of the maximum possible consideration of the diversity of investment activity topics in construction, the presence of explicit and indirect links between them and the environment (artificial and natural) - by combining two main conceptual methodological approaches: "part - whole" and "system - environment".

3 Conclusion

In the structure of control system (see Fig. 2) the quality of control actions on the part of state supervision agencies depends on the properties (structure, qualitative and quantitative parameters) of the control system [16]. In the vast majority of cases, the process of formation of managerial decisions (impacts) is accompanied by the presence of uncertainty in input data and dynamic variability of the indicators of the controlled object state. Improving the efficiency of the supervision system at construction sites will not only reduce the level of injuries and improve the overall level of quality of construction products, but also significantly reduce government costs in this area, without reducing the level of supervision. One of the most effective ways to improve the efficiency of supervision at the facilities of re-profiling in the coming years should be software systems that will be able to form a program of inspections of the construction site, based on the project documentation and regulations of Supervisory units, while taking into account not only the climatic, geographical and other features of the construction site, but also the specifics of the developer carrying out work on the site. In addition, an important role in the implementation of the current supervision, should be given to the author of the project, which provides an opportunity to quickly integrate into the design solutions of individual changes and additions, without re-examination of the entire project. The same adjustments should apply to the possibility of the developer of changes in construction machinery, equipment and mechanization, which differs from that specified in the project, but does not affect the safety of work and the reliability of the building during construction and further operation.

References

1. Gusakov, A.A., Ginzburg, A.V., Veremeenko, S.A.: Organizational and Technological Reliability of Construction Operations. SvR-Argus, Moscow (1994)
2. Bolotova, A.S., Ginzburg, A.V.: Analysis of the organizational and technological reliability of monolithic construction operations. Econ. Entrep. **10**, 647–651 (2016)
3. Bolotova, A.S.: Technological characteristics of monolithic construction operations with particular impact on their safety and quality. In: Construction – Formation of a Living Environment: A Collection of Reports of the 18th International Applied Research Conference, pp. 459–462. Moscow State University of Civil Engineering, Moscow (2015)
4. Bolotova, A.S., Treskina, G.E.: Study of technological characteristics of monolithic construction operations on the basis of systemic analysis. Herald of the Tomsk State Architecture and Civil Engineering University, vol. 2 (2016)
5. Bolotova, A.S., Kiryukhin, S.A.: Developing a model of a quality control business process for monolithic concrete works. In: Construction – Formation of a Living Environment: A Collection of Reports of the 19th International Applied Research Conference, pp. 649–651. Moscow State University of Civil Engineering, Moscow (2016)
6. Shirane, T., Nakamura, K., Nobuhiro, M., Taro, K.: Study of development of urban environments, mainly in the vicinity of underground stations. Procedia Eng. **165**, 326–333 (2016)
7. McMichael, J.: The urban environment and health in a world of increasing globalization: issues for developing countries. Bull. World Health Organ. **78**(9), 1117–1126 (2000)

8. Chavis, D., Wandersman, A.: Sense of community in the urban environment: a catalyst for participation and community development. Am. J. Community Psychol. **18**(1), 55–81 (1990)
9. Vardoulakis, S., Dear, K., Wilkinson, P.: Challenges and opportunities for urban environmental health and sustainability: the HEALTHY-POLIS initiative. Environ. Health **15**(Suppl 1), 30 (2016)
10. Harsritanto, B.I.R.: Urban environment development based on universal design principles. In: The 2nd International Conference on Energy, Environmental and Information System (ICENIS 2017) (2017)
11. Topchiy, D., Skakalov, V., Yurgaitis, A.: Integrated verification construction supervision as a tool to reduce the developer's risks when implementing new and redevelopment projects. Int. J. Civ. Eng. Technol. (IJCIET) **9**(1) (2018)
12. Abramov, I., Poznakhirko, T., Sergeev, A.: The analysis of the functionality of modern systems, methods and scheduling tools. In: MATEC Web of Conferences, vol. 86 (2016)
13. Topchiy, D., Kochurina, E.: Estimation of the degree of influence of environmental factors on construction in a dense urban environment. Syst. Technol. **1** (2018)
14. Topchiy, D., Skakalov, V.: Structural and functional modeling of multi-level and multi-criteria links of organizational and technological, managerial structures and information support when implementing construction control over the course of re-development of industrial facilities. Prospects Sci. **10**, 44–50 (2017)
15. Topchiy, D., Kochurina, E.: Environmental situation in construction, reconstruction and re-profiling of facilities in high-density urban development. In: MATEC Web of Conferences, vol. 193 (2018)
16. Topchiy, D., Tokarskiy, A.: Formation of the organizational-managerial model of renovation of urban territories. In: MATEC Web of Conferences, vol. 196 (2018)

Customized Visualization of Email Using Sentimental and Impact Analysis in R

V. Roopa$^{(\boxtimes)}$ and K. Induja$^{(\boxtimes)}$

Department of Information Technology, Sri Krishna College of Technology,
Coimbatore, India
{Roopa.V, Induja.K}@skct.edu.in

Abstract. In our modern world of social interactions where the analysis of each content on social media is based on the impact of the sentiment it imposes on the forum. The proposed system is used to implement a more personalized and customized report of these impacts. Email is of main focus here where in out of all other social applications, responses to and from the email is the most traditional and ethical way to communicate online. Users share all information, through internet especially emails because of its fast transmission and is considered as the most professional medium. Hence the proposed model focus more on the subjective content of email processed on R libraries created for Natural language processing in a more customized way. Nowadays, crime rate in emails are increasing drastically. Spamming, phishing and email fraudulent are the ways of targeting common people. The sentimental analysis on the impact of the email received is analysed and visualized. The system also proposes a design for establishing a framework that detects the suspicious one by comparing the mail with keywords and also reveals the level of suspiciousness in the particular mail.

Keywords: Sentiment analysis · Text mining · Analysis · Analytic · Spamming

1 Introduction

The usage of online applications for communication have become an essential approach for information exchange. Email system is very ubiquitous one. This is highly preferred communication medium become of its instantaneous and speedy transfer of data from one user to another. Email has the capability of connecting the all sorts of people which means that everyone can mail others by knowing the mail id [2]. It is more intuitive for usage and cost efficient (no charges for per mail). The email system uses many protocols such as SMTP protocol RFC 821 and 822, POP3 etc. Though it connects all people, security is main issue in it. Main security issues for email communication is secrecy, content integrity and identity integrity. Integrity means that anyone can change the content of the mail or recipient's id during mail-transfer without the knowledge of mail holder. Nowadays many illegal activities like [5] trapping, kidnapping, hacking one's own credentials, bomb blasts information are shared through mails. The higher authority may get a mail from a hacker or terrorists intention of stealing his or her personal details else in order to trap the person. Pedophiles [8]

© Springer Nature Singapore Pte Ltd. 2019
M. Singh et al. (Eds.): ICACDS 2019, CCIS 1046, pp. 144–154, 2019.
https://doi.org/10.1007/978-981-13-9942-8_14

mainly start their search from public chats and mails for victims. Only the web based application which is in public use is secure for them. Because analyzing the large sets of chats and mails and finding the suspicious or dubious one is a very tedious task. Vigilance and forensic departments still depend only on our olden methods like google desktop search engines in web. But it is not convenient for our current environment and also it fails to predict the information which is hidden in its interior. Many tools have been developed to analyze and detect but all has the same disadvantage that it is not suitable for unstructured large set of data. In order to avoid the risk in opening the suspicious mails we propose a framework based on text mining process in R language. This model will initially extract mails from a user account and assign it to a corpus. Followed by cleaning the data which includes extraction of punctuations, stop words, numbers and stemming. After cleaning, create a term document matrix which reveals the content in the matrix form. Finally compare the words in mail with the keywords provided. The graph reveals the level of suspiciousness by the frequent use of the words. Sentimental analysis is a natural language processing method to predict the state of mind of public about a product. This paper provides the overall view of detecting the suspicious mail using text mining.

2 Background Theory

Sentimental analysis is mainly based on feature selection. The major concepts of machine learning including supervised and un-supervised learning are also reliable on the data attributes generated. There are various illustrations that these analytical process [6] is an outcome of the major grievances of the social community. Data from various resources is processed in such a way that sentimental and emotional detection analysis is done. Majorly the initial set up was based on the manual and moving on to online survey. The real world applications and its related algorithm are the outcome of the and is even more improvised using big data analytics and visualized using the latest software.

The context based and content based analysis on applications is being done. The usage of Natural language processing and text analysis [12] is an outcome of automation of the social networking. The online portals, emails are to be filtered for specific data sets but they are limited for unauthorized access. The subjective infor-mation is all in the form of text which is the feature for text analysis. Few algorithms on subjective and predictive analytics are implemented [7]. As an outcome deep learning on social applications produced certain rules for their experimental study. The data sets are generated for evaluation of statistical measures. The traditional ensemble methodology also had restrictions on the feature selection and need more analysis on these features to further expand the algorithms. The study involves pre-processing, cleaning and creating of data set which is further classified as training and test data sets. The precision is calculated based on the range from -1 to 1.

The proposed system performs the sentimental analysis to proportionate [12] the relationship in email and produces the visualized results of the customized analytical reports. The email api is in the form of text where in certain attributes are into text mining procedure to form the required data set. The unauthorized access restrictions is to be given importance in this vast social media forum. The same is visualized via implementing analytical algorithms on the data set. The grievances of this social community and the positive aspects of the relationship is of main focus here.

3 Proposed System

The main motive of this paper is to detect suspicious mail and intimate to the vigilance department before any illegal activities happens. This also useful to track the terrorists through their IP address used to send the mails.

Text mining is the process of searching or analyzing for the text pattern provided. The dataset used should be actionable one. Non trivial predictions can be made on new data in a same resource which available already is allowed only in the actionable patterns. Measurement of performance is determined by ratio between success and failures. Text mining has the capability of analyzing structured or unstructured data.

3.1 Main Steps in Text Mining

Here, we discuss about first three steps and plotting the graph. In our recent world, all the data available are unstructured. Many tools and techniques has an issue in handling the unstructured data. Big data comprises of both structured and unstructured data. Nearly 70% of data available are unstructured. In order to reduce the difficulty in analysis process it is preferred to convert unstructured to structured data.

- Unstructured data to structured one
- Cleansing the data
- Text categorization
- Text clustering
- Sentimental analysis

Data cleaning or data transformation involves many process such as converting the upper cases into lowercases, eliminating the stop words, removal of punctuations, numbers and special symbols. Final process of stemming. Then it is processed to the text categorization. Text categorization is nothing but classifying or categorizing the dataset to the predefined classifications. Overall conceptual view can be obtained by categorizing the data. Controlled vocabulary means set of categories in which dataset should be classified. In our practical life, text categorization has many real time applications such as automatic meta data, word sense disambiguation and indexing for retrieval of documents. In our process, the mails are compared with the predefined keywords and get categorized. After categorization, they are plotted in a graph. For graph generation, we use many packages like igraph, ggplot2, graphics. Many graphs are available in R such as dot plots, boxplots, pie chart, scatter plots, 3D plots etc.

3.2 Overloading with Large Set of Data

It's very tedious task to handle the large set of mails or messages by the vigilance department. It also be a bulk details occupying the storage and sometimes may be a disturbance to them. To avoid this the only selected or particular details may store permanently.

3.3 Misunderstand the Suspicious Mail

In some cases, the current generation people prank their friends by sending the mails with the suspicious words. If a person sent a mail which contains a word killing, it will be notified as a suspicious mail. In order to overcome this, the suspicious level has been detected. Only if the suspicious level is beyond the target then it is notified as suspicious mail.

3.4 Differentiating the Words

Two or more words may have the same synonym. But it is difficult for the computer to analyze. Killed and kill are the different words but the meaning is same. It is overcome by stemming process in the text cleaning step.

4 Architecture

4.1 Extracting Unstructured Text

All mails and messages are in the form of unstructured data. In order to perform text mining initially the mail should be imported to the workspace. For our experimental analysis, we have collected the chat logs and mails as datasets from available resources.

4.2 Cleaning

Obviously, the gathered dataset contain may litter data. To remove those data, the cleaning process is very necessary one. By cleaning, all stop words, nonlexical words, numbers, punctuations are excluded from the dataset.

4.3 Creating Document Term Matrix

In text mining, document term matrix plays a vital role. It shows termas rows and document as columns and can also be reverse. It is mainly used to find the presence of each word in the mail easily.

4.4 List of Keywords: NLP

The set of suspicious words have been chosen from many articles and also through internet. This is also called as dictionary which contain a multiset of strings. Here, these words are passed like an argument and compared with the mail received. The presence of those words in mail in sheer numbers then it is suspected (Fig. 1).

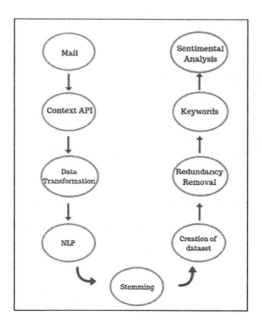

Fig. 1. Architecture model

4.5   Data Set Interpretation

The process of data set interpretation involves the classification of as stop words, tag words, negation words, tokenized words, static words and adult words. The data set is first done using advanced Natural Language processing to generate these classified words. The training and test data is processed further for Sentimental Analysis.

5   Implementation and Discussion

5.1   Implementation of R Package

The R is a programming language which is used for predictive analysis and it visualizes the data in the form of graph. It is an open source which can be accessed by all versions of various operating systems without any pay. In olden days, R tool has been deprecating because of its slow process of analysis method when is applied to a large set of data. But nowadays R become more adaptive to our modern superfast environment. It also performs traditional statistical methods and provide an advanced analytic platform. R language comprises of many packages for each and every process. For text mining the first and foremost package to be installed is tm.Packages essential for text mining are NLP, fpc, biclust, igraph, wordclust, ggplot2, devtool. Natural Language Processing (NLP) is used to make the computer to understand the human language. This is just like computer-human interaction. Biclust performs the text clustering process simultaneously in multiple data.

5.2   Implementation of R Packages & Libraries

Data cleaning is a process of reconstructing the gathered data into suitable forms which can be used in future for analysis purpose. Extra white spaces in the dataset can sometimes cause errors. It is used for implementing the data into graph structure and also perform statistical analysis. Fixed Point Cluster is used for text clustering. ggplot2 meant for plotting graph. Also generate complex-multi layered graph. Basically, R system has some fundamental packages in order to run r commands. Installation of those is must. Some of them are compiler, utils, grid, grDevices, datasets, stats etc.

The collection of large datasets which consists of many mails and messages are stored somewhere in the device which means outside the R studio. In order to import or extract the dataset into R, readCorpus command is used. Else simply import by direct click. Package named gmailR is used to access gmail account for reading receiving mails and import into R (Fig. 2).

```
inspect(opinions.tdm[1:25,])

<<TermDocumentMatrix (terms: 10, documents: 3
Non-/sparse entries: 30/0
Maximal term length: 10
Weighting              : term frequency (tf)

                   Docs
Terms          13-1314 3ea4.pdf 14-46 bqmc.pdf

   trap                    10              2
   assassinate              6              4
   murder                   1              2
   killing                  4              1
   sexually                12             10
   raped                    7             26
   free laptop              1              3
```

Fig. 2. Text Mining Results shows the analysis, sometimes stop words and extra whitespaces consumes more time where text uses less time. Also it occupies more memory space. Rarely, the efficiency may decrease because of those words. So it is essential to eliminate the extra white spaces, stop words and nonlexical words.

The data set is created and is been converted to the specific data frames. The ease of access of the data set for processing is done using:

Converting mail to data frame:
myCorpus<-Corpus(VectorSource(mail$text))
dim(mail)

Eliminating punctuations
myCorpus<-tm_map(myCorpus, removePunctuation)

Removal of numbers
myCorpus<-tm_map(myCorpus, removeNumbers)

Remove stop words
myCorpus<-tm_map(myCorpus,removeWords, myStopwords)

Stemming

Text mining process mainly comprises of analysis part. In order to analyze the inner depth of each word and understand its meaning, stemming is takes place. It compares the words with their base or root words.

Stem words
myCorpus <-tm_map(mycorpus,stemDocument)

Stem completion
myCorpus<-tm_map(myCorpus,stemCompletion,dictionary=keywords)

In order to generate the document term matrix, initially the package required for creating dtm should be installed with the upgraded version. As per our requirements we can generate the term document matrix or document term matrix. In document term matrix, the matrix consists of documents as rows and terms as columns as mentioned.

Create DTM
dtm<-DocumentTermMatrix(mail)
inspect(dtm[1:25,110:135])
Analyzing frequent terms
findFreqTerms(dtm,25)

The detailed analysis of customizing email reports based on the analytical results and various suspicious mail, and other predictive results are analysed. The created document term matrix with the keywords provided. The matrix reveals the number of times the single keyword appears in a mail. If the keyword occurs many times in mail, then the mail is suspected with the high dangerous level. Finally, the results that which is more suspicious detected and graph is plotted for the dataset which contain multi number of mails. Wordcloud and ggplot2 are used to plot the resultant graphs.

Plot graph
m<-as.matrix(dtm)
word.freq<-sort(rowSums(m),decreasing = S)
wordcloud(words = names(word.freq),freq = word.freq,min.freq = 3,random. Order = T)

Few of the extracted content of email are as follows (Fig. 3):

ExtractedSubject
FW: Wow
il_296
Re: Chris Stevens
FVV: Cairo Condemnation - Final
il_296
Meet The Right Wing Extremist Behind Anti-Muslim Film That Sparked Deadly Riots
FW: Anti-Muslim film director in hiding, following Libya, Egypt violence
il_296
FVV: Secretary's remarks
more on Libya
AbZ and Hb5 on Libya and West Bank/Gaza
il_296
hey
il_296
RE: Not a dry eye in NEA
il_296
Fw: The Youth of Libya
Fw: One More Photo
Fw: S today
il_296
Fwd: more on libya
Fwd: more on libya
Fw: H: Magariaf on attack on US in Libya. Sid
Fw: H: Magariaf on attack on US in Libya. Sid
Re: Proposed Quad Deal
il_296
Re: Fwd: more on libya

Fig. 3. Subjective predictions from data set

6 Results

The customized report of email gives us the periodicity of the spam mails is given from Fig. 4 and the subjective predictions can be used to create the filters for those content specific email. This further is the alert for the users on restricting the online content. The positive aspects of the above predictions is also generated in the form of word cloud as Fig. 5 where in frequent users establishes a stronger relationship. This positivity is also a measure of the marketing and other business based strategies as well.

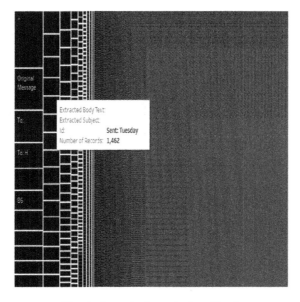

Fig. 4. Impact of reports from Email

The fig also gives the measure of intense spam mails that are received on a constant mode. The proposed system hence is successful in visualizing the outcome in a more personalized and customized approach (Figs. 6 and 7).

Fig. 5. Word cloud of email sentiment analysis

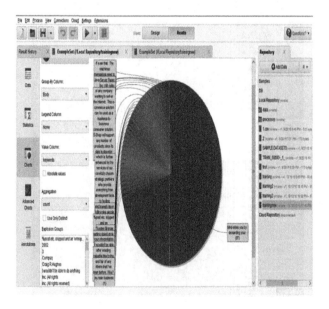

Fig. 6. Spam detection report

Addresses on CD	Click to remove
All natural	Click to remove mailto
Amazing	Compare rates
Apply Online	Compete for your business
As seen on	Confidentially on all orders
Auto email removal	Congratulations
Avoid bankruptcy	Consolidate debt and credit
Be amazed	Copy accurately
Be your own boss	Copy DVDs
Being a member	Credit bureaus
Big bucks	Credit card offers
Bomb	Cures baldness
Billing address	Dear email
Billion dollars	Dear friend
Brand new pager	Dear somebody
Bulk email	Different reply to
Buy direct	Dig up dirt on friends
Buying judgments	Direct email
Cable converter	Direct marketing
Call free	Discusses search engine listings
Call now	Do it today

Fig. 7. Subjective content of spam mail

7 Conclusion and Future Work

Email is the most successful mode of communication and is mandatory in superfast world to widen the social connectivity, The proposed system establishes a customized analytical method to process and to analyze the receiving mails. Here, we implement a text mining frame work which detect the suspicious level of mail. The system also visualizes the sentiment on both personalized and business strategies. It helps the vigilance department for detecting the criminal offence that communicates through the email system. This system can be further customized for improving the ease of sentiments towards the online content. In our paper, we have discussed and done experimental works on the email system using text mining framework for detecting the suspicious mail and also to analyse specific content before becoming suspicious. The visualized results are the outcome of the NLP processed data set. The library packages are customized and is imported using R. The email api is processed on these libraries and the reports are hence generated. The impact of sentiment is personalised and also customized. The proposed model can be extended further for including library files for selective predictions also. Tableau is used for visualizing the data set and generating the analytic reports. Data set is more approachable when its impact is on detailed visualization. The system also detects the extend of impact of spam and suspicious mail when its given a subjective approach. The ease to online forums and participation is clearly visualized and can be extended further for generating the personalized and customized reports are also generated.

References

1. Peng, R.D.: Overview and history of R. Computing for Data Analysis Course, Johns Hopkins University
2. Hershkop, S.: Behavior-based email analysis with application to spam detection. Columbia University

3. Ma, J., Saul, L.K., Savage, S., Voelker, G.M.: Learning to detect malicious web sites from suspicious URLs. University of California, San Diego
4. Chakraborty, G.: Applications of text analytics and sentiment mining. Oklahoma State University
5. Zanasi, A.: Text mining tools. Modena and Reggio Emilia University, Italy. Appendix: Springer-Author Discount
6. Medhat, W., Hassan, A., Korashy, H.: Sentiment analysis algorithms and applications: a survey. Ain Shams Eng. J. **5**, 1093–1113 (2014)
7. Ghosh, S., Roy, S., Bandyopadhyay, S.K.: A tutorial review on text mining algorithms. Int. J. Adv. Res. Comput. Commun. Eng
8. Pendar, N.: Toward spotting the pedophile telling victim from predator in text chats. In: IEEE Internet Computing, pp. 235–241 (2007)
9. Stolfo, S.J., Hershkop, S.: Email mining toolkit supporting law enforcement forensic analyses. Columbia University
10. Vadher, B.: EMail data mining: an approach to construct an organization position-wise structure while performing email analysis. Master's Projects, Paper 63, San Jose State University (2010)
11. Zhao, Y.: Text mining with R – an analysis of Twitter data
12. Haddia, E., Liua, X., Shib, Y.: The role of text pre-processing in sentiment analysis. IEEE

Role of Lexical and Syntactic Fixedness in Acquisition of Hindi MWEs

Rakhi Joon[(✉)] and Archana Singhal

Department of Computer Science, University of Delhi, Delhi, India
rjoon30@gmail.com, archanasinghal1970@gmail.com

Abstract. Multi Word Expressions (MWEs) are one of the most widely used term in linguistics which mainly deals with combination of words rather than single word. In Hindi language, MWEs have become significant and popular for text processing and research related activities. The nicety of any term in linguistics is justified by using statistical measures. Many of these statistical measures are based on frequency of occurrence of a particular word pattern in a corpus. Syntactic fixedness is one of the important statistical measure, which can be used for measuring the degree of lexical and syntactic restrictiveness in the MWEs extraction and analysis process. This paper mainly focuses on evaluating the degree of lexical and syntactic fixedness and justifying their role for Hindi MWEs. The corpus used for experimental purpose is collected from the famous Hindi novel "Godaan". Total 36 text files of the novel are used for the evaluation purpose. The degree of lexical and syntactic fixedness are measured for many classes of 2-grams Hindi MWEs and results are analyzed for accuracy.

Keywords: Linguistics · Hindi multiwords · Lexical fixedness syntactic fixedness · Statistical measures · NLP

1 Introduction

MWEs are the words whose linguistic behavior is unpredictable from the component words they are formed from. The non-compositionality and idiosyncratic behavior [4] of MWEs reveal many different types of analysis including semantics, lexical, syntactic, and so on. Idiomatic expressions are widely used in both spoken and written languages. In computational lexicon, idioms are very challenging for developing large scale and linguistically plausible NLP systems [18]. The MWEs phrases can be classified on the basis of idiosyncratic and institutionalized phrases. The idiosyncratic phrases are further classified to form semantically fixed expressions, semi fixed expressions and syntactically flexible expressions. The Semantically Fixed expressions are of two types, lexical and syntactic fixedness based expressions as shown in Fig. 1. The main focus of this work is based on the lexical and syntactic flexibility measurements. Semantic non-compositionality plays a vital role in formation of any MWE, so MWEs are normally called non-compositional words. In semantic non-compositionality, semantically related words cannot replace the constituent words. For example, the Hindi multiword "आँखे खुलना *(Aankeh Khulna)*" means "सचेत होना *(Sachet Hoona)*", but the semantically related words of this is "नेत्र खुलना *(Netra*

© Springer Nature Singapore Pte Ltd. 2019
M. Singh et al. (Eds.): ICACDS 2019, CCIS 1046, pp. 155–163, 2019.
https://doi.org/10.1007/978-981-13-9942-8_15

Khulna)" which does not mean the same. In the same way another Hindi multiword is "अपना हाथ जगन्नाथ *(Apna   hath   Jagganath)"* means "स्वंय के द्वारा किया गया कार्य ही महत्वपूर्ण होता है *(Sayyam ke dwara kia gaya karya hi mehatvapurn hota hai)"* and the semantically related words "अपना हाथ भगवान *(Apna hath Bhagwan)"*, "अपना हस्त जगन्नाथ *(Apna hasth Jagganath)"* do not convey the same meaning.

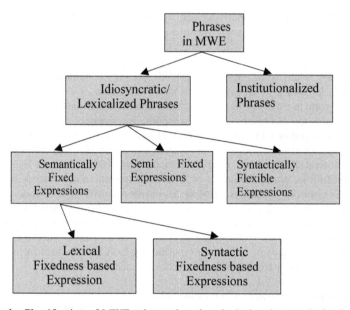

Fig. 1. Classification of MWEs phrases based on lexical and syntactic fixedness.

Non-compositionality is also one of the reasons for the need of description of MWEs in Lexicon [16]. There is very less coverage of MWEs in lexical resources of most of the languages. Some automated methods are required to be designed for the inclusion of MWEs in the lexical resources. Syntactically fixed expressions are less identified in many languages. Various word combinations solely based on the grammatical form allows no syntactic variations. For example, "आंख दिखाना *(Aankeh dikhana)"* and "आँखे दिखा देना *(Aankeh dikha dena)"* both are syntactically different but meaning is same, whereas "एक और एक ग्यारह होते हैं *(Ek or Ek Gyarah hote hai)"* means "एकता में बल होता है *(Ekta me bal hota hai)"* but "ग्यारह एक और एक होते हैं *(Gyarah Ek or Ek hote hai)"* does not convey the same meaning. The syntactic behavior mainly deals with the syntactic fixed expressions.

In the proposed work the MWEs are extracted and their fixedness is measured for 2-grams MWEs. The corpus used for experiments is "Godaan", famous Hindi novel written by Munshi Premchand. Separate results are shown for both lexical and syntactic phrases and the comparison is done for both the fixedness types. Earlier the other statistical measures, Point wise Mutual Information (PMI), Dice Coefficient (DC) and Modified Dice Coefficient (MDC) were analyzed [19] and now in the present work one more statistical measure, i.e. Fixedness is measured for both lexical and syntactic phrases. The various formulas for Fixedness measurement are discussed in Sect. 3.

Rest of the paper is organized in the following manner: Sect. 2 gives the brief overview of the work done by various authors in this area. Section 3 describes the statistical measures of Idiosyncrasy. In Sect. 4, experimental setup and result analysis are described which is followed by the concluding section.

2 Literature Survey

The proposed work is mainly based on calculating the statistical measures of the semantically fixed expressions. The basics of MWEs were explained in [1–4] which mainly include the linguistic concepts and lexicographic treatment designed for MWEs in a particular language along with various grammatical features of MWEs, like lexicosyntactic idiomaticity, semantic idiomaticity, pragmatic idiomaticity and statistical idiomaticity. The criterion of non-compositionality often appears in definition of fixed expressions [5], which is one of the important features for calculating lexical and syntactic fixedness. The authors in [7, 9, 12] discussed about the semantics for extraction of MWEs. The main focus is given on lexical and syntactic fixedness, which are two main components measuring the degree of institutionalization of an expression. In [8], the frequency based measures were used and MWEs were identified and manually validated for Portuguese text. The syntactic flexibility for MWEs is measured in [10] and the morphological and syntactic idiosyncrasy [11] were also discussed. In [13], the authors mainly focused on the lexical fixedness measure for MWEs extraction, the algorithm designed in the paper was based on non-compositionality and gave a new approach for large scale extraction of MWEs. In [6] and [14], the authors also focused on the lexical as well as syntactic flexibility measures and how these measures can be successfully used for analyzing the difference of idiomatic and non-idiomatic phrases. The linguistic properties were examined by the authors which further pertained to the degree of semantic idiosyncrasy of the expressions. The statistical measures were proposed to quantify each property and measures used to automatically distinguish the classes. In [15] and [21] the authors have discussed about the role of statistical measures in acquisition of MWEs and also examined the linguistic properties of metaphorical and idiomatic MWEs. So in general, the MWEs exhibits the idiosyncratic behavior and thus many statistical measures including fixedness play vital role in statistical analysis of MWEs. The proposed work is an extension to the previous work as discussed by the authors in [19] and [20] where various statistical measures for Hindi MWEs were discussed and some other statistical measures related to previous ones are discussed in this paper.

3 Statistical Measures of Idiosyncrasy

Idiosyncracy mainly deals with the idiomatic behavior of the multiword expressions. The main types of idiosyncrasies to be dealt with are lexical, morphological and statistical [11]. The idiosyncratic properties are measured with the help of various statistical measures including the measures used for institutionalized phrases and fixed expressions. The Institutionalization measure and fixedness measure are discussed in next two subsections.

3.1   Institutionalization Measure Analysis

Institutionalization refers to the phrases that are semantically and syntactically compositional, but statistically idiosyncratic [18]. There are many association measures which can be used for assessing the degree of institutionalization of an expression. One of the measure, PMI was used for calculating the fixedness [14]. PMI is also used in many other NLP applications and it is defined as:

$$PMI(v,n) = log \ \frac{P(v,n)}{P(v)P(n)}$$

$$PMI(v,n) \approx log \ \frac{f(*,*)f(v,n)}{f(v,*)f(*,n)}$$

All the frequency counts were measured over verb-object pairs. Frequency and PMI both were used for calculating the degree of Institutionalization.

3.2   Fixedness Measure Analysis

The statistical measures of lexical, syntactic and overall fixedness were developed in [6] and further improved in [2]. The lexical fixedness deals with the comparing the Association measure (e.g. PMI) with the lexical variants. [2]. The lexical variants of the target were generated by replacing the V or N constituents [17] by a semantically similar word from the automatically build dictionary of [16], the Z-Score was used to calculate the lexical fixedness.

$$fixedness_{lex}(v,n) = \frac{PMI(v,n) - \overline{PMI}}{std}$$

Here, $\overline{PMI}$ is the mean and std is the standard deviation over the PMI of the target and all its variants.

Kullback Leibler Divergence [5] is the relative entropy used to measure how one probability distribution is different from the other. This divergence is used to calculate syntactic fixedness by comparing the behavior of target text with the behavior of a particular Verb-Object combination. Standard measures of information theory like entropy etc. are used to calculate the difference between two probability distributions [2].

$$Fixedness_{syn}(v,n) = D(P(pt|v,n)||P(pt))$$
$$= \sum\nolimits_{pt_k \in P} P(pt_k|v,n)log\frac{P(pt_k|v,n)}{P(pt_k)}$$

Here P is the pattern set which can be composed of determiners, prepositions, etc. known to be relevant to syntactic fixedness. $P(pt_k|v,n)$ is the syntactic behavior of the target expression. P(pt) is the syntactic behavior of Verb-Object pairs.

The target preference of the syntactic patterns were not supported by the *Fixedness$_{syn}$*, so an additional pattern measure was used which mainly determine the dominant pattern of the target.

$$Pattern_{dom}(v,n) = \text{argmax}_{pt_k \epsilon P} f(v,n,pt_k)$$

The overall fixedness is measured by using both lexical and syntactic fixedness.

$$Fixedness_{overall} = \alpha Fixedness_{syn}(v,n) + (1-\alpha) Fixedness_{lex}(v,n)$$

Here, α weights the relative contribution of lexical and syntactic fixedness in predicting the sematic idiosyncrasy.

4   Experimental Setup

The present section discusses about experimental study of the proposed approach.

4.1   Corpus

The experiments are performed on the Hindi Dataset taken from one of the famous Hindi novel by writer, "Munshi Premchand": "Godaan". This novel is one of the famous Hindi novels which is based on social and economic poverty and exploitation of rural India mainly in villages. Due to large Corpus, a number of text files from the novel are collected and used for the experiments. This dataset is very useful as it is based on real life scenarios. It contains number of Multiwords in form of compound nouns, named entities, compound verbs, idioms, phrases, and so on. The dataset contains 36 text files, which are processed to get the final dataset. The dataset contains 173691 total words and out of these 15448 are unique words. The data used for training contains 130159 words and 13050 unique words, while the data used for testing contains 43533 words and 6802 unique words.

4.2   Tools Used

For implementing the procedures, NLTK (Natural Language ToolKit) was used which a platform to do python programming to work with Natural language and other text processing tasks. It provides linguistic resources along with rich class libraries for text related operations. In this paper implementation is done using Python 3 with IDE Eclipse and NLTK 3 is used as the toolkit.

4.3   Proposed Methodology

In this paper, the Hindi MWEs are analyzed for fixedness measure. The proposed methodology include the following steps:

1. The raw text is collected from the Hindi novel "Godaan". Then the filtering is done on the text to get the corpus to be used for experimental purpose.
2. The MWEs were extracted from the corpus, here the main focus is on 2-grams MWEs and the following categories of 2-grams MWEs are extracted: *Adj+Noun, Adj+Prep, Adv+Adj, Adv+Adv, Noun+Adj, Noun+Prep, Noun+Verb, Noun+Noun, Verb+Adv, Verb+Particle, Verb+Prep, Verb+Verb.* Later these categories are used for statistical measures.
3. According to the statistical view of machine learning, the work is enhanced [19] for the fixedness measure:
   a. In the earlier work [19], PMI, DC and MDC statistical measures were calculated and result analysis was done for the same, in this work one more statistical measure, i.e. Fixedness is calculated. Two types of fixedness exists in statistical terms, namely lexical fixedness and syntactic fixedness [2], both of these types are calculated in the proposed work. The results are shown in Table 1.
   b. Result analysis is done using histograms and the comparison of both the types of fixedness is done using boxplot as explained in Sect. 4.4.

The proposed model is mainly based on the calculation of fixedness measure, which is based on the PMI measure and the frequency of different types of Hindi MWEs existing in the corpus. PMI and frequency were measured in the earlier work [19], which is enhanced for fixedness measure in proposed work.

4.4   Result Analysis

The experiments are done for 2-grams Hindi MWEs. The lexical and syntactic fixedness score for 2-grams are calculated as shown in Table 1. For some types lexical fixedness is negative, because the mean value is greater than the PMI value. But the overall value of lexical fixedness is 3.163, which is pretty good. In case of syntactic fixedness, most of the values are near to 0.000 due to involvement of the log values of syntactic behavior.

The values are analyzed for accuracy using histograms and boxplots as shown in Figs. 2 and 3. In Fig. 2, the histogram compares lexical and syntactic fixedness with all possible values of different types of 2-grams Hindi MWEs. Negative values are also shown in the histogram. In Fig. 3, the boxplot mainly depicts the same comparison of domains of both lexical and syntactic fixedness types. One thing common in both the types is that both the values mainly lies near to zero, and this is the reason for lesser consideration of the fixedness measure with other measures of statistical types like PMI, DC, MDC, and so on.

Table 1. Fixedness score for lexical and syntactic expression.

2-grams	Total MWEs	Unique MWEs	Lexical fixedness	Syntactic fixedness
JJ+NN	725	419	0.5225	0.05925
JJ+PSP	8	5	0.4929	0.00021
RB+JJ	30	11	1.2690	0.04826
RB+RB	4	3	0.7061	0.0
NN+JJ	302	110	0.6420	0.05925
NN+PSP	130	76	−2.3936	0.05886
NN+VM	1022	814	−0.9872	0.00445
NN+NN	806	529	0.3443	0.0
VM+RB	6	4	0.6022	0.01198
VM+RP	63	23	−0.5955	0.00474
VM+PSP	32	14	−1.4286	0.06601
VM+VM	253	109	0.5565	0.0
All 2-grams	3381	2117	0.2693	0.0

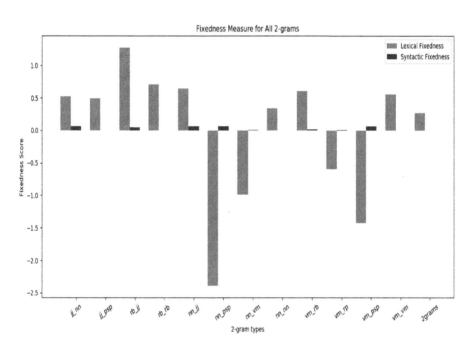

Fig. 2. Comparison of lexical and syntactic fixedness for all 2-gram Hindi MWEs

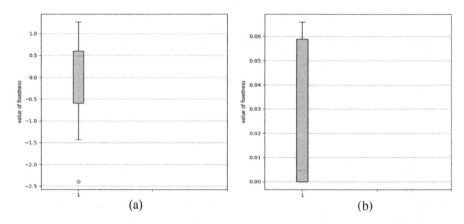

Fig. 3. (a) Variations in lexical fixedness (b) Variations in syntactic fixedness

5   Conclusion and Future Scope

Fixedness measure is the statistical measure used for measuring the degree of lexical and syntactic restrictiveness in a semantically idiosyncratic expression. Lexical fixedness mainly deals with the non-preservance of meaning after substitution of semantically similar words, while syntactic fixedness deals with not undergoing syntactic variation if the expression retain its semantic interpretation [2]. An analysis of lexical and syntactic fixedness is provided to highlight the semantic idiosyncrasy of the Hindi MWEs. There are various linguistically motivated classes of 2-grams Hindi MWEs for which the fixedness is calculated. For some of the classes, lexical fixedness is negative which does not add much relevance to the lexical fixedness measure. The overall lexical fixedness is 0.2693, which is quite relevant and thus there exists some MWEs, which are lexically fixed. For syntactic fixedness measure most of the values are near to 0. So the overall fixedness is also 0.00. Thus, there exists very few Hindi MWEs which are syntactically fixed. Based on the above scenario, it is concluded that lexical fixedness is more relevant than syntactic fixedness for Hindi MWEs. The further extension of this work can be for n-gram MWEs that are not applied in this paper and proposed as a future work.

References

1. Gantar P., Colman L., Escartın C.P., Alonso H.M.: Multiword expressions: between lexicography and NLP. Int. J. Lexicogr. **32**(2), 138–162 (2019)
2. Loukachevitch, N., Parkhomenko, E.: Evaluating distributional features for multiword expression recognition. In: Sojka, P., Horák, A., Kopeček, I., Pala, K. (eds.) TSD 2018. LNCS (LNAI), vol. 11107, pp. 126–134. Springer, Cham (2018). https://doi.org/10.1007/978-3-030-00794-2_13
3. Loukachevitch, N., Parkhomenko, E.: Recognition of multiword expressions using word embeddings. In: Kuznetsov, S.O., Osipov, G.S., Stefanuk, V.L. (eds.) RCAI 2018. CCIS, vol. 934, pp. 112–124. Springer, Cham (2018). https://doi.org/10.1007/978-3-030-00617-4_11

4. Baldwin, T: Compositionality and multiword expressions: six of one, half a dozen of the other? In: Invited Talk Given at the COLING/ACL 2006 Workshop on Multiword Expressions: Identifying and Exploiting Underlying Properties (2006)
5. Svensson, M.H.: A very complex criterion of fixedness: non-compositionality. Phraseol. Interdiscip. Perspect. S. Granger **81**, 81–93 (2008)
6. Fazly, A., Stevenson, S.: Automatically constructing a lexicon of verb phrase idiomatic combinations. In: 11th Conference of the European Chapter of the Association for Computational Linguistics, pp. 337–344 (2006)
7. Van de Cruys, T., Moirón, B.V.: Semantics-based multiword expression extraction. In: Proceedings of the Workshop on a Broader Perspective on Multiword Expressions, pp. 25–32 (2007)
8. Antunes, S., Mendes, A.: An evaluation of the role of statistical measures and frequency for MWE identification. In: The Ninth International Conference on Language Resources and Evaluation–LREC 2014 (2014)
9. Joon, R., Singhal, A.: A system for compound adverbs MWEs extraction in Hindi. In: Proceedings of Eighth International Conference on Contemporary Computing (IC3), Noida, India, pp. 336–341 (2015)
10. Bannard, C.: A measure of syntactic flexibility for automatically identifying multiword expressions in corpora. In: Proceedings of the Workshop on a Broader Perspective on Multiword Expressions, pp. 1–8. Association for Computational Linguistics (2007)
11. Al-Haj, H., Wintner, S.: Identifying multi-word expressions by leveraging morphological and syntactic idiosyncrasy. In: Proceedings of the 23rd International Conference on Computational Linguistics (Coling 2010), pp. 10–18 (2010)
12. Fazly, A., Stevenson, S.: A distributional account of the semantics of multiword expressions (2008)
13. Cruys, T.V., Moirón, B.V.: Lexico-semantic multiword expression extraction. In: Proceedings of the 17th Meeting of Computational Linguistics in the Netherlands. LOT Occasional Series, vol. 7, pp. 175–190 (2007)
14. Fazly, A., Stevenson, S.: Distinguishing subtypes of multiword expressions using linguistically-motivated statistical measures. In: Proceedings of the Workshop on a Broader Perspective on Multiword Expressions, pp. 9–16. Association for Computational Linguistics, Prague (2007)
15. Fazly, A., Nematzadeh, A., Stevenson, S.: Acquiring multiword verbs: the role of statistical evidence. In: Proceedings of the Annual Meeting of the Cognitive Science Society, vol. 31, no. 31, pp. 1222–1227 (2009)
16. Lin, D.: Automatic retrieval and clustering of similar words. In: Proceedings of COLING/ACL 1998, Montreal, Canada (1998)
17. Lin, D.: Automatic identification of non-compositional phrases. In: Proceedings of ACL 1999, University of Maryland, pp. 317–324 (1999)
18. Sag, I.A., Baldwin, T., Bond, F., Copestake, A., Flickinger, D.: Multiword expressions: a pain in the neck for NLP. In: Gelbukh, A. (ed.) CICLing 2002. LNCS, vol. 2276, pp. 1–15. Springer, Heidelberg (2002). https://doi.org/10.1007/3-540-45715-1_1
19. Joon, R., Singhal, A.: A comparative analysis of Hindi MultiWord expressions using relevancy measure-RMMWE. Int. J. Innov. Technol. Explor. Eng. (IJITEE) **8**(8), 3436–3445 (2019)
20. Joon, R., Singhal, A.: Analysis of MWES in Hindi text using NLTK. Int. J. Nat. Lang. Comput. **6**(1), 13–22 (2017)
21. Fazly, A., Stevenson, S.: Automatic acquisition of knowledge about multiword predicates. In: Proceedings of the 19th Pacific Asia Conference on Language, Information and Computation, pp. 31–42 (2005)

Five Input Multilayer Full Adder
by QCA Designer

D. Naveen Sai, G. Surya Kranth, Damarla Paradhasaradhi,
R. S. Ernest Ravindran$^{(\boxtimes)}$, M. Lakshmana Kumar,
and K. Mariya Priyadarshini

Department of Electronics and Communication Engineering,
Koneru Lakshmaiah Education Foundation,
Vaddeswaram, Guntur 522502, India
ravindran.ernest@gmail.com

Abstract. QCA is an upcoming technology with high performance and ultra-low power, less time to designs any circuit while comparing with that of CMOS technology. In existing design the full adder is design with coplanar crossover method. This method requires more number of cells and leading to large area. In the present investigation coplanar crossover and multilayer methods have been implemented with 16 nm dot cells. Five input majority gate is proposed using multilayer full adder architecture and three input majority gate is designed using coplanar crossover method. The offer circuit to perform ultra-low power there by decreasing the area by 20% and more over complexity of circuit is reduced.

Keywords: Polarization · QCA clock · Wire · Full adder ·
Majority gates · Inverter

1 Introduction

QCA is a promising technology that can replaces the CMOS and other existing technology. QCA operating frequency range is in Tera Hertz (THz). In QCA the standard semiconductors materials such as InAs (Indium Arsenide) and GaAs (Gallium Arsenide) structures can be modelled as 3-dimensional quantum wells. CMOS technology is used for implementation of high-speed devices and high integrated circuits. In CMOS, the substrate materials is made up of silicon and Germanium and it takes larger area to design any circuit in CMOS. Whereas, in QCA less area can be utilized to design a circuit within less time when compare to that of CMOS technology.

In general, QCA consist of four quantum dots that are arranged in square pattern, so it is considered as one quantum cell. QCA can be polarized due to columbic repulsion that exist between the electrons which leads to more energy requirement for the quantum dots. In QCA they are two different polarization like logic 0 and logic 1 [1]. In logic 1, when it is represented in binary it stands as +1 and −1 as represented in Fig. 1(a). Four stages resemble to hold, switches, released and relax. In switched stage, the cell begins to polarization with lower prospective block, is elevated. The block are held high in the hold stage whereas in released stage, the barriers are dropped. In the relaxed stage, the blocks continue to drop and keep the cells in a polarized state and the output of the circuit can be observed in this stage [2, 3]. Each of the clock signal is shifted by 90°.

M. Singh et al. (Eds.): ICACDS 2019, CCIS 1046, pp. 164–174, 2019.
https://doi.org/10.1007/978-981-13-9942-8_16

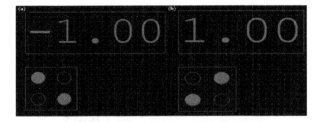

Fig. 1. Different polarizations (a) logic 0 (b) logic 1

When the QCA cells are arranged in a horizontal row then it act as QCA Wire. QCA wire propagates signals from input to output through binary digitals. QCA design consists of different styles like crossover, normal quantum cell, vertical as shown in Fig. 2. In coplanar the crossover only one layer is used to design a circuit in easy way. QCA wire consists of two different angles such as 45° and 90° [4], 45° is known as rotated and 90° is known as regular as shown in Fig. 3(a). In coplanar crossover one can design any circuits very easily but comparatively in multilayer there some fabrication issues which are very complicated to design any circuit. Generally, the coplanar crossover is used to design the circuits because of its high speed and less area.

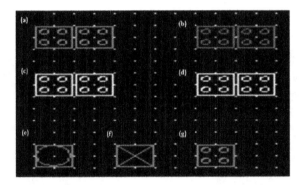

Fig. 2. (a) Four clocks (e) Vertical (f) Crossover (g) Dot cell

2   Existing Method

2.1   Majority Gate

In QCA cell the majority cell is the very crucial part to outline any circuit. The majority gate mostly designed significantly the input of three and five majority cell. With the help of majority gate one can design various circuit for different applications. Fundamentally, it comprises of input cells, output cell and one central cell. The input cell will pass data to central cell and it does some functionality and forward the data to the output cell and the required waveform to the circuit can be received. In the majority gate for three input, QCA consists of three input cells, one output cell and one central cell as shown in Fig. 4(a) [5–7].

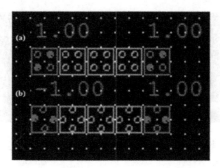

Fig. 3. (a) Normal cell (b) Rotated cell

When the polarization is 0 and it will performance AND logic operation and when the polarization applied as 1 it will perform operation of OR logic. Similarly, majority cell of five input consists of input cells of five, one cell of output and one central as shown in Fig. 4(b). Using QCA, seven-input majority gate can also be designed that will have seven input cells, one output and one central cell as shown in Fig. 5(a).

Majority cell of three input consists of x, y and z the expression are $M(X, Y, Z) = XY + YZ + ZX$. Using this, one can realize a two-input OR gate as $M(X, Y, 1)$.

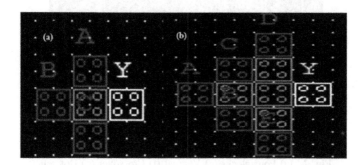

Fig. 4. (a) Three input majority gate (b) Existing method of five input majority gate

2.2 QCA Inverter

QCA inverter can designed by taking the position of rotated cells. Here the cell has located in regular position and the next cell is placed diagonally by 10 nm distance neighboring cell. The electrostatic connection of inverter or NOT gate are shown in Fig. 5(a, b) [5–7]. QCA itself compares the polarization of the electron that were placed are misaligned between the dot cells and it will have the values as 0 and 1. QCA generally shaped by setting the cells with just their corners contacting. Here in the three-cell inverter, composed by utilizing 6 cells that are placed 45° and the cell is automatically inverted, due to the columbic repulsion. Here the basic inverter can be

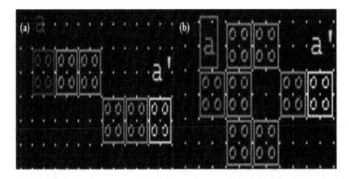

Fig. 5. (a) Three cell inverter and (b) Basic inverter designed structure in QCA tool.

composed by utilizing 8 cells to execute the circuits, with high performance and less destruction in the output.

2.3 Full Adder

The significant measured task like adding, calculation, duplication & separation are generally executed by full adder. An effective adder can be abundant contribution in design of the logical circuits. Addition operation in the three variable Boolean function sum and are the outputs. Full adder can be executed with two half adders. Full adder can be constructed by combining AND, XOR and OR gates. Here, the first half adder is utilized to include the input signal A and B. The output is created by this half adder and the rest of the information (X) is fed to contributions of the second half adder. The complete function gives us the output Sum. In the function of any half adders there will be a carry bit, OR gate is implemented to control the carry output are shown Fig. 6 [9–11].

The Boolean expression of sum and carry are given below

$$\textbf{Sum} = \textbf{A XOR B} = \textbf{A} + \textbf{B} \tag{1}$$

$$\textbf{Carry} = \textbf{A AND B} = \textbf{A}^*\textbf{B} \tag{2}$$

Whereas three input are A, B and C are connecting to the represents the sum and carry. The design consists of Gate 1, Gate 2 and Gate 3 shows the majority cell and connected to the gate 4 and given to the inverting signal level 1. The 2 cell in the level 2 that connecting to the level 1 to level 3. Level 3 makes a contact between two link level 2 and level 1 and it has three different layers and clock zones to see the output of the full adder. For some adder like ripple carry adder it requires an extra additional layer by using crossover and it can also be designed for full adder with less cells which is shown in Fig. 7 [12].

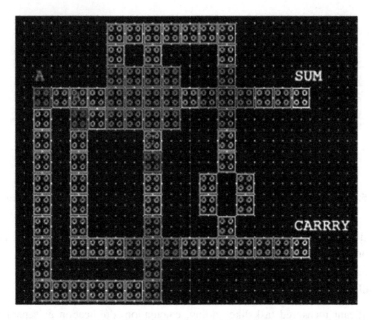

Fig. 6. Existing design of full adder

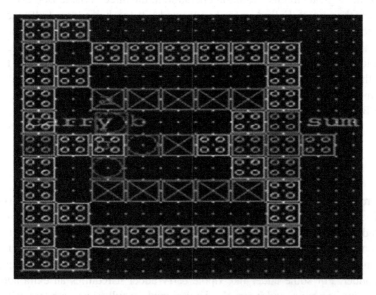

Fig. 7. Existing design of full adder

To design the full adder in QCA, it requires majority cell of two and Inverter, in which two majority gates, 1st five input and another one is three input majority gates respectively. In the full adder, the three inputs are A, B, C and sum and carry are two output signals. From the majority cell at one output SUM can be obtained and from the 2nd majority gate CARRY can be obtained.

3 Proposed Methodology

In proposed methodology, the majority gate and full adder are reduced the size from 18 to 16 nm. Reduce the amount of majority cells and inverter cells, multilayer crossover design utilizing the majority cell of five input (Fig. 8).

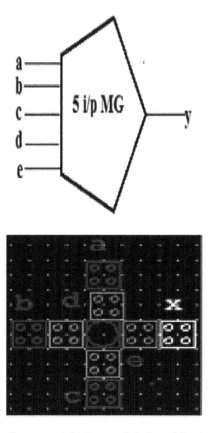

Fig. 8. (a) Block diagram and (b) Proposed design of five-input majority gate

An input majority gate is a Boolean function whose output is 1 just if at least 3 of input one. The majority cell of five input is [9–11]

$$F(X, Y, Z, A, B) = XYZ + XYA + XYB + XAB + YZB + YAB + ZAB \quad (3)$$

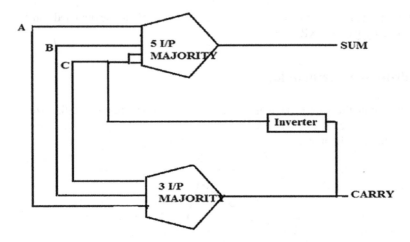

Fig. 9. Full adder using multilayered architecture

Three-input majority cell have actualized utilizing just a single structure. However, a five-input majority gate can be actualized utilizing different designs. The basic cell of our proposed mythology majority cell of five input as appeared in Fig. 8(b). The proportional study creates the construction is more easy when compare to the other five input majority gates. In Multilayer architecture Consists of five layers, Level one source is c, level 3 has three sources is E, D, A and level five has one source is B. Ideal output gotten from level 3. These output isn't encompassed to the alternate cells, and it can easily be accessed. These arrangement not require any regular wire hybrid to conduct to the signal of the output. Consequently, the output can be effectively sustained into the contribution of the other circuits of quantum cellular automata.

These utilization of 5 level to execute a majority gate of five input utilizing multi-layer methodology is been suited because the source are given to the inverter and to the source to levels. However, it is set to the three levels, moreover. All things considered, high-level cell ought to be located in slanting positions of the low cells in its place to directly. Proposed mythology utilizes just a single clocks like green, and from input to output the delay should be reduced. The majority cell of three input and majority cell of five input are shown below: [12–14].

$$SUM = MA5(Carry, A, B, C) \qquad (4)$$

$$CARRY = MA3(A, B, C) \qquad (5)$$

In carry input is created utilizing a conventional majority gate of three input is connected to first level and is straight forwardly communicated to one of the clock zone like clock 0. At that point, the input of carry signal is engendered a lot of utilizing multilevel by engaging a cell in the second level obliquely crossing to the carry signal. The second level is connected to the output carry. The input source of carry is fed to the majority of five input of the level three. Additionally the input source are a, b, c and it connected to the first level and it is connected to the level three.

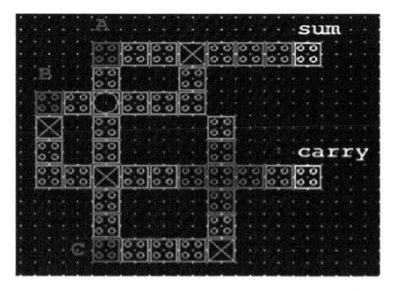

Fig. 10. Proposed design of full adder

The majority cell of five input are generated to the sum bit. The majority of three input is connected to the third level is sustained to the majority cell five input. Hence, somewhere around green and pink are necessary to get the steady output for this mythology for designing the majority of five input. The block diagram of full adder architecture are shown in the Figs. 9 and 10.

4   Result and Discussion

In the proposed method, the cell count and cell size is reduced thereby reducing the area (0.05 µm^2) [11] when compare with that of previous methods. Area, complexity of circuit are reduced and the performance of full adder is increase, cell count required to design the full adder minimal. The mythology to design full adder are simulated in the quantum cellular automata simulated. For design the full adder considerations as to follow bistable simulation: dot size of 16 nm, illustrations of 50000, with merging of 0.00000100, the effect of radius 65 nm, comparative of 12.9, clock high of 9.8 e^{022} i, clock low of 3.8 e^{023} i, clock shift (0 i), clock 2, with level parting of 11.5 and illustrations (100). Most of the mentioned parameters are default values in QCA Designer tool.

From the above wave form observe that when the three inputs are having majority number of value then the output will be represented as 1 (Fig. 11).

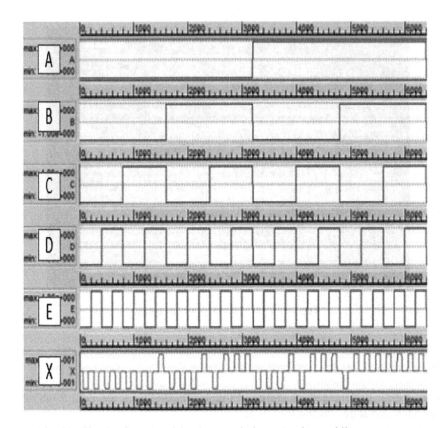

Fig. 11. Simulated results of five-input majority gate using multilayer structure.

From the above waveform as shown in Fig. 12 it is observed that SUM and CARRY functions depend on the input functions A, B, C. whereas SUM function getting one in four cases, when '1' of the input is having '1' then SUM will be '1' and when all the inputs are having '1' then SUM will be '1'. When two inputs are having same value then CARRY will be '1' and all inputs are having '1' then output will be also '1'. From, the waveforms, it is observed that the simulation result shows that there is a coherence vector, cell count is reduced to 42 and area is reduced to 0.04 μm² (Table 1).

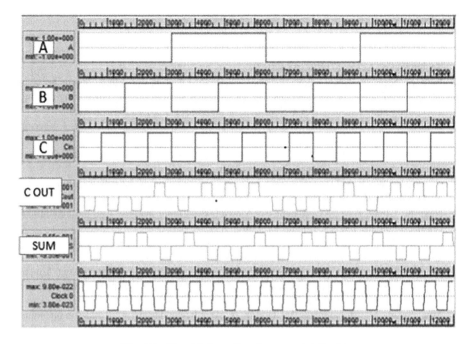

Fig. 12. Simulated results of proposed full adder

Table 1. Comparison of QCA Full-Adders various parameters.

Designs	Area (μm^2)	Cell count	Delay
Existing [12]	0.20	192	Not applicable
Existing [13]	0.17	145	4 clock phases
Existing [14]	0.10	86	3 clock phases
Existing [10]	0.09	83	2 clock phases
Proposed design	**0.05**	**41**	**2 clock phases**

5   Conclusion

QCA is the new technology at Nano scale range circuit configuration level they can make different appropriate for different circuits. In proposed mythology the multilayer crossover is designed with majority cell of five input and adder is designed with quantum cellular automata. The structured is constructed with layers and we combining all the levels and majority cell of five input is designed. The green and pink are two clocks to reduce delay when compare to the existing designs and area is also reduced to 0.02 μm^2. So In future QCA can be the major role to design any circuits or any applications.

References

1. Mehta, U., Dhare, V.: Quantum-dot cellular automata (QCA): a survey. Emerging Technologies. ArXiv:1711.08153 (2017)
2. Rani, S., Sasamal, T.N.: A new clocking scheme for quantum dot cellular automata based designs with single or regular cells. In: International Conference on Power Engineering, Computing and Control, PECCON-2017, 2–4 March 2017, pp. 466–473 (2017)
3. Hennessy, K., Lent, C.S.: Clocking of molecular quantum-dot cellular automata. J. Vaccum Sci. Technol. B **19**(5), 1752–1755 (2001)
4. Snider, G.L., Orlov, A.O., Lent, C.S.: Quantum dot cellular automata line and majority logic gate. Jpn. J. Appl. Phys. **38**, 7227–7229 (1999)
5. Akeela, R., Wagh, M.D.: A five input majority gate in quantum dot cellular automata. In: NSTI – Nanotech, vol. 2 (2011)
6. Navi, K., Chabi, A.M., Sayedsalehi, S.: A novel seven input majority gate in quantum-dot cellular automata. Int. J. Comput. Sci. Issues **9**(1), 84 (2012)
7. Vijayalakshmi, P., Monisha, V.: Design of efficient novel XOR and a code converter using QCA with minimum number of cells. IJIREEICE **5**(5), 62–69 (2017)
8. Jaiswal, R., Sasamal, T.N., Efficient design of full adder and subtractor using 5-input majority gate in QCA. In: Proceedings of 2017 Tenth International Conference on Contemporary Computing (IC3), 10–12 August 2017 (2017)
9. Mohammadi, M., Mohammadi, M., Gorgin, S.: An efficient design of full adder in quantum-dot cellular automata (QCA) technology. Microelectron. J. **50**, 35–43 (2016)
10. Basu, S., Bal, A.: Design of efficient full adder in quantum-dot cellular automata. Int. J. Comput. Appl. **104**(3) (2014). ISSN 0975-8887
11. Sen, B., Rajoria, A., Sikdar, B.K.: Design of efficient full adder in quantum-dot cellular automata. Sci. World J. **2013**, 1–10 (2013). Received 27 March 2013, Accepted 17 May 2013
12. Tougaw, P.D., Lent, C.S.: Logical devices implemented using quantum cellular automata. J. Appl. Phys. **75**(3), 1818–1825 (1994)
13. Zhang, R., Walnut, K., Wang, W., Jullien, G.: A method of majority logic reduction for quantum cellular automata. IEEE Trans. Nanotechnol. **3**, 443–450 (2004)
14. Cho, H., Swartzlander, E.E.: Adder and multiplier design in quantum-dot cellular automata. IEEE Trans. Comput. **58**(6), 721–727 (2009)

Effect of Vaccination in the Computer Network for Distributed Attacks – A Dynamic Model

Yerra Shankar Rao[1], Hemraj Saini[2(✉)], Geetanjali Rathee[2(✉)], and Tarini Charan Panda[3]

[1] Department of Mathematics, Gandhi Institute of Excellent Technocrats, Bhubaneswar 752054, Odisha, India
sankar.math1@gmail.com
[2] Department of Computer Science and Engineering, Jaypee University of Information Technology, Wakanghat 173234, Himachal Pradesh, India
hemraj1977@yahoo.co.in,
geetanjali.rathee123@gmail.com
[3] Department of Mathematics, Revenshaw University, Cuttack 753003, Odisha, India
tc_panda@yahoo.co.in

Abstract. In this reviewed endeavour, a mathematical model is formulated to assess the spread of a distributed attack over a computer network for critical targeted resources. In this paper a mathematical model is formulated, the two sources susceptible, vaccinated, infected, recovered nanonodes in the target population (e-$S_t V_t I_t R_t$) and susceptible, infected, susceptible nanonodes in the attacking population (e-SIS) epidemic model generated in order to propagate malicious object in the network. Further the analysis of the model has been concentrated upon the basic reproduction number. Where threshold value has effectively examined the stability of the network system. This work is verified for both asymptotical stable, that is the basic reproduction number less than on when the infection free equilibrium express the stability and basic reproduction number is more than one when endemic equilibrium is stable. A very general recognized control mechanism is regarded as vaccination strategy, which is deployed in order to defend the malicious object in the computer network. Finally we examine the effect of vaccination on performance of the controlling strategy of malicious objects in the network. The simulated result produced has become compatible with the overall theoretical analysis.

Keywords: Reproduction number · Stability · Vaccination · Malicious objects · DDoS attack

1 Introduction

In the Modern society the ever growing dependence on computer network is accompanied by ever growing concern about the network vulnerability to information attacks and dependability of existing network security system. Many organizations are well recognized to threats to the society. The attacking agents are like worm, virus, etc. Recently our society has witnessed drastic changes catalyses by cyber world. Presently

© Springer Nature Singapore Pte Ltd. 2019
M. Singh et al. (Eds.): ICACDS 2019, CCIS 1046, pp. 175–184, 2019.
https://doi.org/10.1007/978-981-13-9942-8_17

it is threaten by malevolent things, like worm, viruses etc. Frequent use of electronic mails, floppy disk and internet is facilitating in propagation of spiteful virus in the network. Consider the contagious trait; malicious objects spread their tentacles in many ways. To counter the propagation and its dangerous impact, can observe the positive and negative the characteristic of those harmful objects. There are different types of internet based attack, out of which DDoS attack is dangerous and continuous in the cyber security domain. These type of attack is operated by consuming the resources like memory, network bandwidth [19, 20] etc. paralyzing the target sources and consequently which can no longer provide its service to users. The DDoS operates through the host computer systems to attack the target computers. In 2004 for the first time DDoS attack called Cabir, emerged. It used Bluetooth channel of cell phone to infect other phone by running the Symbian Operating System. It is capable of spreading through infected of mobile phones. It drains out the battery of affected devices by intensive scanning operations and blocking the wireless channels. They have not breached in security as it carries a malicious payload. However security threats over Bluetooth DDoS attack [1, 2] cannot rule out. The moment a DDoS attack affects the cell phone placing bough calls, sending spam mails and taking confidential information stored on the cello phone would be easily. DDoS attack might get upper hand over large number of cell phone in which embed Zombie. The wireless botnets can be used as a deterrent against the DDoS attack on base station, cellular switch, and exact IP address or emergence phone numbers.

Several attempts have been made mathematically to understand and analyze such attacks. It has been verified that the epidemic models are useful methods for understanding the transmission of virus malicious affected network in cyber space domain. The malicious objects can disseminate throughout the network rapidly and they pose serious threat. Continuous quarantine method can immunized against DDoS attack. The term vaccination means to compelled termination of infection. From the physiological aspect, vaccination is supposed to be employing in order to lessen the contamination [3, 4] of human ailments e.g. H1N1, Leprosy, Measles, and Smallpox etc. This perception prominently installed in the cyber domain [24, 28–30]. In particular the highest contaminated nodes are separated out from the system domain till the rehabilitation here.

2 Nomenclatures

S_t: Susceptible compartments of target population
I_t: Infected compartments of target population
V_t: Vaccinated compartment of target population
R_t: Recovered compartments of target populations
S: Susceptible nodes from the attacking population
I: Infected nodes from the attacking population
β: Probability of transmission infection rate from susceptible
γ: The rate coefficients from vaccinated to infected class of target population
ε: The rate coefficients from infected to recovered class in target population.
σ: The rate of coefficients from recovered to susceptible class in target population.
α: The rate coefficients from infected to susceptible class in attacking population

3   Mathematical Model and Assumptions

Consider the entire population of nodes is divided in two sections like attacking population and target population [5, 6]. The preliminary object of the attacker is to find more and more sensitive nodes then it unleash attack the precise target population. As the total number of the target population remains constant, the loss of any nodes due to DDoS attack is considered to be replaced instantly by the supporting nodes. The target population remains constant. The vulnerable hosts work on dual approach: one for attacking target and secondly looking for new hosts to begin the attack [7–10]. The susceptible hosts do not recover permanently and it revolt to susceptible. Whereas the target resource of susceptible compartments will move to vaccination compartment with the help of screening or scanning then moves to infected compartments and after treatment of anti malicious object goes to recovery compartments. As soon as these recovered compartments again start net-surfing or receive suspicions emails or other malware factors are accessed, it again becomes susceptible. The repercussion of such attack on critical infrastructure is anticipated. Therefore the target hosts must have much stronger defence mechanism.

Based on assumption we can total population can categorized in to two groups i.e. attacking population and target population. The target population can be divided in to susceptible, vaccinated, infected, and recovered. As well as the attacking population

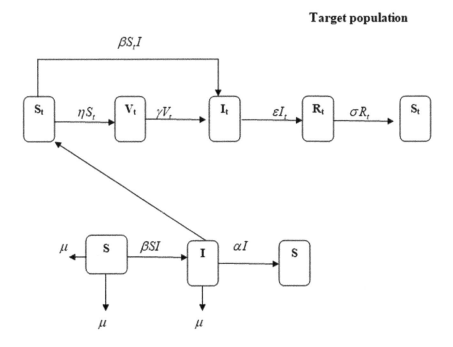

Fig. 1. Schematic diagram for flow of malicious objects in Target/Attacking population

can be categorized into two i.e. either susceptible or infected. The new nodes added in to network is susceptible. Death rate other than attack of malicious objects is constants. The natural death of the nodes as they are once susceptible to any malicious objects decreases. The infectious nodes recover from infection without immunity back to susceptible compartment. Our assumption on transmission of malicious objects in computer network is depicted in Fig. 1.

For the Target population the mathematical model can express as

$$\frac{dS_t}{dt} = -\beta S_t I - \eta S_t + \sigma R_t$$
$$\frac{dV_t}{dt} = \eta S_t - \gamma V_t$$
$$\frac{dI_t}{dt} = \beta S_t I + \gamma V - \varepsilon I_t \tag{1}$$
$$\frac{dR_t}{dt} = \varepsilon I_t - \sigma R_t$$

In similarly for the Attacking population the mathematical model as

$$\frac{dS}{dt} = \mu - \beta SI - \mu S + \alpha I$$
$$\frac{dI}{dt} = \beta SI - \mu I - \alpha I \tag{2}$$

Where $S_t + V_t + I_t + R_t = 1$ and $S + I = 1$
The above system of equation can be represented as

$$\frac{dS_t}{dt} = -\beta S_t I - \eta S_t + \sigma(1 - S_t - V_t - I_t)$$
$$\frac{dV_t}{dt} = \eta S_t - \gamma V_t$$
$$\frac{dI_t}{dt} = \beta S_t I + \gamma V - \varepsilon I_t \tag{3}$$
$$\frac{dI}{dt} = \beta(1 - I)I - \mu I - \alpha I$$

When adding all the equations in the model (2) & (3) we have $S_t + V_t + I_t \leq 1$, $I \leq 1$. This inequality satisfies the condition $\limsup_{t \to \infty} S_t + V_t + I_t \leq 1$, and $I \leq 1$. Thus system (3) is defined on the closed, positive invariant set.

That can further represented as $D = \{(S_t, I_t, V_t, I) : S_t > 0, V_t > 0, I_t > 0, S_t + V_t + I_t \leq 1 : I \leq 1\}$.

As a results we discuss the stability of the model (3) on the set D.

4   Basic Reproduction Number (R₀)

It is the one of the theoretical foundation of the mathematical epidemiology as well as technological epidemiology. It permits for the classification of e- dynamic model. The stability of the system as well as eradication of the malicious objects depends on basic reproduction number. It gives the behaviour of the model stability and prediction of malicious object spread to some extent [21, 23, 25–27].

So, basic reproduction number can play the vital role in both biological as well as technological attack. So it is defined as the t during its life time a single malicious objects affected computer can produce total susceptible class caused by secondary infection. This can approach by Jones. Here it is calculated by two populations

Basic reproduction number for the target population

$$R_{0t} = \frac{\beta}{\varepsilon}$$

Similarly for the attacking population

$$R_{0a} = \frac{\beta}{(\mu + \alpha)}$$

In the epidemiology the value of basic reproduction can be calculated by taking the geometric mean of the attacking and target population reproduction number. Which can expressed as

$$R_0 = \sqrt{\frac{\beta^2}{\varepsilon(\alpha + \mu)}}$$

5   Stability Analysis

The positive invariant set D has two possible equilibriums. First the infection free equilibrium and second is the endemic equilibrium [11–18]. In this section we discuss the locally stability for infection free equilibrium and endemic equilibrium.

For the infection free equilibrium - $(S_t = 1, I_t = 0, V_t = 0, I = 0)$.

On the set D, endemic equilibrium $(S_t^*, V_t^*, I_t^*, I^*)$ can be achieved by considering all the equation of the system to zero.

$$
\begin{aligned}
-\beta S_t I - \eta S_t + \sigma(1 - S_t - V_t - I_t) &= 0 \\
\eta S_t - \gamma V_t &= 0 \\
\beta S_t I + \gamma V - \varepsilon I_t &= 0 \\
\beta(1 - I)I - \mu I - \alpha I &= 0
\end{aligned}
\tag{4}
$$

Solving simultaneously the above equations we have for the endemic state $(S_t^*, V_t^*, I_t^*, I^*)$

$$S_t^* = \frac{\varepsilon\gamma\sigma}{[\eta\gamma\sigma - \varepsilon\sigma\eta - (\beta+\eta) - (\mu+\alpha+\sigma)\varepsilon\gamma]}$$

$$V_t^* = \frac{\varepsilon\eta\sigma}{\eta\gamma\sigma - \varepsilon\sigma\eta - (\beta+\eta) - (\mu+\alpha+\sigma)\varepsilon\gamma}$$

$$I_t^* = \frac{\eta\gamma\sigma}{[\eta\gamma\sigma - \varepsilon\sigma\eta - (\beta+\eta) - (\mu+\alpha+\sigma)\varepsilon\gamma]}$$

$$I^* = \frac{\beta - \mu - \alpha}{\beta}$$

Theorem 1

The infection free equilibrium is locally asymptotically locally stable in the region D if $R_{0a} \leq 1$. And it is unstable if $R_{0a} > 1$.

Proof: Linearization of the system (3) for $S_t = 1, I_t = 0, V_t = 0, I = 0$

$$J_{IFE} = \begin{pmatrix} -\eta - \sigma & -\sigma & -\sigma & -\beta \\ 0 & -\gamma & 0 & 0 \\ 0 & 0 & -\varepsilon & 0 \\ 0 & 0 & 0 & \beta - \mu - \alpha \end{pmatrix}$$

The Eigen values are

$$\lambda_1 = -\eta - \sigma$$
$$\lambda_2 = -\gamma$$
$$\lambda_3 = -\varepsilon$$
$$\lambda_4 = \beta - \mu - \alpha$$

Here first three Eigen values are negative and fourth Eigen value is also negative if $\beta - \mu - \alpha < 0$. i.e.

$$\beta < \mu + \alpha$$
$$R_{0a} < 1$$

Hence the infection free equilibrium is locally asymptotical stable in the region D. While $R_{0a} > 1$, which means $\beta > \mu + \alpha$. So $\lambda_4 > 0$. Therefore the infection free equilibrium is unstable.

Theorem 2

For the endemic equilibrium is asymptotically stable in the region D when $R_{0a} > 1$.

Proof

Linearization of the model about the endemic equilibrium $(S_t^*, V_t^*, I_t^*, I^*)$

$$J_{EE} = \begin{pmatrix} -\beta I^* - \eta - \sigma & -\sigma & -\sigma & -\beta S_t^* \\ \eta & -\gamma & 0 & 0 \\ \beta I^* & \gamma & -\varepsilon & 0 \\ 0 & 0 & 0 & -2\beta I^* - \mu - \alpha \end{pmatrix}$$

Solving we get the Eigen values

$$\lambda_1 = -2\beta I^* - \mu - \alpha$$

The other three Eigen values can be obtained by solving

$$\lambda^3 + A\lambda^2 + B\lambda + C = 0$$

Where

$$A = \beta I^* + \eta + \sigma + \gamma + \varepsilon$$
$$B = \sigma\eta + (\beta I^* + \eta + \sigma)\gamma + (\beta I^* + \eta + \sigma)\varepsilon + \gamma\varepsilon - \sigma\beta I^*$$
$$C = (\beta I^* + \eta + \sigma)\varepsilon\gamma + \sigma\eta\varepsilon + \sigma\eta\gamma - \sigma\gamma\beta I^*$$

Where A, B and C are positive when $R_{0a} > 1$.
Furthermore $AB > C$.
Hence, by Routh-Hurtwitz condition [22] the endemic equilibrium is locally asymptotically stable.

6   Numerical Simulations

The Fig. 2 using the different parameter, we can obtained that the basic reproduction number for attacking population is below the unity the malicious object gradually eliminated. Which is agree with the Theorem 1. This figure also clearly explain that spread of malicious objects is depressive, which consists with the analysis of theory. Lastly the infected nodes will vanishes and reached the recovered level.

Similarly the Fig. 3 using the different parameters remains unchanged, we can seen that the basic reproduction number for attacking population is above the unity, the all the nodes are maintain positive values between the range. Which indicates the malicious objects does not vanish if the objects are initially present. Hence finally theses state reaches their endemic equilibrium point. It agrees with the Theorem 2. This is consistent and asymptotical stable. To reveal the effect of partial vaccination rate on infected nodes. So, we give the partial vaccination, which all the nodes get vaccinated. However, in the real world network, as a result, we expected the use of vaccination process, the rate of spread malicious objects slowly down and decrees the infected nodes in the network.

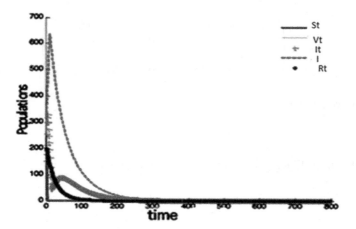

Fig. 2. Dynamic behaviour of the model for infection free equilibrium ($R_{0a} \leq 1$)

In order to simulate the behaviour of spread of the malicious objects the parameters in the experiments are practical values for dies the malicious object in the computer network in real life. Here by using the Range kutta fourth and fifth order to solve the system of ordinary differential equation with the help of MATLAB. Here by applying the MATLAB we can observe the behaviour of different nodes with respect to time. This simulated result agrees with the real life situation.

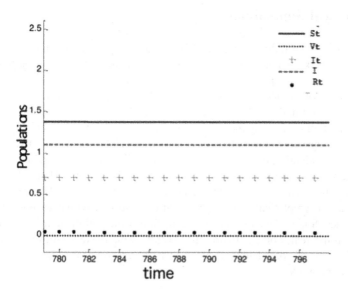

Fig. 3. Dynamic behaviour of the model for endemic equilibrium ($R_{0a} > 1$)

7 Conclusion

The aim of this work is to model the malicious object control in the network. It also finds out the particular workable means of controlling the spread of malicious object in the network. Here a dynamic two population e-epidemic model has been generated for the transmission of the malicious object in the network. The investigation over the dynamic behaviour of the specified model with partial immunizations has been systematically expressed. The derivation of the basic reproduction number which determines the worm extinguished has been solidified. Again the fact behind basic reproduction number is that it exclusively depends on the stability of the system. Considering the consequence of the analysis the infection free equilibrium as well as endemic equilibrium which are locally asymptotically stable have become confirmed. The defence measure i.e. vaccination (filter, scanning) against malicious object in the network has been successfully deployed. Latest version of antivirus with latest signature has made the DDoS attack minimum in the network. The numerical simulation results have optimistically explained the positive impact of increasing the security of DDoS attack. We imagine that our analysis can provide a quantity of close into malicious object counter measure. In the real world, the result can supportive to antivirus companies on related organization to make cost useful countermeasure to work well. Finally the foremost future endeavour will be verifying the model in scale free network. And it can be extended to time delay parameter.

References

1. Gan, C., Xiaofan, Y., Qingyi, Z., Li, H.: The spread of computer virus under external computers. Nonlinear Dyn. **73**(3), 1615–1620 (2013)
2. Gelenbe, E., Gellman, M., Loukas, G.: Defending networks against denial-of-service attacks. In: Unmanned/Unattended Sensors and Sensor Networks, vol. 5611, pp. 233–244. International Society for Optics and Photonics (2004)
3. Li, M.Y., Graef, J.R., Wang, L., Karsai, J.: Global dynamics of an SEIR model with a varying total population size. Math. Biosci. **160**, 191–213 (1999)
4. Kermac, W.O., McKendrick, A.G.: Contribution of mathematical theory to epidemic. Proc. R. Soc. Lond. Ser. Contain. Pap. Math. Phys. Character **14**(843), 94–122 (1933)
5. Haldar, K., Mishra, B.K.: A mathematical model for the distributed attack on the target resources in the computer network. Commun. Nonlinear Sci. Simul. **19**, 3149–3160 (2014)
6. Mishra, B.K., Haldar, K.: e-epidemic models on attack and defence of malicious objects in networks, theories and simulations of complex social system. In: Dabbaghian, V., Mago, V. (eds.) Theories and Simulations of Complex Social Systems. Intelligent System Reference Library, vol. 52, pp. 117–143. Springer, Heidelberg (2014). https://doi.org/10.1007/978-3-642-39149-1_9
7. Song, X., Chen, L.: Optimal harvesting and stability for two species competitive system with stage structure. Math. Biosci. **170**, 173–186 (2001)
8. Toutonji, O., Yoo, S.M.: Passive benign worm propagation modelling with dynamic quarantine defence. KSII Trans. Internet Inf. Syst. **3**(1), 96–107 (2009)
9. Mishra, B.K.: Jha, N: SEIORS model for the transmission of malicious objects in computer network. Appl. Math. Model. **34**, 710–715 (2010)

184   Y. S. Rao et al.

10. Wang, L., Li, M.Y.: A criteria for stability of matrices. Math. Anal. Appl. **225**, 249–264 (1998)
11. Dagon, D., Zou, C., Lee, W.: Modelling bonnet propagation using time zones. In: Proceedings of 13th Network and Distributed System Security Symposium NDSS, vol. 6, pp. 2–13 (2006)
12. Bailey, N.: The mathematical theory of epidemic. Wiley, New York (1957)
13. LaSalle, J.: The Stability of Dynamical Systems. Regional to Conference Series in Applied Mathematics. SIAM, Philadelphia (1976)
14. Mishra, B.K., Pandey, S.K.: Dynamic model of worms with vertical transmission in computer network. Appl. Math. Comput. **217**, 8438–8446 (2011)
15. Rao, Y.S., Rauta, A.K., Saini, H., Panda, T.C.: Mathematical model for the cyber attack in the computer network. Int. J. Bus. Data Commun. Netw. **13**(1), 58–65 (2017). https://doi.org/10.4018/ijbdcn.2017010105
16. Nayak, P.K., Rao, Y.S., Panda, T.C.: Calculation of basic reproduction number by graph reduction method and stability analysis in SEIQRS E epidemic model in computer network. J. Eng. Appl. Sci. **12**(23), 7332–7338 (2017)
17. Rauta, A.K., Rao, Y.S., Panda, T.C., Saini, H.: A probabilistic approach using poisson process for detecting the existence of unknown computer virus in real time. Int. J. Eng. Sci. **4**, 47–51 (2015)
18. Rao, Y.S., Rauta, A.K., Saini, H., Panda, T.C.: Influence of educational qualification on different types of cyber crime: a statistical interpretation. Indian J. Sci. Technol. **9**(32), 1–7 (2016)
19. Saini, H., Rao, Y.S., Panda, T.C.: Cyber-crimes and their impacts: a review. Int. J. Eng. Res. Appl. **2**, 202–209 (2012)
20. Liu, X., Takeuchi, Y.: SVIR epidemic model with vaccination strategies. J. Theor. Biol. **253**, 1–11 (2008)
21. Driessche, P.V.D., Watmough, J.: Reproduction numbers and sub threshold endemic equilibria for compartmental models of diseases transmission. Math. Biosci. **180**, 29–48 (2002)
22. Routh-Hurwitz Criterion. http://web.abo.fi/fak/mnf/mate/kurser/dynsyst/2009/R-hcriteria.pdf
23. Kribs-Zaleta, C., Velasco-Hernandez, J.: A simple vaccination model with multiple endemic states. Math. Biosci. **164**, 183–201 (2000)
24. Gan, C., Yang, X., Liu, W., Zhu, Q., Zhang, X.: An epidemic model of computer viruses with vaccination and generalized nonlinear incidence rate. Appl. Math. Comput. **222**, 265–274 (2013)
25. Anwar, S.: Wireless nanosensor networks: a basic review. Int. J. Emerg. Technol. Adv. Eng. **5**(12), 151–154 (2015)
26. Mishra, B.K., Tyagi, I.: Defending against malicious threats in wireless sensor network: a mathematical model. Int. J. Inf. Technol. Comput. Sci. **6**, 12–19 (2014)
27. Peng, M., Mou, H.: A novel computer virus model and its stability. J. Netw. **9**, 367–374 (2014)
28. Yang, L.X., Yang, X., Tang, Y.Y.: A bi-virus competing spreading model with generic infection rates. IEEE Trans. Netw. Sci. Eng. **5**, 2–13 (2018)
29. Zheng, R., Lu, W., Xu, S.: Preventive and reactive cyber defense dynamics is globally stable. IEEE Trans. Netw. Sci. Eng. **5**, 156–170 (2018)
30. Yang, L.X., Li, P., Yang, X., Wu, Y., Tang, Y.Y.: On the competition of two conflicting messages. Nonlinear Dyn. **91**, 1853–1869 (2018)

Ransomware Analysis Using Reverse Engineering

S. Naveen$^{(\boxtimes)}$ and T. Gireesh Kumar$^{(\boxtimes)}$

TIFAC-CORE in Cyber Security, Amrita School of Engineering, Coimbatore,
Amrita Vishwa Vidyapeetham, Coimbatore, India
infantnaveen13@gmail.com, t_gireeshkumar@cb.amrita.edu

Abstract. Ransomware threat continues to grow over years. The existing defense techniques for detecting malicious malware will never be sufficient because of Malware Persistence Techniques. Packed malware makes analysis harder & also it may sound like a trusted executable for evading modern antivirus. This paper focuses on the analysis part of few ransomware samples using different reverse engineering tools & techniques. There are many automated tools available for performing malware analysis, but reversing it manually helped to write two different patches for Wannacry ransomware. Execution of patched ransomware will not encrypt the user machine. Due to new advanced evading techniques like Anti-Virtual Machine (VM) & Anti-debugging, automated malware analysis tools will be less useful. The Application Programming Interface (API) calls which we used to create patch, were used to create Yara rule for detecting different variants of the same malware as well.

Keywords: Advanced Encryption Standard (AES) ·
Application Programming Interface (API) · Cryptors · Decompile ·
Disassembly · Dynamic analysis · Dynamic linked library · Malware ·
Message-Digest Algorithm 5 (MD5) · Packed executable · Packers ·
Ransomware · Static analysis · Virtual Machine (VM) · Yara rule ·
.NET executables

1 Introduction

Ransomware is a type of malicious software that threatens to publish the victim's data or perpetually block access to it unless a ransom is paid [1,2]. Once the ransom is paid the attacker will provide the needed key for decrypting the files. Most of the ransomware today continue to release a new version of the same malware which may improvise the cryptographic algorithm due to the public release of the decryption tool. Also, an upgraded malware variant may harden the analysis. Ransomware is mainly classified into two types. They are, (1) Crypto Ransomware that encrypts files using various cryptographic encryption algorithms. Most of the ransomware will not encrypt files without extension, this is because malware executable has hardcoded extensions type which needs

© Springer Nature Singapore Pte Ltd. 2019
M. Singh et al. (Eds.): ICACDS 2019, CCIS 1046, pp. 185–194, 2019.
https://doi.org/10.1007/978-981-13-9942-8_18

to be encrypted. The files which have extensions .exe, .dll types will not be encrypted so that it won't tamper the integrity of the Windows operating system. (2) Locker Ransomware will lock the computer & the user machine will be left with only a few functionalities such as interaction for making the payment.

Wannacry Ransomware Message Window: Figure 1 shows the machine affected by wannacry. The window guides the user for making payment saying that the user files have been encrypted. The wannacry demands 300 dollars & once the payment is done the decryption key will be provided.

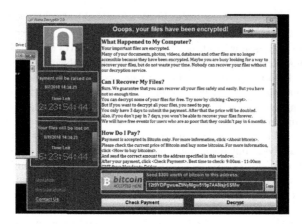

Fig. 1. Payment message

2   Malware Analysis Current Approaches

Static Analysis-Reviewing Assembly Code: This involves analyzing the executable statically without execution. Typically, a static analysis involves analyzing assembly code with the help of a dis-assembler. String pushed on the stack will reveal API calls. If the malware is packed, the actual strings will be known only at run-time.

Dynamic Analysis-Examining Malware in Run-Time: This involves debugging the malware in run-time by executing in an isolated environment. Some malware may try to detect the presence of VM & if it detects VM, malware will not perform any malicious actions & it will simply exit. This hardens the run-time analysis. Also, it has an anti-debugging technique which is used to prevent debugging the malware, so the instruction which is used to detect the debugger needs to be patched before debugging the program. Dynamic Analysis can be effectively handled with the help of software breakpoints or by stepping through the functions. In the case of packed or obfuscated, the actual control flow will be revealed only in run-time [11–13].

Automated Malware Analysis Tools: This involves a simple one-click event. The malware can be submitted & the analysis report will be generated by the automated tools. In this study, we mainly focus on addressing the techniques which can be efficiently used for malware analysis & also the method to write two patches for wannacry ransomware.

Limitations of Static Analysis: In case of packed or obfuscated malware, Static Analysis will not be useful. The actual strings & original control flow will be known at run-time.

Advantages of Dynamic Analysis: Dynamic analysis can efficiently track the behavior of malware. Even in case of packed malware, the malware needs to be unpacked in run-time to achieve its goal. Hence, dynamic always will help to reveal the core-functionality.

3   Problem Formulation

There is no single standard technique to reverse engineer malware because each malware requires a different approach. Modern malware can evade modern antivirus detection by packing the executable. The program source code has been compiled & final raw executable of a program delivered to our machines & there is no access to the source code until there is a chance to decompile the executable. Hence, the executable with machine instructions (Op-Codes) can be converted to Assembly instructions & disassembled assembly instructions can be understood. This is the reason for choosing reverse engineering & dis-assembler which make a reverse engineer life easier. Analyzing packed executable makes it harder to locate Original Entry Point [9].

4   Analysis Task

Table 1 shows the samples analyzed [5]. Once VM is ready with all the necessary tools, a snapshot of the VM is captured so that even when the machine is affected by malware, the changes can be rolled back to the state of the snapshot.

Proposed Architecture: The proposed architecture is shown in Fig. 2. In this study, IDA (Interactive Disassembler) is chosen as the Reverse Engineering Tool which is used to debug the executable files. But, IDA cannot perform efficient static analysis on a few packed malwares. So, different debugger needs to be chosen for unpacking & then the unpacked file can be loaded inside IDA. Some of the tools used for examining malware are PE Studio, CFF Explorer, PE Explorer [8, 10]. IDA tool makes the procedure easier because IDA has the feature to generate decent Pseudo C code for the assembly code.

Host Machine VM: Host Machine was chosen as Linux because incase Virtual Machine escape, there won't be any harm to the host machine.

Table 1. Ransomware samples with hash value

Ransomware samples	MD5-HASH
blueHowl.exe	82a06c622ba85f44f138889e233c5efa
cerber.exe	8b6bc16fd137c09a08b02bbe1bb7d670
mamba.exe	409d80bb94645fbc4a1fa61c07806883
$ucy locker.exe	c850f942ccf6e45230169cc4bd9eb5c8
wannacry.exe	84c82835a5d21bbcf75a61706d8ab549

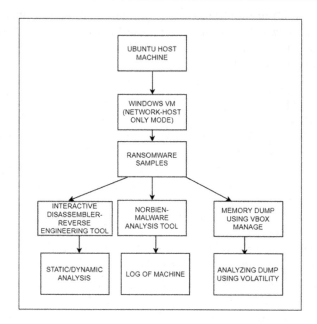

Fig. 2. Ransomware analysis architecture

IDA Reverse Engineering Tool

- It is preferred by many malware analysts around the globe.
- It has an interactive variety of plugins.
- IDA Python makes scripting capability for IDA in the Python programming language.
- IDA Python provides full access to both the IDA API & any installed Python module [7].

Noriben-Automated Malware Analysis Script

- Noriben Script collects the logs of the malware samples in just one click.
- Noriben python script run parallel to the malware to log all the activities done inside the machine [6].

Memory Dump

- During malware execution, live memory dump can be captured using Vbox-manage [3].
- Vboxmanage is the command line interface of VirtualBox which can be used to capture the memory of VM.
- Memory Dump of each sample helps to locate rogue process live with the help of Volatility tool.

Experimental setup

- Install Ubuntu as host operating system.
- Install Windows on top of Ubuntu inside VirtualBox.
- Noriben can be cloned from GitHub Repository.
- Install Python 3.x version which is recommended for Noriben.

Configure Windows VM. VirtualBox Configuration of Windows VM is configured in Host-Only Mode in order to isolate the network traffic.

5 Results and Discussion

This section includes the working of various ransomware samples using various reverse engineering techniques. The interesting result is an efficient Yara rule made out of the patch.

Analysis Of WannaCry-Steps Involved

- Examining WannaCry Executable in Resource Hacker Tool: Wannacry is loaded inside the resource hacker tool to check for the internal resources which are present. Resource Hacker contains information like strings, images, dialogs, menus, VersionInfo & Manifest resources. While examining the header of each file, one of the file stars with ASCII value PK, so a zip file present inside the executable. It drops the needed resource in the path of wannacry executable. The dropped text file contains the instruction for decryption in various languages. These dropped files were extracted from a password protected zip. This password can be retrieved from the stack memory by setting up a break point during run-time. Wannacry is not obfuscated or packed. This makes the analysis part much easier [14].
- Exported Zip File Of WannaCry: The files present inside resource hacker can be exported.
- Noriben Script: Noriben should be triggered before executing malware samples in order to collect the entire trace of the malware.
- Wannacry Decryptor: Wannacry encrypted even the shared files of the VirtualBox that were present in the Host machine. The decryptor executable can be used to decrypt files after the ransomware payment. The shared folder has "write" permission so malware encrypts files that are present in the shared folder, outside the VM. The shared folder was actually present on the Linux host machine.

- Simple Method for Static Analysis: Strings command will be useful & reveals useful information about the malware. Example strings filename | grep exe i.e strings wannacry.exe | grep exe. This will reveal the executables utilized by malware. Note: This works for the unpacked version of the malware.
- Wannacry Permission: The malware uses "attrib + h" command to make the path of the wannacry executable hidden. Also, using 'icacls' command, file permissions can be modified so that the malware has access to all the users present in the machine.
- Wannacry Crypto APIs: The malware uses Microsoft Crypto APIs to generate RSA crypto keys. If the 00000000.pky (Public Key) file does not exist, then ransomware generates a new 2048-bit RSA key & saves the public key to 00000000.pky. The malware then saves the generated private key to 00000000.eky, encrypted with the embedded public key (Table 2).
- Wannacry Kernel 32 API's: The malware imports 'Kernel32.dll' from the Imports section. 'Kernel32.dll' handles memory management, input/output operations, & interrupts. 'Kernel32.dll' is mostly used by most of the ransomware in order to tamper files.
- Wannacry RunTime Stack Trace: During Runtime, examining the stack frame with a breakpoint will reveal the password for the zip file. The password for the zip file can be clearly seen in the stack as "WNcry@2ol7". This can be verified manually by extracting the zip contents with the help of resource hacker tool [4, 16].

Table 2. Wannacry dropped crypto keys during execution

Crypto keys	MD5Hash
00000000.eky	d1e774274d7c3ace1980d270b442e555
00000000.pky	787ba63b931b2405028ae668b8acdd3d
00000000.res	a61474425e516e54b87ab9e4b7a3bd2b

WannaCryPatch

The interesting phase of this project was the patch created for ransomware, that enable us to locate the major API calls for creating Yara rule. This rule can detect different variants of the same ransomware & few other ransomware as well.

- Load the ransomware inside hex editor & locate kernel32 string section which contains API's like 'CreateFileW', 'DeleteFileW'.
- Patch the API calls of kernel32 dll to NO-OPs (OpCode-90). Executing the patched executable will not encrypt the machine.
- Also, if we patch the API 'CreateFileW' of kernel32 alone, the patched executable will not encrypt. So we have created two different patches for the same ransomware. The reason for the second patch to work is, the malware

creates a file, copies the file content for encryption & delete the original file. Since we have modified the create file operation the malware will not achieve its functionality.

Analysis of Cerber-Steps Involved

- Static Analysis Of Cerber: Static Analysis using Pe Studio reveals the blacklisted API's used by the malware.
- IDA Fails: Examining Start Function of the executable shows stack pointer analysis failed in IDA because the malware is packed. Executing packed executable will trigger an unconditional jump to Original Entry Point & then actual execution starts. During Static Analysis of packed malware, reverser needs to find the original entry point for unpacking [15].
- Unpacking While hitting new DLL's: Immunity Debugger can be configured to pause whenever it imports a new DLL in order to extract the unpacked executable from the memory map of the tool. The reason for switching different debugger is to unpack easily.
- Bmp Image From Memory Also, resources like Bmp image can be retrieved from the memory map. The image retrieved was used by the malware for modifying desktop background after encryption.
- Dll Used By Cerber While Encryption: The malicious process present in live memory is mshta.exe.Syclla tool can be used to analyze the DLL's used by the process.
- Unpacking Cerber Payload: We have examined the memory map to locate unpacked executable. We have tried to retrieve a partially unpacked file from the memory map.
- Packed Malware Flow Graph: Flow graph of the Packed Cerber Executable shows there are few branch instructions & also instructions are linear because the actual flow graph can be seen once it is unpacked.
- Report Of Unpacked exe From Virus Total: While Examining the exported file inside PEStudio, ESET antivirus reports the pattern matches with the cerber malware family.

Analysis of Mamba (Hdd Crypter)-Steps Involved

- Pseudocode Of Main Using IDA Tool: The pseudocode of the main function reveals the malware requires command line argument. If there is no command line argument i.e argument vector 1, then the key doesn't exist & the malware will exit.
- Dll Used Upon OS Architecture: Generally, malware will be compiled in x86 Architecture so that it can run on both x86 & x64. This malware checks the OS Architecture for using Dlls prior to the operating system type.
- Static Analysis Over String Section: PeStudio reveals malware use disk cryptor for encrypting hard drives. Disk cryptor is open source & this makes malware author modify disk cryptor code at ease.
- Privilege Required: The malware needs administrator privilege. The malware doesn't encrypt files instead it encrypts the entire Hard Drive.

- Elevated Privilege: The malware cannot work without administrator privilege.
- TimeStamp: The timestamp of the malware shows it was compiled in 2016 but this may be intentionally modified by malware author also to hide its design date.
- Encryption With Argument Vector: To test its drive encryption, input key is passed in argument vector 1 & now the key has been set so it starts encrypting. It also creates a directory in C drive for dropping the necessary DLL's & exe's.

Analysis of $ucy locker-Steps Involved

- Decompiled .net exe: The malware file type is in .NET Framework-Microsoft Intermediate Language (MSIL) So, The source can be retrieved using .net decompilers.
- Extensions Which are to be Encrypted: List of file types which needs to be encrypted is hard coded. The malware will encrypt only the files which belong to these extensions.
- Payment Check: The malware checks whether payment is made or not with the help of payment check button.
- Crypto Background: The malware uses AES in CBC mode for encryption.
- Registry Key: The malware creates an entry in the registry inside windows system polices to look like legitimate windows entry & also check for presence of task manager. It disables windows task manager if it is exist.

Analysis of Blue Howl-Steps Involved

- The malware file type is in .NET Framework-Microsoft Intermediate Language (MSIL). So we can able to retrieve source code with the help of .net decompiler.
- The malware has QR code which can be scanned for the payment. While Decoding the QR code it shows the bitcoin URL address. The URL request for 0.2 BTC. The bitcoin payment provides anonymity. The files will be destroyed after 72 h. So the payment should be done within three days. It creates a registry key similar to legitimate one by creating a entry under windows path & naming it as Windows Update so that it will be hard to locate during registry analysis.
- It checks for a list of live process & if these processes exist in memory, it will be killed. Once the windows explorer is killed the user will have restricted access to the windows GUI. The malware also kills the Task Manager.

Ransomware Detecting Using Yara Rules

- Yara rules are pattern-based detection tool.
- Yara helps to identify & classify malware samples.
- Rule works on Boolean condition.
- The rules are created based on the string section.
- Yara rule should be tested well else it may result in false positives.

- A simple & efficient Yara rule can detect different variants of the same malware at ease.

Table 3. Comparative results

Ransomware samples	Source code	Packers	Encryption	Performance speed
blueHowl.exe	Yes	No	User files	Medium
cerber.exe	No	Yes	User files	High
mamba.exe	No	No	Entire hard disk	High
$ucy locker.exe	Yes	No	User files	Medium
wannacry.exe	No	No	User files	High

Rule for Detecting Wannacry Ransomware. The API's used to build yara rule are DeleteFileW, MoveFilW, ReadFile, WriteFile, CreateFile & one more dll MSVCP60.dll is used. Also we have used regular expression for API's to match both Unicode & ASCII.

Note: This rule detects different variants of the same wannacry ransomware. This simple rules are made out API calls & one dll file.

Limitations of Work. In this project we focused only on crypto ransomware & also we haven't performed in-depth analysis on packed malware (Table 3).

6 Conclusion and Future Work

The project explains various reverse engineering tools & techniques to perform efficient malware analysis. Also, an efficient Yara rule made out of the success-full patch. Malicious binaries are the biggest threat in the evolving cyber world. An in-depth analysis will help the analyst to build a powerful defense mechanism to overcome against distributing malware attacks. Hence, the analysis of all these ransomware samples gives a clear picture of the inner-working.

In future, there will be an increase in malware production since the entire world is moving around computers, so a betterment in current reverse engineering tools & techniques will make a malware analyst life much easier & also helps to design a countermeasure for the malicious files. Also, use of Machine Learning/Artificial Intelligence approach to detect new malware will ease the work of malware analysts.

References

1. Continella, A., et al.: ShieldFS: a self-healing, ransomware-aware filesystem. In: Proceedings of the Annual Computer Security Applications Conference, ACSAC, Los Angeles, CA (2016)
2. Gazet, A.: Comparative analysis of various ransomware virii. J. Comput. Virol. **6**(1), 77–90 (2010)
3. Memory dump of VM using vboxmanage blog. https://www.andreafortuna.org/forensics/how-to-extract-a-ram-dump-from-a-running-virtualbox-machine/
4. Stack strings recovery fireeye blog. https://www.fireeye.com/blog/threat-research/2014/08/flare-ida-pro-script-series-automatic-recovery-of-constructed-strings-in-malware.html
5. Forked malware samples repository. https://github.com/NaveenEzio/malware-samples/tree/master/Ransomware
6. Noriben github repository. https://github.com/Rurik/Noriben
7. Running scripts from the command line with idascript blog. http://www.hexblog.com/?p=128
8. 9 best reverse engineering tools for 2018 blog. https://www.apriorit.com/dev-blog/366-software-reverse-engineering-tools
9. Monnappa, K.A.: Learning Malware Analysis: Explore the Concepts, Tools, and Techniques to Analyze and Investigate Windows Malware (2018)
10. Malware initial assessment tool. https://www.winitor.com/
11. Gregory Paul, T.G., Gireesh Kumar, T.: A framework for dynamic malware analysis based on behavior artifacts. In: Satapathy, S.C., Bhateja, V., Udgata, S.K., Pattnaik, P.K. (eds.) Proceedings of the 5th International Conference on Frontiers in Intelligent Computing: Theory and Applications. AISC, vol. 515, pp. 551–559. Springer, Singapore (2017). https://doi.org/10.1007/978-981-10-3153-3_55
12. Ali, P.D., Kumar, T.G.: Malware capturing and detection in dionaea honeypot. In: Power and Advanced Computing Technologies (i-PACT) (2017)
13. Nieuwenhuizen, D.: A behavioural-based approach to ransomware detection. MWR labs whitepaper (2017)
14. Wannacry ransomware analysis blog. https://www.fireeye.com/blog/threat-research/2017/05/wannacry-malware-profile.html
15. Unpacking cerber ransomware video. https://www.youtube.com/watch?v=g3Cf3cfBxKM
16. Stack solver tool github repository. https://github.com/fireeye/flare-floss

Semantic Textual Similarity and Factorization Machine Model for Retrieval of Question-Answering

Nivid Limbasiya$^{(\boxtimes)}$ and Prateek Agrawal

Department of Computer Science and Engineering,
Lovely Professional University, Jalandhar, Punjab, India
nlimbasiya24@gmail.com, prateek061186@gmail.com

Abstract. Question and Answering (QA) in many collaborative social networks such as Yahoo!-answers, Stack Overflow have attracted copious users to post and transfer knowledge between users. This paper proposes an Adaptive global T-max Long Short-Term Memory-Convolutional Neural Network (ALSTM-CNN) method to retrieve semantically matching questions from historical questions and forecast the best answers by saving their effort and time. Moreover, a novel Field-aware Factorization Machine (FFM) classifier is adapted to rank the high-quality answers from large sparse data. This method has certain advantages include: (a) effectively learns the similarity based on simple pertained models with various multiple dimensions, (b) does not uses handcrafted features. This algorithm shows robust performance for various tasks (i.e., measuring textual similarity and paraphrase identification), when it employs on datasets such as Semantic Textual Similarity (STS) benchmark, Sentence Involving Compositional Knowledge (SICK), Microsoft Research Paraphrase Corpus (MRPC) and Wikipedia Question Answer dataset. The performance of our proposed method is compared with different classifiers and the result shows a better accuracy measure than other state-of-the-art methods.

Keywords: Convolutional neural network · Factorization machine ·
Long short-term memory networks · Machine learning ·
Natural language processing · Question-answering · Semantic textual similarity

1 Introduction

QA archives plays an important role in the information resources on the Web. Some of the sources include Stack Overflow, Quora, Yahoo!-answers and Never are examples of the collaborative social network [1]. Two major type of domains in QA i.e.) closed domain QA and open domain QA. The closed domain QA handles only a finite number of the questions but the open domain QA system can answer anything and everything according to user questions. The advantages of Q&A retrieval are: (i) input is used as a Natural language rather than the keyword; (ii) system obtained several possible answers directly rather than long document and so we can increase the efficacy of finding the required answer. To endure the lexical problem, Chen *et al.* [2] introduced a translation language model (T2LM) to improve the performance of question retrieval and word to

© Springer Nature Singapore Pte Ltd. 2019
M. Singh et al. (Eds.): ICACDS 2019, CCIS 1046, pp. 195–206, 2019.
https://doi.org/10.1007/978-981-13-9942-8_19

question similarity. Wang *et al.* [3] initialize a framework model by handling three problems such as word order, polysemy, and lexical gap mainly retrieves the question in CQA platform. Semantic representation of question and answer could be learned by using neural network architecture [4], which reduce the lexical gap and data sparseness problem. Two novel categories powered model [5] were introduced to learn the better word embedding in CQA page for question retrieval to eliminate the limited words in the query and lexical gap. A Hybrid approach [6] has been used to address the lexical gap and a fusion of various language modelling technique for retrieving the question in CQAs platform. Dai *et al.* [7] presented a question intends identification method to enhance the efficacy of the question answering system. Unified probabilistic ranking method [8] was introduced to combine the weighted key concepts and intent their paraphrases to address the problem of word mismatch problem in CQA archives. Statistical machine translation method [9] was presented to enhance the question retrieval and question representation through non-negative matrix factorization. Word mismatch problem could be mitigated by using a Question-type-specific method [10]. From various models, it is observed that several pre-trained models are used with different aspects for similarity measurement and their semantic relationship between the words are determined by the paraphrase identification. But the existing models are inconsistent due to the varying embedding models and datasets. We propose a method with multiple aspect of embedding learned from different embedding models that predict the answer based on the combination of max pooling and LSTM approach. In this, the semantically matching quality answers are extracted for the appropriate input question task. For measuring the relation between the sentences, the features are extracted with multiple level models that enhances the better prediction ability in question-answer community. ***The significant contribution of the paper as follows:-***

(1)   We transform word to word vector through pre-trained word embedding. Here, we use five pre-trained word embedding's i.e. word2vec, fastText, GloVe, Baroni and SL999.

(2)   We construct multi-aspect word embedding from word vector by using convolution neural network.

(3)   We adapt two schemes, such as Adaptive global T-Max pooling and LSTM. Adaptive global T-Max pooling is used to extract the feature based on the maximal value, which is used for prediction purpose. Then long short term memory is used to predict the best answer based on the prior answer.

(4)   We concatenate both max pooling and LSTM layer, which is fed to the field-aware Factorization Machine for ranking.

The outline of this paper is as follows: - Sect. 2 describes the related work. Section 3 elucidate the methodology and architecture of our proposed model, Sect. 4 report and discuss the experimental setting and results. Finally, Sect. 5 concludes our work.

2   Related Work

Several approaches are proposed earlier to solve the textual matching with various deep learning models are discussed in this section. Wu *et al.* [11] introduced an unsupervised Semantic Information Space (SIS) to evaluate non-overlapping contents of sentences. Ji *et al.* [12] introduced a new discriminative term-weighting metric (TF-KLD) trained on MRPC dataset to measure the semantic similarities at the sentence level. Shao *et al.* [13] introduced a basic CNN to determine the STS task amongst a pair of sentences and achieve better performance. To predict the best answer, Elalfy *et al.* [14] introduced a hybrid approach consists of two module i.e.) content and non-content module. The first module consists of three types of features include answers content feature, answer-answer feature, and question-answer feature. Then, the non-content module uses the reputation score function to forecast the best answer. However, the non-content module in this approach affects the prediction accuracy. Zhao *et al.* [15] presented Heterogeneous Social Network Learning (HSNL) to determine the quality answer on the user's need. This method not only obtain the textual content of the question-answer but also defines the social information cues to improve the community based question answering (cQA) task. Although, the method utilizes the social information, it uses simple items and ignores the rich content information. Tian *et al.* [16] introduced a universal method with the combination of both traditional NLP methods and deep learning to determine the semantic similarity. However, the translation is critical and does not guaranteed an accurate prediction of answers for the query. He *et al.* [17] presented a CNN based that uses multiple granularities and window sizes followed with the multiple pooling layers to address the sentence similarity measurement. First, CNN was used to exploit the multiple similarity function to model every sentence. Then multiple similarity metrics are used to distinguish our sentence model at various granularities. The structural information within the sentences are ignored in this multiple perspective CNN modelling approach. Hu *et al.* [18] analysed the physician's quality answer in HQA service based on multimodal deep belief network based learning framework. This model overcomes the problem of data sparsity, which occurred due to the short text answers. But, the insufficiency of labelled data leads to increase of processing of manual labeling of data.

The above analysis still have some limitations i.e.) lexical gap, word mismatch, data sparsity and word ambiguity are incompatible with existing method and datasets. This will encourage us to develop a new method, called Adaptive global T-max pooling Long-Short Term Memory-Convolution Neural Network (ALSTM-CNN) to recover semantically equivalent questions and predict the best response. Our main concern is to recover the question and to provide best quality answers to the question based on the need of user's information. Here the, Novel FFM classifier is used to forecast the high-quality answers from the subject experts, which perform both regression and classification. This classifier shows the better performance by using performance measures such as Recall, F1 measure, and Accuracy.

3 Methodology

Our proposed method includes three steps of modelling: (i) Pre-trained word vector modelling (Sect. 3.1); (ii) Two schemes for prediction (Sect. 3.2); (iii) Modelling of ranking function (Sect. 3.3). The proposed method determines the similarity/relation between the question and answer by using multiple sets of pre-trained word embedding

Figure 1 elucidates the general architecture of the proposed model to predict the best answer. Initially, word is converted into word vector through m-pre-trained word embedding's. Then convolution neural network is used to construct the multi-aspect word embedding from the word vector. To forecast the quality answer, we adapt two schemes: Adaptive global T-Max pooling and LSTM. The adaptive global T-Max pooling is used to extract the feature based on the maximal value. Then the long short term memory to predict the answer based on the prior information. Next, we concatenate both max pooling and LSTM layer to enhance the prediction performance in terms of both question retrieval and best answer prediction. Finally, we adapt field-aware factorization machine for answer ranking task.

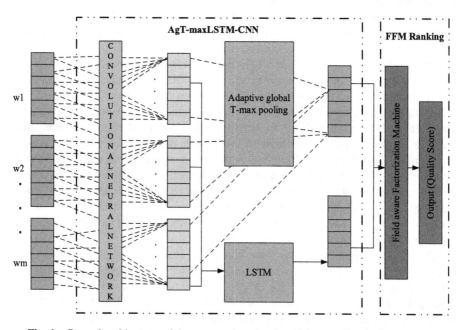

Fig. 1. General architecture of the proposed retrieval model to predict the best answer

3.1 Pre-trained Word Vector Modelling

Words can transform into word vector thorough m-pre-trained word embedding. The word embedding utilizes several pre-trained word embedding's i.e. word2vec, fastText, GloVe, Baroni and SL999. Initially, we apply input in the form of short text with words.

$$B = \{w_1, w_2, \ldots, w_m\} \tag{1}$$

Next, transformation of a word ω into word vector though m pre-trained word embedding's as follows:

$$Q_w^{concat} = Q_w^1 \oplus Q_w^2 \oplus \ldots \oplus Q_w^m \tag{2}$$

Where $\oplus$ be the concatenation operator, Q_w^k denotes word embedding vector of w in the kth pre-trained embedding. Q_w^{multi} be the multi aspect word embedding can be learned from the word vector Q_w^{concat}, H represents the convolution filters, f be the weight vector of each filter with the dimensions is same as that of Q_w^{concat} and a bias value b. Then Q_w^{multi} is given by,

$$Q_w^{multi} = [Q_w^{f1}, Q_W^{f2}, \ldots, Q^{fH}] \tag{3}$$

$$Q_w^{fj} = \sigma(Q_W^{concat} f_j^T + b_{f1}) \tag{4}$$

σ Represents the function of the logistic sigmoid. Next section expresses how to recover the question and best answer selection from its multi-aspect word embedding vector.

3.2   Two Scheme for Prediction

Given input sentence using the above equations Eqs. (2–4), we obtain a sequence of multi-aspect word embedding's $C^{multi} = [Q_{w1}^{multi}, Q_{w2}^{multi}, \ldots \ldots, Q_{wm}^{multi}]$. To forecast the best answer from the multiple-aspect word embedding's, we exploit two schemes, namely, Adaptive global T-max pooling and Long Short-Term Memory networks.

Adaptive Global T-Max Pooling

The objective of Adaptive global T-max pooling is to reduce the number of parameters i.e.) the output is smaller than the input. Here, the computational cost is reduced by decreasing the number of parameters. Normal max pooling can handle a single maximum value but our proposed Adaptive global T-max pooling can handle k maximum values instead of using single values. At last, we obtain the maximum score from the CNN network by using this Adaptive global T-max pooling. It is represented as,

$$Q_{sc}^{T-max} = \max[Q_w^{f1}, Q_W^{f2}, \ldots, Q^{fH}] \tag{5}$$

By taking the consideration of Adaptive global T-max pooling, it suppresses the property of word order. So that, we construct an LSTM sentence embedding Q_u^{lstm} to aid the sentence embedding Q_{sc}^{T-max}. Moreover, multi-aspect word embedding can transfer into a fixed length vector due to the application of the LSTM unit to each input Q_{wu}^{multi} with a prior step h_{t-1}.

By taking the consideration of Adaptive global T-max pooling, it suppresses the property of word order. So that, we construct an LSTM sentence embedding Q_u^{lstm} to aid the sentence embedding $Q_{sc}^{T-\max}$. Moreover, multi-aspect word embedding can transfer into a fixed length vector due to the application of the LSTM unit to each input Q_{wu}^{multi} with a prior step h_{t-1}.

Long Short-Term Memory networks (LSTM) is the special kind of recurrent neural network (RNN) capable of training long-term dependencies. It solves numerous task as compared with RNN and it minimizes the Vanishing gradient problem. It has three crucial layers that are input layer, hidden layer, and output layer. Figure 2 depict the structure of LSTM. In this, input to the LSTM are prior hidden layer h_{t-1}, current input x(t) and prior memory state C_{t-1}. At every time step t, LSTM defines six vectors in R.

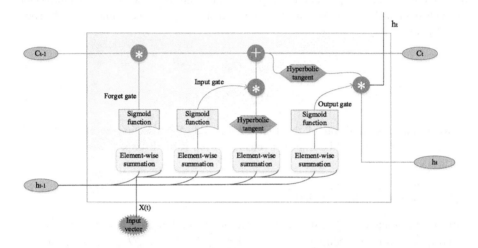

Fig. 2. Structure of LSTM

The input gate i(t) and the candidate gate c(t) can permit the incoming signal to change the state of the cell or block it. These gates are computed in the Eqs. (6) and (7) as follows,

$$i(t) = \sigma(w_i Q_w^{multi} + V_i h_{t-1} + b_i) \tag{6}$$

$$u(t) = \tanh(w_u Q_w^{multi} + V_u h_{t-1} + b_u) \tag{7}$$

Forget layer is used to forgot or remember the useless prior information and acquiring the new information from the input i(t). The forget layer can be calculated using Eq. (8).

$$f(t) = \sigma(w_f Q_w^{multi} + V_f h_{t-1} + b_f) \tag{8}$$

To get the new cell state, we just multiply the old cell state by forget layer and then add it with i(t) ∘ u(t). It is computed in Eq. (9).

$$c(t) = f(t) \circ c_{t-1} + i(t) \circ u(t) \tag{9}$$

LSTM output is based on the cell state, but will be a filtered model. For this purpose, we apply, hyperbolic tangent to Ct and then we need to do the elementary wise multiplication along with output gate o(t) thereby achieving our current hidden state ht.

$$o(t) = \sigma(w_o Q_w^{multi} + V_o h_{t-1} + b_o) \tag{10}$$

$$h(t) = o(t) \circ \tanh(c(t)) \tag{11}$$

$$Q_u^{lstm} = h_m \tag{12}$$

Where σ is the function of logistic sigmoid and $\circ$ represents the element-wise multiplication; w_i, V_i, b_i are the two weight matrices and one bias vector for input gate i. The Hyperbolic tangent function is tanh. i denotes the input gate, o denotes the output gate, f represents the forgot gate h represents the hidden state and c represents the memory cell. At last, we obtain the best answer prediction Q_{sc}, which is the sum of both the Adaptive global T-max pooling and the long short-term memory network.

$$Q_{sc} = Q_{sc}^{T-\max} + Q_{sc}^{lstm} \tag{13}$$

3.3   Ranking Function

FFM machines have recently undergone considerable interest due to their good performance on large-scale data. The performance of the factorization machine is not good, so, we adopt a method called field aware factorization machine to improve the best answer prediction. FFM mainly used to classify large sparse data, which has many latent vectors for each feature. In contrary to FM, every feature is compatible with a single vector, then the FFM feature is compatible with a set of vectors. Compared to other models, its computational cost and memory cost is considerable.

$$y(x) = g_0 + \sum_{k=1}^{n} g_k x_k \sum_{k=1}^{n} \sum_{m=k+1}^{n} (v_{k,f_m} \times v_{m,f_k}) x_k x_m \tag{14}$$

Where k, m = 1, 2, 3, ... n, n denotes each samples dimensions, g_0 be the global bias, g_k be the weight, f_1, f_2 represents the number of fields and v_k be the latency vector. $v_k f_m$ denotes the vector embedded with feature k when it combined with other feature that belongs to field m. In contrary with FM, FFM is robust and flexible. This method is used to enhance the system performance.

4 Experimental Result and Analysis

The proposed method uses four datasets i.e.) STSB [19], SICK [20], MRPC [21] and Wikipedia Question-Answer Dataset [22]. In this, the sematic relatedness is evaluated under STB, SICK and QA dataset and for paraphrase identification, we use MRPC dataset. Based on the STS 2013, we use two task, one is CORE and another one is TYPED comprised with pair of glosses, news headlines, and machine translation evaluation datasets. The SICK dataset comprises of 10,000 English sentence pairs that are enriched with the lexical, syntactic, and semantic features and ignores other aspects of existing sentential datasets. The MRPC dataset consists of 5801 paraphrase sentence pairs extracted from the new sources of web. The annotation of the sentence pairs is made by the human with the binary classification of paraphrases or not. Wikipedia Question-Answer Dataset consists of manually annotated question and answers from the Wikipedia articles related to the topics of animals, languages, music instruments, and artists. Matrix similarity approach was used to solve the paraphrase identification problem, which evaluate the similarity of two text segments.

$|V|$ represents the sentence length and vocabulary size. Table 1 show the overall evaluation of the three datasets. Here, we use five pre-trained word embedding model. (a) **word2vec** comprises 300-dimensional vector and 3 million vocabulary size. (b) **GloVe** consists of 300-dimensional vector trained by aggregated global word-word co-occurrence statistics from the corpus (840 billion tokens). (c) **fastText** used to get a 300-dimensional vector. (d) **Baroni:** learned a 400-dimensional semantic embedding model using context-predict approach. (e) **SL999** is a 300-dimensional embedding model trained under skip-gram objective with negative sampling on word pairs. This proposed method has evaluated under three performance metrics for best answer prediction include Precision (P), recall (R) and accuracy (ACC).

Table 1. Overall evaluation of the three datasets.

Dataset	Training set	Validation	Test set	LENGTH (l)	Vocabulary ($|V|$)
STSB	5,800	1,511	1,385	13	15,201
SICK	5,503	603	4,940	11	2,322
MRPC	3,599	603	1,800	24	18,014
Wikipedia QA	61,888	7,993	13,661	14	–

The performance evaluation is shown in Table 2. In this "All" defines the combination of using five embedding model together and their effectiveness with their proportion of vocabulary in embedding model. Compared with the handcraft features, the performance of this five pre-trained word embedding is good. Here, the STSB and MRPC vocabulary availability is substantially increased using these five pre-trained word embedding but in question set and SICK $|V|$ is not increased. Table 3 gives the performance measures for the proposed work. There are four datasets taken for evaluation. In this, recall, accuracy and F1-measure are measured and the result show that MRPC achieves the better performance than the other three datasets.

Table 2. Comparison of multiple pre-trained word embedding on datasets STSB, SICK and MRPC

Word embedding	STSB		SICK			MRPC		Wikipedia QA dataset	
	Pearsons	$|V|\%$	Pearsons	Acc	$|V|\%$	Acc/F1	$|V|\%$	Acc	$|V|\%$
word2Vec	79.2	76.11	88.12	85.03	99.01	76.11/83.33	69.01	78.9	78.5
fastText	80.15	85.43	88.56	84.43	99.34	74.31/81.75	89.04	79.6	82.1
Glove	81.12	92.43	89.28	85.67	99.88	75.2/83.695	90.02	82.24	81.4
SL999	81.44	95.54	88.45	85.77	99.89	77.49/84.17	95.17	83.2	82.7
Baroni	80.89	91.66	87.04	85	98.95	75.76/83.6	89.48	81.2	92.3
All	**84.56**	96.78	**89.99**	**85.87**	99.45	**79.8/85.9**	96.99	**82.42**	**89.12**

Table 3. R, ACC and F1 measure obtained from the four different datasets

Performance measures/dataset	STSB	SICK	MRPC	Wikipedia question answer dataset
R	84.04	89.12	87.65	80.7
ACC	80.24	82.42	82.12	79.8
F1	84.21	80.92	86.74	79.7

Table 4. Result of the test set with Pearson score r, F1, and Accuracy (highest score for each dataset is in boldface)

Methods	STSB		SICK		MRPC		Wikipedia question answer dataset	
	R	ACC	R	ACC	ACC	F1	R	ACC
Semantic information space [11]	80.9	–	–	–	–	–	–	–
Discriminative term-weighting metric (TF-KLD) [12]	–	–	–	–	80.41	85.96	–	–
Convolution neural network [13]	78.40	–	–	–	–	–	–	–
Universal model (traditional NLP + deep learning) [16]	83	–	–	–	–	–	–	–
Multi-perspective CNN [17]	–	–	86.86	–	78.60	84.73	–	–
Skip though [23]	–	–	86.55	–	75.8	83	–	–
RNN-encoder decoder [24]	–	–	–	–	–	–	79.4	80.2
ALSTM-CNN	**84.04**	**80.2**	**89.12**	**87.42**	**82.12**	**86.74**	**84.2**	**83.1**

Table 4 shows the comparison of the four databases by using several methods. Here, our proposed method ALSTM-CNN shows the better prediction for quality answers. Performance of unsupervised knowledge-based method [15, 16] is low, so our ALSTM-CNN method use five pre-trained word embedding's to improve the semantic textual similarity performance. In ref [21, 22] sentence similarity model is used to improve the performance but it is affected due to word ambiguity problem. Kiros et al. [29] introduce a skip gram vector for synthetic and semantic representation but it is affected due data sparsity. To tackle this problem, we trained our method using five pre-trained models. In RNN-Encoder Decoder [30] determine the rank of the answerability score in the comments from the customer's feedback but produces irrelevant answer predictions for the input query. But our method AgT-maxLSTM-CNN, only based on neural architecture. The max pooling ignores the property of word order, so we use LSTM to enhance the performance. Compare with other models, our FFM classifier attains zero log loss value. This value mainly used to measure the performance of a classification method. Table 5 describes the comparison different classifiers to the proposed model. In this, precision, recall, F1 measure and accuracy measures are estimated. In the Naïve Bayes classifier, the standard deviation is greater than 5% for both F1 and recall.

Table 5. Comparison of different classifiers with the proposed FFR classifier

Classifiers	Recall	Precision	F1 measure	Accuracy
SVM	71.56	81.14	76.98	77.78
LR	80.44	72.55	77.34	75.11
NB	74.02	67.32	70.22	72.01
FM	76.84	80.05	79.04	79.01
FFM (proposed)	**80.03**	78.13	**79.12**	**79.01**

So the NB classifier is not fit for the classification task. To improve the classification performance, we use the FFM classifier. FFM classifier can outperform the existing classifiers.

5   Conclusion

In this paper, we presented an ALSTM-CNN architecture for measuring textual similarity, and paraphrase identification to recover semantically matching questions from historical questions and forecast quality answers. In addition, FFM is used to forecast the quality answers and AgT-max acquire k maximum values rather than a single maximum value. Compared with the existing methods, this method does not use handcraft features, it is only based on neural architecture and the recurrent neural network, LSTM is easier to train. Moreover, LSTM can solve the difficult task and effective at capturing long-term temporal dependencies. The experimental result indicates that the proposed approach achieves a better performance gain in terms of accuracy, precision and F-score measure. In this approach, we uses several embedding models for similarity measurement which will increases the memory space, processing time and cannot be applied for transfer language task. The future work is extended for other problems such as quality question prediction, transfer type of learning task and user level satisfaction by improving the prediction quality of the answers. In addition, the model can be extended for the other task such as information retrieval, detection from the newspaper and plagiarism datasets.

References

1. Xue, X., Jeon, J., Croft, W.B.: Retrieval models for question and answer archives. In: Proceedings of the 31st Annual International ACM SIGIR Conference on Research and Development in Information Retrieval, pp. 475–482 (2008)
2. Chen, M., Li, L., Xie, Q.: Translation language model enhancement for community question retrieval using user adoption answer. In: Asia-Pacific Web (APWeb) and Web-Age Information Management (WAIM) Joint Conference on Web and Big Data, pp. 251–265 (2017)
3. Wang, P., Zhang, Y., Ji, L., Yan, J., Jin, L.: Concept embedded convolutional semantic model for question retrieval. In: Proceedings of the Tenth ACM International Conference on Web Search and Data Mining, pp. 395–403 (2017)
4. Zhou, G., Zhou, Y., He, T., Wu, W.: Learning semantic representation with neural networks for community question answering retrieval. Knowl.-Based Syst. **93**, 75–83 (2016)
5. Zhou, G., He, T., Zhao, J., Hu, P.: Learning continuous word embedding with metadata for question retrieval in community question answering. In: Proceedings of the 53rd Annual Meeting of the Association for Computational Linguistics and the 7th International Joint Conference on Natural Language Processing, pp. 250–259 (2015)
6. Chen, L., Jose, J.M., Yu, H., Yuan, F.: A hybrid approach for question retrieval in community question answering. Comput. J. **60**(7), 1019–1031 (2016)
7. Dai, F., Feng, C., Wang, Z., Pei, Y., Huang, H.: Intent identification for knowledge base question answering. In: 2017 Conference on Technologies and Applications of Artificial Intelligence (TAAI), pp. 96–99. IEEE (2017)
8. Zhang, W.N., Ming, Z.Y., Zhang, Y., Liu, T., Chua, T.S.: Capturing the semantics of key phrases using multiple languages for question retrieval. IEEE Trans. Knowl. Data Eng. **28** (4), 888–900 (2016)
9. Zhou, G., Xie, Z., He, T., Zhao, J., Hu, X.T.: Learning the multilingual translation representations for question retrieval in community question answering via non-negative matrix factorization. IEEE/ACM Trans. Audio Speech Lang. Process. (TASLP) **24**(7), 1305–1314 (2016)
10. Wu, Y., Hori, C., Kashioka, H., Kawai, H.: Leveraging social Q&A collections for improving complex question answering. Comput. Speech Lang. **29**(1), 1–19 (2015)
11. Wu, H., Huang, H., Jian, P., Guo, Y., Su, C.: BIT at SemEval-2017 task 1: using semantic information space to evaluate semantic textual similarity. In: Proceedings of the 11th International Workshop on Semantic Evaluation (SemEval 2017), pp. 77–84 (2017)
12. Ji, Y., Eisenstein, J.: Discriminative improvements to distributional sentence similarity. In: Proceedings of the 2013 Conference on Empirical Methods in Natural Language Processing, pp. 891–896 (2013)

13. Shao, Y.: HCTI at SemEval-2017 task 1: use convolutional neural network to evaluate semantic textual similarity. In: Proceedings of the 11th International Workshop on Semantic Evaluation (SemEval 2017), pp. 130–133 (2017)
14. Elalfy, D., Gad, W., Ismail, R.: A hybrid model to predict best answers in question answering communities. Egypt. Inform. J. **19**(1), 21–31 (2018)
15. Fang, H., Wu, F., Zhao, Z., Duan, X., Zhuang, Y., Ester, M.: Community-based question answering via heterogeneous social network learning. In: Thirtieth AAAI Conference on Artificial Intelligence (2016)
16. Tian, J., Zhou, Z., Lan, M., Wu, Y.: ECNU at SemEval-2017 task 1: leverage kernel-based traditional NLP features and neural networks to build a universal model for multilingual and cross-lingual semantic textual similarity. In: Proceedings of the 11th International Workshop on Semantic Evaluation (SemEval 2017), pp. 191–197 (2017)
17. He, H., Gimpel, K., Lin, J.: Multi-perspective sentence similarity modeling with convolutional neural networks. In: Proceedings of the 2015 Conference on Empirical Methods in Natural Language Processing, pp. 1576–1586 (2015)
18. Hu, Z., Zhang, Z., Yang, H., Chen, Q., Zuo, D.: A deep learning approach for predicting the quality of online health expert question-answering services. J. Biomed. Inform. **71**, 241–253 (2017)
19. Agirre, E., Cer, D., Diab, M., Gonzalez-Agirre, A., Guo, W.: *SEM 2013 shared task: semantic textual similarity. In: Second Joint Conference on Lexical and Computational Semantics (*SEM). Proceedings of the Main Conference and the Shared Task: Semantic Textual Similarity, Proceedings of *SEM, vol. 1, pp. 32–43 (2013)
20. Marelli, M., Menini, S., Baroni, M., Bentivogli, L., Bernardi, R., Zamparelli, R.: A SICK cure for the evaluation of compositional distributional semantic models. In: LREC, pp. 216–223 (2014)
21. Fernando, S., Stevenson, M.: A semantic similarity approach to paraphrase detection. In: Proceedings of the 11th Annual Research Colloquium of the UK Special Interest Group for Computational Linguistics, pp. 45–52 (2008)
22. Smith, N.A., Heilman, M., Hwa, R.: Question generation as a competitive undergraduate course project. In: Proceedings of the NSF Workshop on the Question Generation Shared Task and Evaluation Challenge (2008)
23. Kiros, R., et al.: Skip-thought vectors. In: Advances in Neural Information Processing Systems, pp. 3294–3302 (2015)
24. Liu, M., Fang, Y., Choulos, A.G., Park, D.H., Hu, X.: Product review summarization through question retrieval and diversification. Inf. Retrieval J. **20**(6), 575–605 (2017)

Krisha: An Interactive Mobile Application for Autism Children

Amrita Tulshan[(⊠)] and Nataasha Raul

Computer Science Department, Sardar Patel Institute of Technology,
Mumbai, India
{amrita.tulshan,nataasharaul}@spit.ac.in

Abstract. The intelligent system has presumed a new hope in almost every field, a hope of improving things and making those things effortless for each person. In the same way, hope rose in the direction of distressed and impaired people like disabled people, handicapped people, autistic children, and many others. According to the study, Autism Spectrum Disorder (ASD) is easily found in 1 among 68 children. The main aim of our work is to help autism children to be adaptive, adjustable and interactive with outer world. For this we conducted survey and on the basis of the survey result analysis it was understood that the major problem the autism child suffers from is the Life skills and Emotional skills. So, we designed a Krisha mobile application which is friendly and easy to use, have games after every module so that autism child can enjoy learning and also have interactive interface that coincide with the current environment to keep them motivated and busy. The evaluation and the testing of the application were done. The result of which states that the autism children are benefitted in learning Life skills more than the Emotional skills.

Keywords: Autism children · Human machine interface · Mobile application

1 Introduction

In the current world scenario technology privilege has been constantly changing the face of the world. Similarly intelligent systems had covered most of the fields. In almost every field it has taken a considerable place. In a nutshell we have got an acceleration button to make our lives effortless. So considering impact of mobile applications system in the day to day life of a normal person, this mobile application was an outcome of the question that why can't we use these type of mobile apps for the betterment of impaired people. For all the currently existing medium of interactions, mobile was found to be the most accessible and helpful for this application. These mobile phones are the "cool new" contraptions, not at all like the past, complex and "I - am-not-ordinary looking" helping gadgets. These mobile phones are said to fill in as a specialized gadget in the pocket, a learning gadget in a hurry and even a lifeline for a few. Autism spectrum disorder is a mental disorder (ASD). Autism Spectrum Disorder (ASD) is a turmoil which seems right off the bat in youth and there is no clear real-child behind the reason. At present time, there is no remedy for this. In spite of the way that the type can turn into a mentally unbalanced grown-up, early analysis will take into

© Springer Nature Singapore Pte Ltd. 2019
M. Singh et al. (Eds.): ICACDS 2019, CCIS 1046, pp. 207–218, 2019.
https://doi.org/10.1007/978-981-13-9942-8_20

account more successful treatment. The survey regarding this application was intended to find out that were the existing application are lacking in achieving the goal whether it may be accuracy or any other concern. Therefore this application is based on the conclusion of a survey which was conducted on two autism center and over mentors/parents of 19 autistic children.

This paper is organized as follows: Sect. 2 is literature Survey in which all past study and work is described and white spaces on which the further work can be done. Section 3 is Methodology which explain the work flow of our approach. Section 4 explains the survey and field work carried out by us and it's analysis. Section 5 is detailing about the experimentation setup and its result. Section 6 is feedback of application designed and Sect. 7 gives conclusion and future work.

This mobile based application main aim was to improve autism children emotional skills and make them independent allow them to stand on their own feet mentally. And after taking feedback survey from parents/guardian our work were appreciated, as parents found application easy and very effective in their children lives.

2 Literature Survey

An intelligent system is a machine with an inserted, Internet-associated PC that has the ability to accumulate and dissect information and speak with different frameworks [1]. So to use this technology in disabled persons life and from among all other disease and disabled people one is Autism Children suffering from Autism Spectrum Disorder (ASD). Autism Spectrum Disorder (ASD) is a deep rooted handicap that can be distinguished from the get-go in kids influencing their advancement abilities particularly concerning correspondence and connecting with others [2]. For autistic child that experience the ill effects of discourse disability, communicating can be very difficult. Flow look into in remedial innovation for an autism spectrum disorder is pointed toward enhancing keeping up eye to eye connection, deciding outward appearances and different practices that affect social intelligence. Today innovation can be a protected and propelling method for drawing in mentally autism child in social collaboration exercises [3]. The diversions created for ASD patients are based off online virtual extreme introvert creations created found on the site 'Autism Spectrum Disorder Games'. The point of these recreations is to help youngsters with ASD with social collaboration and relational abilities. The Emotion Game has opportunity to get better in making it a more intuitive diversion for a kid with ASD. Additionally further research and work should be possible to include confront acknowledgment out of sight which would allow the player to reflect the face they have made and affirm their capacity to translate and reflect human demeanors [4]. One of the routes for them to understand daily use language is only through PECS. There is programming for tablets in light of PECS for tablets, however they for the most part don't appear to handle one of the greatest obstacles of the PECS framework: The learning of appropriate syntax. We display an as of now running contextual analysis where an Android application in view of PECS with fundamental sentence structure capacities is being utilized by various gatherings of extremely introverted kids to decide whether a change in their dialect obtaining can accomplished over more customary strategies [5].

In the continuing with orchestrating assistive technology used for autism kids experiences learning inabilities and correspondence boundaries. This exploration assess different supporting innovations and discovers Picture Exchange Communication System (PECS) to be better decision for coordinating with the application. The advancement results indicated empowering effects of the Autism App in supporting mentally unbalanced kids to adjust to ordinary life and enhance the standard of their life [6]. The next app is CaptureMyEmotion that allows autism child to record their voice or sounds and even they can click their photos. With this app child can able to discuss or express it's emotion and even identify one selves. A very good concept is used to overcome the emotion skill but still not found absolute solution out of that [7]. Consistently we see increasingly as often as possible the joining of versatile applications to the educating - learning process by instructors in their classroom; as for kids, the utilization of uses in portable innovation was progressive, opening another skyline for them [8]. The app for this disorder is FillMeApp. FillMeApp is an intelligent portable diversion application which is a supplementary learning material expected for youngsters with Autism that encourages them propel in their learning procedure [9]. Picture Exchange Communication System is the regular academic approach used to build up the relational abilities of kids with a mental imbalance. Shockingly, its inconveniences significantly increment the weight on guardians and harm the experience of clients. To beat these issues, one more app get into picture that is multidisciplinary group created iCAN, a tablet-based APP framework that includes embracing the fruitful parts of the paper-influenced PECS to approach and joining preferences of an electronic gadget into a few highlights to influence the figuring out how to process less demanding again the concept of PECS with some improvement that is not shown in last application [10]. Further experiment has been used concept of virtual technology and mixed it with very famous application like mobile application. Through this system kids will able to learn daily routine activities. This paper has considered four main home rooms like Bathroom, Kitchen, Bedroom, and Living Room. Main new thing this paper has added is that all the activities of kids will be tracked. Through this they will give chance their parents or mentors idea about their life and weak point for improvement [11]. Advancement of such applications will prompt better mindfulness and better wellbeing for people. As a proof of idea, Android application is created for attention to HIV/AIDs just to check that this app is helping in other diseases also [12]. On the other hand the MOSOCO is a portable assistive application that utilizations increased reality and the visual backings of approved educational modules. The discoveries from this examination uncover new practices of the employments of portable assistive advances, all things considered, and circumstances [13]. To date, present day innovation has been appeared to be a valuable learning device in light of the fact that basically it offers understudies fun vivified introductions, utilization of expansive screens, redundancy of particular learning errands, utilization of procedures, exhibited viability for example, video displaying, visual inciting, sound training, execution criticism, fortification, and self-administration [14].

In the last paper design interface of application has been used. Means how should be user experience design of app for autism children should be. Talna app focused mainly on calculation and numeracy. Some call cards and cue cards has been used. Through this app kids will able to understand, calculative in numbers and solved their own maths problem. In this app techniques are very interactive and innovative [15]. There are number of Google apps or Apple store but none of them covered or cured this autism disability completely. Main part of our life that is emotion part and life skills part are left that has been covered in this paper where all the weaknesses will be considered but it is not possible to concentrate on all the weakness so this paper focuses on two skills.

3   Methodology

It starts with profile page. First user has to fill all the personal information and create a profile page then user can access menu page which is divided into four modules. After submitting personal information from users they can access to main menu first then four modules which are as follows:

Module 1: Emotions
Module 2: Daily routine Activities
Module 3: Games on Emotions
Module 4: Progress Report

Even user can access to any of the module and can further go through that. Children first learn about emotions and then further they can play games on it. Next modules are based on daily routine activities application in that users can set alarm for their every activities and start their routine day. Every daily routine steps for children has been mentioned in that. After accessing all modules one module shows progress report for their daily routine activities. Progress report will be displayed after every 21 days and even notification will pop up in application. Figure 1 shows system architecture of application. Table 1 is a Dataset information on which is used for further research results and on the basis of that results whole system research has been done and application designed and executed. Dataset gives information about numbers of people who were children guardians and number of children belong to which group according to their age.

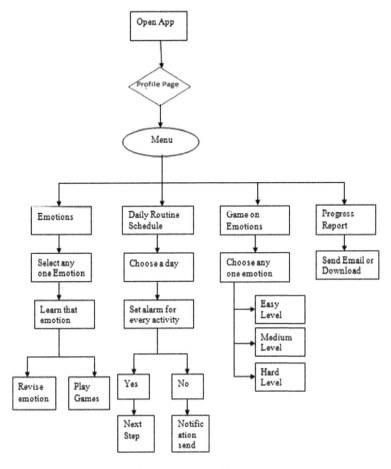

Fig. 1. System architecture

Table 1. Dataset information include no of people attended survey and age of child

Serial no.	Number of people attended survey	Age groups of children
1.	6	5 to 10 years
2.	8	10 to 15 years
3.	1	15 to 20 years
4.	4	20 to 25 years

4 Field Work

The review of this paper was directed to learn at various organizations, meeting the teachers, educators, and specialists, conveying surveys. The data therefore gathered was used to build up the application. It estimates autism Spectrum Disorder to affect one in

68 children and many mobile apps are available from Google Play store or Apple store to help these children and their career. We took a survey at two autism center that are Ashiyana Autism Center and Anandi Autism Center. Survey questions paper had total 50 questions. So the survey was for autistic children's parents. The parents/mentors were personally asked each and every. They were thrilled to share so many things with their open hearts to describe every corner about their child's problems and how much they all are suffering due to those problems. If screenshots are necessary, please make sure that you are happy with the print quality before you send the files.

4.1   Discussion During Survey

This discussion was based on the parent's survey. At the time of survey two main factors were observed that are:

1. Life Skills
2. Emotional Skills

These two skills are important for humans to live a normal life. So, after conducting the survey the conclusion which was drawn was to design and develop an application which overcomes the accuracy gap in both the skills and makes autistic children more aware about the surroundings.

4.2   Result Analysis for Survey

Tables 2 and 3 shows how much percent of children responded to emotional skills and life skills. After this survey results of emotional skills and life skills are displayed in Figs. 2 and 3. Initially, we focused on these two topics for this mobile application. To understand more psychological thoughts of autistic children, some questions were included on primary methods and on receptive language like (if suppose a child wants something then how he/she will say you and what language is used by them to express anything they love and even what actions are used to explain the things well) and primary method graph have been describe in Fig. 4 and receptive language graph have been describe in the Fig. 5. So according to survey children know their name and family member's name correctly. They were able to answer simple and basic question as well. They were also able to identify the names of body parts and common object names. If they wanted something, then they mostly looked at that objects or used 2–3 words in combinations and another way is vocalizing or grunting. In this way, they communicate they don't a respond to any unknown person and even avoid to interrupt with them. Not even with peers of their age.

Table 2. Percent of emotional skills knowledge an autism children has (from survey form)

Emotional skills	How much percent child respond		
	Yes	May be	No
Emotional self awareness	31.11%	12.9%	37.8%
Recognizing other's people emotions	51.58%	15.8%	32.62%
Emotion regulation ability	57.01%	6.48%	36.83%

Table 3. Percent of emotional skills knowledge an autism children has (from survey form)

Life skills	How much percent child respond		
	Yes	May be	No
Know yourself	43.86%	12.4%	43.85%
Respecting others/communication	49.72%	12.28%	38%
Communication/get organized	48.85%	11.41%	39.87%

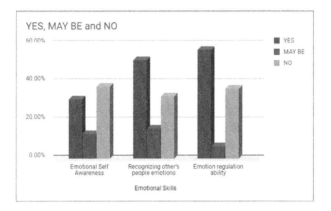

Fig. 2. Survey results show emotional skills knowledge in autistic disease

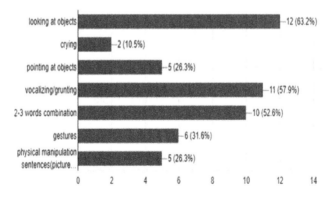

Fig. 3. Primary methods used by autism children for letting what he/she wants

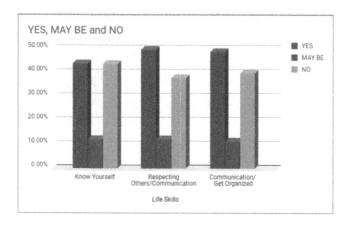

Fig. 4. Survey results show life skills knowledge in autistic disease

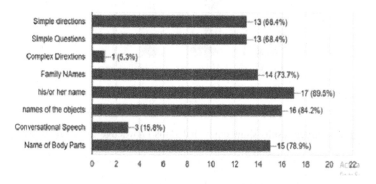

Fig. 5. Receptive language (what autistic child understands)

5 Model Design and Implementation

This mobile based application will run on Android 9 pie version. And model used is Nexus.

- Profile Page: This page will be fill up by parents or mentors to understand Children properly. Type of personal information is asked and Shown in Fig. 6.
- Menu Page: Through this page users will able to access individual category Shown in Fig. 7. There will be four modules.
- Daily Routine Schedule: In this users need to choose one day daily as shown in Fig. 7 and Follow below points.
- Monday: It has more sub categories like morning, afternoon, evening, night. And that categories were also divided into sub more categories. In these way particular activities has alarm set to put it into action.

- Emotions: Happiness, Afraid, Shocking, Angry, Sadness are emotions which are present in mobile application. Then select one from menu page, then they can learn any one of emotion from all the five as Shown in Fig. 8.
- Game on Emotions: In Game section there will be three levels Easy Level, Medium Level, Hard Level and If easy level is choose then easy questions will be provided to children then they have to answer that particular question. In the same way as level will increase, difficulty of questions will gradually increase. As shown in Fig. 9.
- Report Card: In this 21 days of progress report will be present. To know weaknesses of children Fig. 9.

Fig. 6. Profile page, menu, daily routine schedule, emotions design has been describe

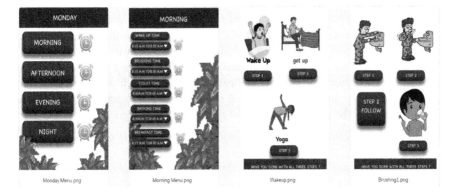

Fig. 7. Monday, morning activity, wake up, brushing design has been describe

Fig. 8. Emotions like happiness, angry, shocking, sadness, afraid.

Fig. 9. Games on emotions related to every topic

6 Results of Feedback Regarding Use of Mobile Application Prototype

This application was used by autism children and after one month feedback was asked by parents. Parents were very satisfied with the application. Parents found that autism children now communicate with itself and showing their interests in others emotions and feelings. Whatever actions common man do daily is depend 70% on their emotions. Parents also describe about the application interface which was very easy to use and softly handle by autism children. And children are now started becoming independent which was the main reason behind this application. Figure 10 says bar graph explanation for mobile application.

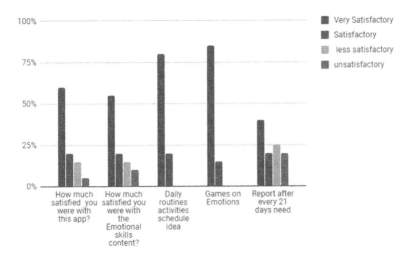

Fig. 10. Feedback form results on mobile application

7 Conclusion and Future Work

The research has vital endowment, regarding both innovation and in personality study, to propel dynamic learning of the autism children. It is to encourage empowering correspondence and habitual among those kids who experiences Autism. Future work is needed that there must be some sound or voice behind after every module. If emotion like Happiness is selected then that module consider voice and pronunciations to make it more interactive. According to feedback parents/guardian found that this mobile based application for children in case of Daily Routine Activities is useful up to 75% and in case of learning Emotional Skills 55%. This itself says that it will definitely come up with positive results in autism children.

References

1. Jameson, A., Riedl, J.: Introduction to the transactions on interactive intelligent systems. ACM Trans. Interact. Intel. Syst. **1**(1) (2011). Article 1
2. Dugger, C.E.: The effects of early intervention on children with autism spectrum disorders. Research papers (2012). Paper 206. Spring 4-2012
3. Davis, N.O., Carter, A.S.: Parenting stress in mothers and fathers of toddlers with autism spectrum disorders: association with child characteristics. J. Autism Dev. Disord. **38**, 1278–1291 (2008)
4. Bhatt, S.K., De Leon, N.I., Al-Jumaily, A.: Augmented reality game therapy for children with autism spectrum disorder. Int. J. Smart Sens. Intell. Syst. **7**(2), 519–536 (2014)
5. Figueroa, A.M., Juárez-Ramírez, R.: Orchestrating assistive technology: enabling autistic people to communicate with others. In: 2014 IEEE International Conference on Consumer Electronics, Tijuana, Baja California, México (2014)
6. Soomro, N., Soomro, S.: Autism children's app using PECS. Ann. Emerg. Technol. Comput. (AETiC) **2**(1) (2018)

7. Leijdekkers, P., Gay, V., Wong, F.: CaptureMyEmotion: a mobile app to improve emotion learning for autistic children using sensors. IEEE (2013)
8. Morenonz, H.B.R., Rojas, E.M.: Digital education using apps for today's children
9. Eder, S., Diaz, J.M.L., Madela, J.R.S., Mag-usara, M.: Fill me app: an interactive mobile game application for children with autism, iJIM **10**(3) (2016)
10. Tang, H.-H., Jheng, C.-M., Chien, M.-E., Lin, N.-M., Chen, M.Y.: iCAN: a tablet-based pedagogical system for improving the user experience of children with autism in the learning process. IEEE (2013)
11. Rambhia, T., Dhodi, M., Patel, V., Kalbande, D.R.: Design of an intelligent system of autism. In: 2018 International Conference on Communication, Information & Computing Technology (ICCICT), 2–3 February 2018. IEEE (2018)
12. Kulkarni, P., Gondane, S., Salagar, M.: Education and creating social awareness for sensitive topics using mobile applications. IEEE (2013)
13. De Leo, G., Gonzales, C.H., Battagiri, P., Leroy, G.: A smart-phone application and a companion website for the improvement of the communication skills of children with autism: clinical rationale, technical development and preliminary results. J. Med. Syst. **35**(4), 703–711 (2011)
14. Escobedo, L., et al.: MOSOCO: a mobile assistive tool to support children with autism practicing social skills in real-life situations. In: Proceedings of the CHI 2012, pp. 2589–2598. ACM Press (2012)
15. Lin, N.-M.: Research of improving communication of children with autism via tablet. Master thesis, National Taiwan University (Unpublished)

Advanced Spatial Reutilization for Finding Ideal Path in Wireless Sensor Networks

A. Basi Reddy[1(✉)], P. Liyaz[1(✉)], B. Surendra Reddy[1(✉)],
K. Manoj Kumar[1], and K. Sathish[2]

[1] Computer Science and Engineering Department, SV College of Engineering,
Opp. LIC Training Center, Karakambadi Road,
Tirupati 517507, Andhra Pradesh, India
basireddy.a@gmail.com, liyaz.liyaz2009@gmail.com,
suril253@gmail.com, kandalamanojkumar@gmail.com
[2] Computer Science and Engineering Department,
Sreenivasa Institute of Technology and Management Studies,
Murukambattu, Chittoor 517127, Andhra Pradesh, India
sathishl234u@gmail.com

Abstract. The extensions in wireless sensor networks has stated that the research communities to turn up into the study of spatial reusability concepts. Because of restricted capacity in wireless links, the keen task is to select the optimal route for packet transmission. The optimal route selection which is achieved is verifiable by using the tremendous end-to-end efficiency rate. Wireless Sensor Networks routing is ideal confront because of essential features that differentiate these kind of networks are differ from other wireless networks like cellular networks or mobile ad hoc networks. This paper proposed an enhanced spatial reusability process using single path and any path routing protocols. Task of the single path routing is to reduce the cost of the nodes in wireless links, although the work of any path routing is to aid the intermediary node, one who observes the packet to take part in packet forwarding. Empirical outputs have shown the potency of our proposed work in terms of cost reduction functionalities.

Keywords: Wireless sensor networks · Wireless links · Packet forwarding · Cost minimization · Single path and any path routing protocols

1 Introduction

Recently, the research on wireless technologies has developed a greater impact among the network users [1]. Wireless networks is an emerging technology in which users can make use of its from anywhere at any time. The study towards wireless networks have enabled the researchers by its functionalities like fault tolerance, self-configuration and scalability. The research over multi-hop wireless networks consists of voluminous amount of wireless devices that covers mesh networks and mesh gateways [2]. Thus, a phenomenal growth has been seen in the development of wireless devices and networks.

© Springer Nature Singapore Pte Ltd. 2019
M. Singh et al. (Eds.): ICACDS 2019, CCIS 1046, pp. 219–227, 2019.
https://doi.org/10.1007/978-981-13-9942-8_21

Energy availability and reliability are the most prominent issues faced in the multi-hop wireless sensor networks. The real-time applications deployed using multi-path routing systems demands optimal reliability and the quality of service. In order to achieve better reliability, the availability of energy among the nodes is a significant factor. Hence, reliability is directly proportional to the energy availability. The task of multipath routing is to get hold of the destination using single path or any path routing systems. In case of any misbehavior occur in node, and then the re-routing process is initiated [3]. Relatively, each node cooperates with other nodes to form the path and behaves like broadcast for transmitting the packets. The uncertainty of the topology node or link failures could results detached routes.

In fact, the paths are formed without any knowledge about the nodes [4]. Thus, the presence of failure nodes can't be detected in an untimely phase. The transformation of packets between failure nodes can affect the performance of the networks. Similarly, the concept of multipath scheme is to supply the energy without any interference at the same time. There are two paths, namely, primary paths and protection paths. Both these paths will not synchronize with other nodes while transmitting the packets. To resolve this, the concept of network interference is achieved. Since the multipath routing inquires more than one route to process the data. Henceforth, Route searching is a vital task in multipath routing scheme. Routing in wireless networks operates based on the received requests in both dynamic and static routing. The two paths, viz, primary path and protection path are used for routing analysis. Primary path deals with failure nodes whereas protection path deals with reserved request [8].

The shared nodes could affect the network performance, if any failure node is detected. It effectively assists to save the energy. The multipath routing strategy has a to provide better in transmitting different types of multimedia applications such as video, voice and data, has been evinced in several prior studies, as in [6]. For every received request, it performs two paths for processing the data. If some network criteria are satisfied, it is feasible to utilize an even link to secure more number of primary paths. Reutilization of a secured link is the ability to protect the multiple paths. In wireless mesh networks, this work discuss about the reusability [7]. The received user's request is further reused for energy consumption in the networks.

The rest of the paper is organized as follows: Sect. 2 depicts the related work; Sect. 3 describes the proposed work; Sect. 4 describes the experimental analysis and concludes in Sect. 5.

2 Literature Survey

This section depicts the related works carried out by other researchers. The author in [10] studied about the video streaming process that specifically deals with bandwidth and energy constrained analysis. In this single video frame is subdivided into different frames and then each frame is transmitted to its sub-stream process. It is deployed over Directional Geographical Routing (DGR) which studied about the parameters load balance and bandwidth. The author in studied about the multipath routing scheme which devised that Quality of the Service in the perspective of hop count, bandwidth and end-to-end lag in MANET environments [11]. The primary path may get disrupted when the route discovery processes are properly initiated. A new path is designed for incessant data transmission systems. And thus, they achieved high reliability and low overloaded systems.

Similarly, the author in [12] studied the performance of the network under diverse path routing in order to enhance the packets delivery ratio, reliability and maximizing the effect of multipath routing design. The author in [13] presented an end-to-end throughput rate using multipath routing process with less inference among the networks. The author in [14] presented about the node disjoint paths in indoor environments in terms of route discovery and message control overhead. Relatively, an enhancement of end-to-end reliability process is studied by author in [15]. A copy of data is being sent to the different paths and also the diversity in frequency is manipulated in multi-radio environment.

Similarly, the author in [16] studied about the multipath routing that helps to raise the rate of throughput. Another research in [17] for discovering and resolving for dynamic path deterioration in wireless networks, they presented hindrance-sensible multi-radio routing protocol. When radical link deterioration happens, the protocol which we proposed that dynamically rebuilds an initiated path of source. One more method for the multipath design used to be studied in [18]. In wireless ad-hoc network, they studied the problem of detecting the minimal intensity disjoint paths. They have concentrated in static ad-hoc networks. They used all total nodes along the primary paths so-called common nodes after finding a primary path in each request. To form disjoint paths, they shared those common nodes to locate another path.

The author in [19] suggested a multipath routing protocol known as AODV-DM that assisted to detect more number of multiple paths with lower intervention. An insulating region is formed around the primary path after finding a primary path. It contains all the edges in the first path within the hindrance range of each node [20]. To shorten the possible network interference with the detected primary path, a protection or secure path must be opted and well-documented outside the secluding region. By the use of insulating region, most of the network connections would be removed. From the reviews, the challenges in spatial reusability analysis are:

- Restricted wireless communication media which involve optimal route selection process in order to embellish the end-to-end throughput.
- Data transmission rate is higher in case of delivering single packets.

3 Proposed Work

3.1 Motivation

The progresses made in wireless networks permitted the wireless users to adopt the wireless services. In order to achieve best data transmission process, the selection of optimal route between sender and receiver node is a vital thing. Though, the prior routing protocols exhibits a better route selection, but it ended up with the issue of high end-to-end throughput. End to End throughput is the amount of data travelled from sender node to the receiver node within stipulated period of time. To overcome from this issue, the spatial reusability concept has been explored by several researchers. Most of the wireless networks environment suffers from the spatial wastage towards the communication process. This motivates us to excavate into the research of spatial reutilization in multi-hop wireless networks environment.

3.2 Devised Spatial Aware Path Routing Protocols

This section depicts the general workflow of our proposed spatial aware path routing protocols. This is achieved by two protocols, namely Singe path routing protocols and any path routing protocols. The proposed algorithm is explained as follows:

$$Z_i = \frac{1}{ij * pij}$$

(a) System Model:
Let us consider a set of static N nodes which are connected via multi-hop wireless networks with fixed transmission rate. The deployment of single path routing protocols incurs Expected Transmission Count Metric (ETX) that states probability transmission rate from the node i to node j. Thus, probability of transmitting packets from node i to node j is given as

$$t_{ij} = Z_i * T_{data} + Z_i * pij * T_{ack}$$

Similarly, anypath routing calculated from the set of forwarder nodes Fi. With the use of forwarder nodes, the expected number of transmissions by node i is given as:

$$Z_i F_i = \frac{1}{1 - \left(J \in F_i (1 - P_{ij}) \right)}$$

Based on the propagation medium, the two distant wireless links can work if they spatial distant from each other. Let us explain about the working of Anypath routing protocols and Single path routing.

(b) Spatial reutilized attentive-single path routing protocols (SR-SPRP)
The primary task of the Single path routing protocol is to choose the optimal paths that yields better performance at lower cost. The proposed steps involved in Single Path Routing Protocols are:

(i)   Input: Path p, Link cost $(t_{ij})\in$ p, Link graph G = (P, E)
(ii) In accord to decreasing order, the links in set P are arranged.
(iii) Estimating the Link delivery time for the set I (collection of non-interfering paths) of wireless links as:

$$C(I) = \max\{t_{ij}/(i,j)\} \in I$$

(iv) For every set I, the spatial resuability aware path delivery time is given as:

$$C = \sum c(I) i \varepsilon I$$

(v)   Consider each path as conflict graph G = (V, E) where V represents links and E represents interferences.

(vi) Thus, every path P in the non-interfering set I, we compute G where E = {(i, j), (i′, j′)} that holds infererence among the links.

(vii) Output: Optimal non-interfering paths with its optimal costs.

(c) Spatial reutilized attentive - Anypath routing protocols (SR-APRP)

The role of anypath routing protocols is to pick the set of source, intermediate and destination nodes, so as to achieve better packet delivery with cost minimized factor. The proposed steps involved in anypath routing protocols are:

(i)   Input: Network Graph G = (N, E), source node and destination node.

(ii) Estimating the distance cost $\overrightarrow{C} = (C_i) i \varepsilon Q$ with forwarder lists $\overrightarrow{F} = (F_i) i \varepsilon Q$

(iii) When the node cost is lower, it implies that the destination node is at reachable position.

(iv) Using recursive function, the probability among node i and node j is given as:

$$\varphi(i,j) = \{1, iFj = i\}; otherwise \sum \omega_{ik} * \varphi(k,j) iFj \varepsilon Q^{C_i} < c_i K \varepsilon F_i$$

(v)   Consider each path as conflict graph G = (V, E) where V is the links and E is the interferences.

$$tF_i = \varphi(src, i) * t_i F_i$$

(vi) Thus, every path P in the non-interfering set I, we compute G where E = {(i, j), (i′, j′)} that holds infererence among the links.

$$C_{src} = \sum c(I) i \varepsilon I$$

(vii) Output: Optimal non-interfering paths with its optimal costs.

(d) Spatial reutilized attentive - Anypath routing protocols (SR-APRP)

The primary role of anypath routing scheme protocols is to elite the set of source, intermediate and destination nodes, so as to achieve better packet delivery with cost minimized factor. The proposed steps involved in anypath routing protocols are:

(i)   Input: Network Graph G = (N, E), source node and destination node.

(ii) Estimating the cost of distance $\overrightarrow{C} = (C_i) i \varepsilon Q$ with forwarder lists $\overrightarrow{F} = (F_i) i \varepsilon Q$

(iii) When the node cost is lower, it implies that the destination node is at reachable position.

(iv) Using recursive function, the probability betwixt node i and node j is given as:

(v)   Thus, the delivery of packet from source node i to the destination node j is given as:

(vi) The total cost of packet delivering from source to destination node is:

(vii) Output: A group of participating nodes Q, and the equivalent form of cost C and forwarder lists F (Fig. 1).

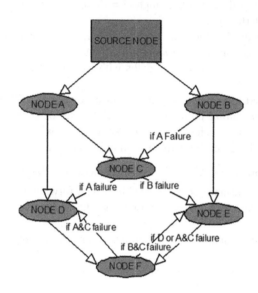

Fig. 1. Proposed workflow

4 Experimental Analysis

This section depicts simulation analysis of our proposed routing protocols. The Table 1 depicts the simulation parameters used in our network environment. Specifying in detail that, we indiscriminately choose 200 source-to-destination matches or pairs for single-path and any path routing, respectively, from those that are results in distinct routing verdicts from the analyzed routing methods for accuracy. The output of every source-to-destination pair was attained over 100 runs, each one of which endured 10 min.

Table 1. Simulation of parameters

Parameter	Value
Number of nodes	100
Area	2000 m * 2000 m
CTS/RTS	Off
Rate of transmission	11 Mbps
Traffic Generation	CBR
CBR	5 Mbps
Size of packet	1500 bytes

With the defined set of nodes, the no. of edges get decreased when the area size increases. Consider an instances 303 requests are satisfied under the area of 1000 m * 1000 m and 53 requests are satisfied under the area of 2500 * 2500 m. The obtained outputs are further as compared with the outcomes of SAAR and AODVDM methods. The results depicts that AODVDM incurs high time in insulating region and the SAAR schemes works incurs high time in multi path routing systems shown in Fig. 2.

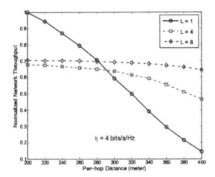

Fig. 2. Normalized network throughput in multi-hop distance.

The proposed SSAAR model satisfies more request than in SAR and AODVDM by examining encumbrance and protection links reutilization. It is inferred from Fig. 3. that AODV-DM able to satisfy less number of requests because it cover all the edges that interfere with primary or protection path and it can also cover majority links in the networks. If the interfered edges in the graph are hided, the ratio of the AODV-DM scheme will reduced and the nodes in the same area size are also increases.

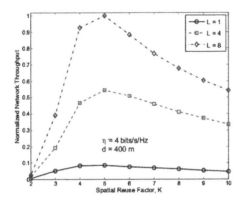

Fig. 3. Normalized network throughput using spatial reuse factor

5   Conclusion

The technology development towards wireless sensor networks has seen phenomena growth which attracts variety of wireless users. Routing is the significant task in view of intrinsic behavior shows the difference between networks and other wireless networks. The wireless networks services are restricted in many ways. Spatial reusability is the concept introduced to overcome the issue of optimal path selection. Thus, we proposed an enhanced spatial reutilized process using single path and any path routing protocols. The duty of single path routing is cost reduction in wireless links, whereas the duty of any path routing is to aid the intermediate node who observes the packet to take part in packet forwarding. Experimental outcomes have proven the efficacy of our proposed work in terms of cost reducing functionalities. The proposed technique is validated via simulating the packets and evaluating with throughput rate and spatial reuse factor in pair-wise. The similar computation model becomes significant in larger networks. And better performance achieved in 2-hop interference than the 1-hop interference.

References

1. Shabu, S.J., Kumar, M.: "K" preserving user's privacy in personalized search. Int. J. Appl. Eng. Res. (IJAER) 9(22), 16269–16276 (2014)
2. Kumar, K.M., Vikram, M.: Disclosure of user's profile in personalized search for enhanced privacy. Int. J. Appl. Eng. Res. (IJAER) 10(16), 36358–36363 (2015)
3. Kandala, H., Tripathy, B.K., Manoj Kumar, K.: A framework to collect and visualize user's browser history for better user experience and personalized recommendations. In: Satapathy, S.C., Joshi, A. (eds.) ICTIS 2017. SIST, vol. 83, pp. 218–224. Springer, Cham (2018). https://doi.org/10.1007/978-3-319-63673-3_26
4. Yuvaraju, B.V., Venkiteela, L., Kumar, K.M.: A presumptuous encephalon electronic brain computing in gaming gadgets. In: 2018 International Conference on Soft-Computing and Network Security (ICSNS), Coimbatore, India, pp. 1–6 (2018)
5. Kumar, K.M., Kandala, H., Reddy, N.S.: Synthesizing and imitating handwriting using deep recurrent neural networks and mixture density networks. In: 2018 9th International Conference on Computing, Communication and Networking Technologies (ICCCNT), Bangalore, pp. 1–6 (2018)
6. Devi, K.J., Moulika, G.B., Sravanthi, K., Kumar, K.M.: Prediction of medicines using LVQ methodology. In: 2017 International Conference on Energy, Communication, Data Analytics and Soft Computing (ICECDS), Chennai, pp. 388–391 (2017)
7. Bhavana, G., Kumar, K.M.: Cardiac disease monitoring based on ZigBee technology. In: 2017 International Conference on Energy, Communication, Data Analytics and Soft Computing (ICECDS), Chennai, pp. 392–395 (2017)
8. Razvi, S.A., Neelima, S., Prathyusha, C., Yuvasree, G., Ganga, C., Kumar, K.M.: Implementation of graphical passwords in internet banking for enhanced security. In: 2017 International Conference on Intelligent Computing and Control Systems (ICICCS), Madurai, pp. 35–41 (2017)

9. Kumar, K.M., Tejasree, S., Swarnalatha, S.: Effective implementation of data segregation &; extraction using big data in E - health insurance as a service. In: 2016 3rd International Conference on Advanced Computing and Communication Systems (ICACCS), Coimbatore, pp. 1–5 (2016)

10. Praveen Kumar, R., Manoj Kumar, K., Tejasree, S., Aswini, R.: Review on cost effective and dynamic security provision strategy of staging data items in cloud. Res. J. Pharm. Biol. Chem. Sci. (RJPBCS) **7**(6), 1592–1597 (2016). ISSN: 0975-8585

11. Rajendran, P.K., Asbern, A., Manoj Kumar, K., Rajesh, M., Abhilash, R.: Implementation and analysis of MapReduce on biomedical big data. Indian J. Sci. Technol. (IJST) **9**(31), 1–6 (2016). ISSN/E-ISSN: 0974-6846/0974-5645

12. Kilaru, S., Lakshmanachari, S., Kishore, P.K., Surendra, B., Vishnuvardhan, T.: An efficient probability of detection model for wireless sensor networks. In: Satapathy, S.C., Prasad, V. K., Rani, B.P., Udgata, S.K., Raju, K.S. (eds.) Proceedings of the First International Conference on Computational Intelligence and Informatics. AISC, vol. 507, pp. 585–593. Springer, Singapore (2017). https://doi.org/10.1007/978-981-10-2471-9_56

13. Broch, J., Maltz, D.A., Johnson, D.B., Hu, Y.-C., Jetcheva, J.G.: A performance comparison of multi-hop wireless ad hoc network routing protocols. In: Proceedings of 4th Annual ACM/IEEE International Conference Mobile Computing Network, pp. 85–97 (1998)

14. Chachulski, S., Jennings, M., Katti, S., Katabi, D.: Trading structure for randomness in wireless opportunistic routing. In: Proceedings of SIGCOMM Conference Applications, Technologies, Architectures and Protocols Computer Communications, pp. 169–180 (2007)

15. Johnson, C.D.B., Maltz, D.A.: Dynamic source routing in adhoc wireless networks. Mobile Comput. vol. 353, pp. 153–181 (1992)

16. Perkins, C.E., Bhagwat, P.: Highly dynamic destination sequenced distance-vector routing (DSDV) for mobile computers. In: Proceedings of Conference Communication Architecture, Protocols Applications, pp. 234–244 (1994)

17. Laufer, R.P., Dubois-Ferriere, H., Kleinrock, L.: Multirate anypath routing in wireless mesh networks. In: Proceedings of INFOCOM, pp. 37–45 (2009)

18. Lin, Y., Li, B., Liang, B.: CodeOR: opportunistic routing in wireless mesh networks with segmented network coding. In: Proceedings of IEEE International Conference Network Protocols, pp. 13–22 (2008)

19. Kim, T.S., Hou, J.C., Lim, H.: Improving spatial reuse through tuning transmits power, carrier sense threshold, and data rate in multihop wireless networks. In: Proceedings of 12th Annual International Conference Mobile Computing Networking, pp. 366–377 (2006)

20. Draves, R., Padhye, J., Zill, B.: Routing in multi-radio, multihop wireless mesh networks. In: Proceedings of 10th Annual Internatioanl Conference on Mobile Computing and Networking, pp. 114–128 (2004)

An Efficient Preprocessing Step for Retinal Vessel Segmentation via Optic Nerve Head Exclusion

Farha Fatina Wahid[1]([⊠]) and G. Raju[2]

[1] Department of Information Technology,
Kannur University, Kannur 670567, Kerala, India
farhawahid@gmail.com
[2] Department of CSE, Faculty of Engineering, Christ (Deemed to be University),
Bengaluru 560764, Karnataka, India
kurupgraju@gmail.com

Abstract. Retinal vessel segmentation plays a significant role for accurate diagnostics of ophthalmic diseases. In this paper, a novel preprocessing step for retinal vessel segmentation via optic nerve head exclusion is proposed. The idea relies in the fact that the exclusion of brighter optic nerve head prior to contrast enhancement process can better enhance the blood vessels for accurate segmentation. A histogram based intensity thresholding scheme is introduced in order to extract the optic nerve head which is then replaced by its surrounding background pixels. The efficacy of the proposed preprocessing step is established by segmenting the retinal vessels from the optic nerve head excluded image enhanced using CLAHE algorithm. Experimental works are carried out with fundus images from DRIVE database. It shows that 1%–3% of improvement in terms of TPR measure is achieved.

Keywords: Fundus image enhancement · Retinal vessel segmentation ·
Optic nerve head · Preprocessing

1 Introduction

Medical image enhancement, as a preprocessing step, gained much attention due to its remarkable ability to achieve better segmentation. At the initial stage of medical image analysis, images captured from different medical devices are in raw format and may consist of noise and other unwanted artifacts [1, 2]. Eye fundus images captured using specialized fundus camera may contain these issues during acquisition. Hence, enhancement of fundus images is a topic of interest nowadays.

There are mainly two types of image enhancement techniques - contrast enhancement and edge enhancement [2, 3]. The basic working of any contrast enhancement algorithm is to transform image intensity values concentrated near a narrow range to values that span a wider range [2]. Generally, fundus images are of low contrast and low bright in nature. Majority of the ophthalmic diseases are due to the abnormalities in the structure of blood vessels present in an eye fundus. These abnormalities are mainly caused due to the variations in vessel attributes such as width,

© Springer Nature Singapore Pte Ltd. 2019
M. Singh et al. (Eds.): ICACDS 2019, CCIS 1046, pp. 228–239, 2019.
https://doi.org/10.1007/978-981-13-9942-8_22

diameter, tortuosity, bifurcation, etc. Excessive dilation of blood vessels present in the posterior section of the retina is another factor for retinal disorders [4, 5]. These disorders are identified by the medical experts using the features of blood vessels such as vessel color, shape and contrast [4–6]. Hence, it is essential to enhance the blood vessel in a fundus image in order to identify different ophthalmic diseases including diabetic retinopathy, hemorrhage, hypertension, retinal artery occlusion, arthrosclerosis, arteriolar narrowing etc. [6].

The enhancement of blood vessel is deteriorated by the presence of optic nerve head in an eye fundus as it has bright white color due to the exposure of hyper reflective tissues [7]. This conflict in contrast of blood vessels and optic nerve head may be one of the factors that adversely affect enhancement efficiency of the existing works.

In this work, an optic nerve head exclusion method for fundus image enhancement is proposed. As the intensity values of optic nerve head are mostly concentrated on the right end of the histogram, it is easily distinguishable from intensity values of the relatively darker vessel as well as non-vessel regions. The uniformity in the image contrast of the non-vessel pixels is achieved by eliminating the effect of brighter optic nerve head via histogram based intensity thresholding scheme. This preprocessed image is further enhanced using Contrast Limited Adaptive Histogram Equalization (CLAHE) algorithm for better retinal vessel segmentation.

The paper is articulated as follows. Section 2 gives an overview of the state of the art preprocessing methods for retinal vessel segmentation followed by proposed optic nerve head exclusion strategy in Sect. 3. Experimental results and discussion are explained in Sect. 4 and Sect. 5 concludes the paper.

2   Overview of Preprocessing Methods

For accurate segmentation of retinal vessels, an efficient preprocessing plays a vital role. Contrast enhancement of fundus images is the basic preprocessing step for retinal vessel segmentation. There are several algorithms proposed in various literatures for effective enhancement of fundus images. Majority of the fundus image segmentation considers CLAHE algorithm for preprocessing [8–10]. CLAHE algorithm works by dividing an image into contextual regions and computing histograms locally on each contextual region followed by clipping. Clipping is done in order to remove high peaks in the histogram which may represent noise. This is followed by histogram stretching and bilinear interpolation [11]. In [8], the authors enhanced retinal blood vessels using CLAHE and median filter. Further, segmentation is carried out using mean-C thresholding. An accuracy of 0.955 and 0.954 are obtained for images from Digital Retinal Images for Vessel Extraction (DRIVE) and Child Heart and Health Study in England (CHASE_DB1) databases respectively. In [9], preprocessing is carried out using 2D wavelet transform assisted morphological gradient operation based CLAHE and vessel segmentation using morphological gray level hit or miss transform. The authors claimed that they attained maximum accuracy of 95.65% and average accuracy of 94.31% for DRIVE database.

Morphological operators are another commonly used technique for fundus image enhancement. Top hat transformation, bottom hat transformation and bowler hat transformations are being used for fundus image enhancement [12–14]. In [12], a multi-scale morphological top-hat transformation and combination of Gabor and matched filter are used for enhancing low-contrast and blurred fundus images. The authors claimed that the quality of vessel enhancement is improved using their proposed method. Morphology based global thresholding and centerline detection methods are used in [13] for retinal blood vessel segmentation. Accuracies of 95.88% and 95.27% are obtained for DRIVE and STARE databases respectively.

Gabor filters with different parameter values are also an effective enhancement scheme for fundus images used in many works [12, 15, 16]. In [15], fundus images are initially enhanced using 30 element Gabor filter and a Gaussian fractional derivative. Blood vessels are isolated from these enhanced images using threshold and series of morphology based decision rules. An average accuracy of 0.9503 is obtained for images from DRIVE database.

Exposure based Sub Image Histogram Equalization (ESIHE), an enhancement scheme developed for low exposure gray scale images, is also used for enhancing fundus images. The ESIHE algorithm works by dividing the input image into sub-images of different intensity levels using an exposure threshold. The contrast enhancement rate is controlled by clipping the histogram using the average intensity value as a threshold. The independently equalized histograms are then integrated to obtain the final enhanced image [17, 18].

3 Proposed Preprocessing Framework via Optic Nerve Head Exclusion

In this section, the proposed preprocessing methodology for fundus image segmentation by optic nerve head exclusion is described. One of the specialties of fundus images is that optic nerve head stands out with respect to vessels and non-vessels as it's the brightest portion of the fundus image. On comparison with the remaining portions of the image, pixel count of optic nerve head is relatively less. However, the brightness of optic nerve head is a major factor that affects accurate segmentation of blood vessels in the fundus image. Here, a novel optic nerve head exclusion method is proposed to enhance the fundus image for accurate vessel segmentation. By reducing the effect of brighter pixel values of optic nerve head in the contrast enhancement process, better vessel segmentation can be achieved. The prime focus is to replace the brighter pixels with the non-vessel background and hence to form a uniformity among the non-vessel pixels in the image.

Initially, green channel of the fundus image in RGB color model is extracted. Green channel is selected as this channel exhibits maximum contrast and is selected by majority of the blood vessel segmentation algorithms [13, 19]. On the extracted green channel image, histogram is computed as it gives the distribution of pixel intensity values. On the histogram, brighter portions of the image representing the optic nerve head are easily distinguishable.

3.1   Optic Nerve Head Extraction

Extraction of the optic nerve head is achieved by a thresholding scheme where a threshold is set based on the distribution of intensity values in the fundus image. i.e., as the pixel count of optic nerve head is comparatively less; a brighter intensity value is found, whose count is greater than all other brighter pixel intensities in the histogram distribution. This brighter intensity value acts as the threshold value for extracting the optic nerve head. Figure 1 shows the optic nerve head extraction based on a threshold value for *02_test* image in DRIVE database.

Fig. 1. Optic nerve head extraction

3.2   Optic Nerve Head Exclusion

Once the optic nerve head is extracted from the fundus image, it's intensity values are replaced with the neighboring background pixels in order to eliminate its influence in the enhancement process. This task is crucial as one has to know the position of the optic nerve head, whether it's on the left or right part of the fundus image. So, in the proposed frame work, the centroid positions of the input fundus image and its corresponding optic nerve head are computed. The decision rule for the optic nerve head location is as follows:

> **if** $I_{xc} < O_{xc}$
> *Optic nerve head lies on the right side*
> **else**
> *Optic nerve head lies on the left side*
> **end**

Here, I_{xc} and O_{xc} are the x co-ordinate of the centroid position of the fundus image and optic nerve head respectively. Figure 2 shows the pictorial representation of the centroid positions of fundus image and its corresponding optic nerve head.

Based on the decision rule, the neighboring background pixels for replacing the optic nerve head are selected by the traversal of the image row pixels containing the y co-ordinate of the optic nerve head centroid, O_{yc}. If the optic nerve head is found to be on the left side of the image, traversal takes place from left to right and vice versa.

When the traversal reaches to the end of the optic nerve head, an $n \times n$ neighborhood is extracted. Finally, the mean value of this neighborhood replaces the optic nerve head pixels.

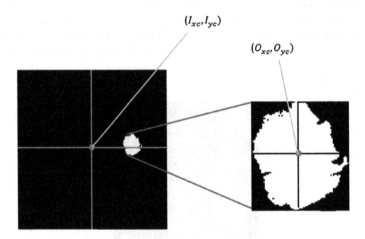

Fig. 2. Centroid positions of the fundus image and its corresponding optic nerve head

Let $row_{O_{yc}}$ represent the reference row containing O_{yc} and p_1 represents the first pixel in $row_{O_{yc}}$ after the traversal of optic nerve head. Using p_1 and O_{yc}, an $n \times n$ neighborhood is extracted as follows.

$$neigh_{ext} = img_{green}([p_1, p_2 \ldots, p_n]; [(O_{yc} - n/2), \ldots, (O_{yc} + n/2)]) \qquad (1)$$

where img_{green} is the green channel of the input fundus image, n is the size of the neighborhood to be extracted, $p_1, p_2, \ldots, p_n \in row_{O_{yc}}$ in the direction of traversal. Figure 3 depicts the pictorial representation of the neighborhood for optic nerve head replacement.

From $neigh_{ext}$, the pixel for replacing optic nerve head is computed as given in Eq. 2.

$$pixel_{replace} = mean(neigh_{ext}) \qquad (2)$$

In order to reflect the exclusion of optic nerve head from the color retinal fundus image, it is to be eliminated separately from all the three channels. General formula for neighborhood extraction is given in Eq. 3.

$$neigh_{ext} = img_{channel}([p_1, p_2, \ldots, p_n]; [(O_{yc} - n/2), \ldots, (O_{yc} + n/2)]) \qquad (3)$$

where $channel \in \{red, green, blue\}$.

The generalized block diagram for the proposed preprocessing methodology is given in Fig. 4.

The algorithm for the proposed optic nerve head exclusion is as follows.

Algorithm I

Step 1: Read a color retinal fundus image, img

Step 2: Extract green channel of img, img_{green}

Step 3: Compute histogram of img_{green}, $hist_{green}$

Step 4: Extract optic nerve head from img_{green} using $hist_{green}$

    Step 4.1: Obtain intensity, $i \in hist_{green}$ satisfying the condition,

$$\{\exists\, i \in hist_{green} \,|\, hist_{count}(i) > c \wedge \forall x \in hist_{green},$$
$$x \neq i,\, hist_{count}(x) > c \;\rightarrow (x < i)\},\ c \text{ is a predefined constant.}$$

    Step 4.2: Set i as the threshold, θ, for optic nerve head extraction.

$$\theta \leftarrow i$$

    Step 4.3: Obtain binary optic nerve head of img_{green} as

$$img_{od} \leftarrow img_{green} > \theta$$

Step 5: Extract background neighborhood pixels of optic nerve head from img_{green} for optic nerve head replacement.

    Step 5.1: Check whether optic nerve head lies on the left or right side of img_{od}

        Step 5.1.1: Compute centroid of img_{od}, (I_{xc}, I_{yc}) and its corresponding optic nerve head, (O_{xc}, O_{yc}).

        Step 5.1.2: if $I_{xc} < O_{xc}$

$$od_{pos} \leftarrow right$$

        else

$$od_{pos} \leftarrow left$$

    Step 5.2: Traverse $row_{O_{yc}}$, $O_{yc} \in row_{O_{yc}}$ of img_{green} from od_{pos} to opposite direction.

    Step 5.3: Obtain $p_1 \in row_{O_{yc}}$, such that all optic nerve head pixels in $row_{O_{yc}}$ is traversed.

    Step 5.4: With p_1 and O_{yc} as reference pixels, extract $n \times n$ neighborhood for optic nerve head replacement.

$$neigh_{ext} \leftarrow img_{green}([p_1, p_2, \dots, p_n];\ [(O_{yc} - {^n\!/_2}), \dots, (O_{yc} + {^n\!/_2})])$$

Step 6: Obtain the pixel for optic nerve head replacement using $neigh_{ext}$

$$pixel_{replace} \leftarrow mean(neigh_{ext})$$

Step 7: Obtain $img_{green\_without\_od}$ by replacing all optic nerve head pixels in img_{green} by $pixel_{replace}$.

$$img_{green\_without\_od} \leftarrow img_{green}(img_{od} == 1) = pixel_{replace}$$

Step 8: Similarly replace optic nerve head pixels in the red and blue channel to obtain final color fundus image excluding optic nerve head.

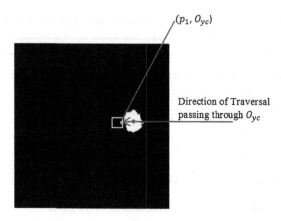

Fig. 3. Neighborhood extraction for optic nerve head replacement

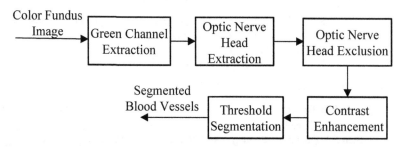

Fig. 4. Generalized block diagram for proposed preprocessing methodology for vessel segmentation.

4 Experimental Results and Discussion

The proposed optic nerve head exclusion is a preprocessing step to be carried out before contrast enhancement process. In order to prove the efficacy of the proposed preprocessing framework, the resultant image obtained after optic nerve head exclusion is further enhanced using CLAHE algorithm and retinal vessels are segmented using thresholding based segmentation algorithm proposed in [8].

The algorithm is tested on standard test images obtained from DRIVE database [20]. DRIVE database contains 40 images divided into equal sets of training and testing samples. For all the images, manual segmented vessels are provided. The working of the proposed algorithm is dependent on two parameters, namely constant, c and the size of neighborhood, n. c is used to extract optic nerve head from the retinal fundus image. n plays a significant role in the pixel intensity used for replacing the extracted optic nerve head from the input fundus image. In this work, the value of c and n are empirically fixed to 100 and 11 respectively. For the segmentation algorithm considered, the parameters are set to values as in [8].

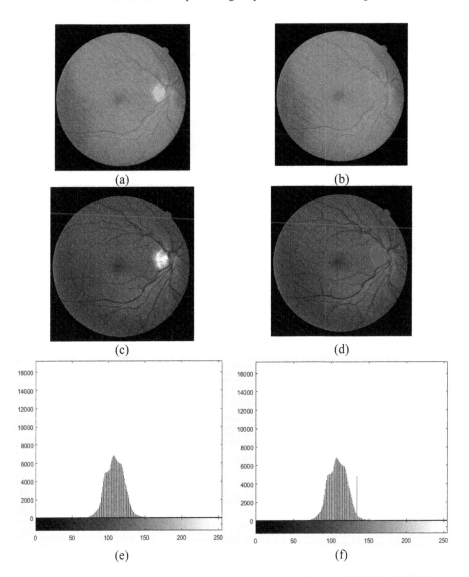

Fig. 5. Results obtained for image *02_test* from DRIVE database. (a) Original RGB image (b) optic nerve head excluded RGB image (c) original image in green channel (d) optic nerve head excluded image in green channel (e) histogram of original image in green channel (f) histogram of optic nerve head excluded image in green channel (g) enhanced image before optic nerve head exclusion (h) enhanced image after optic nerve head exclusion (i) vessels segmented before optic nerve head exclusion (j) vessels segmented after optic nerve head exclusion. (Color figure online)

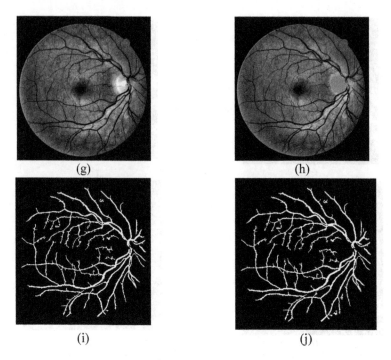

Fig. 5. (*continued*)

The segmentation results of images obtained before and after optic nerve head exclusion are evaluated using the measures- True Positive Rate (TPR) and True Negative Rate (TNR). TPR and TNR can be computed as follows.

$$TPR = \frac{TP}{TP + FN} \tag{4}$$

$$TNR = \frac{TN}{TN + FP} \tag{5}$$

where TP, TN, FP and FN denotes true positive, true negative, false positive and false negative values obtained from the automated segmented vessels on comparison with the manual segmented vessels from the database.

Table 1 gives the segmentation results of randomly selected images from DRIVE database before and after optic nerve head exclusion from the green channel of image based on TPR and TNR measures. Figure 5 shows the results obtained for the image 02_*test* from DRIVE database. It provides optic nerve head excluded image in both RGB color model as well as green channel of the image.

Table 1. Segmentation results of selected images from DRIVE database

SI no.	Image ID	With optic nerve head		Without optic nerve head	
		TPR	TNR	TPR	TNR
1	02_test	0.7589	0.9778	0.7657	0.9807
2	12_test	0.7138	0.9751	0.7453	0.9830
3	16_test	0.7291	0.9796	0.7550	0.9829
4	18_test	0.7811	0.9757	0.7947	0.9785
5	21_training	0.7548	0.9768	0.7684	0.9815
6	22_training	0.6738	0.9826	0.6802	0.9851
7	27_training	0.6889	0.9763	0.6987	0.9813
8	30_training	0.6395	0.9845	0.6656	0.9876
9	32_training	0.7127	0.9810	0.7275	0.9842
10	33_training	0.7309	0.9780	0.7424	0.9818

From Fig. 5(b) and (d), it is clearly visible that the proposed preprocessing methodology is efficient in excluding the brighter optic nerve head from the input fundus image, thereby providing a better input for contrast enhancement process. When enhancement is carried out on the optic nerve head excluded image, vessels will get better enhanced as the high intensity values from the image are eliminated. The histograms of the fundus image before and after optic nerve head exclusion are given in Fig. 5(e) and (f) respectively. The relatively high peak on the right side of histogram in Fig. 5(f) indicates the replaced optic nerve head pixels.

The results obtained for random images from DRIVE database in Table 1 proves that the proposed algorithm is capable of providing 1%–3% improvement in terms of TPR measure. It indicates that a better enhancement is achieved using CLAHE algorithm when optic nerve head is excluded. The better enhanced image leads to more accurate retinal vessel segmentation. The TNR measure on the other hand reveals that optic nerve head exclusion from the image does not lead to increased false positive value.

5 Conclusion

In this paper, a novel preprocessing step for retinal vessel segmentation via optic nerve head exclusion is proposed. Since optic nerve head is the brightest portion of the eye fundus, its influence in the enhancement of retinal vessels is superior. This superiority adversely affects the enhancement process via histogram equalization as stretching of intensity values will be minimal. Hence, a histogram based thresholding scheme is introduced to extract the intensity values representing optic nerve head and eliminate its influence by replacing it with background non-vessel pixel intensities. On the resultant image, CLAHE algorithm is applied to obtain a better enhanced fundus image. Experiments carried out with fundus images from DRIVE database prove the efficacy of the proposed preprocessing method for vessel enhancement. Further, the vessels extracted from the enhanced fundus image are found to give better segmentation results in terms of true positive and true negative rates.

Manifestation of the proposed framework with different enhancement techniques can be explored for further research. Also, various retinal vessel segmentation methods incorporated with the proposed preprocessing framework is expected to provide more accurate retinal vessel segmentation.

Acknowledgement. The authors would like to acknowledge the University Grants Commission (UGC), New Delhi, India for the financial support extended under Maulana Azad National Fellowship (MANF) scheme.

References

1. Kumar, I., Bhadauria, H., Virmani, J., Rawat, J.: Reduction of speckle noise from medical images using principal component analysis image fusion. In: 2014 9th International Conference on Industrial and Information Systems (ICIIS) (2014)
2. Gonzalez, R., Woods, R.: Digital Image Processing. Pearson, London (2006)
3. Jain, A.: Fundamentals of Digital Image Processing. Prentice-Hall of India, New Delhi (2006)
4. Fraz, M., et al.: Blood vessel segmentation methodologies in retinal images – a survey. Comput. Methods Programs Biomed. **108**, 407–433 (2012)
5. Rezaee, K., Haddadnia, J., Tashk, A.: Optimized clinical segmentation of retinal blood vessels by using combination of adaptive filtering, fuzzy entropy and skeletonization. Appl. Soft Comput. **52**, 937–951 (2017)
6. Khan, K., et al.: A review of retinal blood vessels extraction techniques: challenges, taxonomy, and future trends. Pattern Anal. Appl. **22**(3), 767–802 (2018)
7. Almazroa, A., Burman, R., Raahemifar, K., Lakshminarayanan, V.: Optic disc and optic cup segmentation methodologies for glaucoma image detection: a survey. J. Ophthalmol. **2015**, 1–28 (2015)
8. Dash, J., Bhoi, N.: A thresholding based technique to extract retinal blood vessels from fundus images. Future Comput. Inf. J. **2**, 103–109 (2017)
9. Pal, S., Chatterjee, S., Dey, D., Munshi, S.: Morphological operations with iterative rotation of structuring elements for segmentation of retinal vessel structures. Multidimension. Syst. Signal Process. **30**, 373–389 (2018)
10. Mapayi, T., Viriri, S., Tapamo, J.: Comparative study of retinal vessel segmentation based on global thresholding techniques. Comput. Math. Methods Med. **2015**, 1–15 (2015)
11. Zuiderveld, K.: Contrast Limited Adaptive Histogram Equalization in Graphics Gems IV. AP Professional, Boston (1994)
12. Lu, C., et al.: Vessel enhancement of low quality fundus image using mathematical morphology and combination of Gabor and matched filter. In: 2016 International Conference on Wavelet Analysis and Pattern Recognition (ICWAPR) (2016)
13. Jiang, Z., Yepez, J., An, S., Ko, S.: Fast, accurate and robust retinal vessel segmentation system. Biocybernetics Biomed. Eng. **37**, 412–421 (2017)
14. Sazak, Ç., Nelson, C., Obara, B.: The multiscale bowler-hat transform for blood vessel enhancement in retinal images. Pattern Recogn. **88**, 739–750 (2019)
15. Aguirre-Ramos, H., Avina-Cervantes, J., Cruz-Aceves, I., Ruiz-Pinales, J., Ledesma, S.: Blood vessel segmentation in retinal fundus images using gabor filters, fractional derivatives, and expectation maximization. Appl. Math. Comput. **339**, 568–587 (2018)

16. Farokhian, F., Yang, C., Demirel, H., Wu, S., Beheshti, I.: Automatic parameters selection of Gabor filters with the imperialism competitive algorithm with application to retinal vessel segmentation. Biocybernetics Biomed. Eng. **37**, 246–254 (2017)
17. Singh, K., Kapoor, R.: Image enhancement using exposure based sub image histogram equalization. Pattern Recogn. Lett. **36**, 10–14 (2014)
18. Yadav, S., Kumar, S., Kumar, B., Gupta, R.: Comparative analysis of fundus image enhancement in detection of diabetic retinopathy. In: 2016 IEEE Region 10 Humanitarian Technology Conference (R10-HTC) (2016)
19. Câmara Neto, L., Ramalho, G., Rocha Neto, J., Veras, R., Medeiros, F.: An unsupervised coarse-to-fine algorithm for blood vessel segmentation in fundus images. Expert Syst. Appl. **78**, 182–192 (2017)
20. Staal, J., Abramoff, M., Niemeijer, M., Viergever, M., van Ginneken, B.: Ridge-based vessel segmentation in color images of the retina. IEEE Trans. Med. Imaging **23**, 501–509 (2004)

An Upper Bound for Sorting R_n with LE

Sai Satwik Kuppili[1], Bhadrachalam Chitturi[1,2(✉)], and T. Srinath[1]

[1] Department of Computer Science and Engineering, Amrita Vishwa Vidyapeetham,
Amritapuri, India
satwik.kuppili@gmail.com, bhadrachalam@am.amrita.edu,
srinathnairt@gmail.com
[2] Department of CS, University of Texas at Dallas, Richardson, Texas, USA

Abstract. A permutation on a given alphabet $\Sigma = (1, 2, 3, \ldots, n)$ is a
sequence of elements in the alphabet where every element occurs precisely
once. S_n denotes the set of all such permutations on a given alphabet.
$I_n \in S_n$ be the Identity permutation where elements are in ascending
order i.e. $(1, 2, 3, \ldots, n)$. $R_n \in S_n$ is the reverse permutation where elements are in descending order, i.e. $R_n = (n, n-1, n-2, \ldots, 2, 1)$. An
operation has been defined in OEIS which consists of exactly two moves:
set-rotate that we call Rotate and pair-exchange that we call Exchange.
Rotate is a left rotate of all elements (moves leftmost element to the
right end) and Exchange is the pair-wise exchange of the two leftmost
elements. We call this operation as LE. The optimum number of moves
for transforming R_n into I_n with LE operation are known for $n \le 10$;
as listed in OEIS with identity A048200. The contributions of this article are: (a) a novel upper bound for the number of moves required to
sort R_n with LE has been derived; (b) the optimum number of moves
to sort the next larger R_n i.e. R_{11} has been computed. Sorting permutations with various operations has applications in genomics and computer
interconnection networks.

Keywords: Permutations · Sorting · Cayley graphs · Upper bound ·
Set-rotate · Pair-exchange

1 Introduction

Sorting a permutation can be either in an increasing or a decreasing order. In
this article, increasing order is employed. The alphabet for the permutations is
$\Sigma = (1, 2, 3, \ldots, n)$. LE operation consists of two generators: (i) *Rotate* that
cyclically left shifts the entire permutation and (ii) *Exchange* that swaps the
elements at the two left most positions. The application of (i) and (ii) yields
the corresponding *moves* L and E respectively. 1-based indexing is employed,
thus, the two leftmost indices are one and two. S_n is the set of all permutations
over Σ. R_n is the reverse permutation of Σ, i.e. $R_n = (n, n-1, \ldots, 3, 2, 1)$. The
identity permutation $I_n = (1, 2, 3, \ldots, n-1, n)$. The problem of transforming R_n
into I_n (i.e. sorting R_n) with LE operation is of theoretical interest and has been

© Springer Nature Singapore Pte Ltd. 2019
M. Singh et al. (Eds.): ICACDS 2019, CCIS 1046, pp. 240–249, 2019.
https://doi.org/10.1007/978-981-13-9942-8_23

studied. The problem appears in OEIS [1] as follows "A048200 Minimal length pair-exchange/set-rotate sequence to reverse n distinct ordered elements".

The optimum number of moves to sort R_n with LE appears with a sequence number of A048200, OEIS [1] where the values are known only for $n \leq 11$ [1] ($n = 11$ is our contribution). We establish the first upper bound on the number of moves required to sort R_n with LE.

A Cayley graph Γ corresponding to an operation O with a generator set G consists of $n!$ vertices each corresponding to a unique permutation that denotes it. An edge from a vertex u to another vertex v indicates that when a generator $g \in G$ acts upon permutation u yields v. Applying a generator is commonly known as making a *move*. An upper bound k to sort any $\pi \in S_n$ indicates that the distance between any two permutations in Γ is at most k. An exact upper bound equals the diameter of Γ [3]. Cayley graphs are shown to posses various desirable properties in the design of computer interconnection networks [3,8]. Various operations to sort permutations have been posed [8]. A permutation models a genome where a gene is presumed to be unique and an operation like transposition, reversal etc. models the corresponding mutation. Thus, transforming permutations with various operations has applications in genomic studies.

Jerrum showed that when the number of generators is greater than one, the minimum sequence of generators (also called as distance) to sort a permutation is hard to compute [2]. LE operation has two generators and the complexity of transforming one permutation in to another with LE operation is not known. Exchange move is a reversal of length two, in fact it is a prefix reversal of length two. Chen and Skiena studied sorting permutations of length n with reversals of size p [5]. For both permutations and circular permutations for all n and p, they characterized the number of equivalence classes of permutations. For sorting all circular permutations of length n that can be sorted by reversals of length p an upper bound of $O(n^2/p + pn)$ and a lower bound of $\Omega(n^2/p^2 + n)$ were shown. For sorting permutations with (unrestricted) prefix reversals the operation that has $n - 1$ generators, the best known upper bound is $18n/11 + O(1)$ [4]. In *LE* operation, Rotate cyclically shifts the entire permutation whereas in [6] a modified bubblesort is considered, where, in addition to the regular moves, a swap is allowed between elements at positions 1 and n. Given an operation O, all the moves of O constitute its generator set. Jerrum showed that when the number of generators is greater than one, the minimum sequence of generators to sort a permutation is hard to compute [2]. LE operation has two generators and the complexity of transforming one permutation into another with LE operation is not known. We call O symmetric if for any move of O its *inverse* also belongs to O. Exchange is inverse of itself whereas Rotate does not have an inverse. Thus, LE is not symmetric. Further, LE is very restrictive due to the presence of Rotate move compared to the other operations that are frequently applied in genetic studies e.g. [7]. The methodology of this article might be helpful for problems whose generator set does not have a Rotate generator. Research in the area of Cayley graphs pertaining to their efficacy in modelling a computer interconnection network, their properties in terms of diameter, presence of greedy cycles in them etc. has been active [11–15].

Two permutations are *equivalent* if one can be transformed into another by applying a finite number of Rotate moves. In order to show that LE operation generates the entire symmetric group S_n, we need only show that any two elements can be swapped.

Transformation of strings also has been extensively studied [16,17]. Several string transformation problems including the burnt pancake distance problem are shown to be NP-hard [17]. An operation called as short reversal on strings has been defined [7] that has exactly two types of generators. The computation of short reversal distance has been reduced to the computation of a Maximum Independent Set on the corresponding graph that is computed from the two given input strings [9] an efficient algorithm for it has been designed in [10].

Observation 1. *Any two elements can be swapped with LE operation.*

Proof. Consider two arbitrary elements a and b in a permutation π. WLOG assume that a is to the left of b. So $\pi = (\ldots, u, a, v, \ldots, x, b, y, \ldots)$. First we perform a sequence of Rotate moves to yield $(a, v, \ldots, x, b, y, \ldots, u)$. Here we perform a sequence of (Exchange followed by Rotate) to yield $(a, b, y, \ldots, u, v, \ldots, x,)$. After Rotate, Exchange, Rotate this yields $(b, \ldots, u, v, \ldots, x, a, y)$ where a is between x, y. We follow the same procedure to place b between u and v. Then we will get a permutation that is equivalent to the permutation in which a and b are swapped. Rotate moves accomplish the rest of the task.

Let π be the one based index array containing the input permutation. The element at an index i of π is denoted by $\pi[i]$. Initially for all i, $\pi[i] = R_n[i]$. A *block* is a sublist (continuous elements of a permutation) that is sorted. Let EL denote Exchange move followed by a Rotate move. Further, let $(EL)^p$ be p consecutive executions of EL. Let L^p be p consecutive executions of L. We define a permutation $P_{r,n} \in S_n$ as follows. The elements $1, 2, 3, \ldots, r$ are in sorted order. However, $(n, n-1, \ldots, r+1)$ that we call $U(P_{r,n})$ is inserted in between. Thus, $(1, 2, 3, \ldots, r)$ is split into two blocks with $U(P_{r,n})$ in between. Further, the starting position of $U(P_{r,n})$ in $P_{r,n}$ is $x + 2$ where $r = 2^k - x$ and $2^{k-1} < r \leq 2^k$. Let $M(n)$ be the number of moves required to sort R_n with LE. Let $f(x)$ denote the number of additional moves required to sort R_n with LE when compared to R_{n-1}. Therefore, number of moves required to sort R_n with LE is sum of all $f(x)$ where x ranges from 1 to n.

2   Algorithm

The algorithm that we design is called Algorithm LE. The algorithm first transforms R_n into $P_{3,n}$ by executing $n-2$ L moves and an E move. Subsequently, $P_{i+1,n}$ is obtained from $P_{i,n}$ by executing the moves specified by Lemma 2. Thus, eventually we obtain $P_{n,n}$ which is I_n. Pseudo Code for the Algorithm LE is shown below.

Algorithm LE
Input: R_n. Output: I_n. Initialization: $\forall i \pi[i] = R_n[i]$. All moves are executed on π.

Algorithm 1 Algorithm LE

---

for $r \in (2, \ldots, n-1)$ **do**
   if r=2 **then**
      Execute L^{n-2}
      Execute E move
   else
      if $r = 2^k$ for some k **then**
         Execute $(EL)^{n-r}$
      else
         $x \leftarrow (\min_k \text{ s.t. } 2^k \geq r)$
         Execute L^{x-r}
         Execute $(EL)^{n-r-1}$
         Execute L move
         Execute $(EL)^{2r-x-1}$
         Execute L move
      end if
   end if
end for

Lemma 1. *The starting position of $U(P_{r,n})$ in $P_{r,n}$ is $x + 2$ where $r = 2^k - x$ and $2^{k-1} < r \leq 2^k$.*

Proof. Executing $n-2$ L moves and an E moves on R_n yields $(1, 2, n, n-1, \ldots, 3)$ which is $P_{3,n}$. Since, $3 = 2^2 - 1$, $x = 1$. Thus, $x + 2 = 1 + 2 = 3$. If we observe the starting position of $U(P_{3,n})$ in $P_{3,n}$ is $x + 2 = 3$. Hence, lemma is true for $r = 3$. Assume, that lemma is true for $r = 2^k - x$. So, $P_{r,n}$ is $(1, 2, \ldots, x + 1, n, n-1, \ldots, r+1, x+2, x+3, \ldots, r)$ where starting position of $U(P_{r,n})$ in $P_{r,n}$ is $x+2$ where $r = 2^k - x$ and $2^{k-1} < r \leq 2^k$. Executing L^x yields $(x+1, n, n-1, \ldots, r+1, x+2, x+3, \ldots, r, 1, 2, \ldots, x)$. Then executing $(EL)^{n-r-1}$ yields $(x+1, r+1, x+2, x+3, \ldots, r, 1, 2, \ldots, x, n, n-1, \ldots, r+2)$. Then executing R yields $(r+1, x+2, \ldots, r, 1, 2, \ldots, x, n, n-1, \ldots, r+2, x+1)$. Then executing $(EL)^{r-x-1}$ yields $(r+1, 1, 2, \ldots, x, n, n-1, \ldots, r+2, x+1, x+2, \ldots, r)$. Then executing L yields $(1, 2, \ldots, x, n, n-1, \ldots, r+2, x+1, x+2, \ldots, r, r+1)$ which is $P_{r+1,n}$. Since $r = 2^k - x$, $r+1 = 2^k - (x-1)$. Therefore, the starting position of $U(P_{r+1,n})$ in $P_{r+1,n}$ should be $(x-1)+2 = x+1$. In $P_{r+1,n}$ the starting position of $U(P_{r+1,n})$ is in fact $x + 1$. Hence by mathematical induction Lemma 1 holds for all values of r.

Lemma 2. *The number of moves required to obtain $P_{r+1,n}$ from $P_{r,n}$ is (a) $2n - 2r$ if r= 2^k for some k. (b) $r - 2^k + 2n - 2$ otherwise.*

Proof. Case (a): $r = 2^k$ for some k.
According to Lemma 1 the starting position of $U(P_{r,n})$ in $P_{r,n}$ is 2. Therefore, $P_{r,n}$ is $(1, n, n-1, \ldots, r+1, 2, 3, \ldots, r)$. Executing $(EL)^{n-r}$ yields $P_{r+1,n}$. Therefore, number of moves to obtain $P_{r+1,n}$ from $P_{r,n}$ when r is in the form of 2^k is $2 * (n - r) = 2n - 2r$.

Case (b): $2^{k-1} < r < 2^k$.

Let us suppose $r = 2^k - x$ where $2^{k-1} < r < 2^k$. According to Lemma 1 the starting position of $U(P_{r,n})$ in $P_{r,n}$ is $x+2$. Therefore, $P_{r,n}$ is $(1, 2, \ldots, x+1, n, n-1, \ldots, r+1, x+2, x+3, \ldots, r)$. Executing L^{2^k-r} i.e. L^x yields $(x+1, n, n-1, \ldots, r+1, x+2, x+3, \ldots, r, 1, 2, \ldots, x)$. Then executing $(EL)^{n-r-1}$ yields $(x+1, r+1, x+2, \ldots, r, 1, 2, \ldots, x, n, n-1, \ldots, r+2)$. Then executing R yields $(r+1, x+2, \ldots, r, 1, 2, \ldots, x, n, n-1, \ldots, r+2, x+1)$. Then executing $(EL)^{2r-2^k-1}$ i.e. $(EL)^{r-x-1}$ yields $(r+1, 1, 2, \ldots, x, n, n-1, \ldots, r+2, x+1, x+2, \ldots, r)$. Then executing L yields $P_{r+1,n}$. Therefore, number of moves to obtain $P_{r+1,n}$ from $P_{r,n}$ when r is not in the form of 2^k is $2^k-r+(2*(n-r-1))+1+(2*(2r-2^k-1))+1 = r - 2^k + 2n - 2$.

3   Analysis

Lemma 3. *The number of moves required to obtain $P_{3,n}$ from R_n is 1 more than the number of moves required to obtain $P_{3,n-1}$ from R_{n-1}.*

Proof. $P_{3,n}$ is obtained from R_n by executing $n - 2$ L moves and an E move, i.e. a total of $n - 1$ moves. $P_{3,n-1}$ is obtained from R_{n-1} by executing $n - 3$ L moves and an E move, in a total of $n - 2$ moves. Therefore, the number of moves required to obtain $P_{3,n}$ from R_n is 1 more than the number of moves required to obtain $P_{3,n-1}$ from R_{n-1}.

Lemma 4. *The number of moves required to obtain $P_{r+1,n}$ from $P_{r,n}$ is 2 more than the number of moves required to obtain $P_{r+1,n-1}$ from $P_{r,n-1}$ $\forall r \in (3, \ldots, n - 2)$.*

Proof. (a) According to Lemma 2, if $r = 2^k$ for some k, the number of moves required to obtain $P_{r+1,n}$ from $P_{r,n}$ is $2n - 2r$ where as the number of moves required to obtain $P_{r+1,n-1}$ from $P_{r,n-1}$ is $2(n-1) - 2r = 2n - 2r - 2$. Therefore, the number of moves required to obtain $P_{r+1,n}$ from $P_{r,n}$ is 2 more than number of moves required to obtain $P_{r+1,n-1}$ from $P_{r,n-1}$.

(b) According to Lemma 2, if $2^{k-1} < r < 2^k$ for some k, the number of moves required to obtain $P_{r+1,n}$ from $P_{r,n}$ is $r-2^k+2n-2$ where as the number of moves required to obtain $P_{r+1,n-1}$ from $P_{r,n-1}$ is $r-2^k+2(n-1)-2 = r-2^k+2(n)-4$. Therefore, the number of moves required to obtain $P_{r+1,n}$ from $P_{r,n}$ is 2 more than number of moves required to obtain $P_{r+1,n-1}$ from $P_{r,n-1}$.

From (a) and (b) it follows that Lemma 4 holds for all $r \in (3, 4, \ldots, n - 2)$.

Lemma 5. *If $x = 2^k + 1$ for some k then $f(x) = 2x - 5$.*

Proof. Sorting of R_{x-1} involves $(P_{3,x-1}, P_{4,x-1}, \ldots, P_{x-1,x-1})$ as intermediate permutations. According to Lemma 3, the number of moves required to obtain $P_{3,x}$ from R_x is 1 more than the number of moves required to obtain $P_{3,x-1}$ from R_{x-1}. According to Lemma 4, the number of moves required to obtain $P_{r+1,x}$ from $P_{r,x}$ is 2 more than number of moves require to obtain $P_{r+1,x-1}$ from $P_{r,x-1}$

$\forall r \in (3, 4, \ldots, x - 2)$. Since, $x = 2^k + 1, x - 1 = 2^k$. According to Lemma 2 the number of steps required to obtain $P_{x,x}$ i.e. I_x from $P_{x-1,x}$ is $2x - 2(x - 1) = 2$. Therefore, number of additional moves required for sorting R_x when compared to R_{x-1} when $x = 2^k + 1$ for some k is $f(x) = 1 + 2(x - 4) + 2 = 2x - 5$.

Lemma 6. *If $x = 2^k + 2$ for some k, $f(x) = 3x - 6$.*

Proof. Sorting of R_{x-1} involves $(P_{3,x-1}, P_{4,x-1}, \ldots, P_{x-1,x-1})$ as intermediate permutations. According to Lemma 3, the number of moves required to obtain $P_{3,x}$ from R_x is 1 more than the number of moves required to obtain $P_{3,x-1}$ from R_{x-1}. According to Lemma 4, the number of moves required to obtain $P_{r+1,x}$ from $P_{r,x}$ is 2 more than number of moves require to obtain $P_{r+1,x-1}$ from $P_{r,x-1}$ $\forall r \in (3, 4, \ldots, x - 2)$. Since, $x = 2^k + 2, x - 1 = 2^k + 1 = 2^{k+1} - (2^k - 1) = 2^{k+1} - (x - 3)$. According to Lemma 2, the number of steps required to obtain $P_{x,x}$ i.e. I_x from $P_{x-1,x}$ is $(x - 1) - 2^{k+1} + 2x - 2 = (x - 1) - 2x + 4 + 2x - 2 = x + 1$. Therefore, number of additional moves required for sorting R_x when compared to R_{x-1} when $x = 2^k + 2$ for some k is $f(x) = 1 + 2(x - 4) + (x + 1) = 3x - 6$.

Lemma 7. *If x not in the form $2^k + 1$ or $2^k + 2$ then $f(x) = f(x - 1) + 5$.*

Proof. Recall, $f(x)$ gives us number of additional moves required to sort R_x with LE when compared to R_{x-1}. From Lemmas 3 and 4, we can say that difference between number of moves required to obtain $P_{x-2,x-1}$ from R_{x-1} and the number of moves required to obtain $P_{x-2,x-2}$ i.e. I_{x-2} from R_{x-2} is same as the difference between number of moves required to obtain $P_{x-2,x}$ from R_x and the number of moves required to obtain $P_{x-2,x-1}$ from R_{x-1}
(a) According to Lemma 4, the number of moves required to obtain $P_{x-1,x}$ from $P_{x-2,x}$ is 2 more than number of moves require to obtain I_{x-1} from $P_{x-2,x-1}$.
(b) Let z be the number of moves require to obtain I_{x-1} from $P_{x-2,x-1}$. Since $x - 1$ cannot be of the form 2^k for some k, according to Lemma 2 $z = (x - 2) - 2^k + 2(x - 1) - 2 = x - 2^k + 2x - 6$. Similarly, the number of moves require to obtain I_x from $P_{x-1,x}$ is $(x - 1) - 2^k + 2(x) - 2 = x - 2^k + 2x - 3 = z + 3$. The number of moves require to obtain I_x from $P_{x-1,x}$ is 3 more than the number of moves require to obtain I_{x-1} from $P_{x-2,x-1}$.
Therefore, from (a) and (b), $f(x) = f(x - 1) + 2 + 3 = f(x - 1) + 5$.

Theorem 1. *An upper bound for number of moves required to sort R_n with LE is $\frac{11}{6}n^2$.*

Proof. According to Lemma 5, the value of $f(x)$ when $x = 2^k + 1$ for some k is $2x - 5$.

Therefore, for some k,

$f(2^k + 1) = (2 * (2^k + 1)) - 5 = 2^{k+1} - 3$

According to Lemma 6, the value of $f(x)$ when $x = 2^k + 2$ for some k is $3x - 6$.

$f(2^k + 2) = (3 * (2^k + 2)) - 6 = 3 * 2^k$

According to the Lemma 7,

$$f(2^k + 3) = f(2^k + 3) + 5$$
$$f(2^k + 3) = (3 * (2^k)) + 5$$
$$\text{Similarly, } f(2^k + 4) = (3 * (2^k)) + 5 + 5$$
$$f(2^k + 5) = (3 * (2^k)) + 5 + 5 + 5$$

$$\vdots$$

$$f(2^k + 2^k) = (3 * (2^k)) + (5 + 5 + \ldots + (2^k - 2)times)$$

$$\text{Let } A(k) = f(2^k + 3) + f(2^k + 4) + \ldots + f(2^k + 2^k)$$
$$= (3 * 2^k * (2^k - 2)) + (5 + 10 + 15 + \ldots + (2^k - 2)terms)$$
$$= (3 * 2^k * (2^k - 2)) + \frac{1}{2}(5 * (2^k - 2) * (2^k - 1))$$
$$= \frac{11}{2}2^{2k} - \frac{27}{2}2^k + 5$$

$$\text{Let } B(k) = f(2^k + 1) + f(2^k + 2) + A(k)$$
$$= f(2^k + 1) + f(2^k + 2) + f(2^k + 3) + \ldots + f(2^k + 2^k)$$

From Lemmas 5 and 6,

$$B(k) = 2^{k+1} - 3 + (3 * 2^k) + \frac{11}{2}2^{2k} - \frac{27}{2}2^k + 5$$
$$= \frac{11}{2}2^{2k} - \frac{17}{2}2^k + 2$$
$$B(\log_2(\left\lceil \frac{n}{2} \right\rceil)) = f(\left\lceil \frac{n}{2} \right\rceil + 1) + f(\left\lceil \frac{n}{2} \right\rceil + 2) + \ldots + f(\left\lceil \frac{n}{2} \right\rceil + \left\lceil \frac{n}{2} \right\rceil)$$

Therefore, for $M(n)$ the total number of moves to sort R_n we obtain the following recurrence relation.

$$M(n) \leq M(\left\lceil \frac{n}{2} \right\rceil) + B(log_2(\left\lceil \frac{n}{2} \right\rceil))$$

$$= \sum_{k=1}^{\log_2 n} B(\log_2(\left\lceil \frac{n}{2^k} \right\rceil))$$

$$= \sum_{k=1}^{\log_2 n} \frac{11}{2} 2^{2\log_2(\left\lceil \frac{n}{2^k} \right\rceil)} - \frac{17}{2} 2^{\log_2(\left\lceil \frac{n}{2^k} \right\rceil)} + 2$$

(Ignoring the lower order terms)

$$\leq \sum_{k=1}^{\log_2 n} \frac{11}{2} * 2^{2\log_2(\left\lceil \frac{n}{2^k} \right\rceil)}$$

$$\leq \sum_{k=1}^{\log_2 n} \frac{11}{2} * 2^{2\log_2(\frac{n}{2^k}+1)}$$

$$= \sum_{k=1}^{\log_2 n} \frac{11}{2} * (\frac{n}{2^k} + 1)^2$$

(Ignoring the lower order terms)

$$\approx \sum_{k=1}^{\log_2 n} \frac{11}{2} * (\frac{n^2}{2^{2k}})$$

$$\leq \sum_{k=1}^{\infty} \frac{11}{2} * (\frac{n^2}{2^{2k}})$$

$$= \frac{11}{2} * \frac{n^2}{3}$$

$$= \frac{11}{6} * n^2$$

Therefore, an upper bound for number of moves required for R_n with LE is $\frac{11n^2}{6}$.

4   Exhaustive Search Results

An exhaustive search algorithm based on BFS, i.e. *Algorithm Search*, has been implemented to identify the optimum number of moves to sort R_n for a given n. It yielded a novel value i.e. 67 for $n = 11$. The known values for $n = 1 \ldots 11$ are $(0, 1, 2, 4, 10, 15, 23, 32, 42, 55, 67)$. We maintain a list of already visited permutations and we terminate upon reaching I_n. Each intermediate permutation is acted upon by the moves E and R yielding the corresponding permutations. BFS gives us the minimum number of moves to reach I_n from R_n. We avoid two consecutive E move (that nullify each other). Notation: *Node* contains a permutation $\in S_n$ and its distance from R_n corresponds to the optimal moves. Employing this algorithm, with a better processor and larger RAM one should be able to obtain optimum number of moves for higher values of n.

Algorithm Search
Initialization: The source vertex δ contains the permutation R_n and its path is initialized to null. It is enqueued into BFS queue Q.
Input: R_n. Output: Optimum number of moves to reach I_n.

Algorithm 2 Algorithm Search

---
  while (Q is not empty) **do**
    Dequeue u from Q
    if (u is visited) **then**
      continue
    end if
    Mark u as visited
    if (u is I_n) **then**   ▷ Array is sorted
      return length of $u.path$
      break
    end if
    if (Last move on $u.path \neq E$ or $u.path =$ null) **then**
      Execute E on $u \rightarrow v$
      if v is not visited **then**
        $v.path \leftarrow u.path$ followed by E
        Enqueue v to Q
      end if
    end if
    Execute R on $u \rightarrow v$
    if v is not visited **then**
      $v.path \leftarrow u.path$ followed by R
      Enqueue v to Q
    end if
  end while

---

5   Conclusions and Future Work

The first known upper bound for sorting R_n with LE operation is shown. The future work consists of identifying a tighter upper bound and obtaining optimum number of moves for sorting R_n for larger values of n. An upper bound for sorting any permutation in S_n with LE operation is open. Let I_n^* be the set of all permutations that are equivalent to I_n. An upper bound for transforming R_n into a $\pi \in I_n^*$ with LE operation is open where any convenient π can be chosen.

References

1. The On-Line Encyclopedia of Integer Sequences. oeis.org
2. Jerrum, M.R.: The complexity of finding minimum-length generator sequences. Theor. Comput. Sci. **36**, 265–289 (1985)
3. Akers, S.B., Krishnamurthy, B.: A group-theoretic model for symmetric interconnection networks. IEEE Trans. Comput. **38**(4), 555–566 (1989)
4. Chitturi, B., Fahle, W., Meng, Z., Morales, L., Shields, C.O., Sudborough, H.: An (18/11)n upper bound for sorting by prefix reversals. Theor. Comput. Sci. **410**(36), 3372–3390 (2009)
5. Chen, T., Skiena, S.S.: Sorting with fixed-length reversals. Discrete Appl. Math. **71**(1–3), 269–295 (1996)
6. Feng, X., Chitturi, B., Sudborough, H.: Sorting circular permutations by bounded transpositions. In: Arabnia, H. (ed.) Advances in Computational Biology. AEMB, vol. 680, pp. 725–736. Springer, New York (2010). https://doi.org/10.1007/978-1-4419-5913-3_81
7. Chitturi, B., Sudborough, H., Voit, W., Feng, X.: Adjacent swaps on strings. In: Hu, X., Wang, J. (eds.) COCOON 2008. LNCS, vol. 5092, pp. 299–308. Springer, Heidelberg (2008). https://doi.org/10.1007/978-3-540-69733-6_30
8. Lakshmivarahan, S., Jho, J.-S., Dhall, S.K.: Symmetry in interconnection networks based on Cayley graphs of permutation groups: a survey. Parallel Comput. **19**, 361–407 (1993)
9. Chitturi, B.: Perturbed layered graphs. In: ICACCP (2019)
10. Chitturi, B., Balachander, S., Satheesh, S., Puthiyoppil, K.: Layered graphs: applications and algorithms. Algorithms **11**(7), 93 (2018)
11. Mokhtar, H.: A few families of Cayley graphs and their efficiency as communication networks. Bull. Aust. Math. Soc. **95**(3), 518–520 (2017)
12. Zhang, T., Gennian, G.: Improved lower bounds on the degree-diameter problem. J. Algebr. Comb. **49**, 135–146 (2018)
13. Chitturi, B., Das, P.: Sorting permutations with transpositions in $O(n^3)$ amortized time. Theor. Comput. Sci. **766**, 30–37 (2018)
14. Erskine, G., James, T.: Large Cayley graphs of small diameter. Discrete Appl. Math. **250**, 202–214 (2018)
15. Gostevsky, D.A., Konstantinova, E.V.: Greedy cycles in the star graphs. Discrete Math. Math. Cybern. **15**, 205–213 (2018)
16. Fertin, G., Labarre, A., Rusu, I., Vialette, S., Tannier, E.: Combinatorics of Genome Rearrangements. MIT Press, Cambridge (2009)
17. Chitturi, B.: A note on complexity of genetic mutations. Discrete Math. Algorithms Appl. **3**(03), 269–286 (2011)

Image Filtering with Iterative Wavelet Transform Based Compression

Vikas Mahor[(⊠)], Srishti Agrawal, and Rekha Gupta

Department of Electronics, MITS, Gwalior, India
vikas@mitsgwalior.in, agrawal.srishti9@gmail.com,
rekah652003@yahoo.com

Abstract. This paper attempts to propose a methodology to reduce the size of high definition colored images taken by the professional photographers. In this digital era as technology is advancing so fast, high definition photos are captured. But these pictures take a lot of memory space. Therefore data and image compression techniques are in great requirement. The major goal is to find computationally efficient algorithm to significantly reduce the storage size with capability to retrieve the quality of image. The proposed work effectively uses Discrete Wavelet Transform (DWT) and only low frequency part of the image is transmitted, after that further iterations are performed to increase the compression ratio. Numbers of iterations are decided by making a trade-off between compression ratio (CR) and Peak Signal to Noise Ratio (PSNR) value. Arithmetic coding is applied for further compressing the image. To improve the image quality (PSNR) further at higher iteration, filters has been applied. Switching weighted median filter and simple median filter has been studied. Analysis on different window size of median filter has also been done to achieve improved PSNR value.

Keywords: Peak Signal to Noise Ratio (PSNR) · Arithmetic coding ·
Discrete Wavelet Transform (DWT) · HAAR transform ·
Compression ratio (CR) · Median filter ·
Switching weighted median filter (SWMF)

1 Introduction

This instruction file for Word users (there is a separate instruction file for LaTeX users) may be used as a template. Kindly send the final and checked Word and PDF files of your paper to the Contact Volume Editor. This is usually one of the organizers of the conference. You should make sure that the Word and the PDF files are identical and correct and that only one version of your paper is sent. It is not possible to update files at a later stage. Please note that we do not need the printed paper.

1.1 Checking the PDF File

The researches that are done in the compression techniques have originated from the ever increasing demand for efficient transmission of data and reduced storage space. As the profession of photography is increased a lot and using DSLR and CSC cameras

© Springer Nature Singapore Pte Ltd. 2019
M. Singh et al. (Eds.): ICACDS 2019, CCIS 1046, pp. 250–262, 2019.
https://doi.org/10.1007/978-981-13-9942-8_24

take high resolution pictures. If the image is uncompressed then it will require considerable storage space and more transmission bandwidth hence the cost of storage and transmission increases. Even though there is advancement in technology, increased processor speed and digital communication system performance there is always a huge demand for less data storage space and transmission bandwidth.

Image compression is certainly different than raw binary data compression. If image is compressed by using general software the result will be less absolute. The reason is that an image have certain type of statistical properties and that can decoded only by specifically designed encoders. In Lossless image compression the image when reconstructed will be the exact replica of the original image. This type of compression is needed mostly in text data compression and medical imaging. In contrast to this in most applications there is no need to get the exact image, an approximate image will be enough. This compression is called as lossy compression [1].

In an image most of the neighboring pixels are correlated and that is why they have contain the redundant information. In compression the task is to remove these redundant pixels, as long as the quality of compressed image is acceptable. In image compression there are two types of reductions - redundancy reduction & irrelevancy reduction. In the former, the output image is produced by removing duplicate information from the image while in the irrelevancy only that part is omitted which cannot be perceived by the Human Visual System (HVS) [5]. The HSV has some tolerance to prevent distortion that also depends on the content of the image and its viewing condition.

In recent decades many compression techniques have been proposed. The current standard for still image compression (e.g., JPEG) use Discrete Cosine Transform (DCT) [5]. It compacts the energy at the top left corner of transformed image. At the top-left corner of the image low frequency coefficients are present because there is peak energy in this region and the value of coefficient decreases rapidly to the bottom right corner in the matrix, these coefficients contains the high frequency [2].

Recently discrete wavelet transform (DWT) is highly used in image compression. The JPEG-2000 compression came due to the research in wavelet. In comparison from the DCT, wavelet transform coefficients are localized in both frequency and time domains and hence gives the additional property of temporal resolution [4]. In addition to this wavelet transform possess the orientation property. Because of these attractive features wavelet transform provides better compression ratio than DCT compression technique [10].

This paper proposes a compression technique for high resolution colored images. Different types of sensitive images are taken to better analyze the result. DWT is applied on the image and its low frequency part is used for further compression. Haar is used as a mother wavelet. Multiple iterations are done by managing good CR and PSNR value. Lossless Arithmetic coding also called variable length coding is used as it gives better CR than Huffman coding. Filtering operation is performed to increase the PSNR of the reconstructed image. The aim is to seek higher compression with acceptable image quality.

1.2 Discrete Wavelet Transform (DWT)

The DWT uses the features of time & frequency correlation of the image data by contractions & translations of the mother wavelet that is used at the input [14]. It provides multi-resolution analysis that includes progressive transmission & zooming the image without any requirement for more storage, it is also applicable on different scales [3]. It has another useful feature called as symmetric nature which means that the complexity will be same in the forward and inverse transforms, which helps in fast compression & fast decompression process. It has most suited characteristics in the image compression including the HVS's characteristics, greater compaction of energy, robust transmission and provides higher compression ratio [5].

The different properties of wavelet functions in image compression are compact support which helps in efficient implementation, symmetry which is useful for avoiding dephasing, orthogonality which allows splitting without duplicating information, regularity, and the degree of smoothness which is related to the filter order or length [10].

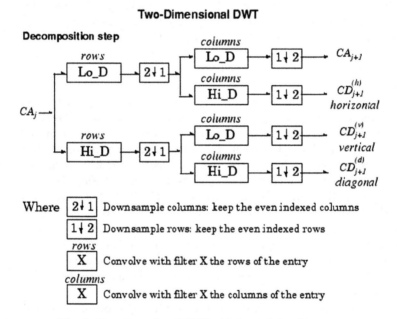

Fig. 1. Two dimensional DWT with four sub band images.

In this research Haar transform is used because of its properties. Haar transformation is real and orthogonal due to which it divides the image in rows and columns each having low and high frequency sub bands and they are orthogonal to each other. DWT decomposes the image by using filter banks [11]. Digital images are actually a matrix which consists of rows and columns (Fig. 1) shows that at each decomposition in DWT, level filtering is done in two stages. The stage 1 contains Low Pass Filter and High Pass Filter which is applied on rows, while the stage 2 contains the same configuration but it is applied on the columns. Result will be four different sub bands of the image which are LL, HL, LH and HH (Fig. 2). The LL is called the approximate sub band and has low frequency and contains most of the image information while rest three sub bands LH, HL and HH are called as vertical, horizontal and diagonal components of the image. They have high frequency and the details in these three sub bands are so small that they are set to be zero [3]. In this research only LL sub band is taken for further work.

If input image size is M * N, then the size of sub bands (LL, HL, LH, HH) is M/2 * N/2. In case of two-level decomposition, the output size is M/4 * N/4 [3].

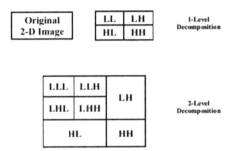

Fig. 2. Two dimensional DWT with four sub band images.

1.3 Arithmetic Coding

One of the type of lossless coding is arithmetic coding it is also called as variable length coding. This type of coding is useful especially when the sources contains small alphabets, like binary sources, and alphabets with high probabilities. It is proved that this approach is useful when for the various reasons in the lossless compression, the modeling & the coding aspects are kept to be separate [9]. The base of arithmetic coding is probability value. It takes the input as a stream of data and after that probability of the symbol is calculated. The input is a real number between 0 and 1. Context formation includes decision & context generation, then it is encoded in arithmetic encoder. Arithmetic encoder is based on recursively probability distribution. The output when it is decoded reproduces the exact original data stream. The range is limited to low and high value. If probability value is 1 then it is taken as more possible symbol (MPS) else it is taken as least possible symbol (LPS). Basic function of an arithmetic encoder is to return value of MPS and LPS in accordance with the decision taken out from the formation of the context. The intervals of MPS and LPS dynamically changes [6].

2 Median Filter

One of the type of non-linear filter is median filter. They are mostly used for removing salt and pepper noise. Median filter is gives best results when the aim is to simultaneously reduce noise & preserve edges. This filter behaves like low pass filter which blocks all high frequency component of the images like noise and edges, thus blurs the image. The window size of median filter (i.e., m × n) is always odd [15]. Sliding Window size of the median filter is decided according to the noise density in the image. If the noise density is low and large window is taken then it will destroy the fine image details due to its rank ordering process [7].

For the filtering of high density corrupted image need large window size so that the sufficient number of noise free pixels will present in the window. A center pixel either it is corrupted or not by the impulse noise it is replaced by the median value. Due to this reason this filter blurs the image. The window size 3 × 3, 5 × 5, 7 × 7, and 9 × 9 median filter are mainly applicable. Output of the median filter is given by:

$$y(i,j) = median\{x(i - s, j - t), x(i,j)/(s,t) \in W, (s,t) \neq (0,0)\} \qquad (1)$$

where {x} is the noisy image and y(i, j) is the recovered image with preserve edges.

3 Switching Weighted Median Filter (SWMF)

Switching weighted median filter [8] makes use of predefined threshold value for the detection of the noisy pixel. If the difference between the center pixel and median value of the neighboring pixels in the window is more than the predefined threshold then that center pixel is called as a noisy pixel and it is replaced by median value of the neighboring pixels, otherwise center pixel is considered as noise free and it will not change [9]. Difference in between the center pixel and median value is given by:

$$\Delta x = |x(i,j) - x\_med| \qquad (2)$$

where median value in the window x_med is given by

$$x\_med = \{x(i - N, j - N), \ldots, w\_c * x(i,j), \ldots, x(i - N, j - N)\} \qquad (3)$$

Here w_c is the weight of the center pixels.

Let {X} is the noisy image and (2N + 1) × (2N + 1) is the sliding window size that are centered at (i, j). The adjustment of the center pixel is given by following equation,

$$y(i,j) = \begin{cases} x_{med}, & \Delta x \geq T_i \\ x(i,j), & \Delta x < T_i \end{cases} \qquad (4)$$

y(i, j) is the recovered image with preserve edges.

4 Proposed Algorithm

In this, we have considered image compression and filtering on different types of images, all images have the same resolution 1600 * 1600. As shown in the (Fig. 3), first the image is read by MATLAB function, which converts it into matrix form. Then colored image is converted into RGB. After that DWT is applied on the matrix by using DWT function using Haar as the mother wavelet, which provides four different frequency components i.e. LL, HL, LH, HH. The sub band LL is the approximation part which has low frequency and contains most of the detail information of the image and therefore it is used for further work [13]. While the LH, HL, HH are detail sub-band and contains the high frequency components and shows horizontal, vertical and diagonal details in the images. As the information in these sub bands are so small that they are neglected and set to be zero. Then this LL sub band is passed again in DWT for further compression. Four iterations are done to get the desired CR and PSNR (Fig. 4) shows the decomposition. The image resolution after fourth iteration reduced to 200 * 200.

Then LL component after fourth iteration is first converted into array from matrix form and then it is fed to arithmetic encoder. The arithmetic encoder takes input as data stream and then probability of symbol is calculated. The output of arithmetic encoder calculates the probability of data hence further compress the image. The compressed image out of arithmetic encoder is transmitted.

At receiver, the received image is first passed through arithmetic decoder which reproduce the exact data stream. The output of decoder is first converted into matrix again. Then this matrix image is decompressed using Inverse Discrete Wavelet Transform (IDWT) by taking received image as a LL part and rest of the frequency components are taken as zero matrix (or black image). The decompressed image is then passed through Median & Switching weighted median filters.

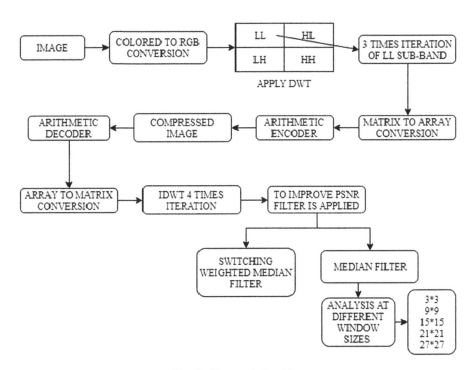

Fig. 3. Proposed algorithm

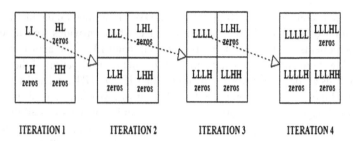

<table>
<tr><td>ITERATION 1</td><td>ITERATION 2</td><td>ITERATION 3</td><td>ITERATION 4</td></tr>
</table>

Fig. 4. Four level decomposition of image after applying Discrete Wavelet Transform

5   Quality Parameters

5.1   Peak Signal to Noise Ratio (PSNR)

It is the ratio of square of the peak value in the image to the mean square error. It shows how well the high intensity regions of the image come through the noise. If $o(i,j)$ is considered as original image and $x(i,j)$ is considered as corrupted image, the PSNR of the corrupted image is given by [4, 5].

$$PSNR = 10 \, \log_{10} \frac{(Imax)^2}{\frac{1}{MN} \sum_{i=1}^{M} \sum_{j=1}^{N} (o(i,j) - x(i,j))^2} \tag{5}$$

Here, M and N is the resolution of image. o is the original image and x is the recovered image. I_{max} is the maximum possible intensity for a pixel, that is 255 in case of unsigned integer 8 bit and 1 in case of double number.

5.2   Compression Ratio (CR)

Compression ratio is also called as compression power. It is actually a terminology used in computer science which is used to quantify reduction in data size after data compression algorithm. CR is analogous to physical compression ratio which is used to calculate physical compression of substances [5, 9].

$$COMPRESSION \ RATIO = \frac{UNCOMPRESSED \ SIZE}{COMPRESSED \ SIZE} \tag{6}$$

When the size of compressed image decreases the CR increases because they are inversely proportional [6].

6 Simulation Results and Discussions

Simulation is performed on four different types of images in MATLAB software, all having resolution 1600 × 1600 in. (Fig. 5) shows the colored images of landscape, hyper pigmented skin and nature object. Compression ratio and PSNR are taken as quality parameters.

For all the colored image database the resolution taken is 1600 × 1600. And after fourth iteration the resolution is reduced to 200 × 200 [12]. For Landscape image Table 1 shows that the as the number of iterations increases from 1 to 4 the CR shows 23 times improvement; as the CR increases the PSNR decreases but the quality of image is acceptable. Upto three iterations the quality of image as acceptable but after fourth iteration in the image the pixels start to show distinctly. The Table 6 shows that the CR from iteration 3 to 4 is huge, so if the quality of image at iteration 4 can be retrieved then we can get more compression with acceptable image quality. For this

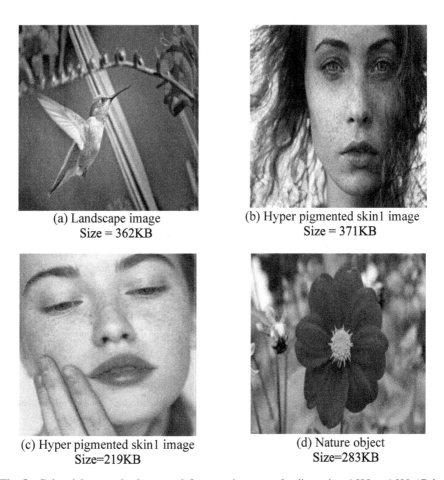

(a) Landscape image
Size = 362KB

(b) Hyper pigmented skin1 image
Size = 371KB

(c) Hyper pigmented skin1 image
Size=219KB

(d) Nature object
Size=283KB

Fig. 5. Colored Images database used for experiment work, dimension 1600 × 1600 (Color figure online)

filters are applied and SWMF and median filter are analyzed. The result shows that the median filter gives 5% improvement after fourth iteration, (Fig. 6(a)) shows the result.

For all the colored image database the resolution taken is 1600 × 1600. And after fourth iteration the resolution is reduced to 200 × 200. For Landscape image Table 1 shows that the as the number of iterations increases from 1 to 4 the CR shows 23 times improvement; as the CR increases the PSNR decreases but the quality of image is acceptable. Upto three iterations the quality of image as acceptable but after fourth iteration in the image the pixels start to show distinctly. The Table 6 shows that the CR from iteration 3 to 4 is huge, so if the quality of image at iteration 4 can be retrieved then we can get more compression with acceptable image quality. For this filters are applied and SWMF and median filter are analyzed. The result shows that the median filter gives 5% improvement after fourth iteration, (Fig. 6(a)) shows the result. But the SWMF does not show much improvement. SWMF gives 1.6% improvement after first iteration. So if the user wants to get less compression then SWMF gives best result on the other hand for more compression Median filter provides good image quality.

The window size of median filter taken for all images is 21 × 21, Table 7 shows that at 21 × 21 window size maximum PSNR is obtained. The landscape image is reduced from 362 KB to 41.4 KB with acceptable image quality or PSNR value.

For hyper pigmented skin1 image Table 2 shows the results, the CR is increased by 23.9 times. The size of the images reduced from 371 KB to 50.2 KB (Fig. 6(b)) shows the result after fourth iteration. The median filter gives 1.7% improvement. One of the added benefit after using median filter is that it removes most of the hyper pigmented pixels from the image after fourth iteration hence it beautifies the image. But it cannot be used for medical purpose. The SWMF at first iteration gives 0.5% improvement.

For hyper pigmented skin2 image Table 3 shows the results, the CR is increased by 22 times. The size of the images reduced from 219 KB to 35.9 KB (Fig. 6(c)) shows the result after fourth iteration. The median filter gives 4% improvement. In this image also median filter beautifies the image after fourth iteration by removing the hyper pigmented pixels. But it cannot be used for medical purpose. The SWMF at first iteration gives 0.5% improvement.

Table 1. CR vs PSNR of 1 and 4 iteration for Landscape image and percentage improvement after applying filter

Iterations	CR	PSNR1 (dB)	PSNR2 (dB) SWMF	% age impv.	PSNR3 (dB) median	% age impv.
1	3.24	42.0872	42.7705	1.6%	31.5562	–
4	74.57	25.2905	25.2933	0.01%	26.6043	5%

Table 2. CR vs PSNR of 1 and 4 iteration for Hyper pigmented skin1 image and percentage improvement after applying filter

Iterations	CR	PSNR1 (dB)	PSNR2 (dB) SWMF	% age impv.	PSNR3 (dB) median	% age impv.
1	3.02	42.4302	42.6600	0.5%	28.9467	–
4	72.43	25.4515	25.4528	0.01%	25.9042	1.7%

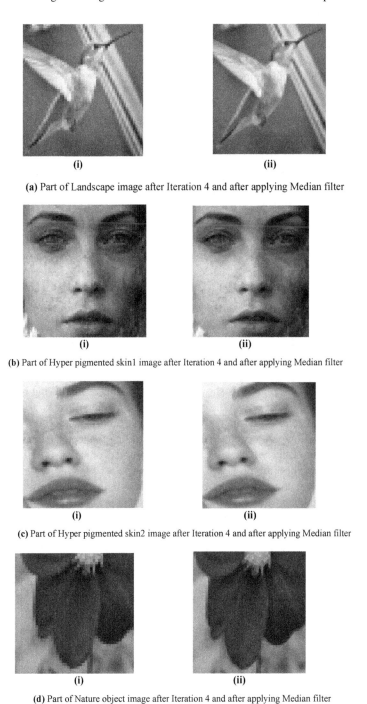

(a) Part of Landscape image after Iteration 4 and after applying Median filter

(b) Part of Hyper pigmented skin1 image after Iteration 4 and after applying Median filter

(c) Part of Hyper pigmented skin2 image after Iteration 4 and after applying Median filter

(d) Part of Nature object image after Iteration 4 and after applying Median filter

Fig. 6. (i) and (ii) shows part of images for highlighting fine details of reconstructed image after 4 iteration and applying median filter on 4 iterated image. (a), (b), (c) and (d) shows Landscape, hyper pigmented skin1, hyper pigmented skin2, nature object images respectively.

For nature object image Table 4 shows the results, the CR is increased by 23 times. The size of the images reduced from 283 KB to 44.2 KB (Fig. 6(d)) shows the result after fourth iteration. The median filter gives 3.6% improvement. The SWMF at first iteration gives 0.8% improvement.

Table 3. CR vs PSNR of 1 and 4 iteration for Hyper pigmented skin2 image and percentage improvement after applying filter

Iterations	CR	PSNR1 (dB)	PSNR2 (dB) SWMF	% age impv.	PSNR3 (dB) median	% age impv.
1	3.40	49.8641	50.1089	0.5%	37.8797	–
4	74.80	31.9796	32.1153	0.4%	33.1807	5%

Table 4. CR vs PSNR of 1 and 4 iteration for Nature object image and percentage improvement after applying filter

Iterations	CR	PSNR1 (dB)	PSNR2 (dB) SWMF	% age impv.	PSNR3 (dB) median	% age impv.
1	3.17	45.5520	45.9294	0.8%	33.7831	–
4	72.99	27.9897	27.9900	0.01%	28.9978	3.6%

From Tables 1, 2, 3 and 4 it is shown that median filter is not giving results at first iteration. The reason is that due to the characteristic of median filter, large window size destroys the fine details of the image due to its rank ordering process. And we have taken 21×21 window size which is very large according to the noise density after first iteration. In median filter whether the pixel is corrupted or not it is replaced by the median value of neighboring pixels. So when the image is of low noise density and the window size is large the image gets blurred and PSNR decreases drastically. So the window size of median filter varies according to the noise density.

From Tables 5 and 6 as the iteration increases the CR increases and as the CR increases, number of pixels in the final image decreases since only LL part i.e. the low frequency part of the image is sent for further process, which results in lesser significant pixels (that can be used to decompress image into almost original image) in the final compressed image. Since there are lesser significant pixels in the compressed image therefore decompressed image does not resembles the exact original image, it means quality of image decreases in decompressed image. And as the degree of compression further increases then number of significant pixels decreases and so quality of decompressed image decreases and thus decreases the PSNR value.

Table 5. Iteration vs PSNR for different images

Iteration	PSNR landscape	PSNR hyper pigmented skin1	PSNR hyper pigmented skin2	PSNR nature object
1	42.0872	42.4302	49.8641	45.5520
2	35.5004	35.4327	43.0769	38.6730
3	29.8059	29.8917	37.2840	32.9185
4	25.2905	25.4515	31.9796	27.9897

Table 6. Iteration vs CR for different images

Iteration	CR landscape	CR hyper pigmented skin1	CR hyper pigmented skin2	CR nature object
1	3.2441	3.0240	3.4036	3.1719
2	9.7139	9.2808	10.0785	9.5707
3	24.5773	23.2514	26.8431	24.3420
4	74.5725	72.4310	74.8013	72.9969

Table 7 contains data of PSNR for different window size of median filter for different images on fourth iteration. As the window size increases, more and more neighboring pixels will be used for filtering and thus output will more resemble the original image. But as the window size increases further after certain limit then pixels which may not be consider as same as center pixel will be used to filter it and thus quality of image started decreasing. From the above tables and plots, it can be concluded that window size 21×21 is that limit which gives better quality of image and thus better PSNR value than other window sizes. Therefore window size 21×21 can be used to get high PSNR.

Table 7. Window size of MEDIAN FILTER vs PSNR on Iteration 4 for different images

Window size	PSNR landscape	PSNR hyper pigmented skin1	PSNR hyper pigmented skin2	PSNR nature object
3×3	25.3637	25.4924	32.0468	28.0480
9×9	25.7744	25.7002	32.4228	28.3721
15×15	26.3453	25.8908	32.9449	28.8126
21×21	26.6043	25.9042	33.1807	28.9978
27×27	26.2828	25.4186	32.9209	28.7744

7   Conclusion

This research has presented a new algorithm for high resolution colored images. The method uses Discrete Wavelet Transform and four iterations are performed. The result shows that the approach used in this provides better image quality with high compression ratio. As the number of iteration increases CR increases but PSNR decreases. At fourth iteration filter is applied to improve the PSNR. Two filters are studied and results show that at higher iteration median filter works better while at lower iteration switching weighted median filter works better. Therefore a trade-off is made between CR and PSNR to get the best result. Median filter is also studied at different window sizes and it is concluded that 21×21 window size gives improved PSNR value.

References

1. Ning, T., Huang, C.H., Jensen, J.A., Wong, V., Chan, H.: Optical emission spectrum processing using wavelet compression during wafer fabrication. IEEE Trans. Semicond. Manuf. **30**(4), 380–387 (2017)
2. Kekre, H.B., Natu, P., Sarode, T.: Color image compression using vector quantization and hybrid wavelet transform. Procedia Comput. Sci. **89**, 778–784 (2016). Twelfth International Multi-Conference on Information Processing
3. Vijaya Kumar, C.N., Kumar, D., Anil Kumar, R.: Performance analysis of image compression using discrete wavelet transform. Int. J. Adv. Res. Comput. Sci. Softw. Eng. **7**(3), 186 (2017)
4. Rawat, S., Verma, A.K.: Survey paper on image compression techniques. Int. Res. J. Eng. Technol. **4**(3) (2017)
5. Siddeq, M.M., Rodrigues, M.A.: A novel image compression algorithm for high resolution 3D reconstruction. 3D Res. **5**, 7 (2014)
6. Kumar, G., Brar, E.S.S., Kumar, R., Kumar, A.: A review: DWT-DCT technique and arithmetic-Huffman coding based image compression. Int. J. Eng. Manuf. **5**, 20 (2015)
7. Murugan, V., Balasubramanian, R.: An efficient Gaussian noise removal image enhancement technique for gray scale images. Int. Sci. Index World Acad. Sci. Eng. Technol. Int. J. Comput. Electr. Autom. Control Inf. Eng. **9**(3) (2015)
8. Mahor, V., Pattanaik, M.: An aging-aware reliable FinFET-based low-power 32-Word x 32-bit register file. Circ. Syst. Signal Process. **36**(12), 4789–4808 (2017)
9. Nair, M.S., Mol, P.A.: An efficient adaptive weighted switching median filter for removing high density impulse noise. J. Inst. Eng. India Ser. B **95**, 255–278 (2014)
10. Sayood, K.: Introduction to Data Compression, pp. 81–88, 473–512, 3rd edn. Elsevier, Boston (2005)
11. Lo, S.-C.B., Li, H., Freedman, M.T.: Optimization of wavelet decomposition for image compression and feature preservation. IEEE Trans. Med. Imaging **22**(9), 1141–1151 (2003)
12. Grgic, S., Grgic, M., Zovko-Cihlar, B.: Performance analysis of image compression using wavelets. IEEE Trans. Ind. Electron. **48**(3), 682–695 (2001)
13. Kundu, S., Mahor, V., Gupta, R.: A highly accurate fire detection method using discriminate method. In: 2018 International Conference on Advances in Computing, Communications and Informatics (ICACCI). IEEE (2018)
14. Daubechies, I.: The wavelet transform, time-frequency localization and signal analysis. IEEE Trans. Inf. Theory **36**(5), 961–1005 (1990)
15. Mahor, V., Pattanaik, M.: A state-of-the-art current mirror-based reliable wide fan-in FinFET domino OR gate design. Circ. Syst. Signal Process. **37**(2), 475–499 (2018)

Multiresolution Satellite Fusion Method for INSAT Images

B. Bharathidasan and G. Thirugnanam[(✉)]

Department of Electronics and Instrumentation Engineering,
Annamalai University, Chidambaram, Tamil Nadu, India
ggtt_me@yahoo.com

Abstract. Image fusion is the procedure in which two input images are fused so as to develop the image quality. The input images have to be the images of the comparable prospect with assorted superiority measures. The superiority of the output image will be superior to any of the input images. In this paper, satellite image fusion performance based on Wavelet Packet Transform (WPT) is proposed. Two level decomposition WPT is done on two images to obtain sub-images. The ensuing coefficients are fused by new fusion rule to acquire the fused image. The worth of this method has explained by different images such as the INSAT 3D, INSAT 3A, LANDSAT and PAN images. In this paper the proposed WPT based fusion technique is compared with Discrete Wavelet Transform (DWT) based image fusion. Simulation results accomplished that the proposed method performs finer for image fusion when compared with DWT. Image fusion methods made a comparison against DWT and WPT quality and quantity. Investigational output ended that the proposed WPT design carry out finer for image fusion in association with DWT.

Keywords: Image fusion · INSAT images · Wavelet packet · Wavelet transform

1 Introduction

Image Fusion scheme of intermingle the momentous facts from a locate of films of the equal vision into an fashionable illustration, and the consequent mixed image is extra enlightening and comprehensive of the original pictures. Original pictures possibly will be the many sensors, many modal and many focal points [1]. The fused image is hypothetical to remain every noteworthy truth from the original images. This fusion let alone introduce bygone that donate to an wrong perception. The main vital fundamental procedure of this procedure is image listing. Image listing is the method of changes into different sets of statistics into one put in order arrangement. This technique perceive request in the area of steering leadership, objective uncovering, and credit, medical judgment, satellite descriptions for distant discern, military, and resident observation, etc. [2]. This image mixing methods are divided into pixel, feature, and choice values.

Original pictures possibly will be the many sensors, many modal and many focal points. The fused image is hypothetical to remain every noteworthy truth from the

© Springer Nature Singapore Pte Ltd. 2019
M. Singh et al. (Eds.): ICACDS 2019, CCIS 1046, pp. 263–271, 2019.
https://doi.org/10.1007/978-981-13-9942-8_25

original images. This fusion let alone introduce bygone that donate to an wrong perception. The main vital fundamental procedure of this procedure is image listing. Image listing is the method of changes into different sets of statistics into one put in order arrangement. This technique perceive request in the area of steering leadership, objective uncovering, and credit, medical judgment, satellite descriptions for distant discern, military, and resident observation. This image mixing methods are divided into pixel, feature, and choice values.

Pixel fusion mechanism directly on the picture elements of foundation images even as trait fusion methods meaning on facial appearance full out from the input images. The wavelet clutch the specter and point, anywhere the previous scheme unsuccessful. DWT is unequaled of the lengthily functional tackle [5]. The fusion of DWT policy is choose the highest sub-sets in all prominent vastness. The failing of wavelet is receptive in the surrounding area of the in order. In this work, the resolution of various investigation is attain by wavelet packet transform.

Input pictures possibly will be the many sensors, many modal and many focal points. The fused image is hypothetical to remain every noteworthy truth from the original images. This fusion let alone introduce bygone that donate to an wrong perception. The main vital fundamental procedure of this procedure is image listing. Image listing is the method of changes into different sets of statistics into one put in order arrangement. This technique perceive request in the area of steering leadership, objective uncovering, and credit, medical judgment, satellite descriptions for distant discern, military, and resident observation. This image mixing methods are divided into pixel, feature, and choice values.

In this document, the scheme based on new fusion proposed rule and WPT domain. The fusion statute amalgamates with the typical-personalized to search out further exact significant facial appearance [4]. Hence, this fusion technique is execute for fusion here. The effort is ordered as continue. The WPT and mixing are described in part 2 and 3. In segment 4, projected fusion regulation is accessible. The imitation consequences are accessible in sector 5. Lastly, the close is agreed in Sect. 6.

2 Wavelet Packet Transform

The main difference between WPT and DWT is that, in the WPT, the fundamental filter bank can be decomposed either in low pass branch or in high-pass branch whereas in DWT, the low pass filter only decomposed for further decomposition. This produces the subjective tree structure with each tree corresponding to a wavelet packet bases. Two level wavelet packet decomposition produces sixteen sub-bands. Out of sixteen sub-bands, one approximation (LLA2) and fifteen detail coefficients (LLH2 to HHD2) are obtained [6] (Fig. 1).

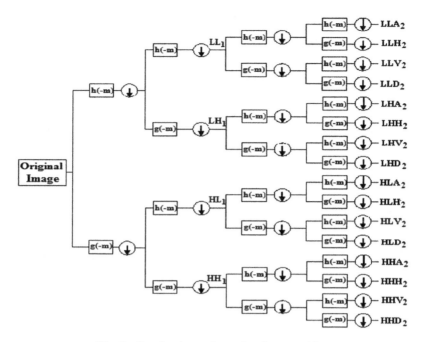

Fig. 1. Two level wavelet packet decomposition

3   Image Fusion

This is the combination applicable in sequence from two or more original pictures into a one image so that it contains all the points from every input images [3, 8]. Here in the paper, fusion is in work for affiliate an INSAT-3D vegetation statistics around India and INSAT 3A manifest rainfall details in India. The ensuing fused image accommodates equally the plant life and precipitation information. An innovative fusion development with WPT come close to is finished.

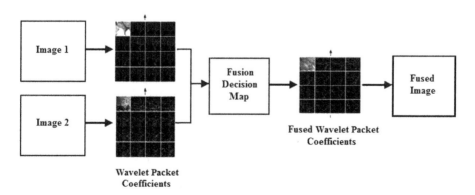

Fig. 2. Systematic process of wavelet packet based image fusion

The lump figure of a broad Wavelet Packet establishes fusion of imaging system is accessible in Fig. 2. INSAT 3D is measured as Image 1, and INSAT 3A is in use as Image 2. Wavelet Packet Transform is practical on Image 1 in addition to functional on Image 2 independently. 16 coefficients are engender in two point productivity of Image 1 and 2. Out of these 16 sub-bands, single is a low frequency approximation coefficient and lasting 15 subsets are high frequency detail sub bands. The planned fusion imperative is used on each 15 facet sub sets [9]. The low-occurrence fusion estimate collective, the standard is functional to two pictures. Lastly, a fused 16 sub set image is acquire, and opposite WPT is completed to obtain the fused image as revealed in Fig. 2.

4 Fusion Rule

Less frequency sub sets situate for the setting of an image, so the process of the less frequency constant from observable and IR images is the foundation of image fusion [7]. In this work, less frequency sub sets of INSAT 3D and INSAT 3A images are centered for the blend of the two frameworks. The calculation is as proceeds:

$$W_j^a = \alpha * W_{Aj}^a + \beta * W_{Bj}^a \tag{1}$$

W - Coefficient of the picture, A and B situate for INSAT 3D and INSAT 3A images in that order, j is the level of wavelet and the values of $\alpha + \beta = 1$.

Bearing in mind that higher frequency sub sets situated for the facts, the author adopted high frequency coefficients of the better component to set aside additional fine points.

$$W_j^d = \begin{cases} W_{Aj}^d, & \left| W_{Aj}^d \right| \geq \left| W_{Bj}^d \right| \\ W_{Bj}^d, & \left| W_{Aj}^d \right| \leq \left| W_{Bj}^d \right| \end{cases} \tag{2}$$

5 Result and Discussion

The INSAT 3D RGB of size 256 × 256 enlighten the plant life in India is considered as Image 1 and the Image 2 indicate rainfall in India is acquired from INSAT 3A of size 256 × 256 as shown in Figs. 3 and 4. Image 1 and 2 are transformed to Y, U, V apparatus, and Y element is measured for fusion. The Y constituent of INSAT 3D and INSAT 3A are revealed in Figs. 5 and 6, in that order. Both the INSAT images are decaying to 2 quantities by means of Wavelet Packet Transform. The resulting one level sub-bands for image 1 and image 2 are shown in Figs. 7 and 8. Two level sub-bands using WPT are shown in Figs. 9 and 10. The proposed Fusion rule is useful on each 16 sub sets in 2 pictures. Approximation coefficient fusion, the middling is found out amid low-frequency components in 2 pictures. Similarly, for the elevated more occurrence elaborated coefficients fusion order is useful. Fused Wavelet Packet coefficients image is attained after the fusion as shown in Fig. 11, and reverse WPT is obligatory to acquire Y component's multiple images as illustrated in Fig. 12. Finally Y constituent fused image is misused to an RGB mixed image as delineated in Fig. 13 (Tables 1 and 2).

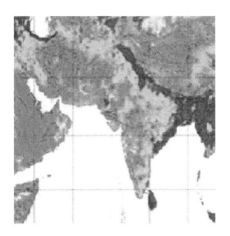

Fig. 3. Input Image 1

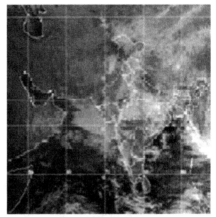

Fig. 4. Input Image 2

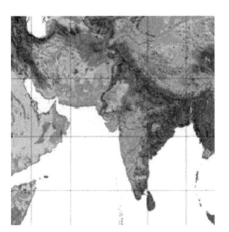

Fig. 5. Y constituent of Image 1

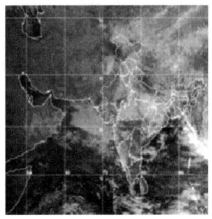

Fig. 6. Y constituent of Image 2

Fig. 7. One level WPT analysis for Image 1   **Fig. 8.** One level WPT analysis for Image 2

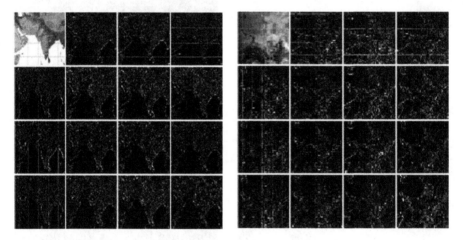

Fig. 9. Two level WPT decomposition for
Image 1

Fig. 10. Two level WPT decomposition for
Image 2

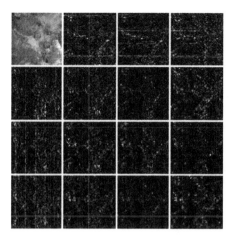

Fig. 11. Fused WPT coefficients

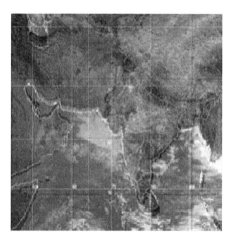

Fig. 12. Y constituent of fused image

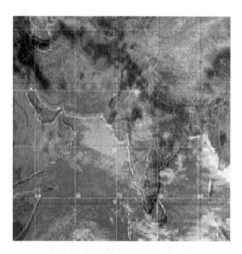

Fig. 13. Fused image

Table 1. Assessment measures of PSNR for wavelet and wavelet packet transform.

Images	Wavelet transform	Wavelet packet transform
Proposed INSAT	41.2910	45.9327
LANDSAT	39.1875	43.4233
PAN-MS	40.2910	44.7331

Table 2. Assessment measures of normalized correlation for wavelet and wavelet packet

Images	Wavelet transform	Wavelet packet transform
Proposed INSAT	0.9117	0.9459
LANDSAT	0.9025	0.9362
PAN-MS	0.9019	0.9312

6   Conclusion

This work has demonstrated a WPT based new fusion techniques for INSAT colour images. This process holds together INSAT 3D and INSAT 3A facts of protectorate pictures. Replication outputs declared the power of the projected Wavelet Packet scheme to image fusion of satellite image wavelet based schemes. The projected manner revealed designate successful for the mixing in the subsistence of intrusion.

References

1. Nikolov, S., Hill, P., Bull, D., Canagarajah, N.: Wavelets for image fusion. In: Petrosian, A. A., Meyer, F.G. (eds.) Wavelets in Signal and Image Analysis, vol. 19, pp. 213–241. Springer, Dordrecht (2001). https://doi.org/10.1007/978-94-015-9715-9_8
2. Vekkot, S., Shukla, P.: A novel architecture for wavelet based image fusion. World Acad. Sci. Eng. Technol. **57**, 372–377 (2009)
3. Li, H., Manjunath, B.S., Mitra, S.K.: Multisensor image fusion using the wavelet transform. Graph Models Image Process. **57**(3), 235–245 (1995)
4. Pu, T., Ni, G.: Contrast based Image Fusion using the Discrete Wavelet Transform. Opt. Eng. **39**(8), 2075–2082 (2000)
5. Xiong, Z., Ramchandran, K., Orchad, M.T.: Wavelet packet image coding using space-frequency quantization. IEEE Trans. Image Process. **7**, 160–174 (1998)
6. Petrovic, V., Xydeas, C.S.: Area level fusion of multi-focused images using multi-stationary wavelet packet transform. Int. J. Comput. Appl. **2**(1), 975–983 (2010)
7. Chandana, M., Amutha, S., Kumar, N.: A hybrid multi-focus medical image fusion based on wavelet transform. Int. J. Res. Rev. Comput. Sci. **2**, 1187–1192 (2011)
8. Tu, T., Huang, P.S., Hung, C., Chang, C.: A fast intensity-hue-saturation fusion technique with spectral adjustment for IKONOS imagery. IEEE Trans. Geosci. Remote Sens. **1**(4), 309–312 (2004)
9. Saleta, M., Catala, J.L.: Fusion of multispectral and panchromatic images using improved IHS and PCA mergers based on wavelet decomposition. IEEE Trans. Geosci. Remote Sens. **42**(6), 1291–1299 (2004)
10. Wald, L., Ranchin, T., Mangolini, M.: Fusion of Satellite images of different spatial resolution: assessing the quality of resulting images. PE&RS **63**(6), 691–699 (1997)
11. Nunez, J., Otazu, X., Fors, O., Prades, A., Pala, V., Arbiol, R.: Image fusion with additive multiresolution wavelet decomposition: applications to spot1 landsat images. J. Opt. Soc. Am. A **16**, 467–474 (1999)
12. Rockinger, O.: Image sequence fusion using a shift invariant wavelet transform. In: Proceedings of IEEE International Conference on Image Processing, vol. 13, pp. 288–291 (1997)
13. Ajazzi, B., Alparone, L., Baronti, S., Carla, R.: Assessment pyramid-based multisensor image data fusion. Proc. SPIE **3500**, 237–248 (1998)
14. Chipman, L.J., Orr, T.M., Graham, L.N.: Wavelets and image fusion. Proc. SPIE **2529**, 208–219 (1995)
15. Blum, R.S., Liu, Z.: Multi-Sensor Image Fusion and Its Applications. CRC Press/Taylor & Francis Group/NW, Boca Raton/Routledge/Evanston (2006)
16. Chipman, L., Orr, T., Graham, L.: Wavelets and Image Fusion. Proc. SPIE **2569**, 208–219 (1995)
17. Yocky, D.: Multiresolution wavelet decomposition image merger of landsat thematic mapper and SPOT panchromatic data. Photogram. Eng. Remote Sens. **62**(9), 1067–1074 (1996)

A Combinatorial Fair Economical Double Auction Resource Allocation Model

Ritu Singhal$^{(\boxtimes)}$ and Archana Singhal

Department of Computer Science, I.P. College, University of Delhi, Delhi, India
rsinghal@ip.du.c.in, archanasinghal1970@gmail.com

Abstract. Role of cloud computing is emerging extensively as it not only reduces hardware maintenance cost, but high end servers provide all the facilities with very high speed and versatile resources required to run an application. Pricing and fairness play very important role in the market as marketing is done online and everything is handled virtually without physical presence. Role of cloud providers become very significant as they are controlling the competitive market by providing the required resources within the budget of a customer. At the same time importance of customers can't be neglected as market can only flourish with the customer's satisfaction. In online market fair distribution of resources is also a necessity for sustainability. The proposed model maintains fairness by giving priority to the genuine providers over the providers who want to monopolies or spoil the market. It also encourages customers who want to use resources for more time with fair bid values. Instead of rejecting non-genuine providers having bid very close to genuine providers, they are allowed to participate after genuine providers according to their degree of closeness with genuine providers. It will lead to increased resource availability and hence increased customers and provider's participation ratio. The proposed model is implemented in CloudSim environment and compared with two popular existing models. The evaluation of proposed model has clearly shown improved utilization of resources and fair allocation with increased participation of customers and providers both.

Keywords: Cloud computing · Resource allocation ·
Combinatorial double auction · Winner determination problem

1 Introduction

Online market is 24 × 7 available and most convenient market for accessing resources from anywhere in the world at any time, removing all physical barriers. In the online competitive market where a lot of companies are providing the door step facilities, pricing play very important role with certain quality of service features. The providers want to earn more profit and at the same time wish to remain in market for long time with their credentials. On the other hand customers wish to pay according to his budget for required resources. In this direction fixed price model is not successful due to ups and downs in the market. Now a day's dynamic pricing scheme is used at a number of places according to demand and supply. It is used for air reservation, railway

© Springer Nature Singapore Pte Ltd. 2019
M. Singh et al. (Eds.): ICACDS 2019, CCIS 1046, pp. 272–281, 2019.
https://doi.org/10.1007/978-981-13-9942-8_26

reservation, booking of taxies, buses and so on by various companies. But this is one sided affair and customer is just a passive entity having no say in the system.

Cloud computing is different from current market scenarios as it provide virtual resources at rent to those who want to store a huge data at online storage for access at anytime and anywhere. Data can also be shared among a group or users who. Cloud computing provides these facilities on cheaper rate without need of physical space, maintenance and technical knowledge.

In the competitive market, auction is coming out as a good solution over dynamic pricing where users and provider both can become active entities. Combinatorial double auction model in cloud computing gained a lot of attention as instead of bidding for individual resources, the price will be asked for the whole bundle of resources required in form of bundle bid. After submission of bids for the auction, the auctioneer runs winner determination algorithm to decide winning providers and customers.

Rest of the paper is organized into five sections. Section 2 presents related work on cloud computing and resource provisioning in auction market. Section 3 describe the proposed approach for auction market in cloud computing. In Sect. 4, evaluation criteria and in Sect. 5 experimental studies are discussed. A detailed scenario is explained in Sect. 6. Finally, Sect. 7 concludes the paper.

2 Literature Survey

Singhal et al. [1] suggested a generic cloud model as a solution to resource scarcity in conventional education system. Cloud computing eliminates physical barriers for the students of special need. Singhal et al. developed an audio repository application for helping visually impaired using cloud computing resources [2]. Sandholm et al. [3] theoretically analyzed the complexity of finding optimal solution for different types of auctions with multiple numbers of items. Hassanzadeh et al. [4] tried to maximize the overall profit after including fairness factor in a combinatorial double-sided auction model with improved resource utilization. Zaman et al. [5] proposed combinatorial auction-linear programming and combinatorial auction-Greedy methods for auction and compared them with fixed pricing scheme. Results have shown improved allocation and higher revenue for the cloud providers. In Samimi et al. [6], non-genuine providers are rejected and not given any chance to participate in auction even if a provider's bid is very close to genuine provider. It will lead to less provider participation and hence less available resources in the market. Also, virtual machines are differentiated only on the basis of CPU capacity. All machines are given same unit price which is not justified according to real market scenario. In Tafsiri et al. [7], no provider is rejected and providers auctioning high grade infrastructures at very low cost are prioritized in spite of being non-genuine providers, leading to unfairness in the system.

Singhal et al. [9] proposed an algorithm that prioritizes the genuine provider over others. Calculation the bid density and unit price of resources is based on CPU only. This model does not take customer time in consideration.

The proposed model also prioritizes the genuine provider over others. The calculation of the bid density and unit price of resources are based on CPU, memory, bandwidth and storage. Customer's time is also taken into consideration. Customers bid densities are calculated using bid for unit time. Customers having same bid densities then are arranged according to decreasing order of time.

3 Proposed Approach

The proposed model is a cloud based combinatorial double auction model named as "Combinatorial Fair Economical Double Auction Resource Allocation Model (CFE-DARA)". The proposed model includes three entities as Cloud user, Cloud provider, and Auctioneer. The cloud providers offer their bundle of resources and cloud users request for the required bundle of resources with the corresponding bundle bids. Resources are allocated in form of virtual machines (VMs), which are differentiated according to their configuration of CPU, memory, storage and bandwidth. An Auctioneer conducts the auction and determines the winners. This problem is known as winner determination problem.

The proposed approach in place of rejecting non-genuine providers they are allowed to participate but are penalized by giving them chance after the genuine provider according to their genuineness. Combinatorial double auction allocation problem resource allocation has to be done efficiently to maximize the overall profit of the system along with fair deal with customers and providers. A heuristic approach is considered for resource allocation and calculating unit prices for each resource from bundle bid satisfying customer expectation according to his budget and resource requirement. Resources are allocated after matching bids from the sorted lists of providers and customers. If bid of provider is less than or equal to the customer's bid then resource availability is checked. If resources are not available with the first provider then next is given the chance and so on. The best price offered for each virtual machine required by a customer is determined on the basis of matching of configuration and lowest price offered by a provider. Different virtual machines can be taken from different providers to minimize customers total cost and maximizing total profit. Higher configuration machine can also be allocated to a customer if required low configuration machine is not available and its bid is within the range of provider's bid.

Once providers and customers submit their list of resources and corresponding bids, their bid densities are calculated. Then genuine bid range of providers is calculated. Then the providers are arranged according to their genuineness of the bids. The range of genuine bid prices is determined according to the configuration of the systems, and average of the bid prices provided by all the providers. The genuine providers will be given highest priority. Other providers are arranged according to their distance with genuine providers. This distance is calculated by finding the difference between bid densities of non-genuine providers with the mean bid density of all the providers. Providers with less distance will be given priority. It ensures that provider having marginal difference in bids will be next to genuine providers ensuring market spoilers putting in the last. When all the resources of genuine providers are exhausted, only then other providers will be given chance to participate according to their genuineness.

In [6, 7] for calculation of bid densities of customers, time is multiplied with bid. Bid and time are directly proportional to the bid density i.e. increasing the value of either bid or time will increase bid density. It implies that in some cases, customer that uses resources for more time but with very low bid value might have higher density as compared to those customers asking for same resources for less time with higher bid. In this case customer giving fewer prices and asking resources for more time will be winning the deal and keep resources for long time. It will result in unfair resource allocation from customer point of view and might lead to reduced customer participation. Instead of giving all the resources to a single customer for more duration in lesser price, the same can be allocated to more customers asking resources for shorter duration in higher prices. It will increase the customer participation as well as profit of the system.

To handle this type of situation, the bid density and unit price for each VM is calculated according to the bundle bid for unit time. Then customers are arranged according to bid density for unit time from higher to lower. If bid density for unit time is same for more than one customer then customer who are asking resources for more time will be given priority over customers asking resources for less time.

As bid is submitted for the entire bundle having different types and different quantities of VMs, it is important to find the weightage and unit price of each VM among the entire bundle. Unit bid price calculation will be based on both, their weightage and required quantity. It will ensure that VM with high configuration will cost more as compare to the machine with lower configuration. Weight of ith type of virtual machine for k^{th} participant according to its configuration is calculated as given below in Eq. 1.

$$W_{VM_{ik}} = CPU_i * W_{CPU} + Mem_i * W_{Mem} + St_i * W_{St} + Bw_i * W_{Bw} \qquad (1)$$

Where W_{CPU}, W_{Mem}, W_{St}, and W_{Bw} are the weightage given to CPU, memory, storage, and bandwidth respectively. These weights are based on number of criterions i.e. utility and price. They are dynamic in nature and their value can be changed according to the market demand. The CPU_i, Mem_i, St_i and Bw_i are the capacity values of CPU, memory, storage and bandwidth respectively for VM of types i.

After finding individual weight of each type of virtual machine we find its weightage with respect to all VMs available for that participant as given below in Eq. 2.

$$Wt_{VM_{ik}} = W_{VM_{ik}} / \sum_{j=1}^{r} W_{VM_{jk}} \qquad (2)$$

Where i is the type of machine and r is the total type of VM available for participant k. Total average weightage of all the VMs of each participant is 1.

After calculating weight, bid densities [7] are calculated. The bid density D_{Pk} of provider k is calculated using bid for unit time as given below:

$$D_{Pk} = \frac{Bid_k}{\sum_{j=1}^{r} \left(Wt_{VM_{jk}} * Qty_{VM_{jk}} \right)} \qquad (3)$$

Similarly bid density D_{Ck} for customer k is calculated using unit bid as given below:

$$D_{Ck} = \frac{Bid_k}{\sum_{j=1}^{r} \left(Wt_{VM_{jk}} * Qty_{VM_{jk}} \right)} \tag{4}$$

Where Bid_k is the bundle bid for unit time, $Qty_{VM_{jk}}$ and $Wt_{VM_{jk}}$ are quantity and weight of a VM of type j for a participant k and r is the total type of VMs for that participant.

The unit price of each VM according to its weightage is calculated as given below.

$$P_{VM_{ik}} = Bid_k * Wt_{VM_{ik}} / \sum_{j=1}^{r} \left(Wt_{VM_{jk}} * Qty_{VM_{jk}} \right) \tag{5}$$

Where i is type and r is the total number of virtual machines for k^{th} participant.

The trade price of winner participant is the average of unit price of the VM supplied by provider and unit price of the virtual machine requested by the customer.

Trade price $TP_{VM_{k_1 v_1}}$ for winner customer k_1 for the VM type v_1 is given as follows:

$$TP_{VM_{k_1 v_1}} = \left(P_{VM_{k_1 v_1}} + P_{VM_{k_2 v_2}} \right) / 2 \tag{6}$$

Where, $P_{VM_{k_1 v_1}}$ is the unit price for VM of type v_1 of customer k_1 and $P_{VM_{k_2 v_2}}$ is the unit price for VM of type v_2 of winner provider k_2 given to customer k_1 for VM type v_1. The type of VM v_2 will be either of same type or higher type.

The profit of the winner customer k_1 for r_1 type of VMs for the required time is calculated as follows:

$$PF_{C_{k_1}} = \sum_{v_1=1}^{r_1} \left(TP_{VM_{Ck_1 v_1}} - P_{VM_{Ck_1 v_1}} \right) * Qty_{VM_{Ck_1 v_1}} * time_{C_{k_1}} \tag{7}$$

Similarly, the profit of the winner provider k_2 is calculated as follows:

$$PF_{Pk_2} = \sum_{v_2=1}^{r_2} \left(P_{VM_{pk_2 v_2}} - TP_{VM_{pk_2 v_2}} \right) * Qty_{VM_{Pk_2 v_2}} * time_{Pk_2} \tag{8}$$

Where $Qty_{VM_{Pk_2 v_2}}$ is the quantity of VM of type v_2 of provider k given to customer C_{K1} against VM of type v_1. The r_1 is the total number of VMs required by customer and r_2 is the total number of VMs allocated by the provider. Here x is the total number of winner customers and $time_{C_{k_1}}$ is the time for customer C_{K1} for the required VMs.

Total profit of the system for x number of winner customers and y number of winner providers is given in equation number (9):

$$PF_{total} = \sum_{k_1=1}^{x} PF_{C_{k_1}} + \sum_{k_2=1}^{y} PF_{P_{k_2}} \tag{9}$$

The winner determination algorithm of proposed CEFDARA model is given below:

CFEDARA Winner Determination Algorithm

Inputs: *List of n Customers* $\{C_1, C_2, \ldots C_n\}$ *with their bundle bid* $\{Bid_1, Bid_2, \ldots Bid_n\}$ *for required resources and list of m providers* $\{P_1, P_2, \ldots Pm\}$ *with their corresponding bundle bids* $\{Bid_1, Bid_2, \ldots Bid_m\}$ *of available resources.*

Output: *Resource allocation table for all the winning customers with their corresponding providers and trade price and Profit.*

Steps:

1. *Calculate bid densities for all the customers and providers based on bundle bids for unit time.*
2. *Find genuine providers and arrange them in increasing order of their bid density. Remaining providers are arranged in ascending order according to their distance/degree of closeness with the genuine providers and the list is appended at the end of list of genuine providers.*
3. *Customers are arranged in decreasing order of their bid density to give priority to the customers offering higher bid. If bid density is same for more than one customer then customer who are asking resources for more time will be given priority.*
4. *Choose the customer from the top of sorted list of customers i.e. customer offering highest bid. Choose provider(s) from the sorted list of providers starting from the top i.e. providers offering the required resources of the selected customer with lowest price. If all required resources of customer are available with some provider (s) declare winning customer and providers. After winner determination, calculate trade price according to agreement's terms and conditions and allocate resources to customer.*
5. *Update the available resources of winner provider(s).*
6. *Choose the next customer in the sorted list and move to step 4 until the complete customer's list is exhausted.*
7. *Calculate the resource utilization of winner providers. Also, calculate total profit for winner customers as well as for winner providers and hence the total profit of the system.*

Next section presents the evaluation criterion of the proposed model.

4 Evaluation Criteria

The proposed model is evaluated according to fairness, truthfulness, economic efficiency, and customers and provider's participation ratio as explained below.

1. Fairness in distribution

The proposed approach maintains the fairness by giving equal opportunity to providers and customers both participating in auction. The customers giving higher bid for the required resources will be given priority over other customers giving lower bid for the same resources. Genuine providers are given first chance in the auction. But if they don't have required resources then only other providers will be considered.

2. Truthfulness

Truthfulness is very important criterion to prioritize providers in auction who gives genuine bids for their product. Proposed algorithm maintains the truthfulness of the system by giving priority to genuine providers. After winning the auction, genuine providers will be allocated to highest paid customers, awarding them with more profit. When all resources of genuine providers are allocated then others are given chance to participate in order of their degree of closeness with genuine providers.

3. Economic efficiency

Proposed approach keeps all providers for auction so number of resources for auction increases and results in economic efficiency of the model.

4. Participation ratio

As more number of providers is encouraged for participating in auction and no provider is rejected, it leads to improved participation rate of providers as well as customers due to more availability of resources. It will increase the participation ratio. Next section presents the simulation of proposed model to evaluate the performance of the system.

5 Experimental Study

The experiments were carried in CloudSim environment [8]. Results were analyzed for 6000 iterations that include random values of providers and customers from 5 to 60 with different range of bids. Resource types used are 13 types of VMs.

Figure 1 indicates that resource utilization is considerably improved over [6] and better than the model given by [7], while maintaining overall profit of the system as shown in Fig. 2. More customers are satisfied in proposed approach as shown in Fig. 3, as more resources are utilized during the auction. Figure 4 indicates that provider's participation is drastically improved over [6] and marginally better than the model given by [7].

Figure 5 demonstrates that the proposed approach prioritizes the genuine providers over other providers as 63% of the total profit is shared by genuine providers. Also, these non-genuine providers sharing 37% of the profit are those providers whose bids are closer to genuine ones.

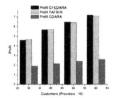

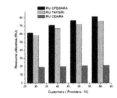

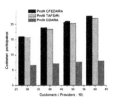

Fig. 1. Total profit   **Fig. 2.** Resource utilization   **Fig. 3.** Customers participation

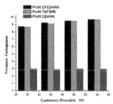

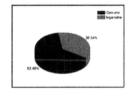

Fig. 4. Providers participation   **Fig. 5.** Proposed approach   **Fig. 6.** Tafsiri et al.

Pie chart in Fig. 6 shows that 76% of the profit is shared by the providers who are not genuine, while only 24% of the total profit is shared by genuine providers. It clearly indicates that in [7], importance is given to providers with lowest bid without taking care of their genuineness, to earn more profit.

6   A Scenario

In this section a scenario is presented where the proposed approach achieves more profit than Tafsiri et al. [7]. In spite of arranging the providers according to the genuineness as first priority, the proposed approach, succeeded in maintaining the profit of overall system. There are number of cases where the proposed approach achieves more profit than [7]. Following scenario depicts one such type of case.

Table 1. Calculation of final trade price and profit in proposed approach

CID	Bid	PID (VM type, quantity, unit price)	Trade price	Profit
9	0.63	4 (5, 3, 0.008258)	0.1091	0.3026
10	0.41	4 (1, 3, 0.003068)	0.0699	0.2004
15	0.63	2 (2, 1, 0.0111133), 4 (7, 2, 0.01741), 3 (12, 2, 0.010565)	0.1790	0.2815
8	0.364	2 (2, 1, 0.0111133), 3 (13, 1, 0.02078)	0.2489	0.1660
7	0.42	4 (7, 1, 0.01741), 2 (11, 1, 0.022271), 1 (2, 1, 0.026421)	0.1790	0.1637

The scenario includes 5 providers and 15 customers. After applying winner determination algorithm under proposed approach, 7 customers got the required resources, while in Tafsiri et al. [7], 4 customers were allocated resources. So, proposed algorithm leads to more profit due to more allocation count. Table 1 shows allocation of resources for winner customers and providers for proposed approach, and Table 2 represents allocation of Tafsiri et al. [7].

In proposed approach, list of customers are sorted in descending order of bid densities and list of providers is a sorted based on their genuineness, where the market spoilers having very low bids are penalized and placed in the last. As move down in the customer's and provider's list, bid of customer is decreased and bid of the provider is increased, customers of lower bid are matched with providers left with comparatively high bid leading to less profit penalizing providers with very high bid. The participants with low bids will also be penalized as their trade price will be less and they will get less profit. Involving more providers lead to more resource allocation and improvement in overall profit of the system.

Table 2. Calculation of final trade price and profit in Tafsiri et al.

CID	Bid	PID (VM type, quantity, unit price)	Trade price	Profit
9	0.63	4 (5, 3, 0.008258)	0.109129	0.302613
10	0.41	4 (1, 3, 0.003068)	0.069867	0.200398
8	0.364	2 (2, 1, 0.011133), 3 (13, 1, 0.02078)	0.178996	0.166044
3	0.542	2 (2, 1, 0.011133), 2 (11, 1, 0.22271), 3 (13, 2, 0.02078)	0.215416	0.236537

In Tafsiri et al. [7] profit of overall system decreases due to rejection of those customers who offers lower bid as their bid is compared with providers offering higher bids as providers are arranged from lower to higher.

Next section concludes the proposed approach.

7 Conclusion

The proposed model CFEDARA, is an efficient market-based economical, fair resource allocation double auction model that allows both customers and providers to participate on egalitarianism basis. This approach promotes truthful providers and penalizes market spoilers to promote fairness in the system, simultaneously benefiting users by satisfying their resource requirements within their budget. The proposed model is dynamic and implemented in CloudSim environment. Criteria for evaluation are incentive driven and include fairness, truthfulness, economic efficiency, and participation ratio. It is evaluated on randomize number of providers, customers and bid patterns over 6000 iterations with versatile combination of the range of customers and providers from 5 to 60. This approach is analysed on a number of combinations that include less number of providers and more customers, more providers and less customers, high number of providers as well customers and low number of both the providers as well as customers. The results based on all combination specified above, have shown significant improvement over CDARA model in terms of economic efficiency. It has shown increased participation of providers and customers incorporating genuineness and truthfulness as compared to the approach given by Tafsiri et al., while maintaining the overall profit and resource utilization. The trustworthiness and fairness is incorporated efficiently by promoting genuine providers over other providers, while maintaining demand and flow market strategy with good profit margins.

References

1. Singhal, R., Singhal, A., Sonia: Towards a generic E-Cloud architecture for universities. Int. J. Web Appl. **8**(2), 36–43 (2016)
2. Singhal, R., Singhal, A., Bhatnagar, M., Malhotra, N.: Design of an audio repository for blind and visually impaired: a case study. In: Mandal, J.K., Bhattacharyya, D., Auluck, N. (eds.) Advanced Computing and Communication Technologies. AISC, vol. 702, pp. 77–85. Springer, Singapore (2019). https://doi.org/10.1007/978-981-13-0680-8_8
3. Sandholm, T., Suri, S., Gilpin A., Levine D.: Winner determination in combinatorial auction generalizations. In: Proceedings of the First International Joint Conference on Autonomous Agents and Multiagent Systems: Part 1, pp. 69–76. ACM (2002)
4. Hassanzadeh, R., Movaghar, A., Hassanzadeh, H.R.: A multi-dimensional fairness combinatorial double-sided auction model in cloud environment. In: 2016 8th International Symposium on Telecommunications (IST), pp. 672–677. IEEE (2016)
5. Zaman, S., Grosu, D.: Combinatorial auction-based allocation of virtual machine instances in clouds. J. Parallel Distrib. Comput. **73**(4), 495–508 (2013)
6. Samimi, P., Teimouri, Y., Mukhtar, M.: A combinatorial double auction resource allocation model in cloud computing. Inf. Sci. **20**(357), 201–216 (2016)
7. Tafsiri, S.A., Yousefi, S.: Combinatorial double auction-based resource allocation mechanism in cloud computing market. J. Syst. Softw. **137**, 322–334 (2018)
8. Calheiros, R.N., Ranjan, R., Beloglazov, A., Rose, C.A., Buyya, R.: CloudSim: a toolkit for modeling and simulation of cloud computing environments and evaluation of resource provisioning algorithms. Softw. Pract. Exp. **41**(1), 23–50 (2011)
9. Singhal, R., Singhal, A.: A combinatorial economical double auction resource allocation model (CEDARA). In: ComITCon 2019 (2019)

Issues in Training a Convolutional Neural Network Model for Image Classification

Soumya Joshi[1], Dhirendra Kumar Verma[2(✉)], Gaurav Saxena[2], and Amit Paraye[2]

[1] Medicaps Institute of Technology and Management, Indore, India
joshisoumya21@gmail.com
[2] Computer Division, Department of Atomic Energy,
Raja Ramanna Centre for Advanced Technology, Indore, India
{dhirendrav, saxenagaurav, aparaye}@rrcat.gov.in

Abstract. Convolutional neural networks (CNN) are a boon to image classification algorithms as it can learn highly abstract features and work with less parameter. Overfitting, exploding gradient, and class imbalance are the major challenges while training the model using CNN. These issues can diminish the performance of the model. Proper understanding and use of corrective measures can substantially prevent the model from these issues and can increase the efficiency of the model. In this paper the conceptual understanding of the basic CNN model along with its key layers is provided. The paper summarizes the results of training the deep learning model using CNN on publicly available datasets of cats and dogs. Finally the paper discusses various methods such as data augmentation, regularization, dropout, etc. to prevent the CNN model from overfitting problem. The paper will also help beginners to have a broad comprehension of CNN and motivate them to venture in this field.

Keywords: Convolutional neural networks · Deep learning ·
Image classification · Data augmentation · Image dataset

1 Introduction

Deep learning is widely used in the field of pattern analysis and now it has become the major techniques in the fields of image recognition, classification, and speech recognition [1]. Deep learning consists of various computational models. These models include various processing layers for learning representations of data with multiple levels of abstraction [2].

Convolutional Neural Network (CNN) is a common method in the area of depth learning. CNN are generally known as deep neural network (DNN) and belongs to the category of supervised learning [3]. Convolutional neural networks are a boon to image and natural language processing as they are easier to train and have less parameters [4]. While making a training model for image classification CIFAR-10, CIFAR-100, MNIST, and ImageNet are the standard datasets used for checking the accuracy of the model. Apart from these standard datasets one can define his own dataset using labeled

M. Singh et al. (Eds.): ICACDS 2019, CCIS 1046, pp. 282–293, 2019.
https://doi.org/10.1007/978-981-13-9942-8_27

images. We also created a new dataset for evaluating the accuracy of the model. The structure of the model is also discussed in this paper.

The issues faced during execution of the training model hampers the performance of the model and can appear quite intricate at first. Overfitting and exploding gradient are the issues we faced during training of the model; these issues are elaborated in this paper.

2 Convolutional Neural Network

Convolutional Neural Networks (CNNs) are a kind of multi-layer neural networks. CNN requires very less preprocessing on images to recognize visual patterns and operates directly at pixel level. CNNs are capable of recognizing patterns with high variability, and with robustness to loss and basic geometric transformations [5]. CNNs are generally used in image recognition, powering vision in robots, self-driving vehicles, medical image analysis, etc.

In this section we explained the layers of CNN. A CNN usually contains an input layer, one or more hidden layers, and an output layer. Major layers in the CNN model are depicted in Fig. 1.

2.1 Convolutional Layer

Convolutional layer is the basic building block of a CNN that does most of the computational heavy lifting [6]. A convolutional layer is applied by taking an image as an input matrix of pixels and then applying learnable filters of a fixed size i.e. n × n to each n × n block of input matrix. A filter is used for identifying the presence of specific features or patterns present in the original input image. Convolutional layer reduces training parameters of the image and focuses only on the necessary details of the image.

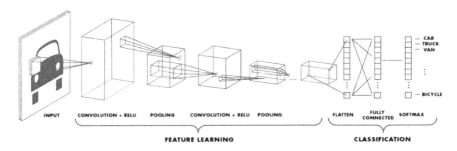

Fig. 1. CNN layers. Image downloaded from https://in.mathworks.com/solutions/deep-learning/convolutional-neural-network.html

2.2   Pooling Layer

The Pooling layer can be seen between Convolution layers in CNN architecture. This layer basically reduces the amount of parameters and computation in the network, controlling overfitting by progressively reducing the spatial size of the network [7]. Max pooling is the widely used pooling layers which takes a 2×2 or larger size filter and a stride. It then applies it to the input volume and produces the maximum number in every sub-region that the filter convolves around on the image. Other methods to perform pooling are average and L2-norm pooling [8].

2.3   Flattening

In this step, all the pooled feature maps are taken and put inside the single vector and feed into a fully connected layer.

2.4   Fully Connected Layer

Similar to a regular Neural Network fully connected layer provides full connections to all activations in its previous layer. Activations are calculated through matrix multiplication followed by a bias offset [6].

2.5   Dropout Regularization

In dropout layer randomly selected neurons are ignored while training. The contribution of dropped out neurons to the activation is removed and their weight updates are also not applied to the neuron while backward pass [9].

2.6   Activation Functions

Activation function calculates a "weighted sum" of inputs to the neurons, adds a bias and then decides whether a neuron should be activated or not. Every activation function takes a single number and performs a certain fixed mathematical operation on it. There are several activation functions such as Sigmoid, ReLU, Tanh, Softmax, etc. depending upon the properties of the problem we can choose the appropriate activation function for easy and quicker convergence of the network [10].

3   Building and Training the Model

3.1   Preparing Dataset

We used CIFAR-10 and CIFAR-100 datasets for training the network. CIFAR (Canadian Institute for Advanced Research) is one of the most widely used dataset for machine learning research.

The CIFAR-10 dataset contains 60,000 32×32 color images in 10 different classes including airplanes, cars, birds, cats, deer, dogs, frogs, horses, ships, and trucks [11]. CIFAR-100 is similar to CIFAR-10 dataset, the only difference is that number of classes are 100, containing 600 images each. The dataset is loaded into training set and test set before the training starts.

3.2   Network Structure

The input to the network is a 32 × 32 image. CNN exploit spatially local correlation by enforcing a local connectivity pattern between neurons of adjacent layers [12].

The network has a multi-layer architecture consisting of total four convolutional layers and two fully connected layers. The network starts with convolutional layer including 32 filters and 3 × 3 kernel size. Rectified Linear Unit (ReLU) activation function is used after convolutional layers. Pooling is performed using MaxPooling2D function to down-sample the input representation. Max pool windows size is fixed to 2 × 2 at all pooling places.

Figure 2 shows the structure of the CNN that we trained using CIFAR100 dataset.

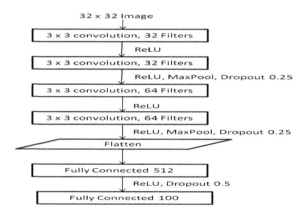

Fig. 2. Network architecture

3.3   Training the Model

The process of image classification consists of training and testing stages. In the training process a unique description is created for each class. The classification may be binary classification or multi-class classification. In testing the test images are categorized in different classes for which system is supposed to be trained. Assignment of images to a particular class is done based on training features [13].

Before training the model can be configured with different parameters. We set the values of loss, optimizer, and metric to 'Categorical Cross entropy', 'Stochastic Gradient Descent', and 'Accuracy', respectively.

CIFAR10 only has one set of labels including airplane, automobile, bird, cat, deer, dog, frog, horse, ship, and truck. CIFAR100 has both coarse labels and fine labels. We trained the model for 150 epochs using CIFAR100 dataset and observed the values of training loss, training accuracy, validation loss, and validation accuracy.

We trained our CNN model using Keras library with TensorFlow as backend. Hardware platform to train the model include a server having dual Intel Xeon 8 core processors with 3.20 GHz clock frequency, 128 GB RAM, NVIDIA TESLA K80 GPU with 2496 CUDA cores and 24 GB memory.

4   Result and Analysis

We trained our CNN models for 100 and 150 epochs for CIFAR10 and CIFAR100 datasets respectively with slight changes in network structure. Both datasets consists of 32 × 32 color images.

Table 1. represents the observations that we recorded for CNN model trained using CIFAR10 dataset. Figure 3 depicts the results in graphical format.

Table 1. CNN model performance with LR = 0.01 for CIFAR10

S. no	No. of epochs	Training loss	Training accuracy	Validation loss	Validation accuracy
1	10	1.1346	59.73	1.1116	60.91
2	20	0.8428	70.53	0.9937	65.33
3	30	0.5979	79.24	0.9161	68.80
4	40	0.4116	85.87	0.9340	69.85
5	50	0.2849	90.23	0.9698	70.51
6	60	0.2022	93.28	1.0505	70.35
7	70	0.1539	94.98	1.1186	70.03
8	80	0.1184	96.15	1.1312	70.56
9	90	0.0955	97.03	1.2352	70.74
10	100	0.0770	97.64	1.2531	70.54
11	110	0.0667	97.97	1.2866	70.80
12	120	0.0562	98.30	1.3270	70.52
13	130	0.0500	98.46	1.3772	70.41
14	140	0.0474	98.52	1.4319	70.61
15	150	$1.1921e{-}07$	10.00	$1.1921e{-}07$	10.00
16	160	$1.1921e{-}07$	10.00	$1.1921e{-}07$	10.00
17	170	$1.1921e{-}07$	10.00	$1.1921e{-}07$	10.00
18	180	$1.1921e{-}07$	10.00	$1.1921e{-}07$	10.00
19	190	$1.1921e{-}07$	10.00	$1.1921e{-}07$	10.00
20	200	$1.1921e{-}07$	10.00	$1.1921e{-}07$	10.00

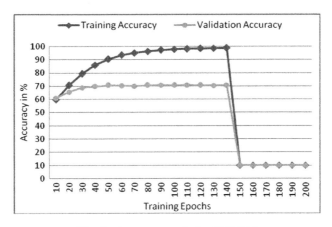

Fig. 3. Accuracy graph for CIFAR10

We observed the performance of the model for epochs at different intervals. The performance metric used during training is Accuracy (Figs. 4, 5 and 6).

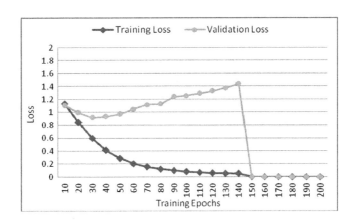

Fig. 4. Loss graph for CIFAR10

Table 2. Model performance with LR = 0.001 for CIFAR10

S. No	No. of epochs	Training loss	Training accuracy	Validation loss	Validation accuracy
1	10	1.7412	0.3873	1.6627	0.4201
2	20	1.5152	0.4621	1.4441	0.4864
3	30	1.3759	0.5138	1.3141	0.5342
4	40	1.2822	0.5473	1.2445	0.5616
5	50	1.2124	0.5742	1.1873	0.5825

(*continued*)

Table 2. (*continued*)

S. No	No. of epochs	Training loss	Training accuracy	Validation loss	Validation accuracy
6	60	1.1560	0.5943	1.1467	0.5925
7	70	1.1036	0.6116	1.1094	0.6099
8	80	1.0545	0.6325	1.0833	0.6141
9	90	1.0085	0.6506	1.0568	0.6245
10	100	0.9679	0.6643	1.0463	0.6332
11	110	0.9243	0.6793	1.0155	0.6424
12	120	0.8872	0.6923	1.0072	0.6455
13	130	0.8491	0.7086	0.9902	0.6514
14	140	0.8054	0.7207	0.9749	0.6594
15	150	0.7745	0.7343	0.9688	0.6598
16	160	0.7358	0.7480	0.9581	0.6670
17	170	0.7010	0.7596	0.9445	0.6751
18	180	0.6643	0.7726	0.9421	0.6745
19	190	0.6333	0.7842	0.9410	0.6729
20	200	0.6015	0.7958	0.9320	0.6799
21	300	0.3468	0.8869	0.9631	0.6919

If we observe the Training and Validation accuracy of the model from Table 1 it is clear that these values increases up to 140 epochs, after that it declines sharply as more training is given to the model. Initially we keep Learning Rate (LR) to 0.01 after that we changed the value of Learning Rate to 0.001 and again trained the model for 300 epochs, results are shown in Table 2. Similarly we created another CNN model using CIFAR100 dataset and trained it for 200 epochs with Learning Rate 0.01. Results are shown in Table 3.

Table 3. CNN model performance for CIFAR100

S. No	No. of epochs	Training loss	Training accuracy	Validation loss	Validation accuracy
1	10	3.2296	21.81	3.1256	25.19
2	20	2.5775	34.44	2.4795	37.82
3	30	2.1733	42.62	2.2425	42.50
4	40	1.8657	49.15	2.0445	46.62
5	50	1.6190	54.53	1.9870	48.60
6	60	1.4141	59.10	1.9777	49.20
7	70	1.2748	62.44	1.9723	49.77
8	80	1.1551	65.84	2.0238	49.97
9	90	1.0610	68.03	2.0116	50.46
10	100	0.9870	69.88	2.0590	50.41
11	110	0.9234	71.52	2.1032	50.16

(*continued*)

Table 3. (*continued*)

S. No	No. of epochs	Training loss	Training accuracy	Validation loss	Validation accuracy
12	120	0.8747	72.98	2.1264	49.83
13	130	0.8237	74.35	2.1670	49.38
14	140	0.7908	75.27	2.2004	49.58
15	150	0.7908	75.27	2.2004	49.58
16	160	0.7228	77.20	2.1932	50.73
17	170	0.6981	77.85	2.2030	50.03
18	180	0.6880	78.26	2.2038	50.32
19	190	0.6643	79.02	2.2239	50.65
20	200	0.6475	79.69	2.2745	49.82

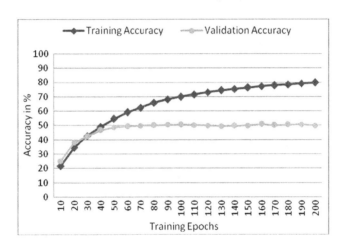

Fig. 5. Accuracy graph for CIFAR100

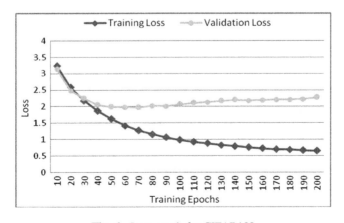

Fig. 6. Loss graph for CIFAR100

We also created our own dataset including five most popular breeds of dogs in the world. The dataset contains a total of 2500 images including 2000 training images and 500 testing images. All the images are 32 × 32 in size. Figure 7 shows the sample images from our dataset.

Classes	Images
Labrador	
Retriever	
German shepherd	
Poodle	
Chihuahua	

Fig. 7. Sample images from own dataset

We have recorded the observations for training loss and accuracy as well as validation loss and accuracy for 150 epochs. Table 3 shows the details of observations (Figs. 8 and 9).

Table 4. CNN model performance for own dataset

S. No	No. of epochs	Training loss	Training accuracy	Validation loss	Validation accuracy
1	10	1.6051	24.7	1.6105	18.4
2	20	1.5988	25.6	1.6116	21
3	30	1.5938	24.05	1.614	20
4	40	1.5766	27.15	1.6176	22.2
5	50	1.5695	28.2	1.6206	20.2
6	60	1.5491	32.5	1.6451	20
7	70	1.5213	34	1.6417	19.8

(continued)

Table 4. (*continued*)

S. No	No. of epochs	Training loss	Training accuracy	Validation loss	Validation accuracy
8	80	1.4921	35.95	1.6693	19.4
9	90	1.3768	44.2	1.753	18.6
10	100	1.303	48.7	1.7502	20.4
11	110	1.0817	58.4	1.9601	20.4
12	120	0.9537	66.1	1.9833	21.2
13	130	0.7897	73.5	2.0041	19.6
14	140	0.6543	79.45	2.0689	19.8
15	150	0.6210	79.48	2.0921	20.4

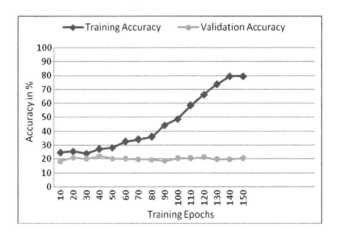

Fig. 8. Accuracy graph for own dataset

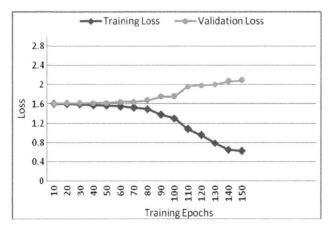

Fig. 9. Loss graph for own dataset

If we observe the training and validation accuracy values in Tables 1, 2, and 3, it is clear that training accuracy of the model is always higher as compared to validation accuracy. This is because training accuracy is the accuracy of a model on examples it was constructed on, and validation accuracy is the accuracy on examples it hasn't seen. After certain training epochs the accuracy of the model (both training and validation) reaches to a saturation point after that it does not show any further improvements. It can be observed from Table 1 that accuracy of the model increases to a certain number of epochs after that it declines sharply. For this sharp decline we noticed two important factors. First is; giving too much training to the model makes it perform worst for classifying new data, Second is; keeping learning rate high make the model to decline its performance after certain training epochs. Later we reduced the learning rate of the model to 0.001 and again trained the model. This time the accuracy of the model found to be increased at much slow rate, but the problem of sharp decline in the accuracy was not encountered even up to 300 training epochs (Table 4).

We can say that increasing training time for the CNN model doesn't necessarily improves the performance of the model and can cause other issues such as overfitting and exploding gradient. The behavior of the model observed in Table 1 is actually the overfitting problem. Learning Rate is another important factor which should be given carefully during the training of the model. We made slight changes in the structure of the models and trained repeatedly for different epochs and observed similar pattern in the performance graphs of validation and accuracy.

5   Issues in Training a CNN Model

One of the most important aspects of CNN model is how well the model generalizes to unseen data. Overfitting is one of the most common issue in CNN networks, it occurs when the model fits well enough to the training dataset but the model is not capable for generalizing new examples which are not the part of training dataset. This happens because the model starts to memorize the training examples, but it has not learning actually. Overfitting can be controlled by adding more data to the training set, using data augmentation techniques, reducing architecture complexity, regularization, and early stopping. Other issues in training a CNN model are exploding gradient and class imbalance.

Exploding gradient is identified when training model cannot learn from the training data after a certain number epochs and results in overflow and NaN loss values of the error gradient. Exploding gradients can make learning unstable [14]. Redesigning the network model, gradient clipping, and choosing appropriate activation functions can help to overcome exploding gradients. Class imbalance is another situation where the sample distribution of classes is significantly non-uniform. Training the model using imbalanced classes is a long-standing and significant challenge for machine learning [15]. We used CIFAR10 and CIFAR100 datasets both of these datasets do not have class imbalance.

6 Conclusion

The main purpose of the work presented in this paper, is to apply the concept of Convolutional Neural Networks in image classification. CNNs are widely used in automatic image classification in many fields.

In this paper we summarized the basic CNN model layers and shared our observations on Training accuracy, Validation accuracy, Training and Validation loss, Training time, Learning Rate, and Overfitting problem. The paper also shares the structure of CNN model that we trained on for classification of different natural objects. We also discussed other common issues and their solutions for better performance of a CNN model.

References

1. Mohamed, A.-R., Dahl, G.E., Hinton, G.: Acoustic modeling using deep belief networks. IEEE Trans. Audio Speech Lang. Process. **20**(1), 14–22 (2012)
2. LeCun, Y., Bengio, Y., Hinton, G.: Deep learning. Nature **521**(7553), 436–444 (2015)
3. Hu, G., Wang, K., Peng, Y., Qiu, M., Shi, J., Liu, L.: Deep learning methods for underwater target feature extraction and recognition. Comput. Intell. Neurosci. **2018**, 10 (2018). Article ID 1214301
4. http://ufldl.stanford.edu/tutorial/supervised/ConvolutionalNeuralNetwork/
5. http://yann.lecun.com/exdb/lenet/
6. http://cs231n.github.io/convolutional-networks/
7. https://medium.com/@udemeudofia01/basic-overview-of-convolutional-neural-network-cnn-4fcc7dbb4f17
8. https://adeshpande3.github.io/A-Beginner%27s-Guide-To-Understanding-Convolutional-Neural-Networks-Part-2/
9. https://machinelearningmastery.com/dropout-regularization-deep-learning-models-keras/
10. https://www.analyticsvidhya.com/blog/2017/10/fundamentals-deep-learning-activation-functions-when-to-use-them/
11. https://www.cs.toronto.edu/~kriz/cifar.html
12. https://en.wikipedia.org/wiki/Convolutional_neural_network
13. Jaswal, D., Vishvanathan, S., Soman K.P.: Image classification using convolutional neural networks. Int. J. Adv. Res. Technol. **3**(6) (2014)
14. Goodfellow, I., Bengio, Y., Courville, A.: Deep Learning (Adaptive Computation and Machine Learning) (2016)
15. https://arxiv.org/pdf/1804.10851.pdf

An Approach to Find Proper Execution Parameters of n-Gram Encoding Method Based on Protein Sequence Classification

Suprativ Saha[1][(✉)] and Tanmay Bhattacharya[2]

[1] Department of Computer Science and Engineering, Brainware University,
Barasat, Kolkata 700125, India
reach2suprativ@yahoo.co.in
[2] Department of Information Technology, Techno India,
Saltlake, Kolkata 700091, India
dr.tb1029@gmail.com

Abstract. Various protein sequence classification approaches are developed to classify unknown sequences in to its classes or familes with an certain accuracy. Features extraction from protein sequence is a key technique to implement all approaches. N-gram encoding method is a popular feature extraction procedure. But to maintain the low computational time and high accuracy level of classification, it requires to fix up the upper limit of 'N' of N-gram encoding method. On the other hand, the standard deviation value of protein sequence is one of the important feature value which is extracted by N-gram encoding method. This feature can be extracted by two different ways like standard deviation calculation using standard mean value and using floating mean value. It is also important to find proper method to calculate the value of standard deviation. In this paper, an investigational proof has done to find upper limit of N-gram encoding method as well as find the proper technique to calculate the standard deviation value as a feature which are extracted from unknown protein sequence.

Keywords: Neural network based classifier ·
N-gram encoding method · Standard mean value · Standard deviation ·
Floating mean value

1 Introduction

Computational intelligence techniques involving bioinformatics plays a big role to extract the information from the biological data. Various projects of bioinformatics like Human Genome Project (1990–2003), different genome or protein sequencing projects etc. [1] discover huge amount of gene or protein data. Size of this achieved sequence is increasing constantly. The protein contains a sequence of 20 amino acids. Within the three significant characteristics of protein like sequence, structure, and function, protein sequence is most vital for identifying

© Springer Nature Singapore Pte Ltd. 2019
M. Singh et al. (Eds.): ICACDS 2019, CCIS 1046, pp. 294–303, 2019.
https://doi.org/10.1007/978-981-13-9942-8_28

the unknown protein. Now a days, UniProtKB database contains more than 90 million protein sequences of various categories of organism [2]. An accurate classification of a protein sequence into protein family, classes or sub classes is a very important and open problem in the field of bioinformatics and computational biology because no one previous method archives 100% classification accuracy on the standard data sets [3]. The process of feature extraction is important techniques to find distinctive characteristic from protein sequences. This article works to find proper upper limit of N-gram encoding method (a feature extraction procedure) as well as find the proper technique to calculate the value of standard deviation. Here, a brief literature survey on various classification techniques involving data mining, proposed by different researchers are presented in Sect. 2. Section 3 describes the method of N-gram encoding method. The final result and investigational proof are shown in Sect. 4, finally Sect. 5 presents the conclusion.

2   Literature Review

Different researchers proposed various classification techniques for classifying the unknown sequences upon features extraction procedure. A Neural network based classifier with 90% accuracy was proposed by *Wang et al.* [4]. 2-gram encoding method and 6-letter exchange group method are used for extracting feature value. *Zainuddin et al.* [5] were used N-gram encoding method in replace of 2-gram encoding method. To improve the accuracy *Nageswara Rao et al.* [6] proposed back-propagation technique. Fuzzy ARTMAP model was proposed by *Mohamed et al.* [7]. Here molecular weight, isoelectric point, hydropathy composition, hydropathy distribution and hydropathy transmission of the protein sequence was used as feature value with 93% accuracy. To reduce the computational time, rank-based algorithm were applied by *Mansoori et al.* [8] the upon fuzzy ARTMAP model. *Cai et al.* [9] proposed a classification model involving rough set theory which is 97% accurate. A 91% accurate classifier was elaborated by *Saha et al.* [10,11] which involves the combination of neural network system, fuzzy ARTMAP model and Rough set classifier.

Spalding et al. [12]was proposed String kernel-based model based on a Local pair-wise method like BLAST, FASTA etc with 87.5% accuracy. *Zaki et al.* [13] proposed a technique to extract the feature value using Hidden Markov Model, which was applied to the classifier that can train the data in high dimensional space. The combination of feature extraction phase and classification phase were formed String weighted based classified with 99.03% accuracy. *Ali et al.* [14] proposed a classification approach based on the functional properties of the protein sequence which is extracted by Fast Fourier transform approach. The classification accuracy of the previous model was 91% when it was applied on full four levels of SCOP database. The accuracy level was enhanced up to 96% when it was applied on restricted level of SCOP. Tree-Based Classifier was proposed by *Boujenfa et al.* [15] with 93% accuracy. Hidden Markov Based Classifier was proposed by *Desai* [16] with 94% accuracy level, which executes 3 phase of extraction like Training, Decoding, and Evolution.

A new classifier using Structural Analysis of Protein was proposed by *Rahman et al.* [17] with 98% accuracy level. A classifier Using Feature Hashing involving K-gram encoding methods followed by Rank based algorithm were invented by *Caragea et al.* [18] with 82.83% accuracy. A classifier combination of Support vector machine and Genetic algorithm, based on SVM hybrid framework were also proposed by *Zhao et al.* [19]. The accuracy level was 99.24%.

3   N-Gram Encoding Method: A Feature Extraction Approach

A protein Sequence contains the combination of twenty amino acids which is recognized by twenty letters of english alphabets. N-gram encoding method is an approach to extract features from the protein sequences. In N-gram encoding method, value of 'N' can be vary from 2 to n. Individual features are extracted in every gram value. At first, occurance of amino acid is calculated where window size is 'n'. After that, mean value and the standard deviation is generated based on the occurance of amino acid group using the following formulas.

$$MN = \frac{\sum_{k=1}^{f} z_k}{f} \qquad SD = \sqrt{\frac{\sum_{k=1}^{f}(z_k - MN)^2}{f - 1}}$$

Where, 'MN' denoted mean value and 'SD' for standard deviation. 'f' means the number of unique patters extracted from sequence and $z = ac/(\text{len(str)} - (g-1))$.'ac' pointed number of occurrence of distinct pattern, len(str) denotes the length of the sequence and 'g' indicates gram value [20].

According to the previous formula standard deviation is derived from the mean value of every occurrence. Now there are two types of procedure to calculate mean value, (1) standard mean value and (2) floating mean value extraction procedure. In this scenario value of standard deviation also varies in two forms depends on forms of mean value. So, every forms of mean value along with standard deviation are considered as feature values in neural network based classifier.

4   An Experimental Result Along with Problem Analysis

The N-gram encoding method is highly appreciable approach, which is used in neural network based classifier. A lot of classifiers along with their own feature extraction procedures already described in literature review section. After analyzing every technique, it is observed that, generally a classifier is evaluated by its computational time and also accuracy. In this scenario, it is vital part of research, to maintain the low computational time and high the accuracy level. In N-gram encoding method, to identify saturation point to 'n-gram', provides reducible computational time which is describe by *Saha et al.* [20]. Besides that, it is also most important to find the best approach between standard mean extraction procedure and floating mean extraction procedure, which can increase the accuracy level of classification.

4.1 Experimental Analysis Based on the Value of Standard Deviation Calculated by Standard Mean Value

In this section, an experimental analysis is shown where standard deviation of each gram encoding method for every protein classes are calculated based on the standard mean value of protein sequence [20].

Table 1. Experimental result sample of 6 different classes (Standard mean value is used to calculate Standard deviation)

Class_name	Standard deviation								
	2-gm	3-gm	4-gm	5-gm	6-gm	7-gm	8-gm	9-gm	10-gm
DsbB-l	0.0039	0.0008	0	0	0	0	0	0	0
FaeA-l	0.00291	0.0009	0	0	0	0	0	0	0
DsbB-l	0.00434	0.0009	0	0	0	0	0	0	0
FaeA-l	0.00274	0.0006	0.0002	0	0	0	0	0	0
DsbB-l	0.00822	0.0024	0.0008	0.0005	0	0	0	0	0
FaeA-l	0.00276	0.0005	0.0002	0	0	0	0	0	0
MMF_WH1*	0.00537	0.0012	0.0004	0	0	0	0	0	0
MMF_WH1*	0.00289	0.0006	0.0002	0.0001	0	0	0	0	0
MMF_WH1*	0.00302	0.0006	0	0	0	0	0	0	0
MiaE-like	0.0039	0.001	0.0002	0	0	0	0	0	0
MiaE-like	0.00391	0.0009	0	0	0	0	0	0	0
MiaE-like	0.00388	0.0009	0	0	0	0	0	0	0
PRP4-l	0.0025	0.0006	0.0002	0.00008	0	0	0	0	0
SOCS box-l	0.00405	0.001	0.0002	0	0	0	0	0	0
PRP4-l	0.00287	0.0006	0.0002	0	0	0	0	0	0
SOCS box-l	0.0038	0.0011	0.0004	0.0002	0	0	0	0	0
PRP4-l	0.00272	0.0006	0.0002	0	0	0	0	0	0
SOCS box-l	0.00334	0.0006	0	0	0	0	0	0	0

MMF_ WH1 means Marine Metagenome Family WH1

Table 1 represents sample actual experimental result of the standard deviation, which is extracted from 2-gram encoding method to 10-gram method against 6 different protein families. Table 2 represents the whole statistical value of experiment where 497 different protein sequences are used to analysis the aim. Among 497 protein sequences, it is already experimentally proved by *Saha et al.* [20], that after executing '5-gram' encoding method all standard deviation value is going to zero. So, it can conclude that after 5-gram encoding approach, any types of markable classification measurement is not found. From Tables 1 and 2, it is also observed that, '2-gram' encoding method provides most markable classification measurement. On the other hand, '3-gram', '4-gram' and '5-gram' also provides some markable classification measurement but it gradually decreases.

Table 2. Summary report of the experimental results of 6 different protein classes (Standard deviation is extracted using standard mean value)

Class_name	No of non-zero standard deviation value									
	Tot_Seq	2-gm	3-gm	4-gm	5-gm	6-gm	7-gm	8-gm	9-gm	10-gm
DsbB-l	63	63	59	42	21	0	0	0	0	0
MiaE-l	83	83	80	49	38	0	0	0	0	0
FaeA-l	78	78	76	48	32	0	0	0	0	0
MMF_WH1*	84	84	84	44	31	0	0	0	0	0
SOCS box-l	108	108	101	66	29	0	0	0	0	0
PRP4-l	81	81	77	59	28	0	0	0	0	0
Total	**497**	**497**	**477**	**308**	**179**	**0**	**0**	**0**	**0**	**0**

MMF_ WH1 means Marine Metagenome Family WH1

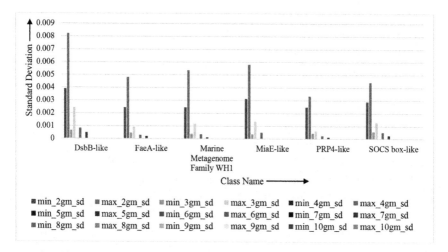

Fig. 1. Graphical representation of standard deviation based on protein class name (calculated through standard mean value) of N-gram encoding method (Value of n varies 2 to 10)

Figure 1 represents, the range of standard deviation extracted from each gram encoding method corresponding 6 different classes. Two types of observation are shown here. First, in '2-gram encoding method' provides high level of distinguishable measurement of classification for each and every protein classes but it belongs in the overlapping fashion. Range of standard deviation of every classes are overlapped, so that it is impossible to classify a particular class for an unknown protein sequence using only '2-gram encoding method'. So, it's obvious to implement others encoding methods like 3-gram, 4-gram etc. Second observation is that from 6-gram to 10-gram encoding method no range bar is shown here. It means minimum and maximum standard deviation valueafter 5-gram encoding method are zero or same. So it can not consider as features of classification. Figure 2 also proves the same.

Figure 2 plots the average value of SD corresponding n-gram encoding method for every protein classes where value of n varies from 2 to 10. This figure clearly shown that 2-gram encoding method provides high markable measurement of classification but 3-gram, 4-gram and 5-gram also consider for the measurement of classification. On the other hand it is shown that from 6-gram to 10-gram encoding method, no markable measurement of classification is found.

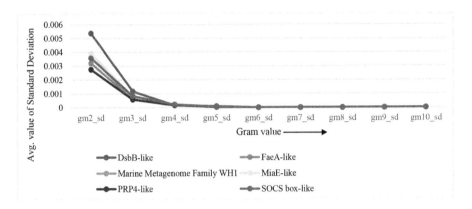

Fig. 2. Graphical representation of standard deviation based on gram value (calculated through standard mean value) of N-gram encoding method (Value of n varies 2 to 10)

On the basic of above experimental results it can conclude that, if standard deviation is extracted by the standard mean value then after 5 gram encoding method, there is no requirement to implement any encoding method. In such way the value of n can be fixed to 5 as a fixed up point of n-gram encoding method. In this way time require to compute n-gram encoding method shall reduce. As well as the accuracy level also increases to implement 2 to 5 gram in replace of implementing only 2-gram encoding method.

4.2   Experimental Analysis Based on the Value of Standard Deviation Calculated by Floating Mean Value

In this section, the floating mean value of protein sequence is used to calculate SD of each gram encoding method for every protein classes. A sample actual experimental result of standard deviation, which is extracted from 2-gram to 10-gram encoding method corresponding 6 different protein classes is presented in Table 3.

A summary of the statistical analysis is also pointed in Table 4. Here, among 497 protein sequences, all values of standard deviation for each and every gram encoding method is non-zero value. This provides a remarkable differentiation with the experimental analysis of previous [20]. In this case, the upper limit of n-gram encoding can't conclude from the statistical analysis of Tables 3 and 4.

Table 3. Experimental result sample of 6 different classes (Floating mean value is used to calculate Standard deviation)

Class_name	Standard deviation (SD)								
	2-gm	3-gm	4-gm	5-gm	6-gm	7-gm	8-gm	9-gm	10-gm
DsbB-like	0.0082	0.0035	0.0034	0.0034	0.0035	0.0035	0.0035	0.0035	0.0036
DsbB-like	0.0066	0.0036	0.0033	0.0033	0.0033	0.0034	0.0034	0.0034	0.0034
DsbB-like	0.0102	0.0046	0.0036	0.0035	0.0035	0.0035	0.0035	0.0036	0.0036
FaeA-like	0.0041	0.0019	0.0018	0.0018	0.0018	0.0018	0.0018	0.0018	0.0018
FaeA-like	0.0036	0.0014	0.0012	0.0012	0.0012	0.0012	0.0012	0.0012	0.0012
FaeA-like	0.0043	0.0022	0.0021	0.0020	0.0020	0.0021	0.0021	0.0021	0.0021
MMF WH1*	0.0039	0.0015	0.0013	0.0013	0.0013	0.0013	0.0013	0.0013	0.0013
MMF WH1*	0.0046	0.0019	0.0017	0.0017	0.0017	0.0017	0.0017	0.0017	0.0017
MMF WH1*	0.0049	0.0028	0.0027	0.0028	0.0028	0.0028	0.0028	0.0028	0.0028
MiaE-like	0.0057	0.0030	0.0028	0.0028	0.0028	0.0028	0.0028	0.0029	0.0029
MiaE-like	0.0051	0.0024	0.0022	0.0022	0.0022	0.0022	0.0022	0.0022	0.0022
MiaE-like	0.0058	0.0030	0.0028	0.0029	0.0029	0.0029	0.0029	0.0029	0.0029
PRP4-like	0.0037	0.0012	0.0010	0.0010	0.0010	0.0010	0.0010	0.0010	0.0010
PRP4-like	0.0040	0.0014	0.0012	0.0011	0.0012	0.0012	0.0012	0.0012	0.0012
PRP4-like	0.0046	0.0025	0.0024	0.0024	0.0024	0.0024	0.0024	0.0025	0.0025
SOCS b-like	0.0049	0.0019	0.0017	0.0017	0.0017	0.0017	0.0017	0.0017	0.0017
SOCS b-like	0.0053	0.0023	0.0019	0.0019	0.0019	0.0019	0.0019	0.0019	0.0019
SOCS b-like	0.0050	0.0020	0.0015	0.0015	0.0014	0.0015	0.0015	0.0015	0.0015

MMF_ WH1 means Marine Metagenome Family WH1

Table 4. Summary report of the experimental results of 6 different protein classes (Standard deviation is extracted using standard mean value)

Class_name	No of non-zero value of standard deviation									
	Tol_ Seq	2-gm	3-gm	4-gm	5-gm	6-gm	7-gm	8-gm	9-gm	10-gm
DsbB-like	63	63	63	63	63	63	63	63	63	63
FaeA-like	78	78	78	78	78	78	78	78	78	78
MMF WH1*	84	84	84	84	84	84	84	84	84	84
MiaE-like	83	83	83	83	83	83	83	83	83	83
PRP4-like	81	81	81	81	81	81	81	81	81	81
SOCS box-like	108	108	108	108	108	108	108	108	108	108
Total	**497**	**497**	**497**	**497**	**497**	**497**	**497**	**497**	**497**	**497**

MMF_ WH1 means Marine Metagenome Family WH1

Because in every gram value some distinguishable measurement of classification is found.

Figure 3 represents, the range of standard deviation extracted from each gram encoding method of 6 protein classes. Two types of observation are

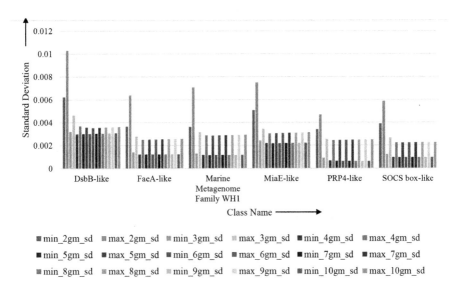

Fig. 3. Graphical representation of standard deviation based on class name (calculated through floating mean value) of N-gram encoding method (Value of n varies 2 to 10)

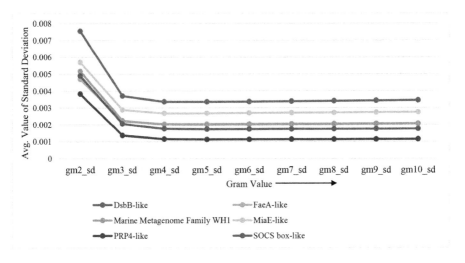

Fig. 4. Graphical representation of standard deviation based on gram value (calculated through floating mean value) of N-gram encoding method (Value of n varies 2 to 10)

also shown here. First, as like previous in 2-gram encoding method also gives high level of markable measurement of classification for each and every protein classes but it also belongs in the overlapping fashion. Second observation of the previous section is little bit differ from it. Here, from 6-gram to 10-gram encoding method all range bars are present but they are belongs to the same range. It means minimum and maximum value of standard deviation from

6-gram to 10-gram encoding method is approx. same. So it can not consider in features of classification.

Figure 4 plots the average value of standard deviation corresponding n-gram encoding method for every protein classes where value of n varies from 2 to 10. This figure clearly shown that 2-gram encoding method provides high distinguishable measurement of classification but 3-gram, 4-gram and 5-gram also consider for the measurement of classification. On the other hand it is shown that after 5-gram encoding method all the lines of every classes are parallel. It means, from 6-gram encoding method to n-gram encoding method (where $n > 6$) all distinguishable measurement of classification is same as like 5-gram encoding method. In this case implementation of its only takes unnecessary more time without increasing accuracy level of classification.

On the basic of above experimental results it can conclude that, if standard deviation is extracted by the standard mean value then after 5 gram encoding method all the value of SD goes to zero but in respect to the approach to calculate SD using floating mean, all value of SD is not zero. But range of SD is same so that no distinguishable measurement of classification is found. So, there is no requirement to implement any encoding method above 5-gram. In such way the value of n can be fixed to 5 as a saturation point of n-gram encoding method. In this way the computational time of n-gram encoding method shall reduce. As well as the accuracy level also increases to implement 2 to 5 gram in replace of implementing only 2-gram encoding method.

5   Conclusion

Several execution procedures and problem of N-gram encoding method are analyzed in this paper. After analyzing two different procedures of N-gram encoding method it can be concluded that, calculation of standard deviation based on the floating mean value provides better significant of classification than the calculation of standard deviation based on the standard mean value. The overlapping values of standard deviation in every gram value are less in calculation of SD based on floating mean value. In this way proper execution procedure of N-gram encoding method is fixed as well as classification accuracy is also increased. On the other hand, in both execution procedures, after 5-gram, no disguisable measurement of classification is found. In this scenario, it is also concluded that, saturation point of N-gram encoding method is fixed to 5-gram. In this way computational time of classification decreases without disturbing the accuracy of classification.

References

1. Bentley, D.R.: The human genome project-an overview. Med. Res. Rev. **20**(3), 189–196 (2000)
2. Apweiler, R., et al.: UniProt: the universal protein knowledgebase. Nucleic Acids Res. **32**(DATABASE ISS.), D115–D119 (2004)

3. Vipsita, S., Shee, B.K., Rath, S.K.: An efficient technique for protein classification using feature extraction by artificial neural networks. In: Proceedings of the Annual IEEE India Conference (INDICON), Kolkata, India, pp. 1–5 (2010)
4. Wang, J.T.L., Ma, Q.H., Shasha, D., Wu, C.H.: Application of neural networks to biological data mining: a case study in protein sequence classification. In: KDD, Boston, pp. 305–309 (2000)
5. Zainuddin, Z., et al.: Radial basic function neural networks in protein sequence classification. Malays. J. Math. Sci. **2**, 195–204 (2008)
6. Nageswara Rao, P.V., Uma Devi, T., Kaladhar, D., Sridhar, G., Rao, A.A.: A probabilistic neural network approach for protein superfamily classification. J. Theor. Appl. Inf. Technol. (2009)
7. Mohamed, S., Rubin, D., Marwala, T.: Multi-class protein sequence classification using Fuzzy ARTMAP. In: IEEE Conference, pp. 1676–1680 (2006)
8. Mansoori, E.G., Zolghadri, M.J., Katebi, S.D., Mohabatkar, H., Boostani, R., Sadreddini, M.H.: Generating fuzzy rules for protein classification. Iran. J. Fuzzy Syst. **5**(2), 21–33 (2008)
9. Cai, C.Z., Han, L.Y., Ji, Z.L., Chen, X., Chen, Y.Z.: SVM-Prot: web-based support vector machine software for functional classification of a protein from its primary sequence. Nucleic Acids Res. **31**, 3692–3697 (2003)
10. Saha, S., Chaki, R.: Application of data mining in protein sequence classification. IJDMS **4**(5), 103–118 (2012)
11. Saha, S., et al.: A brief review of data mining application involving protein sequence classification. In: Meghanathan, N., Nagamalai, D., Chaki, N. (eds.) Advances in Computing and Information Technology. AISC, vol. 177. Springer, Berlin (2012). https://doi.org/10.1007/978-3-642-31552-7_48
12. Spalding, J.D., Hoyle, D.C.: Accuracy of string kernels for protein sequence classification. In: Singh, S., Singh, M., Apte, C., Perner, P. (eds.) ICAPR 2005. LNCS, vol. 3686, pp. 454–460. Springer, Heidelberg (2005). https://doi.org/10.1007/11551188_49
13. Zaki, N.M., Deri, S., Illias, R.M.: Protein sequences classification based on string weighting scheme. Int. J. Comput. Internet Manage. **13**(1), 50–60 (2005)
14. Ali, A.F., Shawky, D.M.: A novel approach for protein classification using fourier transform. Int. J. Eng. Appl. Sci. **6**, 4 (2010)
15. Boujenfa, K., Essoussi, N., Limam, M.: Tree-kNN: a tree-based algorithm for protein sequence classification. IJCSE **3**, 961–968 (2011). ISSN: 0975-3397
16. Desai, P.: Sequence classification using hidden markov models. Electronic thesis or Dissertation (2005). https://etd.ohiolink.edu/
17. Rahman, M.M., Arif Ul Alam, A.-A.-M., Mursalin, T.E.: A more appropriate protein classification using data mining. JATIT, 33–43 (2010)
18. Caragea, C., et al.: Protein sequence classification using feature hashing. Proteome Sci. **10**(Suppl 1), S14 (2012). https://doi.org/10.1186/1477-5956-10-S1-S14
19. Zhao, X.-M., Huang, D.-S., Cheung, Y., Wang, H., Huang, X.: A novel hybrid GA/SVM system for protein sequences classification. In: Yang, Z.R., Yin, H., Everson, R.M. (eds.) IDEAL 2004. LNCS, vol. 3177, pp. 11–16. Springer, Heidelberg (2004). https://doi.org/10.1007/978-3-540-28651-6_2
20. Saha, S., Bhattacharya, T.: A novel approach to find the saturation point of n-Gram encoding method for protein sequence classification involving data mining. In: Bhattacharyya, S., Hassanien, A.E., Gupta, D., Khanna, A., Pan, I. (eds.) International Conference on Innovative Computing and Communications. LNNS, vol. 56, pp. 101–108. Springer, Singapore (2019). https://doi.org/10.1007/978-981-13-2354-6_12

Hyperglycemia Prediction Using Machine Learning: A Probabilistic Approach

Vishwas Agrawal[1(✉)], Pushpa Singh[2], and Sweta Sneha[3]

[1] Cochin University of Science and Technology, Kochi, India
vishwas283@gmail.com
[2] IEC College of Engineering and Technology, Greater Noida, India
pushpa.gla@gmail.com
[3] Kennesaw State University, Kennesaw, GA, USA
ssneha@kennesaw.edu

Abstract. The incidence of diabetes is on the rise all over the globe. Therefore, a proper approach is necessary to identify the diabetic patients at the earliest and provide appropriate lifestyle intervention in preventing or postponing the onset of diabetes. Hyperglycemia and hypoglycemia are two important consequences of diabetes computed on the basis of blood glucose level. In this paper, we propose a machine learning approach to identify the probability of occurrence of hyperglycemia with the impact of physical activity (exercise). This prediction will be helpful in order to reduce the risk factor of hyperglycemia by timely taken preventive step and changing their lifestyle.

Keywords: Diabetes · Machine learning · Hyperglycemia ·
Blood glucose level · Exercise · Probability

1 Introduction

Recent developments in science and technology offer several prospects for the enhancement of health care delivery in diagnosis, management, and even prevention of various diseases. The healthcare decision support system has focused on automated and intelligent predictions of diseases, based on a person's lifestyle and certain other parameters. Significant efforts have been made for the enhancement of computer aided diagnosis applications, because even minute errors in medical diagnostic systems can result in ineffective medical treatments. In computer-aided diagnosis (CAD), machine learning is an important instrument that can contribute significantly towards disease prediction and diagnosis. The machine learning approach is significant in the effective prediction of chronic disease occurrence in disease-frequent communities [1]. Diabetes is a chronic disease that is classified as either Type 1 or Type 2. In Type 1 diabetes, the pancreas does not yield sufficient insulin, whereas in Type 2, the body either cannot effactually use the insulin it creates or an insufficient amount of insulin is released into the bloodstream. The key environmental reasons that raise the risk of Type 2 diabetes are over nutrition and an inactive lifestyle, with resulting overweight and obesity [6].

However, minor variations in blood sugar levels are quite normal for a non-diabetic person. A blood glucose level of around 60–140 (mg/dL) is considered healthy.

M. Singh et al. (Eds.): ICACDS 2019, CCIS 1046, pp. 304–312, 2019.
https://doi.org/10.1007/978-981-13-9942-8_29

Extremely high blood glucose levels (more than 250 mg/dL) is termed as hyperglycemia and chronically low blood glucose levels (less than 60 mg/dL) is referred as hypoglycemia. In India, diabetes is an emergent problem, accounting for here are 8.7% of the diabetic population belong to the age group of 20 to 70 years. Diabetes is driven by different permutations of parameters and factors that include: rapid urbanization, junk food, inactive lifestyle, use of tobacco, and growing life expectancy and many other socioeconomic reasons. Diabetes is a condition which can be treated but not be curable [11].

Minimizing the occurrence of hyperglycemia in patients with diabetes is a challenging task which required the continuous monitoring of blood glucose level. It is very important that people having diabetes could be able to predict a chance to occurrence of hyperglycemia on the basis of blood glucose level. Recently a machine learning technique has been functional to diabetes diagnosis and estimation. The Machine learning technique is suitable when there is a vast volume of sample data and there are no rules for prediction.

In this paper, we propose a method that utilizes machine learning techniques to predict chances of occurrence of hyperglycemia and how one can reduce this chance of occurrence. A sample of blood glucose levels, which is collected in the different time stamp of several days are analyzed through machine learning approach. The outcome is compared with physical activity of that patient for efficient prediction or probability of affecting hyperglycemia.

2   Related Works

Diabetes is the seventh foremost reason of death, a main reason of heart disease and stroke, and the foremost reason of grown-up blindness, kidney failure etc. [8]. Reference [10] presented a detailed review to spread the knowledge of mechanism, pathophysiology and management of diabetes to control this killer disease. Monitoring of blood glucose level is very important in case of diabetes. Neural network models for predicting the time course of the blood glucose concentration in subjects with type 1 diabetes have been investigated in a number of studies [9]. Reference [12] proposed a technique to predict the individual risk of hypoglycemia by using sparse data. The sparse data were used to modify the performance of machine learning algorithms and compute most accurate predictions. Reference [2] conducted a methodical analysis of the applications of machine learning, data mining methods and tools in the arena of diabetes research with respect to: Prediction and Diagnosis, Diabetic Complications, Genetic Background and Environment, and Health Care and Management.

Reference [3] used machine learning techniques on the Pima Indian Diabetes dataset using R tool to classify the patients into diabetic and non-diabetic. They applied supervised machine learning algorithms like SVM, k-NN, RBF, ANN and MDR.

Reference [7] discussed a machine learning method for forecasting blood glucose levels and hypoglycemia prediction. A Support Vector Regression (SVR) was trained on patient specific data and diabetes experts at predicting blood glucose levels. Their model can predict 23% of hypoglycemic events 30 min in advance.

High glucose level can increase the risk of heart attack, kidney disease, nerve disease, etc., while low glucose level can increase the risks of severe confusion and disorientation, unconsciousness, seizures, coma, etc. Heart attack and strokes can be controlled by reducing the blood glucose level [13]. Reference [5] linked the incidence of cardiovascular complications with hyperglycemia. The hyperglycemia is one of the growing health problems which need to timely identified in order to be cured. This motivates the author to predict chances of occurrence of hyperglycemia. So that people can get treated timely and reduce the risk factor due to the consequence of hyperglycemia.

3 Dataset and Model Description

The AIM-94 Diabetes dataset was taken from UCI Machine Learning Repository. The dataset is available in comma separated value (CSV). The objective of dataset to analyze the and understand about potential features. The dataset was cleaned for irregularities and missing values. The dataset have id, date-time and value, column to represent as features of dataset. The column 'id' varies from 1–70 and uniquely identifies each patient. 'Date-time' column is the merged column of 'date' and 'time' columns in the dataset, representing when the timestamp of when the blood glucose sample was taken and 'value' is the value of blood glucose level of particular patient 'id'. The dataset consists of 29262 rows and 4 columns where the first three columns represent the input features discussed above and fourth column named 'Category', consists of one label three target labels, classified according to blood glucose value (bgv):

Table 1. Rule to define categories

Condition	Label
If bgv $\geq$ 200	'Hyperglycemia'
If bgv $\geq$ 80 and bgv < 200	'Normal'
If bgv < 80	'Hypoglycemia'

According to rule mentioned in Table 1, there are following observation in dataset of each category: Hyperglycemia = 3874, Hypoglycemia = 17786 and normal = 7602. But this classification is not sufficient to have these target labels. The categories like 'Hyperglycemia', 'Hypoglycemia' and 'Normal' is predicted on the basis of blood glucose value.

In this paper, we have focused on the prediction of chances of occurrence to have hyperglycemia on the basis of the mean value of bgv, which was observed in the different time stamp. Further, we have visualized the relationship between patient 'id' and corresponding blood glucose level: 'value' in Fig. 1 through the scatter matrix diagram in order to understand the dataset and in the next section we take a look on the impact of various physical activities on the chances of occurrence of hyperglycemia.

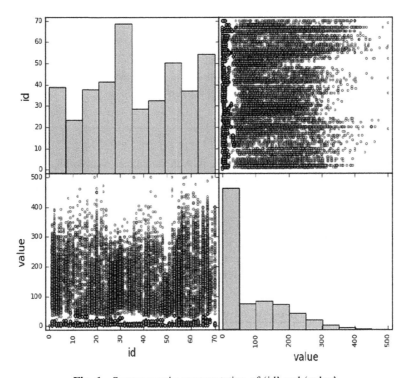

Fig. 1. Scatter matrix representation of 'id' and 'value'

4 Hyperglycemia Prediction Through Machine Learning

Machine learning is a branch of artificial intelligence that permits computers to "learn" from previous cases and to detect patterns from huge, noisy or complex datasets. Machine learning can be categorized in to three further types: supervised, unsupervised and reinforcement learning. Here we have used supervised learning, where the target class has been labeled according to the rule given in Table 1.

In this paper, we propose a simple machine learning approach that could predict a case of hyperglycemia for a person suffering from Type 1 diabetes. If the average blood glucose level of a particular patient is found to be greater than 140, then it's fair to assume that the person could develop hyperglycemia. This chance of occurrence is represented in a probabilistic manner as shown in (1).

$$P_{hyper} = \frac{Mean(bgv) \times 100}{bgv_{hyper}} \tag{1}$$

Here Mean (bgv) is the mean value of blood glucose values of a particular patient 'id', which was observed at different timestamps and bgv_{hyper} is the threshold blood glucose value for hyperglycemia which has been taken as $bgv_{hyper} = 250$. The CSV file is grouped according to 'id' of the patients and to compute the mean value of bgv, the proposed model consists following steps:

1. Read the CSV file having id, date-time, and bgv
2. The CSV file is group by according to 'id' of the patient
3. Compute the mean value of bgv of each patient 'id'
4. if bgv $\geq$ 140 then
5. Compute the P_{hyper} according to Eq. (1)
6. Print the P_{hyper} with their respective 'id'.

The above steps are implemented in python language. Matplotlib, Numpy, and Pandas are important libraries set up that we need to import to fulfill the stated objective. Matplotlib library is used for visualization (plotting) in the python programming language and its numerical mathematics extension NumPy library which is used for scientific computing. Pandas library is used to import CSV file in python. The read_csv method of the pandas library is used to read a CSV file as a data set.

The Mean value 'bgv' with respect to patient 'id' is marked as 'H' and shown in Fig. 2. In Fig. 2, 'H' represents as "Hyperglycemia".

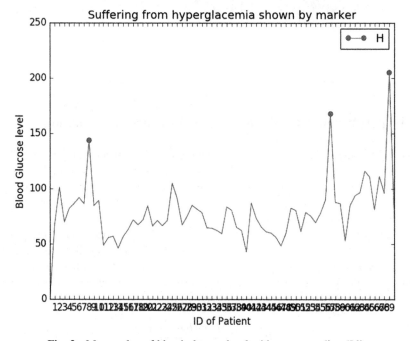

Fig. 2. Mean value of blood glucose level with corresponding 'Id'

Further, we have computed the chances of occurrence of a patient to be hyperglycemia and predicted in Table 2 and visualized in Fig. 3.

According to the proposed work, the chances of occurrence of hyperglycemia can be easily predicted. As per Table 2, patient with id 8 has 57% chance of occurrence,

Table 2. Chances of occurrence of hyperglycemia

S. no.	Patient ID	Mean (bgv)	P_{hyper}
1.	8	143.740113	57.496%
2.	57	167.593985	67.0376%
3.	69	205.254902	82.102%

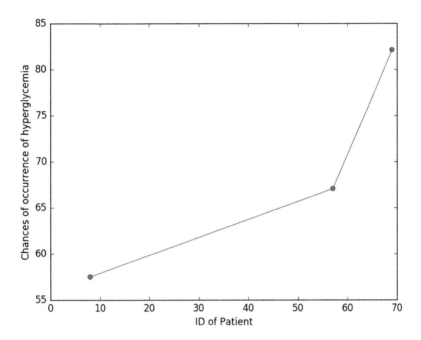

Fig. 3. Chances of occurrence of hyperglycemia (%)

patient with id 57 has a 67% chance of occurrence and patient with id 69 has 82% chance of occurrence of hyperglycemia. This chance of occurrence varies according to the value of bgv_{hyper}.

4.1 Impact of Exercise on Hyperglycemia

Physical activity or exercise is one of the most effective methods to maintain healthy blood glucose levels. Exercise helps in the controlling of blood glucose level in type 2 diabetes, lessens cardiovascular risk factors and also helps in reducing the weight [4]. Here, we discuss the effect that exercise can have in deciding whether a diabetic person can suffer from hyperglycemia. The physical activity of a person can be classified as: regular typical exercise (RE), more than the usual exercise (ME), less than the usual exercise (LE) and no exercise (NE). We assume that all of these categories of physical activity minimize risk factor (R_{min}) by certain factors which are mentioned in Table 3.

Table 3. Categories of physical activity with risk factor

S. no.	Exercise habit	R_{min}
1.	ME	0.25
2.	RE	0.5
3.	LE	0.75
4.	NE	1

An overall chance of occurrence of hyperglycemia when the physical activity of a patient is taken into consideration is represented in (2).

$$P_{hyper} = \frac{Mean(bgv) \times 100}{bgv_{hyper}} \times R_{min} \tag{2}$$

A Comparison of hyperglycemia prediction when the impact of exercise is considered and when it is not is represented in Fig. 4. Data associated with Fig. 4 is depicted in Table 4.

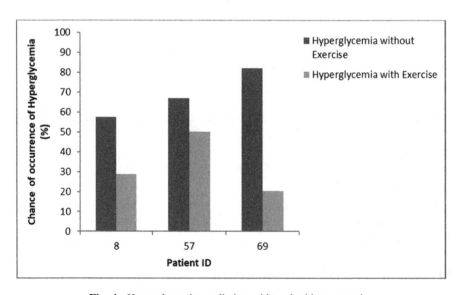

Fig. 4. Hyperglycemia prediction with and without exercise

Table 4. Comparison of hyperglycemia with and without physical activity

S. no.	Patient ID	Exercise habit	P_{hyper} (with exercise)	P_{hyper} (without exercise)
1.	8	RE	28.748%	57.496%
2.	57	LE	50.2782%	67.0376%
3.	69	ME	20.5255%	82.102%

5 Result and Discussion

In this paper, we propose a scheme to predict the chances of occurrence of hyperglycemia with the impact of physical activity. According to Fig. 4, exercise or physical activity reduces the chances of occurrence of hyperglycemia significantly. For example, for the patient id 8, chances of occurring hyperglycemia is 28.748% with exercise and 57.496% is without exercise. Physical activity is important to help prevent hyperglycemia because it helps in reducing the weight, and if the person is insulin resistant, it can help your body increase its sensitivity to insulin.

The above method can be extended to the study the impact of other factors such as: if the blood glucose sample is taken before or after meal/breakfast/dinner/snacks, eating habits and insulin dosage among others.

6 Conclusion

This paper explored the probable chances of occurrence of hyperglycemia through the approach of machine learning. For this purpose, mean blood glucose value of a diabetes patient was analyzed and the chances of occurrence of hyperglycemia on the basis of the threshold blood glucose level were computed. Further, the impact of physical activity was also taken into consideration to accurately predict of hyperglycemia.

References

1. Chen, M., Hao, Y., Hwang, K., Wang, L., Wang, L.: Disease prediction by machine learning over big data from healthcare communities. IEEE Access **5**, 8869–8879 (2017)
2. Kavakiotis, I., Tsave, O., Salifoglou, A., Maglaveras, N., Vlahavas, I., Chouvarda, I.: Machine learning and data mining methods in diabetes research. Comput. Struct. Biotechnol. J. **15**, 104–116 (2017)
3. Kaur, H., Kumari, V.: Predictive modelling and analytics for diabetes using a machine learning approach. Appl. Comput. Inform. (2018). https://doi.org/10.1016/j.aci.2018.12.004
4. Lin, X., et al.: Effects of exercise training on cardiorespiratory fitness and biomarkers of cardiometabolic health: a systematic review and meta-analysis of randomized controlled trials. J. Am. Heart Assoc. **4**(7), e002014 (2015)
5. Mapanga, R.F., Essop, M.F.: Damaging effects of hyperglycemia on cardiovascular function: spotlight on glucose metabolic pathways. Am. J. Physiol. Heart Circ. Physiol. **310** (2), H153–H173 (2015)

6. Nathan, D.M., et al.: Medical management of hyperglycemia in type 2 diabetes: a consensus algorithm for the initiation and adjustment of therapy: a consensus statement of the American Diabetes Association and the European Association for the Study of Diabetes. Diabetes Care 32(1), 193–203 (2009)

7. Plis, K., Bunescu, R.C., Marling, C., Shubrook, J., Schwartz, F.: A machine learning approach to predicting blood glucose levels for diabetes management. In: AAAI Workshop: Modern Artificial Intelligence for Health Analytics, no. 31, pp. 35–39, March 2014

8. Rice, D., Kocurek, B., Snead, C.A.: Chronic disease management for diabetes: Baylor Health Care System's coordinated efforts and the opening of the Diabetes Health and Wellness Institute. In: Baylor University Medical Center Proceedings, vol. 23, no. 3, pp. 230–234. Taylor & Francis, July 2010

9. Robertson, G., Lehmann, E.D., Sandham, W., Hamilton, D.: Blood glucose prediction using artificial neural networks trained with the AIDA diabetes simulator: a proof-of-concept pilot study. J. Electr. Comput. Eng. 2011, Article ID 681786, 11 p. (2011). https://doi.org/10.1155/2011/681786

10. Siddiqui, A.A., Siddiqui, S.A., Ahmad, S., Siddiqui, S., Ahsan, I., Sahu, K.: Diabetes: mechanism, pathophysiology and management-a review. Int. J. Drug Dev. Res. 5(2), 1–23 (2013)

11. Sokol-McKay, D.A.: What is Diabetes? http://www.visionaware.org/info/your-eye-condition/diabetic-retinopathy/what-is-diabetes/125. Accessed 25 Dec 2018

12. Sudharsan, B., Peeples, M., Shomali, M.: Hypoglycemia prediction using machine learning models for patients with type 2 diabetes. J. Diabetes Sci. Technol. 9(1), 86–90 (2015)

13. World Health Organization: Avoiding heart attacks and strokes: don't be a victim-protect yourself. World Health Organization (2005)

Text Caption Generation Based on Lip Movement of Speaker in Video Using Neural Network

Dipti Pawade, Avani Sakhapara, Chaitya Shah[✉], Jigar Wala,
Ankitmani Tripathi, and Bhavikk Shah

Department of IT, K.J. Somaiya College of Engineering, Mumbai, India
{diptipawade,avanisakhapara,chaitya.shah,jigar.wala,
ankitmani.t,bhavikk.shah}@somaiya.edu

Abstract. In this era of e-learning, it will be a great help to deaf people if there can be a system which will generate text caption for various videos. Most of the automatic caption generation system is based on audio to text conversion and thus its accuracy is inversely proportional to the noise in the video. So we have proposed a system which will generate the caption for video based upon the lip movement of the person speaking in the video. Using Facial landmark detector we have extracted facial features of the lip region from frames of the video. These features are fed to the three-dimensional convolutional neural network (3D CNN) to get the text output for the particular frame. The system is trained and tested on GRID dataset.

Keywords: Visual speech processing · Neural network ·
Facial landmark detector · Lip reading

1 Introduction

According to WHO, over 5% of the world's population is suffering from hearing disability. This population is around 466 million across the world. In today's e-learning world, it becomes very difficult for them to get knowledge out of the various videos available on the Internet. Such people can get knowledge through visual aids but cannot get the explanation given through its audio part. For deaf people, there are certain specially developed learning resources containing video tutorials in sign language with captions. But the availability of these kind of resources is very limited. Keeping these needs in mind, YouTube provides automatic caption generation facility for the videos. But YouTube generates the caption using speech processing in which audio signal is converted into text. One of the problems faced with such automatic captioning is that, the caption generation accuracy becomes progressively poor with the increase in noise in the audio. So to address this issue, we have designed a generalized solution in the form of web portal using visual speech processing. This visual speech processing based automatic video caption generation system takes any video input and extracts the frames from it, in which the speaker is pronouncing the words. The facial features of the lip region are extracted from these frames and are fed to 3D CNN to

© Springer Nature Singapore Pte Ltd. 2019
M. Singh et al. (Eds.): ICACDS 2019, CCIS 1046, pp. 313–322, 2019.
https://doi.org/10.1007/978-981-13-9942-8_30

predict the spoken words. For the experimental purpose, we have considered videos containing single speaker, speaking in English language. This paper majorly focuses on the visual speech processing of videos to generate the text captions. In Sect. 2, we have done the survey on the available literature. Further in Sect. 3, implementation of our 3D CNN model architecture along with its layer description is discussed. In Sect. 4, using GRID dataset, the system performance is measured by varying the learning rates of the model. Finally in Sect. 5, conclusion is drawn stating the worth of our study.

2 Related Work

Lip reading is a method that converts visual speech features to text. Automatic lip reading is possible using deep learning techniques which consist of two steps viz. extraction of features from video frames and applying a deep learning model to gathered data. Using feature extraction, the important data that is required to provide information of the speech is extracted. Various features are responsible for carrying speech information like distances between the lip points, change in intensity with respect to time, visibility of teeth etc. After the feature extraction, the extracted information is then used to train a deep learning model. In this step, a learning algorithm decides how the model will be trained to produce the accurate output. Still, there is research going on in this field and researchers are looking for a more robust solution to address this problem. In this section we have discussed the major contribution of various researchers in this area.

Rathee [1] has presented a method of visual speech recognition for 10 Hindi words using Artificial neural network. Here, the mouth and lip detection were done using openCV more precisely Eigen faces, Fischer faces and Haar Cascade Classifier were used. To train the classifier two sets of images were used viz. positive set (that contains lip/face) and negative set (that does not contain lip/face). Then intensity equalization was done and images were converted into hue scale for better results. Key-points of lip were corner lip points and upper middle and lower middle point. The geometric features used in the proposed approach are the height of upper and lower lip, parabolic parameters for the lower and upper lip. A Learning vector quantization with 300 input neurons, corresponding to 300 geometric features and ten output neurons corresponding 10 Hindi words Roti, Papad, Dhoodh, etc. were used. 4800 words were used for training and 200 words for testing out of these 194 words were correctly identified by the neural network implemented. In [2], a speaker independent lip-reading system is designed by Almajai et al. using the Resource Management database of 1090 words. Maximum Likelihood Linear Transform is used along with Speaker Adaptive Training (SAT) for feature extraction which are standard techniques in Automated Speech Recognition. When training acoustic models for recognition, SAT is used for normalizing the effects of variation in the acoustic features of different speakers. It helps to separate inter-speaker variability from intra-speaker variability and helps in extracting speaker independent features. Then they have trained Hidden Markov Model (HMM) by feeding the extracted features over the phonemes and visemes units. They have used the fisher mapping of 45 phonemes to 14 visemes including silence to classify the words. Wand et al. [3] have used Long-Short Term Memory (LSTM) [4] for visual speech recognition. They feed raw mouth images as input to the merged LSTM network. The performance of this merged LSTM network is experimentally evaluated and then it is compared to the standard Support Vector Machine (SVM) classifier. These evaluations are performed using some speaker-dependent tasks on data from 19 speakers of GRID corpus [5]. For the standard SVM model, the feature extraction methods used were Eigen lips and Histograms of Oriented Gradients (HOG). The best word recognition rate of 79.6% is reported from the experiments using this end-to-end neural network-based architecture. In [6] another end-to-end visual speech recognition system based on LSTM networks is proposed by Petridis et al. The model has two streams of input, in the first stream the raw mouth image from video frame is fed and in the second stream an image formed from the difference of the two consecutive frames of mouth is fed. These two streams are passed through an LSTM network and then they are merged together using a Bidirectional LSTM (BLSTM) network which labels the given frame. The model was evaluated on two datasets OuluVS2 and CUAVE. For OuluVS2, they have used 40 speakers for training and 12 for testing and got an accuracy of 84.5% over utterances. For CUAVE dataset 18 speakers were selected for training and validation and 18 speakers were selected for testing also. The same visual model achieved an accuracy of 78.6% over utterances. They have also tried to replace LSTMs with HMM and use Discrete Cosine Transform (DCT) for feature extraction and dimensionality reduction. This baseline model achieved the best accuracy of 74.8%. Stafylakis et al. [7], have proposed an end-to-end deep learning architecture for word-level visual speech recognition. The proposed system uses 3D spatiotemporal convolutions along with max pooling to produce a sequence of reduced features. This sequence is fed to a BLSTM network as an input to the first stream and the reverse of this sequence is fed as an input to the second stream of the BLSTM. They have used a database of 500 target words spoken in the BBC TV broadcasts. The model is evaluated using a baseline multi-tower VGG-M model that forms the standard for model evaluation. They have then tried 6 different models following the same architecture with minor adjustments to provide better accuracy. The best word accuracy of 83.0% is attained by the proposed network. Rathee et al. [8] have presented a visual speech recognition system for 20 Hindi words using a neural network with back-propagation. Here the landmark points are detected by active shape modeling, active appearance model, active contour model, localized active contour model, and Gauss newton deformable part template model. The lip texture features are extracted using Local Binary Pattern (LBP) features, Gabor features, a histogram of gradients features and scale invariant robust feature. Among these features, LBP features have been widely adopted for texture feature representation. Since here the temporal behavior is to be explored, so LBP features were extracted in Three Orthogonal Planes (TOP). Dataset generation was done by capturing the faces of 20 subjects using a USB webcam while uttering 10 Hindi words, which were quite different in terms of utterances. The videos were acquired at a frame rate of 15 frames per second. Learning algorithm Backpropagation neural network was used based on the Deepest-Descent method. Another approach of lip reading is based on DBN-HMM (Deep Belief Network Hidden Markov Model) neural networks to perform visual speech recognition [9]. In the feature extraction process, Fatemeh et al. have used PCA to extract lip coordinates and then they have concatenated 10 context frames to form the hybrid features of the visual lip areas. The extracted features are fed to a DBN for classification. For testing and training purposes the CUAVE database is used where speakers utter digits 0–9 in both ascending and descending order. Also, it has different styles of speaking like tilted head or moving side by side etc. The classification is only done for digits 0–9. An HMM model is used as a baseline model for evaluation. A PRR of 77.65% was obtained by the model for the multi-speaker task while a PRR of 73.40% was obtained on the speaker-independent task.

3   Implementation Overview

As shown in Fig. 1, Visual Speech Processing consists of following three interdependent steps which has their separate influence on the overall process: (1) Preprocessing (2) Training and Validation (3) Testing.

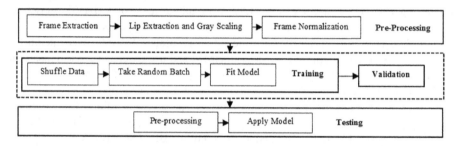

Fig. 1. Implementation overview

3.1   Preprocessing

The main objective of the preprocessing task is to extract the most relevant speech information from the frames. Preprocessing also helps to reduce the dimensionality of the data. It contributes to the simplification of the learning process by providing the relevant features and removing noise that could contribute the errors. In Visual Speech Processing, the preprocessing must be able to extract the geometric features of the mouth during speaking. This includes the movement of the important points (landmarks) between frames. The goal of this task is to identify a set of features that must be extracted such that the model performs well. The features must be selected such that most of the visual features that contribute to speech are selected and most of the noise is removed. The preprocessing task consists of three main subtasks: (1) Frame Extraction, (2) Lip Extraction and Grayscaling, (3) Normalize the frames.

3.1.1   Frame Extraction
In this subtask, the video data is processed to extract all the frames containing the portion of the video when a particular word was being spoken. These frames are collectively labeled as the word. These frames are further processed and serve as an input to the model. The frame extraction helps in separating each word and also to

create a standard format for data so that multiple datasets can be processed through the same pipeline. Figure 2(a) gives the sample frame extracted from the input video.

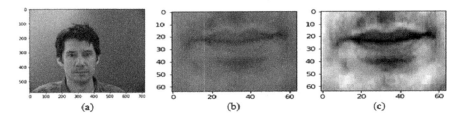

(a)   (b)   (c)

Fig. 2. (a) Frame in the video (b) Lip extracted using dlib facial landmark detector (c) GrayScale image (Color figure online)

3.1.2   Lip Extraction and Grayscaling
Lip Extraction is done to remove unnecessary features and traits from the input data. To extract lips we used two different methods, viz. Haar-Cascade classifier [10] and Facial Landmark detector [11]. The Facial Landmark detector performs very well as compared to Haar-Cascade classifier, hence we use it as a standard for lip extraction. Facial Landmark Detection is basically a technique of localizing key points on a face. These points include salient regions of a face like eyes, nose, mouth, jawline etc. For our system, we have considered only the mouth i.e. lip portion of the face. The Facial landmark detection algorithm is applied to the frames extracted in the previous step to get 68 (x, y) coordinates that are used to represent the facial structure in general. But our region of interest is only the mouth area so it is extracted by forming a rectangle that encloses the mouth region and cropping the image into the rectangle.

The cropped frame is in color format have various extra details, e.g. color of lips, luminance, hue etc. The features that are important in identifying the position and shape of the lips, like edges, corners, etc. can get hidden because of color and luminance. Hence, it is important to convert the lip frames into gray scaled images. Figure 2(b) shows the extracted lip region and Fig. 2(c) is a grayscale image for the same.

3.1.3   Frame Normalization
Each word spoken will not have the same number of frames. Smaller words will have fewer frames and larger words will have more number of frames. In order to create an input feature for the model, the number of frames for each word must be the same. To do this we expand each frame such that each frame is copied an equal number of times. Let's say that the standard number of frames is assumed to be 'n', and a total number of frames in a word is 'k'. We generate a number 'm', such that

$$m = \mathrm{ceil}(n/k) \tag{1}$$

We copy each frame 'm' number of times. Then we copy the last frame n%k times, so the total number of frames becomes 'n'. Figure 3 shows the 16 normalized frames for word "Lay" which only takes 10 frames.

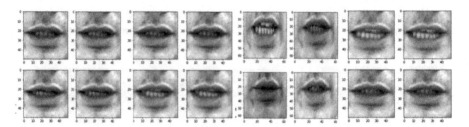

Fig. 3. 16 normalized frames for word "Lay" which only takes 10 frames

3.2 Training and Validation

There are various training techniques that greatly influence the output of the model and also the accuracy with which the model performs on unseen data. The parameters like batch size, number of frames per word, learning rate, number of epochs, shuffle, etc. have a huge effect on the model output. The training technique is divided into three parts: (1) Shuffle Data, (2) Take random batch, (3) Fit Model.

3.2.1 Shuffle Data
Training the model with a predefined order can create bias in the learning model. Thus the data is randomly shuffled for better efficiency.

3.2.2 Take a Random Batch
Here the random set of data points of the provided batch size i.e. 256 is selected. Such random batch selection helps in removing bias due to order. The batch is then ran through the network such that the model tries to minimize the error over the provided batch. This helps in fast convergence of the learning model and cost is reduced rapidly.

3.2.3 Fit Model
The model is the heart of any machine learning application. Figure 4 depicts our model architecture which consists of convolutional layers to extract features and then softmax layer to predict the one hot classification of the words. The model has an input of 16 frames of images of size 50×50 with one color channel. The first layer of the model is a convolutional layer of 48 filters, of size $3 \times 3 \times 3$. The second layer of the model is a maxpooling layer with $3 \times 3 \times 3$, the third layer of the model is another convolutional layer of 256 filters of size $3 \times 3 \times 3$. The fourth layer of the model is a maxpooling layer with $3 \times 3 \times 3$. The fifth and sixth layers are convolutional layers each having 512 filters of size $1 \times 3 \times 3$. The activation function used for each layer is relu. Next layer introduces a dropout of 0.25 to avoid overfitting of the above layers. The last layer is a dense layer with softmax activation to perform learning from features extracted from the above CNN. We have used cross-entropy loss function for our training. The model is trained using two learning rates. Initially, a low learning rate is used (10^{-8}) for 10 epochs. After that, the model is trained using 10^{-4} learning rate for 35 epochs.

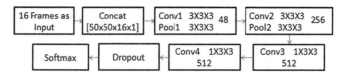

Fig. 4. Model architecture

Validation

Validation is the process where a trained model is evaluated with a testing dataset. The testing dataset is a separate portion of the same dataset from which the training set is derived. The purpose of using the testing dataset is to test the generalization ability of the model. During validation, we check the accuracy and loss of the model.

3.3   Testing

Testing is the process of checking the output of a machine learning model on real data. The model can be considered successful only when it performs well during testing. While testing we provide a video of a sentence spoken and we get the predicted words in the sentence. Testing consists of two main parts: Preprocessing and Applying Model.

3.3.1   Preprocessing

During this subtask, the entire preprocessing pipeline is followed for each word apart from the labeling that was done during the frame extraction.

3.3.2   Apply Model

In this subtask, we simply provide the words as an input to the model and get its prediction. The prediction is probability distributed among 52 classes. And largest one is taken as predicted word. We also calculate the top-k predictions to plot the recall versus rank graph and check for words that the model confuses more often. A visualization of these calculations is shown in the results section.

4   Results and Discussion

For the experimental purpose, we have used the GRID dataset to train and evaluate the model. The GRID dataset consists of 40 different speakers with each speaker speaking sentences consisting of 6 words viz. a verb, a color, a preposition, an alphabet, a digit and an adverb. During our preprocessing phase, we divide the entire dataset to words with the corresponding phrase. Each word and it's phrases become a single data point for our model. We have a total of 196276 data points. The testing is carried out on 10% of data points corresponding to each word. This data is basically used for training the 3D Convolutional Neural Network (CNN). Table 1 shows 10 most frequently confused word along with the proportion by which it is confused. From a total number of 'u' available from test dataset, the model predicts 'q' 0.519 (51.9%) of times. This is bound to happen as some of the literals are homopheme which cannot be identified by visual features only.

Table 1. 10 most frequently confused word pair

Expected literal	U	sp	three	p	e	Z	x	now	in	eight
Observed literal	Q	at	green	b	in	Set	s	again	at	K
Portion of expected literal confused	0.52	0.27	0.20	0.19	0.19	0.18	0.17	0.14	0.13	0.12

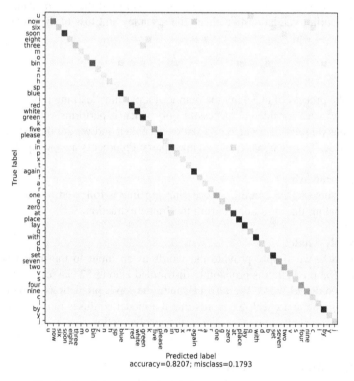

Fig. 5. Confusion matrix for all 52 words in the vocabulary

Through the experimental results, it has been observed that the model gives 82.07% accuracy on test data. Figure 5 shows the confusion matrix for all 52 words in the vocabulary. The visible diagonal clearly shows that the model successfully classifies most of the words. The other square around the diagonal represents words which are homophones. There are two points which are mirror images of each other along the diagonal. These points correspond to the word 'at' and 'in'. Figure 6(a) and (b) shows frames corresponding to the words 'at' and 'in' for two different speakers (two different videos) from the dataset. From the frames shown in Fig. 6(a) and (b), we can clearly see that the lip position for 'at' and 'in' is almost similar for both the speakers.

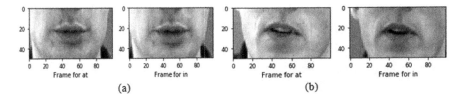

Fig. 6. Frames for words 'at' and 'in' (a) for speaker 1 and (b) for speaker 2

Figure 7 shows the accuracy plot during the training phase. It has been observed that choosing higher learning rate of 10^{-3} to 10^{-2} doesn't help in model convergence. Thus we found that learning rate 10^{-8} initially with 10 epochs and then changing it to 10^{-4} for remaining epochs helps to converge the model better and received a training accuracy of 99.26% for the training set and 98.7% for the validation set. Similarly, the loss plots given in Fig. 8 shows a significant dip when the learning rate is increased. Thus the model is getting confused.

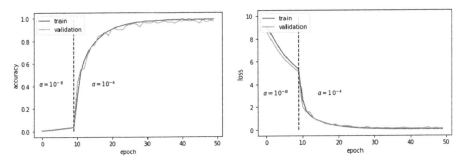

Fig. 7. Model accuracy plot   **Fig. 8.** Model loss plot

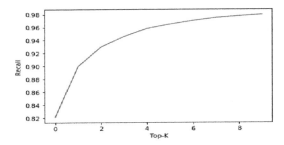

Fig. 9. Recall vs rank plot

The Recall vs Rank plot given in Fig. 9, shows a rapid increase in the Recall value with an increase in rank. The model gives 90% accuracy for top-2 predictions. This accuracy increases to 98% for top-10 predictions. This shows that even if in some cases the model does not produce the highest probability for the expected word, but in other cases it does provide a higher probability to the expected word. This supports the learning efficiency of the model and we can conclude that the model has learned to identify similarities between the utterances of the similar words.

5 Conclusion and Future Work

In this paper, we have discussed automatic text caption generation system from the lip features of the speaker in video clips using the word level classification based on 3D CNN. During preprocessing video clip is divided into frames from which lip region is extracted and is converted into grayscale. After frame normalization, it is fed as input to 3D CNN model to generate the text captions. Through the experimental results, we have observed the model accuracy as 82.07% and misclassification as 17.93% on the test data set. The accuracy of the system is 99.26% for the training set and 98.7% for the validation set. Even though the system shows better performance but still to detect homophones for which the lip movement looks same is an issue to be addressed. For the same, a dataset of more speakers with many more words can be used, which will increase the accuracy of the model and generalize better on real world data. The work can further be extended to do sentence level prediction using a sequence to sequence model.

References

1. Rathee, N.: A novel approach for lip reading based on neural network. In: International Conference on Computational Techniques in Information and Communication Technologies (ICCTICT) (2016). ISSN 978-1-5090-0082-1
2. Almajai, I., Cox, S., Harvey, R., Lan, Y.: Improved speaker independent lip reading using speaker adaptive training and deep neural networks. In: International Conference on Acoustics, Speech, and Signal Processing (ICASSP) (2016)
3. Wand, M., Koutnk, J., Schmidhuber, J.: Lipreading with long short-term memory. In: IEEE International Conference on Acoustics, Speech and Signal Processing (ICASSP) (2016)
4. Hochreiter, S., Schmidhuber, J.: Long short-term memory. Neural Comput. **9**, 1735–1780 (1997)
5. Cooke, M., Barker, J., Cunningham, S., Shao, X.: An audio-visual corpus for speech perception and automatic speech recognition. J. Acoust. Soc. Am. **120**(5), 2421–2424 (2006)
6. Petridis, S., Li, Z., Pantic, M.: End-to-end visual speech recognition with LSTM. In: IEEE International Conference on Acoustics, Speech and Signal Processing (ICASSP), pp. 2592–2596 (2017)
7. Stafylakis, T., Tzimiropoulos, G.: Combining residual networks with LSTM for lipreading. arXiv preprint arXiv:1703.04105 (2017)
8. Rathee, N.: Investigating back propagation neural network for lip reading. In: International Conference on Computing, Communication and Automation (ICCCA) (2016)
9. Fatemeh, V., Farshad, A., Ahmad, N.: LipReading via deep neural networks using hybrid visual features. Image Anal. Stereol. **37**(2), 159–171 (2018)
10. Castrillón, M., Déniz, O., Hernández, D., et al.: Mach. Vis. Appl. **22**, 481 (2011). https://doi.org/10.1007/s00138-010-0250-7
11. Zafeiriou, S., Tzimiropoulos, G., Pantic, M.: 300 W: special issue on facial landmark localisation "in-the-wild". Image Vis. Comput. **47**, 1–2 (2016). https://doi.org/10.1016/j.imavis.2016.03.009

Legendre Wavelet Quasilinearization Method for Nonlinear Klein-Gordon Equation with Initial Conditions

Kotapally Harish Kumar[✉]

Research and Development, Datafoundry Pvt Ltd., Divyasree Technopolis,
Bangalore 560037, India
harish296228@gmail.com

Abstract. A new numerical method using Legendre wavelet together with the quasilinearization for solving nonlinear Klein-Gordon equation with initial conditions is proposed. In the proposed scheme both time as well as spatial derivatives of the Klein Gordon equation are approximated using wavelet without the help of Laplace transform, a contrast to the schemes available in the recent literature. Numerical studies assure that the less number of grid points are required to produce better accuracy and more stable with faster convergence than the Laplace transform based Legendre wavelet method. Further, While solving them numerically in the last section, a comparison is provided between Python and Matlab. The order of accuracy in Python and Matlab are same but Python takes much lesser time to produce the output compared to Matlab [Table 5].

Keywords: Chebyshev wavelet · Collocation method ·
Legendre wavelet · Klein-Gordon equation · Matlab · Python ·
Quasilinearization

1 Introduction

This article proposes a new numerical method based on quasilinearization and Legendre wavelet for the nonlinear Klein-Gordon equation of the form

$$u_{tt} - u_{xx} + g(u) = f(x,t), \quad 0 \le x \le 1, \ t \ge 0, \tag{1}$$

with initial conditions $u(x,0) = f_1(x)$, $u_t(x,0) = f_2(x)$, $0 \le x \le 1$. Equation (1) is a significantly important partial differential equation with greater interest as it serves as mathematical model in various areas of science and engineering. Equation (1) becomes Phi-four equation and Sine Gordon equation for the selection $g(u) = u^3 - u$ and $g(u) = \sin u$ respectively. To solve Klein Gordon equation with initial conditions, variety of analytical as well as numerical methods are available in the literature namely Adomian decomposition method [1], B-Spline

© Springer Nature Singapore Pte Ltd. 2019
M. Singh et al. (Eds.): ICACDS 2019, CCIS 1046, pp. 323–332, 2019.
https://doi.org/10.1007/978-981-13-9942-8_31

collocation method [4] differential transform method [2], Finite Difference Arithmetic Mean (FDAM) [3], Homotopy perturbation method [5], Laplace transform based Legendre wavelet method (LLWM) [11], Taylor matrix method (TMM) [7], and variational iteration method [8]. A brief literature survey is provided in [11]. Due to the complexity involved in handling the nonlinearity in Klein Gordon equation, considerable attentions are devoted to develop new numerical schemes. Recently Yin et al. [11] developed an interesting numerical scheme based on Legendre wavelet coupled with Laplace transform. In that approach Klein Gordon equation was converted into an algebraic system using Legendre wavelet, Laplace transform and block pulse function and the non-linearity system was handled by successive approximation, which gives only linear convergence. Though this approach produce good accuracy than the other methods available in the literature it requires a very stringent stopping criteria to stop the iterative procedure for certain problems. Consequently the approach is computationally sensitive. The main aim of the present article is to improve the efficiency of Legendre based wavelets by a new formulation which provides faster convergence rate. This formulation is also observed to be less sensitive to the stopping criteria, hence an efficient alternative to the available Laplace transform based Legendre wavelet method (LLWM) [11]. The proposed formulation is done with the help of quasilinearization method. In the proposed scheme the non-linearity in the Klein Gordon equation is handled by the quasilinearization method which has quadratic convergence. At each step the linear partial differential equation is converted into algebraic system by approximating both the time as well as spatial derivatives using only Legendre wavelets. This approach also produces higher accuracy than LLWM [11] with less number of wavelets, which is an added advantage. All the numerical examples are solved using Matlab and Python though the accuracy produced by both methods are of same order, Python produces output much faster than Matlab in the all the numerical examples [Table 5].

The organization of the article is as follows. Legendre wavelet collocation method in combination with quasilinearization is detailed in Sect. 2 for Klein Gordon equation. Numerical Implementation is detailed in Sect. 3 for the proposed equation. Further, in Sect. 4 proposed method is applied to different types of examples with the help of Matlab and Python and a comparison has been made with the existing articles [7,11]. By stating the observations made in the numerical simulation, the analysis is concluded in Sect. 5.

2   Wavelet Based Collocation Method

2.1   Legendre Wavelet [9–12]

One of the wavelet with better approximation property, among the commonly used wavelets, is Legendre wavelet. Consider the Legendre Wavelet definition which was defined in Legendre Wavelet [9–12].

2.2   Wavelet Collocation Method

Since the proposed scheme is iterative, at each step of the iteration one needs to solve a linear hyperbolic partial differential equation. Present section details the numerical method for linear hyperbolic partial differential equation using Legendre wavelet collocation method. One assumption is made while developing the proposed method, that is the partial derivatives and all other functions appears in the linear partial differential equation are members of $L^2(0,1)$. Thus

$$\frac{\partial^2 u}{\partial t^2} = \sum_{i=1}^{N} \sum_{j=1}^{N} b_{i,j} \psi_i(x) \psi_j(t) = \Psi^T(t) B \Psi(x) \tag{2}$$

Where $B = [b_{i,j}]$, $\Psi(x) = [\psi_i(x)]^T$ and $\Psi(t) = [\psi_j(t)]^T$ for $1 \leq i,j \leq N$. Throughout this article, the points, members of the set $\{(x_i, t_j) : x_i = t_i = \frac{i-0.5}{N}, 1 \leq i,j \leq N\}$ are chosen for collocation. From (2) one can get $u(x,t)$ and it can be represented as follows.

$$u(x,t) = \Psi^T(t)(P^T)^2 B \Psi(x) + u_t(x,0)t + u(x,0), \tag{3}$$

where P discussed in [13] and it is named as operational matrix for integration. Consequently

$$\frac{\partial^2 u}{\partial x^2} = \Psi^T(t)(P^T)^2 B D^2 \Psi(x) + t\frac{d^2}{dx^2}(u_t(x,0)) + \frac{d^2}{dx^2}u(x,0), \tag{4}$$

where D is discussed in [14] and it is named as operational matrix of derivative. The expressions of u_{tt}, u and u_{xx} given in Eqs. (2), (3) and (4), respectively are substituted in the corresponding linear hyperbolic PDE to obtain N^2 set of equations. Legendre coefficients $b_{i,j}$'s are obtained after solving the above system. After substituting these coefficients in the Eq. (3) the solution of the linear partial differential equation is obtained easily.

Table 1. LLWM [11] vs proposed methods

Example	Grid size $N \times N$		Stop condition		Error		
	LLWM [11]	LWM	LLWM [11]	LWM	LLWM [11]	LWM-M	LWM-P
1	4×4	3×3	-	$1.0e^{-04}$	$6.0e^{-15}$	$2.2e^{-16}$	0.0
2	9×9	4×4	-	$1.0e^{-04}$	$1.0e^{-11}$	$6.2e^{-15}$	$5.4e^{-15}$
3	10×10	9×9	$1.0e^{-12}$	$1.0e^{-04}$	$1.2e^{-11}$	$4.2e^{-11}$	$4.8e^{-11}$
4	11×11	10×10	$1.0e^{-10}$	$1.0e^{-04}$	$1.5e^{-09}$	$1.3e^{-09}$	$1.2e^{-11}$

Table 2. Numerical results of Example 2

Method	MFDCM [15]	LLWM [11]	LWM-M	LWM-P
Grid points	361	81	4×4	4×4
t				
0.1	$5.3e^{-10}$	$3.0e^{-16}$	$4.0e^{-16}$	$2.9e^{-16}$
0.3	$5.5e^{-08}$	$4.3e^{-15}$	$6.3e^{-16}$	$3.7e^{-16}$
0.5	$5.6e^{-07}$	$9.4e^{-14}$	$4.6e^{-15}$	$4.0e^{-15}$
0.7	$7.0e^{-07}$	$7.3e^{-13}$	$6.6e^{-15}$	$5.3e^{-15}$
0.9	$7.9e^{-07}$	$3.9e^{-12}$	$4.0e^{-15}$	$2.3e^{-15}$

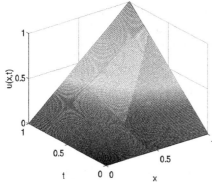

Fig. 1. Numerical solution of Example 1

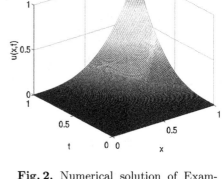

Fig. 2. Numerical solution of Example 2

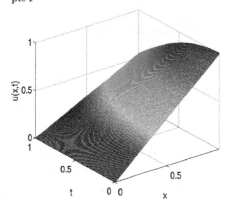

Fig. 3. Numerical solution of Example 3

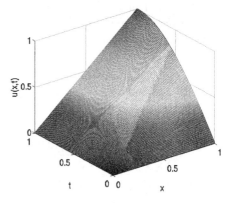

Fig. 4. Numerical solution of Example 4

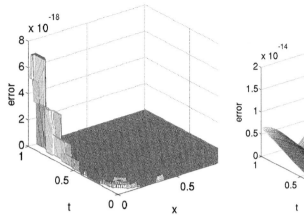

Fig. 5. Relative error of Example 1

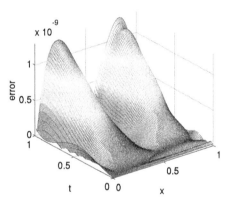

Fig. 6. Relative error of Example 2

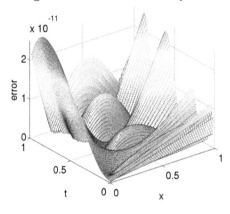

Fig. 7. Relative error of Example 3

Fig. 8. Relative error of Example 4

3   Numerical Implementation

After applying quasilinearization approach to Klein Gordon equation (1) the following sequence of linear PDE is obtained.

$$\frac{\partial^2 u_{n+1}}{\partial t^2} - \frac{\partial^2 u_{n+1}}{\partial x^2} + g(u_n) + g'(u_n)(u_{n+1} - u_n) = f(x,t) \quad n = 0, 1, 2 \cdots \quad (5)$$

with initial conditions $u_{n+1}(x,0) = f_1(x)$, $u_{n+1_t}(x,0) = f_2(x)$, $0 \le x \le 1$. This section provides how to couple the Legendre wavelet collocation method with quasilinearization method to solve Klein Gordon equation. Let B^T denotes transpose of the matrix B. Using the collocation points and the Eqs. (3) and (4) for u_{n+1} can be written as

$$u_{n+1}(x,t) = P_2^T B_{n+1}\phi + K_1 + K_2 \tag{6}$$

$$\frac{\partial^2 u_{n+1}}{\partial x^2} = P_2^T B_{n+1} D_2 + K_3 + K_4 \tag{7}$$

where $K_1 = f_2(x_i)t_j$, $K_2 = f_1(x_i)$, $K_3 = t_j \frac{df_2(x_i)}{dx^2}$, $K_4 = \frac{df_2(x_i)}{dx^2}$, $B_{n+1} = [b_{i,j}]$, $\phi = [\Psi(x_i)] = [\Psi(t_j)]$, $P_2 = P^2\Psi(t_j)$, $D_2 = D^2\Psi(x_i)$ and $\{(x_i, t_j) : x_i = t_i = \frac{i-0.5}{N}, 1 \leq i,j \leq N\}$. Here B_0 is obtained from the initial approximation u_0. The Eq. (5) can be written as after using collocation points

$$\phi^T B_{n+1}\phi - P_2^T B_{n+1} D_2 + K_5 \circ (P_2^T B_{n+1}\phi) = K_6 \tag{8}$$

where $K_5 = g'(u_n(x_i, t_j))$, $K_6 = (K_3 + K_4 - K_5 \circ (K_1 + K_2)) + f(x_i, t_j) - g(u_n(x_i, t_j)) + K_5 \circ K_8$, $K_8 = [u_n(x_i, t_j)]$ and 'o' denotes the Hadamard product. To get B_{n+1} one can solve (8) with initial guess u_0. Using vectorization (8) can be brought into $L\theta = b$ where $\theta = [vec(B_{n+1})]^T$ and $b = [vec(K_6)]^T$ and

$$L = \left[\phi^T \otimes \phi^T - D_2^T \otimes P_2^T + K_7(\phi^T \otimes P_2^T) \right]$$

"vec" represents vectorization of a matrix, '⊗' denotes Kronecker product and K_7 is diagonal matrix contains elements of K_5 in it's diagonal position. Then suitable stopping criteria can be used to obtain the numerical solution of Klein Gordon equation.

4   Numerical Experiments

In this section the proposed method for the Klein Gordon equation are tested with various choices of example problems which were discussed in [11]. The performance of LLWM [11], LWM-P and LWM-M are compared in terms of accuracy, number of grid points and stopping criteria. In all the numerical simulations carried out in this section, the initial guess $u_0 = 0$ is considered. The following notations and abbreviations are used throughout the section.

1. LWM-M – Legendre wavelet method with Matlab code.
2. LWM-P – Legendre wavelet method with Python code.
3. LWM – Both LWM-M and LWM-P.
4. N – Denotes the number of Legendre wavelets
5. t_{LWM-P} is the time taken by LMP-P Method.
6. t_{LWM-M} is the time taken by LMP-M Method.

Example 1. Consider the non-linear Klein-Gordon equation discussed in [11]

$$u_{tt} - u_{xx} + u^2 = x^2 t^2 \tag{9}$$

with the initial conditions of the problem $u(x,0) = 0, u_t(x,0) = x$. From Table 1, it is interesting to note that LLWM [11] produce the accuracy 6×10^{-15} for four wavelets whereas our proposed methods (LWM) produce better accuracy just for three wavelets ($M = 3, k = 1$). Figures 5 and 1 shows the LWM solution and the relative error respectively. From Table 5 one can observe that the time taken by Python is much lesser time that matlab.

Table 3. Numerical results of Example 3

Method	TMM [7]	LWM-M	LWM-P
Grid points	50	6×6	6×6
t			
0.2	$5.6542e^{-07}$	$2.6300e^{-07}$	$2.37644e^{-07}$
0.4	$3.2841e^{-06}$	$7.5503e^{-08}$	$7.4879e^{-07}$
0.6	$4.6197e^{-06}$	$3.0752e^{-08}$	$3.0584e^{-08}$
0.8	$5.6879e^{-05}$	$3.1494e^{-07}$	$2.8208e^{-07}$
1.0	$2.2334e^{-04}$	$1.4324e^{-06}$	$1.3096e^{-06}$

Table 4. Numerical experiment results of Example 5 at $t = 0.1$

Method	TMM [7]	LWM-M	LWM-P	TMM [7]	LWM-M	LWM-P
Grid points	50	4×4	4×4	50	4×4	4×4
x	$c = 0.01$	$c = 0.01$	$c = 0.01$	$c = 0.05$	$c = 0.05$	$c = 0.05$
0.1	$5.88e^{-05}$	$3.16e^{-10}$	$6.22e^{-10}$	$5.91e^{-05}$	$9.07e^{-09}$	$1.79e^{-08}$
0.3	$1.20e^{-06}$	$1.67e^{-09}$	$2.14e^{-09}$	$2.91e^{-06}$	$4.28e^{-08}$	$5.60e^{-08}$
0.5	$5.18e^{-06}$	$3.45e^{-09}$	$4.05e^{-09}$	$3.76e^{-06}$	$8.77e^{-08}$	$1.075e^{-07}$
0.7	$4.65e^{-06}$	$5.85e^{-09}$	$6.54e^{-09}$	$7.00e^{-06}$	$1.49e^{-07}$	$1.68e^{-097}$
0.9	$7.51e^{-05}$	$9.48e^{-09}$	$1.02e^{-08}$	$7.36e^{-05}$	$2.42e^{-07}$	$2.63e^{-07}$

Example 2. Consider the non-linear Klein-Gordon equation discussed in [11, 15]

$$u_{tt} - u_{xx} + u^2 = x^6 t^6 + 6xt(x^2 - t^2) \tag{10}$$

with the initial conditions of the problem $u(x, 0) = 0, u_t(x, 0) = 0$. This problem was solved numerically using LLWM in [11] and MFDCM in [15]. From Tables 1 and 2, it is interesting to note that LLWM produce the accuracy 1×10^{-11} for 81 grids and MFDCM produce the accuracy 5.3×10^{-10} for 361 grids whereas the proposed LWM-P produce the accuracy 5.4×10^{-15} using just 16 grids. Figures 6 and 2 shows the LWM solution and the relative error respectively.

Example 3. Consider the non-linear Klein-Gordon equation discussed in [7, 11]

$$u_{tt} - u_{xx} + u^2 = x \cos t + x^2 \cos^2 t \tag{11}$$

with the initial conditions of the problem $u(x, 0) = x, u_t(x, 0) = 0$. This problem was solved numerically using LLWM in [11] and TMM in [7]. Table 3 gives a comparison of L_∞ error at various points of these methods as well as the proposed LWM. From Table 1, it is interesting to note that LLWM produce the accuracy 1.2×10^{-11} for 100 grids whereas the proposed method (LWM-M) produce the accuracy 4.2×10^{-11} for just 81 grids. To produce this accuracy LLWM uses the stringent stopping criteria 1×10^{-12} whereas our proposed methods (LWM) require only 1×10^{-4}. Figures 7 and 3 shows the LWM solution and the relative error respectively.

Table 5. Time comparison LWM-M vs LWM-P

Example	Grid size	t_{LWM-P} (s)	t_{LWM-M} (s)	$Error_{LWM-P}$	$Error_{LWM-M}$
1	3×3	0.30	1.25	0.0	$2.20e^{-16}$
2	4×4	0.31	2.45	$2.35e^{-15}$	$6.24e^{-15}$
3	9×9	0.46	5.10	$6.81e^{-11}$	$4.23e^{-11}$
4	10×10	0.51	6.21	$3.07e^{-09}$	$1.34e^{-09}$
5	11×11	0.56	7.19	$5.52e^{-05}$	$1.72e^{-06}$

Example 4. Consider the non-linear Klein-Gordon equation discussed in [11]

$$u_{tt} - u_{xx} + u^2 + \frac{\pi^4}{4}u = x^2 \sin^2\left(\frac{\pi}{2}t\right) \tag{12}$$

with the initial conditions of the problem $u(x,0) = 0, u_t(x,0) = \frac{\pi}{2}x$. From Table 1, it is interesting to note that LLWM [11] produce the accuracy 1.5×10^{-09} for 121 grids whereas the proposed method produces the accuracy 1.2×10^{-11} for just 100 grids. To produce this accuracy LLWM uses the stringent stop condition 1×10^{-10} whereas proposed methods (LWM) uses just 1×10^{-4}. Figures 8 and 4 shows the LWM solution and the relative error, respectively.

In the following example the proposed scheme is tested with spatial derivative with coefficient other than one.

Example 5. Consider the non-linear Klein-Gordon equation discussed in [7]

$$u_{tt} - 2.5u_{xx} + u + 1.5u^3 = 0 \tag{13}$$

The initial conditions of the problem (Example 5) are taken from [7]. Table 4 presents the L_∞ error, using both TMM [7] and proposed methods (LWM), at various points for different choices of c. It is interesting to note that though our proposed methods (LWM) took much less number of grids than TMM, Our proposed methods (LWM) produce better accuracy than TMM. Figure 5 shows the LWM solution. From Table 5 one can observe that though both the proposed methods (LWM-M and LWM-P) produce same order of error, Python code is almost 12 times faster than Matlab code in-terms of time.

Remark 4.1

1. In all the examples, the following stopping criteria is used $\|u_{n+1} - u_n\| \leq 10^{-04}$. $u_0 = 0$ is used as initial guess for the proposed method.

2. Chebyshev wavelet is replaced by Legendre wavelet for all the proposed examples, and it was observed that the orders of the errors are same for all the examples.
3. MATLAB R2010b and Python 2.7 are used for solving the numerical experiments in the article.
4. In all the examples, computational time required by LWM-P is much lesser than LWM-M.

5   Conclusions

The present article proposes an efficient numerical method based on quasilinearization combined with Legendre wavelet method for Klein-Gordon equation with initial conditions. The proposed scheme is less sensitive to the stopping criteria and hence having faster convergence than LLWM [11]. Consequently it is computationally more stable than LLWM. The order of error remains same with Matlab and Python [Table 5]. Further, the proposed scheme produces higher accuracy with less number of grids than those in some of the recent literature [7,11,15].

Acknowledgement. The author would like to thanks Prof. V. Antony Vijesh, IIT Indore for his valuable comments and his guidance. The initial Matlab simulations were done when the author was Research Scholar at IIT Indore.

References

1. El-Sayed, S.M.: The decomposition method fo studying Klein-Gordon equation. Chaos Solitons Fractals **18**, 1025–1030 (2003). https://doi.org/10.1016/S0960-0779(02)00647-1
2. Kanth, A.S.V.R., Aruna, K.: Differential transform method for solving linear and nonlinear Klein-Gordon equation. Comput. Phys. Commun. **180**, 708–711 (2009). https://doi.org/10.1016/j.cpc.2008.11.012
3. Noraini, K., et al.: Numerical solution of linear Klein-Gordon equation using FDAM scheme. In: AIP Conference Proceedings, p. 020021 (2017). https://doi.org/10.1063/1.4983876
4. Hepson, O.E., Korkmaz, A., Dag, I.: On the numerical solution of the Klein-Gordon equation by exponential B-spline collocation method. Communications **68**(1) (2016). https://doi.org/10.31801/cfsuasmas.425491
5. Odibat, Z., Momani, S.: A reliable treatment of homotophy perturbation method for Klein-Gordon equations. Phys. Lett. A **365**, 351–357 (2007). https://doi.org/10.1016/j.physleta.2007.01.064
6. Yin, F., Song, J., Lu, F.: A coupled method of Laplace transform and Legendre wavelets for nonlinear Klein-Gordon equations. Math. Methods Appl. Sci. **37**, 781–792 (2014). https://doi.org/10.1002/mma.2834
7. Bülbül, B., Sezer, M.: A new approach to numerical solution of nonlinear Klein-Gordon equation. Math. Prob. Eng. **2013**, 7, Article ID 869749 (2013). https://doi.org/10.1155/2013/869749

8. Yusufoğlu, E.: The variational iteration method for studying the Klein-Gordon equation. Appl. Math. Lett. **21**, 669–674 (2008). https://doi.org/10.1016/j.aml.2007.07.023

9. Kumar, K.H., Vijesh, V.A.: Wavelet based iterative methods for a class of 2D-partial integro differential equations. Comput. Math. Appl. **75**(1), 187–198 (2018). https://doi.org/10.1016/j.camwa.2017.09.008

10. Vijesh, V.A., Kumar, K.H.: Wavelet based quasilinearization method for semilinear parabolic initial boundary value problems. Appl. Math. Comput. **266**, 1163–1176 (2015). https://doi.org/10.1016/j.amc.2015.05.139

11. Yin, F., Tian, T., Song, J., Zhu, M.: Spectral methods using Legendre wavelets for nonlinear Klein or Sine-Gordon equations. J. Comp. Appl. Math. **275**, 321–334 (2015). https://doi.org/10.1016/j.cam.2014.07.014

12. Vijesh, V. A., Kumar, K. H.: Wavelet based numerical simulation of non linear Klein/Sine Gordon equation. J. Comb. Syst. Sci. **40**(1), 225–244

13. Razzaghi, M., Yousefi, S.: The Legendre wavelets operational matrix of integration. Int. J. Syst. Sci. **32**, 495–502 (2001). https://doi.org/10.1080/00207720120227

14. Mohammadi, F., Hosseini, M.M.: A new Legendre wavelet operational matrix of derivative and its applications in solving the singular ordinary differential equations. J. Franklin Inst. **348**, 1787–1796 (2011). https://doi.org/10.1016/j.jfranklin.2011.04.017

15. Lakestani, M., Dehghan, M.: Collocation and finite difference-collocation methods for the solution of nonlinear Klein-Gordon equation. Comput. Phys. Commun. **181**, 1392–1401 (2010). https://doi.org/10.1016/j.cpc.2010.04.006

Runtime Verification and Vulnerability Testing of Smart Contracts

Misha Abraham[✉] and K. P. Jevitha

Amrita School of Engineering, Amrita Vishwa Vidyapeetham, Coimbatore, India
abrahammisha@gmail.com, kp_jevitha@cb.amrita.edu

Abstract. Smart contracts are programs that help in automating agreement between multiple parties involving no external trusted authority. Since smart contracts deal with millions of dollars worth of virtual coins, it is important to ensure that they execute correctly and are free from vulnerabilities. This work focuses on smart contracts in Ethereum blockchain, the most utilized platform for smart contracts so far. Our emphasis is mainly on two core areas. One involves the runtime verification of ERC20 tokens using K framework and the other involves the comparison of tools available for detecting the vulnerabilities in smart contract. The six core functions of ERC20, namely allowance(), approve(), total-supply(), balanceof(), transferfrom() and transfer() were considered for runtime verification. ERC20 contracts were tested with ERC20 standard and the results showed that only 30% in allowance() function, 50% in transferfrom() function, and 90% in transfer() function, were compliant to the standard. The other focus area involves the comparison of existing tool that could identify vulnerabilities in smart contract. Five tools were taken for the comparison, namely Oyente, Securify, Remix, Smartcheck and Mythril and were tested against 15 different vulnerabilities. Out of the 5 tools taken, Smartcheck was found to detect the highest number of vulnerabilities.

Keywords: Blockchain · Smart contract · Vulnerabilities ·
Runtime verification · ERC20 token · K framework

1 Introduction

A blockchain is essentially a distributed database of records of all transactions or digital events that have been shared among participating parties. It is also known as a distributed ledger which uses cryptographic methods to store information and provides better security [1]. Applications like financial transactions, Internet of Things etc., uses blockchain technology. It was initially implemented by Satoshi Nakamoto on bitcoin platform [2]. Ethereum is one among the best blockchain platform which enables decentralized applications. As stated by Vitalik Buterin, Ethereum is a blockchain platform which can understand programming languages. Unlike bitcoin, Ethereum provides one common platform for all the use cases.

© Springer Nature Singapore Pte Ltd. 2019
M. Singh et al. (Eds.): ICACDS 2019, CCIS 1046, pp. 333–342, 2019.
https://doi.org/10.1007/978-981-13-9942-8_32

Smart contracts are the decentralized applications that are designed to run on Ethereum using Ethereum Virtual Machine (EVM). Once a smart contract is deployed in the blockchain, it cannot be modified or updated. This can be both advantage as well as disadvantage. As an advantage, it provides better security by preventing the users from editing/modifying the smart contract that are deployed into the Ethereum blockchain. The disadvantage is that if there are any bugs/vulnerabilities in smart contract, they can be addressed only by deleting the entire smart contract from the blockchain. As Dijkstra stated "testing shows the presence not the absence of bugs" there is a requirement to formally verify the smart contract code to provide better compliance of the contract to its standard.

In this work we focus on using runtime verification to verify smart contract functionality against ERC20 standard to ensure that the contract behaves as they are designed for. This is done by taking ERC20 standard rules written in K language [4] and the EVM semantics (KEVM). It works by symbolically executing the bytecode of the contract in the KEVM and identifying its compliance with ERC20 standard using the K framework [3, 5, 6]. We have also examined the tools, to detect security vulnerabilities in smart contracts in Ethereum, which can analyze solidity code to identify vulnerabilities in smart contract. In our work, we compared 5 different tools, namely Oyente, Securify, Remix, Smartcheck and Mythril against 15 vulnerabilities.

The paper is organized as follows. In Sect. 2, background study of Smart contract and K framework is explained in detail. Section 3 describes the related work done in the field of formal verification and vulnerability assessment of smart contracts. Section 4 explains the proposed work on runtime verification and vulnerability testing of smart contracts, the results of which are explained in Sect. 5. Finally Sect. 6 concludes about the work done and briefly explain about the scope of this work in future.

2   Background Study

2.1   Smart Contract

Smart contracts are used to eliminate the need of trusted third parties and are usually written using programming languages like Solidity, Vyper, Java etc., Smart contracts work in the same way as that of classes in object oriented programming and they are made up of functions and fields [8]. The smart contract code is arranged in a low-level stack-based bytecode. Since the bytecode is openly available, it may be said that the smart contract code can be examined by each and every node in the network. So if the contract is vulnerable everyone in the network can see and understand the vulnerability and can exploit it easily.

Apart from creating decentralized applications, a smart contract can also be used to create tokens for the purpose of developing their own economy on top of Ethereum [7]. In order to standardize token creation, Ethereum community has come up with token standards like ERC20, ERC721 etc., ERC stands for Ethereum Request for Comment, and 20 is the number assigned to the request. It includes six core functions, namely allowance(), approve(), totalsupply(), balanceof(), transferfrom() and transfer() [9]. The use of ERC20 standard makes the risk of tokenization less since every token adhere to the same standards. It also makes the token interaction less complex and also brings in uniformity to the network. If the tokens doesn't match with the ERC20 standard it will not be possible to use the ERC20 compliant wallets like metamask. So it is necessary to check for the compliance of the core functions of ERC20 tokens with the ERC20 standard functions.

2.2   K Framework

K is a framework in which programming languages can be defined and programs can be symbolically executed according to semantics of the language written in K. In order to write semantics of a language in K, we need to define three sections, namely configurations, computations and rules [10]. The configuration part contain the initial values of parameters to be used while writing the semantics. In computations part, we will define the computations that are to be performed to the parameters declared in configuration part. Finally, the rule contains the conditions that should be satisfied while executing the program. The execution of language in K framework will take two inputs. One is the semantics of the language written in K and the other is the program that is written in that language. Executing the program using K will run the program according to the semantics defined in K.

3   Related Work

This section describes the formal verification of smart contracts and also the security vulnerabilities present in smart contracts.

3.1   Formal Verification of Smart Contracts

This section gives an overview of related work on formal verification of smart contracts. In Karthikeyan et al. [19], they focused mainly on formal verification of smart contracts at the source level and also at the EVM level. This is done by converting the solidity code and bytecode into solidity* and bytecode* which can be used to verify the smart contract properties. They have also explained in detail about the conversion of solidity code and bytecode to solidity* and bytecode* respectively. Another formal verification method is given in [20] in which they characterized trace vulnerabilities efficiently by analyzing a smart contract multiple times. The main focus was on three main properties of trace vulnerabilities such as finding contracts that sends ether to arbitrary users, locks funds indefinitely and the contracts that are vulnerable to suicidal attack. They created a tool to detect the above mentioned trace vulnerabilities and named it as MAIAN. It is also known to be the first tool that utilizes symbolic analysis and indicates the trace properties for vulnerability detection in smart contracts. In [16], the authors focuses on creating a semantics for ethereum virtual machine and is known to be the first completely executable formal semantics of the EVM in which the smart contracts can be executed in the form of bytecodes. It deals with identifying the vulnerabilities such as integer overflow and unhandled exceptions.

3.2   Security Vulnerabilities

This section explains about the related work on analysis of security vulnerabilities in smart contracts from various research papers and articles. In Atzei et al. [11], the levels chosen to represent the vulnerabilities are in the following manner: solidity, EVM and blockchain. It is classified into different levels to group all the vulnerabilities in each and every level. So, if a new vulnerability is found, it can be matched to any of these levels. Another classification is given by Alharby and Moorsel [8, 14, 15] in which they found four major issues in smart contracts. They are security, performance, coding and privacy issues. In security issues, they identified the bugs and vulnerabilities where as in privacy they identified the issues like data exposure to unauthorized people. In coding issues they found out flaws in smart contract code and methods to improve them. Finally performance deals with the capacity of blockchain code. Some research papers and articles mainly focused on tools that could detect security vulnerabilities. Ethereum community found Oyente as the first and most important investigation tool in terms of security. It was developed by Luu et al. [16] and uses symbolic execution to identify the security vulnerabilities.

4   Methodology

4.1   Runtime Verification of Smart Contracts

In order to perform runtime verification ERC20 contracts were taken and checked for its compliance with ERC20 standard. For this purpose, K framework was used. Three main inputs to K are contract specification, ERC20 contract bytecode and a trusted input to execute the bytecode. Contract specification states what the contract "should do" in K language. The contract bytecode is the low level code of the smart contract

Table 1. Contracts and its description.

ERC20-token contracts	Description
Storj (STJ)	Decentralized cloud storage network
Odyssey (OCN)	Decentralized sharing economy and peer-to-peer ecosystem
Dentacoin (DCN)	Blockchain designed for improving the quality of dental care worldwide
Wax	Decentralized platform designed to serve video gamers to trade virtual assets
Populous (PPT)	Peer-to-peer invoice discounting platform
Rchain (RHOC)	Decentralized applications platform powered by Rho virtual machine
ICON (ICX)	Decentralized transactions network
Gifto (GTO)	Decentralized universal gifting protocol
OpenZeppelin	OpenZeppelin is a library for secure smart contract development
Dragonchain (DRGN)	Simplifies the integration of real business applications on blockchain

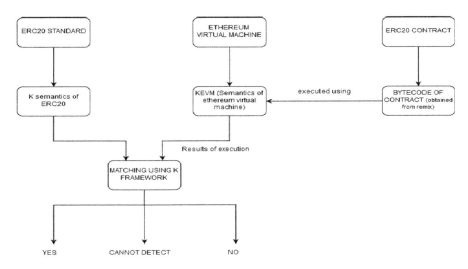

Fig. 1. Runtime verification of smart contracts.

which ethereum virtual machine can understand. And the trusted input is the semantics of the ethereum virtual machine in which the bytecode can be executed. Contracts that were taken for compliance check with ERC20 standard are shown in Table 1. 60 functions from these 10 ERC20 contracts were matched with six core functions of ERC20 standard, namely allowance(), approve(), totalsupply(), balanceof(), transfer-from() and transfer(). The results would show whether an ERC20 contract follow the ERC20 standard. The above process is shown step-by-step in Fig. 1.

The bytecode of each smart contract is obtained from Remix, an online interface for solidity [22]. The contract when written in the interface have to be compiled. Successful compilation of a contract will produce details like bytecode, assembly code, application binary interface etc., The bytecode in Ethereum are executed using ethereum virtual machine and involves gas. So a semantics of ethereum virtual machine is used for executing the bytecode. In our work, we have used K semantics of ethereum virtual machine for symbolically executing the smart contract. The execution result and the ERC20 contract standard in K are given as input to the K framework which then check for its compliance.

4.2 Vulnerability Testing

According to the research paper [16] out of 19,366 existing Ethereum contracts, 8,833 are vulnerable in many ways. We selected 15 different, namely timestamp dependence, use of untrusted input, transaction-ordering dependence, reentrancy, insecure coding patterns, unexpected ether flows, mishandled exceptions, tx.origin usage, blockhash usage, gas costly patterns, DoS by external contract, unchecked external call, locked money, unprotected functions and integer overflow/underflow whose occurrence is very frequent and conducted a study on the tools that could detect these vulnerabilities. Smart contract with above vulnerabilities were taken from different websites given in

[16, 23–25]. The results of this work would allow us to have an idea about the tools to be used to detect the above mentioned vulnerabilities. It would also allow us to identify the tool which could detect highest number of vulnerabilities. The above process falls into 3 steps as depicted in Fig. 2.

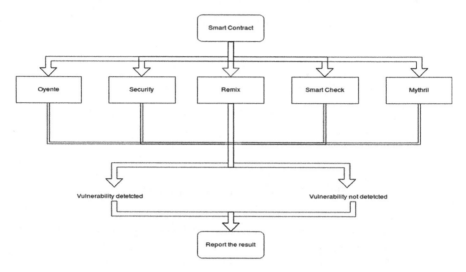

Fig. 2. Vulnerability testing of smart contracts.

5   Analysis and Results

5.1   Analysis of Contracts Based on ERC20 Standard Using K Framework

Among the 10 contracts chosen 6 contracts were not compliant with the ERC20 standard and 4 contracts were compliant with the ERC20 standard, the results of which are shown in Table 2. The analysis also showed that 3 contracts were not compliant with allowance() function, 5 contracts were not compliant with trans ferfrom() function

Table 2. Results of compliance check of contracts with the standard.

Smart contracts	Compliant/Non compliant
Storj	Non compliant
Odyssey	Compliant
Dentacoin	Non compliant
Wax	Non compliant
Populous	Compliant
Rchain	Compliant
ICON	Non compliant
Gifto	Non compliant
OpenZeppelin	Compliant
Dragonchain	Non compliant

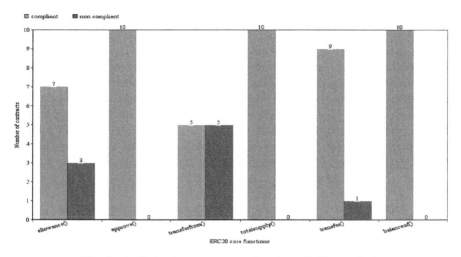

Fig. 3. Analysis of smart contracts based on ERC20 standard.

and 1 contract were not compliant with transfer() function. The Fig. 3 shows the analysis result of 60 functions with the ERC20 standard.

5.2 Analysis of Smart Contract Vulnerability Testing Tools

The analysis on security detection methods helped in understanding different tools and was able to classify them based on solidity analysis or bytecode analysis performed. As shown in Table 3, it was found that Securify and Mythril was the tools that performed both solidity and bytecode analysis. The tools like oyente, Remix and smartcheck performed only solidity analysis.

Table 3. Comparison of tools based on detection method and number of vulnerabilities detected.

Security tool	Method	Bytecode analysis	Solidity analysis	No. of bugs detected
Oyente	Symbolic execution		√	5
Securify	Formal verification	√	√	4
Remix	Formal verification		√	5
Smart check	Symbolic execution		√	7
Mythril	Formal verification	√	√	4

The analysis was also done based on the vulnerability detection capabilities of different tools. Comparison results are briefly explained in Table 4. Oyente was able to detect transaction ordering dependence, timestamp dependence, mishandled exceptions, reentrancy and integer overflow/underflow. Securify was able to detect transaction-ordering dependence, reentrancy, unexpected ether flows and use of untrusted input. Remix an online tool was able to detect timestamp dependence, reentrancy, tx.origin usage, blockhash usage and gas costly patterns. Smartcheck was able to identify timestamp dependence, reentrancy, tx.origin usage, gas costly patterns, DoS by external contract, locked money and unchecked external call. Mythril detected reentrancy, tx.origin usage, unprotected functions and integer overflow/underflow.

Table 4. Results of comparison of tools based on vulnerabilities detected.

Vulnerabilities	Oyente	Securify	Remix	Smart check	Mythril
Transaction-ordering dependence	√	√			
Timestamp dependence	√		√	√	
Mishandled exceptions	√				
Reentrancy	√	√	√	√	√
Insecure coding patterns					
Unexpected ether flows		√			
Use of untrusted input		√			
tx.origin usage			√	√	√
Blockhash usage			√		
Gas costly patterns			√	√	
DoS by external contract				√	
Locked money				√	
Unchecked external call				√	
Unprotected functions					√
Integer overflow/underflow	√				√

6   Conclusion and Future Work

A runtime verification and security analysis of the existing Smart contract was performed and it was discovered that many of the contracts were not compliant with standards like the ERC20 standard. Also the solidity code which was used to write smart contracts in ethereum was vulnerable in many aspects. Some of vulnerabilities are integer overflow, timestamp dependency, invalid random entropy sources, exception handling, unnecessary usage of delegate call, denial of service and callstack depth problem.

The Runtime verification of smart contracts was performed using K framework. 60 functions from 10 contracts were taken and it was found that, some of the functions does not follow ERC20 standard. Also, a comparison of the tools that are developed for identification of vulnerabilities was performed and analyzed different vulnerabilities detected by different tools. Our research showed Smart check as one of the best vulnerability testing tool which can detect seven vulnerabilities. The above two research helped us to perform runtime functionality verification of smart contracts and also to check for vulnerabilities in smart contract.

There are several lines of research arising from this work which should be pursued.

Firstly, on developing a platform in which all vulnerabilities in smart contract can be detected instead of using different tools. A second line of research, which follows from Sect. 4.1, is to write k rules for ERC721 which can be used to check the functionality of ERC721 contracts. Finally, performance checking of semantics of Ethereum Virtual Machine.

References

1. Zheng, Z., et al.: An overview of blockchain technology: architecture, consensus, and future trends. In: 2017 IEEE International Congress on Big Data (BigData Congress). IEEE (2017)
2. Nakamoto, S.: Bitcoin: a peer-to-peer electronic cash system (2008)
3. K Framework - An Overview. https://runtimeverification.com/blog/k-framework-an-overview/. Accessed 22 Sept 2018
4. Rosu, G.: ERC20-K: Formal Executable Specification of ERC20. https://runtimeverification.com/blog/erc20-k-formal-executable-specification-of-erc20/. Accessed 21 Sept 2018
5. Formal verification of ERC-20 contracts. https://runtimeverification.com/blog/erc-20-verification/. Accessed 21 Sept 2018
6. How Formal Verification of Smart Contracts Works. https://runtimeverification.com/blog/how-formal-verification-of-smart-contracts-works/. Accessed 21 Sept 2018
7. Sajana, P., Sindhu, M., Sethumadhavan, M.: On blockchain applications: hyperledger fabric and ethereum. Int. J. Pure Appl. Math. **118**, 2965–2970 (2018)
8. Alharby, M., van Moorsel, A.: Blockchain-based smart contracts: a systematic mapping study. arXiv preprint arXiv:1710.06372 (2017)
9. https://theethereum.wiki/w/index.php/ERC20TokenStandard. Accessed 22 Aug 2018
10. https://runtimeverification.com/blog/k-framework-an-overview/. Accessed 1 Aug 2018
11. Atzei, N., Bartoletti, M., Cimoli, T.: A survey of attacks on ethereum smart contracts (SoK). In: Maffei, M., Ryan, M. (eds.) POST 2017. LNCS, vol. 10204, pp. 164–186. Springer, Heidelberg (2017). https://doi.org/10.1007/978-3-662-54455-6_8
12. Egbertsen, W., et al.: Replacing paper contracts with Ethereum smart contracts (2016)
13. Kosba, A., et al.: Hawk: the blockchain model of cryptography and privacy-preserving smart contracts. In: 2016 IEEE Symposium on Security and Privacy (SP). IEEE (2016)
14. del Castillo, M.: The dao attacked: code issue leads to $60 million ether theft. Saatavissa (viitattu 13.2.2017). http://www.coindesk.com/dao-attacked-code-issue-leads-60-million-ether-theft. Accessed 15 Sept 2018
15. Reentrancy Woes in Smart Contracts. http://hackingdistributed.com/2016/07/13/reentrancy-woes/. Accessed 22 Aug 2018
16. Luu, L., et al.: Making smart contracts smarter. In: Proceedings of the 2016 ACM SIGSAC Conference on Computer and Communications Security. ACM (2016)
17. Kalra, S., et al.: ZEUS: analyzing safety of smart contracts. In: NDSS (2018)

18. Delmolino, K., Arnett, M., Kosba, A., Miller, A., Shi, E.: Step by step towards creating a safe smart contract: lessons and insights from a cryptocurrency lab. In: Clark, J., Meiklejohn, S., Ryan, P.Y.A., Wallach, D., Brenner, M., Rohloff, K. (eds.) FC 2016. LNCS, vol. 9604, pp. 79–94. Springer, Heidelberg (2016). https://doi.org/10.1007/978-3-662-53357-4_6
19. Hildenbrandt, E., et al.: KEVM: a complete semantics of the ethereum virtual machine (2017)
20. Bhargavan, K., et al.: Formal verification of smart contracts: short paper. In: Proceedings of the 2016 ACM Workshop on Programming Languages and Analysis for Security. ACM (2016)
21. Nikolic, I., et al.: Finding the greedy, prodigal, and suicidal contracts at scale. arXiv preprint arXiv:1802.06038 (2018)
22. https://remix.ethereum.org. Accessed 13 Sept 2018
23. https://github.com/smartdec/smartcheck/tree/master/src/test/resources/rules. Accessed 07 Aug 2018
24. https://github.com/eth-sri/securify/tree/master/src/test/resources/solidity. Accessed 07 Aug 2018
25. https://github.com/trailofbits/not-so-smart-contracts. Accessed 07 Aug 2018

A Smart Embedded System Model for the AC Automation with Temperature Prediction

F. M. Javed Mehedi Shamrat[1(✉)], Shaikh Muhammad Allayear[1(✉)],
Md. Farhad Alam[2(✉)], Md. Ismail Jabiullah[3(✉)],
and Razu Ahmed[4(✉)]

[1] Department of Multimedia and Creative Technology,
Daffodil International University, Dhaka, Bangladesh
{shamrat777,drallayear.swe}@diu.edu.bd
[2] Department of Business Administration,
Daffodil International University, Dhaka, Bangladesh
farhadalam@daffodilvarsity.edu.bd
[3] Department of Computer Science and Engineering,
Daffodil International University, Dhaka, Bangladesh
drismail.cse@diu.edu.bd
[4] Department of Software Engineering, Daffodil International University,
Dhaka, Bangladesh
razuahmed@gmail.com

Abstract. A model of an automated temperature prediction on smart AC system for a room has been designed, developed and implemented with an embedded system. In a room, temperature of object (like human being) with the environment is detected, identified and analyzed, with an ideal temperature. Based on data, a mathematical formula can be derived and an algorithm has been formed by using the mathematical formula of the predicted temperature data and the values of the two sensors, where sensors are used for object temperature detection and the AC perform automatically turned on or turned off. Python programming language with its default library has been used to code for the successful implementation of the algorithm. This proposed embedded system can be implemented in any smart AC room where anyone can utilize the AC system automatically switched on/off with the predicted temperature. Exploit this embedded system in all over the places including for disabled peoples, personal room, conference room, hall room, classroom and transports, where manually control of Air conditioner is not feasible.

Keywords: Automation · Temperature prediction · Embedded system ·
Smart AC · Thermal sensor · Raspberry pi zero · IR sensor · IR remote

1 Introduction

Temperature prediction in Air Conditioners is highly challenged in today's life. Automation in air condition is currently important topics in the area of IoT. It's extremely difficult to change the temperature haphazardly by physically for handicapped peoples, in sleeping hours, meeting time and in generally where a large number

© Springer Nature Singapore Pte Ltd. 2019
M. Singh et al. (Eds.): ICACDS 2019, CCIS 1046, pp. 343–355, 2019.
https://doi.org/10.1007/978-981-13-9942-8_33

of peoples exist there must be issue for comfort temperature for all. Many of the researchers work with room environment not with the object temperature, so the result what is found is may be more efficient if temperature prediction only depend on object temperature. If there are one or two people in a place, there can be possible to give an idle temperature for all but if there are more than two peoples there is turmoil to give comfort temperature depend on room temperature.

2 Literature Review

In current years some research paper has been published, where researchers have shown how to reduce the use of electricity during the use of air condition. But they have a few works on Smart AC system by predicting in AC temperature.

The system can recognize the surface temperature of occupants by a non-contact discovery at the limit of 6 m far. Separating human from other moving or potentially static article by warmth variable is about inconceivable since human, creatures and electrical machines produce heat. The wild warmth properties which can change and exchange will add to the location issue. Incorporating the ease MEMS based warm sensor can comprehend the first of human detecting issue by its capacity to recognize human in stationary [1].

The system naturally controls cooling by methods for changing temperature settings in forced air systems. Inside gadgets of climate control systems in this manner doesn't need to be supplanted [2].

Other researchers worked for a Smart AC system that can be controlled by wireless devices. They considered a remote sensor conveyed in the objective zone for detecting the encompassing temperature. The remote sensor issues control directions to a remote cooling framework when the privately detected surrounding temperature surpasses a specific attractive temperature range [3].

The Authors of [4] utilized model-prescient control method to learn and make up for the measure of warmth because of inhabitants and gear. They utilized measurable strategies together with a numerical model of warm elements of the space to assess warming burdens because of occupants and gear and control the AC appropriately.

Paradoxically, this paper presents strategy by methods for transmitting the temperature directions through a remote sensor arrange [5] to control forced air system task for inhabitants' warm solace. The remote system is likewise used to get condition data including the temperature, dampness, and air speed at spots around inhabitants. Along these lines, utilizing the proposed control setup does not need to change inside gadgets of existing climate control systems.

According to use research gap, an approach for detecting human object temperature from an environment and predict an idle temperature is proposed. For developing our experiment, we have used python programming with its default library, develop algorithm, Raspberry pi zero, Thermal sensors, IR sensors, IR remote. We have developed an embedded system by using these equipment's, which works with object temperature and automatic on-off depend on either object is exist in room or not. Finally it produce result of temperature depend of the criteria of number of object, object value, environment temperature, object is in environment or not.

3 Proposed System

To design the proposed embedded system, first detect objects, and take the body temperature from the object and predict a comfort temperature for all by analyzing the collected data to form a fully automated smart AC system. The ideal value of the room temperature is considered as 18 °C for the proposed research work. It is noted that the World Health Organization recommends a minimum indoor temperature of 18 °C, with a 2–3 °C warmer minimum temperature for rooms occupied by sedentary elderly, young children and the handicapped [6]. Below 16 °C temperature, there is an increased risk of respiratory diseases, while below 12 °C temperature the risk is of increased problem of the cardiovascular strain [10]. The main motto of this work is to set an ideal temperature that predicts temperature with automation of the AC system so that one can ignore manually to operate the room AC. A set of hardware components is used here to build up the proposed embedded system. Figure 1 represents the flowchart of the system and In Fig. 2 we have shown our proposed model.

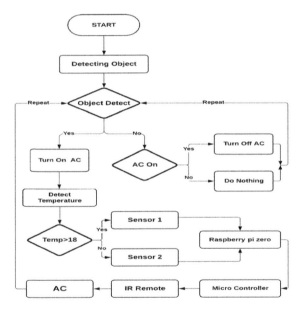

Fig. 1. Flowchart diagram of the proposed system.

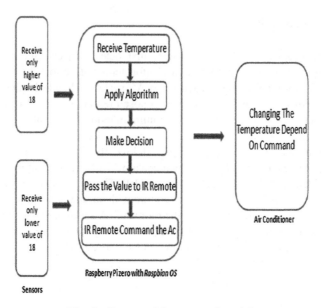

Fig. 2. Process of the proposed model.

3.1 Mathematical Exploration

To design the algorithm of proposed embedded system, first temperature data and object data are collected by using thermal sensors1 and sensor2 to set up a predicted temperature. The sensors play the role of distinctive sorts of significant worth. Sensor 1 is used to identify the temperature more than 18 (temp > 18) and sensor 2 is used to recognize the temperature under (temp < 18). Here, the ideal temperature is considered as 18 °C [6].

Algorithm 1: Mathematical Exploration

```
 1: Sensor1= s1
 2: Sensor2 = s2
 3: Object = x
 4: Temperature = t
 5: No of object in environment = n
 6: Read the value from s1 (t.value>18)
 7: Read the value from s2 (t.value<18)
 8: S1.value = x1.t, x2.t,......, xn.t;
 9: S2.value = x1.t, x2.t,......, xn.t;
10:    ∑s1= x1.t + x2.t +.....+xn.t /n;
11:    ∑s2= x1.t + x2.t +.....+xn.t /n;
12:    Predict Temperature (PT) = (∑s1 + ∑s2) /2
13:    Compare Temperature (CT) = PT - 18°C
14:    If CT value is equal or more than 20 (CT>=20)
15:         PT = CT - 5
16:    If CT > 10 & CT < 20(10<CT<20)
17:         PT = CT - 2
18:    If CT > 1 & CT < 10 (1<CT<10)
19:         PT = CT - 1
20:    If CT value is equal or more than -5 (CT>= -5)
21:         PT = CT + 3
22:    If CT value is equal or more than -5 (-1 <CT< -5)
23:         PT = CT + 1
24:    If CT value is 0
25:         PT = 18 °C
26:    After a required sec.
27:    Repeat [process ()]
```

4 Description of Used Component's

Developing the proposed embedded smart AC system, following hardware components are used. Here, the components with their Figures and description are presented.

4.1 Thermal Sensor

This sensor is an 8×8 cluster of IR warm sensors from Panasonic. When it is associated with the microcontroller (or raspberry Pi) it will restore a variety of 64 singular infrared temperature readings over I2C. This part will gauge temperatures going from 0 °C to 80 °C (32 °F to 176 °F) with a precision of ±2.5 °C (4.5 °F). It can distinguish human item present in the room from a separation of up to 7 m or 23 ft. Program codes are formed for utilizing this breakout on an Adriano or a perfect or on a Raspberry Pi with Python. On the Pi, with a touch of picture preparing assistance from the SciPy python library by which it can insert the 8×8 frameworks and get some truly decent outcomes. The AMG8833 is the up and coming age of 8×8 warm IR sensors from Panasonic, and offers higher execution than its forerunner the AMG8831 [7]. Figure 3 is a warm sensor that is utilized for the framework.

Fig. 3. Thermal sensor AMG8833.

4.2 Raspberry Pi Zero

The *Raspberry* Pi is an ease, MasterCard estimated PC that connects to a PC screen or TV. It is an able little gadget that empowers individuals of any age to investigate processing, and to figure out how to program in dialects like Scratch and Python. It contains 1 GHz single-center CPU, 512 MB RAM, Mini HDMI port, Micro USB OTG port, Micro USB control, HAT-perfect 40-stick header, Composite video and reset headers, CSI camera connector [8]. Figure 4 is an image of Raspberry pi zero.

Fig. 4. Raspberry pi zero.

4.3 IR Sensor

An infrared sensor is an electronic instrument that is used to distinguish certain properties of its condition. Infrared sensors are similarly prepared for evaluating the glow being released by an inquiry and perceiving development [9]. In Fig. 5 we showed the IR sensors which pass the value and receive the value for command the ac.

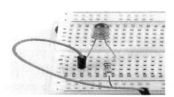

Fig. 5. Infered sensor.

4.4 IR Remote

Infrared remote control a handheld, remote gadget used to work sound, video and other electronic gear inside a room utilizing light flags in the infrared (IR) run. Top notch remotes have three or four incredible IR transmitters set at various points to give the room signals [10]. In Fig. 6 we displayed the picture of an IR remote.

Fig. 6. IR remote.

4.5   Microcontroller (NodeMCU V-3 Development)

The NodeMCU is an open-source firmware and improvement pack that causes us to Prototype our IOT item inside a couple Lua content lines. Open-source, Interactive, Programmable, Low cost, Simple Smart, and WI-FI empowered. The Development Kit dependent on ESP8266, coordinates GPIO, PWM, IIC, 1-Wire and ADC across the board. Power your improvement in the quickest manner blends with NodeMCU Firmware! USB-TTL included, plug and play, 10 GPIO, each GPIO can be PWM, I2C, 1-wire, FCC CERTIFIED WI-FI module, PCB reception apparatus [11]. In Fig. 7 we showed the picture of microcontroller.

Fig. 7. Microcontroller.

By assembling all these components, proposed embedded system has been designed and developed. Figure 8 represents the process diagram of entire smart AC system.

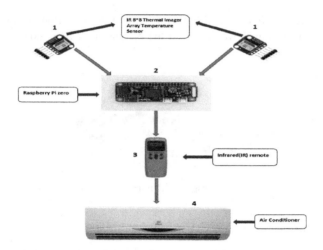

Fig. 8. Diagram of the entire system.

5 Algorithmic Approach for the Proposed System

To design the programming segment of the proposed model, all the tasks are summarized and putted in a sequence of actions so that one can translate them in a programming code. An algorithmic approach for the set of actions is presented below (Fig. 9):

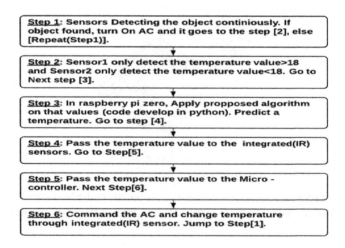

Fig. 9. Algorithmic process step by step.

Based on the above discussion, the formation of the purpose algorithm for the programming standpoint according to Algorithm 2:

Algorithm 2:Entire System Working procedure

```
1: import library;
2: Scanning ← Search Object;
3: Process(){← Working Function;
4: While(Scanning until object found )
5:          If(Scanning = = object)
6:                  Turn on air condition;
7:                   Break;
8:             Else
9:                Turn off air condition ← when ac power(1);
10:           Continue;
11:     end while
12:     If(Object(true)){
13:         Sensor1 scan ← Detect Object Temperature;
14:         Sensor2 scan ← Detect Object Temperature;
15:         If(object temperature >18°C){
16:             Read by Sensor1[ Temp Value ];
17:         Else
18:             Read by Sensor2[ Temp Value ];
19:     S1 = Sensor1[ ].value ← Object[x1.t, x2.t,.........xn.t];
20:     S2 = Sensor2[ ].value ← Object[x1.t, x2.t,.........xn.t];
21:     sumOfS1= ∑S1 ← Object [x1.t + x2.t + ...........+xn.t /n];
22:     sumOfS2= ∑S2 ← Object [x1.t + x2.t +...........+xn.t /n];
23:     Predict Temperature (PT) = (∑S1 + ∑S2) /2;
24:     Compare Temperature(CT)=[PT−18°C] ← Idle value 18°C;
25:         While (CT !=0)
26:                     If (CT >= 20){
27:                     PT= (CT − 5) °C;
28:                     Set.Tmp(PT);
29:                     }
30:                     Else If(CT >10 && CT<20){
31:                     PT= (CT − 2) °C;
32:                     Set.Tmp(PT);
33:                     }
34:                     Else If (CT<10 && CT>1){
35:                     PT = (CT − 1) °C;
36:                     Set.Tmp(PT);
37:                     }
38:                     Else If(CT>=-5){
39:                     PT = (CT +  3) °C;
```

```
40:                    Set.Tmp(PT);
41:                    }
42:                    Else If(CT>-1 && CT<-5){
43:                    PT= (CT + 1) °C;
44:                    Set.Tmp(PT);
45:                    }
46:                    end while
47:          While(CT == 0)
48:          PT = 18°C
49:          Set.Tmp(PT);
50:       }}
51:       Else
52:    Scanning ← Search Object;
53:    Repeat(Process())←After every 10 sec delay;
```

6 Result and Conclusion

The proposed technique has been designed and developed in default IDE and also can build up Anaconda application. A small conference room is selected for test the system, where 12 persons were available in the room. They all are of different temperatures, and the temperatures are detected by two thermal sensors (Sensor1, Sensor2). Then a data table is prepared by what exactly the sensor has provided. The fracture values like 28.5 to 29, 28.3 to 28 are skipped in this case. Several experiments have been observed to test the algorithm of the proposed system. Compare these results of the experiments with another, the result of the proposed system is found in the expected range.

6.1 Experiment 1

Total 12 objects are measured for the temperatures that are presented in Table 1 and the corresponding graphical representations are presented as diagram and are shown in Figs. 10 and 11.

Table 1. Object with temperature by implemented sensors.

No of object	Object temperature in °C	Predict temperature
1	19	
2	20	
3	28	
4	30	
5	17	
6	25	20 °C
7	16	
8	22	
9	20	
10	19	
11	17	

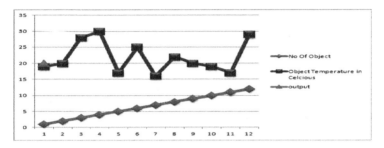

Fig. 10. Diagram of Table 1 data.

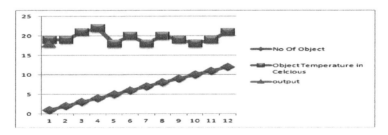

Fig. 11. Diagram of Table 2 data

In Fig. 10 we showed the Line chart of the Table 2 data and output.

Utilizing the estimation of the table distinguishes by the sensors and the output gets by utilizing of our calculation. In Fig. 10 Line graph of the unthinkable information and Output have been demonstrated.

Table 2. Object with temperature by implemented sensors, after program required time.

No of object	Object temperature in °C	Predict temperature
1	19	
2	19	
3	21	
4	22	
5	18	
6	20	18 °C
7	18	
8	20	
9	19	
10	18	
11	19	

6.2 Experiment 2

In Fig. 11 we showed the Line chart of the Table 2 data and output.

In experiment 1 we get temperature data from objects by using sensors from a small conference room and save it in a Table 1 and deploy our proposed Algorithm 1 on it, we have found a predict temperature 20 °C from experiment 1, then after 20–30 s we again collected data and stored raw data in the Table 2 in experiment 2, and deploy Algorithm 1 on it and get a predict temperature 18 °C. If we concentrate on the Figs. 10 and 11, we can easily judge that the temperature of object is changing dynamically, after experiment 1 system predict a temperature (20 °C) and deploy it, then after 20 to 30 s when we collected data in experiment 2 there we can see the changing ratio of temperature of the object in Fig. 10 and we can also see the difference between the Tables 1 and 2 data. Generally what temperature predict by the system using Algorithm 1 that is comfort temperature for all we can easily see it from Fig. 11. Every predict temperature is near to close of comfort temperature 18 °C.

7 Conclusion

A smart AC system room by automation and temperature prediction has been designed, developed and implemented by the python programming language. Several experiments have been performed to analyses the approach and found at satisfactory level. It can be applied in any manual AC system room to convert it into smart AC system environment by using machine learning, artificial intelligence and expert system.

References

1. Parnin, S., Rahman, M.M.: Human location detection system using micro-electromechanical sensor for intelligent fan. In: International Conference on Mechanical, Automotive and Aerospace Engineering (2016)
2. Ku, K.L., Liaw, J.S., Tsai, M.Y., Liu, T.S.: Automatic control system for thermal comfort based on predicted mean vote and energy saving. IEEE Trans. Autom. Sci. Eng. 12(1), 378–383 (2015)
3. Aftab, M., Chau, C.-K., Armstrong, P.: Smart air-conditioning control by wireless sensors: an online optimization approach. Masdar Institute of Science and Technology Abu Dhabi, UAE
4. Babu, D.V., Yadav, D.K., Yadav, N.K., Verma, V.K.: MEMS based smart & secure home automation system with multi-way control & monitoring facility using smart phone. J. Chem. Pharm. Sci. 9357–9359 (2015)
5. Aswani, A., Master, N., Taneja, J., Culler, D., Tomlin, C.: Reducing transient and steady state electricity consumption in HVAC using learning-based model-predictive control. Proc. IEEE 100(1), 240–253 (2012)
6. Wang, J.Y.H., Chuah, Y.K., Chou, S.W., Lo, T.H.: Non-invasive Zigbee wireless controller for air conditioner energy saving. In: Proceedings of IEEE 7th Conference on WiCOM, Wuhan, pp. 1–4 (2011)
7. Thermal camera. https://learn.adafruit.com/adafruit-amg8833-8x8-thermal-camera-sensor/overview. Accessed 28 Sept 2018
8. Raspberry pi zero. https://learn.adafruit.com/introducing-the-raspberry-pi-zero?view=all. Accessed 28 Sept 2018
9. IR sensor. https://learn.adafruit.com/ir-sensor?view=all. Accessed 28 Sept 2018
10. IR remote. https://learn.adafruit.com/using-an-ir-remote-with-a-raspberry-pi-media-center?view=all. Accessed 28 Sept 2018
11. Microcontroller. https://learn.adafruit.com/programming-microcontrollers-using-openocd-on-raspberry-pi?view=all. Accessed 28 Sept 2018
12. Sun, B., Luh, P.B., Jia, Q.S., Jiang, Z., Wang, F., Song, C.: Building energy management: Integrated control of active and passive heating, cooling, lighting, shading, and ventilation systems. IEEE Trans. Autom. Sci. Eng. 10(3), 588–602 (2013)

Rough-Set Based Hotspot Detection in Spatial Data

Mohd Shamsh Tabarej[(✉)] and Sonajharia Minz

School of Computer and Systems Sciences, Jawaharlal Nehru University,
New Delhi 110067, India
mstabarej@gmail.com, sonaminz@jnu.ac.in

Abstract. A special type of cluster is called hotspots in the sense that objects in the hotspot are more active as compared to all others (appearance, density, etc.). The object in a general cluster has a similarity which is less than the object in the hotspot. In spatial data mining hotspots detection is a process of identifying the region where events are more likely to happen than the others. Hotspot analysis is mainly used in the analysis of health and crime data. In this paper, the health care data set is used to find the Hotspot of the health condition in India. The clustering algorithm is used to find the hotspot. Two clustering algorithm K-medoid and Rough K-medoid are implemented to find the cluster. K-medoid is used to find the spatial cluster, Rough K-medoid finds the cluster by removing boundary points and in this way find cluster which is denser. Granules are created on the clusters created using K-medoid and Rough K-medoid and point lying in each granule is counted. Granule containing points above a particular threshold is considered as a potential hotspot. To find the footprint of the hotspot convex hull is created on each detected hotspot. Also in this paper hotspot and footprint is defined mathematically.

Keywords: Clustering · K-medoid · Rough-set · Rough K-medoid · Granules · Convex hull · Footprint · Hotspot

1 Introduction

In the modern world of information technology, every place and object gradually become location aware. With the growing use of location, analysis of spatial data has become more vital. An extensive understanding of spatial data by finding the hotspot of health condition can greatly impact the disease prevention, a planning and resource allocation, modelling and forecasting, disease control programs and evolution of disease prevention. Therefore, hotspot discovery is vital in heath data. Hotspot is an area where the density of certain activity is high as compared to others [9, 10]. Hotspot can be found for a certain activity like a certain disease, crime, vegetation etc. Spatial data is represented by two types of attribute spatial attribute and non-spatial attribute. The spatial attribute describes the location of the object and non-spatial attribute describe characteristics of the object. Spatial data is represented in raster as well as in vector form. Images are a good example of the spatial data represented in raster form. In the vector form, spatial data is represented in the form of point, line, and polygon. In this

M. Singh et al. (Eds.): ICACDS 2019, CCIS 1046, pp. 356–368, 2019.
https://doi.org/10.1007/978-981-13-9942-8_34

paper spatial data in vector form represented by geographical coordinates (latitudes, longitudes) is considered. Spatial data is usually accessed and analyzed using a Geographic Information System (GIS). Characteristic of the spatial data that is spatial autocorrelation and non-stationarity make it more difficult to analyze as compared to commonly assumed independent identically distributed (i.i.d.) data. Machine learning techniques would not perform well with the spatial data as they assume i.i.d. Spatial phenomena regularly change with time, thus adding temporal phenomena to the spatial data and we call it spatio-temporal data. Spatio-temporal data is even more complex to analyze due to its continuous nature.

Organization. Rest of the paper is organized as follows: In Sect. 2 related work is discussed. In Sect. 3 related concepts associated with the model is discussed. In Sect. 4 the proposed algorithms related to the model is discussed. In Sect. 5 experimental set-up and results are discussed. In Sect. 6 conclusions and future research direction is discussed.

2   Related Work

In paper [20], Verma and Baliyan aim at predicting the Taxi hotspot using Particle Around Medoid Clustering. Spatio-temporal data generated by cabs in the metro cities are used for the measurements. This work includes clustering of the data by K-means, k-medians and CLARA and DB-index, Calinski-Harabasz index, Squared Sum of Error and entropy obtained by all the clustering methods are compared. The technique which provides the best result is used for the detection of the hotspot and results shown in this paper shows that K-medians clustering is the best for Spatio-temporal clustering.

In paper [18] Peters, Lampart and Weber proposes a clustering algorithm based on the rough set theory which assigns objects in lower approximation or upper approximation of more than one cluster. Lower members of a cluster are called core objects and are surely belongs to a cluster and upper member are called boundary objects as their membership is uncertain. In this paper Divis-Bouldin index for rough clustering is also introduced.

In the paper, [11] Jamil and Akbar find spatio-temporal hotspot of the taxi services. Time series data obtained from taxi firms in Bandung are used in this study. To find the passenger hotspot Automatic ARIMA model are used. In paper [3] Boldt and Borg finds the statistically significant temporal hotspots of date and time event. Local Indicators of Spatial Association (LISA) statistics are used to find the temporal hotspot. Applicable in crime analysis and implemented in a foremost GIS application.

In paper [13] Meiriza, Malik and Nurmaini (2017) find spatio-temporal hotspot. FIRMS MODIS fire data is used for the analysis. Latitude and Longitude are used to represent the location of the occurrence; the date represents the temporal aspect. DBSCAN clustering is used for the analysis of spatial aspect. District and sub-district are declared as a hotspot and identify hotspot as very high, high and medium potential of risk.

In paper [5] Dong, Qian, Zhang and Zhai finds the hotspot of the passenger based on the trajectory (pick up point, drop of point and time of pickup). They use two-step procedure for pickup hotspot searching. Firstly, travelling similarity model is created to quantify the similarity of travelling behavior and secondly, it uses affinity propagation and simulated annealing to identify the daily passenger hotspot.

In paper [12] Lee and Jang find crash hotspots using aggressive driving behavior. The in-vehicle driving recorder is used for recording data. They use two-step procedure in first they find Aggressive driving behavior extraction- (i) Abrupt change detection, (ii) Auto-encoder, (iii) Two level clustering (Self- organized map and K-means clustering) and in second GIS Analysis– Kernel density analysis and Statistical correlation analysis is performed.

In paper [4] Martino, Pedrycz and Sessa find the hotspot using spatio-temporal clustering method SEFCM which is an extension of extended fuzzy C-Mean. Earth quake data set is used in this analysis for the prediction of the hotspot.

3   Basic Concepts

3.1   Preliminaries

Definition 1. *A **point set** P is the set of all geo-located points such as crime. A point p* $\in P$ *may be represented by a pair of coordinates (latitude, longitude) specifying its spatial location in the study region* [6].

Definition 2. ***Study region** S is defined as the minimum bounding rectangular area containing P in the Euclidean space.*

Definition 3. ***Hotspot** is considered as a special cluster in which certain activity is higher than the normal cluster. Mathematically, hotspot is defined as: Let H be the hotspot function, H: C* $\rightarrow$ *HS where C be the set of cluster* g_1, g_2 *...,* g_K *and HS be the set of hotspots. HS = h_1, h_2 ..., h_k then, $H(g_i) = h_i$, for an arbitrary cluster g_i containing the hotspot h_i and h_i may not exist for every cluster g_i.*
Properties of the Hotspot

- $h_i \subseteq g_i$ *i.e. a spatial cluster may contain a hotspot and* $| h_i | \leq | g_i |$
- $den(h_i) > den(g_i)$ *i.e. the density of hotspot is greater than the density of cluster containing it. As a special case a cluster may be a hotspot only then $den(h_i) = den$ (g_i).*

Definition 4. *A set P is called a **rough set** (inexact)* [16] *with respect to set B if and only if boundary region is non-empty.*

(i) ***Lower Approximation** of P is basically the largest union of all the objects which surely belongs to P. It is also known as the positive region of P. The lower approximation of P with respect to attribute B is denoted by $\underline{BP}$.*
(ii) ***Upper Approximation** of set P consists of all non-empty sets of equivalence classes that intersect with P. It is denoted by $\overline{BP}$.*

The concept of the rough set theory is shown in Fig. 1. The inner region which surely belong to a cluster is a lower approximation, the region which doesn't surely belong to a cluster is called upper approximation.

$$if\ p \in \underline{C_i}\ then\ p \in \overline{C_i}\ and\ p \notin \underline{C_j} \qquad and\ \ if\ p \in \overline{C_i}\ then\ p \in \overline{C_j}$$

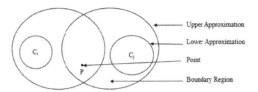

Fig. 1. Rough set concept

Definition 5. *Footprint of a data point or a pattern is defined to be a measure of the geographical coverage, i.e. the extent of the pattern. For example, the area affected by an epidemic. Therefore, depending on the level of the abstraction, the footprint of an epidemic may be country(s), state(s), district(s) household, etc.*

Therefore, mathematically footprint is a function with the domain as a set of spatial data points or a set represented by a spatial pattern. The range of the footprint function may depend on the application. By applying footprint function f, $f(h_i) \ll f(g_i)$ For a specific application let $f(h_i) = \xi_i$ where ξ_i is the footprint of the hotspot h_i.

Example *for the data point shown in Fig. 3(a), footprint of the points is given by convex hull as shown in Fig. 3(b).*

3.2   Measurements

Granule of Study Area [2]. The study region S is divided into a 2-dimensional grid and the number of grid is $N \times N$ where $N = S_{side\ length} / C_{length}$ and C_{length} is the length of each cell and is given by $C_{length} = x_{max} - x_{min}$ for each cell. Now each granule is defined by its coordinate interval and the number of points inside the grid.

$$Granule\ =\ ([x_{min}, x_{max}], [y_{min}, y_{max}], n) \tag{1}$$

where, n is the number of points inside a square grid.

Example: Consider Fig. 2 that shows the granule of the study region S. $C_{length} = 10 - 0 = 10$, $N = 50/10 = 5$, Number of grids $= 5 \times 5 = 25$. A single granule is represented as $((0, 10), (0, 10), 1)$.

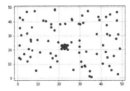

Fig. 2. Granule of the study region S

Convex Hull for a finite point set over the study region S, the convex hull [8, 21] is the set of entire convex combination of its points, each point p_i *in* S is assigned a weight such that weights are non-zero and the sum of all weights is one. For every choice of its weights, the resultant convex combination is a point in the convex hull and the entire convex hull can be formed by choosing weights in all possible ways. Thus the convex hull is defined as:

$$Convs(S) = \left\{ \sum_{i=1}^{|S|} a_i p_i \middle| \left(\forall i : a_i \geq 0 \land \sum_{i=1}^{|S|} a_i = 1 \right) \right\} \qquad (2)$$

Example: Figure 3(a) represents a set of data points over the study region and Fig. 3(b) represents the convex hull on the data points.

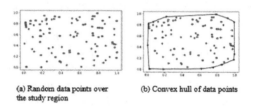

(a) Random data points over   (b) Convex hull of data points
the study region

Fig. 3. Data points and convex hull of data points.

3.3   Determination of Number of Cluster

There are a number of ways to detect the Hotspot such as density based clustering [7], heat-maps [17] to visualize the area with maximum density, etc. Clustering based methodology is used to find an area of maximum density (points). There are a number of clustering algorithm available, we choose K-medoid algorithm for clustering since it is best suited for spatial clustering [20]. These methods use similarity measures to create a cluster. However, these methods need to specify in advance number of clusters to be created. So a method needed to identify the optimal number of cluster based on the available data set.

Davies-Bouldin Index. One of the internal measure for evaluating cluster quality is the Davies-Bouldin index (DB index) [14] which verifies how well the cluster is, based on the quantities and features within the dataset itself. Smaller the value of DB index, better the quality of the cluster.

Silhouette Coefficient [1] refers to the validity and consistency within the data of a cluster. It refers to how well the objects are similar to one another within a cluster and dissimilar for the different cluster. The value 1 will show the best result, a value -1 will show the worst result, and a value 0 shows the overlapping cluster. Negative values indicate that the sample has been assigned to the wrong cluster.

4   The Proposed Algorithm

The problem of hotspot detection is divided into three phases as shown in Algorithm 1. This section provides the detailed description of these three phases.

Algorithm 1 Hotspot Detection Algorithm

Input:

1. Data set $P = (p_1, p_2, ...p_n)$.

2. K = Number of cluster to be formed

Output: Set of Hotspot within clusters

Algorithm:

1. **Clustering Phase** $C_{KM}(P) = (C_{k1}, C_{k2}, ...C_{km})$ where, C_{KM} is K-medoid algorithm and $(C_{k1}, C_{k2}, ...C_{km})$ are the clusters and m is a constant $C_{RKM}(P) = (C_{rk1}, C_{rk2}, ...C_{rkm})$ where, C_{RKM} is Rough K-medoid Algorithm and $(C_{rk1}, C_{rk2}, ...C_{rkm})$ are the clusters.

2. **Hotspot detection Phase** $H(C_{k1}, C_{k2}, ...C_{km}) = (h_{k1}, h_{k2}, ...h_{kj})$ where, $h_{ki}, h_{ki}, ...h_{kj}$ are the hotspots where j is a constant. $H(C_{rk1}, C_{rk2}, ...C_{rkm}) = (h_{rk1}, h_{rk2}, ...h_{rkl})$ where, $h_{rki}, h_{rki}, ...h_{rkl}$ are the hotspots where l is a constant.

3. **Footprint detection Phase** $f(h_{k1}, h_{k2}, ...h_{kj}) = (h_{k1}, h_{k2}, ...h_{kj})$ where, f is the footprint, $f(h_{rk1}, h_{rk2}, ...h_{rkl}) = (h_{rk1}, h_{rk2}, ...h_{rkl})$

4.1 Clustering Phase

K-medoid Clustering algorithm is similar to K-means and medoid shift algorithm [19]. Both of them divide and attempts to minimize squared errors, the distance between a labelled point in a cluster and the centroid of that cluster. The main difference between K-means and the K-medoid algorithm is that K-medoid chooses one of the data points as the centroid [15].

The most popular realization of the K-medoid is the partitioning around medoid (PAM) [20], medoid of the observation is taken as the cluster center. After every iteration medoid is replaced by non-medoid if it improves the total cost. This method provides a locally optimal solution so it is highly sensitive to outliers and noise, it is well suited for small data set but for large data set it doesn't work well. Steps of the PAM is described in Algorithm 2.

Algorithm 2 K-medoid Clustering

PAM: Clustering algorithm based on medoids

Input:

   k = number of cluster

   P = Dataset containing n data points

Output:

   k clusters of data points

Methods:

1: Randomly choose k data points O_{rand} as the center of cluster from D.

2: repeat:

3:    Assign remaining object to the cluster nearest to the medoid.

4:    Randomly select non-medoid O_{new} from each cluster as new medoid.

5:    Compute cost S_{new} and S_{ran} of swapping O_{new} with O_{rand}

6:    If $S_{new} < S_{ran}$ then Swap O_{new} with O_{rand}.

7: until no change

---

362   M. S. Tabarej and S. Minz

Rough K-medoid Clustering using the concept of lower and upper approximation to handle imprecision, noise in data, Peters et al. have proposed a Rough K-medoid algorithm [18] for real-life application. Some abbreviation that are used in Rough K-medoid Algorithm are given in Table 1.

The algorithm for Rough K-medoid clustering is shown in Algorithm 3.

Algorithm 3 Rough K-medoid

1: Randomly take K object of data set P as medoid: m_k and assign to lower approximation of the clusters. The remaining objects are denoted as P'_m where $m = 1, 2, ...(N - K)$.

2: The remaining data points are assigned to clusters in the two step procedure. In first step data point are assigned to upper cluster which is nearest. In the second step objects are assigned to upper approximation of the next nearest cluster or it is assigned to the lower approximation of the closest cluster as follows:

 – Given data point P'_m, obtain its closest medoid m_k as:

$$d(P'_m, m_k) = \min_{1,2,...k} d(P'_m, m_h)$$

 – Assign P'_m to the upper approximation of the cluster k i.e. $P'_m \in \overline{C_k}$

$$Q = h : d(P'_m, m_h) - d(P'_m, m_k) < \epsilon \wedge h \neq k$$

  • If $Q \neq \phi$
  • Then $P'_m \in \overline{C_k}, \forall h \in Q$
  • Else $P'_m \in \underline{C_k}$

3: Now calculate $RC_{current}$

4: Every medoid m_k is swapped with every data point P'_m and calculate the new RC_{new}.

 – If $RC_{new} < RC_{current}$
 – Medoid m_{k0} is swapped with data point P_{m0} and set $RC_{current} = RC_{new}$ and go back to step 2
 – Else stop

Rough Cost is given as:

$RCC(C_k) = w_l \sum_{P_n \in \underline{C_k}} d(P_n, m_k) + W_b \sum_{P_n \in (\overline{C_k} - \underline{C_k})} d(P_n, m_k)$

where $w_l + w_b = 1$

$RC = RCC = \sum_{k=1}^{k} RCC(C_k)$

Table 1. Abbreviation for Rough K-medoid clustering Algorithm [18]

Abbreviation	Meaning
p_n, P	$P = (p_1, p_2, \dots p_n)^T$ are the data set, p_n is the pth data point where, $n = 1,2, \dots n$ (n is number of data points)
$C_k, \underline{C_k}, \overline{C_k}, C_k^B$	For the cluster k: they are cluster, lower approximation, upper approximation and boundary set respectively
m_k, M	Medoid of cluster C_k and M is the set of all medoids
$d(p'_n, m_k)$	Distance between p'_n and medoid m_k
w_l, w_u, w_b	These are the weights for the lower, upper and boundary approximation
$\in$	Threshold
Q, Q'	Set Q and Q' respectively, cluster that are close to an object
RC	Rough Cost

4.2 Hotspot Detection Phase

The study region is divided into Granule. Granule defines the grid and the number of points inside the grid. Average point in a grid and hotspot detection is described in Algorithm 4.

Algorithm 4 Hotspot Detection

Input: A set of cluster
Output: Set of hotspot H of a cluster
Algorithm:
1: Create $Cell_{i,j} = N \times N$ grid of the study region S
2: Find expected number of points over the study region S as $\partial = |C|/(N \times N)$
3: Count the observed number of points of each cell as:
4: for each $cell_{i,j}$ do
5:     for each point $p(x,y)$ do
6:         if $(x_{min} < x < x_{max}) \&\& (y_{min} < y < y_{max})$ then
7:             $cell_{count} = cell_{count} + 1$
8:         $cell_{i,j} = cell_{count}$
9: for each $cell_{i,j}$ do
10:    if $Cell_{i<j} > \partial$ then
11:        $Cell_{i,j} = Hotspot$

4.3 Footprint Detection Phase

To find the footprint of the hotspot detected in hotspot detection phase, convex hull is created on the hotspot as described in Subsect. 3.2 that finds the spatial boundary of the hotspot.

5 Experimental Set-up and Results

5.1 Dataset

Healthcare data provided by www.data.gov.in. The data comprises information about
the different infant immunization that is provided by the health care department of
India. Data set contain information regarding a number of pregnant women received 3
ANC check-ups during pregnancy, Number of pregnant women given TT1 during
current pregnancy, Number of pregnant women given TT2 or Booster during current
pregnancy and Total number of pregnant women given 100 IFA tablets is used for the
experiment in this paperwork. The data is aggregated to district level year wise. Geo-
coding is done on the district level data i.e. (latitude, longitude) of each district is added
to the dataset so that it will be plotted to show spatial cluster.

5.2 Results

Determination of Number of Cluster to find the optimal number of cluster for the
clustering of the data, non-spatial attribute (i.e. remove latitude, longitude) of the data
set is applied to K-medoid algorithm. Value of k was taken from 3 to 23. For each value
of k, Silhouette Coefficient and Devis-Bouldin Index is calculated and plotted against
cluster number k as shown in Fig. 4. Devis-Bouldin index increases as shown in Fig. 4
(a) as the number of k increases from 3 whereas Silhouette Coefficient as shown in
Fig. 4(b) starts to decrease when the cluster increases from 3. For better cluster separation Devis-Bouldin Index should be minimum and Silhouette Coefficient should be
maximum. So the optimum number of cluster for this experiment should be 3.

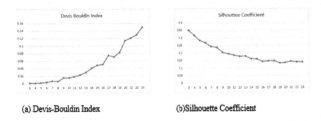

(a) Devis-Bouldin Index   (b)Silhouette Coefficient

Fig. 4. Determination of number of cluster

K-medoid Clustering the Non-spatial attribute of the dataset is clustered using K-
medoid clustering. Latitude, longitude corresponding to each cluster is plotted to show
the spatial distribution of the cluster. Resulting cluster is shown in Fig. 5(a). These
cluster shows a similar health condition. Each cluster is shown in different color and is
distributed spatially around the whole study area. Each cluster as shown in Fig. 5(a) is
taken separately. The study region is divided into a number of grid and the points inside
a grid is counted, grid along with point inside a grid defined the granules. Average no
of points inside a granule is calculated according to Algorithm 4. The Granule which

contains points greater than average no of points is considered as a hotspot. Now, Convex hull is created on a granule to show the footprint of the hotspot.

Output of each cluster shown in Fig. 6. Figure 6(a) shows the data point in cluster 1, Fig. 6(b) shows the data point of hotspot detection phase, and Fig. 6(c) shows spatial extent of the detected hotspot. Respectively, in Figs. 7 and 8 detected hotspots are shown.

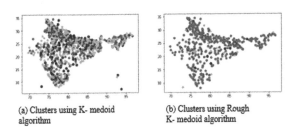

(a) Clusters using K- medoid
algorithm

(b) Clusters using Rough
K- medoid algorithm

Fig. 5. Clustering of the dataset

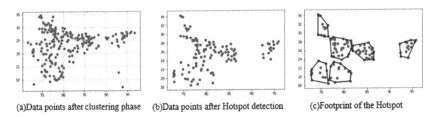

(a)Data points after clustering phase   (b)Data points after Hotspot detection   (c)Footprint of the Hotspot

Fig. 6. Hotspot detection using K-medoid clustering for cluster 1

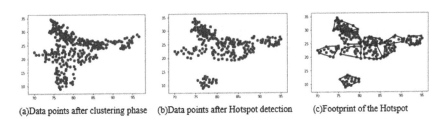

(a)Data points after clustering phase   (b)Data points after Hotspot detection   (c)Footprint of the Hotspot

Fig. 7. Hotspot detection using K-medoid clustering for cluster 2

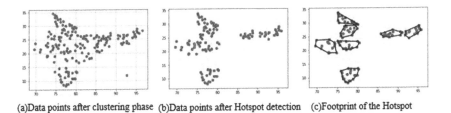

(a)Data points after clustering phase   (b)Data points after Hotspot detection   (c)Footprint of the Hotspot

Fig. 8. Hotspot detection using K-medoid clustering for cluster 3

Rough K-medoid Clustering is applied on a non- spatial attribute of the data set which creates clusters. It divides each cluster into lower and upper approximation. Points in the lower approximation surely belong to a particular cluster and points belonging to the upper approximation are not surely belongs to any cluster. So only those points which belong to lower approximation is considered and corresponding latitude, longitude is plotted for visualization. It also increases the separation between the clusters.

Each lower approximation cluster is divided into a number of grid and the points lying inside a grid is counted. A threshold is applied on the grid count. The grid having points above a threshold are considered as hotspot, steps for hotspot detection are shown in Algorithm 4 and convex hull is created on them to find the footprint of the hotspot. Figure 9(a) shows the point in the cluster 2 using Rough K-medoid clustering, Fig. 9(b) shows the points after hotspot detection phase and Fig. 9(c) shows the spatial extent of the hotspot.

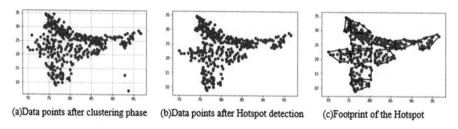

(a)Data points after clustering phase   (b)Data points after Hotspot detection   (c)Footprint of the Hotspot

Fig. 9. Hotspot detection using Rough K-medoid clustering for cluster 2

No hotspot is found in cluster 1 and 3, and the only hotspot is found in cluster 2 and the number of hotspot is also increased in cluster 2.

6   Conclusions and Future Research Direction

In this paper hotspot and footprint is defined mathematically. The significance of the proposed work is to find the hotspot of the health condition of India district wise. Founded hotspot are of irregular in shape and size. This algorithm can be applied to crime, passenger hotspot for the problem of finding the taxi in urban areas, crash hotspot detection, etc.

However, this model lacks the statistical significance test for the detected hotspot to say whether the hotspot is generated by chance or it has statistical significance.

References

1. Aranganayagi, S., Thangavel, K.: Clustering categorical data using silhouette coefficient as a relocating measure. In: International Conference on Computational Intelligence and Multimedia Applications, vol. 2, pp. 13–17. IEEE (2007)
2. Bargiela, A., Pedrycz, W.: Granular computing. In: Handbook on Computational Intelligence: Volume 1: Fuzzy Logic, Systems, Artificial Neural Networks, and Learning Systems, pp. 43–66. World Scientific (2016)
3. Boldt, M., Borg, A.: A statistical method for detecting significant temporal hotspots using LISA statistics. In: 2017 European Intelligence and Security Informatics Conference (EISIC), pp. 123–126. IEEE (2017)
4. Di Martino, F., Pedrycz, W., Sessa, S.: Spatiotemporal extended fuzzy c-means clustering algorithm for hotspots detection and prediction. Fuzzy Sets Syst. **340**, 109–126 (2018)
5. Dong, Y., Qian, S., Zhang, K., Zhai, Y.: A novel passenger hotspots searching algorithm for taxis in urban area. In: 2017 18th IEEE/ACIS International Conference on Software Engineering, Artificial Intelligence, Networking and Parallel/Distributed Computing (SNPD), pp. 175–180. IEEE (2017)
6. Eftelioglu, E., Tang, X., Shekhar, S.: Geographically robust hotspot detection: a summary of results. In: 2015 IEEE International Conference on Data Mining Workshop (ICDMW), pp. 1447–1456. IEEE (2015)
7. Ester, M., Kriegel, H.P., Sander, J., Xu, X., et al.: A density-based algorithm for discovering clusters in large spatial databases with noise. In: KDD, vol. 96, pp. 226–231 (1996)
8. Grubesic, T.H.: On the application of fuzzy clustering for crime hot spot detection. J. Quant. Criminol. **22**(1), 77 (2006)
9. Harries, K.: Mapping crime and geographic information systems (1999). www.ncjrs.gov/html/nij/mapping/ch4_9.html
10. Ishioka, F., Kawahara, J., Mizuta, M., Minato, S.I., Kurihara, K.: Evaluation of hotspot cluster detection using spatial scan statistic based on exact counting. Japan. J. Stat. Data Sci. **2**, 1–22 (2019)
11. Jamil, M.S., Akbar, S.: Taxi passenger hotspot prediction using automatic ARIMA model. In: 2017 3rd International Conference on Science in Information Technology (ICSITech), pp. 23–28. IEEE (2017)
12. Lee, J., Jang, K.: Proactive detection of crash hotspots using in-vehicle driving recorder. In: 2016 3rd Asia- Pacific World Congress on Computer Science and Engineering (APWC on CSE), pp. 193–198. IEEE (2016)
13. Meiriza, A., Malik, R.F., Nurmaini, S., et al.: Spatio-temporal analysis of south sumatera hotspot distribution. In: 2017 International Conference on Electrical Engineering and Computer Science (ICECOS), pp. 198–201. IEEE (2017)
14. Pakhira, M.K., Bandyopadhyay, S., Maulik, U.: Validity index for crisp and fuzzy clusters. Pattern Recogn. **37**(3), 487–501 (2004)
15. Patel, A., Singh, P., et al.: New approach for k-mean and k-medoids algorithm. Int. J. Comput. Appl. Technol. Res. **2**(1), 1–5 (2013)
16. Pawlak, Z.: Rough sets. Int. J. Comput. Inform. Sci. **11**(5), 341–356 (1982)
17. Perrot, A., Bourqui, R., Hanusse, N., Lalanne, F., Auber, D.: Large interactive visualization of density functions on big data infrastructure. In: 2015 IEEE 5th Symposium on Large Data Analysis and Visualization (LDAV), pp. 99–106. IEEE (2015)
18. Peters, G., Lampart, M., Weber, R.: Evolutionary rough k-medoid clustering. In: Peters, J.F., Skowron, A. (eds.) Transactions on Rough Sets VIII. LNCS, vol. 5084, pp. 289–306. Springer, Heidelberg (2008). https://doi.org/10.1007/978-3-540-85064-9_13

19. Sheikh, Y.A., Khan, E.A., Kanade, T.: Mode-seeking by medoidshifts. In: IEEE 11th International Conference on Computer Vision, ICCV 2007, pp. 1–8. IEEE (2007)
20. Verma, N., Baliyan, N.: Pam clustering based taxi hotspot detection for informed driving. In: 2017 8th International Conference on Computing, Communication and Networking Technologies (ICCCNT). pp. 1–7. IEEE (2017)
21. Wikipedia: Convex hull (2018). https://en.wikipedia.org/wiki/Convex_hull

DDoS Attack Detection and Clustering of Attacked and Non-attacked VMs Using SOM in Cloud Network

Nitesh Bharot[(✉)], Veenadhari Suraparaju, and Sanjeev Gupta

Rabindranath Tagore University, Raisen, India
niteshbharot20@gmail.com, veenadhari1@gmail.com,
sanjeevgupta73@yahoo.com

Abstract. Cloud computing has gained more importance in the IT service model that offers cost-effective and scalable processing. It provides virtualized and on-demand services to the user over the internet using several networking protocols with exceptional flexibility. However, with the existing technologies and the vulnerabilities, it leads to the occurrence of several attacks in the cloud environment. Distributed Denial of Service (DDoS) is most dangerous among all the attacks which limit the cloud users to access service and resources. Therefore, the detection of DDoS in the network and the identification of attacked VMs is the most dominating task in the cloud environment. In this work, a novel DDoS attack detection mechanism is presented. The research is carried out as follows: (i) Initially DDoS attack is detected by identifying the maximum number of connections to the network, (ii) then the attacked virtual machine and non-attacked virtual machines will be clustered using Self-Organized Mapping (SOM) based Neural Network (NN). The experimental results exhibit that the presented system can efficiently detect DDoS attacks and cluster attack and non-attack VMs in an attacked cloud network. Moreover, these results demonstrate that the proposed DDoS attack prediction accuracy of 97.63% and precision of 95.4% and it is better than the existing technique.

Keywords: Cloud computing · Artificial neural network · DDoS attack · Self-organizing map · Availability

1 Introduction

In computing, the cloud is the emerging technological advancement that aids in sharing of resources and services over the internet. This combination of the resources, servers, network, connection, and applications are known to be 'cloud' [1–3]. Since the users have to pay only for the services they use, the initial payments of the organization are of very low. Several organizations have a flexible level to achieve the resources or services on demand. The major attributes of cloud computing are On-demand Services availability, Universal Access to resources, Resource Pooling, Scalability and Elasticity and Pay-as-you-go service [4, 5]. Some of the application of cloud are e-learning, e-governance, Enterprise Resource Planning (ERP), etc. [6]. Even though cloud computing offers several applications to the customers, the major challenge that needs to be

© Springer Nature Singapore Pte Ltd. 2019
M. Singh et al. (Eds.): ICACDS 2019, CCIS 1046, pp. 369–378, 2019.
https://doi.org/10.1007/978-981-13-9942-8_35

rectified is the security in the cloud. Various attacks block cloud services to authorized users [7, 8]. Some of the threats that occur in the cloud are network layer oriented threats, physical layer oriented threats, application-oriented threats and web-based threats [9]. There exist various attacks and security threats in the cloud network. The DDoS attack is one of the most dangerous kind of attack which is very difficult to identify and detect [10].

Among all the attacks DDoS is a very treacherous kind of attack which aims at decreasing the service availability and performance by exhausting the resources of service host system [11–13]. The DDoS attack does not directly damage the data, but it intentionally compromises the availability of resources. These kinds of attacks have special effects on the cloud system [14, 15]. The delay in diagnosing the cause of service degradation by the cloud service provider results in the security vulnerability. Over past decades, several efforts have been devoted to identifying the DDoS attacks in the distributed systems [16]. Several attack detection techniques have been developed to protect the network against mischievous users. Such kind of methods has been improved continuously to boost up the detection capability. Several researchers are continually identifying security and privacy loopholes in cloud computing [16–18]. Some of the security measures at different level have been analyzed. Even though these researches are appreciated, but they lack in a comprehensive approach. The major classifications are focused on particular issues such as service delivery models, deployment models, or the cloud infrastructures. Some of the research works did not discuss the threats associated with other distributed computing systems which could become more threatening in cloud environments.

This research paper presents a method to detect the DDoS attack and cluster the attacked and non-attacked VMs in the attacked cloud network. The organization of the rest of the paper is structured as Sect. 2 presents the literature survey on the existing detection methods. Section 3 demonstrates the proposed work the attack detection and classification of variants of DDoS attack. Section 4 shows the result analysis and Sect. 5 gives the concluding remarks over the proposed work and give the future work directions.

2 Literature Review

In the paper [19] DDoS attack defense and mitigation is performed with the aid of intensive request care unit to separate the request. They had used the NSL-KDD data set to classify the attack request from the legitimate requests. 12 important features out of 41 features are used for the request classification. These 12 features are identified using the combined effect of Information gain, Gain ratio, and Chi-squared.

In paper [20] author proposed a threshold based technique for resource allocation. First, the incoming request IP is verified using a blacklist, if the IP does not belong to the blacklist then the administrator will check the available resources against the resources requested. If the number of resources required exceeds the threshold value, then it will be rejected and notified as the attack.

In paper [21], the proposed method categorized users in 3 sections as low, medium and high-risk users. This can be achieved using clustering and semi-supervised learning techniques. The characteristic difference between the user and the attacker is identified and becomes the base for the classification of users. So the attacker will behave like legitimate users. This will increase the attacker's cost.

[22] exploited the penetration testing models to determine the host IP address, operating system, and open ports. The second mode of this research was White box testing. The two attacks performed were DDoS, and Man in the middle Cloud attacks. Both of the attacks evaluated the vulnerabilities of the cloud to the risks such as data breach; identify fraud, compromising integrity, availability, and confidentiality. This research emphasized the liabilities of cloud and the necessity of implementing security measures.

Present solutions for DDoS attack in SDN network are either escalate the control plane or to refine the malicious traffic. [23] proposes a joint solution over the control plane to conquer the DDoS attack on SDN network. They had proposed an SDN shied for this purpose which will deploy special software casket to raise scalability of SDN switches. Results show that SDN shield achieves greater flexibility in comparison to other techniques even with high intensity of the attack.

Most of the attack detection models are based on the flow of packets and sessions of the users. Both the models are vulnerable to either botnets or if the origin of the attack is provisioned with human resource or surrogate servers. To overcome such issue author in [24] proposed a nature-based anomaly detection of DDoS attack. In this work, they had used the cuckoo search (CS) which is based on bio-inspired method. They had defined the attribute metrics to find the behaviors of stream whether it is DDoS or normal. They had modified the CS method to train and search. The modified cuckoo search increases the detection accuracy in comparison to Firefly.

Paper [25] proposed a strengthened approach for the detection of DDoS attack, which is achieved by optimizing the variables of the traffic matrix with the aid of genetic algorithm. It will also escalate the detection rate and accuracy of the system. During the training phase genetic algorithm sets the three parameters as: Traffic matrix (TM) size, packet based window size (WZ) and threshold values 'T_h'. During testing phase construct the TM for the WZ, evaluate the 'σ^2' from the TM and if the 'σ^2' is greater than 'T_h' then alert will be sent otherwise re-evaluate the system.

It is concluded from the above models for the detection of a DDoS attack. An efficient, fast and a robust detection model is required which is capable of detecting and identify the DDoS attack VMs in the cloud infrastructure.

3 Proposed Methodology

The DDoS attack is a type of attack which harnesses the availability of the victim service of an objective system. The proposed method aims at identification of DDoS attack and clustering the attack and non-attack VMs in the network. Once the data center based resource allocation is done to each VMs by the cloudlets, the DDoS attack detection process starts its execution. The flow chart of the proposed method is presented in Fig. 1. The step by step procedure of the proposed research work is given as follows.

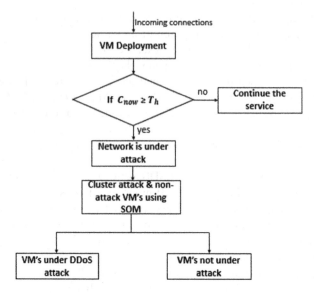

Fig. 1. Flow chart of the proposed method

- **Step1:** Once the data center based resource allocation is done to each VMs by the cloudlets, the DDoS attack detection process is executed.
- **Step2:** In general when network consist of only legitimate request, then there will average a number of connections made with the network. Although if the network is under DDoS attacks then due to flooding a large number of connections are made, which overburdens the network connection limit. If the number of connections 'C_{now}' exceeds the threshold value 'T_h' (Maximum limit for the normal connections), then the network is considered to be under attack.
- **Step3:** Now the attacked VMs and the non-attacked VMs need to be separated in the DDoS attacked cloud network. By the clustering process, the DDoS attack affected VMs and the non-attacked VMs will be clustered. The clustering is done using Self-organized map (SOM) based Neural Network (NN).

3.1 Clustering Using SOM

Kohonen first project is on self-organizing Map (SOM) at the University of Helsinki and it is also called as the Kohonen network [26]. Kohonen considers that a neural network (NN) will be separated into different sections whereas receiving outside input mode and various sections have different output features for respective input mode. In SOM, the high dimensional datasets are estimated onto a one or two-dimensional space. In general, SOM is a two-dimensional matrix of neurons, and each neuron denotes a cluster. SOM operates unsupervised-based learning process where all neurons compare for each input pattern and the neuron that is selected for the input pattern successes it. Then, the winning neuron is triggered, and it updates itself. The neighbor neurons estimate the distribution of the models in the input dataset. After completion of the adaptation process, similar clusters will come adjacent to each other. Topological ordering supports in identifying both dissimilar and similar clusters rapidly. Besides, SOM algorithm is more useful for a large number of datasets, and also it is robust for noisy datasets. Hence, the SOM algorithm is used for data clustering.

SOM contains of a two-dimensional lattice of map units. In SOM, the prototype vector is expressed as,

$$v_i = [v_{i1}, v_{i2}, \ldots, v_{id}] \tag{1}$$

Where, i denotes the unit number and d represents the dimension of input vector.

Based on neighborhood relation, the units are associated with the nearest units. The number of mapping units differs from a few tens to thousands and measures the precision of SOM. At the time of training, SOM creates a flexible net. Mapping of data points are done towards their adjacent units and are placed near to each other. Hence, SOM is constructed as a topology conserve mapping from input space towards a two-dimensional grid. From the available dataset during the SOM training, a constituent vector z is haphazardly selected. Then, the distance among z and all the prototype/model vectors (vi) are estimated. The optimal or perfect analogous unit is represented as b that is the map with model nearest to z,

$$\|z - v_b\| = \min_i \{\|z - v_i\|\} \tag{2}$$

Then, the model vectors revise and best paired unit as well as its adjacent is relocated to the neighbour input vector. For i^{th} unit, the update rule for the model vector is,

$$v_i(t + 1) = m_i(t) + \alpha(t)n_{bi}(t)[z - v_i(t)] \tag{3}$$

Where, t denotes the time, $\alpha(t)$ is the adaptation coefficient and $n_{bi}(t)$ is the winner unit of the adjacent kernel.

$$n_{bi}(t) = \exp\left(-\frac{\|p_b - p_i\|}{2\alpha^2(t)}\right) \tag{4}$$

Where, p_b and p_i are the neuron b and i locations in the SOM grid.

For the discrete number of dataset and stationary neighborhood kernel, SOM error function is expressed as,

$$E = \sum_{i=1}^{N} \sum_{j=1}^{M} n_{bj} \|z_i - v_i\|^2 \tag{5}$$

Where, N and M are the number of training samples and map units respectively. The neighbour kernel n_{bj} is centered at unit b.

Algorithm 1: SOM algorithm

Step 1: Initialize all the weight vectors randomly.
Step 2: Select a random data point from training set and apply it to SOM.
Step 3: Estimate the Best matching unit in the SOM map.
Step 4: Verify the nodes within the neighbourhood of the optimal matching unit.
Step 5: Adopt the nodes weights in the optimal matching unit neighbourhood in the direction of selected data point
Step 6: Repeat step 2 to 5 for N iterations.

In the deployment of virtual machines, the SOM algorithm is used to cluster the virtual machine into with DDoS attack and without DDoS attacks based on the features of both attacks and non-attack VMs.

So, the above mentioned SOM algorithm will cluster the as attacked and non-attacked VMs.

4 Result Analysis

The proposed experiment is conducted using CloudSim in a 64-bit Windows 7 environment with 16 GB RAM. CloudSim is a cloud simulation tool that has identified in the past few years an increasing recognition among both academic research and industrial sectors. The experimentation setup consists of 5 virtual machines and each has a memory RAM capacity of 8 GB, hard drive storage of 495.5625 GB and network bandwidth share per each virtual machines of 50000 Kbit/s. The properties of the datacenter and VMs are summarized in Table 1.

Table 1. Experimental setup and parametric values

Parameters	Values
System architecture	x64
Number of VMs	1000
Operating system	Windows 7
No. of CPU cores/VM	5
CPU speed/VM	1000 MIPS
RAM/VM	8 GB
Network bandwidth share per VM	50000 Kbit/s
Hard drive storage per VM	495.5625 GB

The major objective of the experimentation is to prove the efficacy of the proposed technique. Firstly, it is identified whether the network is attacked by the DDoS attacker group or not. It can be achieved by checking the present number of connections. If the number of connections exceeds the maximum limit then the network is considered under the attack. The within the cloud network the virtual machines which are affected by the DDoS attack are identified and clustered using SOM-based neural network.

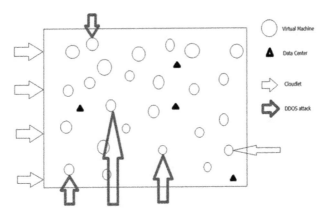

Fig. 2. Cloud environment containing VMs, datacenters and cloudlets along with DDoS attacked VMs

To achieve this experimental setup is created in which, the cloud environment is formed where n number of virtual machines, data center, and cloudlets are affianced. The cloud environment is created which involves virtual machines, data center, and the cloudlets. In the cloud environment, the DDoS attack detection is performed, and the network model is shown in Fig. 2.

The cloud environment includes node, data center, and the cloudlets where also the attacks occur. Table 2 shows the region or area of attack detection in the cloud environment. In this, 1 represents the attack enable and 0 depicts the attack is disable.

Table 2. Region/area of attack detection in cloud

Virtual machine (VM)	Node based attack	Cloudlet based attack	Datacenter based attack	Network based attack
VM 1	0	1	1	1
2VM 2	1	1	1	0
VM 3	1	1	0	0
VM 4	1	1	0	0
VM 5	1	0	0	1
VM 6	0	1	0	1
VM 7	0	1	1	0
VM 8	0	1	1	1
VM 9	1	1	1	1
VM 10	0	1	0	1

The DDoS attack detection rate is increased when increasing the time. The maximum DDoS attack detection rate that is 100% is achieved at the time interval between 11 ms to 32 ms. After that interval, the attack rate gets decreased to a minimum value that is 0%. The Time Vs. Attack rate of the DDoS attack detection is given in Fig. 3.

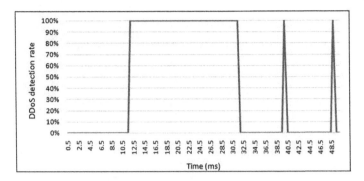

Fig. 3. Time Vs DDoS attack detection rate

By considering the attack rate and cloud activity rate, the attack detection rate is increasing when increased the time. The graph between cloudlet activity and the attack rate is given in Fig. 4.

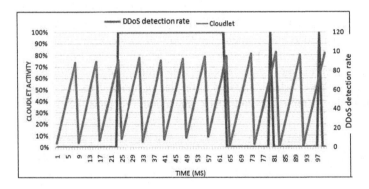

Fig. 4. Cloudlet Vs DDoS detection rate

The performance evaluation of the proposed technique is obtained using cross-validation parameters such as accuracy, precision, sensitivity, and specificity. Based on these parameters, Table 3 shows the comparison of the proposed technique with the existing technique.

Table 3. Performance comparison of the proposed technique

Technique	Accuracy	Precision	Sensitivity	Specificity
Firefly [27]	93.87	92	92	94.83
BAT [27]	91.48	92.30	90.47	92.30
BIFAD [24]	95.63	95.4	95	95.7
Proposed	97.63	96.2	94.4	97.32

5 Conclusion

This work focuses on the DDOS attack detection and clustering of attacked VMs to recover them from the attack. During the clustering process, the attacked and non-attacked virtual machines were separated with the aid of Self organized mapping based neural network. The simulation results demonstrated that the proposed novel technique achieved the maximum DDoS detection rate. Furthermore, these results attained the DDoS attack detection and achieved accuracy of 97.63%. In future work will apply the cryptography algorithm for mitigating the detected attacks in the cloud computing environment and also provide an optimal method to further classify the detected DDoS attack to its variants such as LORDAS attack, SYN FLOOD attack, DNS FLOOD attack, Ping Flood attack, Smurf attack and Nuke attack.

References

1. Zhang, L., et al.: Cloud manufacturing: a new manufacturing paradigm. Enterp. Inf. Syst. **8**(2), 167–187 (2014)
2. Ren, L., Zhang, L., Tao, F., Zhao, C., Chai, X., Zhao, X.: Cloud manufacturing: from concept to practice. Enterp. Inf. Syst. **9**(2), 186–209 (2015)
3. Ren, L., Zhang, L., Wang, L., Tao, F., Chai, X.: Cloud manufacturing: key characteristics and applications. Int. J. Comput. Integr. Manuf. **30**(6), 501–515 (2017)
4. Puthal, D., Sahoo, B.P.S., Mishra, S., Swain, S.: Cloud computing features, issues, and challenges: a big picture. In: 2015 International Conference on Computational Intelligence and Networks (CINE), pp. 116–123. IEEE (2015)
5. Sheikhi, A., Rayati, M., Bahrami, S., Ranjbar, A.M., Sattari, S.: A cloud computing framework on demand side management game in smart energy hubs. Int. J. Electr. Power Energy Syst. **64**, 1007–1016 (2015)
6. Banerjee, S., Paul, R., Biswas, U.: Cloud computing: a wave in service supply chain. In: Handbook of Research on Managerial Strategies for Achieving Optimal Performance in Industrial Processes, pp. 304–324 (2016)
7. Wei, L., et al.: Security and privacy for storage and computation in cloud computing. Inf. Sci. **258**, 371–386 (2014)
8. Li, J., Li, Y.K., Chen, X., Lee, P.P., Lou, W.: A hybrid cloud approach for secure authorized deduplication. IEEE Trans. Parallel Distrib. Syst. **26**(5), 1206–1216 (2015)
9. Islam, T., Manivannan, D., Zeadally, S.: A classification and characterization of security threats in cloud computing. Int. J. Next-Gener. Comput. **7**(1) (2016)
10. Somani, G., Gaur, M.S., Sanghi, D., Conti, M., Rajarajan, M., Buyya, R.: Combating DDoS attacks in the cloud: requirements, trends, and future directions. IEEE Cloud Comput. **4**(1), 22–32 (2017)
11. Yan, Q., Yu, F.R.: Distributed denial of service attacks in software-defined networking with cloud computing. IEEE Commun. Mag. **53**(4), 52–59 (2015)
12. Osanaiye, O., Choo, K.K.R., Dlodlo, M.: Distributed denial of service (DDoS) resilience in cloud: review and conceptual cloud DDoS mitigation framework. J. Netw. Comput. Appl. **67**, 147–165 (2016)
13. Somani, G., Gaur, M.S., Sanghi, D., Conti, M., Buyya, R.: DDoS attacks in cloud computing. Comput. Commun. **107**(C), 30–48 (2017)

14. Poornima, A., Maheshwari, D.: A study on denial of service attacks in cluster based web servers. World Sci. News **41**, 240 (2016)
15. Bhuyan, M.H., Kashyap, H.J., Bhattacharyya, D.K., Kalita, J.K.: Detecting distributed denial of service attacks: methods, tools and future directions. Comput. J. **57**(4), 537–556 (2013)
16. Todorova, M.S., Todorova, S.T.: DDoS Attack detection in SDN-based VANET architectures (2016)
17. Mollah, M.B., Azad, M.A.K., Vasilakos, A.: Security and privacy challenges in mobile cloud computing: Survey and way ahead. J. Netw. Comput. Appl. **84**, 38–54 (2017)
18. Yu, Y., Miyaji, A., Au, M.H., Susilo, W.: Cloud computing security and privacy: standards and regulations (2017)
19. Bharot, N., Verma, P., Sharma, S., Suraparaju, V.: Distributed denial-of-service attack detection and mitigation using feature selection and intensive care request processing unit. Arab J. Sci. Eng. **43**, 959–967 (2018)
20. Bharot, N., Verma, P., Suraparaju, V., Gupta, S.: Mitigating distributed denial of service attack in cloud computing environment using threshold based technique. Indian J. Sci. Technol. **9**(38), 1–7 (2016)
21. Han, Y., Alpcan, T., Chan, J., Leckie, C., Rubinstein, B.I.: A game theoretical approach to defend against co-resident attacks in cloud computing: preventing co-residence using semi-supervised learning. IEEE Trans. Inf. Forensics Secur. **11**(3), 556–570 (2016)
22. Jabir, R.M., Khanji, S.I.R., Ahmad, L.A., Alfandi, O., Said, H.: Analysis of cloud computing attacks and countermeasures. In: 2016 18th International Conference on Advanced Communication Technology (ICACT), pp. 117–123. IEEE (2016)
23. Chen, K.Y., Junuthula, A.R., Siddhrau, I.K., Xu, Y., Chao, H.J.: SDNShield: towards more comprehensive defense against DDoS attacks on SDN control plane. In: 2016 IEEE Conference on Communications and Network Security (CNS), pp. 28–36 (2016)
24. Prasad, K.M., Reddy, A.M., Rao, K.V.: BARTD: bio-inspired anomaly based real time detection of under rated App-DDoS attack on web. J. King Saud Univ. – Comput. Inf. Sci. (2017)
25. Lee, S.M., Kim, D.S., Lee, J.H., Park, J.S.: Detection of DDoS attacks using optimized traffic matrix. Comput. Math Appl. **63**(2), 501–510 (2012)
26. Kohonen, T.: The self-organizing map. Proc. IEEE **78**(9), 1464–1480 (1990)
27. Prasad, K.M., Reddy, A.R.M., Rao, K.V.: BARTD: Bio-inspired anomaly based real time detection of under rated App-DDoS attack on web. J. King Saud Univ.-Comput. Inf. Sci. (2017)

An Efficient Knowledge-Based Text Pre-processing Approach for Twitter and Google+

Tripti Agrawal$^{(\boxtimes)}$ and Archana Singhal

Department of Computer Science, University of Delhi, Delhi 110007, India
tripti.ag@gmail.com, archanasinghal1970@gmail.com

Abstract. People nowadays prefer sharing their opinions towards various products and services frequently on social networking sites (SNSs). These online reviews are huge in size and act as a goldmine for organizations to understand and monitor public reviews of their products and services. But these online reviews are highly unstructured in nature due to the presence of various linguistic features like hashtags, URLs, misspelled words, emoticons and many more. This highly unstructured data makes sentiment classification a challenging task. Hence, data pre-processing is an underlying and fundamental step in sentiment analysis. In the present work, authors have rigorously explored a series of pre-processing steps and observed that the sequence order of pre-processing steps affects the overall results. Hence, a sequence order of pre-processing steps has been proposed and implemented on two different social networks - Twitter and Google+. Twitter has been selected because of its tremendous popularity among netizens and Google+ has been selected because the domain of data for the proposed approach closely matches with the users' interests on Google+. As the existing approach for handling data on Twitter cannot be implemented directly to handle Google+ data, a modified approach for Google+ has been suggested and implemented by the authors. In addition, some new dictionaries for handling linguistic features have been compiled and existing dictionaries have also been modified to improve pre-processing results. The proposed approach is implemented to evaluate the overall results.

Keywords: Data pre-processing · Sentiment analysis ·
Social networks · Twitter · Google+

1 Introduction

Data from user-generated content on social networks have potential commercially significant advantages. Netizens are actively engaged with brands on social networks and generate a huge amount of highly unstructured data by sharing their own experiences with brands and services. The presence of slangs, misspelled words, hashtags, numbers, emoticons along with uninformative data such as

© Springer Nature Singapore Pte Ltd. 2019
M. Singh et al. (Eds.): ICACDS 2019, CCIS 1046, pp. 379–389, 2019.
https://doi.org/10.1007/978-981-13-9942-8_36

URLs, HTML tags, usernames etc. in the text, makes sentiment analysis[1] a challenging task. To identify brand insights quickly and correctly, data needs to be preprocessed before sentiment classification. An efficient data pre-processing leads to the selection of relevant features and the resultant data will have a huge impact on the effectiveness of the classifier.

In the present paper, pre-processing steps have been implemented on various electronic brands data collected from two different social networks - Twitter and Google+. Twitter is one of the most popular social networks with over 326 million (statista 2018) monthly active users whereas, Google+ is another social network with 395 million monthly active users[2].

Out of various social networks, Google+ has been selected because India stands second among the top five countries using Google+.[3] Also, the majority of Indian Google+ users are students and software engineers.[4] And the domain of data collected matches the interests of users on Google+. The reason for the selection of Twitter along with Google+ is the difference in the maximum character length restriction imposed on users. Twitter imposes a maximum limit of 280 characters on user posts whereas Google+ does not impose such character length on users and thus an ideal platform for long-form content and discussions. It has been observed that maximum character limit restriction influences the writing style of users on social networks which in return affects overall pre-processing steps.

It has been observed that the sequence order of pre-processing affects the overall results of pre-processing. In the proposed work, a detailed series of 14 different pre-processing steps have been implemented on Twitter and Google+ data. Also, a new approach to handling Google+ usernames has been proposed and implemented.

Many papers have been published on sentiment analysis. Among various social networks, Twitter has been used as the primary source of data in most of these papers. To the best of authors' knowledge, Google+ data has not been explored much for sentiment analysis task. In the present paper, a modest attempt has been made to study the pre-processing steps of a social network other than Twitter in detail.

Rest of the paper is organized as follows – Sect. 2 outlines existing work on sentiment analysis with a focus on data pre-processing. Section 3 presents the authors approach for data pre-processing in detail. Section 4 shows the experiments and evaluation of implemented approach. The last section concludes the present paper with future work.

2   Related Work

Go, Bhayani and Huang are the pioneers in the field of sentiment analysis of Twitter data. In [6,8,12], authors have implemented basic pre-processing steps

---

[1] https://www.cs.uic.edu/~liub/FBS/SentimentAnalysis-and-OpinionMining.pdf.

[2] https://dustn.tv/social-media-statistics/#google-plus-stats.

[3] https://www.globalmediainsight.com/blog/google-users-statistics/.

[4] https://nextbigwhat.com/google-plus-details-in-india/.

such as removal of hashtags, numbers, replacement of usernames and URLs, handling of repeated characters etc. In addition to basic pre-processing steps, authors in [4], have handled limited emoticons. But in the present paper, authors have implemented all the basic pre-processing steps along with an exhaustive list of emoticons.

In [2,3,9,11,13], authors have explored the role of text pre-processing in sentiment analysis of Twitter and conducted a series of experiments to verify the effectiveness of various pre-processing methods. Experimental results in [9] showed no improvement in accuracy after the removal of Stop words, URLs and numbers whereas, in [3], experiments result showed improvement on URLs reservation. In the proposed approach, stop words, URLs have been removed from the data but numbers are retained.

In [10], authors' discuss different pre-processing methods that affect sentiment classification on Twitter. In addition to basic text pre-processing steps, authors have expanded negations and acronyms using online Slang dictionary. In the present approach, authors have modified existing dictionary to include more acronyms and added frequent spelling mistakes observed in the collected data. Non-negated Apostrophe look-up for expansion along with HTML codes have also been implemented additionally.

In [7], the pre-processing approach is similar to our approach. But our expanding acronym dictionary is quite comprehensive than theirs. Also, a dictionary for expanding HTML codes, combining split acronyms are a few additional steps of our proposed approach. Also, the present approach has been implemented and experimented on two different social networks data.

Detailed data pre-processing steps of the proposed approach are explained in the next section.

3   Proposed Approach

In the proposed approach, the authors' aim is to reduce irrelevant features through a series of pre-processing steps without loss of user context. The proposed approach, first presents how data has been collected from two different social networks. Then, an efficient sequence of pre-processing steps has been proposed and implemented on both social networks data. During pre-processing, some existing dictionaries have been modified. Also, some new dictionaries have been compiled. Finally, to validate the proposed approach, the results of pre-processing steps have been analyzed on the sample data.

3.1   Data Gathering

In this work, authors have collected around 80,853 unique tweets of eight different electronic brands namely Motorola, Apple, Samsung, Oppo, HTC, Xiaomi, Nokia and Huawei. Tweets have been collected using 'rtweet' [14] package in R.

For Google+ data collection, Google+ API [15] has been used. Around 1,09,563 users comments were retrieved for electronic brands mentioned above.

After data collection, details of pre-processing steps are explained in the next section.

3.2   Data Pre-processing

Data pre-processing is the underlying and fundamental step towards sentiment analysis as it facilitates a better understanding of unstructured data. The data is unstructured due to the presence of different linguistic features like hashtags, URLs, misspelled words, emoticons and so on. It has been observed that various social networks data in spite of having almost the same linguistic features differ in the frequency of their usages. The frequencies of frequently used linguistics features of collected data from Twitter and Google+ are shown in Table 1.

Table 1. Frequency of features on Twitter and Google+

Features	Twitter	Google+
HTML tags	0	1,25,067
Emoticons	23,230	10,185
Usernames	46,736	28,135
URLs	57,827	39,149

As shown in Table 1, there exists frequency disparity in the use of linguistic features on Twitter and Google+. The first reason for this is the limitations imposed on users by social networks. For example, on Twitter, 280 characters limit is imposed on users. As a result, users incorporate URLs, hashtags, and emoticons quite frequently in their tweets to convey more in fewer words. On the other hand, Google+ has not imposed such restrictions on users. So, the frequency of hashtags, emoticons is quite comparatively less than that of Twitter tweets. The second reason is the variation in demography of social networks users that segregates their interests and writing patterns on different social networks [1]. For example, the majority of Indian users on Google+ are software engineers, so usage of HTML tags is very high in Google+.

During data pre-processing, it has been observed that the sequence order of pre-processing steps affects the overall pre-processing results. The proposed approach, thus, presents an efficient sequence order of pre-processing steps. Details of these proposed pre-processing steps in order are explained below.

1. Converting to Lowercase. In the first pre-processing step, the text has been converted to lowercase so that dictionary lookup doesn't fail due to the difference in cases. After converting text to lowercase, in the next step, acronyms are combined.

2. Combining Acronyms. Sometimes netizens use spaces in between acronyms such as "w o w", "i o y". Dictionary lookup is done word by word. So due to spaces, split acronyms either won't be expanded to their original form or are wrongly expanded. (Example, in "i o y", 'o' will be wrongly expanded as "oh" and this acronym will be finally expanded as "i oh why"). To avoid such type of errors, in the proposed approach, such split abbreviations are combined by removing in-between spaces. After combining acronyms, "i o y" will become "ioy" which will be expanded as "i owe you", which is the original standard form of this acronym.

After removing spaces between acronyms, the next step is expanding acronyms.

3. Expanding Acronyms. Since usage of acronyms and slang is quite common in the text, it is necessary to expand acronyms to their original words to make sense out of them. Acronyms and slang are expanded to their original words using Internet Slang Dictionary[5]. Each acronym in this dictionary corresponds to an explanation. Example, lol implies "laughing out loud". Though this dictionary is quite comprehensive, netizens style of writing acronyms sometimes lead to unsuccessful dictionary lookup. For example, jk stands for 'just kidding' in the dictionary but if a user uses j/k in place of jk in their text then it won't be expanded correctly because 'j/k' is not present in the dictionary.

In the proposed approach, the dictionary has been modified to handle such type of cases. Also, few misspelled words have also been added to the dictionary such as because, 'cause, coz, bcoz, takin, askin, Sammy (for Samsung) and many more. The modified acronym dictionary has now a total of 5515 different acronyms and slangs words.

4. Expanding HTML Codes. After expanding acronyms, HTML codes are expanded with their meaning. For example, "&", "<", """, "?" and "'" are replaced by "and", "less than", "?" and apostrophe (') respectively. HTML codes replacement has been done in both - Twitter and Google+ data.

After expanding HTML codes, the next step is Negation and non-negation apostrophe look up.

5. Negation and Non-negation Apostrophe Lookup. In this pre-processing step, negation contractions have been expanded to their original form. For example, "can't", "wouldn't", "shouldnt" have been expanded as "cannot", "would not" and "should not" respectively with the help of a dictionary compiled by authors. This dictionary has also been used for non-negation apostrophe look-up. For example, "i'll" will be expanded to "i will".

After this pre-processing step, next step is Emoticon handling.

---

[5] https://www.internetslang.com/.

6. Emoticon Handling. Emoticons usage is ubiquitous across all social platforms. Emoticons express the emotional intent of the messages in a better way. It is common nowadays that users use only emoticons in their texts as they are self-explanatory. Study[6] shows that over 900 million emojis are sent without text each day. Thus, proper emoticon handling during pre-processing is an indispensable step for improving sentiment classification results.

In present work, authors have compiled a comprehensive punctuation-based emoticon dictionary from various online resources. This dictionary consists of 227 unique punctuation based emoticons with their meanings.

During this pre-processing step, all punctuation based emoticons are replaced with their corresponding meaning For example, ":-)" is replaced by "smiling face" and ";-)" is replaced by "eye wink".

After emoticon handling, the next step is removing URLs from the resultant text.

7. Removing URLs. URLs are the web links that are frequently used by users. Since URLs, standalone does not provide any information, they have been removed from the text via regular expression.

After this step, the next step is removing HTML tags.

8. Removing HTML Tags. It has been observed that the frequency of HTML tags is very high in Google+ data as shown in Table 1. HTML tags are used to render the display of text on the web. HTML tags have been removed via regular expression as their removal does not lead to any loss of data.

After removing HTML tags from the text, hashtags are removed as discussed in the next step.

9. Hashtag Removal. A hashtag is a word or an unspaced compound phrase preceded by a hash (#) symbol. Hashtags are mainly used while naming subjects (example, #iphone) or referring currently trending topics (example, #metoo) In this pre-processing step, hashtags have been removed from the data as after manual observation of data, their absence is not making a difference.

The resultant data after this step will be analyzed for replacing usernames.

10. Replacing Usernames. On every social network, every user has a unique username. Anything directed towards a user is indicated by mentioning username in the text.

On Twitter, every username is preceded by '@' and no whitespaces are allowed, as a result, every username is a single word. Thus, replacing usernames is pretty straightforward with the help of regular expressions.

On the other hand, every Google+ username is preceded by '+' and whitespaces are allowed in usernames. Thus, Google+ allows single word as well as

---

[6] https://blog.emojipedia.org/facebook-reveals-most-and-least-used-emojis/.

multiword usernames (for example, "+Ah hong", + "francois o'kennedy" and so on). Presence of multiword usernames in Google+ data makes replacing usernames a challenging task. So, this task has been divided into three subtasks - "PERSON" Entity Identification, followed by extracting usernames and finally username replacement in the text.

Initially, both Stanford Named Entity Recognition[7](NER) and Spacy[8] NER model failed to recognize Google+ usernames as entity "PERSON" and assigned entity label as "OTHERS". Out of these two models, spaCy NER model has been trained with Google+ sample data to enable the model to recognize Google+ usernames. After training, the model is now able to identify Google+ usernames as "PERSON".

After entity recognition, the next subtask is to extract usernames and then usernames replacement. Usually, there are three possibilities for a username - username consisting of first name only (example, ⏐ thcmooiac123) or username consisting of first name and last name (example, +Ah hong) or username consisting of first name, middle name and last name (example, +Mohd. Sarfaraz Ahmed). To cover all these cases, authors have considered unigrams, bigrams, and trigrams. If the only unigram is identified as "PERSON" the single word username is replaced by the word "USERNAME". If bigram is identified as "PERSON" then bigram is replaced by the word "USERNAME" and similarly, if trigram is identified as "PERSON" then trigram is replaced by word "USERNAME".

After replacing usernames, next pre-processing step is filtering repeating letters.

11. Filtering Repeating Letters. Users often repeat letter(s) in a word to express their opinion by putting stress via repeating letters.

For example, '#Iphone looooove you so muchhh'.

In the data collected, though the frequency of repeating characters is not very high, such words exist. So, this has been added as a part of the pre-processing step. In this step, if a letter is repeating more than thrice then it is replaced by exactly three occurrences. The lower bound for replacement of repeating character has been fixed three because there are words that contain repeating letters as a part of their spelling (example, cool).

In the above example, 'loooove' is replaced by 'looove'.

After this pre-processing step, next step is punctuations filtering.

12. Punctuations Filtering. Punctuations except ".", "?", "...", "!" and "+" have been removed from the data. It has been manually observed from the data that there exist a number of texts that would be classified as 'neutral' by the classifier during sentiment classification. But these neutral texts are important for companies for intent analysis, i.e., whether the neutral text is a query related

---

[7] https://nlp.stanford.edu/software/CRF-NER.shtml.
[8] https://spacy.io/.

to their product (so, the question mark has been retained in the data) or a neutral text is a suggestion to a company or is a complaint of their product or service.

Few brand products have "+" in their product version (example, Motorola G5+) and this version information is required in comparative sentences. So, "+" has not been part of punctuation set removed from data.

After punctuation filtering, next step is stop words removal.

13. Stop Words Removal. Stop words are the commonly used words such as "the", "is", "on", "an" and so on. Many researchers consider that these stop words play a negative role in the task of sentiment classification. Also, stop words do not carry any sentiment information and thus are of no use. Hence, stop words have been removed with the help of the nltk Stop Word dictionary.

After stop words removal, the next step is related to dealing with numbers present in the data.

14. Numbers. In general, numbers present in the text are considered of no use for sentiment analysis. In most of the papers, numbers have been removed from the data. But our data has a huge number of products with their numeric version. It has been observed that the numeric version is needed when there is a comparison between different versions of a product.

Example, Samsung note 8 is better than Samsung note 9. If numbers are removed, the above example will become - Samsung note is better than the Samsung note.

So, a distinction is needed and numbers are thus retained in the text. This is the final pre-processing step of our proposed approach.

The next section presents the experimentations and evaluation of the proposed approach.

4   Experiments and Evaluation

In this section, all the above stated pre-processing steps have been implemented on sample data to test whether these pre-processing steps are producing desired results or not. Sample data has been randomly selected from the collected Google+ and Twitter data.

Table 2 shows the results of the pre-processing steps applied to examples taken from the sample data. In the table, the first column has Raw Text from collected data, the second column has the final text after pre-processing and the third column highlights only the main pre-processing steps relevant to the corresponding text. In actual, all the pre-processing steps stated in Sect. 3 are followed. For data in Table 2, stop words are not removed intentionally to retain readability of stated examples. In the example, "Samsung I o y", shown in Table 2, If look-up for expanding acronyms is done before combining acronyms then the resultant text will be "samsung! i oh why" and the original context

Table 2. Results of data pre-processing on raw text

Raw text	Text after pre-processing	Pre-processing steps used
Samsung! I o y	samsung! i owe you	Step 1 - Step 2 - Step3
When you gona offer Deep blue in Poland I'm not going to buy different one!	when you going to offer deep blue in poland i am not going to buy different one!	Step 1 - Step 3 - Step 4
#Iphone :-)	happy face	Step 1 - Step 6 - Step 9
Just w o w	just wow	Step 1 - Step 2
i was going to say that lot next...honest, ;-)	i was going to say that lot next...honest. wink eye	Step 1 - Step 6
+Shahroz Ahmed dudes been so broke and useless on Google plus it& #39;s sad.⟨br/⟩⟨br/⟩He couldn& #39;t afford to buy a clue if you gave him half of the money.⟨br/⟩⟨br /⟩	username dudes been so broke and useless on google plus it is sad.he could not afford to buy a clue if you gave him half of the money	Step 1 - Step 4 - Step 5 - Step 8 - Step 10

of a user will be lost. Also, it is possible that expanding acronyms dictionary lookup will fail just because of sequence order. Similarly in the example "When you gona offer Deep blue in Poland I'm not going to buy different one!", if HTML codes are expanded after apostrophe dictionary lookup then apostrophe expansion will fail because during apostrophe dictionary lookup, i'm is present as " i&#39" and "I'" is not there in apostrophe dictionary and after expanding HTML codes, the result will be "when you going offer deep blue in poland i'm not going to buy different one!". It is concluded from the above examples that the sequentially followed pre-processing steps are the need of the hour to reduce data dimensionality without loss of user context and important features.

A sample of 2000 texts has been manually annotated as "positive", "negative" and "neutral" by two independent annotators. For validation of the proposed approach, the same data has been automatically classified with the help of a lexicon and rule-based sentiment analysis tool - VADER [5]. Out of 2000 texts, 1857 texts have matched accurately with results of manually annotated data.

Accuracy attained in our case is 92.85% which is quite encouraging enough to explore our approach further.

5   Conclusion and Future Work

As public online reviews are highly unstructured in nature due to the presence of various linguistic features, data pre-processing is one of the core steps of sentiment analysis. Authors have observed that the sequence order of pre-processing steps affects the overall results, hence, an efficient sequence ordering for the same has been suggested and implemented by the authors. It was also observed that exactly the same pre-processing steps cannot be applied to every social network. Therefore, not only Twitter but also Google+ data has been analyzed. A new approach for handling usernames on Google+ has also been suggested and implemented in the present work. Some new dictionaries have been compiled and existing dictionaries have also been modified to improve pre-processing results.

In the future, authors will further explore pre-processing steps for negation handling, emoticon handling and hashtags. The manually annotated sample data will be included in the training set and the impact of these pre-processing steps on different classifiers performance will be analyzed in detail.

References

1. Agrawal, T., Singhal, A., Agarwal, S.: A comparative study of potential of various social networks for target brand marketing. In: 2016 International Conference on Information Technology (InCITe)-The Next Generation IT Summit on the ThemeInternet of Things: Connect your Worlds, pp. 305–311. IEEE (2016)
2. Angiani, G., et al.: A comparison between preprocessing techniques for sentiment analysis in Twitter. In: KDWeb (2016)
3. Bao, Y., Quan, C., Wang, L., Ren, F.: The role of pre-processing in Twitter sentiment analysis. In: Huang, D.-S., Jo, K.-H., Wang, L. (eds.) ICIC 2014. LNCS (LNAI), vol. 8589, pp. 615–624. Springer, Cham (2014). https://doi.org/10.1007/978-3-319-09339-0_62
4. Garg, Y., Chatterjee, N.: Sentiment analysis of Twitter feeds. In: Srinivasa, S., Mehta, S. (eds.) BDA 2014. LNCS, vol. 8883, pp. 33–52. Springer, Cham (2014). https://doi.org/10.1007/978-3-319-13820-6_3
5. Hutto, C., Gilbert, E.: Vader: a parsimonious rule-based model for sentiment analysis of social media text. In: Eighth International Conference on Weblogs and Social Media (ICWSM-14). http://comp.social.gatech.edu. Accessed 20 Apr 2016
6. Go, A., Bhayani, R., Huang, L.: Twitter sentiment classification using distant supervision. CS224N Project Report, Stanford, vol. 1, no. 12 (2009)
7. Gupta, I., Joshi, N.: Tweet normalization: a knowledge based approach. In: 2017 International Conference on Infocom Technologies and Unmanned Systems (Trends and Future Directions) (ICTUS), pp. 157–162. IEEE (2017)
8. Haddi, E., Liu, X., Shi, Y.: The role of text pre-processing in sentiment analysis. Proc. Comput. Sci. **17**, 26–32 (2013)
9. Jianqiang, Z.: Pre-processing boosting twitter sentiment analysis? In: 2015 IEEE International Conference on Smart City/SocialCom/SustainCom (SmartCity), pp. 748–753. IEEE (2015)
10. Jianqiang, Z., Xiaolin, G.: Comparison research on text pre-processing methods on Twitter sentiment analysis. IEEE Access **5**, 2870–2879 (2017)

11. Krouska, A., Troussas, C., Virvou, M.: The effect of preprocessing techniques on Twitter sentiment analysis. In: 2016 7th International Conference on Information, Intelligence, Systems & Applications (IISA), pp. 1–5. IEEE (2016)
12. Saif, H., He, Y., Alani, H.: Alleviating data sparsity for twitter sentiment analysis. In: CEUR Workshop Proceedings. (CEUR-WS. org) (2012)
13. Singh, T., Kumari, M.: Role of text pre-processing in Twitter sentiment analysis. Proc. Comput. Sci. **89**, 549–554 (2016)
14. https://cran.r-project.org/web/packages/rtweet/rtweet.pdf
15. https://developers.google.com/+/web/api/rest/latest/comments

Drought Prediction and River Network Optimization in Maharashtra Region

Sakshi Subedi[1,2(✉)], Krutika Pasalkar[1,2], Girisha Navani[1,2],
Saili Kadam[1,2], and Priya Raghavan Nair Lalitha[1,2]

[1] Department of Computer Engineering, University of Mumbai,
Vivekanand Education Society's Institute of Technology, Mumbai, India
{2015sakshi.subedi, 2015krutika.pasalkar,
2015girisha.navani, 2015saili.kadam,
priya.rl}@ves.ac.in
[2] Computer Engineering Department, Vivekanand Education Society's Institute
of Technology, Mumbai, India

Abstract. Drought affects the natural environment of an area when it persists for a longer period, prompting dry season. Thus, such dry season can have many annihilating effects on river networks. The paper address this predominant issue in the form of an alternate solution which re-routes the course of the natural water sources, like rivers, through those areas, where the water supply is minimal in comparison with the demand, in a cost-effective and highly beneficial manner. In the proposed model, Deep Belief Network (DBN) is utilized to foresee the early event of drought in Marathwada region of Maharashtra. Standard Precipitation Index is used to categorize the severity of drought. Using DBN model, the accuracy obtained with root mean square error of 0.04469, mean absolute error of 0.00207 is far better over the traditional methods. The application of Swarm optimization technique is used to address the problem of drought mitigation through providing a re-routed path.

Keywords: Deep Belief Network · Drought prediction ·
Multi-Swarm Optimization technique · River network optimization ·
Standard Precipitation Index (SPI)

1 Introduction

Drought is a cataclysmic event which is caused by the absence of precipitation and high temperature as well as by overuse and overpopulation. It prompts dry climate that holds on for a long term which causes significant issues, for example, crop damage and the lack of water supply in all dimensions specifically air, surface or groundwater. A dry season condition happens when there is under half of the normal precipitation for back to back periods. There are different sorts of drought viz. Meteorological, Agricultural, Hydrological, Socioeconomic, Ecological dry season. As per India Meteorological Department, Maharashtra has gotten 732.5 mm precipitation of its 1007.3 normal ordinary precipitation amid first June to 30th September, 2018 which is 73% of normal precipitation. Of all the district in Maharashtra, Marathwada region has been staggering

© Springer Nature Singapore Pte Ltd. 2019
M. Singh et al. (Eds.): ICACDS 2019, CCIS 1046, pp. 390–398, 2019.
https://doi.org/10.1007/978-981-13-9942-8_37

under drought since 2013. The districts included are Aurangabad, Jalna, Parbhani, Beed, Osmanabad, Nanded, Latur and Hingoli. Out of these, Beed, Jalna, Parbhani, Nanded and Osmanabad are most noticeably bad influenced by drought. Marathwada has the aggregate region of 64590 km^2 and had a population of 18,731,872 according to the 2011 census of India. The normal yearly precipitation over the division is 882 mm, while sugarcane needs 2100–2500 mm of precipitation which is far excessively high. Very nearly three-fourths of Marathwada division is secured by agricultural grounds. Subsequently, it has been a significant issue to foresee drought and relieve it to diminish its negative effects. The proposed framework predicts the early event of drought. For prediction, Standard Precipitation Index (SPI) values are utilized that are the institutionalized measurements of precipitation, temperature. In view of the record, bunching of locales are completed to speak to the dimension of the furthest point of the dry season. So as to invalidate the impact of such occasions requires its forecast as well. Consequently, advanced new stream ways are distinguished to redirect water sources which rely upon different parameters, for example, contamination, water request, normal precipitation, atmosphere and accessibility of substitute water sources. The framework makes utilization of Machine Learning Algorithms to predict drought and optimized path.

2 Literature Review

For improvement in the field of drought prediction, there are methods proposed in several studies in recent years papers [1–7].

Zengchao Hao et al. defined in his work as, R package named "drought" is developed for drought monitoring, prediction and analysis. The package can be installed through R-forged website link "http://r-forge.r-project.org/projects/drought/". This package can be used to calculate the Standardized Precipitation Index (SPI), Standardized Soil Moisture Index (SSMI), and Standardized Runoff Index (SRI) of 6-month timescale. The dataset for their system include parameters such as monthly precipitation, soil moisture and runoff data of Texas, USA from 1932 to 2011. As the prediction of drought requires different index based on region, for the USA, SPI was giving more accurate results. Due to the limitation of space, it covered only basic properties of drought modelling and assessment. Other drought prediction methods and analysis tools such as trend analysis and breakpoint analysis can also be embedded in a package for the future scope.

Nobert A. Agana et al. proposed a drought predictive system using Deep Belief Network (DBN) approach. DBN approach is used for long-term drought prediction and also a performance with standard Multi-Layered Perceptron (MLP) and Support Vector Regression (SVR) model is compared. As per the study, the DBN model provides a correct prediction result as it records lower prediction errors. Therefore it can be more reliable and efficient than MLP and SVR. Use of standardized stream flow index as an only input parameter is its biggest drawback. The requirement of a large dataset for such deep architecture becomes a bottleneck for processing.

Ravinesh C. Deo et al. considered the C implementation of Support Vector Regression (SVM) model for drought prediction, which primarily calculated standardized precipitation and Evapotranspiration Index (SPEI) for hydrometeorological predictors for the year 1915–2012. SVR model is certified as the one of best ML tool for drought prediction according to the survey having error bound within ±0.25. The model is highly efficient in the prediction of drought for the majority of regions considered in the study area. However, its performance in different geographical regions appeared to be different because of the distinct role of regressors used in training of the model.

To achieve better river network optimization, M. Saravanan et al. used Swarm Optimization Techniques. It gives the information such as availability and access to water in drought regions by proposing redirection route of nearby rivers. The proposed model allows room for the implementation of other optimization and deep learning techniques with the help of advanced statistical models. The study has not focused on water quality and other geospatial features. It takes a significant amount of time to analyze the influence and impact of chosen factors for a particular region. Restricted use of geospatial factors influences the relevance of the solution's optimization.

Ravinesh C. Deo et al. proposed that a wavelet-based drought model is designed using extreme learning machine method. The data is screened through the wavelet pre-processing technique to achieve better accuracy to forecast monthly Effective Drought Index. Then, it was analysed and found that wavelet extreme learning machine (W-ELM), wavelet-equivalent artificial neural networks (W-ANN), wavelet-equivalent least squares support vector regression (W-LSVVR) models are significantly better than counterparts that the techniques without using wavelet because they are better to solve regression problems having shorter modelling time and to minimize structural risk by giving good performance using small weight values. It is evidenced in the paper that there is approximately at least a 16% difference in magnitude of predicted drought index value for regions with simulated duration very less.

Daniel Hong et al. discussed that SPI having long duration time scale can predict accurately when compared to short duration time scale data. That is, nine-month SPI values are predicted more accurately than those of three and six months using MLP neural network model. As the number of hidden nodes and input node that will give the best SPI cannot be fixed, a trial and error procedure is adopted for this study.

Anteneh Belayneh et al. performed the surveyed that Standard Precipitation Index is mainly used for calculating the extremity of drought. The ANN models uses feed-forward Multilayer perceptron (MLP) architecture which was trained with the Levenberg-Marquardt (LM) backpropagation algorithm. Only 1–3 leading months prediction is possible, this can't be used for our system.

3 Proposed Model

The reasonable design of the proposed framework as portrayed in Fig. 2 comprises of different segments, for example, Meteorological dataset, SPI value estimation, ML techniques for the forecast, water sources related information, river network optimization dataset, Multi-Swarm Optimization techniques, regression equations and Plotly/Geospace Libraries. In this framework, the meteorological dataset is utilized to recover the estimations of precipitation, normal temperature obtained from India Water

Portal [8]. With these parameters SPI values are determined and drought forecast is finished by Deep Belief Algorithm which utilizes SPI values for computation and groups the districts as drought or non-drought zones. Contingent upon the outcomes, the dry season area will be featured in maps. In order to mitigate drought condition, conceivable re-routing of water assets from closest repositories having adequate water to the drought inclined area will be anticipated utilizing MSO system. In such case, water resources related information and river network optimization dataset are utilized which incorporates territory secured under forest, land available for cultivation and non-cultivation, fallow land [15], latitude and longitude of regions.

The Conceptual design of the Drought prediction and river network optimization system is as depicted in Fig. 1.

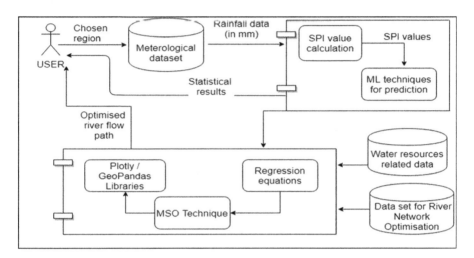

Fig. 1. Conceptual architecture of drought prediction system

4   System Description

The paper aims for an early forecast of drought in Marathwada Region and provides an optimal solution for which the dry season can be avoided. SPI values are utilized for drought prediction. SPI is determined by utilizing the Gamma distribution function for time cycles of 3, 6, 9, 12 months. In view of these records, ANN Deep Belief Network calculation is utilized for the forecast of SPI estimation of each district. According to this predicted value, the extent of drought is determined. After the prediction of drought-prone areas, a Multi-Swarm optimization technique is utilized to foresee the improved new stream ways to divert the water sources.

4.1   Standard Precipitation Index

The Standardized Precipitation Index (SPI) characterize meteorological drought on a range of timescales. For calculation of SPI, precipitation values are required, where

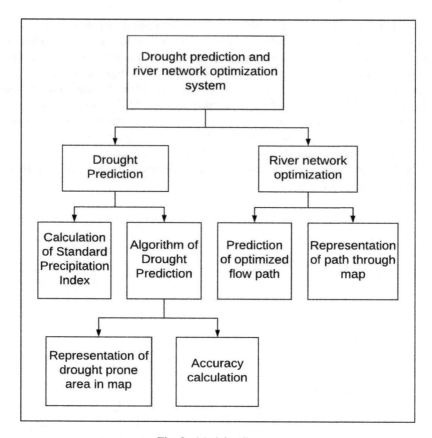

Fig. 2. Modular diagram

Table 1. Drought categories from SPI (source: McKee et al. [10])

2.0+	Extremely wet
1.5 to 1.99	Very wet
1.0 to 1.49	Moderately wet
−0.99 to 0.99	Near normal
−1.0 to −1.49	Moderately dry
−1.5 to −1.99	Severely dry
−2 and less	Extremely dry

precipitation over a period of time is compared to that same period of time throughout the historical record. SPI value represents the probability that the location would have received at least the observed amount of precipitation over the time period. There are different time scales on which SPI can be calculated to monitor drought occurrence. Various time-scales include one month, three months, six months, nine months and twelve months. In this project, we have considered three months time-scale because it is more effective in highlighting available moisture condition. T. B. Mckee et al. classified drought intensities based on SPI values. The Table 1 below shows the classification indicating the values less than −1.0 as drought occurrence.

4.2   Deep Belief Network

Deep Belief Network as shown in Fig. 3 is a class of deep neural network consisting of multiple hidden layers where each layers are connected to each other. They are graphical models and learn from the training data. It is a type of unsupervised pre-trained network such as Restricted Boltzmann Machine. DBN has come into use for time series prediction problems.

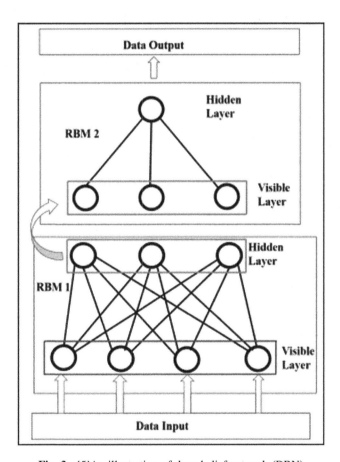

Fig. 3. [5]An illustration of deep belief network (DBN)

4.3   Multi-swarm Optimization

The general approach in multi-swarm optimization is that each sub-swarm focuses on a specific region that is decided by a specific criterion. Factors influencing redirection of river water such as precipitation, Cultivable land, Irrigated land, Sown land, Forest land, Fallow land, Cropland, Population density are considered. The objective fitness function is designed by assigning a weight for each above parameters and weights are captured in variations of parameter values of each location. For identifying location, latitude and longitude is considered. The algorithm proceeds by calculating the fitness values of each considered location. In each iteration, one optimal location with the best fitness value is identified along the rerouting path.

5   Modular Diagram

Drought Prediction and River Network Optimization are the two components as depicted in Fig. 2. First is foreseeing drought in Marathwada Region and the second is to discover new river flow path to rerouting against drought inclined territories.

5.1   Drought Prediction

For the length of 1985–2017, information has been gathered for different meteorological characteristics. For continuous information fetch, OpenWeatherMap API [9] is utilized. Input training set characteristic is precipitation value and a normal temperature of every one of the seven regions of Marathwada districts. SPI is determined dependent on the sources of information which classify the seriousness of drought. A calculation utilized here is Deep Belief Network. The precision of predicted SPI computation additionally decided.

5.2   River Network Optimization

For the relief of regions with most elevated Drought seriousness, Machine learning calculation will be utilized to anticipate advanced new stream ways of adjacent water assets. All conceivable redirecting ways to that area are considered and the best ideal way is picked utilizing Multi-Swarm Optimization system. To apply such different social, prudent, geospatial imperatives are considered.

After the prediction, Multi-Swarm Optimization procedure will be utilized to foresee the advanced new stream ways to occupy the water sources. There are different geological limitations while reorganizing which is likewise considered.

6   Results and Discussion

The SPI calculation is applied to the monthly data of rainfall for each considered district in Marathwada region for the period of 1901 to 2018. The SPI values are evaluated for time-span of 3 months for better performance. Figure 4 represents SPI-3

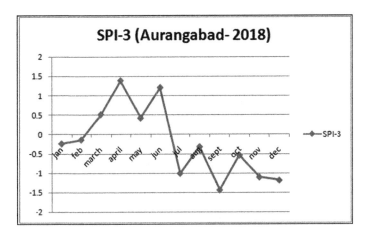

Fig. 4. Shows SPI-3 calculated for Aurangabad district for year 2018

calculation for Aurangabad District for the year 2018. This calculated SPI values is divided into 80% training data and 20% testing data.

For analysis of drought prediction, Root Mean Square Error and Mean Absolute Error performance measures are utilized. The predictive errors for Deep Belief Network model are shown in Table 2. Based on previous studies, it is observed that the Root Mean Square Error and Mean Absolute Error was inferior to our model when considered for SPI calculation for about three months of time scale.

Table 2. 10 year-lead time prediction errors for Aurangabad district

Model	RMSE	MAE
DBA	0.04469	0.00207

The Multi Swarm Optimization technique is applied to the training dataset as per the attributes mentioned in System Description. Among the considered river basins, the optimization algorithm estimated Godavari river basin as an optimized re-routing course flowing in Marathwada region. The re-routed path can be shown as in Fig. 5.

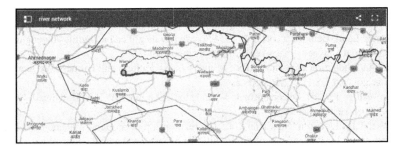

Fig. 5. Rerouted path

7   Conclusion

Prediction of drought has been preeminent significance to defeat the dangerous impact. Its effect can be diminished with by early prediction and giving optimized solution to overcome the drought. Utilizing the Standard Precipitation Index on time scale of 3 months gives efficient prediction results for drought severity. Deep Belief Network model provides a Root Mean Square Error of 0.04469. The river network analysis is done using Multi-Swarm Optimization has permitted tending to the lacking water areas, by proposing a redirection course of an adjacent stream through them wherein Godavari river basin has proven to be the most efficient re-routing path in Marathwada region. In terms of practical utilization of the proposed system, the most primary aspect is to have a long range of precise data thus real time data is continuously fetched from open weather API.

References

1. Hao, Z., Hao, F., Singh, V.P., Ouyang, W., Cheng, H.: An integrated package for drought monitoring, prediction and analysis to aid drought modeling and assessment. https://www.sciencedirect.com/science/article/pii/S1364815216302468
2. Agana, N.A., Homaifar, A.: A Deep learning based approach for long-term drought prediction. https://www.researchgate.net/publication/316943200_A_Deep_Learning_Based_Approach_for_Long-Term_Drought_Prediction
3. Deo, R.C., Salcedo-Sanz, S., Carro-Calvo, L., Saavedra-Moreno, B.: Drought prediction with standardized precipitation and evapotranspiration index and support vector regression models. In: Integrating Disaster Science and Management. Elsevier Inc. (2018). https://www.researchgate.net/publication/325192054_Drought_Prediction_With_Standardized_Precipitation_and_Evapotranspiration_Index_and_Support_Vector_Regression_Models
4. Saravanan, M., Sridhar, A., Nikhil Bharadwaj, K., Mohanavalli, S., Srividhya, V.: River network optimization using machine learning. In: Tan, Y., Shi, Y., Buarque, F., Gelbukh, A., Das, S., Engelbrecht, A. (eds.) ICSI 2015. LNCS, vol. 9142, pp. 409–420. Springer, Cham (2015). https://doi.org/10.1007/978-3-319-20469-7_44
5. Deo, R.C., Tiwari, M.K., Adamowski, J.F., Quilty, J.M.: Forecasting effective drought index using a wavelet extreme learning machine (W-ELM) model (2016). https://www.researchgate.net/publication/303500175_Forecasting_effective_drought_index_using_a_wavelet_extreme_learning_machine_W-ELM_model
6. Hong, D., Hong, K.A.: Drought forecasting using MLP neural networks. In: 2015 8th International Conference on u- and e-Service, Science and Technology (2015). https://www.researchgate.net/publication/303500175_Forecasting_effective_drought_index_using_a_wavelet_extreme_learning_machine_W-ELM_model
7. Belayneh, A., Adamowski, J.: Drought forecasting using new machine learning methods. J. Water Land Dev. 18 (1–v1), 3–12. https://www.mcgill.ca/bioeng/files/bioeng/drought_forecasting_using_new_machine_learning_methods.pdf
8. Area and Production Statistics (APS): Ministry of Agriculture and Farmers Welfare. https://aps.dac.gov.in/LUS/Public/Reports.aspx
9. Openweather Ltd.: 4 Queens Road, Wimbledon, London, SW198YB, United Kingdom. https://openweathermap.org/
10. McKee, T.B., Doesken, N.J., Kleist, J.: The relationship of drought frequency and duration to time scale. In: Proceedings of the Eighth Conference on Applied Climatology, Anaheim, California, 17–22 January 1993, pp. 179–184. American Meteorological Society, Boston (1993)

Classifying Question Papers with Bloom's Taxonomy Using Machine Learning Techniques

Minni Jain, Rohit Beniwal, Aheli Ghosh, Tanish Grover[(✉)],
and Utkarsh Tyagi

Department of Computer Science and Engineering, Delhi Technological
University, New Delhi 110042, India
minnijain91@gmail.com, debjanihome@gmail.com,
tanish1908@gmail.com, utkarsh4430@gmail.com,
rohitbeniwal@yahoo.co.in

Abstract. Constructing well-balanced question papers of the suitable level is a difficult and time-consuming activity. One of the remedies for this difficulty is the use of Bloom's taxonomy. As we know that, Bloom's taxonomy helps in classifying educational objectives into levels of specificity and complexity. Therefore, the primary goal of this research paper is to demonstrate the use of Bloom's taxonomy in order to judge the complexity and specificity of a question paper. The proposed work employs various Machine Learning techniques to classify the question papers into different levels of Bloom's taxonomy. To implement the same, we collected question papers data set, consisting of 1024 questions, from three universities and developed a web app to evaluate our approach. Our result shows that we achieved the best result with Logistic Regression and Linear Discriminant Analysis (LDA) Machine Learning techniques both having an accuracy of 83.3%.

Keywords: Bloom's taxonomy · Classification · Education ·
Linear Discriminant Analysis (LDA) · Machine Learning ·
Neural network · Question paper

1 Introduction

Bloom's Taxonomy was created by Benjamin Bloom during the 1950s. It is a very important parameter to be incorporated in question papers, lesson plans, etc. as most of them unfortunately only test the students' knowledge [1]. However, according to educational psychologists, who evaluated levels of intellectual behavior during learning, classified the levels of reasoning skills as *creating, evaluating, analyzing, applying, understanding, and remembering* [2]. Therefore, not only students should be able to memorize and describe what they have learned, but they should also be able to apply it to new and complex problems. Similarly, the question paper setters must apply bloom's taxonomy principles for all over assessment of the student, as opposed to traditional methods. However, evaluating question papers for their specificity and complexity according to Bloom's taxonomy is a tedious task. Therefore, we propose an

© Springer Nature Singapore Pte Ltd. 2019
M. Singh et al. (Eds.): ICACDS 2019, CCIS 1046, pp. 399–408, 2019.
https://doi.org/10.1007/978-981-13-9942-8_38

approach that uses various Machine Learning (ML) techniques to classify the question papers into different levels of Bloom's taxonomy [3, 4]. To implement the same, we collected question papers data set from three universities and developed a web app to evaluate our approach.

The rest of the paper is organized as follows: Sect. 2 introduces the Bloom's taxonomy; Sect. 3 discusses the related work followed by Sect. 4 which expounds the research approach; Sect. 5 presents the implementation trailed by Sect. 6 which discourses on result and analysis. Finally, Sect. 7 concludes the paper and provides direction for future work.

2 Bloom's Taxonomy

This section discusses the Bloom's taxonomy in detail. It discusses the origin, hierarchal representation, and levels of Bloom's taxonomy. It is a set of three hierarchal models used to classify educational learning objectives into levels of complexity and specificity. The three models cover the learning objectives in cognitive, affective and sensory domains. Bloom's taxonomy is named after Benjamin Bloom, who chaired the committee of educators that devised the taxonomy [1]. The following Fig. 1 shows the hierarchal levels of Bloom's taxonomy.

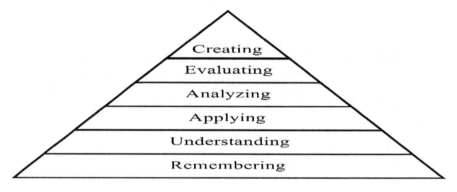

Fig. 1. Hierarchal levels of Bloom's Taxonomy

The six hierarchal levels of Bloom's taxonomy that aims at evaluating knowledge acquisition, intellectual analysis, and skills are *remembering, understanding, applying, analyzing, evaluating, and creating.* The explanation of each level including an example of a question that represents intellectual activity and verbs associated with them are discussed below.

2.1 Remembering

Remembering involves retrieving relevant knowledge from long-term memory [5]. Question: Draw and label a diagram of a typical stream. Verbs: arrange, recognize, define, etc.

2.2   Understanding

Understanding involves determining the meaning of instructional messages, including oral, written, and graphic communication [5].
Question: Explain the process (paraphrase) for finding the perimeter of a rectangular garden
Verbs: describe, explain, classify, etc.

2.3   Applying

Applying involves carrying out or using a procedure in a given situation [5].
Question: Demonstrate how this could work in an industry setting?
Verbs: interpret, solve, demonstrate, etc.

2.4   Analyzing

Analyzing involves breaking material into its constituent parts and detecting how the parts relate to one another and to an overall structure or purpose [5].
Question: Compare and contrast the waterfall model with the prototyping model.
Verbs: distinguish, criticize, analyze, calculate, etc.

2.5   Evaluating

Evaluating involves making judgments based on criteria and standards [5].
Question: Create a new product. Give it a name and plan a marketing campaign.
Verbs: develop, prepare, plan, formulate, etc.

2.6   Creating

Creating involves putting elements together to form a novel, coherent whole or make an original product [5].
Question: Predict the outcome of the following code.
Verbs: judge, predict, rate, support, etc.
Here, we would like to mention that above verbs represent a small subset of the list of verbs, which we collected and applied the various ML techniques on.

3   Related Work

Van Hoeij et al. [6] created a simplified classification tool based on Bloom's taxonomy which could classify the cognitive domains. However, an improved classification procedure might aid in quality assurance of examination. Chang et al. [7] applied Bloom's taxonomy to evaluate and classify cognitive domain of English questions. Their research utilized 14 general keywords for Bloom's Taxonomy. Yusof and Hui [8] used Artificial Neural Networks to categorize cognitive domain according to Bloom's Taxonomy.

Haris et al. [9] applied a rule-based approach to identify different keywords and verbs, which helped to classify the cognitive level of questions. Abdulhadi and Omar [10] proposed a novel method to categorize questions according to Bloom's taxonomy by implementing a combination strategy based on a voting algorithm that combines three ML techniques. In this work, Support Vector Machine (SVM), Naïve Bayes (NB) and k-Nearest Neighbors (k-NN) were used.

However, the proposed work uses nine different ML techniques to classify the question papers into different levels of Bloom's taxonomy.

4   Research Approach

This section expounds the research approach, which is used to classify different question papers according to Bloom's taxonomy. It consists of two sub-sections describing work flow and coding approach of the proposed work.

4.1   Work Flow

The following Fig. 2 shown below represents the workflow of the research approach.

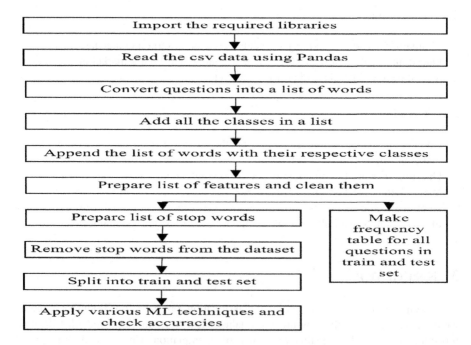

Fig. 2. Work flow of the research flow

4.2   Coding Approach

1. Import the required libraries.
2. Read the dataset csv file.
3. Initialize a panda containing the questions and their respective categories. We collected a dataset of 1042 questions.
4. Import word tokenizer from the NLTK library.
5. Convert the questions in the dataset into a list of words.
6. Prepare a list of stop words.
7. Remove stop words from the dataset.
8. Split the data into train and test.
9. Prepare a list of relevant features.
10. Construct a frequency table for all the questions in training data.
11. Perform step 10 for the testing data.
12. Calculate accuracies of different models.
13. Save the model with the highest accuracy.
14. Use the saved model to classify test papers.

5   Implementation

This section discusses the implementation details of the proposed research approach. It consists of three sub-sections discussing feature extraction, ML techniques used and experimental setup.

5.1   Feature Extraction

We extracted the list of features for each class after carefully examining the various existing related work. To further increase the number of features, we used count vectorizer for frequently occurring words which would help in the classification of questions. From them, the significant features were manually selected and added to the list.

5.2   ML Techniques Used

Here is the description of ML techniques along with parameters used for implementation purpose. After multiple iterations, the parameters were tuned for optimized results.

K-Nearest Neighbours. K-Nearest Neighbours technique predicts the majority of classes of K-nearest neighbors where K is calculated using the distance function given below. In this work, the value of K was taken as 5.

$$Dist(X^n, X^m) = \sqrt{\sum_{i=1}^{D} (X_i^n - X_i^m)^2} \tag{1}$$

Random Forests. Random Forests technique is a combination of many decision trees into one. Since there is overfitting in a single decision tree which leads to less precision, the combined effect of several trees produces a better result. The parameters used were the same as the parameters used in the decision trees.

Decision Trees. Decision Trees classification technique breaks down the data into subsets forming a tree with leaf and decision nodes. The criterion used for splitting in this work was *Gini impurity*. The min_samples_leaf was taken as 2. Let C be the number of classes and p_i be the items labeled with class *i*, then *Gini impurity* is given as:

$$Gini = 1 - \sum_{i=1}^{C} p_i^2 \tag{2}$$

Support Vector Machine (SVM). SVM technique finds the hyperplane that best divides the given data points. This hyperplane is called the decision boundary, and it helps in the classification of testing data. Here penalty parameter for the error term was taken as 1000, and the decision function shape was one-vs-one.

Neural Networks. Neural Networks technique consists of many artificial neurons called units connected in a series of layers, which can improve computation and recognize patterns like a human brain. Input, hidden and output units connected together to form a network. The activation function is applied on the units for processing the input and weights are initialized to train the model to predict values. In this work, the loss function used was *"categorical_crossentropy"* with *"Adam"* optimizer. The number of epochs were taken as 100 and batch size was 5.

Linear Discriminant Analysis (LDA). Here shrinkage parameter was 0.428, the threshold used for rank estimation was taken as 0.0001 for the implementation of LDA technique.

Logistic Regression. Logistic Regression technique finds the relationship between features and the probability of a particular predicted class. The logistic equation is given as:

$$p(X) = \frac{e^{\beta_0 + \beta_1 X}}{1 + e^{\beta_0 + \beta_1 X}} \tag{3}$$

In this work, the inverse of regularization strength was taken 3. The optimization was done by SAGA solver and the penalty type used was l2.

5.3   Experimental Setup

In this sub-section, we collected question papers data set, consisting of 1024 questions, from three universities [11] and developed a web app to evaluate our approach. The hyperlink for the web app is as follows: http://bloom-taxonomy.herokuapp.com.

6 Results and Analysis

The following Figs. 3, 4 and 5 shows the snapshot of the developed web app comprising question papers and their predicted classes belonging to Bloom's taxonomy. The snapshots represent the summary of questions evaluated along with super embedded graphical representation of predicted classes.

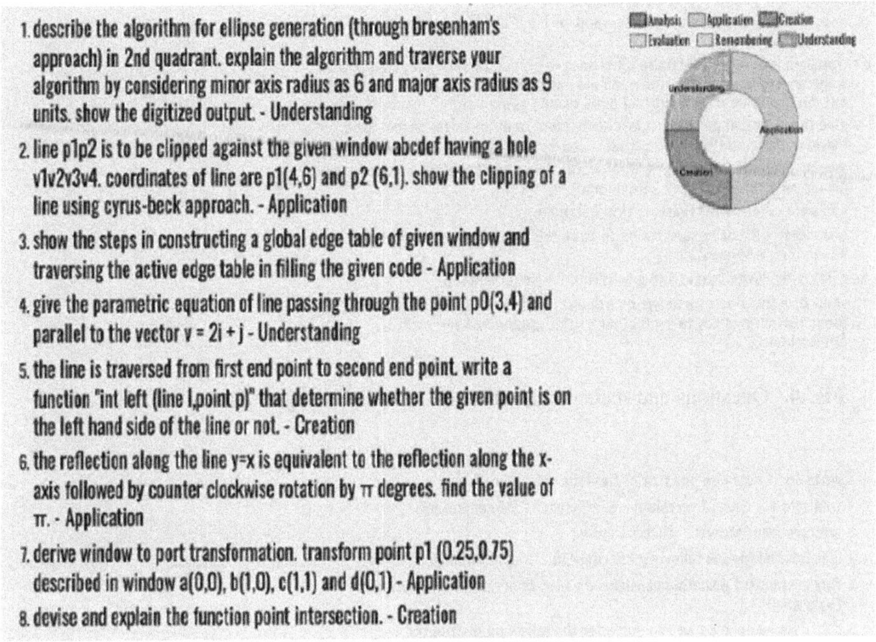

Fig. 3. Questions and their predicted classes corresponding to data set of university 1

From the above figures, we can see that university 1's paper is distributed over four classes, university 2's over three classes and university 3's over five classes.

Considering the result of university 3, we can analyze that that the question paper is sufficiently balanced. *Applying* and *creating* questions make up 11.11%, while *remembering* makes up for 22.22% of the paper. It has many more *understanding* questions (38.88%) than others. *Evaluating* is near-perfectly balanced (16.66%). However, the paper does not have any *analyzing* based questions at all (0.00%).

If a question paper contains two or less than two classes, we can say that it does not ensure accurate or fair grading because of poor distribution of categories. If the paper is divided into 3–4 classes, it can be said to be a good paper, but more questions of other classes should be added. If it has more than four categories, it can be said to be a well-balanced paper.

Also, our proposed work yields the following results when we used the ML techniques discussed above in the implementation section. The results are shown in the following Table 1.

1. prove that the perpendicular from the centre of a circle upon a chord bisects the chord and they are subtended by the chord. - Application
2. reduce the following expression to its simplest form. - Understanding
3. a man bought a watch, a chain, and a locket for $216. the watch and locket together cost three times as much as the chain. and the chain and locket together cost half as much as the watch. what was the price of each? - Understanding
4. prove the formula for the cosine of the sum of two angles. deduce the formulas for the cosine of the double of an angle and the cosine of the half of an angle - Application
5. find the amount of $50 at simple interest at 8% at the end of 5 years, 2 months and 3 days. - Understanding
6. describe the route of the ten thousand, or lay it down on a map. - Understanding
7. translate into latin: who more illustrious in greece than themistocles? who when he had been driven into exile did not do harm to his thankless country, but did the same coriolanus had done twenty years before. - Understanding
8. give the principal parts of cado, cacdo, tono, reperio, curro, pasco, paciscor, marking the quantity of the penult - Understanding
9. give an example of elision. in what words does the accent of the elided vowel disappear with the vowel? - Remembering
10. compare ethens with sparta. - Understanding
11. one meter = 39.37 inches. compute from this datum the value of 4 miles in kilometers. - Application
12. what is the logarithm of 1 in any system? - Remembering
13. show how the area of a polygon circumscribed about a circle may be found. prove that circles are to each other as the squares of their radii - Application

Fig. 4. Questions and their predicted classes corresponding to data set of university 2

1. write short notes on any four of the following. - Creation
2. what are the uses of correlation coefficient? - Remembering
3. interpret your answer. - Understanding
4. calcualte qd for the following distribution - Understanding
5. why is standard deviation considered as the best measure of variability? - Evaluation
6. calculate mean, median and mode for the following distribution. - Application
7. plot the histogram for the above distribution. - Creation
8. arrange the following scores in a frequency distribution. - Remembering
9. describe the steps in preparing a frequency distribution table - Understanding
10. explain the procedure of administering, scoring and interpreting rorschach - Understanding
11. describe wais-iii as an intelligence test. - Understanding
12. explain item difficulty index and item reliability index. - Understanding
13. what is item analysis? - Remembering
14. discuss content validity in detail. - Understanding
15. explain the concept of validity. - Understanding
16. define reliability. - Remembering
17. discuss the various assumptions about psychological testing and analysis. - Understanding
18. explain the concept of half reliability and inter-score reliability. - Understanding

Fig. 5. Questions and their predicted classes corresponding to data set of university 3

Table 1. Accuracy of various Machine Learning techniques

S. No.	Algorithm technique	Accuracy
1.	K-Nearest Neighbors	0.75
2.	Random Forest	0.822
3.	Decision Trees	0.822
4.	SVM	0.822
5.	Neural Network	0.822
6.	Linear Discriminant Analysis	0.833
7.	Logistic Regression	0.833

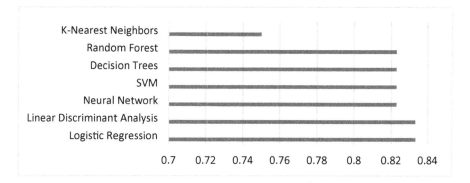

Fig. 6. Graphical representation of achieved accuracies

Figure 6 represents the archived result in the following bar graph.

7   Conclusion and Future Work

In this paper, we employed various ML techniques to classify the question papers into different levels of Bloom's taxonomy. To implement the same, we collected question papers data set, consisting of 1024 questions, from three universities and developed a web app to evaluate our approach. We used ML techniques such as K-Nearest Neighbors, Random Forest, Decision Trees, SVM, Neural Network, Linear Discriminant Analysis (LDA), and Logistic Regression to evaluate our approach. Our result shows that we achieved the best result with Logistic Regression and Linear Discriminant Analysis (LDA) ML techniques both having an accuracy of 83.3%.

Also, it is difficult to increase the accuracy of our model because there is no absolute definition of each level in Bloom's Taxonomy. A question may belong to one or more levels. This causes ambiguity in the model, but there are still some methods, which we can try to improve our approach. These include adding more verbs and phrases to our features, increasing our dataset and taking the length of the question also as a feature in feature set.

The techniques, which we used do not account for the exceptions present in the dataset. We can also use Nature-Inspired algorithms to mine comprehensible and accurate rules for the dataset to improve accuracies further.

References

1. Bloom's, Taxonomy Made Easy: Bloom's taxonomy of educational objectives. Longman (1965)
2. Anderson, L.W., et al.: A Taxonomy for Learning, Teaching, and Assessing: A Revision of Bloom's Taxonomy of Educational Objectives, abridged edn. Longman, White Plains (2001)
3. Beniwal, R., Gupta, V., Rawat, M., Aggarwal, R.: Data mining with linked data: past, present, and future. In: 2018 Second International Conference on Computing Methodologies and Communication (ICCMC), pp. 1031–1035. IEEE (2018)
4. Kumar, A., Bhatia, M.P.S., Beniwal, R.: Ontology driven software development for automated documentation. Webology **15**(2), 1 (2018)
5. Krathwohl, D.R.: A revision of Bloom's taxonomy: an overview. Theory Pract. **41**(4), 212–218 (2002)
6. van Hoeij, M.J., Haarhuis, J.C., Wierstra, R.F., van Beukelen, P.: Developing a classification tool based on Bloom's taxonomy to assess the cognitive level of short essay questions. J. Vet. Med. Educ. **31**(3), 261–267 (2004)
7. Chang, W.C., Chung, M.S.: Automatic applying Bloom's taxonomy to classify and analysis the cognition level of English question items. In: 2009 Joint Conferences on Pervasive Computing (JCPC), pp. 727–734. IEEE (2009)
8. Yusof, N., Hui, C.J.: Determination of Bloom's cognitive level of question items using artificial neural network. In: 2010 10th International Conference on Intelligent Systems Design and Applications, pp. 866–870. IEEE (2010)
9. Haris, S.S., Omar, N.: Bloom's taxonomy question categorization using rules and n-gram approach. J. Theor. Appl. Inf. Technol. **76**(3), 401–407 (2015)
10. Abduljabbar, D.A., Omar, N.: Exam questions classification based on bloom's taxonomy cognitive level using classifiers combination. J. Theor. Appl. Inf. Technol. **78**(3), 447 (2015)
11. Yahya, A.: Bloom's Taxonomy Cognitive Levels Data Set. https://doi.org/10.13140/rg.2.1.4932.3123

Polynomial Topic Distribution with Topic Modeling for Generic Labeling

Syeda Sumbul Hossain$^{(\boxtimes)}$, Md. Rezwan Ul-Hassan,
and Shadikur Rahman

Department of Software Engineering, Daffodil International University,
Dhaka, Bangladesh
{syeda.swe,rezwan35-917,shadikur35-988}@diu.edu.bd

Abstract. Topics generated by topic models are typically reproduced as a list of words. To decrease the cognitional overhead of understanding these topics for end-users, we have proposed labeling topics with a noun phrase that summarizes its theme or idea. Using the WordNet lexical database as candidate labels, we estimate natural labeling for documents with words to select the most relevant labels for topics. Compared to WUP similarity topic labeling system, our methodology is simpler, more effective, and obtains better topic labels.

Keywords: Text mining · Topic model · Topic label · LDA · WordNet

1 Introduction

Statistical topic modeling plays vital roles in many research areas, such as text mining, language processing, and knowledge retrieval. Topic modeling techniques embrace Latent Dirichlet Allocation [1], Probabilistic Latent Semantic Analysis [2] and Latent Semantic Analysis [3]. These techniques can automatically discover the abstract "topics" that occur in an exceeding assortment of documents. They model the documents as a mix of topics, and every topic is sculptural as a likelihood distribution over words. Though the discovered topics word distributions are typically intuitively significant, a serious challenge shared by all such topic models is to accurately interpret the means of every topic. The interpretation of every topic is incredibly necessary once people need to browse, perceive and leverage the topic. However, it is typically terribly exhausting for a user to grasp the discovered topics primarily based only on the polynomial distribution of words.

As an example, here are the highest terms for a discovered topic: {run, drive, car, speed, bike}. It is tough for a user to completely perceive this topic if the user is not terribly acquainted with the document assortment. The situation may deteriorate when the user faces with the variety of discovered topics and also the sets of top terms of the topics are usually overlapping with one another on several sensible document collections.

So as to deal with the above challenge, we design our method by extracting necessary phrase which gives higher tf-idf [4] value for given phrases and working with WordNet [5]. For example, we may extract the phrase "car". If it provides the high

© Springer Nature Singapore Pte Ltd. 2019
M. Singh et al. (Eds.): ICACDS 2019, CCIS 1046, pp. 409–419, 2019.
https://doi.org/10.1007/978-981-13-9942-8_39

value and then working with our process model for generic labeling for this exact phrase. The topic labels will facilitate the user to grasp the topics to some extent. If we choose the word as the label which provides higher value by training model it gives a result however the case will deteriorate when some ambiguous phrase is employed or multiple distinct phrases with poor coherence are used for a topic. To address the drawbacks of the above labels, we need to provide additional contextual data and think about employing the natural label to represent the topics. To figure out the most covering topics and label for polynomial topics we have proposed our model.

This paper is structured as follows: Background is described at Sect. 2 followed by Research Experiment and Result & Discussion at Sects. 3 and 4 respectively. Finally, Sect. 5 summarizes our contribution and furnishes the conclusion.

2 Background

2.1 Topic Model

One similar technique in the field of text mining is Topic Modelling. Topic model is a method to automatically recognize topics in any datasets and to get out hidden patterns shown by a text corpus in our datasets [2]. There are several algorithms for doing topic modeling. The top most are LSA [3], pLSA [6], LDA [1].

2.2 Latent Dirichlet Allocation (LDA)

Latent Dirichlet Allocation (LDA) [1] model, an unsupervised, statistical procedure is introduced as modeling document corpora through finding latent semantic topics within extensive collections of text documents. LDA [1] assumes that the generative manner as every document in a corpus: for every word $w_{d,i}$, in the corpus, it forms a topic z relied on the blend θ attached to the document d and later it produces a word from the topic z. To clarify this fundamental model, the volume of the Dirichlet frequency k (amount of topic sz) is supposed to be acquainted and stable. The Dirichlet prior is used because it has various compatible characteristics that simplify guess and parameter determination algorithms for LDA [1].

2.3 Reason for Using LDA in Our Research

There are several approaches for getting topics from a text like – Term Frequency and Inverse Document Frequency. Latent Dirichlet Allocation (LDA) is that the preferred topic modeling technique [1]. LDA could be a Bayesian version of pLSA [6]. If read the count of topics as count of clusters and therefore the probabilities because the ratio of cluster membership then exploitation LDA could be a method of sentimental clustering your mixed and elements. Distinction this with say k-means wherever every existence will only enter to at least one cluster.

If we select the amount of topics to be less than train datasets exploitation LDA could be a method of minimizing the dimensionality of the first composite versus half knowledge set. With the datasets currently retail to a lower dimensional latent topic area, you will be able to currently attach different machine learning algorithms which can like the smaller variety of dimensions. For instance, you will run your documents through LDA so exhausting cluster them exploitation Density-based special clustering. Of course the most argument you'd usage latent Dirichlet allocation is to uncover the themes lurking in your knowledge. By exploitation LDA on burger orders, you would possibly infer burger topping themes as spicy, salty, savory, and sweet. Probabilistic Latent Semantic Analysis [6] approach is more principled than Latent Semantic Analysis, since it possesses a sound statistical foundation [6]. LDA is similar to pLSA [6], but with dirichlet priors for the document-topic and topic-word distributions. This prevents over fitting, and gives better results.

2.4   Studies Using LDA

While studying for this research, we have found some impressive works done by other researchers. Here in Table 1 we have listed best five studies from our perspective.

Table 1. Five impressive work using LDA

Ref.	Author	Year	Problem domain
[11]	Valle et al.	2018	Birds breeding and bio-geographical shifts
[12]	Guo et al.	2017	Online ratings and reviews analysis
[13]	Feuerriegel et al.	2016	Financial news and stock prices
[14]	Pinoli et al.	2014	Gibbs sampling and gene function
[15]	Lienou et al.	2010	Satellite images

3   Research Experiment

In this section, we have described the overall process of our research work. First of all, we have select our dataset[1]. For dataset, we have chosen some online document to complete our experiment process. For doing so, we have to cross a lot of process for example step by step pre-processing, noun phrase separation, training model, label processing with the help of WordNet. Then we acquire to find out topic label based on our topic model result. Figure 1 shows the overview of our research experiment.

3.1   Text Preprocessing

Quantitative resolution demands that we modify our documents within numerical data. Allowing the reason that word sequence may be influenced of with minimum costs for thought and a 'bag of words' description employed. Research is typical practice (some subset of) any more binary preprocessing [7] moves in constructing the appropriate

---

[1] https://github.com/Sourav-Hasan/topic-modeling-for-generic-labeling/tree/master/datasets.

412   S. S. Hossain et al.

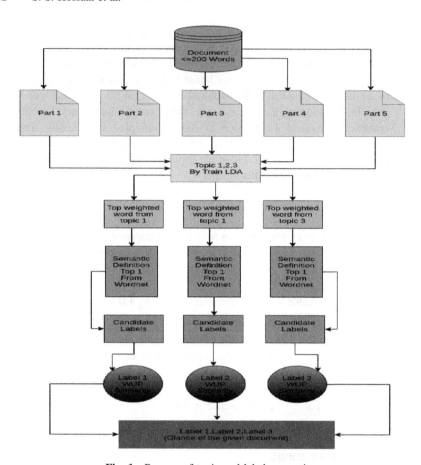

Fig. 1. Process of topic and label generation

document-term matrix. Text preprocessing terms Tokenizing Text, Stop words, lemmatizing words, since certain are the focus of our research work.

3.2   Noun Phrase Choosing

After preprocessing, we only pick the noun and proper noun from the preprocessing result. Using this strategy, the topic is obtained by close top nouns with the largest frequency. The moves involved are as follows: First, tokenization of text is implemented to lemma out the words. The tokenized text is then tagged with parts of speech (NN (nouns), NNP (proper nouns), VB (verbs), JJ (adjectives) etc.) before lemmatizing and stop-words removal as Parts-of-Speech(POS) tagging is flow labeling process and trust on word order. Therefore, removing stop-words results in equivocality and will lose the necessary information expected by POS tagger. The stop-words are removed after POS tagging. In the final stage, words including with their tags and frequencies are put in a hash table and most solid nouns [8] are extracted from those to create a heading for a text.

3.3   Training LDA Model for Generating Topic Set

While training an LDA [1] model, we need to start with a set of documents and any of these is expressed by a fixed-length vector (bag-of-words). Latent Dirichlet Analysis is a probabilistic model, and to obtain cluster assignments, it uses two probability values: P (word | topics) and P (topics | documents). These values are determined based on an initial random distribution, after which they are reproduced for the specific word in the specific document, to determine their topic distribution. In an iterative method, these probabilities are determined multiple times, until the convergence of the algorithm (Fig. 2).

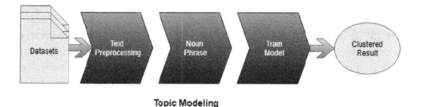

Fig. 2. Training process of model

To perform an LDA [1] model, one first begin by determining the number of 'topics' that are started in your set of documents. Now we will show the model output below (Table 2):

Here we take number of topics = 3 and Number of Words = 2.

Table 2. Result of an example document (see footnote 1)

Topic 1	Topic 2	Topic 3
0.033 * "sweet"	0.094 * "brother"	0.075 * "health"
0.033 * "brother"	0.094 * "sweet"	0.043 * "may"

When we have trained our documents with our LDA model and go through some experiences. We see that passing parameter which bypasses document through the model and it has a big contribution for extracting topics and words behind topics. We also see that LDA model randomly pick frequent words and make topics. So, if we do not set random state = 1 it makes changes model output every time for our document. But this is not our headache this time. So, random state = 1 is enough for our required document.

We have chosen short articles having approximately 200 words which are very relevant with each other very exquisite to find proper topics and words behind. From our understanding, the heart of topic modeling techniques is co-occurrence of terms like we have used LDA model for that. For our experiment, here we only work in between 200 words document and choose only three topics and at first, we take two words under each topic. Because if we take more topics for as our document requirements we get same topics and words again that is called redundant problem.

When we get topics from the documents we only take top weighted word from the topic because its impact is robust for its topic set. Then we search the semantic definition from the lexical database for English parts of speeches which is called WordNet [5]. We select initial definition because that is most appropriate within its terms. After preprocessing the definition, we get the candidate labels and from these candidate labels we measure the candidate labels with the main topic word for conceptual semantic relatedness measurement by WUP [9] similarity. Then actual generic label for each topic come out.

3.4   WordNet Processing

WordNet [5] is a great lexical database of English. Nouns, verbs, adjectives and adverbs are classified into sets of cognitional synonyms (synsets), each meaning a distinct idea. It partially relates a dictionary, in that it classifies words mutually based on their suggestions. However, there are any significant differences. First, it interlinks not just word makes strings of words but special functions of words. As a result, words that are seen in near concurrence to one extra in the system are semantically disambiguated. Second, it specifies the semantic relationships between words, whereas the classification of words in a dictionary does not match any specific decoration other than determining the identity.

In our topic modeling cluster result in our largest valuable words and next works in WordNet term. This WordNet term gives a word definition in our selected word. Suppose our selected word is "Sweet" then WordNet synset gives a definition are below:

S: (n) dessert, sweet, after (a dish served as the last course of a meal).

Then we started again preprocessing in our WordNet definition and also pick up the noun and proper noun phrase.

3.5   WUP Similarity Checking for Choosing Labels

When the WordNet [5] process is finished. Then we started in our WUP similarity process for labeling. Figure 3, WUP [9] similarity process for labeling our topics.

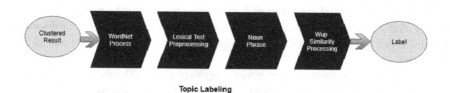

Topic Labeling

Fig. 3. WUP similarity process for labeling

4   Result and Discussion

4.1   Recall, Precision, F-measure

A confusion matrix is needed for our predicted result analysis. So now we are going to discuss on recall, precision, and f-measure [10]. A confusion matrix is a table what is usually practiced to represent the appearance of a classification model on a set of data set for which the true values remain known. All the measures are assumed by using leftmost four parameters. The four parameters are true positive, true negative, false positive and false negative.

True Positives (TP) $\Rightarrow$ these are precisely predicted positive values as means that the value of the exact class is yes and the value of the predicted class is also yes. E.g. if the exact class value symbolizes that this will occurred and predicted class mentions the very same information. True Negatives (TN) $\Rightarrow$ these are precisely predicted negative values as means that the value of the exact class is no and value of the predicted class is also no. E.g. if exact class value symbolizes that this will not occur and predicted class mentions the very same information. False positives and false negatives, those values happen when original class denies with the predicted class. Now by these four parameters, we can calculate Recall, Precision and F1 score for our prediction. Precision is the proportion of perfectly predicted positive audit to the entire predicted positive audit. The precision is the proportion of the quantity of relevant items discovered over the entire quantity of items obtained. Recall is the proportion of precisely predicted positive audits to all audits in actual class - yes. The recall is the proportion of the amount of relevant items obtained across the entire amount of associated items. F-measure is the calculation behind the weighted mean of Precision and Recall. Therefore, as we build a model, this measure helps us to figure out what these parameters mean and how good our model has performed.

In Table 3 we have labeled the documents. First we select candidate key. Then we select final label measuring by WUP.

Table 3.   Label of selected 5 documents

Document (s)	Topics		Top weighted word	Candidate labels	Label
D1	Topic 1	Road, jam	Road	Way, travel, transportation	Transportation
	Topic 2	Traffic, rule	Traffic	Aggregation, thing, vehicle, locality, period, time	Aggregation
	Topic 3	Vehicle, cause	Vehicle	Conveyance, transport, people	Transport
D2	Topic 1	Love, yes	Love	Emotion, regard, affection	Emotion
	Topic 2	Life, year	Life	State, mode, living	Mode
	Topic 3	Cigarette, brush	Cigarette	Ground, tobacco, paper, smoking	Tobacco

(*continued*)

Table 3. (*continued*)

Document (s)	Topics		Top weighted word	Candidate labels	Label
D3	Topic 1	Child, childhood	Child	Person, sex	Person
	Topic 2	Work, event	Work	Activity, something	Activity
	Topic 3	Labour, life	Labour	Class, labor, work, wage	Labor
D4	Topic 1	Role, lesson	Role	Action, activity, person, group	Activity
	Topic 2	Mother, heart	Mother	Woman, birth, child, term, address, mother	Mother
	Topic 3	Child, love	Child	Person, sex	Person
D5	Topic 1	School, activity	School	Institution	Institution
	Topic 2	work, excursion	Work	Activity, something	Activity
	Topic 3	student, thing	Student	Learner, institution	Learner

Here for calculation of recall, precision and f-measure we take words after pre-processing as reference dataset behind each topic. And we need the second dataset to compare with it. So we take candidate labels what we get after lemmatization of reference dataset and given topic word because they have nexus with each other (Table 4).

Table 4. Recall, Precision and F-measure of selected 5 documents

Documents	Topics	Recall	Precision	F-measure
Document 1	Topic 1	75%	50%	0.600
	Topic 2	86.714	54.54%	0.667
	Topic 3	75%	75%	0.750
Document 2	Topic 1	75%	60%	0.667
	Topic 2	75%	75%	0.750
	Topic 3	80%	66.66%	0.727
Document 3	Topic 1	66.667%	50%	0.571
	Topic 2	66.66%	40%	0.500
	Topic 3	80%	57.143%	0.667
Document 4	Topic 1	80%	57.143%	0.667
	Topic 2	100%	66.667%	0.800
	Topic 3	66.667%	50%	0.571
Document 5	Topic 1	50%	50%	0.500
	Topic 2	66.667%	40%	0.530
	Topic 3	50%	50%	0.500

4.2 WUP Similarity

Here we show the score between our topic and label on basis of lexical semantic WUP [9] similarity. This table explains matching score between topics with label. WUP presents good accuracy (Table 5).

Table 5. WUP similarity between topic and label

Documents	Topics	Label	WUP similarity	Average WUP
Document 1	Road	Transportation	0.714	0.845
	Traffic	Aggregation	0.888	
	Vehicle	Transport	0.933	
Document 2	Love	Emotion	0.923	0.789
	Life	Mode	0.545	
	Cigarette	Tobacco	0.900	
Document 3	Child	Person	0.750	0.891
	Work	Activity	0.923	
	Labour	Labor	1.000	
Document 4	Role	Activity	0.800	0.85
	Mother	Mother	1.000	
	Child	Person	0.750	
Document 5	School	Institution	0.857	0.828
	Work	Activity	0.923	
	Student	Learner	0.705	

In Fig. 4, WUP similarity between Score of document is shown through line graphs.

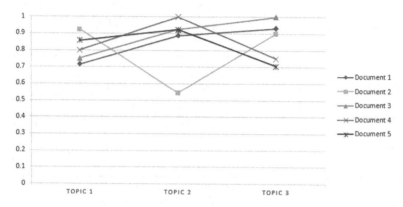

Fig. 4. WUP similarity score of documents

In Fig. 5, Average WUP similarity between Score of document is shown through line graphs.

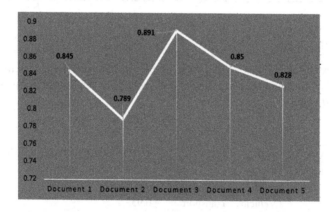

Fig. 5. Average WUP similarity score of documents

5 Future Work and Conclusion

This work has suggested a unique mechanism for genetic labeling detection the topic of the text document by high weight words result and WordNet WUP similarity scores. It has been observed that our proposed method is application to find out the appropriate topic label for the polynomial topic over text in between 200 words and extract the high weight topic with description using WordNet that can concisely convey the generic label for a document. The results shown that the Noun phrase approach is better within the unique mechanisms as it gives the most relevant candidate labels. It can be concluding that the most relevant and suitable word are Nouns for WUP similarity description for choosing word as a label. We have done this experiment on short documents having word count approximate 200. In future, we will do this for large data set.

References

1. Blei, D.M., Ng, A.Y., Jordan, M.I.: Latent Dirichlet allocation. J. Mach. Learn. Res. **3**, 993–1022 (2003)
2. Gildea, D., Hofmann, T.: Topic-based language models using EM. In: Sixth European Conference on Speech Communication and Technology (1999)
3. Deerwester, S., et al.: Indexing by latent semantic analysis. J. Am. Soc. Inf. Sci. **41**(6), 391–407 (1990)
4. Salton, G., Michael, J.: Introduction to Modern Information Retrieval. McGill (1983)
5. Miller, G.A.: WordNet: a lexical database for English. Commun. ACM **38**(11), 39–41 (1995)
6. Hofmann, T.: Probabilistic latent semantic analysis. In: Proceedings of the Fifteenth Conference on Uncertainty in Artificial Intelligence. Morgan Kaufmann Publishers Inc. (1999)
7. Denny, M.J., Spirling, A.: Text preprocessing for unsupervised learning: why it matters, when it misleads, and what to do about it. Polit. Anal. **26**(2), 168–189 (2018)
8. Sajid, A., Jan, S., Shah, I.A.: Automatic topic modeling for single document short texts. In: 2017 International Conference on Frontiers of Information Technology (FIT). IEEE (2017)
9. Wu, Z., Palmer, M.: Verbs semantics and lexical selection. In: Proceedings of the 32nd Annual Meeting on Association for Computational Linguistics. Association for Computational Linguistics (1994)
10. Makhoul, J., et al.: Performance measures for information extraction. In: Proceedings of DARPA Broadcast News Workshop (1999)
11. Valle, D., et al.: Extending the Latent Dirichlet Allocation model to presence/absence data: a case study on North American breeding birds and biogeographical shifts expected from climate change. Glob. Change Biol. **24**(11), 5560–5572 (2018)
12. Guo, Y., Barnes, S.J., Jia, Q.: Mining meaning from online ratings and reviews: tourist satisfaction analysis using latent Dirichlet allocation. Tourism Manag. **59**, 467–483 (2017)
13. Feuerriegel, S., Ratku, A., Neumann, D.: Analysis of how underlying topics in financial news affect stock prices using latent Dirichlet allocation. In: 2016 49th Hawaii International Conference on System Sciences (HICSS). IEEE (2016)
14. Pinoli, P., Chicco, D., Masseroli, M.: Latent Dirichlet allocation based on Gibbs sampling for gene function prediction. In: 2014 IEEE Conference on Computational Intelligence in Bioinformatics and Computational Biology. IEEE (2014)
15. Lienou, M., Maitre, H., Datcu, M.: Semantic annotation of satellite images using latent Dirichlet allocation. IEEE Geosci. Remote Sens. Lett. **7**(1), 28–32 (2010)

Comparative Performance of Machine Learning Algorithms for Fake News Detection

Arvinder Pal Singh Bali$^{(\boxtimes)}$, Mexson Fernandes, Sourabh Choubey,
and Mahima Goel

Asia Pacific Institute of Information Technology SD India, Panipat 132103,
Haryana, India
hgnis.nivra@gmail.com, mexsonfernandes@outlook.com,
sourabhchoubey010@outlook.com, mahima240189@gmail.com

Abstract. Automatic detection of fake news, which could negatively affect individuals and the society, is an emerging research area attracting global attention. The problem has been approached in this paper from Natural Language Processing and Machine Learning perspectives. The evaluation is carried out for three standard datasets with a novel set of features extracted from the headlines and the contents. Performances of seven machine learning algorithms in terms of accuracies and F1 scores are compared. Gradient Boosting outperformed other classifiers with mean accuracy of 88% and F1-Score of 0.91.

Keywords: Fake news · Natural Language Processing · Text classification · Machine learning algorithms · Gradient boosting

1 Introduction

The proliferation of internet and social websites have led to the exponential growth in opinion spams and fake news, in recent times.

The Fake news which diffuse faster than the real news on social websites like Google Plus, Facebook, Twitter etc. [2] have been defined as 'fabricated information' which resemble news media content 'in form but not in organizational process or intent' [1]. Ahmed et al. [3] further subdivided fake news into three distinct categories viz. false news, fake satire news and poorly written news articles.

Fake news is a growing menace in the society. Its detection is a complex task, believed to be much harder than detection of fake product reviews [3]. Fake news poses a grave threat not only to the reliability of certain media outlets but to the government and the society as well. It is reported that more than 62% of U.S. adults get their news from social media. Moreover, the volume of disseminated information and the rapidity in which it is spread in social network sites make it extremely difficult to assess its reliability in a timely manner. Identification of fake contents in the online/offline sources is an important research problem.

The objective of the paper is to compare performances of seven machine learning (ML) algorithms on three standard datasets using a novel set of features and statistically validate the results using accuracies and F1 scores.

The remaining of the paper is organized as follows: A short review of selected papers on fake news identification is presented in Sect. 2. The datasets, the features, the experiments as well as the results are summarized in Sect. 3. In conclusion it has been argued that with an appropriate set of features extracted from the texts and the headlines, Gradient Boosting Algorithm (XGB) can effectively classify fake news with very high accuracy and F1 score.

2 Related Work

Ahmed et al. [3] introduced a new n-gram model to detect automatically fake contents, particularly focusing reviews and news. Results of two different feature extraction techniques viz. tf, tf-idf and six machine learning classification techniques were reported by the authors. Linear classifiers viz. linear Support Vector Machine (SVM), Stochastic Gradient Descent (SDG) and Logistic Regression (LR) achieved better results than nonlinear ones for both fake reviews and news. Shu et al. [4] extensively reviewed the detection of fake news on social media, from a data mining perspective, evaluation metrics and representative datasets. Horne and Adali [5] used stylistic features from Python Natural Language Toolkit, complexity and psychology features, carried out their study on three data sets viz. Buzzfeed election data set, dataset related to political news and Burfoot and Baldwin data set. The authors using SVM classifier concluded that fake news is more akin to satire than to real news. Mean accuracies achieved by the authors were for 78% for the title and 71% for the contents, for a political news data set specifically designed by the authors. Horne et al. [6] presented the NELA2017 dataset, which contains articles from 92 news sources over 7 months, as well as, 130 content-based features that have been used throughout the news literature.

Baly et al. [7] attempted to predict the factuality of reporting of a news, using features that were earlier proposed by Horne et al. for detecting "fake news" articles [6]. These features were used to analyze the characteristics of the article viz. Structure, Sentiment, Topic, Complexity, Bias and Morality. The authors used the features in a SVM classifier, training a separate model for factuality and for bias and reported the results for 5-fold cross-validation. The paper, based on a project sponsored by AI laboratory MIT, demonstrated a new system using ML to determine the accuracy/political bias of a source [11]. Pérez-Rosas et al. [8] introduced two novel datasets for the task of fake news detection, covering seven different news domains. From a set of learning experiments to detect fake news the authors concluded that accuracies of up to 76% could be achieved.

Gilda [9] presented work on datasets from Signal Media and OpenSources.co, applied *tf-idf* to a corpus of nearly 11,000 articles. The test conducted using five classification algorithms viz. SVM, Stochastic Gradient Descent, Bounded Decision Trees, Random Forest and GBoost achieved accuracy of 77.2% using stochastic gradient descent.

The problem was approached by Bajaj [10] from a purely NLP perspective using Convolutional Neural Networks (CNN). The project at Stanford University envisaged to build a classifier that can predict whether a piece of news is fake, based only on its contents. Several architectures were explored, including a novel design that incorporates an attention mechanism in a CNN. However, the results were not promising, compared to conventional ML algorithms.

Liu and Wu argued that the existing ML approaches were inadequate and proposed a model for an early detection of fake news on websites by classifying news propagation paths [12]. Experimental results demonstrate that the proposed model can detect fake news with accuracies 85% and 92% respectively on Twitter and SinaWeibo, the Chinese social website. TriFN proposed by Shu et al. [13] is a tri-relationship embedding framework, based on publisher-news relations and user-news interactions. The authors also reported performance comparison of ML algorithms with TriFN. The algorithms included LR, Naïve Bayes, Decision Tree, Random Forest, XGBoost, AdaBoost, and Gradient Boosting. On BuzzFeed and PolitiFact datasets TriFN recorded 86% and 87% average accuracies. F1 score recorded by TriFN were 0.87 and 0.88 respectively [13]. Eugenio Tacchini et al. in their technical report submitted to UCSC [14] used two classification techniques viz. LR and a novel adaptation of Boolean crowdsourcing algorithm.

3   Experimental Evaluation

3.1   Datasets Statistical Information

The model was tested on three different datasets: (i) OpenSources dataset having 9,408,908 articles out of which 11,161 articles from categories fake and reliable were selected [15] (ii) Kaggle dataset on fake news consisting 20,800 articles [16] and (iii) GitHub repository for fake or real news dataset by George McIntire, having two sections, headlines and text of the news [17]. Description of the labeled datasets is given in Table 1.

Table 1.   Labeled dataset description

Dataset	Fake count	Reliable count	Total
Open sources [16]	5385	5776	11161
Kaggle dataset [17]	10413	10387	20800
George McIntire dataset [18]	3164	3171	6335

3.2   Features

For building a Machine Learning model, feature selection is of utmost importance for optimum performance of the system.

Features used in the proposed model are as follows:

3.2.1   n-grams Count Feature

These features are used for counting occurrences of n-grams in the title and body of the news, and various ratios of the unique n-gram and total word count given by Eq. (1).

$$ratio\ of\ unique\ n\text{-}gram = \frac{total\ unique\ n\text{-}gram}{total\ n\text{-}gram} \tag{1}$$

Equation (1) is the ratio of n-gram where n-gram could be unigram, bigram or trigram [3]. Thereafter it uses specific binary refuting words, like 'fake', 'fraud', 'hoax', 'false', in the headline.

3.2.2   tf-idf: Term Frequency- Inverse Document Frequency

It consists of two terms tf and idf. Term Frequency is how many times a word occurs in a given document given by Eq. (2).

$$tf(t,d) = 0.5 + 0.5 \cdot \frac{f_{t,d}}{\max\{f_{t',d}:t' \in d)\}} \tag{2}$$

Thus, tf(t, d) is raw count of term in a document $f_{t,d}$ divided by max $\{f_{t',d} : t' \in d\}$, the number of words in the document.

Inverse Document Frequency (idf) is the number of times a word occurs in corpus of documents. This facilitates to understand which words are important [3, 21]. Usually the natural log - normalization of the Inverse Document Frequencies given by Eq. (3) is used:

$$idf(t,D) = log\frac{N}{|\{d \in D:t \in d\}|} \tag{3}$$

Here, 'N' is the total number of news articles present in the corpus 'D', N = |D|, $|\{d \in D : t \in d\}|$ is the number of documents where the term 't' appears. Then tf-idf is calculated as: tf (t, d). idf(t, D).

Finally, Cosine similarity of these normalized tf-idf vectors are calculated for headlines and the contents. This gives the measure of how correlated the headlines and their corresponding article contents are. Since cosine similarity considers only those vectors which have non-zero dimension, its calculation is quite fast.

$$Similarity = Cos\ \theta = \frac{A.B}{\|A\|\|B\|} \tag{3}$$

3.2.3   Word Embedding

To get the vector space representation of the words, Word Embeddings are used. Word Embedding replaces each word with real valued vector. Global vector for word representation [18] is used for this task. It is trained on aggregated word-word co-occurrence counts on a given corpus. The pre-trained word vectors contained 6 billion tokens having a vocabulary of 400,000 words and represent each word as a 50-dimensional vector.

3.2.4   Sentiment Polarity Score

It is a basic task in sentiment analysis which could be used as an idea of what tone different articles follow. During dataset exploration, using IBM Watson tone analyzer [19], the fake and reliable news showed clear difference in the Anger analysis.

Therefore, making it a good choice as a feature. Using open source library Natural Language ToolKit (NLTK) [20], sentiment intensities were analyzed for positive, negative, neutral and compound sentiments.

3.2.5   Linguistic

Linguistic features [21] such as readability ease and lexical diversity, represent the texts statistically and also represent context of the sentences in terms of ease of reading it. Readability standard gives an approximation of years of education required to understand a sentence on single reading. By using Flesch-Kincaid, Gunning fog, and other features, the readability standards of the news articles are determined. Also lexical diversity of articles are calculated and used as features.

Feature Matrix: Features and their counts are summarized in Table 2 and explained in the followings:

- The tf-idf vectors and the tf-idf Cosine similarity between headlines and the contents are concatenated in a single feature vector.
- Sentiment analysis for the headings and the contents generate 8 features in total.
- There are 12 Readability features along with 41 count features.
- Total features are 163 with word embedding alone accounting to 101 features.

Table 2. Features and their counts.

Features		Number of feature vectors
Sentiment	Headline	4
	Content	4
Readability		12
Count		41
Cosine Similarity of Normalized *tf-idf* vectors between headline and content		1
Word Embedding	Headline	50
	Content	50
	Cosine similarity between Headline and Content	1
Total number of features		**163**

3.3   Dataset Preprocessing and Model Implementation

Dataset preprocessing and cleaning is one of the important tasks in Natural Language Processing [3]. The removal of extraneous information is crucial. Articles that are used, contained links, numbers, and other symbolic contents that are not required for feature analysis. The statistics of occurrence of word in a corpus is the main source of information for any NLP task. Regular Expressions are used to replace symbolic characters by words, digits by 'number', and dates by 'date'. Source URLs if any are removed from the article content. The text of headline and body are then tokenized and stemmed. Finally unigrams, bigrams and trigrams are created out of the list of tokens. These grams and the original text are used by the different feature extractor modules. The implementation and sequential flow of the classification process is shown in Fig. 1.

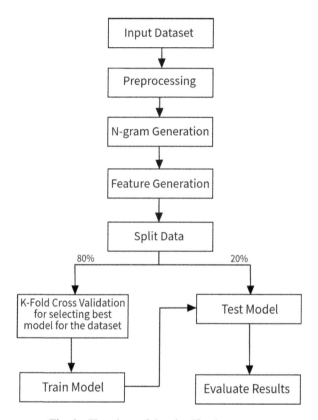

Fig. 1. Flowchart of the classification process

After feature generation, as discussed in Sect. 2, cross validation is used to find the best performing classifier. The best algorithm is then used for training on 80% dataset and rest 20% is used for testing.

3.4 Model Evaluation

Cross validation is a standard technique for assessing how the results of a statistical analysis generalize to an independent data set. To evaluate the models, stratified 10-fold cross-validation [24] was used on the complete dataset.

For model evaluation, seven Machine Learning algorithms viz. Random Forest (RF), Support Vector Classifier (SVC), Gaussian Naïve Bayes (GNB), AdaBoost (AB), K-Nearest Neighbor (KNN), Multi-Layer Perceptron (MLP) and Gradient Boosting

(XGB) [23] were selected. Accuracy and standard deviation are the evaluation metrics for comparison. Accuracy vs n-fold cross validation for the ML algorithms are shown in Figs. 2a, b and c for the three datasets.

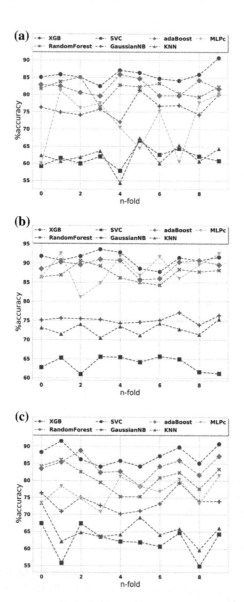

Fig. 2. (a) Accuracy vs. Cross validation (Dataset 1) (b) Accuracy vs. Cross validation (Dataset 2) (c) Accuracy vs. Cross validation (Dataset 3)

It can be readily inferred from Figs. 2a, b and c that the boosting algorithms viz. Gradient Boosting (XGB) and AdaBoost are performing better compared to other classifiers in terms of average accuracies and standard deviations.

The lowest average accuracies recorded are 62.5%, 72.54% and 64.8% when using KNN for Opensource [15], Kaggle [16] and George McIntire [17] datasets. Whereas Gradient Boost (XGB) achieved 87.2%, 92.0% and 87.3% average accuracies for these datasets respectively.

The complete model comparison is shown in Table 3.

Table 3. Model comparison

Classifier	Dataset 1		Dataset 2		Dataset 3	
	A*	SD**	A*	SD**	A*	SD**
XGB	**86.2**	**2.21**	**91.05**	1.67	**87.3**	**2.59**
RF	81.2	2.32	86.63	1.8	82.6	3.1
SVC	62.9	2.31	63.55	1.65	62	3.96
GNB	76.4	2.67	75.24	1.02	73.2	2.73
AB	81.7	2.25	89.25	1.87	83.7	2.75
KNN	62.5	3.28	72.54	1.43	64.8	3.6
MLP	67.1	6.18	88.36	9.93	72.8	6.14

*A: Average Accuracy
**SD: Standard Deviation
Note: All values are in percentage

From n-fold cross validation, the best performing ML algorithm XGB is used for training a model.

3.5 Results and Discussions

The results of the trained models on the test data are tabulated in Table 4. F1 Score defined as the harmonic mean of precision P and recall R is a measure of the accuracy of the test, in statistical analysis for binary classification. It is evident that the models performed remarkably well with XGB as the classifier.

Table 4. Classification report

Dataset	Precision	Recall	F1-score
Dataset 1	0.92	0.92	0.92
Dataset 2	0.93	0.94	0.94
Dataset 3	0.89	0.87	0.89

Finally, to analyze relative significance of the features in the proposed model, F1 Score was calculated for each dataset with exclusion of one the features.

The Loss is calculated as:

$$LOSS = Original\,F1\,Score - New\,F1\,Score \qquad (5)$$

Table 5. Relevance of selected features

Feature excluded		Dataset 1	Dataset 2	Dataset 3
tf-idf	F1-score	0.9	0.94	0.89
	Loss	0.02	0	0
Count	F1-score	0.89	0.92	0.88
	Loss	0.03	0.02	0.01
Word embedding	F1-score	0.8	0.9	0.85
	Loss	0.12	0.04	0.04
Sentiment	F1-score	0.9	0.94	0.89
	Loss	0.02	0	0
Readability	F1-score	0.9	0.93	0.88
	Loss	0.02	0.01	0.01

Table 5, indicates the significance of 'word embedding' as a feature in the proposed scheme for model evaluation. The Original F1 Scores are shown in the Table 4.

While analyzing the results, it may be recalled that Ahmed, Traore and Saad [3] used tf and tf-idf as features, Baly et al. [7] used 141 features earlier used by Horne et al. [6], whereas 163 features proposed in the model viz. Cosine similarity of normalized *tf-idf* vetors, word embedding, sentiment polarity and readability are more generalized and the results Tables 3 and 4 confirm the significance of the features extracted from the news headlines and the contents in this context.

Following is the configuration of the computing environment for carrying out the experiment: Intel Processor - Quad core i7 @ 2.8 GHz, RAM - DDR4 8 GB, 2400 MHz, Nvidia GTX 1050 GDDR5 4 GB, Operating System – 64 bit Ubuntu 18.04.1 LTS, Compiler: Python ver. 3.6.6.

4   Conclusion and Future Scope

Early detection of fake news is of primary importance for public and the society, for redesigning the 'information ecosystem in the 21st century' which would eventually lead to the creation of a system and culture having values that promote truth [1]. The paper demonstrates with extensive experimentation that with a novel set of features extracted from the heading and the text, specifically the XGB classifier can efficiently detect fake news with 88% mean accuracy and 0.91 F1 score, outperforming other ML classifiers. A number of features in addition to the vectors corresponding to the words in the text as well as other linguistic features not explored in this paper, could be added to the feature matrix in future for better accuracies.

Acknowledgements. Comments on the paper by the anonymous reviewers were immensely helpful in revising the paper.

References

1. Lazer, D., et al.: The science of fake news. Science **359**(6380), 1094–1096 (2018)
2. Vosoughi, S., Roy, D., Aral, S.: The spread of true and false news online. Science **359** (6380), 1146–1151 (2018)
3. Ahmed, H., Traore, I., Saad, S.: Detecting opinion spams and fake news using text classification. Secur. Priv. **1**(1) (2017). https://onlinelibrary.wiley.com/doi/full/10.1002/spy2.9
4. Shu, K., Sliva, A., Wang, S., Tang, J., Liu, H.: Fake news detection on social media: a data mining perspective. ACM SIGKDD Explor. Newsl. **19**(1), 22–36 (2017). https://www.kdd.org/exploration_files/19-1-Article2.pdf
5. Horne, B.D., Adali, S.: This just in: fake news packs a lot in title, uses simpler, repetitive content in text body, more similar to satire than real news. Paper Presented at: The 2nd International Workshop on News and Public Opinion at ICWSM; Montreal, Canada (2017). https://arxiv.org/abs/1703.09398
6. Horne, B.D., Khedr, S., Adali, S.: Sampling the news producers: a large news and feature data set for the study of the complex media landscape. In: Proceedings of the Twelfth International Conference on Web and Social Media, ICWSM 2018, Stanford, CA, USA, pp. 518–527 (2018)
7. Baly, R., Karadzhov, G., Alexandrov, D., Glass, J., Nakov, P.: Predicting Factuality of Reporting and Bias of News Media Sources (2018). https://arxiv.org/abs/1810.01765
8. Pérez-Rosas, V., Kleinberg, B., Lefevre, A., Mihalcea, R.: Automatic detection of fake news. In: Proceedings of the 27th International Conference on Computational Linguistics, Santa Fe, New Mexico, USA, 20–26 August, pp. 3391–3401 (2018)
9. Gilda, S.: Evaluating machine learning algorithms for fake news detection. In: 2017 IEEE 15th Student Conference on Research and Development (SCOReD), Putrajaya, pp. 110–115 (2017)
10. Bajaj, S.: The Pope Has a New Baby! Fake News Detection Using Deep Learning. https://web.stanford.edu/class/cs224n/reports/2710385.pdf
11. http://news.mit.edu/2018/mit-csail-machine-learning-system-detects-fake-news-from-source-1004
12. Liu, Y., Wu, Y.-F.B.: Early detection of fake news on social media through propagation path, classification with recurrent and convolutional networks. In: AAAI Publications, Thirty-Second AAAI Conference on Artificial Intelligence (2018). https://aaai.org/ocs/index.php/AAAI/AAAI18/paper/view/16826
13. Shu, K., Wang, S., Liu, H.: Beyond news contents: the role of social context for fake news detection. In: WSDM 2019, 11–15 February (2019). http://www.public.asu.edu/~skai2/files/wsdm_2019_fake_news.pdf
14. Tacchini, E., Ballarin, G., Della Vedova, M.L., Moret, S., de Alfaro, L.: Some like it hoax: automated fake news detection in social networks. Technical report UCSC-SOE-17-05 School of Engineering, University of California, Santa Cruz (2017). https://www.soe.ucsc.edu/sites/default/files/technical-reports/UCSC-SOE-17-05.pdf
15. Opensource Dataset. http://www.opensources.co/
16. Kaggle Dataset. https://www.kaggle.com/jruvika/fake-news-detection
17. GitHub Repository. https://github.com/GeorgeMcIntire/fake_real_news_dataset

18. Pennington, J., Socher, R., Manning, C.D.: GloVe: Global Vectors for Word Representation (2014). https://nlp.stanford.edu/pubs/glove.pdf
19. https://www.ibm.com/cloud/watson-tone-analyzer
20. https://www.nltk.org/
21. Furnkranz, J., et al.: Case study in using linguistic phrases for text categorization on the WWW. In: AAAI Technical report WS-98: (1998). https://www.aaai.org/Papers/Workshops/1998/WS-98-05/WS98-05-002.pdf
22. Seki, Y.: Sentence extraction by tf-idf and position weighting from newspaper articles. In: Proceedings of the 3rd NTCIR Workshop, Tokyo (2002). http://research.nii.ac.jp/ntcir/workshop/OnlineProceedings3/NTCIR3-TSC-SekiY.pdf
23. Chen, T., Guestrin, C.: XGBoost: a scalable tree boosting system. In: Proceedings of the 22nd ACM SIGKDD, pp. 785–794 (2016)
24. Alpaydın, E.: Introduction to Machine Learning, pp. 487–488, 2nd edn. MIT Press, Cambridge (2010)

Pedestrian Intention Detection Using Faster RCNN and SSD

Debapriyo Roy Chowdhury$^{(\boxtimes)}$, Priya Garg$^{(\boxtimes)}$, and Vidya N. More

College of Engineering, Pune, SPPU University, Pune, India
debapriyorcl7.extc@coep.ac.in

Abstract. In the domain of Intelligent Monitoring, Smart Driving and Robotics, Pedestrian intention detection is a prime discipline of object recognition. Currently, several pedestrian detection techniques are proposed however, just a handful are re-ported in the domain of pedestrian 'intention' detection. Due to the complications of the image background and pedestrian posture diversity, pedestrian intention detection is still a challenge which requires concise algorithms. In this paper, Single Shot Detector (SSD) is compared with Faster Region Convolutional Neural Network (Faster RCNN) architecture of deep neural network by applying different Convolutional Neural Network (CNN) models. Experiments have been conducted in a wide spectrum to obtain various models of Faster RCNN and SSD through compatible alterations in algorithm and parameters tuning. In this paper, Faster R-CNN and SSD architecture have been trained and their results are compared. New and simple evaluation performance parameters are suggested namely: Percentage Detection Index, Percentage Recognition Index and Precision score as compared to the traditional mean average precision (mAp) found in literature. While training these architectures with 1350 images, Faster RCNN learned three times faster than SSD with 2% increased accuracy.

Keywords: Pedestrian intention detection · Faster R-CNN · Pre-trained CNN · SSD · Tensorflow

1 Introduction

According to the Global status report on road safety of 2018, 1.35 million annual road traffic deaths have been recorded and the biggest proportion is contributed by pedestrians, cyclist and motorcyclists [1]. Soon, Automatic Driving Vehicles are about to hit the market thereby, the need to control Road Accidents increases dynamically. Pedestrian Behaviour and Movement Prediction can peter out the above-mentioned death figures. In this work, our intent is to detect the pedestrians and predict their movement intention on streets, so as to warn drivers and the surveillance systems regarding upcoming possible risk situations.

Many conventional object detection approaches which deploy Hough transform, Histogram of Oriented Gradient (HoG) [2] and Speeded-Up Robust Features (SURF) like hand-crafted features have attained successful outcomes in Object Recognition. However, under the diversified conditions like sunlight reflections, lightening and

© Springer Nature Singapore Pte Ltd. 2019
M. Singh et al. (Eds.): ICACDS 2019, CCIS 1046, pp. 431–439, 2019.
https://doi.org/10.1007/978-981-13-9942-8_41

weather conditions, various camera angles and image scaling, it is highly challenging to detect pedestrians and their intentions [3].

In the past few years, various Convolutional Neural Network (CNN) algorithms have performed exceptionally well in the field of object detection. They have used CNN as a feature extractor, followed by Support Vector Machine (SVM) as a classifier in general. Noticing favorable outcomes from CNN, many researchers started looking for achieving better accuracy and speed algorithmically. Girshick proposed Region CNN (RCNN) [4, 5] which has overcome the object spatial localization drawback of CNN. RCNN uses Selective Search algorithm to propose approximately 2000 Region proposals (RoI) and then equivalent number of CNNs extract feature from each proposal. Applying CNN and extracting features 2000 times, makes RCNN computationally intensive and time consuming. Fast RCNN [6] eliminates this computation by passing input image to CNN to generate convolutional feature map and then extracting the region proposals using Selective Search algorithm from these feature maps. Further Ross Girshick removed the drawbacks of Fast RCNN, made improvements and built a faster object detection algorithm called as 'Faster RCNN' [6]. Two Enhancements of Faster RCNN are as follows: First, it swaps Selective Search Algorithm with Region proposal Network (RPN) which is fully connected Convolution network, secondly it provides end to end detection proposals [7, 8]. The entire network of Faster RCNN has been involved in Deep Convolutional Neural Network [9], thus overcoming the difficulties related with hand-crafted features.

In this paper, we use Faster RCNN to predict the pedestrian behaviours and intentions. This paper is organized as follows: Sect. 2 describes the related work done in the respective field. Section 3 explains the Pedestrian Detection, SSD and Faster RCNN. Section 4 displays the experimental results and Sect. 5 concludes the paper.

2 Related Work

Pedestrian detection methods include background modelling-based approaches, template matching based approaches, hand-crafted feature-based approaches and CNN based approaches. Even though the Background Modelling approaches worked well for dynamic detection of pedestrians, it failed to detect the static pedestrians [10]. Template Matching approaches used the image contour, texture and grayscale information for object detection [11]. The edge of Template Matching Algorithm is that it worked on original image without feature extraction. To achieve better performance, Hand-crafted feature-based approaches like HoG, Hough Transform, SURF and SIFT came upfront. Outcome of object detection mainly depends upon the quality of features extracted. Feature Detector Approaches have been studied in most possible ways and these approaches are summarized in Table 1 [12, 13].

The implementation and performance of a local invariant feature detector for a particular object detection depends on its rotation, scale and affine invariance requirement. Pedestrian detection does not have the stability of the object; thus, it requires a scale, affine and rotation invariant feature detectors. The performance of a couple of Feature Detectors is summarized in Fig. 1 [12, 13].

Table 1. Different existing Feature Detector Algorithms with their specifications

Feature detector methods	Year	Rotation	Corner	Scale	Blob	Affine
LoG	1998	•				
SIFT	1999	•		•	•	
DoG	2004	•		•	•	•
FAST	2005	•	•	•	•	
SURF	2006	•				
KAZE	2012	•		•	•	
TILDE	2014	•		•	•	

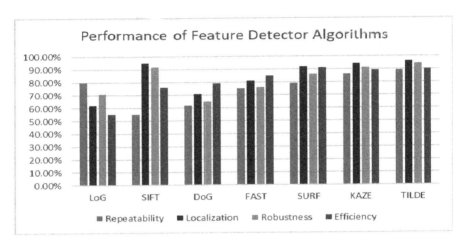

Fig. 1. Performance summary of Feature Detector Algorithms

After comparing KAZE and TILDE with other feature detectors, we come to the conclusion that they result in better object localization capability and efficiency. The scale, affine and rotation invariant performance of these feature detectors is suitable for the pedestrian detection objective. These extracted Feature Vectors are used for training network with the learning algorithms like Gradient Boosting Algorithms, SVM, Decision Tree, Random Forest (RF) and Linear Decrement Analysis (LDA), are experimented for object Classification. To attain a particular objective, choice of feature detector and suitable Machine Learning Algorithm is very essential [14].

The evolution of Deep Learning Algorithms has replaced the feature extraction methods of traditional Machine learning approaches. The divergence of Deep learning Algorithm is its ability to detect objects automatically through multiple layers without involving the feature extraction layer.

3   Overview of Faster R-CNN and SSD

In general, object detection algorithms can be divided into two parts, (a) the network, is dedicated to provide the region proposals (b) A good classifier to classify these region proposals. Therein part (b) is followed by part (a) as an architecture of detection algorithm. In case of SSD, as the name suggests, both the task of object localization and classification are performed together in a single network.

In 2016, Ross Girshick proposed Faster R-CNN which had a great impact in the field of deep learning. In RCNN and Fast RCNN [15], region proposals using selective search algorithm and object detection are disintegrated. Faster RCNN performs region proposal generation and object detection in a single layer convolutional network, thus, the object detection accuracy and computation cost has been reduced compared to its predecessors [16]. Region Proposal Network (RPN) in RCNN and Fast RCNN uses Selective Search Algorithm whereas Faster RCNN uses RPN with CNN. In RCNN, region proposals are about 2000 which further reduce to 300 in Faster RCNN.

The overall approach of Faster RCNN can be split into four segments: Convolutional layers, Region proposal Network, RoI Pooling Layer and Classification.

Invention of Faster R-CNN is great achievement in terms of detection time reduction proposed by Ross B. Girshick in 2016. The architecture combines RPN which generates selective region proposals using CNN instead of selective search algorithm. The Fast R-CNN network does further classification task on selected proposals. The number of proposals greatly reduces from 2000 to 300 in Faster R-CNN along with the improvement in the quality box proposals.

The network structure of faster R-CNN framework is shown below in Fig. 1. There is sharing of fully convolutional layer by both the object classifier and the region proposal network which uses attention mechanism to detect optimal proposals from wide range of aspect ratio and scales. These layers are trained jointly in effective manner.

3.1   Convolutional Layers

The input images are passed through convolutional layer to create Feature Maps. The Convolution layer comprises of Convolution, ReLu and pooling operations. In this Paper, Inception V2 and ResNet pretrained frameworks are used with SSD and Faster RCNN architecture respectively for comparison purpose [17, 18].

3.2   Region Proposal Network (RPN)

The feature maps extracted from the convolutional layers are given as input to RPN. These feature maps are spatially evaluated using a sliding window of size [R × R] to generate Feature Vectors. 9 anchors of different scale and aspect ratio are assigned to every sliding window. All 9 anchors have same center [x, y] and a value Q* is calculated for each of them as shown in Eq. 1. Q* evaluates the common region of these anchors with ground truth bounding boxes.

$$Q^* = \begin{cases} 1 & if \quad IoU > 0.7 \\ -1 & if \quad IoU < 0.3 \\ 0 & otherwise \end{cases} \qquad (1)$$

RPN comprises of two sub-networks: Classification and Regression. The feature vectors gained from the sliding window operation are fed to the regression subnetwork. The regression subnetwork determines the coordinates [a, b, m, n] of the predicted bounding box where a, b, m, n are the coordinates of the bounding box. Classification sub-network deduces the probability of object detection in the bounding box.

3.3 RoI Pooling Layer

Region Proposals extracted from RPN have distinct sizes leading to distinct sized CNN feature maps. Varying feature maps decrease the efficiency of the structure. Region of Interest Pooling will overcome the problem of distinct sized bounding boxes by dragging the feature maps to the same dimensions.

3.4 Classification

The softmax (type of layer in RCNN Architecture) and fully connected layer proposes the class probability for every fixed sized feature map. The bounding boxes are generated by bounding box regression till the attainment of optimum accuracy of classification. Thus, the object detection along with its classification probability is displayed for the input images.

4 Experimental Details

4.1 Experimental Details

Architectures and Setup Used
In this paper, comparison of two different architectures namely SSD and Faster RCNN is reported based on the newly proposed evaluation parameters. There are various CNN models like Coco, Pets, Inception etc. that can be combined with these architectures. Every combination has its own perks and deprivations with respect to accuracy, speed, computation cost and efficiency. These two architectures are implemented on Tensorflow with Anaconda 5.1.0 windows platform and the results are evaluated on Tensorboard.

In this work, SSD and Faster RCNN Architectures are combined with Inception V2 and ResNet CNN Model respectively. The Inception V2 and ResNet CNN Model are pretrained on ImageNet Database.

Training Dataset

The Training Dataset acquired from [19] which shows different classes of pedestrian movement as shown in Fig. 2. The dataset contains 7416 training images and 1752 test images which comprises of different movements of pedestrians along with noisy images. The images are categorized into the following classes: moving towards Left, moving towards Right and moving Front. SSD and Faster RCNN Architectures are trained and compared with the above-mentioned dataset. We have trained the Architectures with 1350 images and used 150 images for validation purpose.

Fig. 2. Samples showing (a) Moving towards left (b) Moving front and (c) Moving towards right

4.2   Experimental Results

Graphs shown in Fig. 3(a) and (b), the x-axis represents the number of iterations and y-axis represents the loss factor. As it can be inferred from the graphs, at training step 3000, the loss factor for Faster RCNN and SSD are 0.08 and 1.13 respectively. Thus, it can be noted that Faster RCNN is 28% faster than SSD. This can be attributed to RPN module used in Faster RCNN.

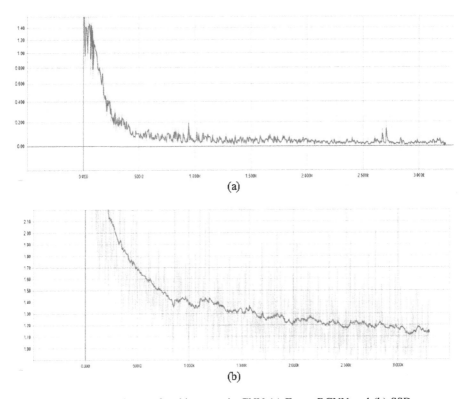

Fig. 3. Loss factor of architectures in CNN (a) Faster RCNN and (b) SSD

Suggested Evaluation Parameters

Percentage Detection index, Percentage Recognition index and Precision Score are the three main parameters applied for the comparison of object detection models.

$$Percentage\ Detection\ Index = \frac{No.\ of\ Detected\ objects}{Actual\ no.\ of\ Objects\ used\ in\ testing} \times 100 \qquad (2)$$

$$Percentage\ Recognition\ Index = \frac{No.\ of\ correctly\ Recognized\ objects}{No.\ of\ Detected\ Objects\ in\ testing} \times 100 \qquad (3)$$

Precision Score shows the probability of the object i.e. pedestrian in our case within the detection window. The performance parameters of the two Architectures for all three classes are shown in Fig. 4.

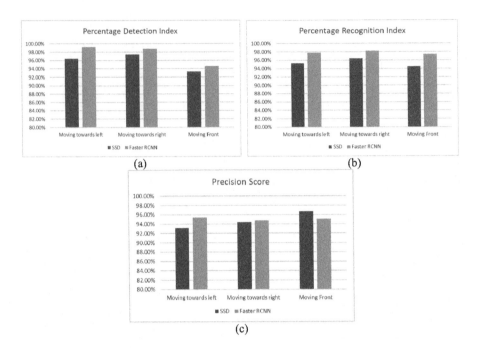

Fig. 4. Comparison of Faster RCNN and SSD with respect to parameters (a) Percentage Detection index (b) Percentage Recognition index and (c) Precision Score

Interpretation of Results

SSD and Faster RCNN are analyzed and compared on the basis of their percentage detection index, percentage recognition index and precision score. While comparing SSD and Faster RCNN, if we consider individual classes, Faster RCNN is better than SSD in every aspect. However, when it comes to precision score there is not much difference between the two, in fact SSD outperforms Faster RCNN by 2.07% in Moving front class. If accuracy is considered, Faster RCNN outperforms SSD by the difference of 2%.

5   Conclusion

In this paper, we have studied SSD and Faster RCNN architecture, along with two different models. SSD architecture was combined with Inception V2 model and Faster RCNN was combined with Resnet CNN model. We have implemented these architectures using Tensorflow framework with Anaconda 5.1.0 windows platform and the results are evaluated on Tensorboard for pedestrian intention detection. For high accuracy and better performance, both the architectures were compared on evaluation factors - Percentage Detection Index, Percentage Recognition Index and Precision Score instead of the conventional mAp parameter. On comparison, SSD is found to be 2% more accurate and 3 times speedy than Faster RCNN. While detecting pedestrian from distant camera viewpoint, Faster RCNN outperforms SSD by 14%. Also, the learning rate of Faster RCNN is 28% faster than the SSD architecture. The overall work done in this paper signifies the superiority of Faster RCNN.

References

1. https://www.who.int/violence_injury_prevention/road_safety_status/2018/en/
2. Dalal, N., Triggs, B.: Histograms of oriented gradients for human detection. In: IEEE Computer Society Conference on Computer Vision and Pattern Recognition (CVPR 2005), vol. 1, pp. 886–893, IEEE Computer Society (2005)
3. Chen, K., Song, X., Zhai, X., Zhang, B., Hou, B., Wang, Y.: An integrated deep learning framework for occluded pedestrian tracking. IEEE Access (2019)
4. Girshick, R., Donahue, J., Darrell, T., Malik, J.: Rich feature hierarchies for accurate object detection and semantic segmentation. In: Proceedings of the IEEE Conference on Computer Vision and Pattern Recognition, pp. 580–587 (2014)
5. Wanguo, W.: Research on RCNN based image recognition of unmanned aerial vehicle inspection power components. J. Earth Inf. Sci. **19**(2), 256–263 (2017)
6. Girshick, R.: Fast R-CNN. In: Computer Science (2015)
7. Ren, S.: Faster R-CNN: towards real-time object detection with region proposal networks. In: Advances in Neural Information Processing Systems, pp. 91–99 (2015)
8. Zeiler, M.D., Fergus, R.: Visualizing and understanding convolutional networks. In: Fleet, D., Pajdla, T., Schiele, B., Tuytelaars, T. (eds.) ECCV 2014. LNCS, vol. 8689, pp. 818–833. Springer, Cham (2014). https://doi.org/10.1007/978-3-319-10590-1_53
9. Sangineto, E., Nabi, M., Culibrk, D., Sebe, N.: Self paced deep learning for weakly supervised object detection. IEEE Trans. Pattern Anal. Mach. Intell. **41**(3), 712–725 (2019)
10. Chengdu, H., Wenguang, H., Bin, Y.: Video pedestrian detection based on codebook background modeling in video. Transducer Microsyst. Technol. **36**(3), 144–146 (2017)
11. Chunfeng, Z., Jiatao, S., Wanliang, W.: A survey of pedestrian detection technology. Telev. Technol. **38**(3), 157–162 (2014)
12. Salahat, E., Qasaimeh, M.: Recent advances in features extraction and description algorithms: a comprehensive survey. In: IEEE International Conference on Industrial Technology (ICIT), pp. 1059–1063. IEEE (2017)
13. Baroffio, L., Redondi, A.E.C., Tagliasacchi, M., Tubaro, S.: A survey on compact features for visual content analysis. APSIPA Trans. Signal Inf. Process. **5** (2016)
14. Yang, H., Wen, J., Wu, X.-J., He, L., Mumtaz, S.G.: An efficient edge artificial intelligence multi-pedestrian tracking method with rank constraint. IEEE Trans. Ind. Inform. (2019)
15. Ullah, A., Xie, H., Farooq, M.O., Sun, Z.: Pedestrian detection in infrared images using fast RCNN. In: Eighth IEEE International Conference on Image Processing Theory, Tools and Applications (IPTA), pp. 1–6 (2018)
16. Manana, M., Tu, C., Owolawi, P.A.: Preprocessed faster RCNN for vehicle detection. In: IEEE International Conference on Intelligent and Innovative Computing Applications (ICONIC), pp. 1–4 (2018)
17. Ning, C., Zhou, H., Song, Y., Tang, J.: Inception single shot multibox detector for object detection. In: IEEE International Conference on Multimedia and Expo Workshops (ICMEW), pp. 549–554 (2017)
18. https://medium.com/@jonathan_hui/ssd-object-detection-single-shot-multibox-detector-for-real-time-processing-9bd8deac0e06
19. Pedestrian Dataset. http://www.rovit.ua.es/dataset/pedirecog/

Implementation of Smart Legal Assistance System in Accordance with the Indian Penal Code Using Similarity Measures

Dipti Pawade, Avani Sakhapara, Hussain Ratlamwala,
Siddharth Mishra[✉], Samreen Shaikh, and Dhrumil Mehta

Department of IT, K.J. Somaiya College of Engineering, Mumbai, India
{diptipawade, avanisakhapara, hussain.r,
siddharth.mishra, samreen.shaikh,
dhrumil.m}@somaiya.edu

Abstract. The rate of crime is increasing rapidly and many citizens of country are the victims of these crimes. It is observed that though the number of crimes taking place is very huge, the actual number of crimes being reported to the legal authorities is very small. This huge difference is because of several reasons where one of the reason is lack of awareness about the civil rights and the laws. Many citizens in India are unaware about the evil practices performed against them and unethical exploitation of them done by others. The citizens are also not aware about various laws in the Indian Penal Code. So inorder to bridge this gap between the laws and the common citizens of India, we have proposed a Natural Language Processing (NLP) system using Word Mover's Distance (WMD) which takes as input the textual description of crime and generates as output, the applicable Indian Penal Code (IPC) sections and the description of the punishments mentioned under these sections. The performance comparison of WMD with cosine similarity is presented. Finally, the accuracy of the system is measured by getting the result generated by the system to be validated by a lawyer personal.

Keywords: Indian Penal Code · Natural language programming ·
Word Mover's Distance · Cosine · Rapid Automated Keyword Extraction

1 Introduction and Related Work

Crimes in India are prevalent in every industry. A common man is usually not literate about his civil rights and ends up being taken advantage. Right from a shopkeeper selling less quantity of goods to illegal business practices by an organization, crime is present everywhere. The helpless citizen unaware of his rights, freedom and social choices often fall prey to exploitation by evil retailers, business holders and other people who show haughty behavior to these people. Due to fear and lack of knowledge, the victims eschew taking any actions to avoid the drudgery of legal works. Even if some of the victims of these unethical works approach the lawyers, some of the lawyers may demand huge fees for just a bunch of advice and if the lawyer turns out to be venal, they pull off in exchange of being well paid by the culprits. The unreported crimes also include other crimes against the silent crowd. According to the survey, the

© Springer Nature Singapore Pte Ltd. 2019
M. Singh et al. (Eds.): ICACDS 2019, CCIS 1046, pp. 440–449, 2019.
https://doi.org/10.1007/978-981-13-9942-8_42

crimes which are not reported significantly involve women and children as the suffering victims [1]. In order to bring to public, knowledge about the enactment of various criminal laws and punishments for the mentioned offences in the Indian Penal Code, we put forth a digital solution which helps the user to know what punishment can be imposed for a particular offence. Our system is based on Closed Domain Question Answering (QA) system [2]. Many researchers have worked on closed domain QA systems in different fields. Pham et al. [3] have designed a system called RASM to understand Vietnamese news articles and implement basic QA system based on these articles. Initially, news articles of ICTNEWS which is a popular news medium are collected. The semantics of articles are computed by using the already present facts in RASM's Facts database. Sample Vietnamese questions are generated for these articles. These questions are then converted to definite clause grammar where in each word's parts of speech and categories are understood. These semantic expressions are converted to Prolog query which fetches the most suitable answer from RASM facts database. Wang et al. [4] have proposed an answer recommendation algorithm for medical community question. Here the answer corpus and passive medical questions are used for training. To avoid zero probability problem, Jelinek-Mercer smoothing method is used. Then feature extraction is carried out. Once features are extracted from the text of answers, quality of the answers is estimated using logistic regression. Devi et al. [5] have proposed QA system that answers questions related to agriculture domain. It uses combination of NLP and semantic web technologies to answer the questions. Initially, Ontology is built by identification of classes and relations between them using Protégé tool. After that questions are taken and basic NLP processes like tokenization, stemming, and Parts of Speech (POS) tagging are applied. Furthermore, in order to make system more intelligent synonyms of words are checked from WordNet [6] to consider all possible cases for the question. This data is then used to form triples which are later used to find SPARQL queries. The computation speed of these queries is then improved with the help of query loosening.

Also there have been some attempts made by the researchers to develop a system for legal assistance based on closed domain QA system which is discussed further. Kamdi et al. [7] have proposed a NLP based, closed domain Question Answering (QA) system, which accepts query related to Indian Penal Code (IPC) sections and Indian Amendment Laws as closed domain Question. The system then tries to retrieve the exact answers for these questions from the stored knowledge-base. In this system, initially a corpus of answers is generated for each IPC section, by retrieving the relevant data from various websites and storing it in a separate text file. Then for preprocessing, the text in the corpus is tokenized, then stop words are removed and finally stemming is applied. Information retrieval is performed by extracting the keywords from user query and preprocessing it, which then generates keywords related to/from the query. The keywords generated are matched with an index-based dictionary to find the text file, to which the keywords relates the most. The answer is then generated from the text in the text file. Pudaruth et al. [8] have proposed web-based QA system for Mauritian Judiciary where users can enter their queries as text. The system then extracts the relevant keywords from user query and returns the relevant sections of law along with list of similar type of cases going on in Supreme Court. In this system, first the legal documents pertaining to Laws and Acts of Mauritian Judiciary, is converted from PDF to text format. The information stored in this document is then broken down into smaller paragraphs. These paragraphs are tagged with information such as name of act/ judgement, section number, description, etc and stored in a separate text file. This tagged information is then stored in relational database. On receiving user query, the relevant keywords are extracted from it and using the relational database the result is fetched and displayed to the user. The user can choose to display the name of Act instead of its textual description. Quaresma et al. [9], has put forth a smart system for Portuguese Judiciary which provides the response to the users question. The system creates a knowledge base by extracting information from the documents. Then syntactical analysis is performed where a new document is created by processing these extracted sentences using Palavras parser [10]. Thereafter in semantic analysis, the collection of new document created using syntactical analysis, is rewritten in order to get another collection of document where each document has a DRS (structure for the discourse representation), a set of conditions and a list of discourse referents. Then semantic and pragmatic interpretation is carried out which comprises of collection of the knowledge base using ontology. Then the user query is accepted on which syntactical analysis, semantic analysis and, semantic and pragmatic interpretation is performed. Finally, the user query processing is carried out where the knowledge base interprets the final query representation through the unification of the discourse entities of the query with documents. Tirpude et al. [11] has proposed a legal assistance system which consists of three distinct modules, viz., Query Processing Module, which is used for the classification of question, Document Processing Module, which is used for information retrieval, and Answer Processing Module which is used for answer extraction. The research is performed on knowledge base which is constructed from legal documents of Indian Laws by, generating a corpus of answers by taking the data from various websites and storing the text for each IPC section along with other amendment laws and parent law in a separate text file. Then the text in the corpus is preprocessed by performing tokenization, removing stop words, applying stemming and rewriting the result as a text sentence. Information retrieval is performed by preprocessing the user query and extracting the keywords from it. These extracted keywords are matched with an index-based dictionary to find the documents which contains the keywords in proximity value of 3. The answer is then generated from the text in the text file.

From the literature survey carried out in this section, we have observed that thorough research has been carried out by different researchers based on QA based system in different domain, still there is lots of scope of research in developing a trustworthy system that can provide the legal assistance especially for Indian Penal Code. Thus we took the challenge and developed the system described in Sect. 3.

2 Similarity Measurement Metrics

In order to generate the IPC sections for the inputted textual description of the crime, the system uses Word Mover's Distance (WMD) and Cosine Similarity (CS) to measure the similarity between the inputted textual description of the crime and the textual description of the IPC section stored in the dataset. The WMD and cosine similarity are discussed further in this section.

2.1   Word Mover's Distance (WMD)

Word Mover's Distance (WMD) is a distance metric used to measure distance between two texts, generated by the total amount of effort needed to move the words from one side to the other, multiplied by the distance the words need to move. It was introduced by Kusner et al. in 2015 [12]. Instead of Euclidean Distance and other bag-of-words or TF-IDF based distance metrics, WMD uses word embeddings to calculate the similarities based on semantics. Word Mover's Distance can be used to measure similarity between two documents or sentences. WMD is derived from a metric known as Earth Mover's distance which is originally derived to compute image similarities. The algorithm first maps each words in the document in a higher dimensional vector space such that each unique word has its corresponding word vector in that space. This vectorization can be achieved using algorithms like word2vec. Then if two vectors are close they represent similar ideas. For example two sentences "Blake loves songs" and "Blake likes music" would be categorized as similar by WMD because vectors of 'loves' and 'likes' would be close and vectors of 'songs' and 'music' would be close representing similar. The vectors are weighted and prioritized using the normalized frequency of their occurrence in the document. The algorithm does not include the words which are of less importance, and the words which are semantically similar are spaced comparatively closer to each other. The WMD between the two documents or sentences is then computed using the resultant euclidean distances between individual weighted word vectors of each document or sentence. The smaller the value of WMD, the more similar the two sentences are.

2.2   Cosine Similarity (CS)

Cosine similarity [13] is a similarity metric which measures the cosine distance i.e. the cosine of angle between the two vectors in a high dimensional space. The cosine similarity between two vectors A and B is given by Eq. (1).

$$Cosine\ Similarity = \cos(\theta) = \frac{A \cdot B}{\|A\| * \|B\|} \tag{1}$$

where,

$A \cdot B \rightarrow$ dot product of vectors A & B
$\|A\| * \|B\| \rightarrow$ product of magnitudes of vectors A & B
$\theta \rightarrow$ Angle between the vectors A & B

Cosine similarity is widely used for comparison of sentences and checking similarity levels between two documents. The value of CS is between 0(zero) and 1. The higher the value of CS, the more similar the two sentences are.

3   Implementation Overview

For the implementation of the proposed system, a reliable and structured dataset on the Indian Penal Code sections and violations available on web portal vakilbabu.com [14] is used. The dataset consist of the IPC sections and corresponding textual description of crime. Out of 511 IPC sections, 130 IPC sections are considered for the implementation of the system. Sample dataset of IPC sections and crime description is provided in Table 1.

Table 1. Sample dataset of IPC sections and crime description

IPC section	Crime description
Section 290	Committing a public nuisance
Section 286	So dealing with any explosive substance
Section 324	Voluntarily causing hurt by dangerous weapons or means

Initially the keywords are extracted for each IPC section description from the IPC dataset using Rapid Automated Keyword Extraction (R.A.K.E.) algorithm [15]. R.A.K.E. consists of following steps:

Step 1. Tokenization: The sentences are broken at various punctuation signs. Each phrase or sentence generated is treated as candidate.

Step 2. Stop word Removal: The stop words are treated as phrase boundaries. The candidates consisting of one or more stop words are refined to generate more candidates from it. The list of all the candidates generated from a sentence is called as candidate set.

Step 3. Calculate word score: As shown in Eq. (2), the score of each word (wd_score) is calculated as,

$$wd\_score = \frac{frequency(word)}{frequency(word) + count(otherwords)} \qquad (2)$$

where frequency(word) = number of times, the word under consideration appears in the candidate set.

count(other words) = total number of other words which appear along with the word under consideration in the candidate set

Step 4. Calculate score of candidate: This score is called as R.A.K.E. score. As shown in Eq. (3), the score of candidate is calculated as,

$$R.A.K.E.\ Score(candidate) = \sum wd\_score\ of\ each\ word\ in\ candidate \qquad (3)$$

Step 5. Keyword generation: The candidates having highest and second highest R.A.K.E. score are added to the final keyword set for an IPC section. The IPC sections and its keyword set are stored in an internal dictionary called as IPC-Keyword dictionary.

Then word2vec model is used to generate vector (section_vector) for each IPC section using the keywords stored in IPC-Keyword dictionary. The criminal description is inputted to the system, on which R.A.K.E. is applied to extract the keywords. These keywords are then converted into vector (input_vector) using word2vec model. Then the similarity between input_vector and each section_vector is calculated using Word Mover's Distance (WMD) and Cosine Similarity (CS) measures as discussed in

Sect. 2. The IPC sections corresponding to section_vector of the two best similarity scores are selected, because most of the times it is highly possible that the user input might contain multiple IPC section violations. The punishment description for these selected IPC sections is fetched from the IPC-Punishment database which contains the textual description of punishment for each IPC section. Finally the applicable IPC section along with the punishment description is given as output by the system. The complete working of the system is demonstrated in Fig. 1.

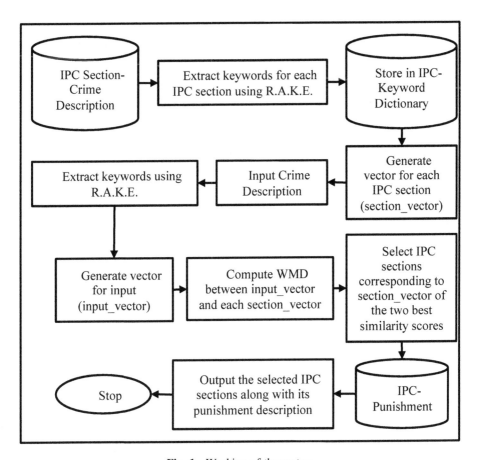

Fig. 1. Working of the system

4 Results and Discussions

For simulation purpose we have tested around 100 cases. The results of the WMD and the cosine similarity for these 100 cases are shown in Table 2.

Here,

True Positives (TP): The cases in which the system predicted sections for a crime, and sections produced by the IPC book are exactly the same.
False Negatives (FN): The cases in which the system predicted sections for a crime and sections produced by the IPC book are not same.
True Negatives (TN) and False Positives (FP): Since the dependent variable (i.e. sections violated) is not categorical, TN and FP is considered as zero.

From the results, it is observed that the accuracy of WMD is 96% whereas the accuracy of CS is 84%. There is 12% increase in accuracy achieved by using WMD. This is because, the number of false predictions in WMD is about a quarter to that in CS.

Table 2. Result of Word Mover's Distance (WMD) and Cosine Similarity (CS)

	Word Mover's Distance (WMD)			Cosine Similarity (CS)		
	Predicted NO	Predicted YES	Total	Predicted NO	Predicted YES	Total
Actual NO	TN = 0	FP = 0	0	TN = 0	FP = 0	0
Actual YES	FN = 4	TP = 96	100	FN = 16	TP = 84	100
Total	4	96	**100**	16	84	**100**

In Table 3, example of crime description and its classification is given. These results are validated by a lawyer.

Table 3. Example of crime description and its classification

Crime description	Applicable section	Actual result	Classification
Maliciously insulting the religion or the religious beliefs of any class	295A	295A	TP
He used extortion towards his employers for money for fulfilling his daily needs	384	363A	FN

In Table 4, the comparison of performance metrics such as accuracy, precision, recall and F1-score for WMD and CS is provided. It is observed that the performance of WMD is better than CS as denoted by F1-score.

Table 4. Comparison of performance metrics of WMD and CS approach

	Accuracy	Precision	Recall	F1 score
WMD	0.96	1	0.96	0.98
CS	0.84	1	0.84	0.91

Table 5, gives the sample test cases, executed for different crime scenario descriptions.

Table 5. Sample test cases

Test case 1:
User Query: My friend was involved in dealing with explosive bombs with dangerous people. **Expected output given by a lawyer:** The IPC sections violation: Section 286 Punishment: Imprisonment for 6 months or fine of 1,000 rupees, or both. **Input keywords generated after R.A.K.E. processing:** "Explosive bombs", "dangerous people", "involved", "friend", "dealing" **Shortest Word Mover's distance between the vectors of keywords from the user's crime description and those of each crime in Knowledge base:** 3.61009 **Maximum Cosine Similarity between the vectors of keywords from the user's crime description and those of each crime in Knowledge base:** 0.35506 **Observed result from Word Mover's distance Approach:** The IPC sections violated were: Section 286 and Section 285 of the Indian Penal Code and the punishment is Imprisonment for 6 months or fine of 1,000 rupees, or both. **Observed Result from Cosine Similarity Approach:** The IPC sections violated were: Section 286 and Section 324 of the Indian Penal Code and the punishment is Imprisonment for 6 months or fine of 1,000 rupees, or both. **Actual IPC Crime Description as mentioned in the Knowledge Base:** Section 286: So dealing with any explosive substance. Section 324: Voluntarily causing hurt by dangerous weapons or means. Section 285: Dealing with fire or any combustible matter so as to endanger human life, etc. **Validation of results by lawyer:** Passed for both the methods.
Test case 2
User Query - A boy was doing a public nuisance by dancing nude on the road, even after he was warned to stop. **Expected output given by a lawyer:** The IPC sections violation: Section 290 Punishment: Fine of 200 Rupees. **Input keywords generated after R.A.K.E. processing:** "public", "dancing", "nuisance", "road", "nude", "warned to stop". **Shortest Word Mover's distance between the vectors of keywords from the user's crime description and those of each crime in Knowledge base:** 3.51459 **Maximum Cosine Similarity between the vectors of keywords from the user's crime description and those of each crime in Knowledge base:** 0.27157 **Observed Result from Word Mover's Distance Approach:** The IPC sections violated were: Section 290 and Section 291 of the Indian Penal Code and the punishment is Fine of 200 Rupees. **Observed Result from Cosine Similarity Approach:** The IPC sections violated were: Section 277 and Section 431 of the Indian Penal Code and the punishment for Section 277 is imprisonment 3 months or fine which may extend to 500 rupees, or both, while punishment for Section 431 is imprisonment 5 years or fine or both.

> **Validation of results by lawyer:** Passed for Word Mover's distance approach, Failed for Cosine Similarity approach.
>
> **IPC Crime Description as mentioned in the Knowledge Base:**
> Section 290: Committing a public nuisance
> Section 291: Continuance of nuisance after injunction to discontinue.
> Section 277: Defiling the water of a public spring or reservoir.
> Section 431: Mischief by injury to public road, bridge, navigable river, or navigable channel, and rendering it impassable or less safe for traveling or conveying property.

5   Conclusion and Future Work

This paper proposes a legal assistance system for the citizens of India where the citizens can get to know the applicable IPC sections for the inputted textual description of the crime. This system allows the citizens to gain knowledge about the relation between the crimes and IPC sections. The system also allows the citizens to identify the malpractices followed by the venal lawyers. As observed from the results, the accuracy of the system using WMD is 96% whereas the accuracy of the system using cosine similarity is 84%. The results generated by the system are validated by a lawyer to test the authenticity of results. From the results, it is inferred that the performance of WMD is better than cosine similarity. Currently the system is designed in accordance with Indian Penal Code Sections and can be used in India only. Furthermore, the system can be extended to be used in other countries and the system performance can be evaluated. Also further the system can be extended to support multiple languages.

References

1. National Crime Records Bureau data, 2015: slight dip in rape, crime against women. The Indian Express (2019). https://indianexpress.com/article/explained/national-crime-records-bureau-data-2015-slight-dip-in-rape-crime-against-women-3004980/
2. Lende, S.P., Raghuwanshi, M.M.: Closed domain question answering system using NLP techniques. Int. J. Eng. Sci. Res. Technol. (IJESRT) 5(4), 632–639 (2016). https://doi.org/10.5281/zenodo.49808
3. Pham, S.T., Nguyen, D.T.: Implementation method of answering engine for vietnamese questions in reading answering system model (RASM). In: 8th Asia Modelling Symposium (AMS), Taipei, Taiwan, pp. 175–180 (2014). https://doi.org/10.1109/AMS.2014.42
4. Wang, J., Man, C., Zhao, Y., Wang, F.: An answer recommendation algorithm for medical community question answering systems. In: IEEE International Conference on Service Operations and Logistics, and Informatics (SOLI), Beijing, China, pp. 139–144 (2016). https://doi.org/10.1109/SOLI.2016.7551676
5. Devi, M., Dua, M.: ADANS: an agriculture domain question answering system using ontologies. In: IEEE Proceedings of International Conference on Computing, Communication and Automation (ICCCA), Greater Noida, India, pp. 122–127 (2017). https://doi.org/10.1109/CCAA.2017.8229784
6. Miller, G.A.: WordNet: a lexical database for English. Commun. ACM 38(11), 39–41 (1995)

7. Kamdi, R.P., Agrawal, A.J.: Keywords based closed domain question answering system for indian penal code sections and indian amendment laws. Int. J. Intell. Syst. Appl. (IJISA) **7** (12), 57–67 (2015). https://doi.org/10.5815/ijisa.2015.12.06

8. Pudaruth, S., Gunputh, R.P., Soyjaudah, K.M.S., Domun, P.: A question answer system for the mauritian judiciary. In: IEEE Proceedings of 3rd International Conference on Soft Computing and Machine Intelligence (ISCMI), Dubai, United Arab Emirates, pp. 201–205 (2016). https://doi.org/10.1109/ISCMI.2016.47

9. Quaresma, P., Rodrigues, I.P.: A question answer system for legal information retrieval. In: ACM Proceedings of Legal Knowledge and Information Systems: JURIX 2005: The Eighteenth Annual Conference, pp. 91–100 (2005)

10. Bick, E.: The Parsing System Palavras: Automatic Grammatical Analysis of Portuguese in a Constraint Grammar Framework. Aarhus University Press, Aarhus (2000)

11. Tirpude, S.C., Alvi, A.S.: Closed domain keyword based question answering system for legal documents of IPC sections and Indian Laws. Int. J. Innov. Res. Comput. Commun. Eng. (IJIRCCE) **3**(6), 5299–5311 (2015). https://doi.org/10.15680/ijircce.2015.0306077

12. Kusner, M.J., Sun, Y., Kolkin, N.I., Weinberger, K.Q.: From word embeddings to document distances. In: ACM Proceedings of 32nd International Conference on Machine Learning (ICML), Lille, France, pp. 957–966 (2015)

13. Dataset. http://www.vakilbabu.com/Laws/Laws.htm

14. Sakhapara, A., Pawade, D., Chapanera, H., Jani, H., Ramgaonkar, D.: Segregation of similar and dissimilar live RSS news feeds based on similarity measures. In: Balas, V.E., Sharma, N., Chakrabarti, A. (eds.) Data Management, Analytics and Innovation. AISC, vol. 839, pp. 333–344. Springer, Singapore (2019). https://doi.org/10.1007/978-981-13-1274-8_26

15. Rose, S., Engel, D., Cramer, N., Cowley, W.: Automatic keyword extraction from individual documents. In: Berry, M.W., Kogan, J. (eds.) Text Mining: Applications and Theory, pp. 1–20. Wiley (2010). https://doi.org/10.1002/9780470689646.ch1

A Review on Facial Expression Based Behavioral Analysis Using Computational Technique for Autistic Disorder Patients

Camellia Ray[(⊠)], Hrudaya Kumar Tripathy, and Sushruta Mishra

School of Computer Engineering, Kalinga Institute of Industrial Technology,
Deemed to be University, Bhubaneswar 751024, Odisha, India
camellia.jhilik@gmail.com, {hktripathyfcs,
sushruta.mishrafcs}@kiit.ac.in

Abstract. Within recent decades the chances of a child being diagnosed with autism spectrum disorder have increased dramatically. Individuals with autism disorder have markedly different social and emotional actions and reactions than non-autistic individuals. It is a chronic disorder whose symptoms include failure to develop normal social relations with other people, impaired development of communicative ability, lack of imaginative ability, and repetitive, stereotyped movements. There exist numerous techniques associated to detect autism disorders in children. Facial expression-based method is an effective technique frequently used by medical experts to detect the emotional patterns of autistic children. Our paper reviews this technique to determine the behavioral analysis of autistic children. Comparative analysis of existing techniques is undertaken to select the most optimal technique of autism detection.

Keywords: Autistic disorder · Facial expression · Emotion recognition · Shanon's entropy · Kinect sensor · $P recognizer · 3D facial model

1 Introduction

Autism Spectrum Disorder is a wide spreading disease which is becoming a matter of awareness in recent times. 'Spectrum' refers to the wide variety of challenges faced by the autistic child. The proportion of the male population suffering from autism is comparatively more than that of females. The autistic disorder needs to be identified earlier so that it can create a roadmap for early treatment. Parents and care providers play an important role in the detection of the challenges faced by the autistic child. They share an intimate relationship with these children and are aware of their behavioral patterns. Autistic based disorder does not occur due to lack of affection from parents rather it may cause due to genetic risk or other environmental factors. It may also happen because of advanced aging of parents, illness during pregnancies, complications during birth, the crisis of oxygen supply in the brain while birth or premature babies. Early diagnosis is possible if parents remain very alert and attentive towards the behavior of their children. Figure 1 shows the different types of Autistic Spectrum Disorder.

© Springer Nature Singapore Pte Ltd. 2019
M. Singh et al. (Eds.): ICACDS 2019, CCIS 1046, pp. 450–464, 2019.
https://doi.org/10.1007/978-981-13-9942-8_43

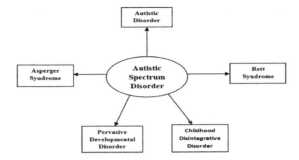

Fig. 1. Types of Autistic Disorder patients

1.1 Types of Autistic Spectrum Disorder

Autism Spectrum Disorder can be categorized into five types based on different symptoms and behavioral patterns. These types of disorders are summarized below.

Pervasive Developmental Disorder (PDD-NOS): Children suffering from PDD-NOS has the autism severe than Asperger Syndrome but not more than Autistic Disorder. They face troubles if there is a change in the routine or problems in understanding languages and relating people. **Asperger Syndrome:** These types of children are intelligent enough to handle their own work but they face social related difficulties. Like other disorders, they also focus on a particular topic by repetitive behaviors. A person having Asperger Syndrome possesses serious issues like anxiety or depressions. **Childhood Disintegrative Disorder (CDD):** CDD is also known as Heller's Syndrome which is commonly diagnosed with abnormal EEG. The disease is considered to be more severe and rarest among others in the spectrum. Children suffering from CDD though develop normally before but gradually they lose their mental stability and social communications.

Rett Syndrome: This syndrome mostly occurs among girls rather than boys. Though the disease has similar behavioral features, but it is not considered under the ASD as they typically occur through genetic mutation [11]. Identical to the CDD, they also start losing their skills like hand movement, brain growth, head growth, and speaking ability. **Autistic Disorder:** It is one of the diseases among Autism Spectrum Disorder. Children suffering from autism faces different challenges in social skills like understanding the feelings of others and joint attention. Repetitive behaviors like flipping objects, smelling things, head banging, spinning in circles and repeating certain words or phrases are usually found in autistic patients.

1.2 Autism

Autism is neither an illness nor a disease and it occurs among 1% of the population. People suffering from this disorder usually don't like changes in their environment and are less social in nature. It is also difficult to determine the disease as each children suffering from autism specifically faces a unique mixture of symptoms. Some of them have signs of lower intelligence while others have higher intelligence [10]. There may be several methods like speech and language therapy, occupational therapy, educational support or other interventions to provide support for living a more fulfilling life. The Autistic disorder is a huge domain where every child faces various problems, among which some are noticeable while a few others are not. However, from all the above problems faced by an autistic child, the one common thread that draws the attention is their social and communicational skills. With the lack of these features, the autistic children face difficulties to express their emotions to others whereas other people also fail to understand their feelings. Since autistic children are more sensitive with little issues, so they may feel pain compared to other normal child. Thus deficit in communication creates miscommunication and misunderstanding, which further results in frustration and discouragement.

In Fig. 2, the autistic child is interacting with the Robot which is already trained through different algorithms to make the child learn how to respond with a facial expression and to recognize emotions on which they lack behind. The therapists are assisting them in the teaching learning process.

Fig. 2. An autistic children taking therapy session (Adapted from [Getting a head start on autism: Science news for students])

During the detection of emotions in autism, the body and speech recognition provides inaccurate emotion detection since they mostly vary in their culture and language. Other emotion detection techniques based on IOT [1], Deep Learning [12–14], EEG [15–18], MRI [20], Gait [19] and Robotic [21–24] are observed to be more precise in normal children than that of autistic affected children. Non-verbal means of representing feelings form the basis of facial recognition to detect emotions by observing facial variations. Thus it can be concluded that facial expression is the most obvious way to show emotions.

2   Literature Survey

Del Coco et al. [7] has detailed a single camera system to analyze the facial expression. The collected data thus help to determine the facial dynamics of an autistic child. Through the technique, the facial complexity is further analyzed and the exact facial response is recommended. With the addition to that, the distinguish of typical and autistic children can be found out automatically, that can help in diagnosis later on. During the detection of action units, Shannon's entropy is required to measure the complexity of signals which is calculated through.

$$H(X) = -\sum_i p(x_i) \log(p(x_i)) \tag{1}$$

H = Shannon's Entropy needs to be measured
X = Each Action Units
$p(x_i)$ = probability of having x_i

Li et al. [1] has described a serious game, that basically acts as a therapy session which when played, the activities are recorded through Microsoft Kinect Sensor and the video game changes the scenes according to their emotional states. This technology helps in recognizing exact emotion through proper action for reaching the goal of the game. The mood of the angry or frustrated autistic children changes due the adaptive change of the situation with music and scenes.

$$\mu_n(x) = \sum_{t=1}^{T} w_t S_{t,n}(x) \tag{2}$$

μ_n = weighted fusion
w_t = total weight
S_t = total support
w_n = class
t = member

The expression (2) depicts detection of emotion by combining different analyzer like textual, speech and skin. That analyzer after integration goes for adaptive changes of mood according to situations. Abirached et al. [2], proposes a serious game that can detect the emotion through various activities with the help of a pipeline centered to produce a generic rig.

$$\lambda = \frac{1}{(t_M - t_0)} \sum_{i=0}^{M} \log \frac{L'(t_i)}{L'(t_{i-1})} \tag{3}$$

t_0 = initial time
$L'(t_i)$ = initial length on later time
t_i = later time
M = the number of evolutionary steps
λ = Lyapunov Exponents
t_M = time required to complete the evolution steps

This technology results in expressing emotion faster with the other facility of customization by its own without sketching facial expression. Heni [3] has implemented behavior detection software to determine the behaviors using a smart-phone with the help of Facial Expression Recognition (FER) and Automatic Speech Recognition (ASR). This technology helps in improving learning skills in a mobile system with good guidance usually provided by the caretakers. It also provides with the facility of monthly emotional improvement reports.

The expression in Eq. 3 measures the expansion of trajectories taking place in different directions of the brain for detecting emotion through Lyapunov Exponents (LLE) through EEG. [16]. Silva in [9] has represented a robot which after interacting with the autistic children as being an assistant can help to synthesize emotions with the help of Intel Real 3D sensor and a robot called ZECA. This technology results in determining negative emotions of the autistic children and the emotions can be con-trolled during violent situations. Manfredonia et al. [26] has used automatic face analysis software known as FACET and compares with the autism knowledge engine called JAKE (Janssen Autism Knowledge Engine) to analyze the facial expressions of an autistic child by facial activation units like happiness, sadness etc. This method helps to interpret the emotions of an autistic child and compares its differences with typical children. Golan et al. [27] have compared the emotions between autistic chil-dren and typically developing controls through facial, vocal and verbal. Later it has been found that ASD comes up with the poorest performance in recognizing surprise and anger in comparison to the typical children.

3   Role of Facial Expression in Autism

Faces, the mirror of feelings plays an important role in emotional communication. As it is the most visualized part, therefore it can be easily captured through camera for analyzing emotions than any other techniques. Facial expression is the pathway to know about the emotions and intentions of other people differing within different age of people. An autistic child (both high functioning and low functioning) of 10 years are worst in labeling emotions while 12 years have a certain lack in labeling.

 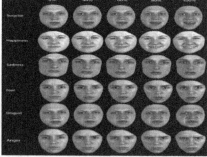

Fig. 3. (a) Demonstration of Facial expression in autistic patients (Adapted from [MIT Lab]), (b) Emotion detection using facial expression (Adapted from [Journal of Neuropsychology (2014)])

As soon as they reach the adulthood they make themselves adaptable in recognizing basic emotion expression, but still struggling for analyzing emotions. This paper consists of a literature review of the different interventions for newly developed technology that targets the recognition of emotional states through various Facial expressions. Several methods have been discussed which can detect the different facial appearance to understand the feeling of others and their intentions [11].

Figure 3(a) illustrates the changes in facial expressions due to variations in situations of an Autistic child which are recorded by the robot. In Fig. 3(b), various emotions are detected through Facial expressions with the change in their facial intensity.

4 Facial Based Emotion Detection Methods for Autistic Patients

The Scalability (20.5%) and Accuracy (20.5%) is higher in the case of non-invasive technique as it can distinguish the facial corners which help in expanding the accuracy for emotions detection while identifying faces. It rises to high security (80.5%) because of the well-ordered procedure of face identification but the time required (80.5%) to complete the task is more. Since there is a chance of facial overlapping, the Reliability (50.5%) is beyond expectation [7]. Table 1 has a brief view of different expression

Table 1. Popular existing facial emotion detection technique

Technology	Process	Authors	Goals	Technique
Multimodal integrated model, active contour model	*Step 1:* Facial expressions recorded while playing games through Kinect sensor. *Step 2:* Analyzed with analyzer. *Step 3:* Report is send to video game. *Step 4:* Perform adaptive situation change	Li et al. [1]	Detection of emotions and helps in changing the mood automatically	Kinect sensor
Active appearance model	*Step 1:* Children trained with AAM model *Step 2:* Choose one AVATAR and one emotion. *Step 3:* Construct desired facial expression. *Step 4:* Gain experience for different facial expression. *Step 5:* Transfer knowledge to real life situation	Abirached et al. [2]	Children learn about various facial expression to express emotion	Game based

(*continued*)

Table 1. (*continued*)

Technology	Process	Authors	Goals	Technique
Viola Jones based algorithm	*Step 1:* Camera is set in the surface. *Step 2:* Parts of faces and corners are detected. *Step 3:* Curvature and density of corners are extracted. *Step 4:* Emotional state detected.	Heni et al. [3]	Emotion detection through FER and Automatic Speech Recognition	Game based
Linear regression model	*Step 1:* Choose and put the absolute expression of perfect emotion to the particular box. *Step 2:* Naming of each expression in two intensities. *Step 3:* Finding exact emotional label. *Step 4:* The exact emotion is find out from the picture shown in screen	Lacroix et al. [4]	Finding out proportion of responses between ASD CA and VMA with the highest response of emotion to detect	Emotion detection task
Augmented reality based model, self-facial model, avatar user interaction model	*Step 1:* Participant select one mask of facial expression for representing emotion of one story narrated by therapist. *Step 2:* Learn to deal with the AR system comfortably. *Step 3:* Retain the skills acquired in the previous process	Chen et al. [5]	Reflection of feelings and status on different situations and determine facial status easily with low cost and accurate observation	Learning system
3D complex facial emotion recognition system	*Step 1:* Choose the appropriate facial expression of 3D character for particular emotion, during the appropriate situation *Step 2:* Elect the particular situation for the facial expression displayed	Cheng et al. [6]	Examining the emotions obtained from answers questioned by Complex Emotion Picture	Learning system

(*continued*)

Table 1. (*continued*)

Technology	Process	Authors	Goals	Technique
Computer vision module	***Step 1:*** Find a semi-rigid object through Histogram of Oriented Gradients (HOG). ***Step 2:*** Detection of Landmark of the face through Conditional Local Neural Field (CLNF) ***Step 3:*** Spotting of new faces through CLNF model	Del Coco et al. [7]	Different Action Units are detected to gain the particular emotion	Non-invasive technique
Active appearance model	***Step 1:*** Monitoring and face detection: Facial action units (AU), the Gabor wavelets, and the scale invariant Feature transform (SIFT). ***Step 2:*** Facial feature extraction. ***Step 3:*** Facial Expression Classification among the most used methods	Fan et al. [25]	Recognition of facial expression to determine emotion	Deep Learning based
Intel Real Sense model, SVM model	***Step 1:*** Extraction of Facial Aus and neck angles. ***Step 2:*** Recognize human facial expression by facial features through facial AU	Silva et al. [9]	Finding of emotion from facial feature	Robotic
$P recognizer	***Step 1:*** Microsoft Kinect sensor captures high quality color 3D images. ***Step 2:*** Microsoft SDK Development toolkit tracks 121 points of human faces ***Step 3:*** Follows euclidean distance algorithm to compare template and candidate emotion	Jazouli et al. [8]	Recognizing the facial expression of emotions automatically	Kinect sensor

detection methods. Kinect Sensor based technique has Accuracy (80.5) higher than non-invasive technique on account of its feature of the sensor. They are also having higher Security (80.8%) with minimum chances of error with electronic features taking a relatively large amount of time (80.5%) while detecting emotions. Since they are already processed it is often difficult to scale up (50.2%), sometimes inattentiveness of autistic children leads to medium reliability (50.8%) [1, 8]. The learning system is an easy going technique; there is more reliability (80.8%). The therapist or researcher can add other features (80.8%) with the system to make them user-friendly during the learning process than non-invasive and Kinect sensor based technique. In Table 2, the distinctive techniques for emotion identification through facial expression are compared in terms of various performance parameters.

Table 2. Analysis of performance metrics for various techniques

	Non-invasive technique	Kinect sensor based technique	Learning system technique	Gaming based technique	Emotion detection task based technique	Robotic technique	Deep learning based EEG technique
Scalability	Low	Medium	High	Medium	Low	Low	Medium
Security	High	High	Low	High	High	Medium	High
Reliability	Medium	Medium	High	Low	High	High	High
Latency	High	High	High	Low	Medium	Low	Medium
Accuracy	Low	High	Medium	Medium	Medium	High	High

As the Learning System depends upon the acquirement of children, it is time taking (80.6%). Accuracy may be slightly lower (50.8%) than the Kinect sensor based technique because of being a learning system [5, 6]. In the Gaming based technique, the children attentively involve themselves in gaming process which helps for emotion detection with pretty less time but the electronic device may be unreliable (80.5%) sometimes than non-invasive, Kinect sensor and Learning system based technique. It is also having medium Accuracy (50.5%) and Scalability (50.5%) due to its unreliability and premade features, whereas higher Security (80.8%) for the attentiveness of autistic children [1–3]. Emotion detection task-based system has lower Scalability (20.5%) and higher Reliability (80.6%). It is having higher Security (80.5%) but accuracy may be slightly (50.4%) lower because of the fact that surprises cannot be detected. In addition to the bunch of tasks that need to perform step by step; it takes a medium amount of time (20.4%) to provide the result [4]. The robotic technique has higher reliability and accuracy for its accuracy for its correct observation and performance. Inbuilt features rise to lower scalability and the teaching-learning process gives rise to lower latency. The continuous presence of therapist during presence leads to medium security. Deep learning based EEG technique has more scalability and latency compared to the robotic technique due to continuous detection of the facial affect of Avatars through 28 trials. Higher security and reliability are there as it extracts EEG signals directly from the brain. Figure 4 shows the graphical view of different emotion detection methods.

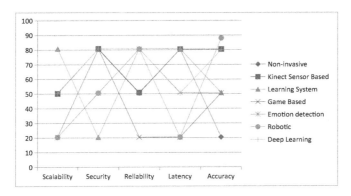

Fig. 4. Graphical representation of the methods for emotion detection through Facial analysis

Table 3. Benefits and limitations of different existing methods

Authors	Method used	Benefit	Limitation
Abirached [2]	1. Generic rig creation through pipeline 2. AAM model	Emotional state identification through facial expression	Lack in friendliness and uses of the model
Li [1]	1. Microsoft Kinect sensor 2. Video game	Control of emotions	Shortfall of sensor accuracy when children moves
Lacroix [4]	Label, Matching, Identification task	Emotional State recognition	Unable to recognize emotions when faced with uncommon situations
Chen [5]	AR system with 3D face modeling	Facial status determination	Shortness of participants with the need of more accuracy
Cheng [6]	3CFER system with 3D humanoid character	Examine the emotions	Fails in identification of emotions like nervousness and embarrassment
Heni [3]	World of Kids FER and ASR	Emotion detection learning concepts	Inaccuracy in ASR when interact with noise
Del Coco [7]	HOG, CLNF, PDM for facial recognition, landmark detection and multi face tracking	Facial actions are extracted to determine emotions	Scarcity in systematic application of data and addition of facial cues like gaze
Jazouli [8]	Microsoft Kinect sensor, $P recognizer	Recognition of facial expression	Absence of database for autistic children, more accuracy in system
Silva [9]	Intel Real 3D sensor ZECA	Recognition of expression	Insufficient accuracy in the sensor
Fan et al. [25]	EEG, Bayes network, SVM, Naive Bayes, ANN, KNN, Random forest, Decision tree	Recognition of facial affects	Deficiency in detecting effectiveness regarding EEG signal

Table 3 will give a reasonable thought of the distinctive strategies utilized in regards to the detection of emotions together through facial appearances with the benefits usually found using the respective methods. Table 4 shows the various algorithms and their purposes of different methodologies.

Table 4. Details of facial emotion based detection

Algorithm used	Purpose	Emotions	Methodology	Number of features
Conditional Local Neural Field Model (CLM) [7]	Extraction of facial data to detect emotions and differences from typical children	Happiness, Fear, Sadness	(i) Support Vector Machine (ii) Support Vector Regression (iii) Conditional Local Neural Field	(i) Histogram of Oriented gradients (HOG)
(i) Hidden Markov Model (ii) Dynamic Bayesian Network [8] (iii) Eigen Face Classification	Recognition of seven basic emotions	Happiness, Anger, Sadness, Surprise, Fear, Disgust, Neutral	(i) $P recognizer, (ii) Microsoft Kinect Sensor	Animation Units (AU), Feature Point Position (FPP)
Augmented Reality Based Model [5]	Judgment of emotions through faces	Happiness, Sadness, Fear, Disgust, Surprise, Anger	(i) Facial Action Coding System (ii) 3D modeling and animation software based pipeline	3D Facial Model feature, Facial feature
(i) Microsoft Kinect Sensor Toolkit (SDK) (ii) Application Programming Interfaces (API) [1]	Reactions to various game scenarios are recorded, monitored and assessed to find emotions	Happy, Excited, Tender, Scared, Anger, Sad, Happy	(i) Kinect Sensor Analyzer, (ii) Therapeutic games	Position of head point, face contour, RGB Data, Depth Data
Linear Regression Model [4]	Choosing the best facial expression that matches with the emotion	Happiness, Fear, Anger, Sadness, Surprise, Neutral	Presentation version 9.90 software	Chronological Age, Verbal Mental Age
Active Approach Model [2]	Make autistic child learn about emotions through facial expression in serious games	Happiness, Sadness, Fear, Disgust, Surprise, Anger	AVATAR	Facial features, Facial intensity and their dynamics

(continued)

Table 4. (*continued*)

Algorithm used	Purpose	Emotions	Methodology	Number of features
N.A. [6]	Recognize emotions through facial expression in Mobile Learning System	Surprise, Pride, Jealousy	(i) 3DCFER (ii) Android 1.5 Platform	Complex Emotion Scale (CE) Complex Emotion Pictures (CEP) Situation Pictures (SP)
Support Vector Machine (SVM) [9]	Identifying various emotions through facial expressions by taking the help of robots	Anger, Fear, Happiness, Sadness, Surprise, Neutral	(i) ZECA (ii) Intel Real Sensor 3D sensor (iii) Mirror Emotion System (iv) Emotion Recognition System	Facial Action Units, Neck Angles
(i) FER (ii) ASR [3]	Recognizing various emotions by recording facial and voice expressions while playing games	Happiness, Sadness, Fear, Disgust, Surprise, Anger	World of Kids	Arousal Level Valence stages, Medium degree of arousal
(i) Machine Learning algorithm (ii) Higuchi algorithm (iii) Artifact removal algorithm (iv) Supervised Machine Learning algorithm [24]	Recognizing facial affects of ASD children	Joy, Sadness, Fear, Surprise, Anger, Neutral	Computer assisted technologies, EEG, Unity Game Engine, Bayes Network, SVM, Naive Bayes, ANN, KNN, Random Forest, Decision tree	Social vignette feature, Baseline feature, Facial expression feature, Statistical feature, HOG based feature, Power feature

5   Discussion

In this paper, we have introduced various methods of detecting emotions through facial expression that includes the mixture of different algorithms in order to find their particular accuracy, scalability, security, reliability, and latency. Autistic children having dysfunction in sensory motors or motor anatomy does not able to cope up with the process of analyzation. But Kinect sensor being a touchless scores positive for autistic children to continue with the process. Kinect sensor when integrated with educatory games helps the autistic children to learn about expressing emotions by establishing a visually based method. The autistic children, being different from normal ones prefer visual learning. Learning system or emotion detection based technique though finds to be highly reliable is a long time learning process and the time required to involve attentively in the learning process totally depends on the capacity of the user. Deep Learning based EEG techniques are also newly emerging techniques to extract signals from brains through electrodes. But autistic children do not prefer to wear caps or electrodes and mostly feels uncomfortable. This puts a barrier for a proper continuation of behavioral analysis. Thus Kinect sensor based technique is the most optimal technique for detecting autism. But every method has its disadvantage. Sometimes inattentiveness of autistic children rises to false detection of faces through sensors and results in wrong emotion classification. So the Kinect based sensor should be accurate enough and provides high sensitivity to capture the faces and compute the facial features points and animation units. The therapists and researcher should be much more attentive to make the children sit in proper position during face detection.

6   Conclusion

Different researches studies have shown that early intervention services on children with autism spectrum disorders show significant improvements in different parts of communication. In our paper we have discussed popular existing facial emotion detection techniques and analysis of performance metrics for various techniques. The various tables and graphs have described as well as compared the different methodologies and their algorithms to find out the better method in the era. The work also deals with all the benefits limitations of different methods to find their respective future scopes. Among all the existing approaches, Kinect sensors were proved to be the best one which when integrated with educatory games comes up with the best emotion detection methodology by providing far interests among autistic children through visual based method. There is a need to focus future research initiatives in the area of ASD in the following areas: (i) Exploration of neurobiological substrates using assessments like neuroimaging, neuropsychological profile, eye movement recording etc. (ii) Development and validation of effective screening and early intervention modules. (iii) Development and validation of psycho education and treatment manuals for parents of children with ASD.

Acknowledgments. The paper is one of the review paper of behavioral analysis of the autistic child before starting my implementation to diagnose the autistic child. I want to express my most profound thankfulness to each one of the individuals who has given me the likelihood to complete the paper. An exceptional appreciation I provide for my guide and my co-guide in invigorating recommendations and support, helped me to organize my point particularly in composing this paper. I would like to express my gratitude to the dean of my college for being a greater part to complete my paper.

References

1. Li, Y., Elmaghraby, A.S.: A Framework for using games for behavioral analysis of autistic children. In: Computer Games: AI, Animation, Mobile, Multimedia, Educational and Serious Games (CGAMES), pp. 1–4. IEEE, Louisville (2014)
2. Abirached, B., et al.: Improving communication skills of children with ASDs through interaction with visual characters. In: 1st International Conference on Serious Games and Applications for Health (SeGAH), pp. 1–4. IEEE, Braga (2011)
3. Heni, N., Hamam, H.: Design of emotional educational system mobile games for autistic children. In: 2nd International Conference on Advanced Technologies for Signal and Image Processing, pp. 631–637. IEEE, Monastir (2016)
4. Lacroix, A., Guidette, M., Roge, B., Reilly, J.: Facial emotion recognition in 4-to 8-year-olds with autism spectrum disorder: A developmental trajectory approach. Res. Autism Spectr. Disord. 8(9), 1146–1154 (2014)
5. Chen, C.H., Lee, I.J., Lin, L.Y.: Augmented reality-based self-facial modeling to promote the emotional expression and social skills of adolescents with autism spectrum disorders. Res. Dev. Disabil. 36(8), 396–403 (2014)
6. Cheng, Y., Luo, S.Y., Lin, H.C.: Investigating the performance on comprehending 3D social emotion through a mobile learning system for individuals with autistic spectrum disorder. In: 5th IIAI International Congress on Advanced Applied Informatics, pp. 414–417. IEEE, Kumamoto (2016)
7. Del Coco, M., et al.: A computer vision based approach for understanding emotional involvements in children with autism spectrum disorders. In: International Conference on Computer Vision Workshops, pp. 1401–1407. IEEE, Venice (2017)
8. Jazouli, M., Majda, A., Zarghili, A.: A $P recognizer for automatic facial emotion recognition using Kinect sensor. In: Intelligent Systems and Computer Vision (ISCV), pp. 402–406. IEEE, Fez (2017)
9. Silva, V., Soares, F., Esteves, J.S.: Mirroring and recognizing emotions through facial expressions for a RoboKind platform. In: 5th Portuguese Meeting on Bioengineering (ENBENG), pp. 1–4. IEEE, Coimbra (2017)
10. Griffiths, S., Jarrold, C., Penton-Voak, I.S., Woods, A.T., Skinner, A.L., Munafò, M.R.: Impaired recognition of basic emotions from facial expressions in young people with autism spectrum disorder. J. Autism Dev. Disord. 47, 1–11 (2017)
11. Trigeorgis, G., et al.: Adieu features?: End-to-end speech emotion recognition using a deep convolutional recurrent network. In: International Conference on Acoustics, Speech and Signal Processing (ICASSP), pp. 5200–5204. IEEE, Sanghai (2016)
12. Gong, Y., Poellabauer, C.: Continuous assessment of children's emotional states using acoustic analysis. In: International Conference on Healthcare Informatics (ICHI), pp. 5200–5204. IEEE, Park City Park City (2017)
13. Tzirakis, P., Trigeorgis, G., Nicolaou, M.A., Schuller, B.W., Zafeiriou, S.: End-to-end multimodal emotion recognition using deep neural networks. IEEE J. Sel. Top. Sig. Process. 11(6), 1301–1309 (2017)
14. Mollahosseini, A., Chan, D., Mahoor, M.H.: Going deeper in facial expression recognition using deep neural networks. In: IEEE Winter Conference on Applications of Computer Vision (WACV), pp. 1–10. IEEE, Lake Placid (2016)
15. Yeung, M.K., Han, Y.M.Y., Sze, S.L., Chan, A.S.: Altered right frontal cortical connectivity during facial emotion recognition in children with autism spectrum disorders. Res. Autism Spect. Disord. 8(11), 1567–1577 (2014)

16. Rodriguez-Bermudez, G., Garcia-Laencina, P.: Analysis of EEG signals using nonlinear dynamics and chaos: a review. Appl. Math. Inf. Sci. Int. J. Nat. Sci. **9**(5), 2309–2321 (2015)
17. Othmana, M., Wahaba, A., Karima, I., Dzulkifli, M.A., Alshaiklia, I.F.T.: EEG emotion recognition based on the dimensional models of emotions. Proc. Soc. Behav. Sci. **97**, 30–37 (2013)
18. Black, M.H., et al.: Mechanisms of facial emotion recognition in autism spectrum disorders: insights from eye tracking and electroencephalography. Neurosci. Biobehav. Rev. **80**, 488–515 (2017)
19. Jamil, N., Khir, N.H.M., Ismail, M., Razak, F.H.A.: Gait-based emotion detection of children with autism spectrum disorders: a preliminary investigation. Proc. Comput. Sci. **76**, 342–348 (2015)
20. Zhou, Y., Yu, F., Duong, T.: Multiparametric MRI characterization and prediction in autism spectrum disorder using graph theory and machine learning. PlosOne **9**(6), 1–14 (2014)
21. Leo, M., Del Coco, M., Carcagn, P., Distante, C.: Automatic emotion recognition in robot-children interaction for ASD Treatment. In: IEEE International Conference on Computer Vision Workshop (ICCVW), pp. 537–545. IEEE, Santiago (2015)
22. Swangnetr, M., Kaber, D.B.: Emotional state classification in patient–robot interaction using wavelet analysis and statistics-based feature selection. IEEE Trans. Hum.-Mach. Syst. **43**(1), 63–75 (2013)
23. Soares, F., et al.: Robotica-Autismo project: technology for autistic children. In: 3rd Portuguese Meeting in Bioengineering IEEE (ENBENG), pp. 1–4. IEEE, Braga (2013)
24. Fan, J., Bekele, E., Warren, Z., Sarkar, N.: EEG analysis of facial affect recognition process of individuals with ASD performance prediction leveraging social context. In: Seventh International Conference on Affective Computing and Intelligent Interaction Workshops and Demos (ACIIW), pp. 38–43. IEEE, San Antonio (2017)
25. Li, B.Y., Mian, A.S., Liu, W., Krishna, A.: Using Kinect for face recognition under varying poses, expressions, illumination and disguise. In: IEEE Workshop on Applications of Computer Vision (WACV), pp. 186–192. IEEE, Tampa (2013)
26. Manfredonia, J., et al.: Automatic recognition of posed facial expression of emotion in individuals with autism spectrum disorder. J. Autism Dev. Disord. **49**(1), 279–293 (2019)
27. Golan, O., Gordon, I., Fichman, K., Keinan, G.: Specific patterns of emotion recognition from faces in children with ASD: results of a cross-modal matching paradigm. J. Autism Dev. Disord. **48**(3), 844–852 (2018)

Smart Learning System Based on EEG Signals

Aaditya Sharma[✉], Swadha Gupta[✉], Sawinder Kaur[✉],
and Parteek Kumar[✉]

Department of Computer Science and Engineering,
Thapar Institute of Engineering and Technology, Patiala, India
aadityaja@gmail.com, swadhagupta15@gmail.com,
sawindekaurvohra@gmail.com, parteek.bhatia@thapar.edu

Abstract. According to recent trends in information technology, classroom learning is transformed to Web based learning. This transformation helps learner to trigger digital technologies anywhere and anytime. This paper plan to build a system that can harness the power of the brain and build smart and meaningful applications to make life easier. The major problem is emerged during online education is loose the learner's active attention after some duration of time. This leads to the user getting distracted without having any mechanism to provide him with a feedback, as a result, online learning is not getting as much effective as classroom learning. Therefore, EEG device is used for data acquisition, to measure EEG signals and also to monitor the attention levels of user. Proposed project will collect the EEG data to calculate various parameters such as concentration level, attention level, etc. These parameters will be used in the smart applications to provide real-time analysis and feedback to the user. This technology will provide real-time feedback user who has enrolled in MOOCs. This should foresee whether the student struggles or not while learning to give convenient alarms.

Keywords: E-learning · EEG · MOOCs · Classroom education

1 Introduction

Advancement in technology leads to open various opportunities to enhance instructional procedures as well as e-learning platforms. Language learning relies upon intelligent guidance, tweaked learning maps, checking frameworks, or more all commitment and inspiration. In conventional classroom educating, an educator can pass judgment on the learning dimension of understudies by their signals and can alter according to students' pace. However, in web-based educating, the educator can't know consistently that student is really understanding the content or not. In this way, it has turned out to be important to consider intelligent tutoring system, where it can survey that how profoundly student is considering while at the same time learning. The analysts are taking a shot at this plan to construct a framework that can consequently gauge cognitive load (CL) progressively and streamline its systems to promote intrinsic cognitive load.

Brainwaves are profoundly connected with one's psychological state, including the level of concentration, emotional state, and degree of relaxation. Electroencephalograms

© Springer Nature Singapore Pte Ltd. 2019
M. Singh et al. (Eds.): ICACDS 2019, CCIS 1046, pp. 465–476, 2019.
https://doi.org/10.1007/978-981-13-9942-8_44

(EEG) are a non-invasive neuroimaging method used to gauge the electrical movement of neurons in the mind utilizing electrodes put on the scalp.

Ongoing advancements in EEG innovation, for example, dry cathodes and remote transmission, have made it conceivable to apply these gadgets in the field of training to screen the psychological status of students occupied with learning.

The EEG device is used for data acquisition and to measure EEG signals and to monitor the attention levels of user as they interact with complex problems. Use of EEG is to capture the alpha and beta brain waves and analyze them with our machine learning models. To accomplish the above vision and goal, knowledge of the CL of a user can play a very crucial rule. CL relates to the effort being and amount of data that the working memory holds at one time. Cognitive load theory can be used by the tutors to design and improve the learning course materials, so that the learning material can be presented at a pace and at a level that is easy for the learner to understand.

1.1 Cognitive Load Theory (CLT)

CLT is based upon the broadly acknowledged model of human data handling. Three primary parts human data processing are shown in Fig. 1.

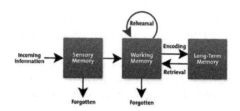

Fig. 1. Cognitive load theory (CLT)

The sensory memory keeps information about the relevant data and later transfer this information to working memory. The transferred information is either processed or discarded. The working memory of the brain can hold up to nine chunks of information at any one time. This is central to Cognitive Load Theory.

The brain starts processing information, after this it categorizes that information and moves it into long-term memory, where it is stored in schemas. The human concepts and their habits are built on these schemas. There are three types of cognitive load:

a. **Intrinsic load:** It is characterized as the essential cognitive load required to carry out a task. It is specifically relative to the trouble of the assignment and contrarily corresponding to the level of aptitude of the user.
b. **Extraneous load:** It is characterized as the squandered cognitive load that does not identify with the essential psychological learning exercises but rather rises reluctantly. It is caused by elements that are not vital to the material to be adapted, for example, introduction techniques or exercises that part consideration between

numerous wellsprings of data. Instructional techniques ought to abstain from overburdening it with extra exercises that don't straightforwardly add to learning.

c. **Germane load:** It is characterized as the load utilized for adapting, for example, for developing schema activities. These components help to encourage the advancement of a student's learning base. Every one of these loads ought to be inside the working memory.

1.2   Methodology Used

In this section, the various methodologies that have been used for the design and analysis of the application have been mentioned. Our project is majorly based CLT and we are also using EEG to collect data from the user. The proposed device when worn by the user will keep on analyzing the alpha and beta waves to measure the attention of the user. It will trigger an alert when the concentration falls under a specific threshold

CL theory is based upon the broadly acknowledged model of data handling. Three primary parts human data processing are the sensory memory, working memory, and long-term memory.

Consistently, we are barraged with heaps of tactile data on daily basis. The sensory memory keeps information about the relevant data and later transfer this information to working memory. The transferred information is either processed or discarded. The working memory of the brain can hold up to nine chunks of information at any one time.

In the human cerebrum, every individual neuron speaks with the others by sending small electrochemical signs. At the point when a huge number of neurons are enacted, each contributing with little electrical flow, they produce a flag that is solid enough to be recognized by an EEG device. The ongoing accessibility of basic, minimal effort and compact EEG observing gadgets makes it conceivable to take this innovation from the lab into schools/universities.

These devices collect the data from human scalp by putting electrodes at number of positions. It is a universally perceived strategy to portray and apply the area of scalp electrodes with regards to an EEG test or trial. This framework depends on the connection between the location of an electrode and the hidden zone of the cerebral cortex. 10% or 20% of the aggregate front–back or right–left separation of the skull. The variation of this standard is known as Modified Combinatorial Nomenclature.

Since EEG signals are exceptionally frail and normally contain a considerable measure of noise. Therefore, these signs should be intensified and separated. To evacuate potential EEG antiquities, regularly band-pass channel 3–100 Hz is connected to the crude EEG signal. A Notch channel can likewise be connected to dispose of electrical noises from the power source, which fluctuates from 50 to 60 Hz relying upon the geological location (Table 1).

Table 1. Summary and research studies

S. No	Paper title	Tools/Technology	Findings	Citation
1	Brain machine interface system automation considering user preferences and error perception feedback	Machine learning, Deep learning, BCI, EEG	Experiments were done to design BCI systems that gradually become autonomous	Penaloza et al. [1]
2	Machine learning based detection of user specific brain states	Machine learning and BCI	System robustly transfers The discrimination of mental states	Blankertz et al. [2]
3	On the need for online learning in brain-computer interfaces	BCI and EEG processing	Performance is increased	Millan [3]
4	Toward brain-computer interfacing	Survey on EEG dataset	Research indicates there are several approaches that may provide alternatives for individuals with severe motor disabilities	Dornhege et. al. [4]
5	General signal processing and machine learning tools for BCI	Machine learning and EEG	Tested various regression and classification machine learning algorithms	Dornhege et al. [5]
6	Speed control of Festo Robotino mobile robot using NeuroSky MindWave EEG headset based brain-computer interface	Neurosky, EEG and BCI	Implementing speed control using neurosky, have been finished with positive results	Katona et al. [6]
7	Evaluating the ergonomics of BCI devices for research and experimentation	BCI, EEG	Compared various ergonomics of 2 different BCI devices	Ekandem et al. [7]
8	EEG-based brain controlled prosthetic arm	BCI, EEG, Robotics	The movement of the finger can be controlled	Bright et al. [8]
9	Brain robot using neurosky mindwave	Robotics, EEG, BCI	ROBOT will move forward when attention and ROBOT will move backward when meditation value crosses a certain limit	Tiwari and Saini [9]
10	A user-friendly wearable single channel EOG-based human-computer interface for cursor control	Neurosky, BCI, EEG	The NeuroSky MindWave headset can control cursor navigations and actions	Ang et. al. [10]

(*continued*)

Table 1. (*continued*)

S. No	Paper title	Tools/Technology	Findings	Citation
11	A wearable real-time BCI system based on mobile cloud computing	Cloud computing, BCI, EEG	Facial expression interface can indicate the user's mental States according to the analysis of EEG data on the server	Blondet *et al.* [11]
12	Replacing the computer mouse	BCI, EEG and machine learning	It shows ways to move mouse cursors and clicks using BCI	Dernoncourt [12]
13	A novel EEG for alpha brain state training, neurobiofeedback and behavior change	EEG, BCI	Alpha brain waves were used to provide real time, Easily interpretable feedback to the user	Stinson and Arthur [13]
14	Brain-controlled home automation system	Raspberry Pi, EEG device, IOT	Able to control various appliance like light bulbs using raspberry pi and AWS	Ghodake and Shelke [14]

1.3   Literature Survey

In human brain, every individual neuron communicates with the others by passing a small electrochemical signs. At the point when a huge number of neurons are enacted, each contributing with little electrical flow, they produce a flag that is solid enough to be recognized by an EEG device. These devices collect the data from human scalp by putting electrodes at number of positions. The positions to gauge EEG signals are characterized by the International 10–20 system. It is a universally perceived strategy to depict and apply the location of scalp electrodes with regards to an EEG test or analysis. This framework depends on the connection between the location of the electrode and the basic zone of the cerebral cortex.

An extensive review of literature was done in order to study already existing work and the kind of research that is being done in the field. Penaloza *et al.* [1] addresses the problem of mental fatigue caused by the excessive use of brain machine interface systems. Blankertz *et al.* [2] talked about how BCI can be used to translate brain signals to commands. Millan [3] mentioned the use of BCI in online learning to improve the learning process. Dornhege *et al.* [4] gave a detailed analysis of the use and improvements in the field of brain computer interface. Dornhege *et al.* [5] addressed the issue of noise in EEG data and how can it be removed or minimized to the maximum. It mentions how signal processing can be used to improve the quality of the data. Katona *et al.* [6] and Ekandem *et al.* [7] mentions the use of neurosky headset. The same headset is being used by the smart learning system. Bright *et al.* [8] mentions how BCI can be used in understanding various human thoughts and shows how it is used in controlling a prosthetic arm. Tiwari and Saini [9] mentions the use of neurosky mindwave eeg device to control a robot. Ang *et al.* [10] and Blondet *et al.* [11] addresses the development in the field of portable and low-cost EEG devices and how such devices can be made. Dernoncourt [12] showed how BCI can be used to control a mouse cursor and replaced the traditional mouse cursor by an EEG device. Stinson and Arthur [13] gave a deep analysis of how EEG devices are being used to detect calmness in the human body and provide feedback to the user about the state of mind. Ghodake and Shelke [14] proposed a home automation system using brain computer interface that uses EEG device.

2 Methodology Adopted

2.1 Investigative Techniques

Experimental investigation technique was enforced on this system to get the best possible accuracy with the as minimum latency as possible. Various machine learning model was used on the data generated to get the best possible result. The devised algorithm was able to give real-time results with best accuracy.

2.2 Proposed Solution

The proposed solution consists of a web application and a device which when worn by the user will keep on analyzing the alpha and beta waves to measure the attention of the user. It will trigger an alert when the concentration falls under a specific threshold along with monitoring the eye movements of the user. This will make sure that the user is able to get constant feedback from the system according to his performance and the system will adopt the appropriate pedagogy to adjust to the users' learning curve and hence improving the overall learning experience of the user (Fig. 2).

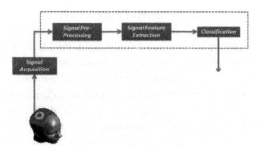

Fig. 2. EEG data processing

3 Design Specifications

3.1 System Architecture

The architecture of our system is divided into 2 parts which are interdependent on each other. One is our MVC structure and other is the web application which talks to the desktop application. Figure 3 shows the basic system architecture and Fig. 4 shows the MVC architecture.

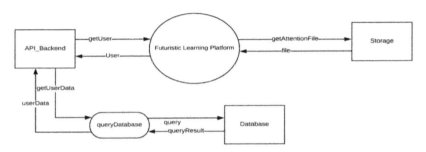

Fig. 3. System architecture

The user comes to the smart learning platform with an EEG device connected to the system. To fetch the required videos by the user several backend APIs are called. The user opens the desktop app where he enters the video id and obtains the analysis of his performance.

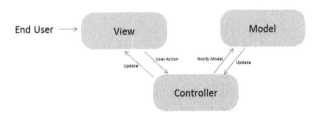

Fig. 4. MVC architecture

Model-View-Controller is a software design pattern or a software development methodology. The main objective of this architecture is to promote code usability and also to implement separation of concerns so that the software becomes easily testable. There are 3 components Model, View, and Controller.

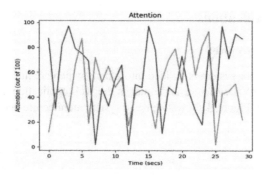

Fig. 5. Analysis of EEG data

The above Fig. 5 is a visual representation of the user attention level compared with the average attention level of all the users.

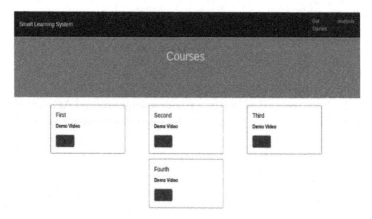

Fig. 6. Screenshot of web app

The above Fig. 6 shows the available courses on the platform. The users can click on the course of their choice and watch online lectures for that particular course.

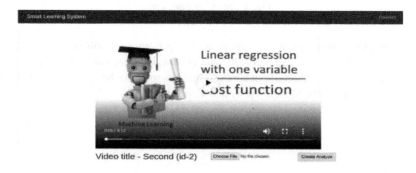

Fig. 7. Video player of web app

The above Fig. 7 shows the screenshot of the video player where the user will watch lectures of the courses of their choice.

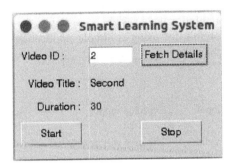

Fig. 8. Desktop app

The Fig. 8 shows the desktop app where the user is the required type the id of the video they are watching to get the analysis of their performance.

4   Experimental Results

4.1   Experimental Setup and Simulation

EEG device: The Neurosky Mindwave EEG device has flexible rubber sensor arms and rounded forehead sensor tip, T-shaped headband, and ear clip contacts. The user will wear the device on the forehead and connect the device with the laptop through Bluetooth.

Web Application: After connecting the device the user has to open the web application on the laptop and start a lecture of choice. There is a desktop app where the user has to enter the id of the video lecture that he is watching to get a detailed analysis of his performance and attention level.

4.2   Experimental Analysis

4.2.1   Data

The data in the application is generated by the EEG device which reads the brain waves and then converts them into numeric data which is further processed by the application to convert it from raw EEG data to usable and clean data.

4.2.2   Performance Parameters

- Time Delay: Time between notification alerts is taken as one of the important performance parameters. The lesser the delay the more the efficiency of the system. The time delay occurs during transmission of the signal from the surveillance area to the app via a server or vice versa.

- Accuracy: The accuracy of the EEG data and the calculation of the performance of the user are also an important parameter that can generate unexpected results if not taken into consideration.
- Ease of use: Ultimately user is the one who will benefit from the system. So, it becomes more important to make a system according to the user's perspective. Our system takes care of this by using a simple application that can be modified according to user behavior.

4.2.3   Test Cases

S. No.	Test Case	Input	Expected output	Actual output	Result
1	The user enters a valid video id	Valid video id	The user will be able to generate an analysis of the attention level	Analysis generated	Successful
2	The user enters an invalid video id	Invalid video id	The desktop app will show −1 in video title and duration	−1 is shown on the desktop app	Successful
3	User presses pause/stop button	Button pressed	Data will not be written to the file	Data is not written on the file	Successful
4	User uploads data	Data file	Graphs will be displayed	Graphs are displayed	Successful

4.2.4   Test Results

All the test cases were successful. The application worked as expected and if there were any bug or corner cases, they were fixed while testing. Figures 9, 10, 11 and 12 shows the screenshots of the test cases.

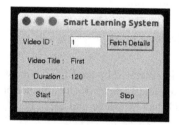

Fig. 9. Valid video id

Fig. 10. Invalid video id

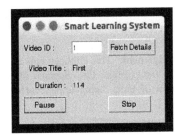

Fig. 11. Pausing the application

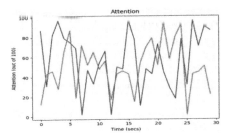

Fig. 12. Uploading the data

5 Conclusion and Future Directions

In this paper we developed a smart learning system based on EEG that has capabilities of monitoring the active attention of learner. The main focus to this paper is to enhance the progress of students by improving attention and concentration level. So, we have used EEG signal to calculate various parameters such as concentration level, attention level, etc. These parametric values further used for real-time analysis and provides feedback to the user. This system improves the learner's active attention during online learning. It may also use to improve learning through MOOCs, making driving safer, etc. Brain Computer Interface is prepared to significantly affect instruction, human services, diversion, security, and numerous different ventures and will no uncertainty advance our lives in manners we can't yet predict for ages to come. Currently, the EEG device gives good accuracy with data and analysis. But following features can be added and improved:

i. By applying machine learning algorithms, we can give better recommendations for the video lectures to the user. This will help them in learning efficiently.
ii. The collected of users can also be used to improve the online courses.
iii. The BCI technology can be used in different projects such as making brain controlled robots, giving attention triggers while driving, manipulating a computer cursor etc.

The EEG technology is still a huge research-oriented field and will continue to make immense leaps and bounds in the future. The tools like NeuroSky Mindwave and other EEG devices provide a low budget and user-friendly solution for conducting EEG oriented research.

Acknowledgement. This Publication is an outcome of the R&D work undertaken in the project under the Visvesvaraya PhD Scheme of Ministry of Electronics & Information Technology, Government of India, being implemented by Digital India Corporation (formerly Media Lab Asia).

References

1. Penaloza, C., Mae, Y., Cuellar, F., Kojima, M., Arai, T.: Brain machine interface system automation considering user preferences and error perception feedback. In: IEEE Transactions on Automation Science and Engineering, vol. 11, no. 4 (2014)
2. Blankertz, B., Dornhege, G., Lemm, S., Krauledat, M., Curio, G., Müller, K.: The Berlin brain-computer interface: machine learning based detection of user specific brain states. J. Univ. Computer. Sci. **12**(6), 581–607 (2006)
3. Millan, J.: On the need for on-line learning in brain-computer interfaces. MIT Press **38**(4), 34–41 (2004)
4. Dornhege, G., Millán, J., Hinterberger, T., McFarland, D., Müller, K.: Toward Brain-Computer Interfacing. MIT Press, Cambridge (2007)
5. Dornhege, G., Krauledat, M., Müller, K., Blankertz, B.: General signal processing and machine learning tools for BCI. In: Toward Brain-Computer Interfacing, pp. 207–233. MIT Press, Cambridge (2007)
6. Katona, J., Ujbanyi, T., Sziladi, G., Kovari, A.: Speed control of Festo Robotino mobile robot using NeuroSky MindWave EEG headset based brain-computer interface. In: 7th IEEE International Conference on Cognitive Infocommunications, pp. 000251–000257 (2016)
7. Ekandem, J., Davis, T., Alvarez, I., James, M., Gilbert, J.: Evaluating the ergonomics of BCI devices for research and experimentation. Ergonomics **55**, 592–598 (2012)
8. Bright, D., Nair, A., Salvekar, D., Bhisikar, S.: EEG-based brain controlled prosthetic arm. In: Advances in Signal Processing (CASP), pp. 479–483 (2016)
9. Tiwari, K., Saini, S.: Brain controlled robot using neurosky mindwave. J. Technol. Adv. Sci. Res. **1**(4), 328–331 (2015)
10. Ang, A., Zhang, Z., Hung, Y., Mak, J.: A user-friendly wearable single-channel EOG-based human-computer interface for cursor control. In: IEEE Engineering in Medicine and Biology Society Conference on Neural Engineering Montpellier, April 2015
11. Blondet, M., Badarinath, A., Khanna, C., Jin, Z.: A wearable real-time BCI system based on mobile cloud computing. IEEE, January 2014
12. Dernoncourt F.: Replacing the computer mouse. In: Presented at the Boston Accessibility Conference, Cambridge, USA (2012)
13. Stinson, B., Arthur, D.: A novel EEG for alpha brain state training, neurobiofeedback and behavior change. Complement. Ther. Clin. Pract. **19**, 114–118 (2013)
14. Ghodake, A., Shelke, S.D.: Brain controlled home automation system. In: 10th International Conference on Intelligent Systems and Control (ISCO), pp. 1–4 (2016)
15. Eldenfria, A., Al-Samarraie, H.: The effectiveness of an online learning system based on aptitude scores: an effort to improve students' brain activation. Educ. Inf. Technol. **2019**, 1–15 (2019)

Optical Character and Font Recognizer

Manan Rajdev, Diksha Sahay, Shambhavi Khare,
and Sumita Nainan[✉]

Electronics and Telecommunication, Mukesh Patel School of Technology
Management & Engineering, Mumbai, India
mananrajdev.nmims@gmail.com, sumita.nainan@nmims.edu

Abstract. Optical Character and Font Recognizer focuses primarily on building a complete model for document processing. The proposed system recognizes
the font style along with the text from an image of certain resolution. The system
uses principles of both machine learning and image processing to obtain the
desired results. The model uses Contour selection for character extraction and
K-Nearest Neighbor approach for character and font recognition. With the
assistance of the proposed system using the mentioned techniques, scanned
documents can be altered or the font style of a particular document can be
known as desired. Many models that perform character recognition are present
but a model that performs both character and font recognition with good
accuracy is difficult to find. The experiment resulted in 87% overall accuracy for
detection of characters.

Keywords: OCR · OFR · Text recognition · K-NN · Contour ·
Character-line extraction

1 Introduction

Optical Character Recognition (OCR) refers to the conversion of printed, handwritten
or typewritten texts that are scanned into machine-encoded texts [5]. This technology
uses an optical mechanism for the automatic recognition of characters from a provided
text material.

Optical Font Recognition involves the detection of the font styles in the documents.
A particular document may comprise of different font styles for the titles and the main
text [3]. Thus, font recognition helps in identification of the multiple fonts that are used
in documents. This technology can be widely used for documents whose special feature
is the font style and the font style detection can be used as a guide for automatic
classification of the documents. This technology holds vast applications in different
fields such as converting scanned documents, PDF files and digital images into editable
format. This technology also has a major application in banking sector, where OCR is
used to process demand drafts or cheques without human involvement. OCR further
simplifies the process by making documents text-searchable, so that the words are
easier to locate and work with in a database [5]. Since the documents are made text
searchable, OCR can be used in the medical field as well, where the professionals have
to deal with huge numbers of data pertaining to a certain patient. Only the desired and

© Springer Nature Singapore Pte Ltd. 2019
M. Singh et al. (Eds.): ICACDS 2019, CCIS 1046, pp. 477–486, 2019.
https://doi.org/10.1007/978-981-13-9942-8_45

required set of data can be stored in the electronic database and accessed when required. OFR on the other hand is of great use in the field of digital designing where new and attractive fonts could be identified easily. It also has a great demand in the corporate sector as the knowledge of font helps in replicating the documents if required. Section 1 introduces the paper briefly followed by the different ideologies and research work that led to the paper are discussed under Sect. 2 and the background of the work in Sect. 3. The implementation is broadly discussed under Sect. 4 describing elaborately as to how the project works thus providing the outputs that are discussed in Sect. 5 under the Results. Further discussions are carried out under Sect. 5 followed by Sect. 6 that finally concludes discussing the efficiency and the future scope of the project.

2 Literature Review

There are several approaches for text detection and recognizing from image, which have been developed in the past. Most methods require principles of both image processing and machine learning. Before the detection of font or characters starts, edge detection can be used to find the areas in an image where text is present. This will help in separating text from graphical designs [1]. The detection of fonts and characters has mainly two approaches; firstly, the priori approach where the recognition of font takes place prior to the recognition of characters or text [2] and secondly, the posteriori approach, which was used in this experiment, where the font recognition occurs after the character recognition which worked efficiently for a Multi-font OCR system [3]. The process of text recognition involved several steps including pre-processing, segmentation, feature extraction, classification, post processing [4]. It can also be done via character extraction and feature matching using texture and topological feature [5]. The 8-connected component method can be implemented in order to find the characters in the image and recognize them after binarization of the image [6]. After the recognition of character, font recognition begins which can be done in three ways. First, using distance profile features with respect to left, right and diagonal directions of a character image [7]. Second, using a weighted Euclidean distance classifier where the text document is taken as an image file. The characters would contain some specific textures, and hence the font recognition is done with the help of texture identification [8]. Third, an approach which aims at the identification of the typeface, weight, slope and size of the text from an image block based on global typographical features [9]. The process of recognition of a character or font after the extraction of features through the methods and approaches discussed above is done through machine learning algorithms. Machine learning can be used to identify certain frequency words and predominant font [10] or it can be used for classification and recognition of separate characters and fonts using different approaches, one of them being Support Vector Machine where data sets are used for training the SVM Database and the trained network is used for classification and further for recognition [11]. The other method is K means clustering which is a simple unsupervised learning clustering algorithm. It can learn the features automatically from unlabeled data and allows the construction of highly effective linear classifiers for both detection and recognition of text [12]. K- Nearest Neighbor can also be used if proper labels are known, as it is supervised learning algorithm [13]. Furthermore, a set of feedforward neural networks can be used to improve the character recognition in case of similar character confusion [14]. Neural networks can also be used to enhance the capability of the system to recognize handwritten text [15]. In the next section, the terminologies of the experiment as well as the approach used are discussed.

3   Background and Terminologies

A brief discussion of the types of OCR and the different approaches are discussed in this section which provides a better understanding towards the implementation of the experiment.

3.1   Types of OCR

There are mainly three types of OCR on the basis of fonts present in an image or document. Each of them have different accuracy and are used for different applications [3].

Mono-font OCR: As the name suggests, it performs character recognition on images having text of a specific font. It requires separate font modules for each font. Accuracy is very high compared to other OCRs but separate modules require a lot of storage. Moreover, documents containing different font styles reduce the accuracy.

Multi-font OCR: It is an intermediate type of OCR in which characters can be recognised from an image of document containing a subset of fonts. The accuracy and complexity depend on the number and the similarity of fonts taken into consideration. As the number of fonts increases, accuracy and complexity increases as well. But if similarity between letters of different font increases, the accuracy decreases.

Omni-font OCR: Image of documents involving characters of combination of fonts can be recognised by such type of OCR. It does not contain a subset of fonts and can recognise various fonts in a single image. The accuracy is very low and complexity is relatively high.

3.2   Approach

Priori: The Priori involves the recognition or identification of fonts taking place prior to the recognition of characters or text i.e. operation of OFR is done prior to OCR [2]. This approach helps in character recognition as knowing the font prior will help in the detection of characters.

Posteriori: The Posteriori involves the recognition or identification of font taking place after the recognition of characters or text i.e. operation of OFR is done after the OCR [2]. This approach acts as an additional feature/application to OCR. It is less complex compared to other approach as the context is already known. The flowchart shown in

Fig. 1 is a graphical representation of the steps involved in posteriori and priori approaches.

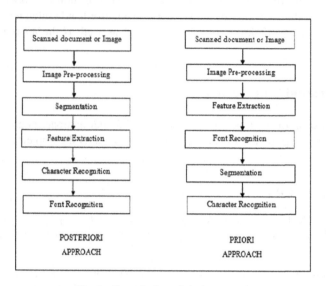

Fig. 1. Posteriori vs. Priori approach

The experiment was performed using Posteriori approach. Once the character was recognized, it was matched with different fonts of the same letter to find its font. The character recognition classifier does not require specific training each time a new font has to be recognized. It would be an ominous classifier which can recognize any letter irrespective of its font. Also, if the document contains more than one font then Posteriori approach plays a better role for character recognition. Moreover, the character recognition plays a more important role in document processing than font recognition.

3.3   Machine Learning Algorithm

The K-Nearest Neighbor machine learning algorithm was used in this paper to classify the characters. In the K-NN algorithm, 'K' stands for number of neighbors [13]. In this experiment a 1-NN machine learning algorithm was used to classify the characters and fonts. It is a supervised algorithm in which the result set is already available and the system knows the set of outputs i.e. letters for OCR and fonts for OFR. All the characters which were used for training were plotted according to their features. The test character was matched with all the available characters and the one which was the closest to the test character's feature was chosen as the result. The metric used for measuring the closeness is Euclidean distance. It measures the distance between the test point and cases from the training classes. If x and y are two points in Euclidean space and it is assumed that $x = (x1, x2, x3, x4 .... xk)$ and $y = (y1, y2, y3, y4 .... yk)$, then the Euclidean distance of line segment x-y is given in Eq. (1)

$$\sqrt{\sum_{i=1}^{k} (x_i - y_i)^2} \qquad (1)$$

The value of K in K-NN plays an important role in the classification process. The Fig. 2(a) shows a K-NN classifier with K = 1 whereas, the Fig. 2(b) has K = 5. In this algorithm, the output of the classifier is the class to which the majority of nearest neighbors belong. The output of Fig. 2(a) would be class 3 while the output of Fig. 2 (b) would be class 1. So, based on the utility and accuracy, the value of K is chosen. For the proper implementation and good accuracy, K was taken as 1 in this experiment.

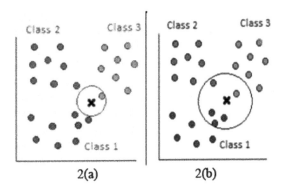

Fig. 2. K K-NN space representation where 2(a) represents K = 1 and 2(b) represents K = 5

4 Implementation

A Multi-font OCR system along with Euclidean distance as a classification function in a nearest neighbor approach (1-NN) algorithm was used for document processing which would perform both the character recognition and the font-style detection of **the digits** belonging to a subset of the existing fonts.

4.1 Character Recognition Implementation

The process consists of 5 major steps as follows:

- Image Pre-processing
- Line Extraction
- Character Extraction
- Training
- Testing

Image Preprocessing: The first step was to convert the test image to gray scale [4]. The conversion of grayscale to binary was based on adaptive threshold i.e. all pixels below a certain threshold value becomes 0 and above the threshold becomes 255.

After the conversion of the image to grayscale, it is smoothened using Gaussianblur function.

Line Extraction: For proper sequencing of the characters in a line and for lines in a paragraph, line extraction plays a crucial role. The image was converted to 1D array where the change in pixel intensity is used to detect the start and end of a line. These lines were extracted and character extraction performed on them simultaneously.

Character Extraction: In the character extraction process a rectangle is drawn around the characters which are to be recognized. The rectangle can be drawn only if the edges of the characters are known for which an edge detection technique was performed. Edge detection is an image processing technique used for finding the boundaries of objects within images [1]. It is used for image segmentation and data extraction in areas such as image processing, computer vision, and machine vision. In the experiment performed, edge detection was done through contour detection. A contour is a closed curve of points or line segments, representing the boundaries of an object in an image. It represents the shapes of objects found in an image.

Character extraction involved finding Contours followed by the bounding rectangle information. The Bounding information is followed by appending the entire contour to form a list. After the appending, the list is sorted from left to right for proper sequencing within a line. Then the individual character images are extracted and resized so that all images are of same dimensions and the converted to 1-D array. The Fig. 3 shows the bounding rectangle formation around the characters which were recognized.

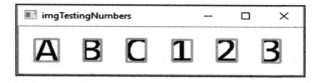

Fig. 3. Rectangular box formation in character extraction step

Training: Character extraction was followed by training the algorithm. A list of valid characters were made in which, the ASCII values of those characters were stored [4]. The image was trained using a particular image consisting of all the alphabets and digits of varying widths shown in Fig. 4. Characters were extracted from the training image and the user was required to press the same key on the keyboard as the character which was extracted and displayed on the screen. This classification list was converted to array of floats and stored as .txt file. The characters which were extracted were converted to 1-D array and stored in another .txt file as flattened image list.

Testing: The process of testing revolved around machine learning algorithm K-NN (with K = 1). This approach was used to classify the characters. Based on the classification and flattened image data, the testing characters were recognized.

```
0 1 2 3 4 5 6 7 8 9
A B C D E F G H I J K L M N O P Q R S T U V W X Y Z
0123456789
ABCDEFGHIJKLMNOPQRSTUVWXYZ
0 1 2 3 4 5 6 7 8 9
A B C D E F G H I J K L M N O P Q R S T U V W X Y Z
0 1 2 3 4 5 6 7 8 9
A B C D E F G H I J K L M N O P Q R S T U V W X Y Z
0 1 2 3 4 5 6 7 8 9
A B C D E F G H I J K L M N O P Q R S T U V W X Y Z
```

Fig. 4. Training image used for OCR

4.2   Font Recognition Implementation

There were 5 fonts which were chosen to be recognized by the OFR namely "Arial, Comic Sans, Calibri, Lucida Sans and Times New Roman". The reason for choosing these fonts was that they are most commonly used by public at various places such as newspapers, magazines, research papers, posters and pamphlets. Using all the letters for font recognition was a tedious task which increased complexity and computation time [7]. Hence, 6 different letters were chosen at random from the image as there were 5 fonts, so even in the worst-case scenario there was a majority. If the number of letters in the image were less than 6 then all of them were chosen. These letters were then stored as temporary images which are sent to the K-NN font classifier. For each of the letters, the classifier was trained on an image which contained the same letters in 5 different fonts. An example of such training image is shown in Fig. 5. The steps for training and testing of the classifier and the algorithm used for font recognition were same as that

```
ABCDEFGHIJKLMNOPQRSTUVWXYZ
a b c d e f g h i j k l m n o p q r s t u v w x y z
ABCDEFGHIJKLMNOPQRSTUVWXYZ
a b c d e f g h i j k l m n o p q r s t u v w x y z
ABCDEFGHIJKLMNOPQRSTUVWXYZ
a b c d e f g h i j k l m n o p q r s t u v w x y z
ABCDEFGHIJKLMNOPQRSTUVWXYZ
a b c d e f g h i j k l m n o p q r s t u v w x y z
ABCDEFGHIJKLMNOPQRSTUVWXYZ
a b c d e f g h i j k l m n o p q r s t u v w x y z
```

Fig. 5. Training image used for OFR; the first pair of rows is the alphabets written in Arial, followed by Calibri, Comic Sans, Lucida Sans and the last pair is Times New Roman

used for character recognition. As there were 6 letters extracted, this process provided 6 outputs. The font output which was in majority among the 5 fonts was chosen as the result of font recognition.

5 Result and Discussion

The section discusses the results obtained after the implementation and few notable discussions regarding the experiment. The input to the system was an image and the output was obtained on a python console as shown in the Fig. 6.

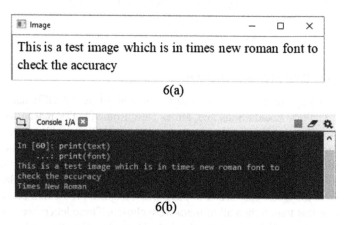

Fig. 6. The input to the system is shown in 6(a) and output in 6(b)

The Table 1 shows the accuracy of the OCR. A database consisting of 100 images (10 images each of uppercase, lowercase and digits and 70 images consisting of all the types of character) was used for the recognition process. It was inferred that uppercase letters were recognized with a better accuracy than the lowercase letters. The overall accuracy obtained was 87%.

Table 1. OCR accuracy table

OCR input	Accuracy
Uppercase	89.7%
Lowercase	86%
Digits	88.2%
Overall	87%

The low accuracy of the OCR was due to many reasons. Firstly, there were letters which were identical to some other character, like letter uppercase 'O' was identical to lowercase 'o' and zero '0', similarly, letter uppercase "I" was identical to lowercase "l" and digit "1". Secondly, during the line extraction, if some of the upper or lower part of the line were cropped, then OCR's accuracy was greatly affected; letters like lowercase "p" and "q", uppercase "Q" could be recognized as uppercase "O" or lowercase "o".

The Table 2 shows the accuracy of the OFR. A database consisting of 100 images was used which consisted of 10 images of each fonts in uppercase and 10 images of each font in lowercase. It can be observed that the accuracy was the highest for Comic Sans font as it could be easily distinguished from the others even through naked eyes. The probability was least for lowercase Calibri and Lucida Sans as most of the lowercase letters in both the fonts were similar.

Table 2. OCR accuracy table

Fonts	Uppercase accuracy	Lowercase accuracy
Arial	84.3%	81.4%
Calibri	83%	77.3%
Comic Sans	94.3%	93.1%
Lucida Sans	87.6%	78%
Times New Roman	91.8%	89.1%

6   Conclusion and Future Scope

Document processing is a complex task, consisting of several steps and employing different techniques according to its purpose. Further enhancement in the Optical Character Recognition (OCR) step will provide the translation of human-readable characters into machine-readable codes, while the Optical Font Recognition (OFR) would help in the detection of the font style of the documents. The advancements in the fields of digital marketing and graphical designing, one may be interested in a particular type of font but might not be aware of what it is. The accuracy of OCR can be increased using techniques like smoothing and snowball training [14]. There is a need for an OCR which can even detect symbols and computerize equations present in various research papers. There is no application or program which can convert an image or PDF to a computerized text provided that the font without changing the format of the document. The subset of fonts used in this paper can also be increased to make an ominous OFR. There is a need for conversion of handwritten texts to computer format [15]. The approach can be extended into handwriting and signature detection which would be of great use in forensics and banking sector.

References

1. Grover, S., Arora, K., Mitra, S.K.: Text extraction from document images using edge information. In: 2009 Annual IEEE India Conference, Gujarat, pp. 1–4 (2009)
2. Shi, H., Pavlidis, T.: Font recognition and contextual processing for more accurate text recognition. In: ICDAR 1997, Ulm, Germany, pp. 39–44, August 1997

3. La Manna, S., Colia, A.M., Sperduti, A.: Optical font recognition for multi-font OCR and document processing. In: DEXA 1999 Proceedings of the 10th International Workshop on Database & Expert Systems Applications (1999)
4. Mizan, C., Chakraborty, T., Karmakar, S.: Text recognition using image processing. Int. J. Adv. Res. Comput. Sci. 8(5), 765–768 (2017)
5. Jana, R., Chowdhury, A.R., Islam, M.: Optical character recognition from text image. Int. J. Comput. Appl. Technol. Res. 3(4), 239–243 (2014)
6. Al-Shabi, M.A.M.: Text detection and character recognition using fuzzy image processing. J. Electr. Eng. 57, 258–267 (2006)
7. Bharath, V., Rani, N.S.: A font style classification system for English OCR. In: 2017 International Conference on Intelligent Computing and Control (I2C2), Coimbatore, pp. 1–5 (2017)
8. Zhu, Y., Tan, T., Wang, Y.: Font recognition based on global texture analysis. IEEE Trans. Pattern Anal. Mach. Intell. 23(10), 1192–1200 (2001)
9. Zramdini, A., Ingold, R.: Optical font recognition using typographical features. IEEE Trans. Pattern Anal. Mach. Intell. 20(8), 877–882 (1998)
10. Khoubyari, S., Hull, J.: Font and function word identification in document recognition. Comput. Vis. Image Underst. 63, 66–74 (1996). https://doi.org/10.1006/cviu.1996.0005
11. Tiwari, U., Gupta, S., Basudevan, N., Shahani, P.D.: Text extraction from images. Int. J. Electron. Electr. Eng. 7(9), 979–985 (2014). ISSN 0974-2174
12. Coates, A., et al.: Text detection and character recognition in scene images with unsupervised feature learning. In: International Conference on Document Analysis and Recognition, Beijing, pp. 440–445 (2011)
13. Patidar, D., Shah, B.C., Mishra, M.R.: Performance analysis of k nearest neighbors image classifier with different wavelet features. In: 2014 International Conference on Green Computing Communication and Electrical Engineering (ICGCCEE), Coimbatore, pp. 1–6 (2014)
14. Wang, J., Jean, J.: Resolving multifont character confusion with neural networks. Pattern Recogn. 26, 175–187 (1993). https://doi.org/10.1016/0031-3203(93)90099-I
15. Kacalak, W., Majewski, M.: Handwriting recognition methods using artificial neural networks. In: Proceedings of the Artificial Neural Networks in Engineering (ANNIE), At St. Louis, Volume: 16 (2016)

Association Rule Mining for Customer Segmentation in the SMEs Sector Using the Apriori Algorithm

Jesús Silva[1]($\boxtimes$), Mercedes Gaitan Angulo[2], Danelys Cabrera[3],
Sadhana J. Kamatkar[4], Hugo Martínez Caraballo[5],
Jairo Martinez Ventura[6], John Anderson Virviescas Peña[7],
and Juan de la Hoz – Hernandez[6]

[1] Universidad Peruana de Ciencias Aplicadas, Lima, Peru
jesussilvaUPC@gmail.com
[2] Corporación Universitaria Empresarial de Salamanca (CUES),
Barranquilla, Colombia
M_gaitan689@cuesw.edu.co
[3] Universidad de la Costa, St. 58 #66, Barranquilla, Atlántico, Colombia
dcabrera4@cuc.edu.co
[4] University of Mumbai, Mumbai, India
sjkamatkar@mu.ac.in
[5] Universidad Simón Bolívar, Barranquilla, Colombia
hugo.martinez@unisimonbolivar.edu.co
[6] Corporación Universitaria Latinoamericana, Barranquilla, Colombia
academico@ul.edu.co, juandelahoz03@gmail.com
[7] Corporación Universitaria Minuto de Dios - UNIMINUTO,
Bello, Antioquia, Colombia
john.virviescas@uniminuto.edu

Abstract. Customer's segmentation is used as a marketing differentiation tool which allows organizations to understand their customers and build differentiated strategies. This research focuses on a database from the SMEs sector in Colombia, the CRISP-DM methodology was applied for the Data Mining process. The analysis was made based on the PFM model (Presence, Frequency, Monetary Value), and the following grouping algorithms were applied on this model: k-means, k-medoids, and Self-Organizing Maps (SOM). For validating the result of the grouping algorithms and selecting the one that provides the best quality groups, the cascade evaluation technique has been used applying a classification algorithm. Finally, the Apriori algorithm was used to find associations between products for each group of customers, so determining association according to loyalty.

Keywords: Data mining · Apriori algorithm · Dates product ·
Association rules · Hidden patterns extraction · Consumer's loyalty

© Springer Nature Singapore Pte Ltd. 2019
M. Singh et al. (Eds.): ICACDS 2019, CCIS 1046, pp. 487–497, 2019.
https://doi.org/10.1007/978-981-13-9942-8_46

1 Introduction

Marketing focuses on the establishment, development and maintenance of continuous relationships between client and seller as a source of mutual benefits for the parties [1]. In this sense, for marketing policies to be effective in a context of highly competitive marketing, the literature proposes to consider relational benefits and customer segmentation [2]. Through the definition of consumer segments that value the benefits of the relationship to varying degrees, a company can design marketing strategies according to the characteristics of each type of customer [3]. Based on what has been described, the purpose of this research is to perform the customer's segmentation according to their level of loyalty on a sample of companies belonging to the SMEs sector in Colombia through the application of Data Mining techniques.

2 Theoretical Review

2.1 RFM Analysis

The RFM (Recency, Frequency, Monetary) analysis is a marketing technique used for the analysis of the customer's behavior [4], which is achieved by examining what the customer has purchased, using three factors: (R) purchase Recency, (F) Frequency of purchase, and (M) amount of purchase in Monetary terms. According to theories and researchers, customers who spend more money or buy more frequently in their company, are those customers who end up being more sensitive to the information and messages that the company is transmitting.

2.2 Data Mining Methodologies

2.2.1 SEMMA

The SAS Institute, developer of this methodology, defines SEMMA as the process of selection, exploration and modeling of large amounts of data to discover unknown business patterns. The name of this terminology is the acronym corresponding to five basic phases of the process: Sample (Sampling), Explore (Exploration), Modify (Modification), Model (Modeling), Assess (Evaluation) [5].

2.2.2 CRISP-DM

The CRISP-DM, which stands for Cross-Industry Standard Process for Data Mining, is a method that has proven to guide the Data Mining works. It was created by the group of companies SPSS, NCR and Daimer Chrysler in the year 2000, and is currently the most used reference guide in the development of Data Mining projects [6]. This method structures the process in 6 phases: Understanding the business, Understanding the data, Preparing the data, Modeling, Evaluation, and Implementation. The succession of phases is not necessarily rigid, and each phase is broken down into several general tasks in a second level.

3   Materials and Methods

The data was provided by the Chamber of Commerce of Barranquilla, Colombia, and corresponds to customer records and sales taken from 2015 to 2018 for a group of companies belonging to the SMEs sector in Colombia, Caribbean region [7].

The data collected were categorized as follows:

- Clients: covers the personal data of clients, provides geographical and demographic descriptors such as ID, RUC, address, age, gender, marital status, telephone, e-mail, workplace, profession, etc.
- Sales: this category has the daily billing records for sale, which provide the description of each purchase made by customers during the period 2015–2018.

The databases that contain the data of interest for the analysis are the following [8]:

- Clients: contains personal information of the company's clients. It has a total of 44,800 customer records.
- Client Type: contains three records representing end customers, distributors, and franchisees.
- Institution: defines if the client belongs to a public institution/company, to a private company, or a natural person.
- Invoice: all the billing information recorded by the company during the study time period. It has a total of 136,278 invoice records.
- Invoice Details: the products that have been purchased in each invoice. It has a total of 403,159 invoice detail records.
- Products: contains the records of all the products that the company sells. It has a total of 11,127 product records.
- Product Groups: the groups or categories to which the products belong. It has a total of 58 product categories.
- Brands: the brands of the products marketed by the company. It has a total of 396 trademark registrations.

The method used to carry out the process of Data Mining was the CRISP-DM ([9] and [10]) which consists of five phases: Sample (Sampling), Explore (Exploration), Modify (Modification), Model (Modeling), Assess (Valuation), each of them covering a set of activities that must be followed to carry out a mining process with high quality results.

For the segmentation of Master PC customers based on their purchasing behavior, these normalized variables were taken into account: Receipt, Frequency, and Amount. Considering that there is a wide range of clustering algorithms, an analysis was performed on some of them, corresponding to the most used in this type of case. This step allowed selecting the segmentation algorithms that were applied in the present research, which are the following: self-organized maps (SOM) of Kohonen, K-means, and CLARA algorithm (Cluster for Large Applications) which is an extension of the k-medoids algorithm [11].

For the selection of the number of groups, the techniques of internal evaluation applied sum of error squared and the silhouette index. After applying the segmentation algorithms, the results determine which of them provide the best results based on the described cascade evaluation method in [12].

4 Results

Based on the results, it was determined that the most appropriate method for customer segmentation in the study sample on the RFM attributes is the CLARA algorithm which belongs to the group of k-medoids methods. As a result, the following loyalty levels were discovered: Group 1 High, Group 2 Low, Group 3 Medium, and Group 4 Very Low, see Table 1.

Table 1. Loyalty groups profile

Group	RFM punctuation			Characteristic
	R	F	M	
High	4	3	4	Customers belonging to this group have a high level of loyalty, with a high level of recency, meaning that their last purchase was made a short time ago, in an average of 1 year ago. It also presents a level of frequency between medium and high, that is, they have bought several times, in an average of once a year, and a high amount that indicates that they have invested a lot of money in their purchases with an average of 982 dollars
Medium	3	1	5	Customers belonging to this group have a Medium level of loyalty, made their last purchase some time ago, in an average of two years and two months. The number of purchases made on average is one time, but have a very high average purchase amount of 830 dollars. This indicates that they have invested a lot of money in their purchases, considering that they have a low purchase frequency
Low	4	1	2	Customers belonging to this group have a Low loyalty level, have a high Recency level, that is, they have made their last purchase a short time ago, in an average of 1 year ago, but the average number of times they have purchased is 1, and the average amount spent is 22.3 dollars, which indicates that they have invested little money in their purchases. Customers of this group could also be considered new customers
Very low	1	1	2	Customers belonging to this group have a Very Low loyalty level, have a very low Recency, which indicates that they have made their last purchase a long time ago, with an average of 3.6 years ago. They also have an average frequency of a single purchase, and a Low amount indicating that they have invested little money in their purchases, with an average of 38.6 dollars. Customers of this group could be considered almost lost customers

4.1   Generating Association Rules (Product-Product) by the Apriori Algorithm

An association rule is a rule of the form X ⇒ Y, where X and Y are sets of elements. The meaning of this rule is that the presence of X in a transaction implies the presence of Y in the same transaction. X and Y are respectively called the antecedent and the consequent of the rule [1, 4, 7].

To generate the association rules, the Apriori algorithm, the most commonly used algorithm for the generation of these rules was applied. The Apriori algorithm is a method to discover sets of frequent elements and generates association rules on a set of transaction data [8]. It first identifies the frequent individual elements through the transactions and then extends to the increasingly large element sets until the resulting element sets reach a specified frequency threshold (support) [13]. This algorithm is implemented within the rules package [9] of R.

In order to elaborate the transaction data set, the following data were used: Invoice, Detail_Invoice, Product, Product Group, and Clients with their respective Loyalty groups. In this way, the data set was made up of an identifier of the transaction and the name of the category of product purchased in the transaction. Finally, a set of data was prepared for each customer loyalty group.

In an initial generation of rules, association rules were generated from 57 product categories, for which an amount that exceeded 20,000 rules was obtained. According to the inspection of the rules, it was possible to see that almost all of them were made up of the following categories: CASES and CHASSIS, HARD DRIVES, MEMORIES, PROCESSORS, MOTHERBOARDS, MONITORS, INTE-EXTE MEMORY READERS, DVD WRITERS AND DVD PLAYERS, SUPPRESSOR REGULATORS.

4.1.1   Generation of Association Rules for Product Recommendation to High Loyalty Customers

For the generation of rules for High loyalty customers, an acceptable level of support was selected according to the distribution of products in the set of transactions and a fairly high confidence level. The values of these parameters are described below in the Table 2.

Table 2. Parameters to generate high loyalty customer association rules

Parameter	Value	Percentage
Support	0.01	1%
Confidence	0.8	80%
Maximum length	3 (items per rule)	
Minimum length	2 (items per rule)	

After applying the Apriori algorithm, a set of 84 rules was obtained but, to guarantee its quality, only those rules that present a lift value greater than 3 were selected, leaving a total of 70 rules. The association rules obtained served as the basis for making recommendations to any High loyalty customer. Figure 1 shows the first 10 with the highest level of confidence, and Table 3 presents the interpretation of some of them.

```
> inspect(head(sort(subrules, by="confidence"),10));
    lhs                            rhs                     support    confidence    lift
1  {FLASH MEMORY,
    PORTATILES}              => {MOUSES Y MINIMOUSE}  0.02951638  0.9317618  9.172869
2  {MOCHILAS Y ESTUCHES,
    SOFTWARE}               => {PORTATILES}           0.03106884  0.9294533 20.890940
3  {FLASH MEMORY,
    PORTATILES}             => {MOCHILAS Y ESTUCHES} 0.02930021  0.9249380 13.191513
4  {IMPRESORAS,
    PORTATILES}             => {MOUSES Y MINIMOUSE}  0.01243933  0.9227405  9.084058
5  {IMPRESORAS,
    MOCHILAS Y ESTUCHES}    => {MOUSES Y MINIMOUSE}  0.01240002  0.9225146  9.081834
6  {MOCHILAS Y ESTUCHES,
    PORTATILES}             => {MOUSES Y MINIMOUSE}  0.03242478  0.9171762  9.029280
7  {FLASH MEMORY,
    PORTATILES}             => {SOFTWARE}            0.02904475  0.9168734 10.649838
8  {MOCHILAS Y ESTUCHES,
    SOFTWARE}               => {MOUSES Y MINIMOUSE}  0.03063651  0.9165197  9.022816
9  {IMPRESORAS,
    MOCHILAS Y ESTUCHES}    => {PORTATILES}           0.01228212  0.9137427 20.537820
10 {IMPRESORAS,
    PORTATILES}             => {MOCHILAS Y ESTUCHES} 0.01228212  0.9110787 12.993852
```

Fig. 1. Main association rules for recommendation of product-customers with High loyalty Original screen in Spanish.

Table 3. Interpretation of the main association rules for recommendation of product-customers with high loyalty

Rule	Interpretation of rules for High loyalty customers
1.	If a high loyalty customer buys product from the [FLASH MEMORY] and [PORTABLE] categories, the likelihood that he/she will also buy [MOUSES AND MINIMOUSES] on the same visit is 93%
2.	If a High loyalty customer buys product from the [BACKPACKS AND CASES] and [SOFTWARE] categories, the likelihood that he/she will also buy [PORTABLE] on the same visit is 92%
3.	If a High loyalty customer buys product from the [FLASH MEMORY] and [PORTABLE] categories, the likelihood that he/she will also buy [BACKPACKS AND CASES] on the same visit is 92%
4.	If a High loyalty customer buys product from the [PRINTERS] and [PORTABLE] categories, the likelihood that he/she will also buy [MOUSES AND MINIMOUSES] on the same visit is 92%
5.	If a High loyalty customer buys product from the [PRINTERS] and [BACKPACKS AND CASES] categories, the likelihood that he/she will also buy [MOUSES AND MINIMOUSES] on the same visit is 92%
6.	If a client of High loyalty buys product from the categories [BACKPACKS AND CASES] and [PORTABLE], the probability that he/she will also buy [MOUSES AND MINIMOUSES] in the same visit is 91%
7.	If a High loyalty customer buys product from the [FLASH MEMORY] and [PORTABLE] categories, the likelihood that he/she will also buy [SOFTWARE] on the same visit is 91%
8.	If a High loyalty customer buys product from the [BACKPACKS AND CASES] and [SOFTWARE] categories, the likelihood that he/she will also buy [MOUSES AND MINIMOUSES] on the same visit is 91%
9.	If a High loyalty customer buys product from the [PRINTERS] and [BACKPACKS AND CASES] categories, the likelihood that he/she will also buy [PORTABLE] on the same visit is 91%
10.	If a High loyalty customer purchases product from the [PRINTERS] and [PORTABLE] categories, the likelihood that he will also buy [BACKPACKS AND CASES] on the same visit is 91%

4.1.2   Generation of Association Rules for Product Recommendation to Average Loyalty Customers

For the generation of rules for average loyalty customers, an acceptable level of support was selected according to the distribution of the product categories in the transaction set and a fairly high confidence level. The values of these parameters are described in Table 4. The initially generated size of the rules was 952. From this total of rules, those with higher quality were selected, i.e. those with the highest lift values.

The base of lift was set to 3, but the number of rules was still being high, which would hinder its interpretation within the marketing area of the company, so finally, those rules that have a lift value greater than or equal to 5 were selected, leaving a total of 125 rules. The association rules obtained will serve as a basis for making recommendations to any customer of Average loyalty. Figure 2 shows the first 10 rules according to the level of trust for the customers of Average loyalty and, in Table 5, the interpretation of some of them is presented.

Table 4. Parameters to generate association rules for average loyalty customers

Parameter	Value	Percentage
Support	0.01	1%
Confidence	0.8	80%
Maximum length	2 (items per rule)	-
Minimum length	2 (items per rule)	-

```
> inspect(head(sort(subrulesMedio, by="confidence"),10));
    lhs                              rhs                              support    confidence  lift
1  {GAMERS-VOLANTES-VIDEOJUEGOS,
    TECLADOS}                     => {PARLANTES}                     0.04988789 0.9569892  7.855531
2  {CAMARAS, WEB , FILMADORAS,
    GAMERS-VOLANTES-VIDEOJUEGOS}  => {MESAS Y SILLAS}                0.06240658 0.9515670  9.029763
3  {MESAS Y SILLAS,
    MOUSES Y MINIMOUSE}           => {TECLADOS}                      0.05493274 0.9514563  8.044541
4  {GAMERS-VOLANTES-VIDEOJUEGOS,
    MESAS Y SILLAS}               => {CAMARAS, WEB , FILMADORAS}     0.06240658 0.9488636  7.152561
5  {GAMERS-VOLANTES-VIDEOJUEGOS,
    PARLANTES}                    => {MESAS Y SILLAS}                0.05997758 0.9441176  8.959074
6  {GAMERS-VOLANTES-VIDEOJUEGOS,
    TECLADOS}                     => {CAMARAS, WEB , FILMADORAS}     0.04914051 0.9426523  7.105740
7  {MESAS Y SILLAS,
    MOUSES Y MINIMOUSE}           => {PARLANTES}                     0.05437220 0.9417476  7.730419
8  {CABLES Y ADAPTADORES,
    GAMERS-VOLANTES-VIDEOJUEGOS}  => {PARLANTES}                     0.05287743 0.9401993  7.717710
9  {AUDIFONOS, MICROFONOS,
    GAMERS-VOLANTES-VIDEOJUEGOS}  => {CAMARAS, WEB , FILMADORAS}     0.05156951 0.9355932  7.052528
10 {GAMERS-VOLANTES-VIDEOJUEGOS,
    PARLANTES}                    => {CAMARAS, WEB , FILMADORAS}     0.05941704 0.9352941  7.050273
```

Fig. 2. Main rules of association for recommendation of product-customers with Average loyalty. Original screen in Spanish

4.1.3   Generation of Association Rules for Product Recommendation to Low Loyalty Customers

For the generation of rules for Low loyalty customers, the values of 0.01 for support and 0.8 for trust were selected as initial parameters, but under these conditions no association rule was found. The reason is that although there are several transactions for this group of customers, they rarely buy several products together, and those that are bought together do not satisfy high confidence levels.

Therefore, other parameters were established maintaining the support level, but decreasing the confidence level by half, which is also an acceptable value, although not as good as in the previous experiments.

The association rules obtained will serve as the basis for making recommendations to any Low loyalty customer. Table 6 shows the final values of the parameters for generating rules.

Despite having decreased the value of the acceptance parameters, only 3 rules were generated, one of which was discarded because the lift value was too low, leaving only 2 association rules. The association rules obtained will serve as a basis for making recommendations to any client with very low loyalty. The generated rules are described in Fig. 3 and the interpretation in Table 7.

Table 5. Interpretation of the main rules of association for recommendation of product - customers with Average loyalty.

Rule	Interpretation of rules for Average loyalty customers
1	If an Average loyalty customer buys product from the categories [GAMERS-FLYERS-VIDEO GAMES] and [KEYBOARDS], the probability that he/she will also buy [SPEAKERS] on the same visit is 95%
2	If an Average loyalty customer purchases product from the [WEBCAMS, VIDEOCAMERA] and [GAMERS-VOANTES-VIDEO GAMES] categories, the probability that he/she will also buy [TABLES AND CHAIRS] in the same visit is 95%
3	If an Average loyalty customer buys product from the [TABLES AND CHAIRS] categories and [MOUSES AND MINIMOUSE], the probability that he/she will also buy [KEYBOARDS] on the same visit is 95%
4	If an Average loyalty customer buys product from the categories [GAMERS-FLYERS-VIDEO GAMES] and [TABLES AND CHAIRS], the probability that he/she will also buy [WEBCAMS, VIDEOCAMERA] on the same visit is 94%
5	If an Average loyalty customer buys product from the categories [GAMERS-FLYERS-VIDEOGAMES] and [SPEAKERS], the probability that he/she will also buy [TABLES AND CHAIRS] on the same visit is 94%
6	If an Average loyalty customer buys product from the categories [GAMERS-FLYERS-VIDEO GAMES] and [KEYBOARDS], the probability that he/she will also buy [WEBCAMS, VIDEOCAMERA] on the same visit is 94%
7	If an Average loyalty customer buys product from the [TABLES AND CHAIRS] categories and [MOUSES AND MINIMOUSE], the probability that he/she will also buy [SPEAKERS] on the same visit is 94%

(continued)

Table 5. (*continued*)

Rule	Interpretation of rules for Average loyalty customers
8	If an Average loyalty customer buys product from the categories [CABLES AND ADAPTERS] and [GAMERS-FLYERS-VIDEO GAMES], the probability that he/she will also buy [SPEAKERS] on the same visit is 94%
9	If an Average loyalty customer buys product from the categories [HEADPHONES, MICROPHONES] and [GAMERS-FLYERS-VIDEO GAMES], the probability that he/she will also buy [WEBCAMS, VIDEOCAMERAS] on the same visit is 93%
10	If an Average loyalty customer buys product from the [HEADPHONES, MICROPHONES] and [SPEAKERS] categories, the probability that he/she will also buy [WEBCAMS VIDEOCAMERAS] on the same visit is 93%

Table 6. Parameters to generate Low loyalty customer association rules.

Parameter	Value	Percentage
Support	0.01	1%
Confidence	0.4	40%
Maximum length	2 (items per rule)	-
Minimum length	2 (items per rule)	-

```
> inspect(head(sort(subrulesBajo, by="confidence"),10));
  lhs                       rhs                      support    confidence  lift
1 {SOFTWARE}             => {SERVICIOS INFORMATICOS} 0.02018943 0.7826087 2.854387
2 {REDES E INTERNET} => {CABLES Y ADAPTADORES}   0.01370887 0.4182510 4.547487
```

Fig. 3. Main association rules for product recommendation for Low loyalty customers.

Table 7. Interpretation of the main association rules for product recommendation for Low loyalty customers

Rule	Interpretation of rules for Low loyalty customers
1	If a Low loyalty customer buys a product from the [SOFTWARE] category, the probability that he/she will also buy [COMPUTER SERVICES] on the same visit is 78%
2	If a Low loyalty customer buys a product in the [NETWORKS AND INTERNET] category, the probability that he/she will also buy [CABLES AND ADAPTERS] in the same visit is 41%

4.1.4   Generation of Association Rules for Product Recommendation to Very Low Loyalty Customers

For the generation of rules for Very Low loyalty customers, the parameters were initially set at 0.01 for support and 0.8 for trust but, as for the previous group, no rule was found under these conditions. The value of the confidence parameter was reduced to 40%, which is an acceptable value, see Table 8.

Table 8. Parameters to generate association rules for Very Low loyalty customers

Parameter	Value	Percentage
Support	0.01	1%
Confidence	0.4	40%
Maximum length	3 (items per rule)	–
Minimum length	2 (items per rule)	–

The final result was a total of 3 rules that meet a lift value greater than 2. In Fig. 4, these rules are presented, and their interpretation in Table 9.

```
> inspect(head(sort(rulesMuyBajo, by="confidence"),300));
  lhs                              rhs                      support    confidence  lift
1 {SOFTWARE}           => {SERVICIOS INFORMATICOS} 0.01143649 0.7857143 2.617234
2 {IMPRESORAS}         => {CABLES Y ADAPTADORES}   0.02755155 0.6556701 8.076568
3 {REDES E INTERNET}   => {CABLES Y ADAPTADORES}   0.01031017 0.4630350 5.703682
```

Fig. 4. Main association rules generated for product recommendation for Very Low loyalty customers.

Table 9. Interpretation of the main association rules for product recommendation for Very Low loyalty customers.

Rule	Interpretation of rules for Very Low loyalty customers
1	If a Very Low loyalty customer buys a product from the [SOFTWARE] category, the probability that he/she will also buy [COMPUTER SERVICES] on the same visit is 78%
2	If a Very Low loyalty customer purchases a product from the [PRINTERS] category, the probability that he/she will also buy [CABLES AND ADAPTERS] on the same visit is 65%
3	If a Very Low loyalty customer buys a product from the [NETWORKS AND INTERNET] category, the probability that he/she will also buy [CABLES AND ADAPTERS] on the same visit is 46%

5   Conclusions

To assess the accuracy of the used algorithms, k-means, k-medoids, and Self Organizing Maps (SOM), classification rules were generated taking, as a decision attribute, the groups created by the algorithms mentioned in this research. Besides, based on the prediction level, the results suggest that the classification of the groups generated by the CLARA of k-medoids algorithm provide a higher accuracy. The groups of customers of the sample of companies in study, by means of data mining, revealed the levels of loyalty as: High, Medium, Low and Very Low. These results will allow the company to develop retention strategies to their customers. The application of the Apriori association algorithm on the set of transactions of each group of customers allowed to create important association rules with quite high confidence levels, especially for the customers that belong to the highest loyalty groups because these customers are those who buy more products in the same transaction.

References

1. Amelec, V.: Increased efficiency in a company of development of technological solutions in the areas commercial and of consultancy. Adv. Sci. Lett. **21**(5), 1406–1408 (2015)
2. Varela, I.N., Cabrera, H.R., Lopez, C.G., Viloria, A., Gaitán, A.M., Henry, M.A.: Methodology for the reduction and integration of data in the performance measurement of industries cement plants. In: Tan, Y., Shi, Y., Tang, Q. (eds.) Data Mining and Big Data, DMBD 2018. LNCS, vol. 10943, pp. 33–42. Springer, Cham (2018). https://doi.org/10. 1007/978-3-319-93803 5_4
3. Lis-Gutiérrez, J.P., Lis-Gutiérrez, M., Gaitán-Angulo, M., Balaguera, M.I., Viloria, A., Santander-Abril, J.E.: Use of the industrial property system for new creations in Colombia: a departmental analysis (2000–2016). In: Tan, Y., Shi, Y., Tang, Q. (eds.) Data Mining and Big Data, DMBD 2018. LNCS, vol. 10943, pp. 786–796. Springer, Cham (2018). https:// doi.org/10.1007/978-3-319-93803-5_74
4. Anuradha, K., Kumar, K.A.: An e-commerce application for presuming missing items. Int. J. Comput. Trends Technol. **4**, 2636–2640 (2013)
5. Larose, D.T., Larose, C.D.: Discovering Knowledge in Data (2014). https://doi.org/10.1002/ 9781118874059
6. Pickrahn, I., et al.: Contamination incidents in the pre-analytical phase of forensic DNA analysis in Austria—Statistics of 17 years. Forensic Sci. Int. Genet. **31**, 12–18 (2017). https://doi.org/10.1016/j.fsigen.2017.07.012
7. de Barrios-Hernández, K.C., Contreras-Salinas, J.A., Olivero-Vega, E.: La Gestión por Procesos en las Pymes de Barranquilla: Factor Diferenciador de la Competitividad Organizacional. Información tecnológica **30**(2), 103–114 (2019)
8. Prajapati, D.J., Garg, S., Chauhan, N.C.: Interesting association rule mining with consistent and inconsistent rule detection from big sales data in distributed environment. Future Comput. Inform. J. **2**, 19–30 (2017). https://doi.org/10.1016/j.fcij.2017.04.003
9. Abdullah, M., Al-Hagery, H.: Classifiers' accuracy based on breast cancer medical data and data mining techniques. Int. J. Adv. Biotechnol. Res. **7**, 976–2612 (2016)
10. Khanali, H.: A survey on improved algorithms for mining association rules. Int. J. Comput. Appl. **165**, 8887 (2017)
11. Ban, T., Eto, M., Guo, S., Inoue, D., Nakao, K., Huang, R.: A study on association rule mining of darknet big data. In: 2015 International Joint Conference on Neural Networks, pp. 1–7 (2015). https://doi.org/10.1109/IJCNN.2015.7280818
12. Vo, B., Le, B.: Fast algorithm for mining generalized association rules. Int. J. Database Theory Appl. **2**, 1–12 (2009)
13. Al-Hagery, M.A.: Knowledge discovery in the data sets of hepatitis disease for diagnosis and prediction to support and serve community. Int. J. Comput. Electron. Res. **4**, 118–125 (2015)

Recommendation of an Integrated Index for the Quality of Educational Services Using Multivariate Statistics

Omar Bonerge Pineda Lezama[1], Rafael Luciano Gómez Dorta[2],
Noel Varela Izquierdo[3], Jesús Silva[4(✉)], and Sadhana J. Kamatkar[5]

[1] Faculty of Engineering, Universidad Tecnológica Centroamericana (UNITEC),
San Pedro Sula, Honduras
omarpineda@unitec.edu
[2] Gerente de calidad, BECAMO, Villanueva, Honduras
rafaellucianog@yahoo.es
[3] Faculty of Engineering, Universidad de la Costa, (CUC), Barranquilla,
Colombia
nvarela2@cuc.edu.co
[4] Universidad Peruana de Ciencias Aplicadas, Lima, Peru
jesussilvaUPC@gmail.com
[5] University of Mumbai, Mumbai, India
sjkamatkar@mu.ac.in

Abstract. In this work, the analysis of the surveys was carried out through a factorial analysis, which facilitates the evaluation of the validity of the selected construct for the case under study, as well as evaluating the quality of the service for each factor, with a view to determining the level of quality of the educational service, for which it integrates elements of descriptive and multivariate statistics with the management of the quality of the educational service. They are used as fundamental statistical techniques, descriptive analysis, factor analysis and analysis of variance. As a final result, it was concluded that the students of five UNITEC careers evaluated the educational service they receive as very satisfactory (4 points), highlighting the tangible elements as the most weighted factor. A significant aspect is that there are no significant differences in the perceptions of students from different careers and different sections.

Keywords: Quality of educational services · Multivariate statistics · Evaluation of customer

1 Introduction

Evaluation of customer satisfaction should be an essential objective in any service organization. There are several questionnaires that have been used for this purpose, however, studies have reported problems in their use [1]. To assess customer feedback clearly requires an appropriate questionnaire design, implement and analyze their results efficiently with depth; however, in most cases the analysis is limited to calculating the frequency responses of the different questions, which is not to develop a

© Springer Nature Singapore Pte Ltd. 2019
M. Singh et al. (Eds.): ICACDS 2019, CCIS 1046, pp. 498–508, 2019.
https://doi.org/10.1007/978-981-13-9942-8_47

limited approach, as the questionnaires will have many interrelated questions. This justifies the need to use appropriate statistical techniques that facilitate better understanding of the information we provide questionnaires.

This paper presents the application of a group of techniques of descriptive statistics and multivariate analysis to assess the level of quality of educational services received by university students, determining factors and critical attributes of these services to design improvement strategies that allow raising the competitive level of college. The procedure used takes into account the concept of service quality and the most recognized measurement models and integrates elements: qualitative research, multivariate statistics and quality.

That's why so this research focuses on the use of statistical tools such as descriptive analysis, factor analysis and analysis of variance with the aim to deepen the complex relationships between attributes that characterize educational services to characterize the critical variables that affect customer satisfaction and generate from here results that allow through a mathematical model to obtain an indicator of the level of satisfaction of its students which facilitates an objective assessment of the implementation of corrective actions and preventive which they are adopted, facilitating the monitoring of the effectiveness and efficiency of the Management System.

2 Research Approach

One of the main problems currently present higher education organizations, is effective management and manipulation of data, generated satisfaction surveys that are implemented in these centers. They provide greater clarity in all its operations and decisions. A consideration of the authors have not yet been adequately developed the potential of these results we could provide, especially with regard to an indicator that allows monitoring and management improvement program.

Activities aimed at retaining customers generate a number of benefits to businesses, therefore it is necessary to identify factors or dimensions that affect customer satisfaction, as this allows you to draw action plans leading to significant improvements for organization. This work is based on the work carried out by different authors relating to improving the quality of educational services [2, 3].

In the literature review we did not work that demonstrate the existence of a scientifically based indicator to measure satisfaction college student found. Therefore, the research question is formulated under the following question: How to develop an indicator to integrate the different dimensions of educational services and enable monitoring and measuring the impact of actions to improve these services?

3 Concept of Service Quality

The quality concept was extended to all phases of the life of a product or service from conception and design to manufacture and subsequent use by the customer, with the slogan "Zero Defects". At present products and services must not only be suitable for use assigned to them, but they also have to match and even exceed the expectations that customers have placed in them. The aim is to satisfy customers from the beginning to the end. This new concept of quality is what is known as "quality of service".

It should be noted that quality in higher education is a complex and multifaceted phenomenon, still insufficient to have only a definition of quality; there is, therefore, one way to define and measure the quality of service. Each of the actors involved in higher education has a particular view of the quality of education (government, students, and academic staff) depending on it for their own needs [3]. To maintain quality and increase accountability, Institutions of Higher Education should strive to develop alternative assessment procedures [2]. Therefore, to improve the quality of services customers should know and understand their needs, once done you should embrace the quality attributes welcomed by customers.

3.1 Quality in Education

Whenever the concept of quality is not absolute but relative, there are many and varied definitions of the quality of education have been changing and adjusting according to the evolution of society. Similarly, several authors [4, 5], mentioned in one way or another that the concept of quality of education has different approaches, among which are the following:

- Quality-excellence and prestige: quantized according to the prestige enjoyed by the academic institution as well as its recognition and makes differs from the others.
- Quality in terms of resources: it has to do with the resources available to institutions, whether physical, economic or human capital character. It is then valued in accordance with appropriate and modern infrastructure and equipment, qualification and teacher productivity and student performance.
- Quality as change (value added): awarded according to the degree of influence that the school exerts on student behavior.
- Quality as conformity of a program with some previous standards minimum quality accreditation processes: they are seeking to secure and ensure the student who has managed to pass all the curriculum along with the minimum requirements that allow their degree.
- Quality as fitness to meet the needs of the recipients or clients: approach that sees the complexity of the quality of education, given the amount of public or stakeholders involved or affected by it as the state, businesses, students, parents, government agencies that govern it, etc.

3.2 Conceptual Models for Measuring Service Quality

A service quality model is merely a simplified representation of reality, which takes into account those basic elements capable alone of explanation for the level of quality achieved by an organization from the point of view of their customers. Numerous models [6–8], have been developed to understand the definition and formation of the perceptions of the quality of services. The most comprehensive model of all reviewed is the SERVQUAL was developed as a result of the absence of literature that should specifically address the problems related to the measurement of service quality, is a measuring instrument construct service quality, it is based on the theoretical model of GAPS. However, although this measurement scale has had a major impact, it has not been without criticism, covering both conceptual and operational aspects. In this context, several studies have appeared in the literature defending and replicating the Servqual model [6, 9], from which an instrument alternative measurement, the SERVPERF [6] scale was proposed, which comprises of the 22 items of the SERVQUAL scale, but used only to measure perceptions of service. In the revisions it was found that the quality concept is closely associated with customer satisfaction. To [10] there are five levels of satisfaction: excitement, satisfaction, irritation, dissatisfaction and anger.

4 Methodology

The methodology developed takes into account the different tasks performed measuring the quality of services and consists of four stages [2]:

1. Selection and validation of the instrument.
2. Evaluation of the quality of educational services.
3. Construction and determination of this indicator.
4. Valuation differences.

5 Results and Research Findings

5.1 Selection and Validation of the Instrument

The selected questionnaire is proposed [2]. It evaluates the different aspects of the educational service provided at universities. The questionnaire evaluates selected 24 questions (see Table 1) with a Likert scale with responses from 1 to 5; 1 strongly disagree and 5 strongly agree.

Table 1. Aspects to evaluate questions

No. of questions	Aspect that evaluates
P1	Modern facilities and equipped
P2	Atmosphere and pleasant surroundings
P3	Attractive and suitable sites for learning
P4	Appearance of physical facilities
P5	Compliance with the program content
P6	Cooperation and understanding from college
P7	Education service provided is adequate
P8	Fulfilling the responsibilities of teachers
P9	Compliance with college applications
P10	Programming activities teachers

(*continued*)

Table 1. (*continued*)

No. of questions	Aspect that evaluates
P11	Compliance with requests made to administrative staff
P12	Feedback activities and concerns students
P13	Available to help students
P14	Updated knowledge of teachers
P15	Communication and trust between teachers and students
P16	Clarification of doubts students
P17	Explaining concepts clearly to students
P18	Strategies to apply knowledge to reality
P19	Acceptance and error correction by the teacher
P20	The university provides individual attention
P21	The teacher provides individualized attention
P22	Knowledge of student needs
P23	The university is interested student training
P24	The teacher is interested student learning

The total was 446 surveys completed, the selected students were racing systems engineering, telecommunications, mechatronics, industrial, civil and marketing and international business. It is intended from this determine an indicator to assess the level of service quality and monitor performance this time, dimensions and analyzing critical variables.

A data obtained through these questionnaires were applied a factor analysis with Statgraphics Centurion software support. According to the selected questionnaire are five factors that explain the main aspects in the quality of this service. Table 2 shows the results of this analysis are shown.

Table 2. Percentage of variance explained by the factors

Factor	Own value	Percentage of variance explained	Accumulated percentage	Index weighting
1	10.477	43.65	43.65	0.68
2	1.636	6.82	50.47	0.11
3	1.553	6.47	56.94	0.10
4	1.047	4.36	61.30	0.07
5	0.73	3.04	64.34	0.05

On the other hand, Table 2 tells us that there are basically five factors that explain the quality of education. It can be seen that the first factor explains 43.65% of the total variability, the second factor explains 6.82%. The five factors explain 64.35%, literature states that the value of the variability explained by the factors selected to be about 70% [11], so that the value of 64.35% can be considered as a reasonable level for validating the instrument used.

5.2   Evaluation of the Quality of Educational Services

Table 3 shows the relationship of the factor with the questions and the variable that represents and is the cornerstone for evaluating the quality of service and subsequent determination of the level of satisfaction with the educational service and the reliability of the instrument which was assessed using the criterion of internal consistency of Cronbach occurs. Factor 1 represents the evaluation of tangibles, factor 2 is concerned with the evaluation of the reliability factor 3 with the responsiveness, the factor 4 and safety factor of 5 to empathy. Similarly show is the average score and standard error, which received each question considering the 446 respondents show.

The worst feature quality was evaluated Question 6 (cooperation and understanding by the university), with a rating of 3.32; As opposed to this was the best evaluated Question 14 (updated knowledge of teachers), with a rating of 4.30. For an overall assessment of the dimension that represents each factor the average mean of the questions which groups each factor was calculated, this calculation is also reflected in Table 3. Thus it is seen that the best dimension was assessed four (Safety) with an average of 4.08; followed by three dimension (responsiveness) with an average rating of 4.06; the dimension one (tangible elements) with a rating of 3.98; three dimension (Reliability) with a 3. 68 and the worst was assessed five dimensions (empathy) with a grade of 3.67. The latter therefore constitutes a factor to address to improve the quality of education.

Table 3. Results of means, standard errors of the factors, of factor loadings and Cronbach

Factors	No.	Items	Average	Standard error	Loads factor	Cronba ch's alpha factor
Tangibility	1	Modern facilities and equipped	3.85	0.051	0.678	
	2	Atmosphere and pleasant surroundings	3.91	0.046	0.674	
	3	Attractive and suitable sites for learning	3.91	0.047	0.660	
	4	Appearance of physical facilities	4	0.045	0746	
		Average tangibility factor and Cronbach	**3.92**			**0.896**
Reliability	6	Cooperation and understanding from college	3.32	0.059	0.616	
	7	Education service provided is adequate	4.02	0.044	0.371	
	9	Compliance with college applications	3.77	0.053	0.660	
	11	Fulfillment of requests	3.62	0.054	0.768	
		Average reliability factor and Cronbach	**3.68**			**0.870**

(continued)

Table 3. (*continued*)

Factors	No.	Items	Average	Standard error	Loads factor	Cronba ch's alpha factor
Answer's capacity	5	Compliance with the program content	4.09	0.046	0.629	
	8	Fulfilling the responsibilities of teachers	3.95	0.05	0.406	
	10	Programming activities teachers	4.25	0.043	0.566	
	12	Feedback activities and concerns	3.98	0.045	0.643	
	13	Available to help students	4.03	0.048	0.668	
		Media responsiveness factor and Cronbach	**4.06**			**0.882**
Security	14	Updated knowledge of teachers	4.3	0.041	0.599	
	15	Communication and trust between teachers and students	4.06	0.045	0.401	
	16	Clarification of doubts students	4.1	0.041	0.587	
	17	Explaining concepts clearly	3.97	0.045	0.551	
	18	Strategies to apply knowledge to reality	3.97	0.044	0.667	
	19	Acceptance and error correction by the teacher	4.07	0.048	0.538	
		Average safety factor and Cronbach	**4.08**			**0.873**
Empathy	20	The university provides individual attention	3.55	0.054	0.682	
	21	The teacher provides individualized attention	3.81	0.049	0.721	
	22	Knowledge of student needs	3.48	0.055	0.775	
	23	The university is interested student training	3.65	0.053	0.705	
	24	The teacher is interested student learning	3.87	0.053	0.676	
		Media empathy factor and Cronbach	**3.67**			**0.887**
		Average factors and total Cronbach	**3.88**			**0.946**

5.3   Construction of the Indicator and Its Assessment

Table 2 shows the contribution made by each factor to the observed variation appears, thus for example Tangibility factor contributes 68% as (43.65/64.34) = 0.68. These factors bound to the average score of each factor are the elements for calculating the satisfaction index is proposed, which is defined using the expressions:

$$P_i = \frac{V_i}{\sum\limits_{i=1}^{n} V_i} \tag{1}$$

$$ESQI = \sum_{i=1}^{n} P_i * \overline{F_i} \tag{2}$$

Where:

$ESQI$:   Index quality of educational services.
P_i: Index weighting for the ith factor $i = 1, 2, \ldots, n$
V_i: Percentage of explained variance for the ith factor $i = 1, 2, \ldots, n$
$\overline{F_i}$:   Is the average factor consists of the middle of the items of the ith factor $i = 1, 2, \ldots, n$

Taking the values of the weighting indices and means of the factors given in Tables 2, 3 and 4 and substituting in Eqs. (1) and (2) the quality index educational service is obtained, Eq. (3):

$$QIES = 0.68 * 3.92 + 0.11 * 3.68 + 0.10 * 4.06 + 0.07 * 4.08 + 0.05 * 3.67 = 3.94 \tag{3}$$

This value (Eq. 3) can be interpreted as the average assessment of quality in educational service from the student's perspective. This analysis is supported by the fact that variations in the answers to each question are relatively similar. The assessment of the variation can be done by standard error also it appears in Table 3.

5.4   Rating Differences

Factor analysis allows factors are analyzed and compared in detail. In this case we select the worst evaluated factor (empathy) and perform the comparison by career and day to better locate the problem and to define more precisely what actions to take. We are doing a multifactorial ANOVA with the support of Statgraphics Centurion software. This can be validated through the multifactorial ANOVA Table 4. For both factors (P-value > 0.05); It is indicating that the effect of these factors is not significant on the empathy factor.

Table 4. Analysis of variance for empathy factor for career and day

Source	Sum of squares	DF	Horsebit	Reason-F	Value-P
Main effects					
A: Day	0.0355162	2	0.0177581	2.91	.1121
B: Carrera	0.0217106	4	0.00542765	0.89	.5118
Waste	0.0487756	8	0.00609695		
Total (corrected)	0.106002	14			

6 Discussion of Results

The results achieved indicate that it is possible by applying a simple methodology to evaluate the perceived quality of education provided by an institution of higher education. The instrument used as part of an investigation of Colombian authors [2] was constructed based on the scale SERVPERF [6] and could be validated to apply in the Honduran context through this work as shown by the results achieved in the reliability analysis and validity performed, the results are similar to those achieved in the work of the aforementioned authors.

Several important works [12, 13], in the context of the topics addressed they have emphasized the importance of higher education institutions worry about how to measure the quality of service from the perspective of students; This work is an effective answer to this need raised. The test work also multidimensionality of the concept quality of educational services, as shown in other published scientific papers [7]. The procedures applied can be generalized to any university.

The work as well as other previous works by the authors [14–17], demonstrates the potential of statistical methods to support the analysis and improvement of business processes.

7 Conclusions

In this paper we have proposed using multivariate factor analysis, through principal component analysis to test the consistency of a proposed in the scientific literature that is applied to measure the quality of educational services questionnaire.

The proposed methodology was applied to the case of evaluating the quality of education at the Universidad Tecnológica Centroamericana (UNITEC), surveying 446 students majoring in systems engineering, telecommunications, mechatronics, industrial engineering and marketing and international business. Applying the factor analysis it was found that the five dimensions proposed in the literature account for 64.34% of the variability in the observed response variable. 24 variables analyzed through the questionnaire might be associated with each of the dimensions set out therein, which is an empirical evidence of the validity of the questionnaire, which also showed high reliability (alpha =).

The indicator of quality of education reflected a rating on a scale of 1 to 5 of 3.94 which can be considered as a state of satisfaction [10] where the dimension best evaluated by students proved the Security (4.08) and the worst evaluated the empathy (3.67), so it is here that should be evaluated immediately opportunities for improvement.

With analysis of variance for the empathy factor was determined that there are no significant differences between careers or between sections so the improvement opportunities that arise should cover equally different careers and sections.

References

1. Van Dyke, T.P., Prybutok, V.R., Kappelman, L.A.: Cautions on the use of the SERVQUAL measure to ASSESS the quality of information systems services. Decis. Sci. **30**(3), 877–891 (1999)
2. Duque Oliva, E., Finch Chaparro, C.: Measuring the perception of service quality education by students AAUCTU Duitama. Free Criterion Mag. **10**(16), 1–12 (2012)
3. Rodriguez-Ponce, E., et al.: The impact of service quality on institutional quality in universities: empirical evidence from Chile. Intersci. Mag. **36**(9), 657–663 (2011)
4. Yao, L.: The present situation and development tendency of higher education quality evaluation in Western Countries. Priv. Educ. Res. 2006-03 (2006). http://en.cnki.com.cn/A_rticlein/DTCJFOTAL-MB-JY200603010.html
5. Bertolin, J., Leite, D.: Quality evaluation of the Brazilian higher education system: relevance, diversity, equity and effectiveness. Qual. Higher Educ. **14**, 121–133 (2008)
6. Cronin, J., Taylor, S.: Measuring service quality: a reexamination and extension. J. Mark. **56**(3), 55–68 (1992)
7. Grönroos, C.: Marketing and Service Management: Managing the Moments of Truth and Service Competition. Díaz de Santos, Madrid (1994)
8. Valarie Zeithaml, A., Parasuraman, A., Berry, L.L.: Total Quality Management Services. Diaz de Santos, Bogota (1993)
9. Carman, J.M.: Consumer perceptions of service quality: an assessment of the SERVQUAL dimensions. J. Retail. **69**(Spring), 127–139 (1990)
10. Larrea, P.: Quality of Service, the Marketing Strategy. Dfaz Santos, Madrid (1991)
11. Hair Jr., J.F., Anderson, R.E., Tatham, R.L., Black, W.C.: Multivariate Analysis, 5th edn. Prentice Hall Iberia, Madrid (1999)
12. Tsiniduo, M., et al.: Evaluation of the factors that determine quality in higher education: an empirical study. Qual. Assur. Educ. **18**, 227–244 (2010)
13. Gonzalez Espinoza, O.: Quality of higher education: concepts and models. Calif. Sup. Educ. **28**, 249–296 (2008)
14. Bonerge Pineda Lezama, O., Varela Izquierdo, N., Pérez Fernández, D., Gómez Dorta, R.L., Romero Marín, L.: Models of multivariate regression for labor accidents in different production sectors: comparative study. In: Tan, Y., Shi, Y., Tang, Q. (eds.) Data Mining and Big Data, DMBD 2018. LNCS, vol. 10943, pp. 43–52. Springer, Cham (2018). https://doi.org/10.1007/978-3-319-93803-5_5
15. Izquierdo, N.V., Lezama, O.B.P., Dorta, R.G., Viloria, A., Deras, I., Hernández-Fernández, L.: Fuzzy logic applied to the performance evaluation. Honduran coffee sector case. In: Tan, Y., Shi, Y., Tang, Q. (eds.) ICSI 2018. LNCS, vol. 10942, pp. 164–173. Springer, Cham (2018). https://doi.org/10.1007/978-3-319-93818-9_16

16. Pineda Lezama, O., Gómez Dorta, R.: Techniques of multivariate statistical analysis: an application for the Honduran banking sector. Innovare: J. Sci. Technol. 5(2), 61–75 (2017)
17. Viloria, A., Lis-Gutiérrez, J.P., Gaitán-Angulo, M., Godoy, A.R.M., Moreno, G.C., Kamatkar, S.J.: Methodology for the design of a student pattern recognition tool to facilitate the teaching - learning process through knowledge data discovery (big data). In: Tan, Y., Shi, Y., Tang, Q. (eds.) Data Mining and Big Data, DMBD 2018. Lecture Notes in Computer Science, vol. 10943, pp. 670–679. Springer, Cham (2018). https://doi.org/10. 1007/978-3-319-93803-5_63

Windows Based Interactive Application to Replicate Artworks in Virtual Environment

Apurba Ghosh[1]([🖂]), Anindya Ghosh[1], and Jia Uddin[2]

[1] Department of Multimedia and Creative Technology,
Daffodil International University, Dhaka, Bangladesh
apurba.mct@diu.edu.bd, anindya.ghosh835@gmail.com
[2] Department of Computer Science and Engineering,
BRAC University, Dhaka, Bangladesh
jia.uddin@bracu.ac.bd

Abstract. This paper demonstrates a Windows based interactive application, which can be used for showcasing artworks in a virtual environment and can be a potential support for artists, curators, art gallery owners, art critics and academic researchers. In this demonstration, we described in details - how this application was developed with the help of a series of highly sophisticated software like- Autodesk 3ds Max, Unity and how it actually comes into action. Bunch of challenges that we faced during the development and implementation of this application - are also mentioned. The proper utilization of this interactive application will bring a significant change in the sector of arts. In addition, this work will add up a new dimension on the way of art appreciation.

Keywords: Virtual art gallery · Interactive application ·
Windows based application · Multimedia for art industry ·
Replication of art works

1 Introduction

Art is something that is always present in any creation. It's not a moral thing like good or bad, neither it's always a substantial form that anyone can see. Art in nature is always present in any visible or invisible form. Those can be the art of creation, the art of living, also the art of destruction is possible. What a so called "Artist" does is, actually grabbing a part of experience of that art and give that a visible form that others can also experience through their senses. Thereby, the media the artist is presenting the art can be very different from person to person, cause that's only a tool of representation. And thus, different art mediums and forms have come to the human civilization. Among all the art mediums, Paintings are one of the oldest. Since the cave paintings era, or maybe even since long before that, drawing and painting has always been a part of our civilization. Human discovered the visible language of communicating ideas and feelings with paintings. So, the importance of such art is always undeniable. Artists are truly documentary makers of history and evolution. Hence it's our sincere duty to preserve and expand the possibilities of art as much as possible.

© Springer Nature Singapore Pte Ltd. 2019
M. Singh et al. (Eds.): ICACDS 2019, CCIS 1046, pp. 509–518, 2019.
https://doi.org/10.1007/978-981-13-9942-8_48

So whenever the thought of making a painting came to human mind, they probably came up with the solution of a canvas with a comparatively plane stone. They could draw the same thing easily on soft land or sand; but they didn't. This simple act of our ancestors prove that, art had always an appeal to be exhibited and preserved for viewers. And from there, the idea of exhibition came. There are numbers of historical proofs that arts were started to be given priority from thousands of years ago. Even the most ancient civilizations had certain appreciation of art that helped them to create new things with more artistic forms. So, whatever tools we are using now a days are actually developed artistic forms of their ancient versions. Alike anything else, even the presentation styles of art today, definitely had its ancient forms. If that is true, there is definitely scope for a better future of the exhibition tools of art.

The most popular way of presenting paintings are through a museum or art gallery, where the paintings are collected and mounted in frames on the wall. People are allowed in that place from time to time to see and know about the arts there. Sometimes the artists are also present there which allows the viewer to know more from him or her. There are both public and private galleries with different motives. Public galleries are mostly free of cost, and they intend to exhibit only. But most private galleries intend to exhibit the artworks as a product and provide the viewers with the opportunity to buy or make some trade deals with the owners. But whatever the motive is, paintings are mostly exhibited this way for thousands of years.

Now, modern electronic technology is emerging day by day. People are being busier too. In many societies, the appreciation for arts are lessened because, people don't give priority of going to a museum to see the artworks comparing with their other productive works. Some may have the wish to attend exhibitions, but misses for time schedule. A lot of people definitely loose the opportunity just because they are from a different country. So, a solution was required.

People now a days have access to a computer, or at least a smart mobile phone, which is quite a powerful computer indeed. So, the best way of facing the limitation of real exhibitions was to find out a virtual solution. Modern computer graphic technology is so advanced that, it can replicate almost anything in three dimension by the help of 3D animation creating software, which enables the possibility of a virtual art gallery. Thus, the tradition of exhibiting arts will be preserved well with the integration of modern technologies and abilities.

Previous researches on 3D animation as a medium of strong multimedia tool have focused on many important aspects. Research on classification of 3D models has already done for 3D animation environments [1]. Specific 3D tool based research for film and television [2, 9], rapid 3D human modeling and animation based on sketch and motion database [3], real water simulation for 3D animation [4] - researches on all those areas have done. Even researches on- emotion based facial animation [5], real-time speech driven facial animation using neural network [6], 3D measurement technologies for computer animation [7], 3D character animation engine [8] have come up with new findings. The area of interactive 3D animation system [10] and experimental teaching of 3D animation [11] have also explored. But none of them pull out the importance of implementing a virtual art gallery with the help of 3D animation [16] technology. Compared to the earlier research works, our endeavor of a windows based application makes a significant number of contributions. Firstly, we are focusing on showcasing real artworks so that the artist community are getting the opportunity to preserve their artworks in a digital form. This application can also be a great help for those art collectors or buyers who have large geographic distance between the artist and artworks. Secondly, our developed work does not require internet connection during operation so that this application can run effectively in those places where high speed internet connection is not available. Thirdly, we are adding a new dimension in the way of showcasing artworks in comparison with the traditional approach [17].

Throughout the rest of this paper we have tried to reveal all the technical complexities and approaches we have followed to develop this application. The development process flow of our work is described in Sect. 2, detailed workflow at the implementation phase is discussed in Sect. 3. Finally Sect. 4 concludes this paper.

2 Proposed Model

Figure 1 demonstrates the stages that are involved in the development of our virtual art gallery application.

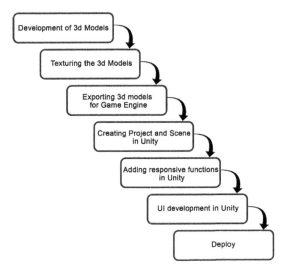

Fig. 1. Development stages of the application

Focusing on the implementation phase, we need to develop the necessary 3d models first. While creating 3d models, they don't have any texture. So it is crucial to assign necessary textures on them at the second stage. Thirdly the 3d models need to be exported for game engine. After finishing the required set ups on game engine at forth stage, 3d models are allowed to be brought inside. Responsive functions which unfold the interactivity features are added with the 3d models in fifth stage. In stage six the user interface (UI) is developed and integrated with the main application. Lastly the application is deployed in stage seven. All those stages with detailed insights are mentioned in next section of this paper.

3 Detailed Workflow During Implementation

This virtual art gallery was planned in such a way that the user can have a unique view of the interior. Most traditional art galleries are too straight in their plans and geometry that in most cases it is a boring space with the artworks hung in walls. So it was our first challenge to come up with a unique shape of the virtual space. Our intensive research on geometry and architecture helped us to figure out an octagonal base for each room of the gallery. Thereby, the first person camera having a wide field of view allows the user to look at a good number of paintings in a master view and undistorted single views when get closer to any artwork. We developed the 2d blueprint for the architecture first. Then following the blueprint stated in Fig. 2, this magnificent art gallery was modeled in Autodesk 3ds max [12]. Modeling in 3ds Max is a very exciting task because it provides multiple ways to solve a matter. The gallery could be made in numerous ways but we followed poly modeling technique with an octagonal base.

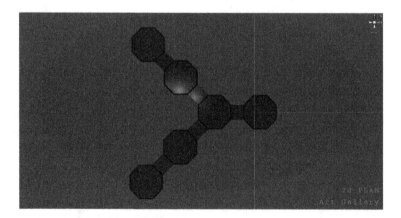

Fig. 2. 2D plan for gallery

The building architecture was needed to be done in such a manner that all its parts can be textured separately later and also respond with lights in game engine according to requirements. So first we modeled one octagonal room with a separate floor and roof. Then we made 5 copies of that room and joint them with corridors which formed a shape quite similar to the letter – Y as shown in Fig. 3.

Once the full gallery was present visually then it was challenge to attach and detach polygons of different objects predicting the texturing procedure of the walls, floor and roofs. Because, in lieu of creating the rooms as different object, they were needed to respond with similar commands. Like the wall texture of one room, should not be different from others. So all the polygons of the walls were attached to one element as if any change on any polygon creates similar change on every wall. And the same were done for the roofs, floors, and corridor moreover every common part of the gallery interior.

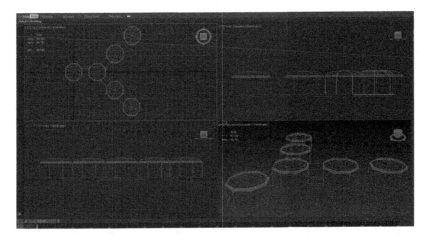

Fig. 3. Topology of the gallery

Another key issue was kept in mind that no matter how complicated the output be, the topology of every 3d model must be clean. It was also important to make a low poly model so that it doesn't have trouble in real-time rendering inside game engine. High poly 3d models reduce the performance of the applications. So as shown in Fig. 3, we managed to get a very low-poly architecture for this project. When the gallery was ready, the time for modeling the frames of the paintings came. In this case, firstly a skeleton of a simple frame was made so that it can be easily scaled to different sizes and ratio. For this we used a normal box object and following poly-modeling technique the frames were made out of it. Manually 17 different sizes of painting-frames were modeled as shown in Fig. 4 and after that the time to texture came.

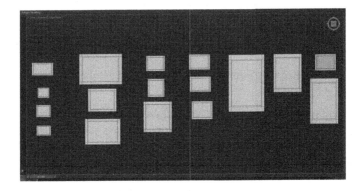

Fig. 4. 3D painting frames of different size

The gallery was needed to be textured in walls, roofs, grills of roofs, floors and corners of wall. So, at first we edited the necessary texture in Adobe Photoshop [14] and then applied them on the objects in 3ds max via material editor. Important to note that not all the images were directly applied to the 3d surface as needed. Sometimes they are stretched too much or unusually tiled or scaled. So, in order to get a distortion free look we used the tile and offset option in material editor, and some cases applied a dedicated 3ds Max modifier named- UVW Map to help us sorting the problem out.

In order to use the 3d models developed with 3ds max to Unity game engine, it was important to export them in perfect format and settings. Otherwise topology and textures may get highly affected during the transformation of work environments. So, the best format in this case is *.fbx format. The short form *.fbx came from the word Filmbox. In our case, we selected each 3d model and exported the selected object in .fbx format. In this process, an important option "Embed Media" was always checked in 3ds max during the export to keep the textures intact as shown in Fig. 5.

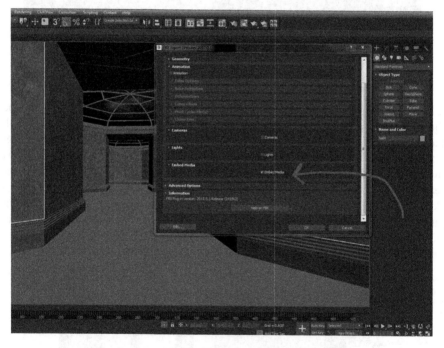

Fig. 5. Exporting in *.fbx format with Embed Media

While working in Unity [13] game engine, creating and managing the project is a very sensitive issue. Each time the Unity game engine gets started, it shows the option to create new project. While creating this project we made a distinct folder for the whole project at first. Because, just when the project is created, Unity automatically creates sub folders inside the project folder and keeps the "Project Settings" saved. These project settings folder is unavoidable to build the final application or even to work with the file in different workstations. An "Asset" folder was also created inside the directory where everything used in this project like- images, sounds, scripts, materials are preserved. This folder is responsive with the Unity interface which allowed us to add or delete items in this project either from inside the game engine or normally from file explorer. While the project is created developer must switch the 3d or 2d option depending on the type of his/her project. We created a 3d project in this case.

When the project was opened for the first time it showed the default scene. In unity, the first scene contains a main camera and a directional light. At that point inside Unity we needed to build our environment. We brought all the materials, textures, fbx models, audio clips everything in the asset folder as shown in Fig. 6. Then brought the gallery model inside the hierarchy just by dragging and dropping.

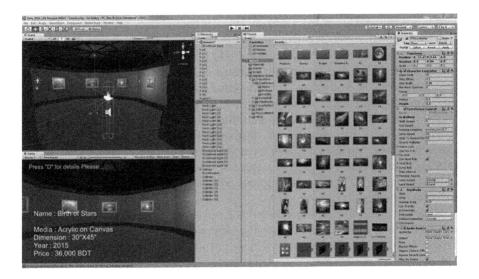

Fig. 6. A glimpse of scene development in unity

Later we added mesh collider to the meshes so that they collide with other rigid body objects in this project. When the gallery was ready we imported standard assets package and inserted a "First Person Character" prefab in the scene. This allows us to walk through the environment like fps games. But before that, deleting the existing main camera was a must. Because every camera is an audio listener and the FPS prefab itself has a camera. Thereby the scene contains 2 audio listener. In Unity, 2 audio listener in one scene is a serious error that will stop the application to work as needed. So, we deleted the main camera and the FPS camera works as the main camera and main audio listener indeed. By then we could walk through our scene. Later on we brought every paintings' 3d models and placed them in the wall with necessary scaling according to ratio. All the paintings were hung keeping the subject matter in mind. Thereby, everything in the scene was added.

When all the paintings were in place, we found the necessity of light in the scene. We deleted the main directional light from the scene and added 48 individual point lights for 48 paintings. The intensity, effective area and color of these lights were customized from the inspector. Later we added one master light on top of every room and made the roof a light emitting material. Thus it also works as the master light of the galley. Besides, the bluish glossy roof brought the concentrated mode for a gallery. Finally the scene became visually ready but still functions were to be added.

In Unity we can make things react with our action. That's the sole purpose of a game engine. So our objective was to add text information for each painting. To do that we first needed to create texts under a canvas in hierarchy. But using Unity's default text could make the information blurry when the screen is scaled. So, we imported a free package called Textmesh Pro, owned by Unity technologies themselves. So, with this text editor we created 48 text panels and wrote the necessary information about each painting in the individual panels. In order to trigger them when the camera gets close to a painting, we created a dummy cylinder before every paintings and kept its mesh renderers off. A trigger condition script is added with these cylinders and the texts were added in the public variable fields. Thus, according to the script's logic – whenever the camera gets to the collider range of any artwork, this trigger gets activated and shows the instruction. The instruction text says to press 'T' key for details and 'V' key for voice over. At that point if we put respective text panels in their public variable holder places in the inspector, the information texts just starts appearing nicely. But still pressing V we can't find the voice over. Because we didn't assign the voice clips in the public variable holders in the inspector of the trigger cylinders. As soon as we dragged and dropped the clips in places, the whole function started to run. Now we could walk inside the gallery, get information in texts with one key and listen voice over with the other.

Here we would like to add that the voice-over was recorded earlier before this process. But still, we had a lack of sound in our project which is the background music. We searched for cool piano music and came in contact with musician Aakash Gandhi [15], who played the 2 piano tracks used in this project. Once we had the soundtrack in hand, we just had to add this in the audio source component of the camera. After some adjustments with normal parameters, we found our desired environment of the virtual art gallery where we could hover and enjoy the artworks along with their information.

For main menu (user interface) we introduced very fundamental elements like-background images, texts, and buttons. Our crucial requirement was just the buttons to be responsive. Figure 7 demonstrates a glimpse of the main menu. If any of the blue buttons are clicked naming- Instruction, About Artist, About Developer, and Credits; the main menu page will just be inactive and another page like this will be active. And if we click the "Back" button on that page, that page will be inactive and the Main Menu page will be active again.

So, the key concept of such button activity is – "On Click" event. In Unity, every button has an "On Click" event in the inspector. There we can reference any canvas or object and can activate and deactivate UI environments with clicks. We can also call functions in "On click" event from the added C# scripts to reference object thereby we can change from one scene to another too. And that's what has done with the "Gallery" and "Exit" buttons.

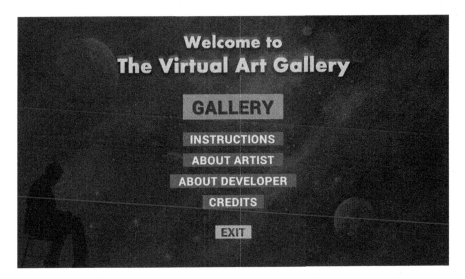

Fig. 7. UI for main menu (Color figure online)

The whole gallery is in one scene, and the whole UI is in another. When the "Gallery" button is pressed, the scene just changes to the next scene in serial. This serial is maintained from Build settings. When "Escape" key is pressed, that just redirects user to the previous scene, means Main Menu. The Exit button quits the application. So, all the scene management functions were added in C# scripts, and then were called by buttons' "On Click" event or key-code functions.

4 Conclusion

This paper describes the detailed demonstration a Windows based application which is interactive in nature. It can effectively showcase artworks particularly paintings in a virtual environment having the potential of being an excellent application for a wide group of users like- artists, art critics, curators and most significantly academic researchers. The entire development process of this application includes some highly sophisticated software like- Autodesk 3ds Max and Unity. Lots of challenges arose while implementing this application and every aspects of these challenges are mentioned in this paper. This application is an excellent combination of 3d technology and game development process. Needless to mention- this application is a very first endeavor of its kind even though it has some limitations like the scopes of customization from the user end is unavailable. However the appropriate utilization of this application even in this stage, can bring notable changes in the sector of arts holding the hand of advanced computing technologies.

References

1. Yuesheng, H., Tang, Y.Y.: Classification of 3D models for the 3D animation environments. In: 2009 IEEE International Conference on Systems, Man and Cybernetics (2009). https://doi.org/10.1109/icsmc.2009.5346642
2. Huang, L., Pei, Y.: Film and television animation design based on Maya and AE. In: 2010 3rd International Congress on Image and Signal Processing (2010). https://doi.org/10.1109/cisp.2010.5646354
3. Xu, X., Leng, C., Wu, Z.: Rapid 3D human modeling and animation based on sketch and motion database. In: 2011 Workshop on Digital Media and Digital Content Management (2011). https://doi.org/10.1109/dmdcm.2011.52
4. Feng, Y., Zhan, S.: Simulation of real water in 3D animation. In: 2011 International Conference on Multimedia Technology (2011). https://doi.org/10.1109/icmt.2011.6001656
5. Zhou, W., Xiang, N., Zhou, X.: Towards 3D communications: real time emotion driven 3D virtual facial animation. In: 2011 Workshop on Digital Media and Digital Content Management (2011). https://doi.org/10.1109/dmdcm.2011.76
6. Hong, P., Wen, Z., Huang, T.S., Shum, H.-Y.: Real-time speech-driven 3D face animation. In: Proceedings of First International Symposium on 3D Data Processing Visualization and Transmission (n.d.). https://doi.org/10.1109/tdpvt.2002.1024147
7. Suenaga, Y.: 3D measurement technologies for computer animation. In: Proceedings Computer Animation 1996 (n.d.). https://doi.org/10.1109/ca.1996.540499
8. Ying, G., Xuqing, L., Xiuliang, W., Yi, F., Shuxia, G.: Design and realization of 3D character animation engine. In: 2009 2nd IEEE International Conference on Broadband Network & Multimedia Technology (2009). https://doi.org/10.1109/icbnmt.2009.5347860
9. San-ao, X.: Application of Maya in film 3D animation design. In: 2011 3rd International Conference on Computer Research and Development (2011). https://doi.org/10.1109/iccrd.2011.5764150
10. Furukawa, M., Fukumoto, S., Kawasaki, H., Kawai, Y.: Interactive 3D animation system for Web3D. In: 2012 IEEE International Conference on Multimedia and Expo Workshops (2012). https://doi.org/10.1109/icmew.2012.122
11. Lam, A. D. K.-T., Su, Y.-Y.: A study on experimental teaching of 3D animation. In: 2016 International Conference on Applied System Innovation (ICASI) (2016). https://doi.org/10.1109/icasi.2016.7539903
12. https://www.autodesk.com/products/3ds-max/overview
13. https://unity.com
14. https://www.adobe.com/products/photoshop.html
15. https://www.88keystoeuphoria.com/about.php
16. https://www.quora.com/What-is-3d-animation
17. https://www.artworkarchive.com/blog/is-the-traditional-art-gallery-still-king

Enhanced Bag-of-Features Method Using Grey Wolf Optimization for Automated Face Retrieval

Arun Kumar Shukla$^{(\boxtimes)}$ and Suvendu Kanungo

Department of Computer Science and Engineering, Birla Institute of Technology,
Mesra, Ranchi, Allahabad Campus, Allahabad, India
aks.jit@gmail.com, s.kanungo@bitmesra.ac.in

Abstract. As images are increasing exponentially over the Internet, the retrieval of such images using content-based approach becomes an important research area. Out of the various models of the image retrievals, recognition of facial images is highly used by many application areas. However, due to the different variations involved in the facial images, it is a challenging problem. Therefore, this work introduces an efficient face recognition method which uses the bag-of-features approach for the same. The proposed bag-of-features based face recognition approach uses Grey wolf optimization algorithm for obtaining the prominent visual words. The enhanced bag-of-features based face recognition approach has been analyzed on a face database of Oracle Research Laboratory against the classification accuracy. The experimental results show that the presented method identifies the faces more accurately than the other metaheuristic based approaches.

Keywords: Image retrieval · K-means clustering · Face identification ·
Bag-of-features · Grey wolf optimization

1 Introduction

Automatic searching of faces on Internet is a demanding application due to the exponential increase in the uses of social platform like Facebook, Instagram, and many more. Moreover, it is also applicable to terrorist identification, tagging of faces, biometric analysis and other application areas. The automatic retrieval of faces can be utilized at different places like for marking of attendance, vigilance purpose, and for surveillance. In literature, various face recognition approaches have been presented like, PCA (principal component analysis) based approaches [1], elastic bunch graph matching algorithm based on fisher face [2–4], LDA based techniques [5], subspace learning [6], learning based techniques [7], and convolutional deep learning [8]. In general approach, face recognition systems first find the facial features from dataset of images followed by the multi-class classifiers for training using these features along with corresponding facial image labels. Such systems are known as face recognition systems based on model [9]. But such approaches are not efficient and depends heavily on the handcraft features, extracted manually. Hence, this study introduces a retrieval

© Springer Nature Singapore Pte Ltd. 2019
M. Singh et al. (Eds.): ICACDS 2019, CCIS 1046, pp. 519–528, 2019.
https://doi.org/10.1007/978-981-13-9942-8_49

method for faces which shows improvement of the performance over the existing system.

A CBIR system has mainly three phases; (i) features extraction from images, (ii) similarity measurement, and (iii) image retrieval. The feature extraction phase extracts the important features in the images. The phase of similarity measurement finds the similarity between the images and the query image using the extracted features which is used to get the query image from the image database. Various research groups have given their views on variety of CBIR based face recognition systems. Walsh Hadamard Transform (WHT) was introduced as a face sketch image retrieval system based on contents and given by Besbas et al. [10]. Shih and Liu [11] used the geometric properties for the retrieval of images. Further, a fuzzy decision and a parallel aggregation of features are used by ElAdel et al. [12] for face recognition. Desai and Sonawa [13] used three approaches of feature extraction (Gist, HOG, DWT) equivalent to a specified question image. Moreover, Sultana and Gavrilova [14] used KNN algorithm as a classifier and color, texture and shape features for identification of faces. However, it is observed in pilot studies that robustness of the multiple feature-based retrieval systems is better than the one feature-based method. In the same way, Wang et al. [15] efficiently merged the shape and texture features for a CBIR. Additionally, local and global attributes are used by Wu et al. [16] for the representation of faces. Therefore, it can be observed that good quality features give better performance for an image retrieval system [17].

In literature, many feature extraction methods were presented and classified into statistics-based approaches and learning-based approaches, especially for image retrieval. In the learning-based algorithms, the attributes of images are extracted through the machine learning models such as, restricted Boltzmann machines [19], auto-encoders [18], and deep learning [20]. These approaches perform good for various image databases but, their computational overheads are extensively greater. However, statistics-based techniques extract the external morphological structures such as shape and size to epitomize the images. These methods mostly do not qualify and degrade the precision of a classifier for a complex textured image. Additionally, some other popular methods that are used to characterize the images are LBP [21], SIFT [22] and HOG [23].

The bag-of-features (BOF) framework is one of the prime image classification methods, used by many classification problems [24]. It is a method emerged from the bag-of-words, used in the classification of documents. BOF converts each image into the histograms of visual words. Visual words are also known as codewords. Images are classified by the classifier on providing the generated histograms. This method performs better and its computational complexity is also efficient in case of the presence of occlusion and various transformations. This method sometimes generates the suboptimal outcomes when it uses k-means to obtain codewords because k-means shows biased behavior for different initial cluster seeds. In such cases, meta-heuristic methods yield better results. Thus, such approaches are extensively in a variety of actual world problems. The meta-heuristic approaches use the different natural phenomena for different optimization problems [25, 26]. The popular meta-heuristic approaches for clustering include GWO (Grey wolf optimization), SMO (spider monkey optimization) [27], ABC [28], GSA [30], and PSO (particle swarm optimization) [29].

GWO [31] is one of the prime techniques inspired from behavior of grey wolves. GWO depicts better convergence precision for standard benchmark problems than other meta-heuristics. Further, it was efficaciously useful for many applications such as image analysis, clustering of data, and many others. To obtain the best solutions, it uses the social behavior of wolves in which the search space is explored first followed by gradual exploitation similar to grey wolf hunting behavior. Keeping this in view in the present study GWO has been used for clustering the extracted keypoints in BOF and generating the visual words. This presented BOF has been verified for face identification on Oracle Research Laboratory (ORL) image dataset. This work is divided into following phases: the brief of GWO is depicted in Sect. 2. Section 3 presents the GWO based BOF method for image retrieval and Sect. 4 shows the experimental and statistical results. Section 5 concludes the paper.

2 Grey Wolf Optimization (GWO)

GWO is an approach inspired from nature and is used for many real-world optimization problems. It shows the leadership hierarchy of gray wolves during the process of hunting. The Grey wolves track a strict social dominance and walk in a 5–12 wolves group. According to their dominance behavior Grey wolves has four major groups which are termed as α (alpha), β (beta), δ (delta), and ω (omega) and their domination is shown in Fig. 1 [31].

In these four groups of Grey wolves, the Alpha group leads the other groups in the process of hunting. The β wolves in pyramid assists wolves of alpha group by taking decisions. The delta group has α and β Grey wolves and dominants omega. This group generally works as scouts, elders, hunters, sentinels, and caretakers. Whereas, omegas are passive to α, β, and δ wolves. Thus, α, β, and δ are the leading groups who performs the hunting. In addition to the group hunting, tracking, encircling, and attacking on the prey are different activities of leading groups of Grey wolves. As per the social behavior, GWO is modeled mathematically and used for different optimization problems. In the subsequent sections, various steps of GWO are presented.

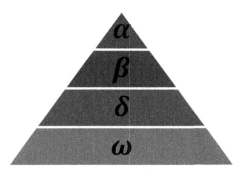

Fig. 1. Hierarchal dominance of the Grey wolves, decreasing from top to bottom [31].

2.1 Social Hierarchy

The GWO considers the best, second best, and the third best solutions as α, β, and δ respectively. Rest of the solutions are considered as ω.

2.2 Encircling Prey

In the encircling phase, the position of wolves changes according to Eq. (2) [31].

$$D = |C.Xp(t) - X(t)| \tag{1}$$

$$X(t+1) = Xp(t) - A.D \tag{2}$$

where, $Xp(t)$ and $X(t)$ show the prey's position and position of Grey wolf at iteration t respectively. The value of coefficient vectors, A and C, are measured as per Eqs. (3) and (4) respectively.

$$A = 2a.r_1 - a \tag{3}$$

$$C = 2.r_2 \tag{4}$$

where, r_1 and r_2 are generated randomly in between 0 and 1. The value of parameter **a** linearly decreases from 2 to 0 which manages the Grey wolf step size (**D**).

2.3 Hunting

The grey wolves perform hunting by Alpha group and is reinforced by β and δ wolves in GWO. This process is mathematically represented by the best 03 solutions as α, β, δ respectively in a iteration while omegas change their positions as per these groups. The following equation shows the mathematical formulations for the same equations [31]:

$$\overrightarrow{D_\alpha} = \left|\overrightarrow{C_1}.\overrightarrow{X_\alpha} - \vec{X}\right|, \overrightarrow{D_\beta} = \left|\overrightarrow{C_2}.\overrightarrow{X_\beta} - \vec{X}\right|, \overrightarrow{D_\delta} = \left|\overrightarrow{C_3}.\overrightarrow{X_\delta} - \vec{X}\right| \tag{5}$$

$$\overrightarrow{X_1} = \overrightarrow{X_\alpha} - \overrightarrow{A_1}.\left(\overrightarrow{D_\alpha}\right), \overrightarrow{X_2} = \overrightarrow{X_\beta} - \overrightarrow{A_2}.\left(\overrightarrow{D_\beta}\right), \overrightarrow{X_3} = \overrightarrow{X_\delta} - \overrightarrow{A_3}.\left(\overrightarrow{D_\delta}\right), \tag{6}$$

$$\vec{X}(t+1) = \frac{\overrightarrow{X_1} + \overrightarrow{X_2} + \overrightarrow{X_3}}{3} \tag{7}$$

where, the coefficient vectors are A_i and C_i. The step size is shown by D_i and X_i depicts the Grey wolf's position at an iteration.

2.4 Attacking Prey

By attacking prey, grey wolves' hunting becomes terminated and they stop moving. Mathematically it is simulated by parameter **A** which decrease linearly according to Eq. (2). The value of **a** is used to calculate by **A** which linearly decreases from 2 to 0.

That's why it is used in the exploitation of the solution space. Therefore, investigation stage becomes narrow due to which the solution sticks into local solution.

2.5 Search for Prey

GWO maintains the divergence behavior using **A** which is kept greater than one or less than −1 which also affects the exploration. Moreover, in all iterations an arbitrary value to **C** is allocated which shows the better investigation in the initial and final generations. It escapes the GWO from stagnation. Various phases of the elementary GWO are presented in Algorithm 1 [31].

3 Proposed Face Retrieval Approach

The presented face identification approach contains four phases as depicted in Fig. 2. First phase, input face images are taken by SURF feature descriptor and for each image corresponding feature vector is produced. In the second phase, GWO is used to perform keypoints clustering and generates the codewords which are utilized for generating the feature histograms for each image in the third step. In the final phase, SVM classifier is trained using the image feature histograms to recognize the face images. All the steps of this system are discussed in the following subsections.

Algo. 1 GWO (Grey Wolf Optimization) [31]

Input: Let there are N search agents X_i (i = 1, 2, . . ., N) of n dimensions.
Output: The best search agent X_α.
Initialize N agents randomly
Assign the values to **a**, **A**, and **C**
Each agent's fitness is to be measured
Select the best agent (X_α), second-best agent (X_β), and third best agent (X_δ)
while termination condition is false **do**
  for i=1 to N **do**
    Update the position of X_i by Eq. (7)
  end for
  Update **a**, **A**, and **C**
  Fitness of search agents are to be calculated
  Update X_α, X_β and X_δ
end while
return X_α

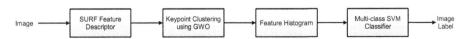

Fig. 2. Presented CBIR based face recognition system.

3.1 Feature Extraction

A significant step of a CBIR system is to extract the relevant and non-redundant attributes in the images. It will help to segregate the variety of faces. In this work, extraction of the attributes from image dataset of faces is carried out using fast and robust features SURF method [32] which utilizes the convolutions of image by means of the image's integrals and box filters. For the detection of interest points within the images this method uses Hessian matrix approximation. This method shows better performance for the images having blurred regions and is rotational and illumination. Hence, the proposed technique finds the features by SURF.

3.2 Enhanced GWO Based Clustering in BOF Method

Further, BOF framework is employed (after extraction of feature vectors form SURF descriptor) for representing feature vectors the meaningful image histogram. The BOF method generally first generates the codewords by performing the clustering using k-means approach on extracted feature vectors. Our work proposes a Grey wolf optimization algorithm-based method to cluster the feature vectors, since, the clustering of data using k-means shows biased behavior towards the initial cluster seeds and the steps for the same has been mentioned below.

1. The population of size N for GWO is randomly initialized. Each search agent has K decision variables which represents the K cluster heads.
2. Each search agent calculates the fitness by using intra-cluster distance which is shown in Eq. (8).

$$Minimize : \sum_{i=1}^{K} \sum_{features} \|feature - agent_i\|^2 \qquad (8)$$

3. Update search agents' positions as per the GWO method.
4. After the termination of the GWO, the best agent represents the K optimal visual words. Further, an image is represented as histograms of these visual words.

3.3 Feature Representation Using Histograms

After obtaining the optimal visual words, images are encoded into histograms of visual words which depicts the frequency count of codewords in an image. Mathematically, histogram ($H_j = \{H_{j1}, H_{j2}, \ldots, H_{jK}\}$) of each image ($I(j)$) is obtained by using Eq. (9).

$$H_{jk} = \sum_{i=1}^{P} \delta_{ik}(j) \quad for\, k = 1, 2, \ldots, K \qquad (9)$$

where, $\delta_{ik}(j)$ is one if visual word (v_k) is close to any visual word.

3.4   Face Recognition

At last the training of a classifier using the obtained histograms and corresponding image labels is performed. For the training of classifier, multi-class SVM is used which is fed by the histograms of images and respective labels. After the training, SVM classifier identifies the face images from test images.

4   Experimental Results

To analysis the efficiency of GWO based BOF method for face identification, Intel core i7 processors having RAM of 8 GB and MATLAB are used. For the face images, Oracle Research Laboratory dataset has been considered which is developed by AT & T, Cambridge which contains 400 images of 40 different individual, i.e. each individual has 10 images of varying expressions. PGM extension of image files, each of size 92×112 pixels and 256 grey levels per pixel were used in this work. The representative face images are depicted in Fig. 3. The considered database is segregated randomly into training and testing sets. As a classifier, SVM is used [33] with Gaussian kernel function [34]. Further, 10-fold cross validation is also used to prevent overfitting problem.

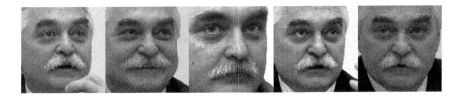

Fig. 3. Examples of face images of one object from the considered dataset [35].

A represented visual words histogram for an image is depicted in Fig. 4. The proposed GWO based BOF method for identification of faces has been tested against GWO, SMO, PSO, k-means, and GSA based approaches. Accuracy, precision, recall, and F-measure are used as performance parameters and are shown in Table 1. Significant values of all the parameters are shown in bold. From the table, it is observed that GWO based BOF method for identification of faces gives improved values for almost all the parameters. The presented approach returns 92.5% overall accuracy which is the best among other methods. Thus, the proposed face identification system outperforms the existing methods.

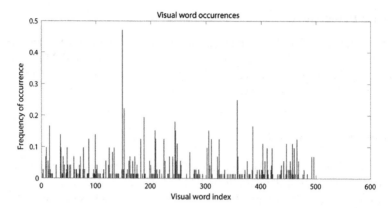

Fig. 4. Represented histogram for an image using the generated visual words.

Table 1. Comparative study of the GWO based BOF approach for face identification using different performance parameters.

S. no.	Approach	Accuracy	Recall	Precision	F1 score
1.	K-means	87.6	86.3	78.1	84.6
2.	SMO	89.1	89.2	89.3	89.1
3.	PSO	91.2	87.2	87.2	89.1
4.	GSA	91.0	86.1	87.0	89.1
5.	GWO	**92.5**	**90.2**	**89.9**	**90.1**

5 Conclusion

In the present paper, Content based method has been proposed for face identification. For the same GWO based BOF framework has been introduced. Oracle Research Laboratory (ORL) database for facial images was used to test the accuracy of the presented approach. Further, features from the images were extracted in this method using SURF descriptor. GWO method does clustering of extracted attributes and generates visual words. Histograms are obtained from these visual words that are further given to classifier SVM. Further, k-means, GWO, SMO, PSO, and GSA based face recognition methods were compared with present system for testing its efficiency and the same has been analyzed against accuracy, F1 score, recall, and precision. Result of this work depicts that the GWO based BOF method for face identification with overall accuracy of 92.5% (highest among other considered methods) outperforms the existing methods. Further, this method can be used for newer solutions to the real-world recognition problems and for added efficient results other parameters of GWO may be adjusted.

References

1. Yi, S., Lai, Z., He, Z., Cheung, Y.-M., Liu, Y.: Joint sparse principal component analysis. Pattern Recogn. **61**, 524–536 (2017)
2. Zafeiriou, S., Petrou, M.: 2.5 D elastic graph matching. Comput. Vis. Image Underst. **115**(7), 1062–1072 (2011)
3. Senaratne, R., Halgamuge, S., Hsu, A.: Face recognition by extending elastic bunch graph matching with particle swarm optimization. J. Multimed. **4**(4), 204–214 (2009)
4. Wiskott, L., Fellous, J.-M., Krüger, N., von der Malsburg, C.: Face recognition by elastic bunch graph matching. In: Sommer, G., Daniilidis, K., Pauli, J. (eds.) CAIP 1997. LNCS, vol. 1296, pp. 456–463. Springer, Heidelberg (1997). https://doi.org/10.1007/3-540-63460-6_150
5. Liu, C., Wechsler, H.: Enhanced fisher linear discriminant models for face recognition. In: 1998 Proceedings of Fourteenth International Conference on Pattern Recognition, vol. 2, pp. 1368–1372. IEEE (1998)
6. Lin, C., Long, F., Zhan, Y.: Facial expression recognition by learning spatiotemporal features with multi-layer independent subspace analysis. In: 2017 10th International Congress on Image and Signal Processing, BioMedical Engineering and Informatics (CISP-BMEI), pp. 1–6. IEEE (2017)
7. Lu, J., Wang, G., Zhou, J.: Simultaneous feature and dictionary learning for image set based face recognition. IEEE Trans. Image Process. **26**(8), 4042–4054 (2017)
8. Ding, C., Tao, D.: Trunk-branch ensemble convolutional neural networks for video-based face recognition. IEEE Trans. Pattern Anal. Mach. Intell. **40**, 1002–1014 (2017)
9. Matthews, I., Baker, S.: Active appearance models revisited. Int. J. Comput. Vis. **60**(2), 135–164 (2004)
10. Besbas, W., Artemi, M., Salman, R.: Content based image retrieval (CBIR) of face sketch images using WHT transform domain. Inform. Environ. Energy Appl. **66**, 77–81 (2014)
11. Shih, P., Liu, C.: Comparative assessment of content-based face image retrieval in different color spaces. Int. J. Pattern Recognit. Artif. Intell. **19**(07), 873–893 (2005)
12. ElAdel, A., Ejbali, R., Zaied, M., Amar, C.B.: A hybrid approach for content-based image retrieval based on fast beta wavelet network and fuzzy decision support system. Mach. Vis. Appl. **27**(6), 781–799 (2016)
13. Desai, R., Sonawane, B.: GIST, HOG, and DWT-based content-based image retrieval for facial images. In: Satapathy, S., Bhateja, V., Joshi, A. (eds.) Proceedings of the International Conference on Data Engineering and Communication Technology. Advances in Intelligent Systems and Computing, vol. 468, pp. 297–307. Springer, Singapore (2017). https://doi.org/10.1007/978-981-10-1675-2_31
14. Sultana, M., Gavrilova, M.L.: Face recognition using multiple content-based image features for biometric security applications. Int. J. Biometr. **6**(4), 414–434 (2014)
15. Wang, X.-Y., Liang, L.-L., Li, Y.-W., Yang, H.-Y.: Image retrieval based on exponent moments descriptor and localized angular phase histogram. Multimed. Tools Appl. **76**(6), 7633–7659 (2017)
16. Wu, Z., Ke, Q., Sun, J., Shum, H.Y.: Scalable face image retrieval with identity-based quantization and multi-reference re-ranking. In: 2010 IEEE Conference on Computer Vision and Pattern Recognition (CVPR), pp. 3469–3476. IEEE (2010)
17. Saraswat, M., Arya, K.: Feature selection and classification of leukocytes using random forest. Med. Biol. Eng. Comput. **52**, 1041–1052 (2014)
18. Xu, J., et al.: Stacked sparse autoencoder (SSAE) for nuclei detection on breast cancer histopathology images. IEEE Trans. Med. Imaging **35**(1), 119–130 (2016)

19. Chang, H., Nayak, N., Spellman, P.T., Parvin, B.: Characterization of tissue histopathology via predictive sparse decomposition and spatial pyramid matching. In: Mori, K., Sakuma, I., Sato, Y., Barillot, C., Navab, N. (eds.) MICCAI 2013. LNCS, vol. 8150, pp. 91–98. Springer, Heidelberg (2013). https://doi.org/10.1007/978-3-642-40763-5_12

20. Cruz-Roa, A.A., Arevalo Ovalle, J.E., Madabhushi, A., González Osorio, F.A.: A deep learning architecture for image representation, visual interpretability and automated basal-cell carcinoma cancer detection. In: Mori, K., Sakuma, I., Sato, Y., Barillot, C., Navab, N. (eds.) MICCAI 2013. LNCS, vol. 8150, pp. 403–410. Springer, Heidelberg (2013). https://doi.org/10.1007/978-3-642-40763-5_50

21. Ojala, T., Pietikäinen, M., Harwood, D.: A comparative study of texture measures with classification based on featured distributions. Pattern Recogn. 29(1), 51–59 (1996)

22. Lowe, D.G.: Distinctive image features from scale-invariant keypoints. Int. J. Comput. Vis. 60(2), 91–110 (2004)

23. Dalal, N., Triggs, B.: Histograms of oriented gradients for human detection. In: IEEE Computer Society Conference on Computer Vision and Pattern Recognition, CVPR 2005, vol. 1, pp. 886–893. IEEE (2005)

24. Csurka, G., Dance, C., Fan, L., Willamowski, J., Bray, C.: Visual categorization with bags of keypoints. In: Workshop on Statistical Learning in Computer Vision, ECCV, Prague, vol. 1, no. 1–22, pp. 1–2 (2004)

25. Hussain, K., Salleh, M.N.M., Cheng, S., Shi, Y.: Metaheuristic research: a comprehensive survey. Artif. Intell. Rev. 2018, 1–43 (2018)

26. Saraswat, M., Arya, K., Sharma, H.: Leukocyte segmentation in tissue images using differential evolution algorithm. Swarm Evol. Comput. 11, 46–54 (2013)

27. Bansal, J.C., Sharma, H., Jadon, S.S., Clerc, M.: Spider monkey optimization algorithm for numerical optimization. Memetic Comput. 6(1), 31–47 (2014)

28. Mohammadi, F.G., Abadeh, M.S.: Image steganalysis using a bee colony-based feature selection algorithm. Eng. Appl. Artif. Intell. 31, 35–43 (2014)

29. Chhikara, R.R., Sharma, P., Singh, L.: A hybrid feature selection approach based on improved PSO and filter approaches for image steganalysis. Int. J. Mach. Learn. Cybernet. 7, 1195–1206 (2016)

30. Rashedi, E., Nezamabadi-Pour, H., Saryazdi, S.: GSA: a gravitational search algorithm. Inf. Sci. 179, 2232–2248 (2009)

31. Mirjalili, S., Mirjalili, S.M., Lewis, A.: Grey wolf optimizer. Adv. Eng. Softw. 69, 46–61 (2014)

32. Bay, H., Ess, A., Tuytelaars, T., Van Gool, L.: Speeded-up robust features (SURF). Comput. Vis. Image Underst. 110, 346–359 (2008)

33. Ali Bagheri, M., Montazer, G.A., Escalera, S.: Error correcting output codes for multiclass classification: application to two image vision problems. In: 2012 16th CSI International Symposium on Artificial Intelligence and Signal Processing (AISP), pp. 508–513. IEEE (2012)

34. Jiang, Y.-G., Yang, J., Ngo, C.-W., Hauptmann, A.G.: Representations of keypoint-based semantic concept detection: A comprehensive study. IEEE Trans. Multimed. 12(1), 42–53 (2010)

35. ORL database of face images, September 2018. https://www.cl.cam.ac.uk/research/dtg/attarchive/facedatabase.html

A Context-Aware Approach to Enhance Service Utility for Location Privacy in Internet of Things

Shivangi Shukla(✉) ⓘ and Sankita J. Patel(✉)

Sardar Vallabhbhai National Institute of Technology, Surat 395007, Gujarat, India
shivangishukla968@gmail.com, sankitapatel@gmail.com

Abstract. The Internet of Things (IoT) is a new revolution of technology that interconnects billions of smart objects to each other offering autonomous services and comfort to everyday human lives. However, the information exchanged to provide services can introduce potential risks in terms of security and privacy. The geographic location of the user is one such information that can breach location privacy of the user. Researchers have provided algorithms to sustain location privacy of the users in IoT. The existing approach provides fixed base points as an obfuscated location to preserve location privacy of the user. However, these fixed base points are sometimes too far or too close to the user's true location that either he cannot utilize services provided by Location Based Services (LBS) or sometimes there is not much distance between actual and obfuscated location. In this paper, the proposed method procures random obfuscated location according to time and location of the context-aware IoT device while retaining service utility. Experiment results compares the existing and proposed algorithm and shows that the proposed algorithm maintains a certain distance with user's true location and the services provided by LBS can still be used.

Keywords: Internet of Things · Location-based services · Security · Privacy

1 Introduction

After the development of computer and internet, Internet of Things (IoT) can be called as next wave in the era of computing and technology. The concept of IoT was first introduced in the year 1998 by Kevin Ashton in MIT Auto-ID lab [1]. Since then IoT has gained more and more attention in the academic and industrial field [2]. IoT is the seamless integration of interconnected physical objects into information network to provide intelligent and automated services to human beings. Its application domain incorporates Home Automation, Smart Healthcare, Intelligent Transport System (ITS), Smart Agriculture etc. [3].

The diverseness of IoT increases the security and privacy concerns because of three reasons: firstly, the traditional internet is used for connection of devices

© Springer Nature Singapore Pte Ltd. 2019
M. Singh et al. (Eds.): ICACDS 2019, CCIS 1046, pp. 529–542, 2019.
https://doi.org/10.1007/978-981-13-9942-8_50

secondly, numerous devices equipped with sensors are connected to the network and lastly, all these devices interact with each other without human interference. The traditional security and privacy countermeasures imposes heavy computations on resource-constraint IoT devices. Hence, defining security, privacy and trust model in IoT is a major challenge.

The privacy concerns needs to be addressed at every step of IoT environment. However, these privacy concerns can be broadly classified into four categories namely privacy of device, privacy during communication, privacy in storage and privacy at processing [4]. The IoT device privacy concern comprehends hiding its identity, location and other personal information for protection against malicious users and intruders. Location privacy of IoT device provides protection to the user's location information from intruders and deceitful third parties.

Location Based Services (LBS) provides convenience and flexibility to IoT devices (say smart cars) by presenting information about nearest restaurants, shopping malls, petrol pumps etc. to the user. However, revealing the exact location of user can breach his privacy. Hence, preservation of the actual location of user is required in IoT environment. But the false location generated should be such that the information provided by LBS is beneficial to the user. Also, the ubiquitous devices of IoT paradigm exchange information to provide autonomous services without human assistance hence, context awareness plays a significant role to allow devices to sense their physical environment such as location, time etc. and change their behavior accordingly [5].

Researchers have provided algorithms to preserve location privacy of IoT users. One of the existing location privacy methods is Dynamic Location Disclosure Agent (DLDA) [6] which uses context-aware adaptive approach to preserve location privacy of IoT devices. This approach produces obfuscated location which is fixed for suburb, state and country level. However, these fixed obfuscated locations have two major drawbacks. Firstly, if the obfuscated location provided to LBS is in different suburb or state then, LBS will provide information (say nearest restaurants or supermarkets) about that suburb or state which will be pointless for the user. Also, if the user's actual location is close to one of these fixed obfuscated locations then there is not much distance between actual and obfuscated location of the user.

In this paper, we aim to amend DLDA agent such that random obfuscated locations are generated for IoT users. Generating obfuscated location with the help of Enhanced Semantic Obfuscation Technique (ESOT) [7] can help in maintaining balance between location privacy of user and utilization of location-based services. The proposed methodology amends the context-aware adaptive approach to use ESOT and compares the location privacy and service utility of LBS. The rest of the paper is organized as follows. Section 2 discusses location privacy techniques. Section 3 discusses the motivation and contribution. Section 4 presents the proposed algorithm. Sections 5 and 6 discusses the experimental work and result analysis respectively and in the end Sect. 7 covers conclusion and future work.

2   Location Privacy Techniques

Disclosing the actual location of users can lead to serious consequences such as stalking, blackmail and physical violence. Regular visits to locations such as AIDS clinic or abortion clinic can also harm an individual's social status and reputation. Location privacy prevents the learning of an individual's location either current or past from other parties [8]. This section briefly discusses the techniques to preserve location privacy.

Location Anonymization Approach: This approach is based on the concept of hiding the user's actual location by making it indistinguishable from other users location. Gedik et al. [9] proposed location privacy framework for mobile clients in which user can specify the minimum level of anonymity he wants. A trusted anonymization server runs message perturbation engine which performs location anonymization for the user. Ying et al. [10] proposed a method named Protecting Location Privacy with Clustering Anonymization (PLPCA) for preserving location privacy in vehicular networks. This method first transforms road map into edge-cluster graph to acquire road and traffic information. Then, it defines a Cloaking Region (CR) having at-least k vehicles and l road segments i.e. k-anonymity and l-diversity. Aryan et al. [11] proposed location preservation algorithm using the concept of both k-anonymization and pseudo-anonymization. However, this approach requires a Trusted Third Party (TTP) to execute the algorithm.

Randomization Noise-Based Technique: To conceal the user's actual location from adversary, this technique adds random noise to it. Wightman et al. [12] proposed three techniques namely N-Rand, N-Mix and N-Dispersion. These algorithms provide better average distance from actual location as compared to classic techniques Rand and Distortion. Wightman et al. [13] proposed θ-RAND technique for proactive applications that continuously track their users. The author compared this technique with N-Rand and instead of using symmetrical geometric area of radius r_{max} defined by user in case of N-Rand, θ-RAND technique generates circle sector of angle θ and radius r_{max}. This technique prevents noise filtering attack as compared to N-Rand technique. The authors extended this work and proposed Pinwheel obfuscation technique [14]. Instead of using circle of maximum radius to generate random points, this algorithm uses pinwheel-like polygons to generate random points. Comparing N-Rand, θ-RAND and Pinwheel, the filtered noise level is 35% in case of N-Rand, 30% in case of θ-RAND and 15% in case of Pinwheel technique [14].

Cryptography Primitive Based Approach: This technique protects the location of user by using encryption techniques. Shao et al. [15] proposed fine-grained privacy preserving LBS framework called FINE to provide location privacy to mobile users. To provide location privacy to user and confidentiality to LBS data, this framework uses ciphertext-policy anonymous attribute based encryption technique. It helps the devices to avoid operations that require massive resources by providing transformation key and proxy re-encryption key. Yi et al. [16] proposed a solution to preserve location privacy where user queries LBS about k

nearest point of interests (POIs). The solution uses Paillier public-key cryptosystem to provide location privacy in k nearest neighbor (kNN) queries.

Dummy Location Selection Approach: This approach replace the user's actual location with dummy location to provide location privacy. Lu et al. [17] proposed privacy-area aware dummy location privacy (PAD) for mobile users. This approach selects dummy location from a virtual grid or circle as per privacy requirements. However, light-weight server is required for integration of PAD into mobile devices. Niu et al. [18] proposed two algorithms namely Dummy-Location Selection (DLS) and enhanced-DLS. The DLS algorithm selects dummy location based on entropy metric and enhanced-DLS enlarges cloaking region to ensure the dummy location selected is as far as possible.

Obfuscation Based Approach: This technique changes the user's actual location to slightly different location. This technique hides the location information but not user's identity. Ardagna et al. [19] proposed spatial obfuscation based technique to preserve location privacy. The authors [19] presented a formal way to determine user's privacy preference and metric for location accuracy. Ardagna et al. [20] proposed different obfuscation operators that can be used individually or in combination to preserve location of the user. The results of [20] show that these operators provide better location privacy than the existing approaches. Zhang et al. [21] proposed a method for preservation of location privacy named path based access control method. This model uses access probability that adjusts itself according to moving path of mobile users in history.

3   Motivation and Contribution

The location privacy algorithms in IoT environment needs to be context-aware i.e. sense their physical requirements and change their behavior according. Also, to procure the services from LBS, the false location generated should trade-off between location privacy and service utility. Consider the following example to have a better view of location privacy and context-awareness requirements of the users in IoT.

Consider a smart car in IoT environment that sends user's locations to other IoT devices in his house, office etc. to manage his daily activities. For instance, it sends user's location to the digital diary in his office to manage his official appointments and meetings. With the help of Intelligent Transport System (ITS) and LBS, it provides information such as optimum navigation paths with lesser traffic jams while he is driving, nearest restaurant with available discounts during his lunch hours, nearest petrol pumps if the petrol in his smart car is not sufficient etc. While driving towards home, this smart car sends user's location to home appliances like cooling system to start its cooling functionality automatically. The user visits a particular hospital periodically and requires the smart car to provide highest privacy level while he visits this hospital. However, all these information provided to user are automated and not assisted by user. But the user has special privacy requirements like while he visits the hospital, highest level of privacy should be provided. Also while searching for nearest restaurant, the user requires moderate level of location privacy. While managing office appointments during working hours, the smart car can send his actual location. All these changes in privacy requirements should be automated and the user need not worry about it.

Elkhodr et al. [6] proposed location privacy approach that is context-aware and provides location privacy to the user. This approach uses DLDA agent to decide privacy level according to physical environment. However, this proposed approach has fixed base points as obfuscated location for suburb, state and country level. These fixed base points are generated as obfuscated location for privacy level 1, 2 and 3. However, these base points have two shortcomings. Firstly, if the user's actual location is close to any fixed points, then there is not much distance between true and obfuscated location of user. Secondly, if user's actual location is too far from these fixed points, then the information by LBS is of no use for the user.

The motive is to produce obfuscated location randomly within a certain range. The defined range will help in generating obfuscated location in such a manner that the user can utilize the services of LBS to some extent. Random generation of obfuscated location will ensure that there is always some distance between actual and obfuscated location which the DLDA [6] can't provide. The technique used in this paper for providing location privacy is based on obfuscation based approach as this approach does not rely on presence of k users (unlike location anonymization approach) and is less costly than cryptography based approach.

Ullah et al. [7] proposed Enhanced Semantic Obfuscation Technique (ESOT) which generates obfuscated location randomly. However, the random points generated lie within a specific range so that it maintains balance between location privacy and service utility.

Our contribution is to modify DLDA [6] by using ESOT [7] to provide following features:

- Four different levels of privacy along with automated change of privacy preferences with varying time and location.
- Generation of obfuscated location randomly.
- Services provided by LBS for these obfuscated location can be utilized by the user.
- These obfuscated locations are never too close to the user.

4   Proposed Algorithm

4.1   Formal Definition

The location privacy preservation techniques has two algorithms: decide privacy level algorithm *FindPrivacyLevel* and generate obfuscated location algorithm *GenerateObfuscateLocation*. The notations used in the algorithms are briefly explained in Table 1.

1. **FindPrivacyLevel** $\left(\left(\mathbf{L}\left(\mathbf{x}, \mathbf{y} \right)_i, \left(\mathbf{CT}' \right)_i \right) \to \mathbf{pl}_{j,i} \right)$. This algorithm takes current location $L\left(x, y \right)_i$ and current time $\left(CT' \right)_i$ of ith user as input and decides the privacy level $pl_{j,i}$. The privacy level can either be $pl_{0,i}$, $pl_{1,i}$, $pl_{2,i}$ or $pl_{3,i}$ based on current time and location of the user. The privacy level $pl_{0,i}$ generates the actual location $L\left(x, y \right)_i$ as obfuscated location $L_{of}\left(x, y \right)_i'$. If the current time $\left(CT' \right)_i$ lies within $\left[T\left(lo, pl_j \right)_i, T\left(up, pl_j \right)_i \right]$ then privacy level is set to $pl_{j,i}$. Also, the privacy level is set to $pl_{3,i}$ if the current location $L\left(x, y \right)_i$ is categorized as sensitive location $L_{se}\left(x, y \right)_i''$. By default, the privacy level is set to $pl_{2,i}$ however, this default privacy level can vary from user to user.

Table 1. Notations used in proposed algorithm

Notations	Description
L	Actual location
(x, y)	Latitude $= x$ and longitude $= y$
$L\left(x, y \right)_i$	The ith user actual location with latitude x and longitude y
$L_{of}\left(x, y \right)_i'$	The ith user obfuscated location with latitude x and longitude y
$L_{se}\left(x, y \right)_i''$	The ith user sensitive location with latitude x and longitude y
pl_i	The ith user location privacy level
$pl_{j,i}$	The ith user location privacy level $j, j \in \{0, 1, 2, 3\}$
$\left(CT' \right)_i$	Current time of ith user
$\left(TR' \right)_i$	Time range of ith user
$T\left(lo, pl_j \right)_i$	Lower time limit of ith user with location privacy level $pl_{j,i}$
$T\left(up, pl_j \right)_i$	Upper time limit of ith user with location privacy level $pl_{j,i}$
R1/R2/R3	Location privacy ranges for generating $L_{of}\left(x, y \right)_i'$ for $pl_{1,i}/pl_{2,i}/pl_{3,i}$
$(POI_{ext})_i$	The ith user Point of Interest (POI) generated by $L_{of}\left(x, y \right)_i'$ of existing algorithm [6]
$(POI_{pro})_i$	The ith user Point of Interest (POI) generated by $L_{of}\left(x, y \right)_i'$ of proposed algorithm
d_{ext}'	Distance between $L\left(x, y \right)_i$ and $(POI_{ext})_i$
d_{pro}'	Distance between $L\left(x, y \right)_i$ and $(POI_{pro})_i$

2. **GenerateObfuscateLocation** $\left(\left(\mathbf{L}\left(\mathbf{x}, \mathbf{y} \right)_i, \mathbf{pl}_{j,i} \right) \to \left(\mathbf{L}_{\mathbf{of}}\left(\mathbf{x}, \mathbf{y} \right)_i' \right) \right)$. This algorithm takes current location $L\left(x, y \right)_i$ as input and based on privacy level $pl_{j,i}$ decided by *FindPrivacyLevel*, it generates random obfuscated location $L_{of}\left(x, y \right)_i'$ within the range of R1/R2/R3 for privacy level $pl_{1,i}/pl_{2,i}/pl_{3,i}$. The location privacy range R1/R2/R3 is according to ESOT [7].

Algorithm 1. *FindPrivacyLevel()*

Input: $L(x,y)_i$, $\left(CT'\right)_i$

Output: pl_i

1: **if** $L(x,y)_i == L_{se}(x,y)_i''$ **then**
2:     Set $pl_i \leftarrow pl_{3,i}$
3: **else if** $T(lo,pl_0)_i \leq \left(CT'\right)_i$ **and** $\left(CT'\right)_i \leq T(up,pl_0)_i$ **then**
4:     Set $pl_i \leftarrow pl_{0,i}$
5: **else if** $T(lo,pl_1)_i \leq \left(CT'\right)_i$ **and** $\left(CT'\right)_i \leq T(up,pl_1)_i$ **then**
6:     Set $pl_i \leftarrow pl_{1,i}$
7: **else if** $T(lo,pl_2)_i \leq \left(CT'\right)_i$ **and** $\left(CT'\right)_i \leq T(up,pl_2)_i$ **then**
8:     Set $pl_i \leftarrow pl_{2,i}$
9: **else if** $T(lo,pl_3)_i \leq \left(CT'\right)_i$ **and** $\left(CT'\right)_i \leq T(up,pl_3)_i$ **then**
10:    Set $pl_i \leftarrow pl_{3,i}$
11: **else**
12:    Set $pl_i \leftarrow pl_{2,i}$
13: **end if**
14: **return** (pl_i)

Algorithm 2. *GenerateObfuscateLocation()*

Input: $L(x,y)_i$

Output: $L_{of}(x,y)_i'$

1: Set R1:= $(200m < R1 < 250m)$
2: Set R2:= $(250m < R2 < 300m)$
3: Set R3:= $(300m < R3 < 350m)$
4: $pl_i \leftarrow FindPrivacyLevel()$
5: **if** $pl_i == pl_{0,i}$ **then**
6:     $L_{of}(x,y)_i' \leftarrow L(x,y)_i$
7: **else if** $pl_i == pl_{1,i}$ **then**
8:     Generate $L_{of}(x,y)_i'$ in range R1
9: **else if** $pl_i == pl_{2,i}$ **then**
10:    Generate $L_{of}(x,y)_i'$ in range R2
11: **else**
12:    Generate $L_{of}(x,y)_i'$ in range R3
13: **end if**
14: **return** $\left(L_{of}(x,y)_i'\right)$

---

5 Experimental Work

Three different metrics are considered for evaluation namely, Context Awareness, Location Privacy and Service Utility. Location privacy is evaluated as the distance between $L(x,y)_i$ and $L_{of}(x,y)_i'$ produced by existing algorithm [6] and proposed algorithm. For context-awareness, $\left(CT'\right)_i$ and $L(x,y)_i$ is taken into consideration to provide four levels of privacy i.e. $pl_{0,i}$, $pl_{1,i}$, $pl_{2,i}$ and $pl_{3,i}$ to the ith user. Service utility metric refers to the utilization of services provided by LBS. LBS provides information like nearest located Automated Teller Machine (ATM), supermarket, restaurants etc. These locations are referred as Point Of Interest (POI). So, $(POI_{ext})_i$ and $(POI_{pro})_i$ are obtained according to $L_{of}(x,y)_i'$ of existing algorithm [6] and proposed algorithm respectively. The distance between $L(x,y)_i$ and attained $(POI_{ext})_i$ or $(POI_{pro})_i$ are compared between existing algorithm [6] and proposed algorithm for Quality of Service (QoS).

The experiment is performed on Cooja simulator and Contiki operating System. The motes of Cooja simulator have low computational capabilities and consume less-energy hence, well-suited to run experiments for IoT environment [22]. It should be noted that $(POI_{ext})_i$ and $(POI_{pro})_i$ are derived from Google Maps.

The user's policies assumed in the experiments are as follows:

- For time $\left(CT'\right)_i = 0$, the ith user requires privacy level $pl_{2,i}$.
- For time $\left(CT'\right)_i = 1$ to $\left(CT'\right)_i = 2$, the ith user requires privacy level $pl_{1,i}$.
- For time $\left(CT'\right)_i = 4$ to $\left(CT'\right)_i = 5$ the ith user requires privacy level $pl_{0,i}$.
- For time $\left(CT'\right)_i = 6$ to $\left(CT'\right)_i = 7$ the ith user requires privacy level $pl_{3,i}$.
- The coordinates L(21.167136, 72.785971) i.e. State Bank of India, Athwa, Surat, Gujarat is categorized as sensitive location $L_{se}(x,y)_i''$ hence, requiring privacy level $pl_{3,i}$. The default location privacy level is provided as $pl_{2,i}$.

The experiment is performed in Surat city of Gujarat, India. The existing algorithm [6] has fixed obfuscated location at suburb, state and country level. However, if we assume base points is in some other state or country, it would be of no use of comparing the service quality of LBS of a city while user resides in some other city. Hence, the base points for all the privacy levels for existing algorithm [6] are assumed to be in Surat. The assumed fixed base points for the existing algorithm [6] are:

- For privacy level $pl_{1,i}$, $L_{of}(x,y)_j'$ is L(21.163256, 72.785540)
- For privacy level $pl_{2,i}$, $L_{of}(x,y)_j$ is L(21.155950, 72.763967)
- For privacy level $pl_{3,i}$, $L_{of}(x,y)_i$ is L(21.150457, 72.761214)

The actual location of ith user $L(x,y)_i$ for Test Case 1 is assumed as L(21.172178, 72.789937) and for Test Case 2 is assumed as L(21.149822, 72.761509). For the diversity of POI, Test case 1 assumes POI as nearest located ATM and Test case 2 assumes POI as nearest located restaurant.

6   Result Analysis

This section analysis the results obtained from experimental work of Test case 1 and Test case 2. For Test case 1, Table 2 shows experiment results of generating

Table 2. Comparison of location privacy for Test Case 1

Current time	Privacy level	Existing algorithm [6]		Proposed algorithm	
		Obfuscated location $L_{of}(x,y)'_i$	Distance between $L(x,y)_i$ and $L_{of}(x,y)'_i$ (in m)	Obfuscated location $L_{of}(x,y)'_i$	Distance between $L(x,y)_i$ and $L_{of}(x,y)'_i$ (in m)
$\left(CT'\right)_i = 0$	$pl_{2,i}$	21.155950, 72.763967	3250	21.174742, 72.790179	291.48
$\left(CT'\right)_i = 1$	$pl_{1,i}$	21.163256, 72.785540	1080	21.174148, 72.790131	219.88
$\left(CT'\right)_i = 2$	$pl_{1,i}$	21.163256, 72.785540	1080	21.174391, 72.790155	244.75
$\left(CT'\right)_i = 3$	$pl_{2,i}$	21.155950, 72.763967	3250	21.174769, 72.790193	280.50
$\left(CT'\right)_i = 4$	$pl_{0,i}$	21.172178, 72.789937	—	21.172178, 72.789937	—
$\left(CT'\right)_i = 5$	$pl_{0,i}$	21.172178, 72.789937	—	21.172178, 72.789937	—
$\left(CT'\right)_i = 6$	$pl_{3,i}$	21.150457, 72.761214	3840	21.175309, 72.790246	342.94
$\left(CT'\right)_i = 7$	$pl_{3,i}$	21.150457, 72.761214	3840	21.175219, 72.790237	329.45

Table 3. Comparison of QoS for Test Case 1

Current time	Privacy level	d'_{ext} (in m) [6]	d'_{pro} (in m) (proposed algorithm)
$\left(CT'\right)_i = 0$	$pl_{2,i}$	3020	308.15
$\left(CT'\right)_i = 1$	$pl_{1,i}$	683.51	308.15
$\left(CT'\right)_i = 6$	$pl_{3,i}$	3300	308.15

obfuscated location for existing algorithm [6] and proposed algorithm. Table 3 shows the comparison of QoS for Test Case 1. The Figs. 1 and 2 shows comparison of location privacy and QoS for Test case 1 respectively. According to existing algorithm [6] in this case, location privacy is provided for all the three levels $pl_{1,i}$, $pl_{2,i}$ and $pl_{3,i}$ but the $(POI_{ext})_i$ obtained as per obfuscated location $L_{of}(x,y)'_i$ is distant from user's actual location $L(x,y)_i$. It should be noted that this distance d'_{ext} will increase as user moves away from the assumed fixed obfuscated location of existing algorithm [6]. However, according to the proposed algorithm for Test case 1, the obfuscated location $L_{of}(x,y)'_i$ are generated within a specific range

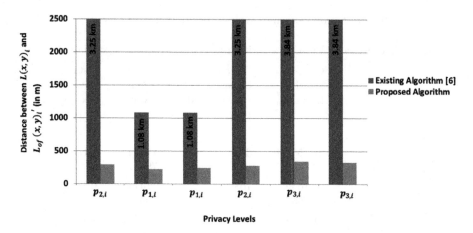

Fig. 1. Comparison of location privacy for Test Case 1

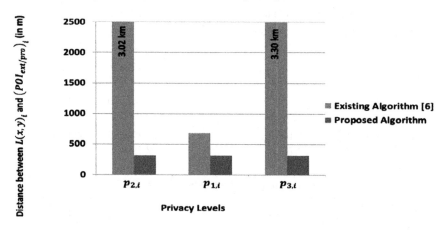

Fig. 2. Comparison of QoS for Test Case 1

from user's actual location $L\,(x,y)_i$ so, the $(POI_{pro})_i$ obtained may not be ideal but the distance d'_{pro} is not too far from the user's actual location $L\,(x,y)_i$.

For Test case 2, Table 4 shows the experiment results of generating obfuscated location for existing algorithm [6] and proposed algorithm. Table 5 shows the comparison of QoS for Test Case 2. The Figs. 3 and 4 compares the location privacy and QoS for Test case 2. According to existing algorithm [6] for this case, the location privacy provided for $pl_{3,i}$ is less than that of $pl_{1,i}$ because the user's actual location $L\,(x,y)_i$ is close to the assumed obfuscated location $L_{of}\,(x,y)'_i$ of privacy level $pl_{3,i}$. Not only for this location but also for all those locations that are close to the assumed obfuscated location, the existing algorithm [6] will not provide sufficient distance between actual location $L\,(x,y)_i$ and obfuscated location $L_{of}\,(x,y)'_i$. However, the proposed algorithm in Test case 2, $L_{of}\,(x,y)'_i$

Table 4. Comparison of location privacy for Test Case 2

Current time	Privacy level	Existing algorithm [6]		Proposed algorithm	
		Obfuscated location $L_{of}(x,y)'_i$	Distance between $L(x,y)_i$ and $L_{of}(x,y)'_i$ (in m)	Obfuscated location $L_{of}(x,y)'_i$	Distance between $L(x,y)_i$ and $L_{of}(x,y)'_i$ (in m)
$\left(CT'\right)_i = 0$	$pl_{2,i}$	21.155950, 72.763967	687.10	21.152346, 72.761751	272.68
$\left(CT'\right)_i = 1$	$pl_{1,i}$	21.163256, 72.785540	2910	21.151864, 72.761699	212.93
$\left(CT'\right)_i - 2$	$pl_{1,i}$	21.163256, 72.785540	2910	21.151863, 72.761711	210.95
$\left(CT'\right)_i = 3$	$pl_{2,i}$	21.155950, 72.763967	687.10	21.152375, 72.761956	278.44
$\left(CT'\right)_i = 4$	$pl_{0,i}$	21.149822, 72.761509	—	21.149822, 72.761509	—
$\left(CT'\right)_i = 5$	$pl_{0,i}$	21.149822, 72.761509	—	21.149822, 72.761509	—
$\left(CT'\right)_i = 6$	$pl_{3,i}$	21.150457, 72.761214	67.16	21.152952, 72.761808	344.31
$\left(CT'\right)_i = 7$	$pl_{3,i}$	21.150457, 72.761214	67.16	21.175219, 72.790237	318.41

Table 5. Comparison of QoS for Test Case 2

Current time	Privacy level	d'_{ext} (in m) [6]	d'_{pro} (in m) (proposed algorithm)
$\left(CT'\right)_i = 0$	$pl_{2,i}$	719.08	408.35
$\left(CT'\right)_i = 1$	$pl_{1,i}$	2440	147.94
$\left(CT'\right)_i = 6$	$pl_{3,i}$	147.94	408.35

maintains the distance from user's actual location $L(x,y)_i$ for privacy levels $pl_{1,i}$, $pl_{2,i}$ and $pl_{3,i}$.

It should be noted that the existing algorithm [6] generates same coordinates as obfuscated location $L_{of}(x,y)'_i$ at different time instances for the same privacy level $pl_{j,i}$. However, the proposed algorithm generates different obfuscated location $L_{of}(x,y)'_i$ at different time instance for the same privacy level $pl_{j,i}$. Also, in case of existing algorithm if the assumed obfuscated location $L_{of}(x,y)'_i$ for $pl_{3,i}$ happens to be close to the sensitive location $L_{se}(x,y)''_i$ then the existing algorithm [6] will not be able to maintain the location privacy required for $pl_{3,i}$.

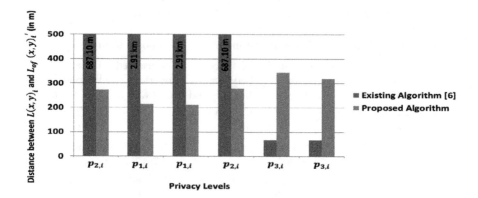

Fig. 3. Comparison of location privacy for Test Case 2

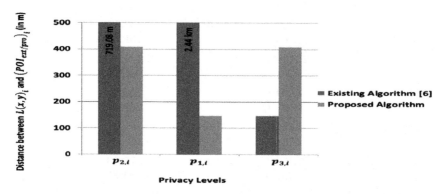

Fig. 4. Comparison of QoS for Test Case 2

To summarize, the proposed algorithm always maintains the distance between $L\left(x,y\right)_i$ and $L_{of}\left(x,y\right)_i^{'}$ within specific range; hence the obfuscated location $L_{of}\left(x,y\right)_i^{'}$ is never too close to user's true location $L\left(x,y\right)_i$. Also, even for the same level of privacy, different coordinates of latitude and longitude are generated at different instance of time. The proposed algorithm generates obfuscated location $L_{of}\left(x,y\right)_i^{'}$ such that the $\left(POI_{pro}\right)_i$ obtained can be utilized by the user, thus, maintaining the balance between location privacy and QoS.

7 Conclusion and Future Work

In IoT applications, millions of connected resource-constraint devices exchange confidential and sensitive information about users and devices. One such information can be the actual location of a user in IoT paradigm. As communication among IoT devices occurs without any human-intervention, necessitates the devices to be context-aware. Proposed algorithm considers contextual information as current time and user's actual location and aims to provide location privacy while retaining service utility for context-aware IoT devices. With the help of ESOT, the proposed algorithm ensures the generated random obfuscated locations can utilize LBS services. The proposed algorithm collects user's requirements and policies and then according to the current environment, it provides location privacy to the IoT devices. For the same level of privacy, different coordinates of latitude and longitude are generated at different time instances. The LBS services can be utilized even at the highest level of privacy. The context-aware adaptive model maintains balance between location privacy and service utility.

In future, this work can be extended by considering other contextual information like network settings and some more user policies for them. Proposed algorithm relies on device computational capabilities, may require enhancement further considering the limitation in computational capabilities in IoT paradigm.

References

1. Bandyopadhyay, D., Sen, J.: Internet of things: applications and challenges in technology and standardization. Wirel. Pers. Commun. **58**(1), 49–69 (2011). https://doi.org/10.1007/s11277-011-0288-5
2. Liu, Y., Zhou, G.: Key technologies and applications of internet of things. In: 2012 Fifth International Conference on Intelligent Computation Technology and Automation (ICICTA), pp. 197–200. IEEE (2012). https://doi.org/10.1109/ICICTA.2012.56
3. Alaba, F.A., Othman, M., Hashem, I.A.T., Alotaibi, F.: Internet of things security: a survey. J. Netw. Comput. Appl. **88**, 10–28 (2017). https://doi.org/10.1016/j.jnca.2017.04.002
4. Kumar, J.S., Patel, D.R.: A survey on internet of things: security and privacy issues. Int. J. Comput. Appl. **90**(11), 20–26 (2014). https://doi.org/10.5120/15764-4454
5. Perera, C., Zaslavsky, A., Christen, P., Georgakopoulos, D.: Context aware computing for the internet of things: a survey. IEEE Commun. Surv. Tutor. **16**(1), 414–454 (2014). https://doi.org/10.1109/SURV.2013.042313.00197
6. Elkhodr, M., Shahrestani, S., Cheung, H.: A contextual-adaptive location disclosure agent for general devices in the internet of things. In: 38th Annual IEEE Conference on Local Computer Networks-Workshops, pp. 848–855. IEEE (2013). https://doi.org/10.1109/LCNW.2013.6758522
7. Ullah, I., Shah, M.A., Wahid, A., et al.: ESOT: a new privacy model for preserving location privacy in Internet of Things. Telecommun. Syst. **67**, 553–573 (2018). https://doi.org/10.1007/s11235-017-0352-x
8. Beresford, A.R., Stajano, F.: Location privacy in pervasive computing. IEEE Pervasive Comput. **1**, 46–55 (2003). https://doi.org/10.1109/MPRV.2003.1186725
9. Gedik, B., Liu, L.: Protecting location privacy with personalized k-anonymity: architecture and algorithms. IEEE Trans. Mob. Comput. **7**(1), 1–18 (2008). https://doi.org/10.1109/TMC.2007.1062
10. Ying, B., Makrakis, D.: Protecting location privacy with clustering anonymization in vehicular networks. In: 2014 IEEE Conference on Computer Communications Workshops (INFOCOM WKSHPS), pp. 305–310. IEEE (2014). https://doi.org/10.1109/INFOCOMW.2014.6849249

11. Aryan, A., Singh, S.: Protecting location privacy in augmented reality using k-anonymization and pseudo-id. In: 2010 International Conference on Computer and Communication Technology (ICCCT), pp. 119–124. IEEE (2010). https://doi.org/10.1109/ICCCT.2010.5640424

12. Wightman, P., Coronell, W., Jabba, D., Jimeno, M., Labrador, M.: Evaluation of location obfuscation techniques for privacy in location based information systems. In: 2011 IEEE Third Latin-American Conference on Communications, pp. 1–6. IEEE (2011). https://doi.org/10.1109/LatinCOM.2011.6107399

13. Wightman, P., Zurbaran, M., Zurek, E., Salazar, A., Jabba, D., Jimeno, M.: θ-Rand: random noise-based location obfuscation based on circle sectors. In: 2013 IEEE Symposium on Industrial Electronics and Applications, pp. 100–104. IEEE (2013). https://doi.org/10.1109/ISIEA.2013.6738976

14. Wightman, P., Zurbarán, M., Santander, A.: High variability geographical obfuscation for location privacy. In: 2013 47th International Carnahan conference on security technology (ICCST), pp. 1–6. IEEE (2013). https://doi.org/10.1109/CCST.2013.6922079

15. Shao, J., Lu, R., Lin, X.: FINE: a fine-grained privacy-preserving location-based service framework for mobile devices. In: IEEE INFOCOM 2014-IEEE Conference on Computer Communications, pp. 244–252. IEEE (2014). https://doi.org/10.1109/INFOCOM.2014.6847945

16. Yi, X., Paulet, R., Bertino, E., Varadharajan, V.: Practical k nearest neighbor queries with location privacy. In: 2014 IEEE 30th International Conference on Data Engineering, pp. 640–651. IEEE (2014). https://doi.org/10.1109/ICDE.2014.6816688

17. Lu, H., Jensen, C.S., Yiu, M.L.: PAD: privacy-area aware, dummy-based location privacy in mobile services. In: Proceedings of the Seventh ACM International Workshop on Data Engineering for Wireless and Mobile Access, pp. 16–23. ACM (2008). https://doi.org/10.1145/1626536.1626540

18. Niu, B., Li, Q., Zhu, X., Cao, G., Li, H.: Achieving k-anonymity in privacy-aware location-based services. In: IEEE INFOCOM 2014-IEEE Conference on Computer Communications, pp. 754–762. IEEE (2014). https://doi.org/10.1109/INFOCOM.2014.6848002

19. Ardagna, C.A., Cremonini, M., Damiani, E., De Capitani di Vimercati, S., Samarati, P.: Location privacy protection through obfuscation-based techniques. In: Barker, S., Ahn, G.-J. (eds.) DBSec 2007. LNCS, vol. 4602, pp. 47–60. Springer, Heidelberg (2007). https://doi.org/10.1007/978-3-540-73538-0_4

20. Ardagna, C.A., Cremonini, M., di Vimercati, S.D.C., Samarati, P.: An obfuscation-based approach for protecting location privacy. Trans. Dependable Secure Comput. 8(1), 13–27 (2011). https://doi.org/10.1109/TDSC.2009.25

21. Zhang, Y., Chen, K., Lian, Y.: A path-based access control method for location obfuscation in mobile environment. In: 2012 IEEE Symposium on Electrical and Electronics Engineering (EEESYM), pp. 570–573. IEEE (2012). https://doi.org/10.1109/EEESym.2012.6258721

22. Get Started with Contiki. http://www.contiki-os.org/. Accessed 31 Jan 2019

Cyberbullying Detection in Hindi-English Code-Mixed Language Using Sentiment Classification

Shrikant Tarwani, Manan Jethanandani, and Vibhor Kant[✉]

Department of Computer Science and Engineering,
The LNM Institute of Information Technology, Jaipur 302031, RJ, India
{16ucs179,16ucs099}@lnmiit.ac.in,
vibhor.kant@gmail.com

Abstract. Cyberbullying is one of the radical emerging problems with the advancements in the Internet, connecting people around the globe by social media networks. Existing studies mostly focus only on cyberbullying detection in the English language, thus the main objective of this paper is to develop an approach to detect cyberbullying in Hindi-English code-mixed language (Hinglish) which is exorbitantly used by Indian users. Due to the unavailability of Hinglish dataset, we created the Hinglish Cyberbullying Comments (HCC) labeled dataset consisting of comments from social media networks such as Instagram and YouTube. We also developed eight different machine learning models for sentiment classification in-order to automatically detect incidents of cyberbullying. Performance measures namely accuracy, precision, recall and f1 score are used to evaluate these models. Eventually, a hybrid model is developed based on top performers of these eight baseline classifiers which perform better with an accuracy of 80.26% and f1-score of 82.96%.

Keywords: Cyberbullying detection · Hinglish text · Sentiment classification · Hybrid model

1 Introduction

With the rapid evolvement of Internet, Social Media can be witnessed as the largest medium of communication among people. The usage of Social media networks on internet is increasing day by day particularly in developing countries like India, China, etc. [1]. Due to this exponential rise in the number of social media users, the problem of hate inducing speech, offensive and abusive posts on social media has come into the picture which can be referred as cyberbullying. Cyberbullying is an emerging issue which has affected a substantial proportion of youth and teenagers in India and all over the world. Comprehending the unfavorable outcomes of cyberbullying, it is vital to observe the usage of such disgraceful language over the Internet on numerous Social media websites present [2].

The humongous amount of data present on these platforms has a very diverse nature and the textual data constitutes a major part of the overall data available on these sites. The text present in the comments by Indian users is generally code-mixed

© Springer Nature Singapore Pte Ltd. 2019
M. Singh et al. (Eds.): ICACDS 2019, CCIS 1046, pp. 543–551, 2019.
https://doi.org/10.1007/978-981-13-9942-8_51

language i.e. Hinglish, a bi-lingual code-mixed version in which the Hindi language words are written in Roman script in lieu of Devanagari Script [3]. For example: 'Main tujhse nafrat karta hun' is in Hinglish language which means 'I hate you'. Hinglish language is pronunciation based with grammar setup derived from Hindi language in addition to overabundant slurs, slang and phonetic variations. In India, most of the cyberbullying instances can be spotted in Hinglish language due to it wide usage on different social media sites. Sentiment analysis on this language is extremely difficult due to various challenges. The major problem is tons of spelling variations of the same word with no lexical database like WordNet for Hinglish words. Moreover, multiple possible interpretations and no fixed grammar rules of this language makes the automatic categorization of the text into cyber-bullying or not difficult. Furthermore, to overcome the limitation of availability of Hinglish comments dataset, here we present an annotated Hinglish Cyberbullying Comments (HCC) dataset created by us consisting of Hinglish comments from social media networks, Instagram and YouTube which are currently very popular among Indian population with numerous active users.

The approaches to detect cyberbullying in any text can be categorized in two types namely Machine learning, Semantic Orientation [4]. Out of the two fundamental approaches machine learning is widely used to serve the requisite purpose. Furthermore, experiment results in the literature shows that the ensemble model approach in machine learning produces accurate and balanced predictions than the other baseline classifier algorithms for sentiment classification [5]. Thus, in this paper, we performed sentiment classification of Hinglish text through a hybrid model developed with the help of machine learning techniques to detect and classify the content into Cyberbullying or Non-Cyberbullying. Based on the performance measures, five models were chosen to develop the voting classifier, the hybrid model from a host of classifiers viz. Logistic Regression, Support Vector Machine, Multinomial Naive Bayes, Bernoulli Naive Bayes, Decision Tree Classifier, AdaBoost Classifier, Perceptron, Passive Aggressive Classifier. The comparison was carried out using the evaluation metrics like accuracy, precision, recall and f1-score. The whole process involving tasks such as subjectivity detection, text preprocessing, feature extraction and sentiment classification is referred as sentiment analysis or opinion mining using Natural Language Processing.

The main contributions of our work can be summarized as follows. First, Building an annotated Hinglish Cyberbullying Comments (HCC) dataset. Second, developing a hybrid machine learning model that outperforms the other baseline models on HCC. The remainder of this paper is organized as follows. Sections 2 discusses the Literature review. Section 3 presents the methodology in detail. Results and evaluations are drawn in Sect. 4 followed by conclusion and future work in Sect. 5.

2   Literature Review

Since the current study is based on machine learning approaches, therefore we studied several works in the literature focusing on sentiment analysis using machine learning. In [6], Support vector machine model is developed to perform subjectivity and sentiment analysis on dataset from Arabic social networks. Online Sentiment classification was performed for mobile reviews in [7], where recurrent neural network model out-performs other classic machine learning models. Hybrid machine learning approaches have also been employed for sentiment classification in [8] for Myspace comments in English. In [9], hybrid model consisting of back-propagation neural network and semantic orientation is developed to perform classification of sentiment conveyed in blogs.

Several studies have been done for cyberbullying detection but most of them are studied only on pure English language. For example, in [10], K-nearest neighbor model and Support Vector Machine model have been implemented on the dataset to classify the category of comment into cyberbullying or not. Several experiments were con-ducted to compare both model's performance with varying amount of data in the training set. In [11], cyberbullying detection was performed to identify vulnerable posted images of attacks using early warning mechanisms. The dataset comprised of more than 3000 images and convolutional neural network was developed for identi-fying potential targets of cyberbullying from the images and its captions. Moreover, SVM fuzzy algorithm was developed in [12] to detect cyberbullying.

Few studies also carried out investigations on Indic languages. Most of them focused on dataset of multiple languages such as Hindi, Bengali, Tamil, etc. based on popular datasets available such as FIRE 2018 [13], etc. and not on Hinglish which is the most popular version used by Indian social media users. In [14], Hindi-SentiWordNet (H-SWN) was developed based on English-Hindi Wordnet and existing SentiWordNet. Sentiment analysis was done on dataset consisting of Hindi movie reviews. Multi-class SVM was developed in [15] to perform multilingual sentiment analysis on the FIRE 2015 dataset consisting of Tamil, Hindi, Bengali and Telugu. In [16], to find the polarity of Hindi reviews into positive, neutral and negative sentences, a Hindi dictionary was developed for this sentence-level sentiment analysis.

3 Methodology

Here in this section, the proposed method of solving the sentiment classification problem for cyberbullying detection is explained comprehensively. Figure 1 shows the details of methodology that are further explained in detail in sub-sections namely 3.1 Data Collection, 3.2 Data Preprocessing, 3.3 Feature Extraction, 3.4 Proposed Hybrid Model below.

3.1 Data Collection

Sentiment analysis of code-mixed language for e.g. say Hinglish is Sentiment analysis of Hinglish text is an unexplored field resulting to limitations of publicly available data to investigate upon. Some data sources like FIRE 2017, FIRE 2018 [13] etc. are available which is a combination of many Indian languages which is less relevant for our work. We created a Hinglish Cyberbullying Comments (HCC) dataset[1] for

---

[1] https://github.com/mananjethanandani/HCC-Dataset

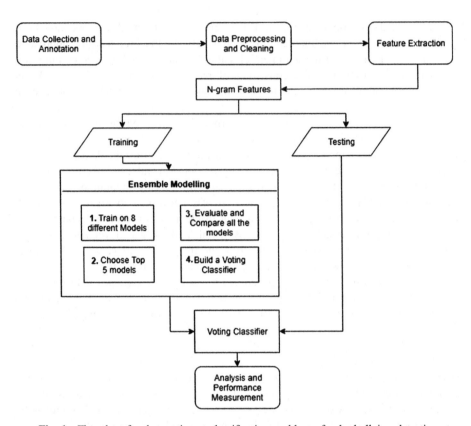

Fig. 1. Flowchart for the sentiment classification problem of cyberbullying detection

sentiment classification of Hinglish text. The user comments in Hinglish were collected from two online social media platforms viz. Instagram and YouTube. These comments were gathered from different viral and popular posts on these social media platforms. All these posts consisted comments written in different languages like Hindi, English, and Hinglish. Out of all these comments, 1010 were filtered comments written in Hinglish along with usernames. Further, these comments were crowdsourced to three NLP researchers for annotation and verification.

The annotation was finalized based on majority voting which decided the comment's category among cyberbullying and non-cyberbullying. Thus, the data repository created consists of 1010 labelled comments out of which the count of cyberbullying and non-cyberbullying comments is 448 and 562 respectively.

3.2   Data-Preprocessing

The comments obtained from the dataset undergone the following pre-processing steps. These steps can be understood using any Hinglish comment from dataset. For e.g. "@mohanbachani muze to uske uper ky comments ache lagte ahai 😊 #badelog"

Step 1 - Removal of emoticons: Thus, through this, the above comment is converted to "@mohanbachani muze to uske uper ky comments ache lagte ahai #badelog"

Step 2 - Tokenization: It is the process of converting a text stream into small individual tokens. The tokenization results to following for the comment: ['@-mohanbachani', 'muze', 'to', 'uske', 'uper', 'ky', 'comments', 'ache', 'lagte', 'ahai', '#badelog']

Step 3 - Removal of URLs, punctuations and user mentions. Replacement of hashtags with corresponding plain text. Thus, after step 3, the comment is preprocessed to ['muze', 'to', 'uske', 'uper', 'ky', 'comments', 'ache', 'lagte', 'ahai', 'badelog']

Step 4 - Conversion of all tweets into lower case. All the tokens are already in lower case in our example comment.

Step 5 - Spelling variation checking: In order to handle the numerous variations in opinion words found in the comments, spelling variation lists were created, an example of which is shown in Table 1.

Table 1. Examples of spelling variations in the HCC dataset

Opinion word	Variations found in the HCC dataset
best	bestt, beesst
mujhe	muze, muje
acha	achha, achaa, ache

Thus, our example is converted to: ['mujhe', 'to', 'uske', 'upar', 'ke', 'comments', 'acha', 'lagte', 'hai', 'badelog']

Step 6 - Removal of Stop Words: Stop words do not contribute to any sentiment. Therefore, their removal is required as they lead to decrease in accuracy. For Hinglish, we created Hinglish stop word list which is used for pre-processing. Since, Hinglish being code-mixed language English stop word list provided in NLTK library is also used. After this step, the example is now changed to: ['upar', 'comments', 'acha', 'badelog'] Further, the creation of stopword list was carried out manually from all the comments of HCC dataset. Table 2 gives a brief of this Step.

Table 2. Examples of stop words present in Hinglish comments

Comment	Stop words
mazza ata h bhaii tri video's dekh Kr... haaa Gazzab	aata, hai, tere, kar
aapki music mst h	Hai
Bhai maza aa gya, luv you😊😊😊😊😊😊	aa, gaya, you

Step 7 - Stemming and Lemmatization: This being important step for english words, the example comment is now converted to: ['upar', 'comment', 'acha', badelog'] (Table 3).

Table 3. Examples of Hinglish comments from HCC dataset converted to standardized comments after data pre-processing steps

Real comments	Standardized comments	Label
@mohanbachani muze to uske uper ky comments ache lagte ahai 😊 #badelog	upar comment ach	Non-Bullying
vai tera level top hain....love you dude...	bhai level top love dude	Non-Bullying
Awesome Video Babaji... Kaafi din baad kuchh majedaar item dekhne ko mila... Keep it up	awesom babaji kaafi din baad kuch majedaar item dekhn mila keep	Non-Bullying
Kutty ki baxhi sharm kr	kutti bachi sharm	Bullying

3.3 Feature Extraction

The following steps are performed on the HCC dataset:

Term Frequency–Inverse Document Frequency (TF-IDF): To find the significance of a word to a document in a corpus, this feature extraction technique is introduced. In order to compute it, two things are required: (i) term frequency (tf): In a document, the occurrence of a word is determined by tf (ii) inverse document frequency (idf): It tells us how important a term is. tf is calculated taking into consideration the importance of each term but few frequent terms such as 'hai', 'bhi', 'kar' in Hinglish context are less significant in most of the documents. Thus, combining the attributes of both tf and idf, the importance of the word could be obtained using the equation written below.

$$TF - IDF = tf * idf \qquad (1)$$

N-gram Features: A set of co-occurring words in a text is referred as N gram. N gram tokenization is generally used for developing features by combining two or more words which usually appear together in the corpus. It carries a great significance which could be understood by following example, here unigram "ache" is positive word. But bigram "ache nahi" is caring negative meaning. In most of the research word, unigram, bigram and trigram are highly recommended for sentiment analysis.

3.4 Proposed Hybrid Model

After all the comments have been classified and annotated manually, and subsequent preprocessing and feature extraction steps, the extracted features were incorporated into the different models to be processed and built. The data was split randomly into the training and validation sets according to holdout method containing 75% and 25% of the data respectively. We performed the experiment using eight different well-known classifiers, the results are discussed in the next section. A hybrid model is developed based on the voting classification algorithm on the dataset that is an ensemble of the top five best performing models from above surpassing the other baseline methods as analyzed in Sect. 4.

4   Results and Discussions

To validate the effectiveness of our proposed work on sentiment classification we have compared our approach with popular classification algorithms namely Logistic Regression, Support Vector Machine, Multinomial Naive Bayes, Bernoulli Naive Bayes, Decision Tree Classifier, AdaBoost Classifier, Perceptron, Passive Aggressive Classifier. The classifiers' performance is reported using evaluation measures such as Accuracy, Precision, Recall and F1 score shown in Table 4. These measures are calculated using Eqs. (2), (3), (4) and (5).

$$\text{Accuracy} = (\text{tp} + \text{tn})/(\text{tp} + \text{tn} + \text{fp} + \text{fn}) \tag{2}$$

$$\text{Precision(P)} = \text{tp}/(\text{tp} + \text{fp}) \tag{3}$$

$$\text{Recall(R)} = \text{tp}/(\text{tp} + \text{fn}) \tag{4}$$

$$\text{F1 score} = 2 * P * R/(P + R) \tag{5}$$

Where *tp, tn, fp, fn* denotes true positives, true negatives, false positives and false negatives respectively.

All the models were tested on validation set of 253 data points randomly chosen from the given dataset. From the results of Table 4, it can be seen that the performance of Logistic Regression, Support Vector Machine, Multinomial NB, Decision Tree Classifier and Passive Aggressive Classifier outperforms other baseline classifiers in terms of accuracy which is greater than 80% for all the 5 classifiers. The F1 score for all the given classifiers is almost equivalent. Also, in the respect of precision and recall, these models performed analogously. The Hybrid Model i.e. the Voting classifier based on these 5 top models mentioned performs better than all the 8 baseline models. Of the 253 comments tested, 202 comments resulted the same i.e. either Bullying comment or Non-Bullying comment as labelled in data collection step.

Table 4. Performance measure results for the HCC dataset

Model	Accuracy	Precision	Recall	F1-score
Logistic Regression	76.39%	70.66%	95.16%	81.10%
Linear SVC	80.26%	77.46%	88.71%	82.71%
Multinomial NB	79.83%	74.84%	93.55%	83.15%
Passive Aggressive Classifier	78.97%	76.98%	86.29%	81.37%
Bernoulli NB	56.22%	54.91%	99.19%	70.69%
Perceptron	76.82%	78.23%	78.23%	78.23%
Adaboost Classifier	74.25%	68.60%	95.16%	79.73%
Decision Tree Classifier	78.11%	73.86%	91.13%	81.59%
Hybrid Model	**80.26%**	**76.71%**	**90.32%**	**82.96%**

From the confusion matrix, we analyzed the detailed classification of comments in terms of the number of true positives, true negatives, false positives and false negatives for all nine classifiers as shown in Fig. 2. The results imply that our proposed method successfully performs sentiment classification on the Hinglish text.

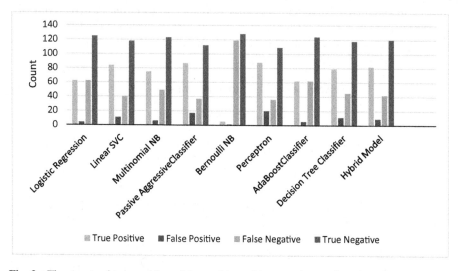

Fig. 2. The counts of true positives, false positives, false negatives and true negatives for all the classifiers

5   Conclusion and Future Work

In this study, we proposed to perform sentiment classification on Hindi-English code-mixed (Hinglish) language written in Roman script. We created a dataset consisting of the comments in Hinglish text taken from social media sites like Instagram and YouTube. The dataset is named as Hinglish Cyberbullying Comments (HCC). Later, we used various tools for the purpose of data preprocessing and feature extraction which included Stemmer and lemmatizer for data cleaning and Tf-Idf vectorizer and N-grams for feature extraction which can be endowed as the best combination for detecting the intention expressed in the Hinglish comment. The results in the above section indicate that the proposed method successfully identifies cyberbullying text and the Hybrid model i.e. Voting Classifier dominates over other eight baseline classifiers in terms of performance. In future, to improve the performance, developing the semantics of the comment can be used to classify sentiment expressed in Hinglish text. Also, the model performance can be enhanced by increasing the training set in terms of size. Moreover, Neural Network models can be developed for detecting cyberbullying in Hinglish text.

References

1. Ravi, K., Ravi, V.: A survey on opinion mining and sentiment analysis: tasks, approaches and applications. Knowl.-Based Syst. **89**, 14–46 (2015)
2. Galán-García, P., Puerta, J.G., Gómez, C.L., Santos, I., Bringas, P.G.: Supervised machine learning for the detection of troll profiles in twitter social network: application to a real case of cyberbullying. Log. J. IGPL **24**(1), 42–53 (2016)
3. Thakur, S., Dutta, K.: Hinglish: code switching, code mixing and indigenization in multilingual environment. Lingua Et Linguistica **1**(2007), 109 (2007). books.google.com
4. Tarwani, N., Chorasia, U., Shukla, P.K.: Survey of cyberbulling detection on social media big-data. Int. J. Adv. Res. Comput. Sci. **8**(5), 831–835 (2017)
5. Ravi, K., Ravi, V.: Sentiment classification of Hinglish text. In: 3rd International Conference on Recent Advances in Information Technology (RAIT), pp. 641–645. IEEE (2016)
6. Abdul-Mageed, M., Diab, M., Kübler, S.: SAMAR: subjectivity and sentiment analysis for Arabic social media. Comput. Speech Lang. **28**(1), 20–37 (2014)
7. Ravi, K., Ravi, V., Gautam, C.: Online and semi-online sentiment classification. In: International Conference on Computing, Communication and Automation (ICCCA 2015), pp. 938–943 (2015)
8. Prabowo, R., Thelwall, M.: Sentiment analysis: a combined approach. J. Inf. **3**(2), 143–157 (2009)
9. Xia, R., Zong, C., Li, S.: Ensemble of feature sets and classification algorithms for sentiment classification. Inf. Sci. **181**(6), 1138–1152 (2011)
10. Ducharme, D., Costa, L., DiPippo, L., Hamel, L.: SVM constraint discovery using KNN applied to the identification of cyberbullying. In: The Steering Committee of the World Congress in Computer Science, Computer Engineering and Applied Computing (World-Comp), pp. 111–117 (2017)
11. Zhong, H., Li, H., Squicciarini, A., Rajtmajer, S., Griffin, C., Miller, D., Caragea, C.: Content-driven detection of cyberbullying on the Instagram social network. In: IJCAI, pp. 3952–3958 (2016)
12. Nahar, V., Al-Maskari, S., Li, X., Pang, C.: Semi-supervised learning for cyberbullying detection in social networks. In: Wang, H., Sharaf, M.A. (eds.) ADC 2014. LNCS, vol. 8506, pp. 160–171. Springer, Cham (2014). https://doi.org/10.1007/978-3-319-08608-8_14
13. Basu, M., Ghosh, S., Ghosh, K.: Overview of the FIRE 2018 track: information retrieval from microblogs during disasters (IRMiDis). In: Proceedings of the 10th Annual Meeting of the Forum for Information Retrieval Evaluation, pp. 1–5. ACM (2018)
14. Pandey, P., Govilkar, S.: A framework for sentiment analysis in Hindi using HSWN. Int. J. Comput. Appl. **119**, 23–26 (2015)
15. Bhargava, R., Sharma, Y., Sharma, S.: Sentiment analysis for mixed script indic sentences. In: 2016 International Conference on Advances in Computing, Communications and Informatics (ICACCI), pp. 524–529. IEEE (2016)
16. Sharma, R., Nigam, S., Jain, R.: Polarity detection of movie reviews in Hindi language. Int. J. Comput. Sci. Appl. **4**(4), 49–57 (2014)

Effective Predictive Analytics and Modeling Based on Historical Data

Sheikh Mohammad Idrees[(✉)], M. Afshar Alam, Parul Agarwal,
and Lubna Ansari

Department of Computer Science and Engineering, Jamia Hamdard,
New Delhi 110062, India
{smidrees.sch,aalam,pagarwal,
lubnaansari_sch}@jamiahamdard.ac.in

Abstract. Advances in all the fields of everyday life, in the past decade have
laid a foundational block for production of huge amount of data. In this age of
algorithms where everything is within the finger tips, this huge amount of data is
of no use unless and until it is not converted to a form which is beneficial and
meaningful for the recipient to do something beneficial. This is taken care of by
the Predictive analytics, which involves use of various statistical models, data
mining techniques, artificial intelligence, machine learning and others to extract
meaningful insights from data. Business ventures are constantly being flooded
with huge amount of data that is generated from time to time. So there is a need
to develop new approaches to foresee the time series data. This research paper
presents the predictive analytics of time series data by taking real world data, to
build an effective model for prediction. The results obtained were quite
interesting.

Keywords: Predictive analytics · Time series analysis · Forecasting ·
ARIMA modeling

1 Introduction

All developing nations at present are undergoing swift changes in the social and
economic structures. Anticipation of future ups and downs will provide a helping hand
in solving the expected problems by providing a strategy plan for future. Making
predictions about the future is always a challenging task to do [1]. Human nature has at
all times been more interested in knowing about future. Forecasting hence, can be
considered as an important ingredient for future planning. Forecasting comprises of a
method for foretelling what is expected to follow in the future by noticing what has
occurred previously in the past and what is happening currently. As an example we can
consider it just like driving a vehicle in frontward direction, only by looking at the rear-
view mirror of the vehicle. All the organizations whether those dealing with medicine,
education, politics, finance, science or government, are currently paying more attention
towards forecasting [2]. To be considered as a good forecast, it should be simple and
easy to understand, precise, trustworthy and cost effective. There is almost no area left

M. Singh et al. (Eds.): ICACDS 2019, CCIS 1046, pp. 552–564, 2019.
https://doi.org/10.1007/978-981-13-9942-8_52

where the forecasts don't find their application, however in general there exist only two categories of techniques for forecasting [3, 4]:

(a) Qualitative models of Forecasting
(b) Quantitative models of Forecasting

We may start the discussion with the "Qualitative models" of forecasting; they are generally of subjective type and mostly based upon the views and opinions of experts. These methods are employed when we have very little preceding data available to ground a forecast. Delphi method, one of the most popular forecasting techniques is a good example of qualitative forecasting models. This method is based upon the expert opinion of a group of experienced experts who are believed to be having sound knowledge about the problem.

However, when we talk about the quantitative forecasting models, they make predictions about the future on the basis of the available existing data. This model analyses the interesting patterns hidden inside the data and identifies an association between the previous and the existing data. They are simply employed to extrapolate the upcoming behavior of a variable based on its previous and existing values. Time series Models, Regression Analysis and others are some of the examples of the Qualitative models of prediction.

This paper presents the predictive analytics of time series data by taking real world data, to build an effective "ARIMA (Auto Regressive Integrated Moving Average) model" for prediction. ARIMA model is among one of the most popular statistical univariate forecasting methods used for prediction of the upcoming values in a time series [5]. The remainder of this paper is organized as follows. Section 2 defines the Predictive analytics along with various steps involved. Section 3 discusses the Time series analysis, while Sect. 4 discusses the various Statistical Predictive models for forecasting. Section 5 presents the methodology of this work. Results and conclusion are discussed in Sect. 6 of this paper.

2 Predictive Analytics

Predictive analytics involves analysing the present and historical data through proper statistical, data mining and machine learning techniques for purpose of making future predictions. Nowadays, Data being a new catalyst for business development is being considered as a new economic asset. Predictive analytics is now able to predict our each move accurately by using data along with appropriate predictive models [5]. However, keeping in view the nature of this present day data, the existing traditional models are not able to make exact predictions. As such the existing techniques need a new overhaul so as to deal with this torrent of data and make precise predictions. An effective analytics platform acts as an eminent source of information that can improve the on-going operations and provide a better insight into the future with more effective decisions and plans. In the present decade, there has been a vast upsurge in the level of data creation due to the widespread growth of social media along with other promising applications across all sectors. The financial sector has been greatly stirred by the big data torrent. The financial sector is considered as one of the most sensitive but complex sector that is held responsible for the overall stability and development of an economy [6, 7]. All investors try to extract maximum profit out of the investments made by them; as such they always attempt to observe the risks associated with their investments. This is where the predictive analytics comes into picture; it aims to use various forecasting models over the existing available data to produce the forecasts that could be used to safeguard the interest of investors.

Examples of predictive modeling are now familiar to everybody. Recommendations on famous online shopping websites like amazon, flipkart and Netflix regarding the purchase of an item, is based upon these predictive models. Online business ventures rely comprehensively upon the predictive models for purpose of marketing and advertisement to target people who are more likely to purchase an item or respond to offers. Predictive modeling is even used by many government agencies [8] to develop models that could predict terror threats communication and other data. Moreover, there has been a considerable amount of work on the statistical and machine learning techniques that underlie beneath these promising applications. An effective predictive modeling consists of a series of stages which are discussed in the subsequent section.

2.1   Predictive Analytics Process

Efficient predictive analysis and modeling involves a series of stages that start from problem identification and end up at the evaluation of the model [9, 10]. These stages are briefly summed up as below and illustrated through Fig. 1.

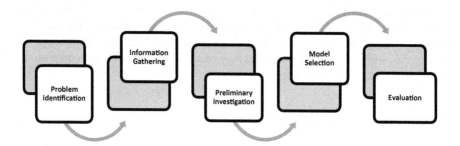

Fig. 1.   Various stages in predictive analytics process

Step 1: Identification of the Problem
To plan for the upcoming events, we need to make accurate predictions about them. The first thing we need to do is to identify who requires these forecasts and for what purposes. This phase is mainly concerned with collection of data. So, an analyst needs to allocate some time to gather data by talking to every person associated with data and to those who will be using the forecasts too. Additionally the analyst needs to maintain the databases for purpose of analysis.

Step 2: Information gathering
This phase involves the selection of various relevant variables that essentially need to be studied for purpose of prediction. Furthermore, the data whether primary data or

secondary data needs to be assembled in this phase. The primary data is not having any former presence, so it needs to be gathered openly from the respondents. This data is of vital significance in prediction process but its consistency is a matter of concern. On the other hand, the secondary data has already been gathered earlier at a particular point of time.

Step 3: Preliminary Investigation
The data collected in phase II needs to be analyzed to check whether it can be beneficial or not. This is done in the preliminary investigation phase. This phase further helps in conveying the hidden patterns embedded inside data apart from aiding in the selection of best model to fit in. This phase eases the process of forecasting by scrutinizing any redundant data.

Step 4: Model Selection
After the step 3 is positively carried out, we need to select the model that could be used to carry out the prediction. This is mainly carried out by analyzing the accessibility and nature of data.

Step 5: Model Evaluation
This step is carried out after the model is put into work for making the predictions. As soon as the prediction model has carried out the predictions, it needs to be evaluated. The authentication of this model is exactly done only after the data for the projecting period becomes available.

3   Time Series Analysis

Time-series denotes a well-organized sequence of data points, which a variable under consideration is supposed to take at identical time segments. The motive of time series analysis is to design models that could define the time series under consideration, to a certain amount of accuracy. The research in the field of time series analysis has seen a multifold increase in the recent years. The need for effective research in time series is given vital importance owing to the reason that it can be used to predict the unpredictability of data in future. So essentially, the time series forecasting may be branded as a method for making calculations about the future by studying the historical data [11]. It is considered as a vital decision making component for the formulation of upcoming strategies and approximations in almost all areas of life including governance, business, banking, education and others [12]. So there is a need for suitable attention while choosing a model for prediction, so as to obtain better forecasting results [13, 14].

A "Time Series can be technically stated as a sequential set of data points, generally observed over successive or identical time intervals. Precisely it is symbolized by means of a set of vectors $X(t), t = 0, 1, 2, 3,\ldots$ where t indicates the time intervened" [15].

$$`Xt : t \in T'$$ where 'T represents the ordered set of time'.

Based on the set of observations of a variable, the time series can either be uni-variate or a multi-variate. A 'time series' covering the observations associated with a single variable is stated to as 'uni-variate type of time series'. On the other hand, the 'time series' with observations associated with greater than one variable is designated as a 'multi-variate type of time series'. A 'time series' can further consist of two kinds [16]:

'Continuous' – When the observations are calculated at every instant of time, then the time series is said to be continuous. In case of economic data the continuous type of time series are found very rarely. Certain examples consist of – 'recordings of temperature of a place', water flow of a particular tributary, and many more.

Discrete – A time series is believed to be discrete, when the observations are recorded at distinct time instants. In a 'discrete time series', the successive observations are recorded at identical intervals of time. These intervals of time could be – "yearly, seasonally, monthly weekly or daily". Some of the examples comprise – population in a region, production rate of a company, stock exchange rate and many more.

Time Series Example:

(1) Daily performance of the Stock Market.
(2) Yearly birth rate in India.
(3) Monthly rainfall over a particular city.
(4) Yearly or monthly sale of vehicles by a particular automaker.

4 Prediction Models

The reliability of a forecast mainly depends upon the accuracy of the data involved and the underlying model that is used to obtain a forecast. Generally, the most popular and commonly used linear models [17, 18, 32] are - "Auto-Regressive models (AR)" and "Moving Average (MA) models". However, when we combine these two model we get a new class of model called as Auto-regressive Moving Average (ARMA). Likewise, there is one more related type of model called as "Auto-Regressive Integrated Moving Average model" (ARIMA) [19, 20]. All of the above mentioned models are discussed as below:

A. AR (p) Model
"Auto regressive (AR) models" are employed to determine the forthcoming nature of a variable in observation, by means of linear arrangement of its past values [21]. *Auto*-regression implies the regression of the variable against itself. Alternatively, this is identified as a function of preceding values. i.e.

$$\text{"}y_t = f(y_{t-1}, y_{t-2}, y_{t-3}, y_{t-4}, \ldots \ldots \epsilon_t)\text{"}$$

An 'Auto regressive model' dependent on 'p' of its former values denoted by AR(p) is symbolized as:

$$\text{"yt = c + }\phi\text{1yt-1 + }\phi\text{2 yt-2 + + }\phi\text{pyt-p + }\epsilon\text{t "}$$
$$\text{yt = c + }i\text{=1}\Sigma p\ \phi\text{1}yt\text{-}I\text{ + }\epsilon\text{t} \tag{1}$$

where ϵt is the error term.

B. MA (q) Model

The AR(p) model used the past values of a variable to base the forecasts, but this is not the case with the "Moving Average (MA)" model. This model utilizes the previous errors terms for prediction. So we can consider the MA model as the function of error terms as:

$$\text{yt = f }(\epsilon\text{t, }\epsilon\text{t-1, }\epsilon\text{t-2, }\epsilon\text{t-3 ,. ...... }\epsilon\text{t-q)}$$

In "regression, the error terms are generated when a series is regressed with its past values:
Regression of yt over" yt-1:

$$\text{yt = }\mu\text{ + }\theta\text{1 }\epsilon\text{ t-1 + }\epsilon\text{1 where }\mu\text{= constant, }\epsilon\text{1 = error}$$

Likewise, the error terms ϵ2, ϵ3 and so on are generated as a result of regression. So in the moving average model we use the error values to make a forecast in place of using the historical values. Thus the "moving average model" can be expressed as:

$$\text{"yt = }\mu\text{ + }\theta\text{1 }\epsilon\text{ t-1 + }\theta\text{2 }\epsilon\text{t-2 + ... + }\theta\text{q }\epsilon\text{t-q + }\epsilon\text{t"}$$
$$\text{yt = }\mu\text{ + }j\text{=1}\Sigma q\ \theta\text{j }\epsilon\text{t-j + }\epsilon\text{t} \tag{2}$$

The error ϵt generated are basically white noise processes in nature, those with constant variance σ2 and mean equal to zero.

C. ARMA (p, q) Model

ARMA model is an outcome of the AR model used along with MA model (AR+MA) [22]. ARMA (p, q) model is generally represented as:

$$\text{"yt = (c + }\phi\text{1yt-1 + }\phi\text{2 yt-2 +... + }\phi\text{pyt-p + }\epsilon\text{t) + (}\mu\text{ + }\theta\text{1 }\epsilon\text{ t-1 + }\theta\text{2 }\epsilon\text{t-2 + .. + }\theta\text{q }\epsilon\text{t-q + }\epsilon\text{t)"}$$
$$\text{yt = c + }\epsilon\text{t + }i\text{=1}\Sigma p\ \phi\text{1}yt\text{-}I\text{ + }j\text{=1}\Sigma q\ \theta\text{j }\epsilon\text{t-j} \tag{3}$$

'p' and 'q' in the Eq. (3) above denote to the auto-regressive and moving average model.

D. ARIMA (p, d, q) Model

Auto-regressive Integrated Moving Average (ARIMA) class of autoregressive model is often recognized by the well-known "Box-Jenkins model". This model handles time series data that is stationary in nature, however in real majority of the time series data exhibits a non-stationary character. So, there is a need to convert the non-stationary data into stationary. This is achieved through means of differencing [22]. The general expression of an "ARIMA model" for yt is as:

$$\text{"} yt = c + \phi 1 yt\text{-}1 + \phi 2\ yt\text{-}2 + \ldots + \phi p yt\text{-}p + \theta 1\ \epsilon\ t\text{-}1 + \theta 2\ \epsilon t\text{-}2 + \ldots + \theta q\ \epsilon t\text{-}q + \epsilon t \text{"}$$

Where yt is "differenced time series" that could possibly have been differenced once or more.

ARIMA (p, d, q) model, has 3 parameters p, d, q, which signify the following:

p - portrays the auto-regressive portion,
d - portrays the level of differencing,
q - portrays moving average portion,

ARIMA model basically incorporates 3 simple methods as:

"Auto-Regressive (AR)"
This states that values in a particular time series has to be regressed upon its own lagged value. This is indicated by the "p value of an ARIMA model".

"Differencing Part (I for Integrated)"
Integration is concluded as the converse of differencing. It specifies the degree on differencing that requires to be done on data.

"Moving Average (MA)"
The letter 'q' represents the moving average part in an ARIMA model. It basically points toward the entire number of lagged values of the error term. As an example, while 'q = 1' it states that there is a presence of an error term, along with auto-correlation having one lag.

5   Data Gathering and Method

This pragmatic study is based on the time series data regarding the sale of vehicles in US. The publically available data is collected from the Data Market [23]. This data is provided by Federal Reserve Bank of St. Louis (citing: U.S. Bureau of Economic Analysis). This dataset contains the historical data of the monthly vehicles sold in thousands for a period of forty three years. The dataset specifies the date and the total number of vehicles sold in that month. Out of this dataset a sub part of historical data containing sales information from January 2005 to June 2018 is chosen for this study. In this study, we have divided the dataset into two slices as the training data and the testing data part. The sales data starting 'January 2005 till December 2015' is taken as training data, while the sales data from January 2016 to June 2018 is taken as testing data in this study. The "training data part" from the time series under consideration is used for design of the model for prediction while the "testing part" has been used for the authentication or validation purposes.

5.1   Approach

The Auto-regressive processes contain some degree of 'volatility or randomness' built in, that seldom makes it capable of predicting the upcoming trends very well. However, one needs to understand that forecasts may never be 100% accurate. The framework for making the prediction is shown in Fig. 2 as:

Fig. 2. Framework for prediction.

After examining the time series data, regarding the vehicles sold during a certain period, the 1st thing that need to be done, is to confirm whether the series is 'stationary' or not. For a non-stationary series, it requires to be differenced for purpose of converting it to stationary. Hence the 'auto-co-relation as well as the partial auto co-relation' of the series needs to be recognized. ARIMA model depend upon the 'stationarity of the time series' [24, 25].

In order to analyse the vehicle time series data very clearly, the first thing we need to do is to plot this time series with respect to time as in Fig. 3. Plotting the time series provides a rough idea about the behavior of the time series. Also we decompose the time series into its constituent as shown in Fig. 4.

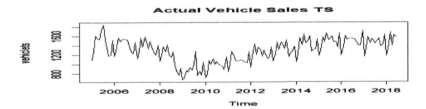

Fig. 3. Actual vehicle sales time series

Decomposition of multiplicative time series

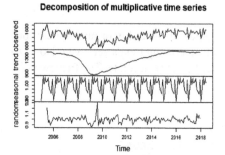

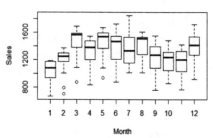

Boxplot for Vehicle TS

Fig. 4. Decomposition of time series

Fig. 5. Box Plots for vehicle TS data

A time series from inside contains a lot of hidden patterns which are revealed through decomposition of the time series. There are mainly four constituents of a time series, which are shown in Fig. 4 above. These four components are- trend, cyclic, seasonal and irregular. We use the Boxplots to examine the impact of seasons on the time series. This helps in investigating for every month under study, how the data is changing through several years of time series. The Fig. 5 shows the box plots for vehicle sales data.

ACF for Vehicle TS

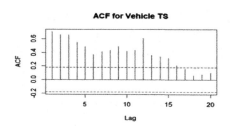

PACF for vehicle TS

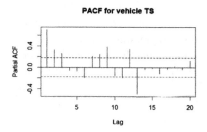

Fig. 6. Plot ACF

Fig. 7. Plot PACF

The next step we need to do is to check whether the series is stationary or not. This is carried out by plotting the 'ACF and PACF' plots for the same. Figures 6 and 7 represent the ACF and PACF plot for the same. While analysing the 'ACF and PACF' plots the series appears to be stationary, alternatively we can use 'dickey fuller test' to screen for stationarity [26–28]. As such we need to take the difference of the lags, which is shown in Fig. 8. Also the ACF and PACF of the difference lag series is shown in Figs. 9 and 10.

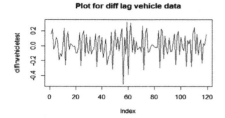

Fig. 8. Plot of differenced lag

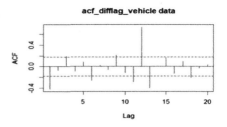

Fig. 9. ACF differenced lag

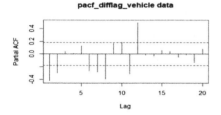

Fig. 10. PACF differenced lag

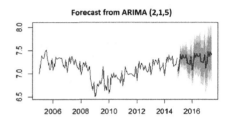

Fig. 11. Forecast with ARIMA

Model Selection

The next phase involves prediction of the series using the previous data or the training data. This is done by selecting an efficient model. In this study we have chosen the ARIMA model to make predictions. We use the ARIMA model with the best parameters as (2, 1, 5) for calculating the next forthcoming values of the series. The best parameters are justified through the use of 'trace' in the auto.arima () function [29] as below:

auto.arima(lnvehicletest, ic = "aic", trace = TRUE)
Best model: 'ARIMA(2, 1, 5)'

6   Results and Conclusion

After the best fit parameters (p, d, q) are picked, the series is forecasted. The predicted series for the vehicle sales data is plotted in Fig. 11.

Since the time series consists of the irregular components, so the anticipated time series may certainly not be 100% accurate [30]. In this study, a evaluation of the forecasted series and the real series shows nearly a 'aberration of 5% mean percentage error'. The monthly predicted values for the vehicle sales are given in Table 1.

Table 1. Forecasted sales value

Month	Actual sales	Predicted sales
2016-01	1188.8	1151.463
2016-02	1374.3	1331.848
2016-03	1614.1	1661.704
2016-04	1524.1	1499.916
2016-05	1552.7	1648.520
2016-06	1548.9	1551.306
2016-07	1546.8	1535.606
2016-08	1539.8	1647.374
2016-09	1462.1	1373.640
2016-10	1397.1	1356.203
2016-11	1399.4	1333.441
2016-12	1717.9	1597.191
2017-01	1164.3	1187.919
2017-02	1352.1	1374.015
2017-03	1582.7	1714.314
2017-04	1449.7	1547.404
2017-05	1543.9	1700.712
2017-06	1502.8	1600.421
2017-07	1441	1584.223
2017-08	1512.1	1699.530
2017-09	1553.1	1417.130
2017-10	1385.6	1399.141
2017-11	1424.5	1375.658
2017-12	1638.7	1647.758
2018-01	1181.7	1225.529
2018-02	1328.1	1417.516
2018-03	1687.6	1768.589
2018-04	1391.3	1596.395
2018-05	1625.1	1754.557
2018-06	1586.7	1651.091

Alternatively we can also employ the 'L-Jung Box test' for authentication of the predicted series. This test is used to examine whether the residuals are random or not.

7 Conclusion

In this paper we have presented the concept of predictive analytics along with the time series data based on the data set available from Data Market provided by Federal Reserve Bank of St. Louis (citing: U.S. Bureau of Economic Analysis) regarding the sale of vehicles. This paper builds an efficient ARIMA model to predict the future value of the time series based on previous data values. We have compared the predicted time series with that of the real/actual time series, which exhibits an aberration of nearly 5%, mean percentage error with respect to actual sales data on average. There are different tests that can be used for validation purposes to check the reliability of the forecasts [31]. In this paper, we have employed the L-jung box testand the augmented Dickey - Fuller test for validation. From this study, it appears that- "ARIMA method is proficient enough for handling time series data". Furthermore, this model can be very productive in solving the actual world forecasting difficulties in various sectors like governance, health sector, finance, education, and other practical domains.

References

1. Brockwell, P.J., Davis, R.A., Calder, M.V.: Introduction to Time Series and Forecasting, vol. 2. Springer, New York (2002). https://doi.org/10.1007/b97391
2. Montgomery, D.C., Johnson, L.A., Gardiner, J.S.: Forecasting and Time Series Analysis, p. 151. McGraw-Hill, New York (1990)
3. https://en.wikipedia.org/wiki/Forecasting. Accessed Aug 2018
4. Kurzak, L.: Importance of forecasting in enterprise management. Adv. Logist. Syst. 6(1), 173–182 (2012)
5. Yaffee, R.A., McGee, M.: An Introduction to Time Series Analysis and Forecasting: With Applications of SAS® and SPSS®. Elsevier, Amsterdam (2000)
6. Idrees, S.M., Alam, M.A., Agarwal, P.: A study of big data and its challenges. Int. J. Inf. Technol. 1–6 (2018)
7. Abdou, E., Mahmoud, S.: The role of technological forecasting in planning future developments. IFAC Proc. Vol. 10(14), 65–68 (1977)
8. Einav, L., Levin, J.: The data revolution and economic analysis. Innov. Policy Econ. 14(1), 1–24 (2014)
9. https://robjhyndman.com/papers/forecastingoverview.pdf
10. http://www.economicsdiscussion.net/demand-forecasting/data-collection-for-demand-forecasting/3583. Accessed July 2018
11. Ashik, A.M., Kannan, K.S.: Time series model for stock price forecasting in India. In: Deep, K., Jain, M., Salhi, S. (eds.) Logistics, Supply Chain and Financial Predictive Analytics. AA, pp. 221–231. Springer, Singapore (2019). https://doi.org/10.1007/978-981-13-0872-7_17
12. Zhang, G.P.: A neural network ensemble method with jittered training data for time series forecasting. Inf. Sci. 177(23), 5329–5346 (2007)
13. Tong, H.: Threshold Models in Non-Linear Time Series Analysis, vol. 21. Springer, New York (2012)
14. Andersen, T.G., Davis, R.A., Kreiß, J.P., Mikosch, T.V. (eds.): Handbook of Financial Time Series. Springer, Heidelberg (2009). https://doi.org/10.1007/978-3-540-71297-8
15. Box, G.E., Jenkins, G.M., Reinsel, G.C., Ljung, G.M.: Time series analysis: forecasting and control. Wiley, Hoboken (2015)
16. Dufour, J.M.: Introduction to time series analysis. Research Paper, McGill University, Canada, pp. 1–16 (2008)
17. Idrees, S.M., Alam, M.A., Agarwal, P.: A prediction approach for stock market volatility based on time series data. IEEE Access 7, 17287–17298 (2019)
18. Khashei, M., Hajirahimi, Z.: A comparative study of series arima/mlp hybrid models for stock price forecasting. Commun. Stat.-Simul. Comput. 1–16 (2018)

19. Green, S.: Time series analysis of stock prices using the box-Jenkins approach (2011)
20. Mostafa, M.M., El-Masry, A.A.: Oil price forecasting using gene expression programming and artificial neural networks. Econ. Model. **54**, 40–53 (2016)
21. Frees, E.W.: Analytics of insurance markets. Annu. Rev. Financ. Econ. **7**, 253–277 (2015)
22. Conejo, A.J., Plazas, M.A., Espinola, R., Molina, A.B.: Day-ahead electricity price forecasting using the wavelet transform and ARIMA models. IEEE Trans. Power Syst. **20** (2), 1035–1042 (2005)
23. https://datamarket.com/data/set/3cy1/total-vehicle-sales#!ds=3cy1&display=line
24. Narayanan, P., Basistha, A., Sarkar, S., Kamna, S.: Trend analysis and ARIMA modelling of pre-monsoon rainfall data for Western India. Comptes Rendus Geosci. **345**(1), 22–27 (2013)
25. Kavousi-Fard, A., Kavousi-Fard, F.: A new hybrid correction method for short-term load forecasting based on ARIMA, SVR and CSA. J. Exp. Theor. Artif. Intell. **25**(4), 559–574 (2013)
26. Claveria, O., Torra, S.: Forecasting tourism demand to Catalonia: neural networks vs. time series models. Econ. Model. **36**, 220–228 (2014)
27. Chand, S., Kamal, S., Ali, I.: Modelling and volatility analysis of share prices using ARCH and GARCH models. World Appl. Sci. J. **19**(1), 77–82 (2012)
28. Pati, J., Kumar, B., Manjhi, D., Shukla, K.K.: A comparison among ARIMA, BP-NN, and MOGA-NN for software clone evolution prediction. IEEE Access **5**, 11841–11851 (2017)
29. Zhang, Q., Li, F., Long, F., Ling, Q.: Vehicle emission forecasting based on wavelet transform and long short-term memory network. IEEE Access **6**, 56984–56994 (2018)
30. Zhang, X., Xue, T., Stanley, H.E.: Comparison of econometric models and artificial neural networks algorithms for the prediction of baltic dry index. IEEE Access **7**, 1647–1657 (2019)
31. Bianchi, F.M., De Santis, E., Rizzi, A., Sadeghian, A.: Short-term electric load forecasting using echo state networks and PCA decomposition. IEEE Access **3**, 1931–1943 (2015)
32. Petrevska, B.: Predicting tourism demand by ARIMA models. Econ. Res.-Ekon. Istraživanja **30**(1), 939–950 (2017)

Efficient Ballot Casting in Ranked Based Voting System Using Homomorphic Encryption

Bhumika Patel[(✉)], Purvi Tandel, and Slesha Sanghvi

Department of Computer Engineering, CGPIT, Uka Tarsadiya University,
Bardoli, India
patelbhumika1007@gmail.com,
{purvi.tandel,slesha.sanghvi}@utu.ac.in

Abstract. Elections conducted on paper consumes many resources. Online voting system is very faster, cheaper and more suitable. Recent in online voting system improve the security guarantees for elections, because of confidentiality of voters and their integrity and validity. For security purpose, three election models are used for online voting: the mix-net model, the blind signature model, and the homomorphic encryption model. However only homomorphic encryption gives direct tallying without decrypting every votes. In this paper, we are focusing on ballot casting and tallying for ranked based voting system using Paillier homomorphic and Elgamal homomorphic encryption schemes and at the end we will compare results of both encryption schemes.

Keywords: Ballot casting · E-voting system · Homomorphic · Paillier · Elgamal · Ranked

1 Introduction

In every, democratic country in the process of voting is a very crucial task where people choose a new government for the next years and make it better in all the ways. Electronic voting systems, compared to traditional paper based elections, promise that election results will be calculated quickly with less chance of human error and will reduce cost. However, there are many issues with the electronic vote casting like system errors, security error and so on. In online voting system, one of the major issue is security votes as it is as given by voters. Either it may be possible by insider or outsider privacy of vote can be breach.

Cryptography technique is the best idea to overcome these issues because only cryptography technique is allowed to encrypt the voter's information and send to the server side. For security purpose, three voting election models are used: Mix-net model, Blind signature model and Homomorphic encryption model.

- Mix-net model [1]:
  In mix-net based voting schemes, multiple mix servers are used to remove connections to the voter. They shuffle and re-encrypt the ballots. The mix servers can be used to anonymize the ballots, because these servers remove the connection of the

© Springer Nature Singapore Pte Ltd. 2019
M. Singh et al. (Eds.): ICACDS 2019, CCIS 1046, pp. 565–576, 2019.
https://doi.org/10.1007/978-981-13-9942-8_53

voter's signature and her/his vote and re-encrypt the ballots. The main disadvantages of these models is that cryptographic operations need many resources, which are not deniable.

- Blind signature model [2]:
  A blind signature is same as digital signature in that one person can get another person to sign a message without information revealing. It is the most famous technique in online voting system. It provide confidentiality of voters. The signature is used to authenticate the voter without revealing the information of ballot. The disadvantages of these model is polynomial in all suitable parameters, is inefficient.
- Homomorphic encryption model [3]:
  Homomorphic encryption differs from typical encryption methods in that it allows computation to be performed directly on encrypted data without decrypting individual data. The result of such computation gets in encrypted form, and after performing all computation final result can revealed by the owner secret key.

In any encryption and decryption method, there are no one can know who won the election without decrypting every votes.

In given three model only homomorphic encryption model can directly tally votes without decrypting individuals vote. Also the vote casting and storing can be secured using homomorphic encryption scheme because, when used other encryption scheme, every time decryption is needed.

Homomorphic encryption is used to encrypting and calculating all votes without decrypting. Benaloh [4] first introducing voting schemes, which is based on homomorphic encryption. Homomorphic encryption is a one type of encryption in that some operation to be performed on the cipher text without decrypting the cipher text. The result of the operations is gives as an encrypted result, which when decrypted is the same as if some operation was performed on the plain text [5]. For the given advantages of homomorphic cryptosystem, we used homomorphic encryption scheme for online voting system.

Online voting system consists of the following stages: initialization stage, registration stage, ballot casting stage and tally and result revealing stage [10]. Figure 1 indicates phases of online voting system.

1.1 Initialization Stage

Beginning of an election, each authority generates a key pair (public key and secret key). The common public key is generated using all public key of authority, and that public key is posted on the public bulletin board in order to encrypt each ballot.

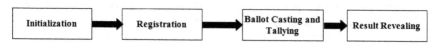

Fig. 1. Phases of online voting system

1.2 Registration Stage

In these stages, each voter must be register with their present valid ID before election. All voter generate a key in registration phase.

1.3 Ballot Casting Stage and Tallying

In these stages, registered voters will cast their votes, after the announcement of voting stage is started. Each vote of voters will be encrypted and will be stored in server side.

Next, tallying stage is to count the ballots and get the final result for each candidate. Each tally authority should apply the algorithm of this stage.

1.4 Revealing Stage

It is last stage of online voting system. In that, results are display.

After studying the phases in online voting system, ballot casting is very crucial task in any democratic country. Because if proper encryption scheme is not implemented, then attacker can change the vote information. So, ballots are encrypted using proper encryption schemes is necessary.

Moreover, for that, some security requirements in any online voting system. These requirements include: Eligibility, Uniqueness, Privacy, Accuracy, Efficiency [4].

- Eligibility: Only authorized voters are allowed to cast their vote.
- Uniqueness: Only single time voting is performed.
- Privacy: Anyone else can access voter's ballot information.
- Accuracy: Only valid ballots is counted.
- Efficiency: Efficiently perform counting of vote.

By considering, above security requirement we implemented ballot casting and tallying stage of online voting system, using Paillier cryptosystem and Elgamal cryptosystem for ranked based voting system, and then we compared both the algorithms to get better efficiency for ballot casting and tallying stage.

In ranked based ballot, casting each voter can assign different numbers of points to candidates, and the winner is the candidate who receives the highest total number of points. Voter also assign the same rank to all candidate or different rank to all candidate based on voter's personal preference. Voters are assign any number of points to any candidate. The only limitation is that the total number of assigned points is equal to the total available points. Available point can be defined based on number of candidates.

2 Preliminaries on Cryptography

2.1 Homomorphic Encryption

Homomorphic encryptions allow complex operations performed on encrypted data without decrypting individual data using homomorphic property [6].

There are two homomorphic properties, which is used for complex computation without revealing information.

- Additive Homomorphic Encryption [6]
  An additively homomorphic scheme is one in that; it will perform multiplication on cipher text which is equivalent to results of sum of the plaintexts. That is,

$$\text{Encrypt}(m_1) \times \text{Encrypt}(m_2) = \text{Encrypt}(m_1 + m_2). \tag{1}$$

where the decryption of both sides the sum of the plaintexts produced.

- Multiplicative Homomorphic Encryption [6]
  A multiplicatively homomorphic scheme is one in that, it will perform multiplication on cipher text which is equivalent to results in the product of the plaintexts. That is,

$$\text{Encrypt}(m_1) \times \text{Encrypt}(m_2) = \text{Encrypt}(m_1 \times m_2). \tag{2}$$

where the decryption of both sides the product of the plaintexts produced.

Types of Homomorphic Encryptions:

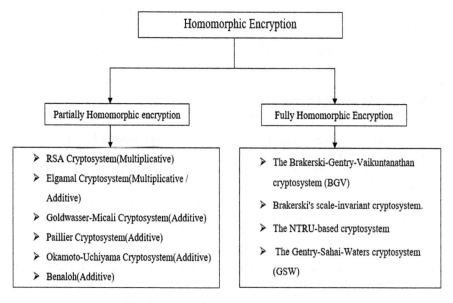

Fig. 2. Types of homomorphic encryption

Homomorphic cryptosystem can be classified into two categories, as given in Fig. 2.

- Partially Homomorphic Cryptosystems: - A cryptosystem is considered as a partially homomorphic if it either additive or multiplicative homomorphism, but not both at a time [7].

- Fully Homomorphic Cryptosystem: - A cryptosystem is considered as a fully homomorphic if it supports arbitrary number of operation on cipher texts [7].

There are many algorithm on partially homomorphic cryptosystems that allow specific operations to be performed (namely addition and multiplication), whereas in case and fully homomorphic cryptosystem, it takes more processing time and implementation complexity is there. Due to such drawbacks, fully homomorphic cryptosystem is not very practical. For electronic voting, homomorphic encryption provides a tool to obtain the tally given the encrypted votes without decrypting the individual votes. Therefore, online voting system only choose the partial homomorphic encryption for ballot casting.

The different cryptographic algorithm can be implemented for ballot casting and tallying like a Paillier and Elgamal cryptosystem. Paillier algorithm has addition property of homomorphic encryption and Elgamal have both property of homomorphic encryption (Addition and Multiplication). For tallying of ballots, only addition property used because of that additive Elgamal cryptosystem is taken for encryption and decryption. In additive Elgamal taken same encryption decryption, process like simple Elgamal but simply some difference in encryption and decryption process.

Paillier algorithm and Elgamal algorithm that support homomorphic properties. There are two keys (Public key and Private key) needed for Paillier and Elgamal to perform encryption, decryption. Given section, describe the procedure of both algorithm.

There are Elgamal and Paillier methods of homomorphic encryption, which is used in ballot casting and tallying without decrypting.

2.2 Elgamal Cryptosystem

Elgamal have satisfied both properties of homomorphic cryptosystem, but additive property is used to tallying the votes [8].

A. Key Generation
In Elgamal key generation phase generates a public key and private key, we need to choose finite cyclic group G with large prime number p and generator, which is primitive root of p. Choose random number x, which is private key of authority and calculate public key using,

$$h = g^x \bmod p. \tag{3}$$

After following these step we can generate public key (p, g, h) and private key (x).

B. Encryption Process
In encryption process, the data is converted into not readable or encrypted format which means it is not gets original message to everyone without private key.

For Elgamal cryptosystem message m that need to be encrypted must be an integer. In First step random number (y) is generated, using that random number for same plain text message different cipher text are generated. In Elgamal cryptosystem two-cipher text generated for one plain text. After generating random number, compute cipher text using given equation.

$$c_1 = g^y \bmod p, \text{ and } c_2 = (g^m * h^y) \bmod p. \tag{4}$$

C. Decryption Process

At decryption side, private key is used for find out the original message. In Elgamal, decryption process is computed using given equation, and finally message m can be computed using discrete logarithm problem.

$$\frac{c_2}{c_1} = g^m. \tag{5}$$

D. Homomorphism Property

Elgamal Homomorphic property in which addition is perform without decrypting every votes.

$$\begin{aligned} E(m_1) * E(m_2) &= (g^{y_1}, g^{m_1} * h^{y_1}) * (g^{y_2}, g^{m_2} * h^{y_2}) \\ &= (g^{y_1 + y_2}, g^{m_1 + m_2} * h^{y_1 + y_2}) \\ &= E(m_1 + m_2). \end{aligned} \tag{6}$$

$$\begin{aligned} E(m_1)^{m_2} &= (g^{y_1}, g^{m_1} * h^{y_1})^{m_2} \\ &= (g^{y_1 . m_2}, g^{m_1 . m_2} * h^{y_1 . m_2}) \\ &= E(m_1 * m_2). \end{aligned} \tag{7}$$

2.3   Paillier Cryptosystem

Paillier algorithm have satisfied additive property of homomorphic cryptosystem. Additive property is useful in ballot casting when we can tallying ballots without decrypting. Paillier is semantically secure [9].

A. Key Generation

In Paillier key generation first of all choose large prime numbers p and q such that $\gcd(pq, (p - 1 * q - 1)) = 1$, then calculate $n = p*q$ and compute $d = \lambda(n)$ and $g = n + 1$. Generate public key (n) and private key (p, q, n)

B. Encryption Process

In Paillier cryptosystem, also different cipher text is generated for same plain text. In that first generated random number and then compute cipher text.

$$c = g^m * x^n \bmod n^2. \tag{8}$$

where m is actual message and x is random number.

C. Decryption Process

In Paillier, we can obtain message m using following computation,

$$m = \frac{L\left(c^{\lambda(n)} \bmod n^2\right)}{L\left(g^{\lambda(n)} \bmod n^2\right)} \bmod n. \tag{9}$$

D. Homomorphism Property

Pallier homomorphic property in which multiplication is performed on cipher text without decrypt plain text, when decrypt that cipher text result is given sum of plain text.

$$
\begin{aligned}
E(m_1) * E(m_2) &= \left(g^{m_1} * x_1^n\right) * \left(g^{m_2} * x_2^n\right) \\
&= g^{m_1 + m_2} (x_1 * x_2)^n \\
&= E(m_1 + m_2).
\end{aligned} \tag{10}
$$

$$
\begin{aligned}
E(m_1)^{m_2} &= \left(g^{m_1} * x^n\right)^{m_2} \\
&= \left(g^{m_1 \cdot m_2} * x^{n \cdot m_2}\right) \\
&= E(m_1 * m_2).
\end{aligned} \tag{11}
$$

3 Implementation

Our proposed work will be focus on ranked based ballot casting, with the help of Elgamal encryption as well as Paillier encryption. Implementation is based on different parameters like number of voters, number of candidates and key size. After performing both ballot casting methods compare those results and prove which is best to ballot casting in which circumstance.

In ranked based voting system, voters allows ranking to all candidates. Each voter can assign either different numbers of points or same number of points to candidates, and the candidate who receives the largest total number of points is the winner. Voters are allowed to assign any points to candidate. The restriction is that the total number of assigned points is equal to the total available points. Available point is defined before the election is started and which is decided on the base of number of candidates. The number of point can be calculated using fractional of $n * \left(n - \left(\frac{n}{2}\right)\right)$ for odd number of candidates and $n * \left(n - \left(\frac{n}{2} - 1\right)\right)$ for even number of candidates. Here n is number of candidates. For example, if number of candidate are 2, 4, 6... The available point is 4, 12, 24...and if number of candidate are 3, 5, 7... the point is 6, 15, 28...

In our example, five voters is given, that gives ranked for three different candidates based on personal preference. There are three candidates so available point decided his 6. After giving, all ranked to candidates that ranked will be converted into binary

Table 1. Ranked based Voting

	C1	C2	C3
Voter1	2	2	2
Voter2	6	0	0
Voter3	3	2	1
Voter4	1	4	1
Voter5	1	2	3

format. Each element of that ranked will be encrypted using Elgamal as well as Paillier cryptosystem.

In Table 1, five voter's gives ranked to different candidates. It gives same ranked to all candidates or different ranked to all candidates, then it ranked will be converted into binary format. Table 2 shows that all ranked will be converted into binary format.

Table 2. Ranked converted into binary format

	C1	C2	C3
Voter1	010	010	010
Voter2	110	000	000
Voter3	011	010	001
Voter4	001	100	001
Voter5	001	010	011

After converting in binary format each element of voter has ranked will be encrypted using Paillier encryption as well as Elgamal encryption. Table 3 gives encrypted ranked of voters.

Table 3. Encrypted ballots

	C1			C2			C3		
Voter1	E(0)	E(1)	E(0)	E(0)	E(1)	E(0)	E(0)	E(1)	E(0)
Voter2	E(1)	E(1)	E(0)	E(0)	E(0)	E(0)	E(0)	E(0)	E(0)
Voter3	E(0)	E(1)	E(1)	E(0)	E(1)	E(0)	E(0)	E(0)	E(1)
Voter4	E(0)	E(0)	E(1)	E(1)	E(0)	E(0)	E(0)	E(0)	E(1)
Voter5	E(0)	E(0)	E(1)	E(0)	E(1)	E(0)	E(0)	E(1)	E(1)

Table 4. Convert into decimal format

	C1	C2	C3
Voter1	$E(0)^4 \times E(1)^2 \times E(0)^1 =$ $E(0 \times 4 + 1 \times 2 + 0 \times 1)$	$E(0)^4 \times E(1)^2 \times E(0)^1 =$ $E(0 \times 4 + 1 \times 2 + 0 \times 1)$	$E(0)^4 \times E(1)^2 \times E(0)^1 =$ $E(0 \times 4 + 1 \times 2 + 0 \times 1)$
Voter2	$E(1)^4 \times E(1)^2 \times E(0)^1 =$ $E(1 \times 4 + 1 \times 2 + 0 \times 1)$	$E(0)^4 \times E(0)^2 \times E(0)^1 =$ $E(0 \times 4 + 0 \times 2 + 0 \times 1)$	$E(0)^4 \times E(0)^2 \times E(0)^1 =$ $E(0 \times 4 + 0 \times 2 + 0 \times 1)$
Voter3	$E(0)^4 \times E(1)^2 \times E(1)^1 =$ $E(0 \times 4 + 1 \times 2 + 1 \times 1)$	$E(0)^4 \times E(1)^2 \times E(0)^1 =$ $E(0 \times 4 + 1 \times 2 + 0 \times 1)$	$E(0)^4 \times E(0)^2 \times E(1)^1 =$ $E(0 \times 4 + 0 \times 2 + 1 \times 1)$
Voter4	$E(0)^4 \times E(0)^2 \times E(1)^1 =$ $E(0 \times 4 + 0 \times 2 + 1 \times 1)$	$E(1)^4 \times E(0)^2 \times E(0)^1 =$ $E(1 \times 4 + 0 \times 2 + 0 \times 1)$	$E(0)^4 \times E(0)^2 \times E(1)^1 =$ $E(0 \times 4 + 0 \times 2 + 1 \times 1)$
Voter5	$E(0)^4 \times E(0)^2 \times E(1)^1 =$ $E(0 \times 4 + 0 \times 2 + 1 \times 1)$	$E(0)^4 \times E(1)^2 \times E(0)^1 =$ $E(0 \times 4 + 1 \times 2 + 0 \times 1)$	$E(0)^4 \times E(1)^2 \times E(1)^1 =$ $E(0 \times 4 + 1 \times 2 + 1 \times 1)$

After encrypting individual elements of votes, that vote will be sent to the server side. Server will receive votes and perform exponential function using property of Elgamal as well as Paillier cryptosystem on encrypted data,

Tallying will be performed on each column of ballots, because each column indicates ranked of each candidate.

Table 5. Tallying ballots

	C1	C2	C3
Voter1	E(2)	E(2)	E(2)
Voter2	E(6)	E(0)	E(0)
×			
	E(8)	E(2)	E(2)
Voter3	E(3)	E(2)	E(1)
×			
	E(11)	E(4)	E(3)
Voter4	E(1)	E(4)	E(1)
×			
	E(12)	E(8)	E(4)
Voter5	E(1)	E(2)	E(3)
×			
Final tallying	E(13)	E(10)	E(7)

All encrypted ballots is converted into encrypted decimal ballots using exponential function with the help of homomorphism property. Table 4 shows that decimal encrypted ballots.

After converting decimal encrypted ballots, votes will be counted one by one on each column using Elgamal homomorphism property and Paillier homomorphism property. Table 5 shows that tallying on ballots using homomorphic property of both algorithm without decrypting individual ballots.

If all ballots are counted then last encrypted ballots, answer was decrypted. Finally, all the ballots will decrypted using decryption process of both algorithms.

4 Result and Analysis

Implementation work is based on Elgamal cryptosystem as well as Paillier cryptosystem. All experiment was performed using a 256-bit key (p and q are 256-bit) in both Elgamal and Paillier algorithm.

All implementation was performed on a laptop with the following specifications requirement: Intel® Core™ i5-4440 CPU @ 3.10 GHz 3.10 GHz Processor with a 64-Bit operating system and 12 GB and implementation is performed on python 2.7.11 version of python language. Pycrypto module which is used in python 2.7 to 3.3, they provide secure hash functions and various encryption algorithms.

Figure 3 indicates total encrypted time of ballot using Elgamal cryptosystem and Paillier cryptosystem of number of voters.

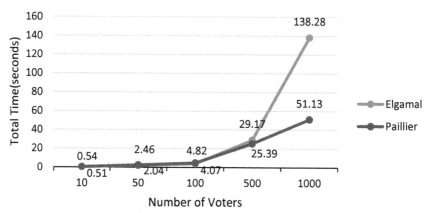

Fig. 3. Ballot encryption time using Elgamal and Paillier

Implementation results show that Elgamal cryptosystem takes less time or equal time compare to Paillier cryptosystem up to 500 voters, but voters are increasing Paillier cryptosystem is gives less time for encrypting ballots. Paillier cryptosystem gives accurate result compare to Elgamal if number of voters is increased.

For Elgamal we are not getting result for 5000 voter but Paillier quickly getting results for 5000 voter, which is approximately 244.70 s.

Figure 4 shows that total counting and decryption time at server side using Elgamal and Paillier cryptosystem. In that for small number of voter Elgamal gives same time or less time compare to Paillier cryptosystem, but when number of voter are increase Elgamal takes larger time than Paillier cryptosystem.

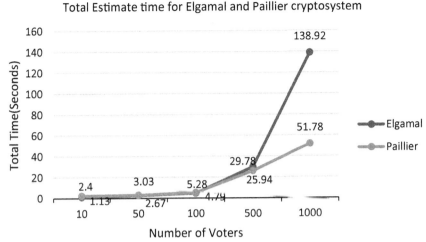

Fig. 4. Total time using Elgamal and Paillier cryptosystem

Implementation results proved that both algorithm produce exactly same result in manually tallying process and after decrypting tallying on cipher text.

5 Conclusion and Future Work

In this paper, the use of Elgamal and Paillier cryptosystem in ballot casting and tallying can utilize homomorphic properties of algorithm to calculate votes. This paper focuses on ranked based ballot casting in that each voters can gives ranked to all candidates. Both algorithms produce different cipher text for same plain text using random number. The Elgamal cryptosystem takes much larger time than Paillier cryptosystem in ranked based ballot casting when number of voters get increase.

In the future, we will provided more security and verification on ballot casting phase. We intend to improve all security requirements and provide verification on each stage.

Verification will be without revealing voter's information in each phase.

References

1. Meter, C.: Design of distributed voting systems. arXiv preprint arXiv:1702.02566 (2017)
2. Wang, K.-H., Mondal, S.K., Chan, K., Xie, X.: A review of contemporary e-voting: Requirements, technology, systems and usability. Data Sci. Pattern Recognit. 1(1), 31–47 (2017)
3. Zhang, L., Zheng, Y., Kantoa, R.: A review of homomorphic encryption and its applications. In: Proceedings of the 9th EAI International Conference on Mobile Multimedia Communications, pp. 97–106. ICST (Institute for Computer Sciences, Social-Informatics and Telecommunications Engineering) (2016)

4. Jabbar, I., Alsaad, S.N.: Design and implementation of secure remote e-voting system using homomorphic encryption IJ Netw. Secur. **19**(5), 694–703 (2017)
5. Geurden, M.: A new future for military security using fully homomorphic encryption (2018)
6. Morris, L.: Analysis of partially and fully homomorphic encryption. Rochester Inst. Technol., 1–5 (2013)
7. Azougaghe, A., Hedabou, M., Belkasmi, M.: An electronic voting system based on homomorphic encryption and prime numbers. In: 2015 11th International Conference on Information Assurance and Security (IAS), pp. 140–145. IEEE (2015)
8. Sharma, T.: E-voting using homomorphic encryption scheme. Int. J. Comput. Appl. (0975–8887) **141**, 14–16 (2016)
9. Yang, X., Yi, X., Nepal, S., Kelarev, A., Han, F.: A secure verifiable ranked choice online voting system based on homomorphic encryption. IEEE Access **6**, 20506–20519 (2018)
10. Shubhangi, S., Chitre, SD.K.: Privacy preservation in e-voting using homomorphic technology. Int. J. Latest Trends Eng. Technol. (IJLTET) **2**(4), 397–402 (2013)

Topic Modelling with Fuzzy Document Representation

Nadeem Akhtar$^{(\boxtimes)}$, M. M. Sufyan Beg, and Hira Javed

Department of Computer Engineering, Zakir Husain College of Engineering
and Technology, Aligarh Muslim University, Aligarh, India
nadeemakhtar@zhcet.ac.in, mmsbeg@hotmail.com,
hirajaved05@gmail.com

Abstract. Latent Dirichlet Allocation (LDA) and its variant topic models have been widely used for performing text mining tasks. Topic models sometimes produce incoherent topics having noisy words with high probabilities. The reason is that topic model suffers from binary weighting of terms, sparsity and lack of semantic information. In this work, a fuzzy document representation is used within the framework of topic modeling that resolves these problems. Fuzzy document representation uses the concept of Fuzzy Bag of Word (FBoW) that maps each document to a fixed length fuzzy vector of basis terms. Each basis term in the fuzzy vector belongs to all documents in the dataset with some membership degree. Latent Dirichlet Allocation is tailored to use fuzzy document representation and results are compared with regular LDA and term weighted LDA over short and long text documents on document clustering and topic quality tasks. LDA with fuzzy representation generates more coherent topics than other two methods. It also outperforms the other methods on document clustering for short documents and produces comparable results with term weighted LDA for long documents.

Keywords: Fuzzy bag of words · Latent Dirichlet Allocation ·
Fuzzy document representation

1 Introduction

Topic Models [1] have been proven useful for analyzing and discovering important statistical pattern in large collection of text documents. Topic models are probabilistic models which discover the latent semantic structure hidden in the large text data. They have wide spectrum of text mining applications such as multi-document summarization [2, 3], Microblog Summarization [4], Sentiment analysis [5, 6], opinion mining [7], social network analysis [8], machine translation [9] etc.

Topic models assume that the documents are mixture of several latent topics and each topic is a distribution over vocabulary words. A probabilistic framework is used to infer topic distribution for each document and word distribution for each topic [1]. Often, topic models produce low quality topics having noisy or unrelated words with high probabilities. This happens due to three reasons. First, high frequency words are given more importance, some of which are domain specific stop-words. Moreover, an

© Springer Nature Singapore Pte Ltd. 2019
M. Singh et al. (Eds.): ICACDS 2019, CCIS 1046, pp. 577–587, 2019.
https://doi.org/10.1007/978-981-13-9942-8_54

informative word may be given less importance due to its low frequency. Second, the document term relationships are very sparse. A document contains only a small number of vocabulary words. For short text like tweets and snippets, this problem is more severe. Third, topic models does not consider semantic association among words.

To alleviate the first problem, the term weighting schemes [10–12] are used to weight the document words according to their importance, assigning important words higher weights and domain specific words lesser weights. The term weighting schemes resolved the first problem but does not consider second and third problems.

In this work, fuzzy document representation is used for the implementation of Latent Dirichlet Allocation (LDA) [13], which is the base of all topic models. Use of fuzzy document representation resolves all the three mentioned problems for topic models. Recently some fuzzy document representation methods [14, 15] are proposed which are shown to perform better on text mining tasks like classification, clustering. In fuzzy representation, each document in the dataset is represented as a fixed length vector of basis terms. Basis terms are some high frequency words in the dataset. Each basis term is assumed to belong to each document with some fuzzy membership value. This membership value is calculated using the semantic similarity between the basis term and all the words in the document. The fuzzy document representation for topic model resolves all three problems. First, fuzzy weights are assigned to basis terms as in term weighted schemes. Second, every basis term belongs to each document with some membership degree removing sparsity problem completely. Third, fuzzy representation also considers semantic association among words.

The contribution of the proposed work is as follows:

- Fuzzy document representation is used for the implementation of LDA topic model. To the best of our knowledge, no other has used this kind of fuzzy representation for topic modeling.
- LDA with fuzzy representation is evaluated over long and short document datasets on two tasks- document clustering and topic quality. It is compared with regular LDA and a term weighted LDA which uses log weights.
- LDA with fuzzy representation outperform both the baselines on topic quality. It also outperform the baselines over short documents on document clustering but perform at par with term weighted LDA.

Remainder of the paper is organized as follows. Next section describes related work. Section 3 presents the proposed method. Section 4 presents experimental settings. Section 5 present results and discussion. Section 6 concludes and discusses future work.

2   Related Work

Regular topic models consider each word in the document having equal weights. This leads to the inclusion of non-informative words which appears frequently in the dataset. Several term weighting schemes [10, 12, 16] have been proposed which significantly improves the performance of text mining tasks including topic modeling. Authors in [11] proposed that high frequency words contributes little to document semantics for discrimination. These high frequency words are either general stop-words or domain specific stop-words. The log-weighted LDA proposed in [11] reduces the weights of such words using information theory by assigning log weights – log(p(w)) to each word w, where p(w) is the probability of the word w in the dataset.

PMI weighted LDA [11] assigns different weights to a word in different documents. A word w in document is assigned weight equal to – log(p(w/d)/p(w)). In [12], authors have used a supervised approach called BDC term weighting scheme to punish domain specific stop-words. In [10], entropy based term weighting scheme is proposed. Authors in [10] also combines entropy based term weighting scheme with log weight and BDC weight to form combined entropy based term weighting scheme called CEW.

The term weighting schemes are evaluated on LDA and its variants on several text mining tasks and have performed better than non-weighted topic models.

3   Proposed Method

In the proposed method, firstly, the documents are represented using fuzzy bag of words representation. Secondly, Latent Dirichlet Allocation is modified to consider the fuzzy memberships of basis terms in the documents.

3.1   Fuzzy Representation of Documents

In bag of word (BoW) representation, each document is represented as a vector of fixed length of vocabulary words. In BoW, each vocabulary word is mapped to the document vector in binary fashion. If the vocabulary word is not present in the document, corresponding word weight is zero otherwise it is equal to the normalized frequency of the word in the document. This binary mapping of vocabulary words to documents results in sparse vectors because a document contains only a small number of words. Also, this binary mapping lacks semantic relationship among words. To alleviate the problems of BoW representation, Fuzzy Bag of Words (FBoW) representations [14–16] may be used, which provides dense document representation which also considers word semantics.

In Fuzzy Bag of Word (FBoW) representation, a document is represented as a vector of basis terms, wherein each basis term value represents the semantic correlation of that basis term with all the words in document. A document is represented as $z = [z_1, z_2, \ldots, z_l]$, where l is the number of basis terms. The ith value z_i is equal to the sum of membership degrees between i^{th} basis term and all words in the document.

$$z_i = \sum_{w_j \in W} A(t_i, w_j) . x_j \tag{1}$$

Where w is the set of all words in the document, t_i is the ith basis term and x_j is the frequency of w_j in the document. The membership function A can be specified in several ways. In this paper, membership function A is used to find semantic similarity between words as described in [14] given by:

$$A(t_i, w_j) = \begin{cases} Cos\{W[t_i], W[w_j]\} & \text{if } Cos\{W[t_i], W[w_j]\} > 0 \\ 0 & \text{otherwise} \end{cases} \qquad (2)$$

Where W[w] is the word embedding for word w. Only the positive cosine similarity values are counted. To find the cosine similarity between word embeddings, pre-trained word2vec vectors trained on Google News dataset [17] are used.

Since in fuzzy document representation, every word belongs to every document with different membership values and LDA assigns a topic to each word of the document, the complexity of LDA for fuzzy document representation will be much higher than the complexity of LDA for BoW representation. To not degrade the LDA performance for fuzzy representation, the document vectors are restricted to use only a small set of basis terms.

In text mining applications, usually the very high frequency and very low frequency words in documents are discarded because they are not useful for text mining applications. Very high frequency words are usually domain specific stop-words and not useful for discrimination among topics of the dataset. Very low frequency keywords does not represent much statistical correlation with other words. The remaining words after discarding very high and very low frequency words are called basis terms of the dataset. Representing documents as vector of basis terms reduces both sparsity and dimensionality.

Fuzzy Bag of Word (FBoW) representation addresses both the sparsity and semantic similarity problem of BoW representation. FBoW removes the sparsity problem as each basis term belongs to each document with some membership degree, whereas in BoW, few vocabulary terms belong to each document due to the use of exact matching. FBoW representation also uses semantic similarity between terms to encode semantic correlation among document words and basis terms, whereas BoW representation only uses statistical correlation among document words.

3.2   Latent Dirichlet Allocation for FBoW Representation

Latent Drichlet allocation has been widely applied for topic modelling of text documents. In LDA, each document in the corpus is supposed to be a mixture of multiple topics. Each word of the document is supposed to come from a different topic. Each document has a multinomial distribution over a fixed number of topics and each topic has a multinomial distribution over a fixed vocabulary words. To generate a word in a document, the generative process of LDA first generates a topic according to the probability distribution of the document over topics and then generates a word according to the probability distribution of the selected topic over vocabulary words.

Gibbs sampling [18] and Markov Chain Monte Carlo (MCMC) [19] is used to approximate the intractable posterior of LDA. The topic for each word of each document is sampled from the conditional distribution of topic, which is given by:

$$p(z_{di} = k | W_{-i}, Z_{-i}) = \frac{n_{k,-i}^w + \beta}{\sum_{w=1}^{W} \left(n_{k,-i}^w + \beta \right)} \times \frac{n_{d,-i}^k + \alpha}{\sum_{k=1}^{K} \left(n_{d,-i}^k + \alpha \right)} \qquad (3)$$

Where z_{di} is the topic assignment for i^{th} word of document d, $n_{k,-i}^w$ is the number of times word w appear with topic k, $n_{d,-i}^k$ is number of times a word in document d is assigned topic k. '$-i$' indicates that the current word is not included in the counts. K is the topics and W is the vocabulary size. α and β are dirichlet hyper-parameter for topic and word distributions respectively.

Inference of LDA with Fuzzy Representation

In LDA inference, eachword is observed with binary weights. The words which are not present in the document are not observed (i.e. observed with zero weight) and which are present in the document are observed with weight 1. In Fuzzy representation, all basis terms are assigned to all documents with some membership degree. The same LDA inference procedure can be used for fuzzy document representation but with fuzzy word weights. When a word w is observed in the document d, it contributes f_{dw} to the counts, where f_{dw} is the fuzzy membership degree of basis term w in document d. The conditional distribution for topic for LDA wit fuzzy representation can be written as:

$$p(z_{di} = k | W_{-i}, Z_{-i}) = \frac{\sum_{v=1}^{n_{k,-i}^w} f_{d_v v} + \beta}{\sum_{w=1}^{W} \left(\sum_{v=1}^{n_{k,-i}^w} f_{d_v v} + \beta \right)} \times \frac{\sum_{v=1}^{n_{d,-i}^k} f_{dv} + \alpha}{\sum_{k=1}^{K} \left(\sum_{v=1}^{n_{d,-i}^k} f_{dv} + \alpha \right)} \qquad (4)$$

Where d_v is the document containing word v.

The LDA parameters θ and φ are estimated using following equations:

$$\theta_{dk} = \frac{\sum_{v=1}^{n_d^k} f_{dv} + \alpha}{\sum_{k=1}^{K} \left(\sum_{v=1}^{n_d^k} f_{dv} + \alpha \right)} \qquad (5)$$

$$\Phi_{kw} = \frac{\sum_{v=1}^{n_k^w} f_{d_v v} + \beta}{\sum_{w=1}^{W} \left(\sum_{v=1}^{n_k^w} f_{d_v v} + \beta \right)} \qquad (6)$$

The Gibbs sampling algorithm is described as follows:

Algorithm 1 Gibbs sampling algorithm

Input: Iterations I, Topics K,hyper-parameters α, β, All D documents with document d having L fuzzy words. L is the number of basis terms.

C^{DK}: Document-Topic Count Matrix C^{KT}: Topic-Term Count Matrix
Randomly Initialize Count Matrices C^{DK}, C^{KT}

For i = 1 to I Do
    For d = 1 to D Do
        For j = 1 to L Do
            Decrement fuzzy counts for the current word
            Draw topic z_{dj} according to equation 4
            Update fuzzy CountsMatrices C^{DK}, C^{KT}
        End For
    End For
    Calculate parameters and $\theta$and Φaccording to equations 5 and 6 respectively.
End For

We call LDA with fuzzy document representation as **F**uzzy **B**ow **L**atent **D**irichlet **A**llocation (FBLDA).

We call LDA with fuzzy document representation as **F**uzzy **B**ow **L**atent **D**irichlet **A**llocation (FBLDA).

4   Experiment Settings

This section describes the evaluation methods and experimental results.

4.1   Datasets

Experiments are performed on two datasets. First dataset is a subset of Reuters-21578 dataset [20]. Only those documents in Reuters-21578 are used which has non empty topic attribute. Some documents have multiple topics. For such documents, only the first mentioned topic is considered for evaluation. The Reuters dataset considered in the experiments has 9094 documents and 82 topics.

To show the effectiveness of the fuzzy representation, experiments are also performed on short text documents. Snippets [21] dataset is used which is collection of 12340 web snippets of average document length 17.5. There are 8 categories of documents in the dataset.

4.2   Preprocessing and Data Split

Both the datasets are preprocessed to remove spurious words and stop-words. Stemming is also performed for LDA and TWLDA because these algorithms use exact word matching. Stemming is not performed for FWLDA because fuzzy membership can be found without performing stemming from word2vec.

Reuters dataset is divided into 80% training and 20% test set. Snippet dataset is available already divided into training and test set. Snippet training set has 10064 documents and test set contains 2276 documents.

4.3   Parameter Settings and Baselines

The proposed method is compared with LDA and a term weighing LDA which uses log weights for terms. In the proposed method, the high frequency 1000 words in the dataset are used as basis terms. The hyper-parameter α and β are set as $1/K$ and 0.01 respectively. K is the number of topics.

4.4   Evaluation Criterion

The proposed method is evaluated on two task.

First task is document clustering. The performance of proposed method is evaluated on how well it clusters the text documents. The topic-word distribution of each topic is considered as cluster signature. To assign a document to a cluster, cosine similarity is calculated between the vector representation of document and cluster signatures. Each document is assigned to exactly one cluster with maximum similarity. To avoid directly mapping the obtained clusters with the ground truth clusters as required in Precision and Recall, Purity and Normalized Mutual Information (NMI) [21] are used. Clustering quality is good if value of Purity and NMI are large.

Second task is evaluation of topic quality, which is measured using PMI score [22], which agrees with human-judged topic coherence. PMI score uses point wise mutual information using an external knowledgebase. In our experiment, English Wikipedia of size 1.3 M articles is used for calculating PMI score. Top 20 words are used for PMI calculation for each topic.

5   Results and Discussion

The Purity, NMI and PMI results are shown in Table 1. Table 2 shows the top 20 words of Snippet topics.

Purity, NMI and PMI results for Snippets dataset shows that topic models with fuzzy document representation produces better topic distributions than topic models with binary and term weighted vector representation on short documents. Log weighted LDA performs better than LDA on document clustering i.e. purity and NMI values are significantly higher. But, PMI values are almost same i.e. topic coherence is almost same for both the method. LDA with fuzzy document representation performs better than log weighted LDA on both document clustering and topic quality task.

Table 1. Purity, NMI and PMI results

Method	Purity	NMI	PMI
Snippets dataset			
LDA	0.3826	0.1694	0.488
logWLDA	0.4570	0.2577	0.476
FBLDA	0.5474	0.3749	0.600
Reuters dataset			
LDA	0.5353	0.3403	4.085
logWLDA	0.7199	0.5408	3.93
FBLDA	0.6484	0.4366	4.643

Table 2. Top 20 words for snippets topics

Topic	FBLDA	Log weighed LDA
1	Web website updates pages homepage online content page articles blog info blogs videos database profiles	Wikipedia encyclopedia wiki political system web party programming united search engine republic intel jobs government military article democratic politics language
2	Game football sports tournament league baseball basketball games sport players tournaments soccer hockey teams tennis	News sports games yahoo football game world tennis match soccer league theorem team tickets espn players online hockey tax statistics
3	Maxwellaol albert USA Greece India linux Chinese Germany America Japan cpu einstein bbc Japanese	Research democracy amazon books market theory stock marketing computing finance social paper parallel financial mathematical definition papers writing degree sector
4	Democratic political government democracy republic politics economic constitutional economy elections country socialist parliament regime policy	Information trade business directory cancer digital global network service security topics online google international internet disease services guide reviews heart
5	Mathematical theoretical theory physics empirical science biogeography hypothesis mathematics scientific biology thesis evolutionary dissertation concepts	Culture school music library resources art history arts students links graduate university education college page book information directory literature philosophy
6	Education health medical nutrition faculty educational academic care teaching patients pharmacy nursing students university programs	Health journal theoretical national law gov research physics department information economic war natural university association human healthy faculty american center

(*continued*)

Table 2. (*continued*)

Topic	FBLDA	Log weighed LDA
7	Technology products software business systems retail technologies companies company solutions manufacturing businesses product market sales	Science computer software management products technology engineering systems design business physical data discovery space development memory fashion database release gov
8	Music film movie movies cinema films artist filmmaking poetry artists theater poems art cinematography comics	Movie film movies imdb music biology oscar band fitness video academy evolution comedy romantic news awards model title action videos

For long text dataset, LDA with fuzzy representation produces better topic distributions in terms of topic coherence. PMI values are significantly larger than both LDA and log weighted LDA. For document clustering task, LDA with fuzzy representation performs better than LDA but lags behind log weighted LDA. For long documents, statistical term co-occurrence relationship is not as sparse as short documents. Moreover, inspection of FBLDA topics shows that some true topics are not found by FBLDA. For this reason, Log weighted LDA performs better than LDA with fuzzy representation.

Fuzzy document representation is able to model short documents for LDA in better ways. Short text documents are very sparse and fuzzy document representation handles sparsity problem by introducing semantic association. Due to consideration of semantic relationships, fuzzy document representation is capable to find coherent topics, but fails to identify all the topics in the dataset. The reason for this is that we include only 1000 high frequency words as basis terms. The basis set may not represent the full coverage of the dataset. The performance of fuzzy document representation may be improved by including more high frequency words into the set of basis term. Increasing the size of basis term set increases the size of each document, which increases the computational cost of running LDA. There is a trade-off between performance and computational cost of LDA based on the size of basis term set.

6 Conclusion

In this paper, a fuzzy document representation method is used to improve the performance of Latent Dirichlet Allocation (LDA). Fuzzy document representation resolves the three problems of LDA - binary weights for all words, sparsity and lack of semantic information. The proposed use of fuzzy document representation with LDA improves the performance on document clustering and topic quality task better than log weighted LDA for short documents. For long documents, it gives better performance than regular LDA on both tasks, but lags behind log weighted LDA for document clustering tasks due to the small size of basis term set. The performance may be improved by increasing the size of basis term set with additional computational cost. In all experiments, fuzzy document representation generates more coherent topics having higher PMI values than both the regular and log weighted LDA.

In the future work, fuzzy documentation representation for LDA may be enhanced for long documents. The set of basis term can be chosen intelligently using for example some clustering method instead of selecting pre fixed number of terms. Another enhancement might be to use a hybrid method of fuzzy representation and term weighting scheme to get the benefit of those methods.

References

1. Blei, D.M.: Introduction to probabilistic topic modeling. Commun. ACM **55**, 77–84 (2011)
2. Wang, D., Zhu, S., Li, T., Gong, Y.: Multi-document summarization using sentence-based topic models (2010)
3. Yang, G., Wen, D., Kinshuk, Chen, N.S., Sutinen, E.: A novel contextual topic model for multi-document summarization. Expert Syst. Appl. **42**, 1340–1352 (2015)
4. Akhtar, N., Siddique, B.: Hierarchical visualization of sport events using Twitter. J. Intell. Fuzzy Syst. **32**(4), 2953–2961 (2017)
5. Akhtar, N., Zubair, N., Kumar, A., Ahmad, T.: Aspect based sentiment oriented summarization of hotel reviews. Procedia Comput. Sci. **115**, 563–571 (2017)
6. Lin, C., He, Y.: Joint sentiment/topic model for sentiment analysis. In: Proceeding of the 18th ACM Conference on Information and Knowledge Management – CIKM 2009, p. 375 (2009)
7. Zhai, Z., Liu, B., Xu, H., Jia, P.: Constrained LDA for grouping product features in opinion mining. In: Huang, J.Z., Cao, L., Srivastava, J. (eds.) PAKDD 2011. LNCS (LNAI), vol. 6634, pp. 448–459. Springer, Heidelberg (2011). https://doi.org/10.1007/978-3-642-20841-6_37
8. Ho, K.T., Bui, Q.V., Bui, M.: Dynamic social network analysis using author-topic model. In: Hodoň, M., Eichler, G., Erfurth, C., Fahrnberger, G. (eds.) I4CS 2018. CCIS, vol. 863, pp. 47–62. Springer, Cham (2018). https://doi.org/10.1007/978-3-319-93408-2_4
9. Hu, Y., Zhai, K., Eidelman, V., Boyd-Graber, J.: Polylingual tree-based topic models for translation domain adaptation (2015)
10. Li, X., Zhang, A., Li, C., Ouyang, J., Cai, Y.: Exploring coherent topics by topic modeling with term weighting. Inf. Process. Manag. **54**, 1345–1358 (2018)
11. Wilson, A.T., Chew, P.A.: Term weighting schemes for latent dirichlet allocation. In: Human Language Technologies: The 2010 Annual Conference of the North American Chapter of the ACL (2010)
12. Kai, Y., Yi, C., Zhenhong, C., Ho-fung, L., Raymond, L.: Exploring topic discriminating power of words in latent dirichlet allocation. In: Proceedings of COLING 2016, 26th International Conference on Computational Linguistics Technical Paper, pp. 2238–2247 (2016)
13. Blei, D., Ng, A., Jordan, M.: Latent dirichlet allocation. J. Mach. Learn. Res. **3**, 993–1022 (2003)
14. Zhao, R., Mao, K.: Fuzzy bag-of-words model for document representation. IEEE Trans. Fuzzy Syst. **26**, 794–804 (2018)
15. Jia, H., Li, Q.: Fuzzy bag-of-topics model for short text representation. In: Cheng, L., Leung, A.C.S., Ozawa, S. (eds.) ICONIP 2018. LNCS, vol. 11305, pp. 473–482. Springer, Cham (2018). https://doi.org/10.1007/978-3-030-04221-9_42

16. Wang, T., Cai, Y., Leung, H.F., Cai, Z., Min, H.: Entropy-based term weighting schemes for text categorization in VSM. In: Proceedings - International Conference on Tools with Artificial Intelligence, ICTAI (2016)
17. Google Code Archive - long-term storage for Google code project hosting. https://code.google.com/archive/p/word2vec/. Accessed 15 Mar 2019
18. Griffiths, T.L.: Gibbs sampling in the generative model of latent Dirichlet allocation. Unpublished note (2002). https://citeseerx.ist.psu.edu/
19. Gilks, W.R.: Markov chain monte carlo. Encyclopedia of biostatistics. Adv. online Publ. (2005)
20. UCI Machine Learning Repository: Reuters-21578 Text categorization collection data set. https://archive.ics.uci.edu/ml/datasets/reuters-21578+text+categorization+collection. Accessed 15 Mar 2019
21. Manning, C.D., Raghavan, P., Schütze, H.: Introduction to information retrieval introduction. Nat. Lang. Eng. **16**, 100–103 (2008)
22. Newman, D., Lau, J., Grieser, K., Baldwin, T.: Automatic evaluation of topic coherence. In: Proceedings of NAACL-HLT (2010)

Security Validation of Cloud Based Storage

Shruti Jaiswal[1]([✉]) and Daya Gupta[2]

[1] Jaypee Institute of Information Technology, Noida, India
dce.shruti@gmail.com
[2] Delhi Technological University, Delhi, India

Abstract. In the era of big data and IoT, rate of data generation is very high which needs lot of space. So it is not feasible to store such huge data locally. Hence, to cater the large storage need cloud based storage models has evolved. With the increasing demand of cloud storage, occurrence frequency of security threats has increased exponentially. The steep rise in threat incidences cannot be ignored, as cloud storage model is being used for storing confidential data. Increased threat rate cause decline in the acceptance rate of cloud-based storage models besides it numerous benefits. In this paper, we are evaluating our existing proposal by applying it on an open source cloud based system. Evaluation is done by comparing the threats identified using our approach and threats reported on it by CVE.

Keywords: Security engineering · Cloud computing · Storage · Risk · Software development

1 Introduction

Cloud computing is defined as a practice of providing computing resources to the customer hosted on the internet on-demand, and in the economy friendly way [1]. Various benefits are provided by different cloud computing models such as fast deployment, fulfilling the need of data storage at lower cost, pay for use, scalability, and many more. Growth of cloud computing is restricted due to data privacy and data protection issues. In contrast to a network system providing security to cloud architecture is very difficult and challenging; because of complex architecture.

Security of computer systems is about preserving the CIA of dedicated system resources. Where, 'C' stands for 'Confidentiality' which confines access to data by application of set of rules, 'I' refers to 'Integrity' which gives assurance that information is consistent, and accurate. 'A' stands for 'Availability' which guarantees the access to data by authorized people. Some proposals are found that addresses the security in cloud system either by identifying the threats to system or by eliciting the security requirements and suggesting mechanism for implementation in ad-hoc manner [2–8].

Hence, to deal with the security breach occurring in the system, a structured security methodology is proposed in our earlier work [9–11] which tries to mitigate the above drawbacks and provide better security. In our earlier works [11] a framework to implement security in cloud based systems is proposed. The proposed framework has

© Springer Nature Singapore Pte Ltd. 2019
M. Singh et al. (Eds.): ICACDS 2019, CCIS 1046, pp. 588–596, 2019.
https://doi.org/10.1007/978-981-13-9942-8_55

steps for elicitation of security requirements and prioritization based on threats to functionalities. Once the security requirements are prioritized, security algorithms are identified based on design constraints. Therefore, in this paper, an open source cloud model is evaluated for confirming the validity of our proposal.

The rest of the paper is organized as follows: Sect. 2, presents a brief overview of cloud architecture; Sect. 3, provides the overview of our previous security engineering framework; Sect. 4, presents the evaluation of open source cloud model; finally, Sect. 5 concludes the paper.

2 Cloud System Architecture

Cloud architecture provided by NIST [1] is depicted in Fig. 1. Conceptual view of the architecture presents the involved actors their roles, how they communicate, and other necessary components of the cloud-based system.

2.1 Involved Actors in Cloud

Cloud Customer: Cloud customer is individual or organization who uses Cloud products and services and later paying for it.

Cloud Provider: Cloud provider owns, manage and operate the Cloud system services, and receive payment from Cloud customers for the provided services.

Cloud Broker: Broker helps consumer in understanding the complexity of cloud services and may create additional value-added cloud services. Cloud Broker acts as the intermediary between customer and provider.

Cloud Auditor: They provide valuable function to the government by conducting the independent performance and security monitoring of cloud services.

Cloud Carrier: They are the organization which is having the responsibility of transferring the data, somewhat similar to the power distributors for the electric grid.

2.2 Service Models of Cloud

Infrastructure as a Service (IaaS): IaaS model provides the computing infrastructure like servers, network equipment, and software. The user can install operating system images to create their customized environment. The Cloud Service Provider (CSP) owns the hardware and is responsible for housing and maintaining them. Some known IaaS Clouds are Rackspace, Amazon EC2, Google Compute Engine.

Platform as a Service (PaaS): PaaS provides the computing platform as on demand, which is used to develop and deploy applications. Besides providing the computing platform, PaaS also offers the solution stack consisting of operating systems, programming language environment, databases and web servers. This model is mainly

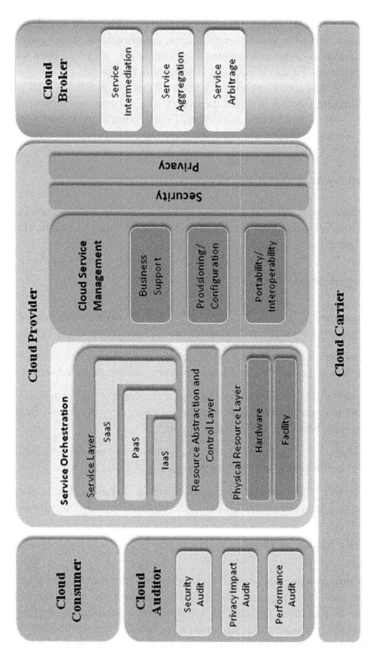

Fig. 1. Cloud reference architecture [1]

suitable for both developers and testers. The motive of PaaS is to decrease the cost and difficulty faced in buying and managing the required hardware and software compo-nents. Clouds in this category are GAE, Windows Azure Compute.

Software as a Service (SaaS): SaaS provides access to application software to Cloud Service User (CSU) which is installed and maintained by CSP. Implementation and Deployment are hidden from the user, only limited set of configuration control is made available to the customer by the provider. Its principal advantage is the reduction in hardware cost and software development and maintenance cost. Major SaaS clouds are Microsoft Office 365, Quickbooks online, etc.

Beside the above trivial services here one new service for storage is considered known as Storage as a Service (StaaS).

Storage as a Service (StaaS): StaaS provides the storage requirements of various other service models. Here we are presenting it as a separate model because of its involvement in each basic service model. Moreover, its growing need gives rise to various security issues inherent in it. Security of storage is among the key challenges as mentioned in studies by various researchers [12–15]. Therefore, it must be considered separately then the trivial service models.

3   Security Engineering Framework

Security is enforced by the developers during the later phase (design phase or further), which results in unnecessary constraints and may leave security loopholes because security requirements analysis is ignored during initial phase (requirements engineering). To handle the security related issues, a new field of Security Engineering has come into existence, that identifies and suggest algorithms to mitigate them in a structured manner [10]. Hence, handling of security issues should be initiated with the activities of requirements engineering activities of development process. Hence, to cater the need a novel framework for handling security in a cloud based system is proposed in our earlier work [11], depicted in Fig. 2. The framework works in three different phases:

- Specification
- Prioritization
- Implementation and Validation

Specification. In this phase activities are executed along with the requirement engineering activities that builds on the understanding of the requirement engineers who are good at eliciting the functional requirements but are not well experienced when it comes to security requirements [16]. In this phase, security requirements are generated based on the threats and vulnerabilities applicable to functional requirements and associated assets of the system.

Prioritization. Identified security requirements are prioritized using risk analysis method to get the ordered list of security requirements that are representing threats with high impact. Single algorithm is not enough to realize all the security requirements. Therefore, prioritization of security requirements is required, and high priority security requirements are handled first. Prioritization would help the developers and users in knowing which security requirement is more critical and need immediate focus.

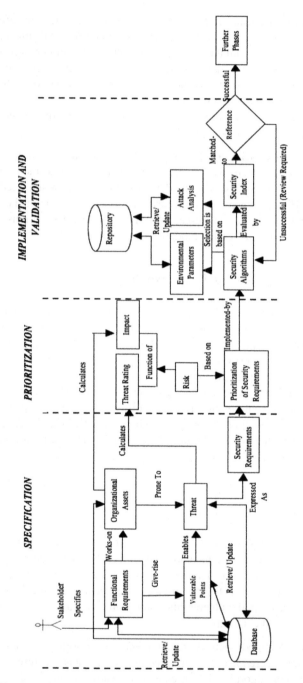

Fig. 2. Framework to implement security in cloud-based systems

Implementation and Validation. Security algorithms are identified in this phase to implement the elicited security requirements based on the environmental parameters (communication, computational) and attack analysis. Attack analysis of different algorithms is done and saved in a repository. Algorithms with highest threat match are selected first and then their performance is checked on given environmental conditions. Thereafter, the selected algorithm is validated by calculating the SI (Security Index) value which shows the effectiveness of selected security algorithms. Basically SI is the percentage of threats mitigated to the threats identified on the system.

For details of each phase and its related activities refer to our earlier work [11].

4 Case Study of Open Source Software: ownCloud

ownCloud is a client–server software for creating file hosting services and using them. Functionality of ownCloud is similar to the popularly known and used Dropbox. Basic difference between the two is that the Server Edition of ownCloud is free and open-source, and thereby allowing users to install and operate it without charge on a private server. Various vulnerabilities are reported for ownCloud by Common Vulnerabilities Exposures (CVE) over the years [17]. Frequency of vulnerability occurrence can be seen from the graph shown in Fig. 3.

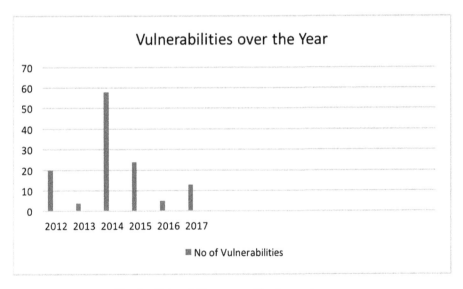

Fig. 3. Vulnerability to ownCloud over the years

We have made a comparison of threats identified for our case study of cloud based storage system with the threats reported by CVE for ownCloud. Result of comparison is shown in Table 1.

Table 1. Threat comparison

SNO.	Possible threats	Threats reported by CVE for ownCloud	Threats identified using security engineering framework
1	Distributed Denial of Service (DDoS)	No	Yes
2	Denial of Service (DoS)	Yes	Yes
3	Password cracking	No	Yes
4	Password reuse	No	Yes
5	MITM	No	Yes
6	Replay attack	No	Yes
7	Data leakage	No	Yes
8	Impersonate	No	Yes
9	Lock in	No	Yes
10	Sniffing	No	Yes
11	*Malicious code**	Yes	Yes
12	Data theft	Yes	Yes
13	Repudiate	No	Yes
14	Social engineer	Yes	Yes
15	Privilege abuse	Yes	Yes
16	Management interface compromise	Yes	Yes
17	Insider	No	Yes
18	Operational log compromise	No	Yes
19	Security log compromise	No	Yes
20	Data deletion	No	Yes
21	Side channel attack	No	Yes
22	Change data	Yes	Yes
23	Modifying network traffic	No	Yes
24	Loss of governance	No	Yes
25	Compliance challenges	No	Yes
26	Legal issues	No	Yes
27	network Issues	No	Yes
28	Natural disaster	No	Yes
29	Loss of encryption keys	No	Yes
30	Resource exhaustion	No	Yes
31	Backup lost stolen	No	Yes
32	Supply chain failure	No	Yes
33	Conflict between customer provider hardening process and cloud environment	No	Yes

(*continued*)

Table 1. (*continued*)

SNO.	Possible threats	Threats reported by CVE for ownCloud	Threats identified using security engineering framework
34	Sabotage	No	Yes
35	Unauthorized physical access	No	Yes
36	Disclose data	No	No
37	Cloud service termination	No	No
38	Cloud provider acquisition	No	No
39	Compromise service engine	No	No

*__Malicious Code__ It refers to the change in the source code with an intention of security breach. It can be created by inserting SQL queries having untrusted data, or by exploiting an existing bug in the code, or by adding camouflaging XML scripts in dynamic web pages. Threats Code Execution, Sql Injection, XSS (Cross Site Scripting), Http Response Splitting, Cross Site Request Forgery (CSRF) are comes under Malicious Code.

From the list of threats reported on ownCloud by CVE and the threats addressed by our framework. Threats identified by our approach is much more than the threats reported by CVE. In addition to this, proper security mechanisms are suggested to handle the reported/identified threats. Hence, we can say that our framework aids the identification of threat and vulnerabilities at right time and try to handle them accordingly. It will also reduce the problems that may occur in future due to security negligence.

5   Conclusion

In this paper we have applied and validated our modified generic framework of security engineering on cloud-based systems. The framework does its work in three phases that are specification, prioritization, and implementation & validation. In specification and prioritization phase security requirements are elicited, analyzed and prioritized. In implementation and validation phase optimal algorithm is selected based on domain constraints, and system security level is tested.

An open source file hosting service provider 'owncCloud' has been evaluated for the purpose of validation of our proposal. And it is found from Table 1, that our proposal identifies more threats as compared to threats listed by CVE. It was established from the case study that more threats can be identified during initial phase if our structured security engineering framework is applied, thus providing more secure system.

References

1. Liu, F., et al.: NIST cloud computing reference architecture: recommendations of the national institute of standards and technology. NIST Special Publication 500-292, Gaithersburg (2011)
2. Honer, P.: Cloud computing security requirements and solutions: a systematic literature review. In: 19th Twenty Student Conference on IT (2013)
3. Rong, C., Nguyen, S., Jaatun, M.: Beyond lighting: a survey on security challenges in cloud computing. Comput Elect. Eng. **39**(1), 47–54 (2013)
4. Sun, D., Chang, G., Sun, L., Wang, X.: Surveying and analyzing security, privacy and trust issues in cloud computing environments. Proc. Eng. **15**, 2852–2856 (2011). Advances in control engineering and information science
5. Che, J., Duan, Y., Zhang, T., Fan, J.: Study on the security models and strategies of cloud computing. Proc. Eng. **23**, 586–593 (2011). International conference on power electronic and engineering application
6. Ficco, M., Palmieri, F., Castiglione, A.: Modeling security requirements for cloud-based system development. Concurrency Comput.: Pract. Experience **27**(8), 2107–2124 (2015)
7. Islam, S., Mouratidis, H., Edgar, R.W.: A goal-driven risk management approach to support security and privacy analysis of cloud- based system. In: Mario Piattini, E.F.-M. (ed.) Security Engineering for Cloud Computing. IGI Global, Hershey (2011)
8. Naveed, R., Abbas, H.: Security requirements specification framework for cloud users. In: Park, J., Stojmenovic, I., Xhafa, F. (eds.) Future Information Technology. LNEE, vol. 276, pp. 297–305. Springer, Berlin (2014). https://doi.org/10.1007/978-3-642-40861-8_43
9. Jaiswal, S., Gupta, D.: Security requirements prioritiztion. Softw. Eng. Res. Pract. 673–679 (2009)
10. Chatterjee, K., Gupta, D., De, A.: A framework for development of secure software. CSI Trans. ICT **1**(1), 143–157 (2013)
11. Jaiswal, S., Gupta, D.: Int. J. Syst. Assur. Eng. Manag. **8**(Suppl 2), 1419 (2017). https://doi.org/10.1007/s13198-017-0612-x
12. Grobauer, B., Walloschek, T., Stocker, E.: Understanding cloud computing vulnerabilities. IEEE Secur. Priv. **9**(2), 50–57 (2011)
13. Fernandes, D., Soares, L., Gomes, J., Freire, M., Iñacio, P.: Security issues in cloud environments—a survey. Int. J. Inf. Secur. (IJIS) **13**(2), 113–170 (2014)
14. Vu, Q.H., Pham, T.-V., Truong, H.-L., Dustdar, S., Asal, R.: DEMODS: a description model for data-as-a-service. In: 26th IEEE International Conference on Advanced Information Networking and Applications, pp. 605–612. IEEE (2012)
15. Xiao, Z., Xiao, Y.: Security and privacy in cloud computing. IEEE Commun. Surv. Tutorials **15**(2), 843–859 (2013)
16. Firesmith, D.G.: Engineering security requirements. J. Object Technol. **2**(1), 53–68 (2003)
17. CVE Details: owncloud: vulnerability statistics. www.cvedetails.com: https://www.cvedetails.com/product/22262/Owncloud-Owncloud.html?vendor_id=11929 (2012)

A Literature Survey on Eye Corner Detection Techniques in Real-Life Scenarios

M. Zefree Lazarus$^{(\boxtimes)}$, Supratim Gupta , and Nidhi Panda

Department of Electrical Engineering,
National Institute of Technology, Rourkela 769008, Odisha, India
zefree.lazarus@gmail.com, sgupta.iitkg@gmail.com, nidhipanda15@gmail.com

Abstract. Accurate iris movement detection and tracking is an important and widely used step in many Human-computer interactive applications. Among the eye features, eye corners are considered as stable and reliable reference points to measure the relative iris motion. In real time scenarios, the presence of spectacles prohibit the current state-of-the-art methods to yield accurate detection as the appearance of eye corners changes considerably due to the glare and occlusion caused by them. We term this problem as the Spectacle problem. In this paper we review the available single and multiple image based spectacle problem removal techniques and highlight the pros and cons of the approaches. For this state-of-the-art report, we investigated research papers, patents and thesis presenting the basic definitions, terminologies and new directions for future researches.

Keywords: Eye corners · Detection · Spectacle problem ·
Specular reflection · Glare · Occlusion

1 Introduction

Eyes are one of the most important human facial features. They provide information about a person's identity, intentions and attention levels [1]. Detection, localization, and recognition of eye features is an important step in face detection, Biometric, Human-computer interaction (HCI) and many other diverse applications. Of all the applications, iris movement estimation is a very challenging task as it involves in continuous tracking of eye features. Many algorithms employ projective geometric parameters like the distance between the camera and the subject to estimate the eye position coordinates. However, these measurements will be erroneous when the subject is free to move his/her head. Hence, a relative measurement of pupil position with respect to other fixed reference point(s) may be appropriate to alleviate the problem [2]. Among the eye features, eye corners

This work was partially supported by the Board of Research in Nuclear Sciences (BRNS), Government of India, under the grant number 34/14/08/2016.

have the advantage of being robust to various facial expressions, gaze direction and eye status [1–8]. Because of these advantages, localization of eye corners is of great importance as they offer robust reference points.

1.1   Eye Corner Detection

Compared to a large amount of iris detection methods, methods related to eye corner detection are limited [2,3,9]. One of the prime reason being lack of proper semantic definition of eye corners. Generally, eye corners near to the nose are called the inner eye corners, and the eye corners towards the ears are called the outer eye corners. In literature there are three semantic definitions of eye corners: (a) The intersection between the upper and lower eyelids [3–6,9–14]; (b) Eye corner is classified as a pit under image topography perspective [2]; (c) The end of the sclera is labeled as the eye corner [7,15]. Based on these definitions, various eye corner detection algorithms are available in the literature, which can be broadly classified into three categories namely: Shape based, Feature based, and Sample based models.

Shape Based Eye Corner Detections. Shape-based models [3,7,8,14–16] explores the geometrical shape details between eyes and other facial features in the human face context. Some algorithms assume an eye template consisting of simple geometric primitives and energy function for feature detection. Though shape based model detects eye corners reliably, they suffer from the following lacunas:

- The efficacy of the detection is mainly influenced by the formulation of the template.
- As the template is predetermined, it may not be able to handle real-time scenarios like head pose change.
- The execution time depends on how close the template is initiated to the eye corners. Therefore these approaches may not yield real-time results.

Feature Based Eye Corner Detections. Feature based methods explore pertinent eye properties like local structure and image intensities to identify the eye corners [17]. No pre-determination and pre-processing of templates is required in these methods. These methods are easy to implement and can be used in real-time operations. In literature, there are two types of feature based corner detection schemes: edge-based and corner detection based. Generally, the edge-based corner detection methods like [6,18] are more reliable than the corner-based methods [2,19]. The main challenge for general purpose corner detectors is the fact that image characteristics of eye corners can largely vary between subjects [9,20]. As a result, reliable detection might be possible only under good imaging conditions.

Sample Based Eye Corner Detections. Sample based eye corner detection methods [9, 21–23] try to extract useful visual features from photometric appearance, based on which eye model is learnt from a large set of training images. With the advent of appearance based approaches, many traditional approaches have been replaced by deep-learning methods like Convolutional Neural Networks (CNN). The major advantage of CNN based approaches is it's precision while the limitation is that the efficiency of the methods totally depends on the representative variability of eye appearance in the training data. Due to the usage of large-datasets for training—which involves high performance computing analysis—the brevity and ease of administration is quite questionable.

1.2 Summary

No matter what the approach is, accurate detection and localization of eye features in an unconstrained environment is an ever challenging task due to the high degree of eye's appearance variability. This variability is caused either by intrinsic dynamic features of the eyes or by external factors like spectacles, hair and ambient environment changes. An extensive literature review on this application lead to the identification of several platform specific factors that influence eye feature detection and accuracy. Here, we mention few of the factors that have significant influence on the detection of eye features: Eyebrows [24–27]; Eyelids [15]; Hair [28]; Head rotation and Pose [1, 17, 29]; Imaging condition and quality [1–3, 10, 17, 24, 28, 30, 31]; Semiclosed eyes [5, 9, 17, 20, 32]; Spectacles [5, 9, 13, 15, 20–22, 24, 26–30, 32–40]; Squinted eyes [11]; Wrinkles, dark circles, swells, and cosmetics [3, 6].

Of the challenges mentioned above, two standout the most: Spectacles and illumination. [2, 3, 10–12, 15, 16] circumambulate these challenges by working on facial images without spectacles only. Among [5, 9, 13, 20–22, 29, 38] - which dealt with spectacle images, papers related to eye corner detection are [9, 13] only. We term the challenges that arise from the usage of spectacles as the spectacle problem [39].

2 Spectacle Problem

Though spectacles occupy fewer area in-terms of number of pixels, it has a huge impact on face feature detection as well as tracking algorithms. Two problems occur when the user wears spectacles (see Fig. 1). They are:

- Occlusion: Occlusion is the phenomena in which eye features are obstructed by the spectacle frame. Depending upon the comfort, nature, and size of spectacle frame used - most or partial amount of eye feature information may be lost [26, 34, 38, 39, 41, 42].
- Illumination changes: Glare and secondary reflections occur due to the variation in illumination projected on to the human subjects. These variations result in an apparent change on the reflectance properties of the spectacles - leading to a visual variation of the eye features [26, 27, 36, 39, 40, 42].

(a)   (b)   (c)   (d)

Fig. 1. Sample images from CASIA NIR-VIS 2.0 database [43] illustrating the Spectacle problem. (a), (b) Glare; (c) Occlusion; (d) Secondary reflection

All the spectacle problem elements individually or cumulatively can vary or obstruct the appearance of the eye features. These factors pose great challenges to the existing eye corner detection strategies. However, little research has been done addressing these issues [24]. One of the major reason being that most of the available databases have been collected under well controlled laboratory conditions with normal lighting, neutral expression and high image quality [1]. Such conditions generally do not represent the real-time challenges like the spectacle problems.

3   Datasets

Table 1 provides a brief overview of the most used databases in the research field of eye feature detection. This review helps the researchers to choose an appropriate database for their specific research.

3.1   Summary of Database Review

– **Illumination:** [52] provides thermal facial imagery, whereas [43] provides facial images captured in NIR illumination. NIR and thermal imaging conditions do not mimic real-time visible conditions. [44,46–48,54] databases are created in visible illumination conditions, but the variation levels are limited. Among the remaining databases, [56,57] images are captured at low, medium and high illumination conditions of an office environment.
– **Accessories (here spectacles):** Structural differences in glasses can change the appearance of an individual. Spectacles used in [42] have almost identical shapes, sizes and colors. Therefore, the variation that the accessories bring is not prominent. [57] database have considered the usage of various spectacle frames: Full-rim, Half-rim, and Rim-less - resulting in a larger accessory variation.
– **Ground-truth:** Most of the available databases focus on face detection and recognition. So, the ground-truth information of the eye feature information is hardly found [7]. Also in case of spectacle problem removal algorithms, we need to have pairs of corresponding face images with and without eyeglasses for verifying the seamlessness of the spectacle removal algorithm outputs.

Table 1. Real-life scenario databases and their variabilities considered.

Name of the database	Variation in				
	Illumination	Pose	Expression	Accessories	Session
MIT database [44]					
ORL database [45]	✓	✓	✓	✓	
AR face database [46]					
CurtinFaces dataset [47]					
FEI face database [48]					
COFW [38]		✓	✓	✓	
300 faces in-the-wild [49]					
XM2VTSDB [50]				✓	✓
KFDB [51]	✓	✓	✓	✓	
LWIR imagery [52]	✓		✓	✓	
CASIA NIR-VIS 2.0 database [43]					✓
YALE database [53]	✓		✓	✓	
CASIAWebFace [54]				✓	
LFW [55]	✓	✓	✓	✓	
CAS-PEAL [42]	✓	✓	✓	✓	
FERET database [56]	✓	✓		✓	✓
Indian database [57]	✓	✓	✓	✓	✓

Such ground-truth images along with spectacle problem free image and eye corner location details is provided in [30, 34, 57].

- **Database size:** Using private large-scale training datasets, several sample-based algorithms achieve huge success in terms of adaptability and performance. While there are many open source implementations of the algorithms, none of the large-scale face dataset with spectacles is publicly available. [56] considered many variation factors but the quantity of images is very less when compared to [57].

4 Spectacle Problem Removal: Previous Approaches

Due to the unpredictability caused by occlusion, glare and secondary reflection formations, the spectacle removal problem is quite challenging than the detection application [1]. Depending upon the number of input images used to rectify the spectacle problem, the methods can be classified as: Single image based and Multiple image based approaches.

5 Single Image Approach

One of the most commonly used single image based approach is the image in-painting based approach [58, 59]. Image inpainting techniques are more suitable for texture synthesis applications only and tend to fail in generating a seamless output image in case of facial images [36]. [60] proposed an anti-glare algorithm, in which they assumed that the reflection occurs proportionately on both the eyes. In real-time scenarios, this reflection assumption does not hold good and therefore limits the usability of the algorithm to synthetic images only. In [61] approach, a user has to physically mark the regions in which there are traces of reflection. This approach is more efficient in terms of output results but, the effort and precision of the user will influence the algorithm. [26] proposed a phase congruency based approach, but the algorithm's efficiency degrades when the user wear a full-rim spectacle-frame (see Fig. 2).

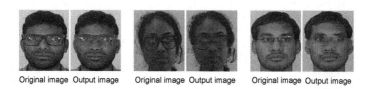

Original image Output image   Original image Output image   Original image Output image

Fig. 2. Sample output images of single image based approach [26].

5.1   Multiple Image Approaches

[27,30] are sample-based approaches that learn from the statistical mapping between face images with and without spectacles to generate a seamless facial image without spectacle problem. The problem with these approaches is that the representational power of these algorithms depends on the training set. [59] adopts a new hybrid approach by combining inpainting and deep learning technique for spectacle problem removal. A more generalized de-occlusion algorithm is reported in [62]. [39] is based on the assumption that facial images subjected to various illumination conditions tend to lie on a low-dimensional Lambertian space. Therefore, a given sequence of multiple images is decomposed into the Low rank and Sparse component. The low-rank layer retains most of the uncorrupted facial features while the sparse layer retains the pixels related to the spectacle problem. Even though the multiple image based approaches perform much better than the single image based approaches, one might experience the following limitations.

Limitations

- Performance of multiple based approaches depend on the facial image alignment. This is a unrealistic assumption as in real-time scenarios, the subject might continuously change his/her head position. Large head movements can cause some time-aliasing artifacts to appear in the output image.
- Because of the usage of a large number of input images: resource, computational, and time complexity of these multiple image based methods is quite large.

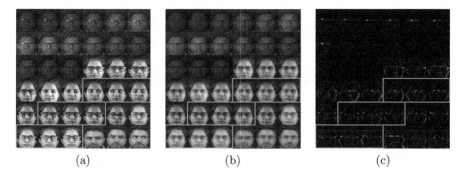

(a)   (b)   (c)

Fig. 3. Result of [39]. Each sub-plot contains (a) original, (b) reconstructed and (c) error component images respectively. The ineffectiveness of recovering the eye feature dynamics is highlighted in yellow. (Color figure online)

- The output images fail to extract the eye image dynamics (see Fig. 3). This would be a serious problem in case of eye tracking applications.

6 Experimentation

In this section, we conduct a landmark localization experiments to highlight the impact of spectacle problem. We have considered CNN based algorithm presented in [23], for determining the influence of illumination level and spectacles on the detection accuracy of facial landmark localization. We have created a ground-truth of manually generated facial landmarks for a subset of 1,600 images from [57] database. For a test-bench containing facial images without spectacles, the images subjected to high illumination level have least average localization error values as compared to the poorly illuminated images (Fig. 4(a)). This showcases the influence of illumination on landmark localization. Similar experiment

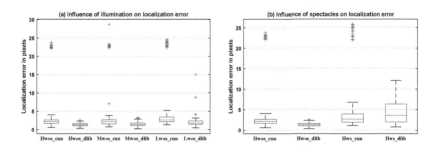

Fig. 4. Error distribution highlighting the influence of (a) illumination and (b) spectacles on the localization of face features. Where H: High, M: Medium, L: Low illumination level; wos: Without spectacles, ws: with spectacles; dlib and cnn methods as proposed in [23].

Fig. 5. Sample images highlighting the influence of spectacles on eye localization.

on a test-bench of images subjected to the same illumination levels reveals that the localization error rate increases for images with spectacle problem (Fig. 4(b)).

Due to the error in landmark localization, application related to human-computer-interaction systems also suffer. In Fig. 5 we present the influence of inaccurate eye feature localization on eye-blink detection as an example.

7   Conclusion

Accurate eye feature detection, localization and tracking is a preliminary but important step in the spectrum of disciplines like human-computer-interaction, biometrics, alertness-level detection applications. In this article, we attempt to present a comprehensive survey on the state-of-the-art eye corner detection techniques. The review focuses on real-life scenarios wherein the subject wear spectacles and the research challenges that comes along with it. Recent developments in the topic related to spectacle problem removal approaches is also presented and discussed. Due to the inherent complexity of the spectacle problem and its wide practical applications in science, society, research and industry, we believe that this area will draw increasing attention from a variety of fields beyond image processing and machine learning.

References

1. Song, F., Tan, X., Chen, S., Zhou, Z.H.: A literature survey on robust and efficient eye localization in real-life scenarios. Pattern Recogn. **46**(12), 3157–3173 (2013)
2. Bengoechea, J.J., Cerrolaza, J.J., Villanueva, A., Cabeza, R.: Evaluation of accurate eye corner detection methods for gaze estimation. J. Eye Mov. Res. **7**(3) (2014). https://bop.unibe.ch/JEMR/article/view/2381
3. Xu, C., Zheng, Y., Wang, Z.: Semantic feature extraction for accurate eye corner detection. In: 2008 19th International Conference on Pattern Recognition, pp. 1–4, December 2008. https://doi.org/10.1109/ICPR.2008.4761409
4. Erdogmus, N., Dugelay, J.L.: An efficient iris and eye corners extraction method. In: Hancock, E.R., Wilson, R.C., Windeatt, T., Ulusoy, I., Escolano, F. (eds.) SSPR/SPR 2010. LNCS, vol. 6218, pp. 549–558. Springer, Heidelberg (2010). https://doi.org/10.1007/978-3-642-14980-1_54
5. Cheung, Y., Peng, Q.: Eye gaze tracking with a web camera in a desktop environment. IEEE Trans. Hum.-Mach. Syst. **45**(4), 419–430 (2015). https://doi.org/10.1109/THMS.2015.2400442

6. Yang, Y., Lu, Y.: A new method of the accurate eye corner location. In: Yao, J., et al. (eds.) RSCTC 2012. LNCS (LNAI), vol. 7413, pp. 116–125. Springer, Heidelberg (2012). https://doi.org/10.1007/978-3-642-32115-3_13
7. Sirohey, S.A., Rosenfeld, A.: Eye detection in a face image using linear and nonlinear filters. Pattern Recogn. **34**(7), 1367–1391 (2001). https://doi.org/10.1016/S0031-3203(00)00082-0. http://www.sciencedirect.com/science/article/pii/S0031320300000820
8. Lam, K.M., Yan, H.: Locating and extracting the eye in human face images. Pattern Recogn. **29**(5), 771–779 (1996). https://doi.org/10.1016/0031-3203(95)00119-0. http://www.sciencedirect.com/science/article/pii/0031320395001190
9. Villanueva, A., Ponz, V., Sesma-Sanchez, L., Ariz, M., Porta, S., Cabeza, R.: Hybrid method based on topography for robust detection of iris center and eye corners. ACM Trans. Multimed. Comput. Commun. Appl. **9**(4), 25:1–25:20 (2013). https://doi.org/10.1145/2501643.2501647
10. Santos, G., Proença, H.: A robust eye-corner detection method for real-world data. In: 2011 International Joint Conference on Biometrics (IJCB), pp. 1–7, October 2011. https://doi.org/10.1109/IJCB.2011.6117596
11. Herpers, R., Michaelis, M., Lichtenauer, K., Sommer, G.: Edge and keypoint detection in facial regions. In: Proceedings of the Second International Conference on Automatic Face and Gesture Recognition, pp. 212–217 (1996, Quarterly). https://doi.org/10.1109/AFGR.1996.557266
12. Alkassar, S., Woo, W., Dlay, S., Chambers, J.: Efficient eye corner and gaze detection for sclera recognition under relaxed imaging constraints. In: 2016 24th European Signal Processing Conference (EUSIPCO), pp. 1965–1969. IEEE (2016)
13. Xu, G., Wang, Y., Li, J., Zhou, X.: Real time detection of eye corners and iris center from images acquired by usual camera. In: 2009 Second International Conference on Intelligent Networks and Intelligent Systems, pp. 401–404, November 2009. https://doi.org/10.1109/ICINIS.2009.109
14. Jesorsky, O., Kirchberg, K.J., Frischholz, R.W.: Robust face detection using the hausdorff distance. In: Bigun, J., Smeraldi, F. (eds.) AVBPA 2001. LNCS, vol. 2091, pp. 90–95. Springer, Heidelberg (2001). https://doi.org/10.1007/3-540-45344-X_14
15. Moriyama, T., Kanade, T., Xiao, J., Cohn, J.F.: Meticulously detailed eye region model and its application to analysis of facial images. IEEE Trans. Pattern Anal. Mach. Intell. **28**(5), 738–752 (2006). https://doi.org/10.1109/TPAMI.2006.98
16. Zhang, L.: Estimation of eye and mouth corner point positions in a knowledge-based coding system (1996). https://doi.org/10.1117/12.251289
17. Pang, Z., Wei, C., Teng, D., Chen, D., Tan, H.: Robust eye center localization through face alignment and invariant isocentric patterns. PloS One **10**(10), e0139098 (2015)
18. Xia, H., Yan, G.: A novel method for eye corner detection based on weighted variance projection function. In: 2009 2nd International Congress on Image and Signal Processing, pp. 1–4, October 2009. https://doi.org/10.1109/CISP.2009.5304434
19. Zhou, R., He, Q., Wu, J., Hu, C., Meng, Q.H.: Inner and outer eye corners detection for facial features extraction based on CTGF algorithm. In: Information Technology for Manufacturing Systems II. Applied Mechanics and Materials, vol. 58, pp. 1966–1971. Trans Tech Publications, July 2011. https://doi.org/10.4028/www.scientific.net/AMM.58-60.1966
20. Valenti, R., Gevers, T.: Accurate eye center location through invariant isocentric patterns. IEEE Trans. Pattern Anal. Mach. Intell. **34**(9), 1785–1798 (2012). https://doi.org/10.1109/TPAMI.2011.251

21. Dibeklioglu, H., Salah, A.A., Gevers, T.: A statistical method for 2-D facial land-marking. IEEE Trans. Image Process. **21**(2), 844–858 (2012). https://doi.org/10.1109/TIP.2011.2163162

22. Zhang, Z., Shen, Y., Lin, W., Zhou, B.: Eye corner detection with texture image fusion. In: 2015 Asia-Pacific Signal and Information Processing Association Annual Summit and Conference (APSIPA), pp. 992–995, December 2015. https://doi.org/10.1109/APSIPA.2015.7415420

23. Kazemi, V., Sullivan, J.: One millisecond face alignment with an ensemble of regression trees. In: 2014 IEEE Conference on Computer Vision and Pattern Recognition, pp. 1867–1874, June 2014. https://doi.org/10.1109/CVPR.2014.241

24. Fernández, A., García, R., Usamentiaga, R., Casado, R.: Glasses detection on real images based on robust alignment. Mach. Vis. Appl. **26**(4), 519–531 (2015). https://doi.org/10.1007/s00138-015-0674-1

25. Jing, Z., Mariani, R., Wang, J.: Glasses detection for face recognition using bayes rules. In: Tan, T., Shi, Y., Gao, W. (eds.) ICMI 2000. LNCS, vol. 1948, pp. 127–134. Springer, Heidelberg (2000). https://doi.org/10.1007/3-540-40063-X_17

26. Jia, X., Guo, J.: Eyeglasses removal from facial image based on phase congruency. In: 2010 3rd International Congress on Image and Signal Processing, vol. 4, pp. 1859–1862, October 2010. https://doi.org/10.1109/CISP.2010.5647366

27. Park, J.S., Oh, Y.H., Ahn, S.C., Lee, S.W.: Glasses removal from facial image using recursive error compensation. IEEE Trans. Pattern Anal. Mach. Intell. **27**(5), 805–811 (2005). https://doi.org/10.1109/TPAMI.2005.103

28. Tian, Y., Kanade, T., Cohn, J.F.: Dual-state parametric eye tracking. In: Proceedings Fourth IEEE International Conference on Automatic Face and Gesture Recognition (Cat. No. PR00580), pp. 110–115, March 2000. https://doi.org/10.1109/AFGR.2000.840620

29. Zhu, Z., Ji, Q.: Robust real-time eye detection and tracking under variable lighting conditions and various face orientations. Comput. Vis. Image Underst. **98**(1), 124–154 (2005). https://doi.org/10.1016/j.cviu.2004.07.012. http://www.sciencedirect.com/science/article/pii/S1077314204001158, Special Issue on Eye Detection and Tracking

30. Wu, C., Liu, C., Shum, H.Y., Xy, Y.Q., Zhang, Z.: Automatic eyeglasses removal from face images. IEEE Trans. Pattern Anal. Mach. Intell. **26**(3), 322–336 (2004). https://doi.org/10.1109/TPAMI.2004.1262319

31. Du, C., Su, G.: Eyeglasses removal from facial images. Pattern Recogn. Lett. **26**(14), 2215–2220 (2005). https://doi.org/10.1016/j.patrec.2005.04.002. http://www.sciencedirect.com/science/article/pii/S0167865505001133

32. Li, S.Z., Chu, R., Liao, S., Zhang, L.: Illumination invariant face recognition using near-infrared images. IEEE Trans. Pattern Anal. Mach. Intell. **29**(4), 627–639 (2007). https://doi.org/10.1109/TPAMI.2007.1014

33. Xiao, Y., Yan, H.: Extraction of glasses in human face images. In: Zhang, D., Jain, A.K. (eds.) ICBA 2004. LNCS, vol. 3072, pp. 214–220. Springer, Heidelberg (2004). https://doi.org/10.1007/978-3-540-25948-0_30

34. Liu, D., Shen, L., Yin, Y., Li, X.: How to recognize facial images with spectacles. In: 2006 6th World Congress on Intelligent Control and Automation, vol. 2, pp. 10153–10156 (2006). https://doi.org/10.1109/WCICA.2006.1713987

35. Wang, Y., Jang, J., Tsai, L., Fan, K.: Improvement of face recognition by eyeglass removal. In: 2010 Sixth International Conference on Intelligent Information Hiding and Multimedia Signal Processing, pp. 228–231, October 2010. https://doi.org/10.1109/IIHMSP.2010.64

36. Yi, D., Li, S.Z.: Learning sparse feature for eyeglasses problem in face recognition. In: Face and Gesture 2011, pp. 430–435 (2011)
37. Liu, L., Sun, Y., Yin, B., Song, C.: Local gabor binary pattern random subspace method for eyeglasses-face recognition. In: 2010 3rd International Congress on Image and Signal Processing, vol. 4, pp. 1892–1896, October 2010. https://doi.org/10.1109/CISP.2010.5647554
38. Burgos-Artizzu, X.P., Perona, P., Dollár, P.: Robust face landmark estimation under occlusion. In: 2013 IEEE International Conference on Computer Vision, pp. 1513–1520, December 2013. https://doi.org/10.1109/ICCV.2013.191
39. Lazarus, M.Z., Gupta, S.: A low rank model based improved eye detection under spectacles. In: 2016 IEEE 7th Annual Ubiquitous Computing, Electronics Mobile Communication Conference (UEMCON), pp. 1–6, October 2016. https://doi.org/10.1109/UEMCON.2016.7777820
40. Mayaluri, Z.L., Gupta, S.: Spectacle problem removal from facial images based on detail preserving filtering schemes. J. Intell. Fuzzy Syst. (Preprint) 36, 1–11 (2019)
41. Burgos-Artizzu, X.P., Zepeda, J., Clerc, F.L., Pérez, P.: Pose and expression-coherent face recovery in the wild. In: 2015 IEEE International Conference on Computer Vision Workshop (ICCVW), pp. 877–885, December 2015. https://doi.org/10.1109/ICCVW.2015.117
42. Gao, W., et al.: The cas-peal large-scale chinese face database and baseline evaluations. IEEE Trans. Syst. Man Cybern. - Part A: Syst. Hum. 38(1), 149–161 (2008). https://doi.org/10.1109/TSMCA.2007.909557
43. Li, S.Z., Yi, D., Lei, Z., Liao, S.: The CASIA NIR-VIS 2.0 face database. In: 2013 IEEE Conference on Computer Vision and Pattern Recognition Workshops, pp. 348–353, June 2013. https://doi.org/10.1109/CVPRW.2013.59
44. Moghaddam, B., Pentland, A.P.: Face recognition using view-based and modular eigenspaces (1994). https://doi.org/10.1117/12.191877
45. Samaria, F.S., Harter, A.C.: Parameterisation of a stochastic model for human face identification. In: Proceedings of 1994 IEEE Workshop on Applications of Computer Vision, pp. 138–142, December 1994. https://doi.org/10.1109/ACV.1994.341300
46. Martinez, A.M.: The AR face database. CVC Technical Report24 (1998)
47. Li, B.Y.L., Mian, A.S., Liu, W., Krishna, A.: Using kinect for face recognition under varying poses, expressions, illumination and disguise. In: 2013 IEEE Workshop on Applications of Computer Vision (WACV), pp. 186–192, January 2013. https://doi.org/10.1109/WACV.2013.6475017
48. Thomaz, C.E.: Fei face database (2012). http://fei.edu.br/~cet/facedatabase.html. Accessed 13 Mar 2018
49. Sagonas, C., Antonakos, E., Tzimiropoulos, G., Zafeiriou, S., Pantic, M.: 300 faces in-the-wild challenge: database and results. Image Vis. Comput. 47, 3–18 (2016). https://doi.org/10.1016/j.imavis.2016.01.002. http://www.sciencedirect.com/science/article/pii/S0262885616000147, 300-W, the First Automatic Facial Landmark Detection in-the-Wild Challenge
50. Messer, K., Matas, J., Kittler, J., Jonsson, K.: XM2VTSDB: the extended M2VTS database. In: Second International Conference on Audio and Video-Based Biometric Person Authentication, pp. 72–77 (1999)
51. Hwang, B.W., Roh, M.C., Lee, S.W.: Performance evaluation of face recognition algorithms on Asian face database. In: Proceedings of the Sixth IEEE International Conference on Automatic Face and Gesture Recognition, pp. 278–283, May 2004. https://doi.org/10.1109/AFGR.2004.1301544

52. Selinger, A., Socolinsky, D.A.: Appearance-based facial recognition using visible and thermal imagery: a comparative study. Technical report (2001)
53. Belhumeur, P.N., Hespanha, J.P., Kriegman, D.J.: Eigenfaces vs. fisherfaces: recognition using class specific linear projection. IEEE Trans. Pattern Ana. Mach. Intell. **19**(7), 711–720 (1997). https://doi.org/10.1109/34.598228
54. Yi, D., Lei, Z., Liao, S., Li, S.Z.: Learning face representation from scratch. CoRR abs/1411.7923 (2014). http://arxiv.org/abs/1411.7923
55. Huang, G.B., Ramesh, M., Berg, T., Learned-Miller, E.: Labeled faces in the wild: a database for studying face recognition in unconstrained environments. Technical report 07–49, University of Massachusetts, Amherst, October 2007
56. Phillips, P., Wechsler, H., Huang, J., Rauss, P.J.: The feret database and evaluation procedure for face-recognition algorithms. Image Vis. Comput. **16**(5), 295–306 (1998). https://doi.org/10.1016/S0262-8856(97)00070-X
57. Lazarus, M.Z., Gupta, S., Panda, N.: An Indian facial database highlighting the spectacle problems. In: IEEE International Conference on Innovative Technologies in Engineering 2018 (ICITE OU), April 2018. http://hdl.handle.net/2080/2992
58. Tan, P., Quan, L., Lin, S.: Separation of highlight reflections on textured surfaces. In: 2006 IEEE Computer Society Conference on Computer Vision and Pattern Recognition (CVPR 2006), vol. 2, pp. 1855–1860 (2006). https://doi.org/10.1109/CVPR.2006.273
59. Liang, A., Pathirage, C.S.N., Wang, C., Liu, W., Li, L., Duan, J.: Face recognition despite wearing glasses. In: 2015 International Conference on Digital Image Computing: Techniques and Applications (DICTA), pp. 1–8, November 2015. https://doi.org/10.1109/DICTA.2015.7371260
60. Sandhan, T., Choi, J.Y.: Anti-glare: tightly constrained optimization for eyeglass reflection removal. In: 2017 IEEE Conference on Computer Vision and Pattern Recognition (CVPR), pp. 1675–1684, July 2017. https://doi.org/10.1109/CVPR.2017.182
61. Levin, A., Weiss, Y.: User assisted separation of reflections from a single image using a sparsity prior. IEEE Trans. Pattern Anal. Mach. Intell. **29**(9), 1647–1654 (2007). https://doi.org/10.1109/TPAMI.2007.1106
62. Zhao, F., Feng, J., Zhao, J., Yang, W., Yan, S.: Robust lstm-autoencoders for face de-occlusion in the wild. IEEE Trans. Image Process. **27**(2), 778–790 (2018). https://doi.org/10.1109/TIP.2017.2771408

Prediction Studies of Landslides in the Mangan and Singtam Areas Triggered by 2011 Sikkim Earthquake

Aadityan Sridharan[1(✉)] and Sundararaman Gopalan[2]

[1] Department of Physics, Amrita Vishwa Vidyapeetham,
Amritapuri, India
aadityans@am.amrita.edu
[2] Department of Electronics and Communication Engineering,
Amrita Vishwa Vidyapeetham, Amritapuri, India
sundar@am.amrita.edu

Abstract. Prediction of field displacements of Earthquake induced slope failure is a common methodology used to estimate the possibility of failure in a ground shaking scenario of interest. Newmark's algorithm has been used extensively over years to arrive at estimates of ground displacements during earthquakes. This method has been proven to be a reliable technique to predict the spatial distribution of earthquake induced landslides. The current study involves selecting 12 horizontal components of strong motion records from 6 recording stations during the main shock of the Sikkim earthquake of magnitude Mw 6.9 that occurred on September 18th 2011. This data is then used in predicting the spatial distribution of the landslides triggered in and around the Mangan and Singtam areas in the district of North and East Sikkim. Displacement values were calculated by rigorous numerical integration of the acceleration records. These values were then regressed in a multiple linear regression model and the resultant equation was found to be statistically significant with an R^2 value of 85.7%. These predicted displacement values were compared with the field data of triggered landslides and was found to predict the slope failures with fair amount of accuracy given the nature of the triggered landslides and the climatic conditions during the earthquake event.

Keywords: 2011 Sikkim earthquake · Landslides ·
Earthquake induced landslides · Arias intensity · Newmark's displacement ·
Mangan · Singtam

1 Introduction

Earthquakes are one of the most damaging events among the natural disasters causing structural hazards, tsunamis and landslides. Earthquake induced landslides are very common in steep topography and there have been incidents of such slope failures burying an entire village [1]. Sikkim is a region high seismic hazard and has been categorized by Indian Meteorological Department [2] as seismic zone 4. While the state has experienced many quakes in the past, the 18th September 2011 earthquake that

© Springer Nature Singapore Pte Ltd. 2019
M. Singh et al. (Eds.): ICACDS 2019, CCIS 1046, pp. 609–617, 2019.
https://doi.org/10.1007/978-981-13-9942-8_57

occurred in the Sikkim Nepal border remains to be one of the most catastrophic among them. Around 334 individual landslides were reported to have been triggered during the earthquake. These landslides were along major roads in Sikkim and hence were responsible for major transportation blocks, and hampered effective disaster relief work in the area after the earthquake [3]. By developing a method to map such areas that are prone to earthquake induced landslides, loss of life and property can be reduced.

Predictive modeling is extensively used in the domain of earth science for various scenarios. Prediction of displacements due to an earthquake event has been used successfully carried out by statistical methods in various cases of such events. These models have been able to predict the spatial variability of earthquake induced landslides with appreciable amount of accuracy [4]. Displacements in the slope is dependent directly and indirectly on various factors like the geotechnical properties of the geological units, topography of the slope, precipitation etc. Newmark's algorithm proposes one such method to predict field displacements by modeling the landslide as a rigid block on an inclined plane [5].

When there is a ground shaking scenario during an earthquake, the horizontal components namely: North-South and East-West, of the earthquake accelerations cause slope failures [6]. While it has been observed that common slope failures are shallow rock slides, overburden debris slides have also been reported under such conditions [7]. Various forms of multiple linear regression models have been proposed in the literature to predict such displacements. Each model employs different combinations of independent variables such as critical acceleration, Arias intensity, moment magnitude, etc. to predict the landslide displacements [4].

Variation of the Newmark's displacements with respect to the arias intensity and critical acceleration is a model proposed by Jibson et al in 1993. The model was constructed by selecting 11 strong motion records with a range of Arias intensity values that signify small and large shaking intensities [8]. In estimating co-seismic landslide displacements Newmark's method has been found to be effective in estimating the dynamic stability of slopes in co-seismic condition [9]. Further research in this direction has been continued by Jibson et al. 2000 by extending the same model for 555 individual earthquake records to model displacements during the 1994 Northridge earthquake [6]. Such rigorous Newmark's analysis is simpler and is fairly accurate in predicting the slope failure in most ground shaking conditions. While other methods involving pseudo-static analysis present a reasonable estimate in predicting the displacements, the models assumes a static earthquake acceleration which is not applicable to dynamic analysis [10]. Finite element modeling (FEM) methods give accurate estimate of slope stability but the amount of data required to process the same would restrict study area to at most one or two hills [11]. This reduces the scope of predicting spatial distribution of landslides in an earthquake condition.

In this paper, a similar analysis based on Newmark's method has been done for predicting the field displacements in and around the Mangan and Singtam areas of north Sikkim during the Sikkim 2011 earthquake. A predictive algorithm that models the Newmark's displacement in terms of critical accelerations and Arias intensity has been developed for this earthquake. Further, field data [12] has been used to verify the predicted displacements and the spatial extent of triggered landslides.

2 Methodology

2.1 Study Area

Mangan is a town in the northern district of Sikkim, the area is connected to the lower areas of the state via the NH-310A. Singtam is a town in the eastern district of Sikkim and is surrounded by NH-710. These national highways are cut in steep slopes and are prone to frequent landslide incidents thus reducing the accessibility of such important towns [13]. The following shows the location of Mangan and Singtam in the state of Sikkim with National borders (Fig. 1):

Fig. 1. The figure shows the state of Sikkim with Mangan and Singtam (Photo credits: http://www.theroyaldemazong.com/sikkim.html)

2.2 Selection of Strong Motion Records

Twelve strong motion records of the main shock were obtained from the Ministry of earth science website [14]. All the six recording stations in Sikkim were considered for the regional analysis and horizontal components of the strong motion records were used in the predictive model. Shaking intensity was also calculated to identify appropriate records, mostly the acceleration time histories that had good Arias intensity values and significant displacement values were used for the predictive modeling. The stations in consideration here are Mangan and Singtam in the North and East Sikkim respectively.

2.3 Newmark's Sliding Block Analysis

Displacements of co-seismic landslides can be predicted by Newmark's sliding block analysis which models the landslide as a sliding block on an inclined plane [4]. When the accelerations due to an earthquake exceed a certain critical acceleration value there will be a slope failure. Newmark defines the formula for the critical acceleration as:

$$a_c = (FS - 1) g \sin\alpha \tag{1}$$

Where a_c is the critical acceleration, FS is the static factor of safety, g is acceleration due to gravity and α is the angle of slope. Co-seismic landslide displacements are calculated by a rigorous double integration of the acceleration values that are above the critical acceleration. The resultant displacement values depict the displacements of the landslide mass. Typically for a landslide the static factor of safety is determined and then the formula given by Eq. (1) is applied to arrive at the critical acceleration values. However, in order to get reasonable displacement values for regional analysis, a range of critical acceleration values from 0.02 g to 0.2 g were selected. For each value of critical acceleration in this range Newmark's displacements are computed in all selected strong motion records.

2.4 Arias Intensity

Intensity is usually determined by the amount ground shaking caused by an earthquake event. Arias intensity was initially proposed to measure the effect of strong ground motion on nuclear reactors. Subsequently this has been used as a reliable measure to predict the spatial distribution of seismically triggered landslides [15].

$$I_a = \pi/(2g) \int a^2 \, dt \tag{2}$$

In the above equation I_a is the Arias intensity, a^2 is the square of acceleration values in the record. The integral has been calculated over the entire duration of the strong motion records which in our case is within the range of 18 s to 64 s. Every record of the earthquake has an individual measure of Arias intensity. Values from both the components were averaged and used for estimation of displacement from the predictive model.

2.5 Formulating the Predictive Model

The values of displacements, arias intensity and the critical accelerations were regressed using multiple linear regression and the coefficients were measured. Due to the random fluctuations found in the values, $\log_{10}$ of the values were regressed [6]. The fit for the model was found to be:

$$\text{Log } D_N = 1.22 \text{ Log } I_a - 2.4483 \text{ Log } a_c - 1.6905 \tag{3}$$

The regression fit is found to have a R^2 value of 85.7% which shows that this is a fairly accurate fit for the data. This model is used to arrive at the predicted displacement in and around the Mangan and the Singtam areas. Here only those acceleration values within the range that give realistic displacements were chosen for substitution in the predictive model. This now helps us to predict the Newmark's displacement using the average Arias intensity values. Based on the predicted values we can estimate the possibility of failure given an earthquake condition.

3   Results and Discussion

Tables 1 and 2 present the predicted displacements for slides around the area of Mangan and Singtam from the predictive model developed in this study

Table 1. The values of predicted displacements given by the model in centimeters for the Mangan area.

Critical acceleration (g)	Arias intensity (m/s)	Predicted displacement (cm)
0.02	0.055	8.55
0.025	0.055	4.955
0.0275	0.055	3.923
0.03	0.055	3.171
0.035	0.055	2.17

Table 2. The values of predicted displacements given by the model in centimeters for the Singtam area.

Critical acceleration (g)	Arias intensity (m/s)	Predicted displacement (cm)
0.02	0.116	21.26
0.025	0.116	12.315
0.0275	0.116	9.752
0.03	0.116	7.88
0.035	0.116	5.4

As it is evident from the table various displacement values are predicted for the range of critical acceleration values in the two areas of Mangan and Singtam. These values were correlated with landslide failures from field data collected shortly after the event shortly after the earthquake. It was found that most of the triggered slides in the Mangan area were shallow rock falls and a few shallow debris slides. But in the Singtam area there were a lot of shallow over burden slides along with rock slides. The average displacement value in the two areas have been calculated as 4.1 cm in Mangan and 10 cm in Singtam (Fig. 2).

According to the field data by the post-earthquake survey conducted by Geological Survey of India [12] around 13 landslides were reported in and around the area of Mangan. 8 of the reported slides are either rock slides or rock fall and 5 slides have

(A)

(B)

Fig. 2. The figures show the field images of a landslide (A) Mangan area and (B) Singtam area. (Reproduced with the permission of Dr Saibal Gosh [12])

been reported to be Debris slides which involve failure of the overburden material. From the Table 1 we can see that predicted displacements are significant, this could correspond to small rock falls identified along the main roads in the area. Similarly in Singtam around 65 slides were reported out of which 36 were characterized as debris slides. Another 19 slides were reported to be rock slides or rock falls while the rest were uncategorized. As it is clearly evident that the predicted displacement in Singtam is more than in Mangan this could signify the reason behind more number of triggered landslides in Singtam than in Mangan which is consistent with literature [6]. Figure 3

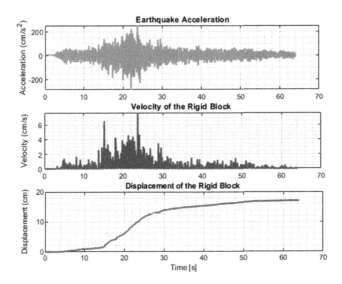

Fig. 3. The plots of earthquake acceleration, velocity and displacement of rigid block for the Newmark's analysis

shows the typical variation of displacement values according to the Newmark's algorithm. Simultaneous values of velocity and acceleration have also been plotted.

The reason for the change in the spatial variation of the landslides could also be due to the fact that these landslides were induced by the earthquake and the failure could have happened at a later time. Hence by just a predictive model made from the main shock we could draw a general conclusion on the supposed slope failures in the field. The current model addresses the relation between Arias intensity and critical acceleration to the Newmark's displacement values. While the entire focus has been on the Newmark's displacement, it is interesting to note the significant relationship among the Arias intensity values and the displacements as well from the Tables 1 and 2. It can be seen that the Arias intensity values of the Singtam area is on an average twice that of Mangan area. Correspondingly the displacement values are proportionately higher for the Singtam area. The seismic ground shaking is usually measured by Intensity values such as this, while the intensity scales are usually qualitative Arias intensity is a quantitative measure that considers the acceleration time history to in the calculation as shown in Eq. (2). Here we can see that it significantly quantifies the slope failures and correlated with Newmark's predicted displacement.

As for a detailed model this data could be combined with larger data to enhance the spatial accuracy of predicted landslides. In doing so researchers can add to the accuracy by detailed field data specific to this case and improve the predictability and accuracy of such models. Field survey of possible areas that could be affected by such events have to be investigated on a regular basis so that there is pre-disaster data which is very close to the date of such disasters. Such models could predict a larger area affected by earthquake induced slope failures and could bring out the relations among other factors that contribute to such slope failures [16]. Post surveys should be more close to the date so that the immediate site conditions can be assessed and accurate estimates of input variables such as volume of slide, saturation, pore pressure etc can be noted. Inaccessible areas must be mapped by more recent remote sensing techniques thus giving an overall picture of the disaster aftereffect. To avoid blockage of roads due to such disasters careful planning and detailed engineering evaluation of the slopes are essential. In states such as Sikkim the roads are sometimes constructed in a way that the slope faces are vulnerable to toppling failure. This can be ensured by road cuts that expose the face angle to be less than 60°. In conditions where this is not possible Geo-materials can be used to ensure further stability, in rock slopes bolting and shotcreting techniques can be deployed to ensure that failure does not pose threat to transportation.

As the data shows that in just two regions of study there are more than 70 landslides, FEM based techniques may not be suitable for modelling all slopes. At the same time dynamic earthquake accelerations have to be considered for coseismic landslide displacements. Hence psudo-static methods might not be efficient for this kind of an anlayisis. Hazard maps generated from the results of such predictive models could be used in disaster risk reduction and could contribute in reducing the loss of human lives [17].

4   Summary and Conclusion

In this paper we have discussed a predictive algorithm based on Newmark's analysis and have correlated the field data with the predicted displacements to estimate the spatial distribution of a few landslides triggered due to Sikkim 2011 earthquake. It was observed that the computed values of displacement correlates with the field data fairly accurately. The 2011 Sikkim earthquake was one of the severe earthquakes experienced by our country and the amount of lives lost shows that we need to equip ourselves with advanced technologies and predictive systems more efficient to reduce the same in a similar situation in the future.

Predictive models such as the one proposed in this work can be further modified by accurate field measurements thereby increasing the value of such models in assessing hazards caused by earthquake induced landslides. Further research could involve scaling the model for larger regions and include independent variables that could add to better prediction of such hazards. Including land use and land cover in the future models can make the predictions more specific to areas that are densely populated and hence more socially significant.

Acknowledgements. The authors would like to show immense gratitude to the chancellor of Amrita University, Mata Amritanandamayi Devi for her constant guidance and for being the inspiration behind this work. We would also like to thank Dr. Saibal Gosh Director (Geology) Engineering Project Evaluation (EPE) Division, DGCO, Geological survey of India (GSI) for his valuable contributions to this work. Mr. Kannan (Former NHPC Engineer) for his constant support in pursuing this study. We would also like to extend our gratitude to Dr. H. M. Iyer (Former Scientist USGS) for the guidance and direction that he has been sharing with us.

References

1. Li, X., He, S.: Seismically induced slope instabilities and the corresponding treatments: the case of a road in the Wenchuan earthquake hit region. J. Mt. Sci. **6**(1), 96–100 (2009)
2. Government of India, Indian Meteorological Department (IMD). www.imd.gov.in
3. Chakraborty, I., Ghosh, S., Bhattacharya, D., Bora, A.: Earthquake induced landslides in the Sikkim-Darjeeling Himalayas–An aftermath of the 18th September 2011 Sikkim earthquake. no. Sept, pp. 1–8 (2011)
4. Dreyfus, D., Rathje, E.M., Jibson, R.W.: The influence of different simplified sliding-block models and input parameters on regional predictions of seismic landslides triggered by the Northridge earthquake. Eng. Geol. **163**, 41–54 (2013)
5. Newmark, N.M.: Effects of earthquakes on dams and embankments. Géotechnique **15**(2), 139–160 (1965)
6. Jibson, R.W., Harp, E.L., Michael, J.A.: A method for producing digital probabilistic seismic landslide hazard maps: an example from the Los Angeles, California, USA. Eng. Geol. **58** (3–4), 271–289 (2000)
7. Keefer, D.K.: Landslides caused by earthquakes. Geol. Soc. Am. Bull. **95**(4), 406–421 (1984)
8. Jibson, R.W.: Predicting earthquake-induced landslide displacements using Newmark's sliding block analysis. Transp. Res. Rec. **1411**(8), 9–17 (1993)
9. Ma, S., Xu, C.: Assessment of co-seismic landslide hazard using the Newmark model and statistical analyses: a case study of the 2013 Lushan, China, Mw6.6 earthquake. Nat. Hazards **96**, 389–412 (2018). no. 0123456789
10. Guo, M., Ge, X., Wang, S.: Slope stability analysis under seismic load by vector sum analysis method. J. Rock Mech. Geotech. Eng. **3**(3), 282–288 (2012)
11. Wang, M., Liu, K., Yang, G., Xie, J.: Three-dimensional slope stability analysis using laser scanning and numerical simulation. Geomat. Nat. Hazards Risk **8**(2), 997–1011 (2017)
12. Ministry of Mines, Government of India, Geological Survey of India (GSI). ww.gsi.gov.in
13. Bhasin, R., et al.: Landslide hazards and mitigation measures at Gangtok, Sikkim Himalaya. Eng. Geol. **64**(4), 351–368 (2002)
14. Strong-motion-data-records-september-2011-sikkim-earthquake. https://www.moes.gov.in/content/strong-motion-data-records-september-2011-sikkim-earthquake
15. Godt, J., et al.: Rapid assessment of earthquake-induced landsliding, pp. 3–6 (2007)
16. Ramkrishnan, R., Karthik, V., Unnithan, M.S., Kiran Balaji, R., Athul Vinu, M., Venugopalan, A.: Stabilization of seepage induced soil mass movements using sand drains. Geotech. Eng. **48**(4), 129–137 (2017)
17. Prakash, E.L., Kolathayar, S., Ramkrishnan, R.: Proceedings of GeoShanghai 2018 International Conference: Geoenvironment and Geohazard (2018)

Quantitative Analysis of Feature Extraction Techniques for Isolated Word Recognition

Chesta Agarwal[(⊠)], Pinaki Chakraborty, Serena Barai,
and Vaibhav Goyal

Division of Computer Engineering, Netaji Subhas University of Technology,
Dwarka, New Delhi, India
chesta.agarwal@gmail.com,
pinaki_chakraborty_163@yahoo.com, {serenab.co.16,
vaibhavg.co.16}@nsit.net.in

Abstract. Isolated word recognition has been a subject of research since the 1940s when speech recognition technology was in a nascent stage. Recurrent neural networks and deep feed-forward networks are currently being explored by researchers to increase the efficiency of the speech recognition systems. However, probabilistic techniques like Gaussian Mixture Model (GMM) and Hidden Markov Model (HMM) have been the state-of-the-art since long. This paper performs a quantitative analysis of feature extraction techniques for isolated word recognition to provide better insights in improving the efficiency of the system. In this regard, a basic architecture of the word recognizer system has been modelled and it has been observed that Mel Frequency Cepstrum Coefficients (MFCC) in combination with Delta and Delta-Delta parameters have 92.4% accuracy for a sufficiently large dataset. Also MFCC features, appended with Delta parameters have 87.0% accuracy which is 36.4% higher than that of Short Time Fourier Transform (STFT) features. The feature extraction techniques have been classified by a Gaussian Mixture Model- Hidden Markov Model (GMM-HMM) classifier. This paper also studies the effect of varying data size and number of features on the recognition model towards efficient word recognition. These recognizers may then be used as a building block for mispronunciation detection in a Computer Aided Pronunciation Training (CAPT) system.

Keywords: Isolated word recognition · Feature extraction ·
Gaussian Mixture Model - Hidden Markov Model ·
Mel Frequency Cepstral Coefficients · Computer Aided Pronunciation Training

1 Introduction

Technological enhancement and recent research in speech technology has opened a wide range of applications of Automatic Speech Recognition (ASR). From executing instructions on voice commands to providing security to individuals by restricting the access to unknown user, speech recognition finds application in a number of ways in our lives. However, most of these technologies rely on efficient speech recognition for their results. Isolated word recognition is the speech to text conversion of an isolated

© Springer Nature Singapore Pte Ltd. 2019
M. Singh et al. (Eds.): ICACDS 2019, CCIS 1046, pp. 618–627, 2019.
https://doi.org/10.1007/978-981-13-9942-8_58

individual word utterance of a speaker. Unlike continuous speech recognition which converts a free form or a conversational speech to text, isolated word recognition is independent of the context of the previous words. Pedronan et *al.* [7] worked on automatic speech recognition of correctly pronounced English words using Machine Learning.

Apart from commercial applications, ASR has also paved its way into the educational domain through Computer Aided Pronunciation Training (CAPT). As a significant step of Mispronunciation Detection in CAPT, it is important to recognize speech utterance and convert it into the plausible text. An incorrect input pronunciation would be linked to an incorrect recognition thereby a successful mispronunciation detection.

Some speech recognition systems recognize only one speaker's voice and are known as speaker dependent systems. Such speakers are trained on the speech samples of that particular speaker only. However, systems trained on multi-user data can recognize words by any speaker. Such systems are speaker independent systems. Speech recognizers use artificial neural networks to classify the speech data. However, with current demand to increase the efficiency of speech recognition of conversational speech, recurrent neural networks and deep neural networks are being explored in this domain. Deep feed forward (non-recurrent networks) also find their application in some speech recognizers along with classification techniques like Vector Quantization (VQ) and Support Vector Machines (SVM). However, probabilistic techniques like Gaussian distribution based Hidden Markov Model have been extensively used because a speech signal can be viewed as a short time stationary signal which can be modelled as a Markov Model. Chuctya et *al.* (2018) [1] explored the isolated word recognition of numbers in Quencha language using Mel Frequency Cepstrum Coefficients (MFCC), Dynamic Time Warping (DTW) and K- Nearest Neighbour (KNN) algorithms.

In this paper we investigate the effect of different feature extraction techniques on the accuracy of isolated word recognition. For this, GMM-HMM model has been used as a base classifier taking input from the varied feature extraction techniques. Section 2 of the paper summarizes the related work. Section 3 gives an overview of the methodology followed in the paper and the architecture of the Word Recognizer system along with the implementation details of the study. The results generated by the Word Recognizer are reported in Sects. 4 and 5 concludes the paper.

2   Related Work

Many researchers have been working on the different approaches to improve the effectiveness of single word recognition techniques. Speech sample has been converted to a sequence of *Phones* and then to the corresponding word. Phone is the base unit of speech perceivable by the human listener. This speech when converted to text is a collection of characters represented by one or more phones (in case of complex sounds). In order to analyze the speech signal, it is first divided into short segments (usually 15–25 ms) called as *Frames*. It is assumed that only one phone is uttered in a single frame which is then parametrized into acoustic features to allow classification.

Different feature extraction techniques have been worked upon to improve the robustness of speech recognition systems, especially in noisy conditions. Ghadee et al. [4] performed experiments on the Mel-Frequency Cepstral Coefficient (MFCC) features for isolated word recognition. Some researchers [5, 6] used an approach which used Mel-frequency spectral coefficients to extract the speech relevant information from an input signal and displayed it to the user in the form of vibrations, colors and other constructs. They recommended Hidden Markov model for the classification post feature extraction. Tuske et al. [13] dropped the short time stationary assumption of the voiced speech and introduced the non-stationary signal analysis to the ASR framework. Based on the MFCC feature extraction approach, they proposed non-stationary gammatone features and claimed them to be comparable to the MFCC parameters in performance. Sledevic et al. [10] presented a comparative evaluation of feature extraction algorithms for a real-time isolated word recognition system based on Field Programmable Gate Array (FPGA). Feature extraction techniques like MFCC, Linear Frequency Cepstral (LFC) and cepstral coefficients were implemented in hardware/software co-design. Experiments were performed to check the robustness of feature extraction algorithms in recognizing the speech records at different signal to noise rates. Mel-frequency cepstral and linear frequency cepstral coefficients show highest accuracy results. This highlights the suitability of word recognition system for application in embedded systems. Following a similar approach, Dhingra et al. [2] used MFCC with Dynamic Time Warping (DTW) classification approach to accommodate different speaking speeds of the speakers for isolated speech recognition. They performed experiments with five speakers speaking ten words each in an acoustically controlled environment. Gedam et al. [3] worked on similar lines and recognized Marathi words using MFCC and DTW techniques. Taking advantage from the close approximation of the Mel-frequency scaling to human auditory system MFCC was used for feature extraction and DTW for feature matching and classification. They used VQ for efficient representation of each speaker. Recognizing the effectiveness and robustness of the MFCC approach, Singh and Rani [9] used the nonparametric frequency domain approach for isolated word recognition in English. Some researchers [11] combined the MFCC based speaker recognition technique with Weighted Vector Quantization approach for efficient pattern matching. Their experiments established the system's capability for correct speaker identification with short speech samples. Vijh et al. [14] suggested improving the accuracy of the recognition system using an artificial neural network to classify the features extracted by the MFCC approach. Tryfou and Omologo [12] enhanced the MFCC features and investigated those under different speech recognition scenarios. On lines similar to Vijh et al. [14], Saini et al. [8] achieved 91.20% accuracy in speech recognition for 40 isolated words. They suggested classifying the MFCC features with the Hidden Markov Model and neural network based approach.

3 Methodology

3.1 Techniques Used

The word recognition system is an important component in most speech recognition systems. It finds special application in a CAPT system. Feature Extraction is one of the preliminary steps of a word recognizer. The Feature Extraction component generates a feature vector for each frame (*i.e.* quasi-stationary signal) depicting the different parameters of the speech signal like amplitude of the signal, energies of frequencies and energy envelope of signal. This section explores the different speech analysis methods, both in time domain and in frequency domain. Amongst the different parameters representing the relevant information about the speech signal overall energy of the signal is the used for speech activity detection and low-rate coding application. This is depicted by Short Term Fourier Transform (STFT) which calculates the energy spectrum of the speech signal.

STFT represents the non-stationary input speech signal by sum of sinusoids thereby exposing the hidden signal properties. The two components of STFT, *viz.* time and frequency, empower STFT to realize the discretized stationary as well as continuous speech parameters. Fourier Transform represents the speech in terms of amplitude and phase as a function of frequency. The short time spectrum of the signal is the magnitude of a Fourier Transform of the waveform after it has been multiplied by a time window function of appropriate duration.

Mel Frequency Cepstral Coefficients (MFCC) are the state-of-the-art feature extraction technique in automatic speech recognition being used since the 1980 s. MFCC is the real cepstrum of a windowed short time signal derived from the Fast Fourier Transform (FFT) of a signal subjected to a log based transform of the frequency axis (Mel-frequency scale), and then decorrelated using a modified Discrete Cosine Transform (DCT-II). The capability of the MFCCs to accurately represent the shape of the human vocal tract in the envelope of short time power spectrum makes it as the most widely used feature extraction technique.

The MFCC feature vector describes only the power spectral envelope of a single frame, but the speech information in the dynamic parameters is not catered by the MFCC parameters. The information in the trajectories of the MFCC coefficients over time generates the differential and acceleration coefficients, popularly known as Delta and Delta-Delta coefficients respectively. Appending these coefficients to the MFCC feature vector increases ASR performance.

The feature vectors identified by the different feature extraction techniques, then needs to be classified to different phones to recognize speech. A Gaussian Mixture Model (GMM) is a probable classification technique. For each phone class, a GMM is fit using all the frames where that phone is found. For classification of a new utterance, frame by frame analysis is done for identifying the GMM with highest likelihood. However, the incompetency of the GMM model to accommodate the temporal dependency in the acoustic signal limits the classification accuracy. The GMM model assumes depends only on the current frame, ignoring the context. This is taken care of by the GMM-HMM model.

The Hidden Markov Model (HMM) is a temporal model which assumes an unknown source state (*e.g.* position of different vocal tract elements). Common HMM architectures for speech recognition having phone models consisting of three states, assumes the uttered phone to be in three distinct phases, *viz.* 'beginning', 'middle' and 'ending' phases. Each of the phase when modelled by GMM, determines the likelihood of an observation (*i.e.* frame) in that state. Thereby, a sequence of frames, each classified as some state, belongs to a phone. However, many frames may be generated by one state, also several states may refer to a single phone, a correlation of which builds up a single word. Automatic training and computational feasibility have made HMM a popular classifier.

3.2 System Architecture

A word recognizer system consists of several modules as represented in Fig. 1. The details of the different modules of our system are as follows:

Sound Recorder: The sound recorder records the speech signal using the Microphone and prepares the signal by removing noise from it. The output of this module is a wave file which is fed to the subsequent module.

Framing and Windowing: The input speech signal is a non-stationary signal and varies with time. An audio signal is constantly changing. So, it is assumed that on short time scales the audio signal is statistically stationary. To capture the variability in the waveform, the signal is segmented into 20–40 ms frames. Shorter frames have a lack of sufficient sample size for a reliable spectral estimate, while longer frames have constantly changing speech signal thereby compromising the quasi-stationary feature of the signal.

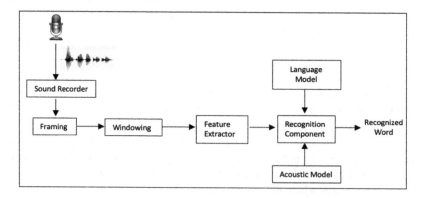

Fig. 1. Block diagram of the word recognition system.

Post frame blocking, the spectral artifacts at frame edges are reduced by subjecting the frames to a windowing function. Windowing is a point-wise multiplication of the frame and the window function. The discussed word recognizer system uses a

Hamming window applied to each frame to minimize the signal discontinuities at the frame edges during signal trimming. Consecutive frames are overlapped at the edges to avoid loss of information at signal boundaries.

Feature Extraction: The segmented frame of the speech signal is subjected to feature extraction to generate a sequence of parameters known as a feature vector. The parameters in the feature vector determine different properties (like energies of the different peaks identified in the frequency distribution of the speech signal) of the input speech signal within the frame. Length of the feature vector depends on the feature extraction technique used for the process (Table 1). The system discussed uses STFT, MFCC and MFCC with Delta and Delta-Delta Parameters as the feature extraction techniques.

The first step in any automatic speech recognition system is to extract features *i.e.* identify the components of the audio signal that are good for identifying the linguistic content and discarding all the other components which carries information like emotion and background noise.

Recognition Component: It is a GMM-HMM based classification component. The input feature vectors are used to train the GMM-HMM model in order to recognise the word being spoken by the different frames of the input speech signal. The recognition model is based on the stochastic properties of the probability based supervised machine learning classification technique.

Table 1. Size of feature vector generated by different feature extraction techniques.

Technique	No. of features
STFT	6
MFCC	12
MFCC + Delta	24
MFCC + Delta + Delta-Delta	36

Knowledge Model: The knowledge model consists of the Acoustic Model and the Language Model which contain the expert data related to the correct word for the speech samples. The Recognition Component trains the model in accordance with the knowledge model.

3.3   Implementation Details

The system has been implemented to recognise words in recorded isolated speech samples with each utterance containing one word. The dataset consisted of the 24 isolated English words with utterances ranging from 15 to 50 per word generating a total of 720 utterances. The 8 kHz speech utterances were framed at 25 ms and subjected to windowing by Hamming window function and a default 26 filter filter-bank. Each of the frames were then fed to a feature extractor algorithm and a feature vector of corresponding length was generated. GMM-HMM model was then used for classification. The model was implemented on the Anaconda Platform using Python language.

4   Results and Discussion

The GMM-HMM model recognized the different words spoken in the utterances provided as input from the dataset. The accuracy of the word recognition is calculated to study the effectiveness of the different feature extraction techniques. The model was first trained on 80% of the dataset while 20% of the dataset was used for testing the model. However, slightly better accuracy was achieved later when 90% of the data was used for training and remaining for the testing stage. Figure 2 depicts the accuracy results in word recognition with STFT feature vector. An accuracy of 53.24% was achieved on a 720 utterance dataset with the STFT feature extraction approach. MFCC closely envelopes the human vocal spectrum, thereby, 61.10% accuracy was achieved on the 720 utterance dataset as depicted in Fig. 3. Enhancing the MFCC features with the Delta features further improves the accuracy to 87.00% (Fig. 4). Appending the Delta-Delta features to the Delta features and MFCC features enhances the word recognition capability of the GMM-HMM classifier to 92.40% as illustrated in Fig. 5.

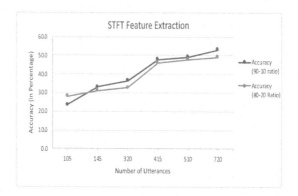

Fig. 2. Accuracy in word recognition when STFT is used for feature extraction.

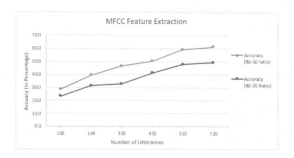

Fig. 3. Accuracy in word recognition when MFCC is used for feature extraction.

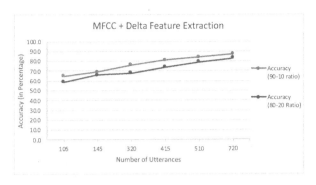

Fig. 4. Accuracy in word recognition when MFCC + Delta is used for feature extraction.

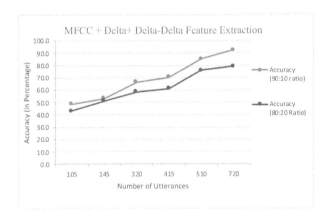

Fig. 5. Accuracy in word recognition when MFCC + Delta + Delta-Delta is used for feature extraction.

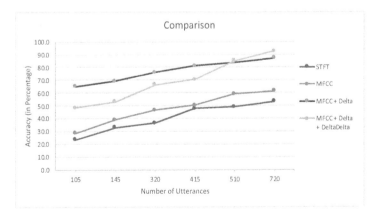

Fig. 6. Comparison of accuracy of results (as per 90:10 training: testing split ratio) of the different feature extraction techniques.

All the feature extraction techniques were analysed by a common classifier, *i.e.* the GMM-HMM model. It has been observed that having 90% of the dataset for training the model gives better recognition results as compared to 80% of the data for training as it helps in fine tuning of the model parameters, thus improved accuracy ranging from 3% to 10%. Small dataset limits the capabilities of the word recognizer which can be enhanced by increasing the sample size. Larger datasets provides a better quality test set ruling out the possibility of overfitting the model parameters.

Different feature extraction techniques have a remarkable impact on the efficiency of the system. MFCC with differential and acceleration coefficients generate 28.76% improved average accuracy when compared to STFT. However, MFCC with Delta coefficients alone raise the accuracy by 36.41% on an average across the different data sizes in comparison to STFT. As illustrated in Fig. 6, MFCC with Delta and Delta-Delta parameters have better accuracy results when the dataset is sufficiently large (720 utterances) and is overshadowed by the MFCC with Delta parameters in most other cases. This is due to a trade-off between the size of feature vector and the available sample size for model-parameter tuning. Larger feature vector generates enhanced results but appending the MFCC features with Delta-Delta parameters to the Delta parameters should be preferred only in case sufficient dataset is available. MFCC alone in comparison with STFT approach gives marginal improvement to the system of about 6.9%.

Saini *et al.* [8] achieved 91.2% accuracy with MFCC technique along with Delta and Delta-Delta coefficients with a dataset of 40 isolated words. They combined the MFCC approach with HMM and artificial neural network classification methods. Vijh *et al.* [14] observed 95% accuracy when MFCC is combined with artificial neural network suggesting the capability of the word recognition system can be further enhanced by incorporating more efficient classifiers.

5 Conclusion

In this paper we have performed a quantitative analysis of different feature extraction techniques for isolated word recognition. Different feature extraction techniques like STFT, MFCC and Delta and Delta-Delta coefficients were evaluated using a GMM-HMM classifier. The paper discusses the architecture of the word recognizer system the effect of the feature extraction techniques on the accuracy of the system. MFCC features when appended with Delta parameters generate correct results in 87.0% of the cases while, MFCC with Delta and Delta-Delta parameters increase the accuracy of the recognizer to 92.4% with sufficiently large dataset. These results and the word recognizer system can be used as an important building block for mispronunciation detection in CAPT.

References

1. Chuctaya, H.F.C., Mercado, R.N.M., Gaona, J.J.G.: Isolated automatic speech recognition of Quechua numbers using MFCC, DTW and KNN. Int. J. Adv. Comput. Sci. Appl. **9**, 24–29 (2018)
2. Dhingra, S.D., Nijhawan, G., Pandit, P.: Isolated speech recognition using MFCC and DTW. Int. J. Adv. Res. Electr. Electron. Instrum. Eng. **2**, 4085–4092 (2013)
3. Gedam, Y.K., Magare, S.S., Dabhade, A.C., Deshmukh, R.R.: Development of automatic speech recognition of Marathi numerals - a review. Int. J. Eng. Innov. Technol. **3**, 198–203 (2014)
4. Ghadee, A., Jonvale, G.B., Deshmukh, R.R.: Speech feature extraction using Mel- frequency cepstral coefficient (MFCC). In: Proceedings of Conference on Emerging Treads in Computer Science, Communication and Information Technology, pp. 503–506 (2010)
5. Gulaker, V.: Speech recognition by human and machine. M.Sc. Thesis, Norwegian University of Science and Technology (2010)
6. Nasreen, P.N., Kumar, A.C., Nabeel, P.A.: Speech analysis for automatic speech recognition. In: Proceedings of International Conference on Computing, Communication and Science (2016)
7. Pedronan, R.C., Manglal-lan Jr., R.A., Galasinao, K.J.B., Salvador, R.P., Acang, J.P.A.: Automatic recognition of correctly pronounced English words using machine learning. ASIA Pac. High. Educ. Res. J. **4**, 82–93 (2017)
8. Saini, N.K., Bohara, V., Balai, L.N.: An approach to extract features from speech signal for efficient recognition of speech. Int. J. Innov. Res. Comput. Commun. Eng. **6**, 144–149 (2018)
9. Singh, P.P., Rani, P.: An approach to extract feature using MFCC. IOSR J. Eng. **4**, 21–25 (2014)
10. Sledevic, T., Serackis, A., Tamulevicius, G., Navakauskas, D.: Evaluation of features extraction algorithms for a real-time isolated word recognition system. Int. J. Electr. Electron. Sci. Eng. **7**, 302–307 (2013)
11. Sunitha, C., Chandra, E.: Speaker recognition using MFCC and improved weighted vector quantization algorithm. Int. J. Eng. Technol. **7**, 1685–1692 (2015)
12. Tryfou, G., Omologo, M.: A reassigned front-end for speech recognition. In: Proceedings of 25th European Signal Processing Conference, pp. 583–587 (2017)
13. Tuske, Z., Golik, P., Schluter, R., Drepper, F.R.: Non-stationary feature extraction for automatic speech recognition. In: Proceedings of IEEE International Conference on Acoustics, Speech and Signal Processing, pp. 5204–5207 (2011)
14. Vijh, S., Singh, P., Gill, M.K.: Feature extraction using MFCC for speech recognition. In: Proceedings of Fourth International Conference on Recent Trends in Communication and Computer Networks, pp. 310–314 (2016)

Mathematical Analysis of Image Information Retained in the Complex Domain Phases Under Additive and Multiplicative Noise

Susant Kumar Panigrahi[1]($^{(\boxtimes)}$) and Supratim Gupta[2]

[1] Koneru Lakshmaiah Education Foundation, Vijayawada 522502, AP, India
susant.panigrahi@yahoo.com, susant146@gmail.com
[2] National Institute of Technology, Rourkela 769008, Odisha, India
sgupta.iitkgp@gmail.com

Abstract. It is often observed that phases in complex transform of images are important ingredients compared to their magnitude for information extraction. Literature indicates that these phases are immune to noise. The aim of this paper is to find the structural (Edge) and statistical information retained by the complex domain phases for the images corrupted with additive white Gaussian noise (AWGN) and multiplicative (speckle) noise. Initially, we measure the edge information preserved by both phase and magnitude only synthesized image using edge mismatch error (EMM), to illustrate the significance of phase in image restoration and reconstruction. A mathematical model for the sensitivity of phase and magnitude is derived to examine the respective rate of deterioration under varying noise strength. Both the mathematical finding and experimental results indicate that the phase of any complex transform is degraded slowly compared to its magnitude. Comparative analysis of effect of noise on these phases is also investigated and reported.

Keywords: Additive white Gaussian noise (AWGN) ·
Edge mismatch error (EMM) · Multiplicative noise ·
Dual tree complex wavelets transform (CWT) ·
Fast discrete curvelet transform (CT) · Noise sensitivity

1 Introduction

Transforming signal (or image) to frequency or frequency-analogous (scale) space may reveal some of the indispensable properties of the signal. These representations or so called (signal) transformations has gained its popularity in many signal and image processing applications [1–3]. Some of the signal representation techniques like: Fourier transform (FT), Dual-Tree Complex wavelet transform (DT-CWT or simply CWT) [4], Curvelet transform (CT) [5] and Stockwell Transform (ST) [6] represents signal using both magnitude and phase (i.e the

© Springer Nature Singapore Pte Ltd. 2019
M. Singh et al. (Eds.): ICACDS 2019, CCIS 1046, pp. 628–642, 2019.
https://doi.org/10.1007/978-981-13-9942-8_59

transformed coefficients are complex in nature). Literature suggests that the complex domain transforms play a significant role in signal representation and restoration compared to real transforms [7]. The phase in complex domain transforms preserve most of the signal feature information compared its magnitude [8–10].

The information retentivity of phase and magnitude can well be understood from their frequency distribution. Investigating the phase and magnitude spectra of any natural image indicates that the phase is almost equally distributed across the spectrum, while the magnitude is only concentrated near the fundamental frequency and decays exponentially with increasing in frequency. In addition, the spectral distribution of magnitude is common to all the natural images [11]. This strengthen the fact that the information which differentiates between images is not embedded in the magnitude spectra, but is preserved in the phase spectra. Moreover according to Kovesi [12] the image features such as step edges, lines, and corners are also retained by the phase or more precisely at the location of phase congruency. Due to its importance in the image representation and/or reconstruction[1], the phase based image analysis has gained its popularity in diverse field of applications [13–16].

In most of the image processing applications, the phase of the clean or noise free image is utilized for feature extraction. Due to the limitations of image acquisition system most of the natural images are affected by noise. These noises can be modeled either additively or multiplicatively [17,18]. It was reported that the complex domain phases, thus observed in different transformation techniques remain more immune to noise that the corresponding magnitude [19]. However, the authors limited their analysis on locally referenced phase in FT and utilized FT phase to detect edges in an image [19]. In this article, the analysis is conducted on various complex domain phases and reported their sensitivity under both additive and multiplicative noises. The following are the main contribution of the article:

i. Quantitative evaluation of different domain magnitude and phase only synthesized images using EMM. This measure will provide the amount of edge information retained by both phase and magnitude.
ii. A concrete mathematical support for the illustration of non-sensitive nature of phase, when image is corrupted with either additive white Gaussian (AWGN) or multiplicative (Speckle) noise.
iii. Experimental verification of proposed mathematical inference on a wide variation of noise strength with different image datasets.

2   Edge Information in Phase

The phase and magnitude spectral distribution of different complex transform retains distinct signal information. In general the important image features such

---

[1] In our earlier work a comparative analysis on different phases reveal the importance of phase based reconstruction over magnitude based reconstruction [9].

as: step edges, lines, and corner are occurred at the location where the frequency components of the image are maximally in phase or congruent [20]. Here, the edge mismatch error (EMM) [21] is adapted to quantify the amount of edge information retained in both phase and magnitude only reconstructed image[2]. This measure was originally proposed to evaluate the discrepancy between the edge map of two images [22]. As in this context we are interested to quantify the similarity in edge map between the original and magnitude (or phase) only reconstructed images, therefore the edge matching index is defined as:

$$EMM = \frac{CE}{CE + \omega \left[\sum_{k \in \{EO\}} \delta(k) + \alpha \sum_{k \in \{ET\}} \delta(k) \right]} \tag{1}$$

with,

$$\delta(k) = \begin{cases} |d_k| & \text{if, } |d_k| < \text{maxdist} \\ D_{max} & \text{Otherwise} \end{cases}$$

Where,

- CE = Number of common edge pixels in original and synthesized image.
- EO = Number of excess original (reference) edge pixels that are missing in reconstructed image..
- ET = Excess number of edge pixels available in reconstructed image but not in original image.
- $|d_k|$ = The Euclidian distance of the k'th excess edge pixel to neighbor edge pixel with in a search area calculated by '$maxdist$'.
- If N is image dimension, then maxdist = $0.025 \times N$.
- $\omega = \frac{10}{N}$, with $\alpha = 2$.

The Most popular Canny's edge detector is considered to find out the edge map of both original and synthesized images [23]. We then determine the percentage of total edge information preserved by both magnitude and phase based reconstructed image individually. Assuming EMM_m and EMM_p be the edge match index (see, Eq. 1) of magnitude and phase only reconstructed image to ground truth edge map, then the percentage of relative edge information preserved by the magnitude and phase of each transform is calculated as:

$$\% \text{ of relative edge information in magnitude} = \frac{(EMM)_m}{(EMM)_m + (EMM)_p} \times 100\% \tag{2}$$

$$\% \text{ of relative edge information in phase} = \frac{(EMM)_p}{(EMM)_m + (EMM)_p} \times 100\% \tag{3}$$

---

[2] The phase only reconstructed image was synthesized from the phase of respective transform (such as FT, CWT and CT) with unity magnitude. Similarly, the magnitude only reconstructed image was synthesized by preserving magnitude information with unity phase.

Table 1. The average % of edge information in magnitude only reconstructed image per total edge information (as a combination of both magnitude and phase) for the considered complex transformations.

	Amount of edge information in							
	Magnitude (%)				Phase (%)			
	FT	CWT	CTW	CT	FT	CWT	CTw	CTu
BSDS [24]	23.74	48.66	37.00	32.93	76.27	51.34	63.00	67.07
Caltech background [25]	31.64	52.3	36.05	32.14	68.36	47.70	63.69	67.86
DTU IMM face [26]	24.94	49.49	30.11	31.19	75.06	50.51	69.89	68.81
TID2008 [27]	30.55	48.21	42.29	38.21	69.45	51.79	57.71	61.79
Zurich building [28]	37.41	43.10	37.23	35.69	62.59	56.90	62.77	64.31

CTw: Fast discrete curvelet transform (FDCT) via. Wrapping, **CTu**: Fast discrete curvelet transform (FDCT) via. USFFT.

Five image database containing various images (≥ 1100) of human faces, buildings, natural scenes and objects with distinct texture information, distributed anonymously (see Table 2 for more information) have been considered to measure the edge similarity (see Eq. 1) between the original image (obtained from each database) and its phase and magnitude only reconstructed images. For each image database the average value of relative edge information as defined in Eqs. 2 and 3 are calculated. The mean relative value of EMM index (in %) is shown in Table 1, which reveals that the phase only reconstructed image retains most of the features compared to its magnitude. In addition, it also indicates that the absolutely referenced phase (ARP) in FT possess more signal information than its magnitude.

3   Noise Sensitivity of Phases

Literature suggests that the most commonly observed noises are either modeled additively or multiplicatively [17,18]. The presence of noise in an image may cause several distortion in the magnitude and phase distribution of complex transforms. Therefore, in this article we derive the noise sensitivity of phase and magnitude (i.e the rate of change of noisy image magnitude or phase in transformed domain with respect to noise magnitude) to measure the amount of distortion occurred due to the change in noise strength.

Now, let us consider x be the noise-free image of size $N_1 \times N_2$ and $y = x + \eta$ be the noisy image corrupted by additive white Gaussian noise with zero mean and σ^2 variance (i.e. η is i.i.d of $\aleph(0, \sigma^2)$), then transformed **T** (either via. FT, CWT or FDCT) noisy image can be represented as given below:

$$\mathbf{T}\left[y(n_1, n_2)\right] = \mathbf{T}\left[x(n_1, n_2) + \eta(n_1, n_2)\right] \tag{4}$$

Where n_1 and n_2 represents spatial locations along row and column directions of the image. Assuming, Curvelet, transforms image in complex domain using basis functions of tight frames, then Eq. 4 can be written in a linear form as:

$$Y(u,v) = X(u,v) + N(u,v) \tag{5}$$

Where, u and v are the spatial frequencies along row and column directions, respectively. Then the Eq. 5 can be rewritten in polar with phase, $\varphi[Y(u,v)]$ and magnitude, $|Y(u,v)|$ of the respective complex transform as given below:

$$\varphi[Y(u,v)] = \arctan\left(\frac{|X|sin(\theta) + |N|sin(\phi)}{|X|cos(\theta) + |N|cos(\phi)}\right) \tag{6}$$

$$|Y(u,v)| = \left(|X|^2 + |N|^2 + 2|X||N|cos(\theta - \phi)\right)^{1/2} \tag{7}$$

Here, θ and ϕ are the phase angle of X and N respectively. Although, literature suggests that the Fourier phase of AWGN remain zero with high probability $(p(\varphi(N(u,v)) = 0.85)$, and the magnitude exhibits the randomness, the derogatory effect of both can not be separated [29]. Thus the sensitivity of the magnitude and phase with respect to those of noise can be used for analysis. These are expressed as:

$$\frac{\partial |Y|}{\partial |N|} = \frac{|N| + |X|cos(\theta - \phi)}{\left(|X|^2 + |N|^2 + 2|X||N|cos(\theta - \phi)\right)^{1/2}} \tag{8}$$

$$\frac{\partial(\varphi[Y])}{\partial |N|} = \frac{|X|sin(\phi - \theta)}{|X|^2 + |N|^2 + 2|X||N|cos(\theta - \phi)} \tag{9}$$

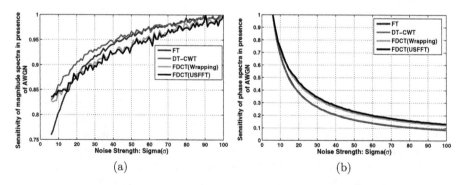

Fig. 1. Noise sensitivity of (a) Magnitude & (b) Phase for different complex transform, when image is corrupted with AWGN (Normalized between $[0,1]$).

The noise sensitivity as derived in Eq. 8 indicates the magnitude deteriorates significantly with increasing in noise strength. On the other hand, it reduces for phase as illustrated in Eq. 9 with increasing in noise strength, σ. We found out the rate of change in absolute difference between the original and noisy image magnitude with respect to the magnitude spectrum of AWGN and also the phase difference per noise magnitude (i.e. the sensitivity as defined in Eqs. 8 and 9). The normalized average value of both measures for different complex transform are shown in Fig. 1, which yields the non-sensitive nature of phase in presence of AWGN.

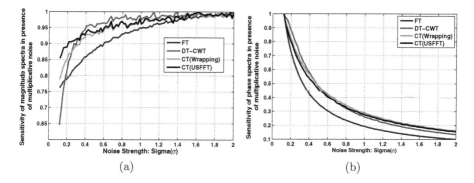

(a)   (b)

Fig. 2. Noise sensitivity of (a) Magnitude & (b) Phase for different complex transform, when image is corrupted with multiplicative noise(Normalized between $[0, 1]$).

Similarly assuming x as reference image, corrupted with random noise η of zero mean and σ^2 variance is also modeled multiplicatively [18]. Then the complex transform of distorted image y is expressed as follows:

$$\mathbf{T}\left[y(n_1, n_2)\right] = \mathbf{T}\left[x(n_1, n_2) \times \eta(n_1, n_2) + x(n_1, n_2)\right] \qquad (10)$$

Then, the noise sensitivity of any corrupted image, Y as can be derived as:

$$\frac{\partial |Y|}{\partial |N|} = |X| \cdot \frac{|N| + cos(\phi)}{\sqrt{(1 + |N|^2 + 2|N|cos(\phi))}} \qquad (11)$$

$$\frac{\partial (\varphi[Y])}{\partial |N|} = \frac{sin(\phi)}{1 + |N| + 2|N|cos(\phi)} \qquad (12)$$

As expected the phase of complex transforms are also immune to multiplicative noise (Eq. 12). However, the image information retained by the magnitude degrades significantly with increasing in noise magnitude (Eq. 11). The experimental results on Lena image as shown in Fig. 2 supports the theoretical validation.

4 Experiment

The noise sensitivity of both phase and magnitude are distinct while the image is exposed to either additive Gaussian or multiplicative noise. To demonstrate

Table 2. Database specification.

Database	Original image type	No. of images	Image resolution	Other specifications
Berkley Segmentation Data Set (BSDS) [24]	Wide range of natural scene	300	481 × 321 321 × 481	5–9 binary edge maps per image segmented by human subjects are available
Caltech database [25]	Background images	550	223 × 147 378 × 251	Assorted scenes around the Caltech campus and in the vision lab.
IMM face database [26]	Human face with different orientation	240	640 × 480	7 female and 33 male subjects without eyeglasses
TID 2008 database [27]	Natural scenes and artificial images	25	512 × 384	24 natural scene images and 1 artificial image
Zurich database [28]	Building images	115	240 × 320	Each building have 5 different view point, with varying illuminations

this effect, several experiments have been carried out quantitatively, using peak signal to noise ratio (PSNR) and structural similarity measure index (SSIM) [30] on different image databases.

4.1 Database

The choice of image database plays an important role for extraction of information from phase or magnitude, when image is corrupted with noise. In this context five standard image database containing various images (≥ 1100) of human faces, buildings, natural scenes and objects with distinct texture information, distributed anonymously are considered for the experiment. Table 2 represents few essential information regarding each database. In order to maintain uniformity in comparision, the dimension of the images are changed to 512×512 pixels array.

4.2 Experimental Process

The reference images in each database were contaminated with simulated AWGN of zero mean and varying noise strengths of seven different standard deviations, $\sigma = 10, 20, 30, 40, 50, 60$ and 70. Similarly, the images are degraded with speckle of noise strength $\sigma = 0.1, 0.3, 0.6, 1, 1.3, 1.6$, and 2 with uniform distribution.

Two images were reconstructed from the magnitude of noisy image and phase of original image (known as noisy magnitude based reconstruction) and viceversa (called as noisy phase based reconstruction) for different complex domain transformations. The information retained in the reconstructed images were calculated using SSIM and PSNR.

(a)   (b)   (c)

Fig. 3. (a) Original Barbara image, (b) Image corrupted with AWGN of $\mu = 0$ & $\sigma = 20$, (C) Noisy image corrupted with Speckle noise of $\sigma = 1$.

(a)   (b)   (c)   (d)

Fig. 4. Fourier (FT) synthesis: (a) Reconstructed image from the magnitude of noisy image (Fig. 3b) and phase of original image (Fig. 3a)-[Noisy Magnitude based Reconstruction], while (b) Reconstructed vice-versa-[Noisy Phase based Reconstruction], (c) Synthesized image from magnitude of corrupted image (Fig. 3c) and phase of original image (Fig. 3a)-[Noisy Magnitude based Reconstruction], while (d) Synthesized otherwise-[Noisy Phase based Reconstruction]

5   Results and Discussion

Figure 4 illustrates effect of noise on the magnitude and phase based reconstructed images, qualitatively. Here, the Fourier magnitude and phase of original image (Fig. 3a) and noisy image (Fig. 3b) corrupted with AWGN are swapped to reconstruct the images in Figs. 4a and b (Known as Fourier (FT) synthesis). Similarly, the images in Figs. 4c and d are synthesized using noisy image, distorted with multiplicative noise. It can be seen that the images which are reconstructed using phase of noisy images (Figs. 4b and d) are more visually similar to original image.

(a)   (b)   (c)   (d)

Fig. 5. Wavelet (CWT) synthesis: (a) Noisy magnitude based reconstructed image & (b) Noisy phase based reconstructed image for AWGN and (c) Noisy magnitude based reconstructed image & (d) Noisy phase based reconstructed image for speckle noise.

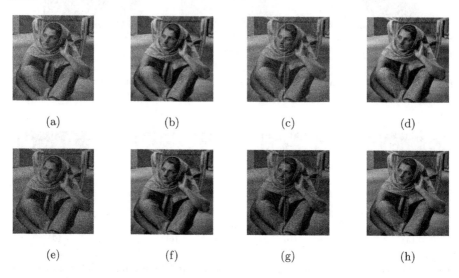

(a)   (b)   (c)   (d)

(e)   (f)   (g)   (h)

Fig. 6. Curvelet (CT) synthesis via. wrapping [2,5]: (a) Noisy Magnitude based reconstructed image & (b) Noisy phase based reconstructed image for AWGN and (e) Noisy Magnitude based reconstructed image & (f) Noisy phase based reconstructed image for Speckle noise. **Curvelet (CT) synthesis via. USFFT** [2,5]: (c) Noisy magnitude based reconstructed image & (d) Noisy phase based reconstructed image for AWGN and (g) Noisy magnitude based reconstructed image & (h) Noisy phase based reconstructed image for speckle noise.

We also investigate the noise sensitivity of locally referenced phases in CWT and CT for qualitative assessment. The results for CWT (known as wavelet synthesis) and CT (known as Curvelet synthesis) magnitude and phase swapped reconstructed images are shown in Figs. 5 and 6 respectively. Since, the second generation fast discrete Curvelet transform has two digital implementations such as: wrapping and USFFT [2,5], we considered the effect of noise on the respective phases of both implementations in Fig. 6. It may be observed that the locally

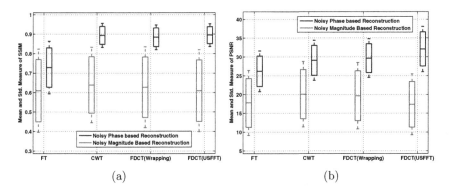

Fig. 7. Mean and standard deviation of (a) SSIM and (b) PSNR measure between original Barbara image (Fig. 3a) and its reconstructed image from noisy observations with AWGN.

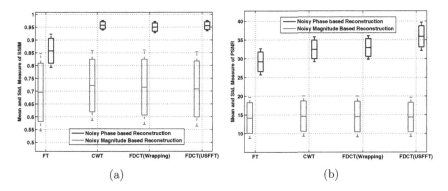

Fig. 8. Mean and standard deviation of (a) SSIM and (b) PSNR measure between original Barbara image (Fig. 3a) and its reconstructed image from noisy observations with multiplicative noise.

referenced phases in CWT and CT also immune to noise and preserves most of the original image features, while magnitude degrades significantly.

In order to quantify the image information retained by the individual reconstructed images, we have computed the PSNR and SSIM measure for Barbara image (Fig. 3a) contaminated with both AWGN and speckle noise, respectively. Here, a linear variation in noise strength was considered and the mean & standard deviation of each measure was computed for various complex transformations. Figures 7a and b illustrate effect of SSIM and PSNR measures computed for noisy magnitude and phase only reconstructed images corrupted under AWGN. The high variation and low mean score for magnitude based reconstructed image indicates that it deteriorates severely as noise strength increases. However, phase based synthesized images remain immune to it, with minimum variations from the mean value. A similar conclusion can also be drawn for speckle noise (with uniform distribution), as its noisy magnitude based recon-

Table 3. Average value of SSIM & PSNR measure between original and noisy magnitude and phase based reconstructed image, for AWGN.

	Structural similarity index measure								Peak signal to noise ratio							
	FT		DT-CWT		CTw		CTu		FT		DT-CWT		CTw		CTu	
Noise strength	Mag.	Phase	Mag.	Phase	Mag.	Phase	Mag.	Phase	Mag.	Phase	Mag.	Phase	Mag.	Phase	Mag.	Phase
BSDS image database [24]																
$\sigma = 10$	0.941	0.949	0.939	0.982	0.946	0.977	0.936	**0.983**	30.03	34.32	32.84	37.12	32.49	36.74	29.03	**40.12**
$\sigma = 20$	0.823	0.869	0.818	0.953	0.831	0.942	0.815	**0.958**	23.53	30.17	26.31	33.03	25.82	32.70	22.99	**35.04**
$\sigma = 30$	0.706	0.799	0.709	**0.924**	0.719	0.906	0.702	0.913	19.74	28.02	22.48	30.85	21.95	30.56	19.45	**32.38**
$\sigma = 40$	0.607	0.743	0.623	**0.896**	0.625	0.872	0.611	0.881	17.07	26.62	19.77	29.41	19.2218	29.14	16.93	**30.65**
$\sigma = 50$	0.528	0.697	0.553	**0.870**	0.550	0.842	0.537	0.851	15.01	25.62	17.67	28.35	17.119	28.10	14.96	**29.41**
$\sigma = 60$	0.463	0.658	0.497	**0.846**	0.488	0.815	0.478	0.823	13.33	24.86	15.97	27.53	15.415	27.30	13.36	**28.46**
$\sigma = 70$	0.411	0.695	0.450	**0.825**	0.437	0.791	0.429	0.799	11.92	24.24	14.53	26.86	13.98	26.64	12.01	**27.70**
Caltech image database [25]																
$\sigma = 10$	0.914	0.955	0.921	**0.986**	0.926	0.982	0.917	0.983	28.76	37.79	32.06	40.81	31.09	40.78	29.01	**41.71**
$\sigma = 20$	0.764	0.895	0.771	**0.966**	0.778	0.956	0.762	0.956	22.53	33.66	25.72	36.83	24.77	36.71	22.94	**37.22**
$\sigma = 30$	0.627	0.843	0.644	**0.945**	0.645	0.930	0.627	0.929	18.92	31.40	22.04	34.57	21.10	34.44	19.38	**34.80**
$\sigma = 40$	0.519	0.797	0.547	**0.925**	0.541	0.905	0.525	0.903	16.37	29.87	19.44	33.01	18.51	32.90	16.86	**33.18**
$\sigma = 50$	0.437	0.758	0.474	**0.906**	0.461	0.882	0.447	0.880	14.395	28.73	17.43	31.82	16.51	31.73	14.90	**31.97**
$\sigma = 60$	0.375	0.724	0.417	**0.888**	0.399	0.861	0.388	0.858	12.79	27.83	15.79	30.88	14.88	30.79	13.30	**31.01**
$\sigma = 70$	0.325	0.695	0.372	**0.872**	0.351	0.841	0.341	0.839	11.43	27.10	14.41	30.10	13.50	30.02	11.94	**30.23**
IMM face database [26]																
$\sigma = 10$	0.880	0.919	0.903	0.964	0.908	0.961	0.874	**0.973**	30.19	35.04	32.13	37.38	32.22	37.18	29.01	**42.11**
$\sigma = 20$	0.660	0.843	0.692	0.944	0.702	0.935	0.652	**0.950**	23.41	32.48	25.06	35.25	25.09	35.03	22.88	**38.80**
$\sigma = 30$	0.484	0.791	0.523	0.930	0.533	0.916	0.483	**0.932**	19.54	31.18	21.11	34.17	21.11	33.92	19.31	**36.99**
$\sigma = 40$	0.366	0.752	0.409	**0.919**	0.415	0.901	0.370	0.917	16.84	30.29	18.38	33.40	18.37	33.14	16.77	**35.75**
$\sigma = 50$	0.286	0.722	0.331	**0.910**	0.335	0.888	0.295	0.904	14.78	29.61	16.29	32.81	16.28	32.52	14.81	**34.81**
$\sigma = 60$	0.231	0.698	0.276	**0.901**	0.278	0.876	0.242	0.893	13.10	29.06	14.61	32.31	14.59	32.01	13.21	**34.05**
$\sigma = 70$	0.191	0.678	0.235	**0.893**	0.235	0.866	0.204	0.882	11.70	28.61	13.20	31.88	13.18	31.57	11.86	**33.41**
TID 2008 image database [27]																
$\sigma = 10$	0.940	0.943	0.943	0.979	0.949	0.975	0.937	**0.980**	30.39	33.44	32.76	36.58	32.75	36.04	29.04	**40.01**
$\sigma = 20$	0.822	0.853	0.824	0.940	0.836	0.937	0.816	**0.945**	23.83	29.25	26.15	32.52	25.10	32.07	23.01	**34.98**
$\sigma = 30$	0.706	0.779	0.715	0.920	0.725	0.900	0.702	**0.921**	19.99	27.13	22.29	30.35	22.07	29.99	19.46	**32.34**
$\sigma = 40$	0.610	0.721	0.628	**0.892**	0.632	0.865	0.610	0.878	17.28	25.81	19.57	28.91	19.31	28.61	16.94	**30.64**
$\sigma = 50$	0.531	0.673	0.559	**0.866**	0.558	0.836	0.537	0.848	15.19	24.85	17.47	27.86	17.18	27.61	14.97	**29.39**
$\sigma = 60$	0.467	0.634	0.503	**0.843**	0.497	0.809	0.478	0.822	13.49	24.11	15.76	27.04	15.46	26.84	13.37	**28.45**
$\sigma = 70$	0.415	0.602	0.457	**0.821**	0.447	0.784	0.430	0.799	12.06	23.53	14.33	26.36	14.02	26.21	12.02	**27.69**
Zurich building database [28]																
$\sigma = 10$	0.936	0.949	0.958	**0.987**	0.960	0.983	0.952	0.984	28.89	35.47	33.04	38.09	32.10	38.12	29.06	**40.07**
$\sigma = 20$	0.839	0.894	0.866	**0.966**	0.867	0.955	0.854	0.956	22.64	31.29	26.62	33.97	25.57	33.95	23.01	**35.13**
$\sigma = 30$	0.737	0.843	0.773	**0.944**	0.766	0.926	0.754	0.927	19.00	29.26	22.86	31.71	21.79	31.70	19.46	**32.54**
$\sigma = 40$	0.647	0.799	0.691	**0.921**	0.675	0.898	0.666	0.899	16.44	27.72	20.20	30.17	19.13	30.18	16.93	**30.83**
$\sigma = 50$	0.571	0.768	0.622	**0.898**	0.597	0.872	0.593	0.872	14.46	26.57	18.15	28.98	17.08	29.03	14.97	**29.56**
$\sigma = 60$	0.507	0.728	0.563	**0.877**	0.531	0.848	0.530	0.848	12.85	25.66	16.47	28.04	15.40	28.12	13.36	**28.57**
$\sigma = 70$	0.453	0.698	0.513	**0.856**	0.476	0.826	0.478	0.825	11.49	24.93	15.06	27.27	14.01	27.36	12.01	**27.75**

Mag.: Noisy magnitude based reconstruction: reconstructed image from magnitude of noisy image (corrupted with AWGN) and phase of original image, phase: noisy phase based reconstruction: reconstructed image from phase of noisy image and magnitude of original image.

structed image is severely distorted, however most of the structural (SSIM) and statistical (PSNR) information of original image is retained by noisy phase based synthesized image (see Fig. 8).

Table 4. Average value of SSIM & PSNR measure between original and noisy magnitude and phase based reconstructed image, for Multiplicative noise.

BSDS Image Database [24]																
	Structural Similarity Index Measure								Peak Signal to Noise Ratio							
	FT		DT-CWT		CTw		CTu		FT		DT-CWT		CTw		CTu	
Noise strength	Mag.	Phase	Mag.	Phase	Mag.	Phase	Mag.	Phase	Mag.	Phase	Mag.	Phase	Mag.	Phase	Mag.	Phase
$\sigma = 0.1$	0.989	0.992	0.990	0.996	0.991	0.996	0.989	**0.997**	31.95	42.09	32.27	44.82	32.26	44.45	31.66	**49.32**
$\sigma = 0.3$	0.922	0.956	0.922	0.986	0.929	0.982	0.922	**0.987**	22.27	35.09	22.64	38.04	22.61	37.65	22.11	**41.17**
$\sigma = 0.6$	0.779	0.904	0.793	**0.969**	0.802	0.961	0.793	0.966	16.16	31.56	16.56	34.55	16.51	34.22	16.07	**36.89**
$\sigma = 1.0$	0.604	0.854	0.642	**0.951**	0.646	0.939	0.639	0.945	11.65	29.48	12.08	32.46	12.02	32.17	11.62	**34.33**
$\sigma = 1.3$	0.502	0.828	0.550	**0.940**	0.550	0.926	0.545	0.933	9.346	28.60	9.782	31.56	9.719	31.28	9.340	**33.24**
$\sigma = 1.6$	0.421	0.807	0.474	**0.931**	0.471	0.916	0.468	0.923	7.521	27.98	7.961	30.92	7.894	30.66	7.534	**32.48**
$\sigma = 2.0$	0.338	0.786	0.393	**0.921**	0.388	0.904	0.386	0.912	5.561	27.40	6.007	30.31	5.938	30.06	5.589	**31.75**
Caltech image database [25]																
$\sigma = 0.1$	0.973	0.984	0.981	0.996	0.983	0.995	0.980	**0.996**	30.05	43.92	30.74	47.13	30.65	47.25	30.22	**49.05**
$\sigma = 0.3$	0.867	0.949	0.871	**0.987**	0.880	0.982	0.869	0.982	20.48	37.52	21.13	41.10	21.02	40.93	20.66	**41.82**
$\sigma = 0.6$	0.675	0.903	0.705	**0.973**	0.710	0.964	0.697	0.963	14.46	34.12	15.07	37.81	14.96	37.57	14.63	**38.12**
$\sigma = 1.0$	0.484	0.860	0.545	**0.959**	0.540	0.945	0.529	0.943	10.03	32.03	10.61	35.73	10.50	35.49	10.18	**35.88**
$\sigma = 1.3$	0.387	0.837	0.457	**0.951**	0.446	0.934	0.439	0.932	7.758	31.12	8.327	34.81	8.212	34.56	7.906	**34.91**
$\sigma = 1.6$	0.315	0.819	0.388	**0.944**	0.374	0.925	0.368	0.923	5.961	30.47	6.516	34.14	6.400	33.90	6.094	**34.21**
$\sigma = 2.0$	0.246	0.801	0.316	**0.937**	0.301	0.916	0.296	0.914	4.031	29.86	4.571	33.50	4.456	33.27	4.152	**33.56**
IMM face database [26]																
$\sigma = 0.1$	0.992	0.994	0.995	0.996	0.995	0.996	0.993	**0.998**	36.54	45.25	36.81	47.14	36.82	47.03	36.17	**53.36**
$\sigma = 0.3$	0.939	0.968	0.958	0.983	0.960	0.982	0.946	**0.988**	26.90	38.12	27.17	40.24	27.18	40.08	26.63	**45.52**
$\sigma = 0.6$	0.799	0.931	0.851	0.969	0.855	0.966	0.827	**0.976**	20.75	35.30	21.03	37.61	21.03	37.43	20.59	**42.07**
$\sigma = 1.0$	0.599	0.898	0.686	0.958	0.690	0.954	0.656	**0.966**	16.21	33.83	16.50	36.30	16.51	36.10	16.14	**40.15**
$\sigma = 1.3$	0.477	0.881	0.576	0.953	0.579	0.947	0.545	**0.960**	13.89	33.23	14.19	35.77	14.19	35.56	13.85	**39.35**
$\sigma = 1.6$	0.383	0.868	0.485	0.949	0.486	0.942	0.453	**0.956**	12.06	32.81	12.36	35.40	12.35	35.18	12.04	**38.77**
$\sigma = 2.0$	0.292	0.855	0.388	0.945	0.387	0.937	0.357	**0.951**	10.09	32.41	10.40	35.05	10.39	34.83	10.09	**38.24**
TID2008 image database [27]																
$\sigma = 0.1$	0.988	0.991	0.990	0.996	0.991	0.995	0.988	**0.996**	31.87	41.34	32.14	44.24	32.15	43.21	31.5382	**49.16**
$\sigma = 0.3$	0.917	0.948	0.920	0.984	0.927	0.979	0.917	**0.984**	22.20	34.12	22.50	37.45	22.51	36.88	21.9896	**41.02**
$\sigma = 0.6$	0.772	0.888	0.787	**0.966**	0.796	0.956	0.783	0.963	16.08	30.54	16.41	33.96	16.40	33.46	15.9573	**36.75**
$\sigma = 1.0$	0.598	0.833	0.634	**0.948**	0.639	0.933	0.627	0.941	11.56	28.49	11.92	31.87	11.90	31.46	11.5072	**34.21**
$\sigma = 1.3$	0.496	0.804	0.542	**0.937**	0.543	0.919	0.533	0.929	9.253	27.63	9.624	30.97	9.597	30.59	9.2216	**33.13**
$\sigma = 1.6$	0.416	0.783	0.466	**0.928**	0.464	0.909	0.456	0.918	7.419	27.03	7.798	30.34	7.768	30.01	7.4087	**32.38**
$\sigma = 2.0$	0.334	0.761	0.385	**0.918**	0.381	0.897	0.374	0.907	5.458	26.46	5.845	29.72	5.811	29.41	5.4664	**31.63**
Zurich building database [28]																
$\sigma = 0.1$	0.972	0.975	0.989	0.997	0.990	0.996	0.987	**0.998**	30.35	42.51	31.35	45.68	31.31	45.27	30.73	**48.62**
$\sigma = 0.3$	0.906	0.944	0.924	**0.990**	0.930	0.983	0.919	0.984	20.85	35.53	21.75	39.01	21.66	38.73	21.18	**40.65**
$\sigma = 0.6$	0.771	0.903	0.805	**0.977**	0.809	0.965	0.798	0.965	14.86	32.33	15.68	35.54	15.58	35.28	15.15	**36.57**
$\sigma = 1.0$	0.607	0.864	0.666	**0.964**	0.659	0.946	0.654	0.946	10.46	30.21	11.22	33.42	11.11	33.18	10.70	**34.15**
$\sigma = 1.3$	0.509	0.851	0.579	**0.956**	0.566	0.935	0.565	0.934	8.201	29.02	8.928	32.47	8.817	32.24	8.414	**33.09**
$\sigma = 1.6$	0.430	0.827	0.505	**0.949**	0.488	0.926	0.489	0.925	6.417	28.62	7.118	31.79	7.005	31.59	6.609	**32.36**
$\sigma = 2.0$	0.349	0.811	0.424	**0.941**	0.404	0.917	0.407	0.915	4.496	27.75	5.146	31.14	5.052	30.97	4.662	**31.65**

The variation in original feature information for noisy phase and magnitude based reconstructed images are summarized in Table 3 for additive noise and in Table 4 for multiplicative noise on different image databases. The average SSIM and PSNR values are shown in these tables are used for the quantitative analysis of phase and magnitude sensitivity with respect to noise, when image is corrupted with either additive or multiplicative noise. The following few facts may be highlighted from these results-

a. While magnitude is distorted, phase is remains less sensitive to noise.
b. Most of the statistical (PSNR) and structural (SSIM) information of undistorted image is retained by the complex domain phase.
c. The locally referenced phases in DT-CWT and FDCT (or CT) preserves more signal energy (with high PSNR) and retains most image structural information compared to globally referenced phase of FT.
d. Wavelet phase retains more structural information of image, while curvelet phase (computed via. USFFT) is more immune to noise (with high PSNR value).
e. The two implementation methods of curvelet transform differs from each other by the choice of spatial window in frequency domain. Since wrapping is an approximation method of curvelet transform that wraps the coefficients around the rectangular window at the origin, hence loses some of the signal information. Therefore, though wrapping (CTw) is a fast method of implementation among the two, its phase is less immune to noise compared to USFFT (CTu).

6 Conclusion

For both one and multidimensional signal processing the magnitude and phase of complex transform play different roles in signal reconstruction. In this article we quantitatively investigate their information retention capability using edge mismatch error (EMM). The results indicate that the phase only reconstructed image retains most of the image information than magnitude only reconstruction. Moreover between ARP (in FT) and RRP (in CWT and FDCT), Fourier phase preserves more edges compared to its magnitude.

This article also provides a theoretical and experimental analysis to understand the effect of noise on both phase and magnitude of different complex transforms. A simple derivation of sensitivity (i.e. the rate of change of magnitude or phase of noisy image per noise magnitude) mathematically supports the importance of phase over magnitude, for image reconstruction from noisy observations. Our analysis not only examines the effect of noise on phase and magnitude for signal independent additive noise, but also investigates their behavior for correlated multiplicative noise. The experimental results indicate that phases preserve structural similarity more than that by magnitude. It is also observed that the phase based reconstructed image is less degraded by noise than magnitude based synthesized image, with high PSNR value. Therefore, this analysis would motivate to consider phase over magnitude for signal understanding, representation and characterization.

References

1. Kingsbury, N.: Image processing with complex wavelets. Philos. Transact. Royal Soc. London A: Math. Phys. Eng. Sci. **357**(1760), 2543–2560 (1999)
2. Ma, J., Plonka, G.: The curvelet transform. Signal Process. Mag. IEEE **27**(2), 118–133 (2010)
3. Brown, R., Lauzon, M.L., Frayne, R., et al.: A general description of linear time-frequency transforms and formulation of a fast, invertible transform that samples the continuous s-transform spectrum nonredundantly. Signal Process. IEEE Transact. **58**(1), 281–290 (2010)
4. Selesnick, I.W., Baraniuk, R.G., Kingsbury, N.C.: The dual-tree complex wavelet transform. Signal Process. Mag. IEEE **22**(6), 123–151 (2005)
5. Candes, E., Demanet, L., Donoho, D., Ying, L.: Fast discrete curvelet transforms. Multiscale Model. Simul. **5**(3), 861–899 (2006)
6. Stockwell, R.G., Mansinha, L., Lowe, R.: Localization of the complex spectrum: the S transform. Signal Process. IEEE Transact. **44**(4), 998–1001 (1996)
7. Kovesi, P.: Phase preserving denoising of images. Signal **49**(3), 1 (1999)
8. Oppenheim, A.V., Lim, J.S.: The importance of phase in signals. Proc. IEEE **69**(5), 529–541 (1981)
9. Panigrahi, S.K., Gupta, S.: Quantitative evaluation of image information retention by relative phases. In: 2013 Students Conference on Engineering and Systems (SCES), pp. 1–6. IEEE (2013)
10. Panigrahi, S.K., Gupta, S., Sahu, P.K.: Phases under Gaussian additive noise. In: 2016 International Conference on Communication and Signal Processing (ICCSP), pp. 1771–1776. IEEE (2016)
11. Torralba, A., Oliva, A.: Statistics of natural image categories. Netw. Comput. Neural Syst. **14**(3), 391–412 (2003)
12. Kovesi, P.: Phase congruency detects corners and edges. In: The Australian Pattern Recognition Society Conference, DICTA 2003 (2003)
13. Zitova, B., Flusser, J.: Image registration methods: a survey. Image Vis. Comput. **21**(11), 977–1000 (2003)
14. Tanaka, H., Yoshida, Y., Fukami, K., Nakano, H.: Texture segmentation using amplitude and phase information of Gabor filters. Electron. Commun. Jpn. Part III Fundam. Electron. Sci. **87**(4), 66–79 (2004)
15. Gupta, S., Panigrahi, S.K.: Joint bilateral filter for signal recovery from phase preserved curvelet coefficients for image denoising. arXiv preprint arXiv:1804.05512 (2018)
16. Panigrahi, S.K., Gupta, S., Sahu, P.K.: Curvelet-based multiscale denoising using non-local means & guided image filter. IET Image Process. **12**(6), 909–918 (2018)
17. Buades, A., Coll, B., Morel, J.M.: On image denoising methods. CMLA Preprint, vol. 5 (2004)
18. Zhao, Y., Liu, J.G., Zhang, B., Hong, W., Wu, Y.-R.: Adaptive total variation regularization based sar image despeckling and despeckling evaluation index. IEEE Trans. Geosci. Remote Sens. **53**(5), 2765–2774 (2015)
19. Skarbnik, N., Zeevi, Y.Y., Sagiv, C.: The importance of phase in image processing. Ph.D. thesis, Technion-Israel Institute of Technology, Faculty of Electrical Engineering (2009)
20. Morrone, M.C., Owens, R.A.: Feature detection from local energy. Pattern Recogn. Lett. **6**(5), 303–313 (1987)

21. Panigrahi, S.K., Gupta, S.: Automatic ranking of image thresholding techniques using consensus of ground truth. Traitement du Signal **35**(2), 121 (2018)
22. Sezgin, M., et al.: Survey over image thresholding techniques and quantitative performance evaluation. J. Electron. Imaging **13**(1), 146–168 (2004)
23. Pellegrino, F.A., Vanzella, W., Torre, V.: Edge detection revisited. Syst. Man Cybern. Part B Cybern. IEEE Transact. **34**(3), 1500–1518 (2004)
24. Martin, D., Fowlkes, C., Tal, D., Malik, J.: A database of human segmented natural images and its application to evaluating segmentation algorithms and measuring ecological statistics. In: Proceedings of Eighth IEEE International Conference on Computer Vision 2001, ICCV 2001, vol. 2, pp. 416–423. IEEE (2001)
25. Fei-Fei, L., Fergus, R., Perona, P.: Learning generative visual models from few training examples: an incremental Bayesian approach tested on 101 object categories. Comput. Vis. Image Underst. **106**(1), 59–70 (2007)
26. Nordstrøm, M.M., Larsen, M., Sierakowski, J., Stegmann, M.B.: The imm face database-an annotated dataset of 240 face images. Technical report Technical University of Denmark, DTU Informatics, Building 321 (2004)
27. Ponomarenko, N., Lukin, V., Zelensky, A., Egiazarian, K., Carli, M., Battisti, F.: Tid2008-a database for evaluation of full-reference visual quality assessment metrics. Adv. Mod. Radioelectr. **10**(4), 30–45 (2009)
28. Shao, H., Svoboda, T., Van Gool, L.: Zubud-zurich buildings database forimage based recognition. Computer Vision Lab, Swiss Federal Institute of Technology, Switzerland, Technical Report, vol. 260 (2003)
29. Richards, M.A.: The discrete-time Fourier transform and discrete Fourier transform of windowed stationary white noise. Technical Memorandum, November 2013
30. Wang, Z., Bovik, A.C., Sheikh, H.R., Simoncelli, E.P.: Image quality assessment: from error visibility to structural similarity. Image Process. IEEE Transact. **13**(4), 600–612 (2004)

Comparative Study of Segmentation Techniques Used for Optic Disc Segmentation

Shivesh Madhawa Shukla[✉], Amit Kaul, and Ravinder Nath

Department of Electrical Engineering, National Institute of Technology,
Hamirpur, India
shivmshuk@gmail.com

Abstract. Fundus image, picture of posterior portion of eye, facilitates non-intrusive diagnosis of various eye diseases. Glaucoma is progressive neurode-generative ocular disorder, second leading cause of blindness in the world. For diagnosis of Glaucoma using fundus image, cup to disc ratio is the method preferred by researchers. Various methods like Active Contour, K-mean Clustering and Thresholding method are used to segment cup and disk from fundus images. In this paper a comparative study of the above mentioned methods has been presented. These methods were independently tested on two public databases namely DRISHTI-GS, and DRIONS-DB. Based upon the results obtained it was found that active contour technique is best among these methods.

Keywords: Fundus image analysis · Glaucoma · Computer-aided diagnosis · ONH segmentation

1 Introduction

Non-intrusive diagnosis of diseases is rapidly gaining attention of researchers. Retina is extension of brain; many eye and systemic diseases like Cataract, Glaucoma, and Diabetic Retinopathy (DR) can be identified with help of fundus images. After cataract, glaucoma is the second leading cause of blindness but glaucoma is leading cause of irreversible blindness with nearly 12 million people affected and nearly 1.2 million people blind from this disease[1]. However, person to ophthalmologist ratio is 10,000:1 [1]. Thus, there is need to develop computer-aided diagnosis methods to facilitate ophthalmologists.

Segmentation of optic disc is not limited to glaucoma but it is one of the fundamental steps in retinal image processing. Only after segmentation of optic disc, fundus images can be further processed for presence of exudate which is one of the prime indicators of diabetic retinopathy. Optic disc has unique features like colour, intensity, size, brightness, shape and vessel information, in spite of this localization and segmentation of optic disc is very challenging task. Initial attempts to localize and segment optic disc employed shape based template matching in which optic nerve head is supposed to be circular [2, 3] or elliptical [4]. Lalonde *et al.* localized optic disc using

---

[1] https://www.nhp.gov.in/disease/eye-ear/glaucoma.

© Springer Nature Singapore Pte Ltd. 2019
M. Singh et al. (Eds.): ICACDS 2019, CCIS 1046, pp. 643–654, 2019.
https://doi.org/10.1007/978-981-13-9942-8_60

Haar discrete wavelet transform and template matching based on Hausdorff to segment optic nerve head. Lu [5] and GeethaRamani et al. [6] used template matching method to localize optic disc and morphological method to segment it. Circular average filter is used in [7] to localise optic disc and combination of morphological operations and active contour technique to segment optic disc. In [8] active contour model is utilised to detect optic disc boundary in fundus image. In [9] region growing technique is used to segment optic disc. Feature based detection method combined with scale space algorithm were used to mark boundary of optic disc in [10]. Combination of circular Hough transform and morphological operation is used to segment optic disc in [11]. Moreover if some features like colour, intensity are missing in fundus image then the results obtained using these methods has less accuracy.

Anatomical information, like converging of retinal vessels to a point inside optic disc is utilised by few researchers to localize optic disc. In [12] 2-D localisation approach is converted into two 1-D localization problem. Horizontal coordinate is a point that has maximum ratio of sum of edge difference to sum of pixel intensity inside window. Similarly vertical coordinate is determined by finding location where multiplication of sum of edge sum with sum of pixels intensity inside window comes out to be maximum. This method is very fast in localizing optic disc but lacks accuracy when fundus image has many vertical sub vessels, optic disc is not bright and in case of image artifacts.

Recent trends in research include combining various existing method with aim of achieving higher accuracy. Sudhan et al. [13] utilised Bat algorithm, Otsu's based multi-thresholding, K-mean, and level set approach for optic disc segmentation. Choukikar et al. [14] performed image enhancement using histogram equalization on grayscale images, and segmented optic disc using gray level thresholding. In [15] tri-level thresholding based on Firefly Algorithm (FA) in combination of Kapur's entropy and K-means clustering method is used to segment optic disc. In [16] morphological operations, K-means clustering, and Connected Component Analysis (CCA) is used to segment optic disc. Nugroho et al. [17] extracted red channel form colour fundus image and applied average filter to remove noise. Subsequently used bottom hat transform to remove blood vessels in fundus image. Joshi et al. [18] combined local image information in multidimensional space around each point of interest to increase robustness of algorithm around OD region. Multi stage strategy called r-bends in combination with local spline fitting is used to mark cup boundary. In [19] contrast adjustment, morphological operation, and filtering is used to process fundus image and remove vasculature from fundus image. Region growing technique is used to segment optic disc and centre of optic disc is taken as seed point. In [20] uses Circular Hough Transform to roughly segment optic disc. This approximated optic disc is now used to compute initial optic disc and cup shape. Cascaded shape regression method iteratively learns the final shape of optic disc and cup from given initial shape. In [21] on contrast enhanced red channel, combination of Hough transform, morphological operation and K-means clustering is used to mark region of interest. Feature extraction was done using combination of Markov Random Field Least Estimates and Grey Level Co-Occurrence Matrix. Finally classification of image was done using support vector machine. In [22] comparative study between two methods has been done. First method utilizes Gabor convolution to detect glaucoma using histogram features. Second method utilizes structural and non-structural features for detection of Glaucoma. The histogram feature method has maximum accuracy. In [23] classification is done using cascade correlation neural network, local mesh pattern is used to generate features, segmentation of optic disk and optic cup is performed using fuzzy C-means clustering algorithm.

2   Threshold Method

Down sampling of image to resolution 400×600 saves computational time and has negligible effect on optic disc segmentation [5]. Mask is generated by convolving red channel of retinal image with Gaussian low pass filter keeping standard deviation equal to 0.8 [24]. The resultant image is then threshold using Otsu's global threshold [25]. Now generated mask is multiplied with red channel to generate desired image. Red channel of any coloured image has maximum brightness and green channel has maximum contrast. In red channel optic disc is clearly visible while in case of green channel edges generated due to blood vessels will reduce efficiency of segmentation methods.

Histogram equalization refers to technique of adjusting pixel intensity to enhance contrast of an image. Let I be an image having 'r' rows and 'c' column and image intensity varying between 0 to $L - 1$ were largest possible value of L is 256 for grayscale image. Let N_n denote normalised histogram of image (I) for all possible intensities.

$$N_n = \frac{\text{Number of pixel with intensity n}}{\text{Total number of pixel}} \qquad (1)$$

Thresholding means binarize an image with respect to an intensity level. The pixels having intensity below desired intensity is set to 0 and pixels having intensity above desired intensity is set to 1. In red channel of fundus image, optic disc is visible as cluster of bright pixels thus thresholding can be used for segmenting optic disc. Fundus images having prominent blood vessels inside optic disc region leads to cluster of 0 intensity pixels inside optic disc region.

Grayscale image $(G_{x,y})$ generated by extracting red channel of fundus image has pixels intensity varying in between 0–255. The threshold (Th) is set to 251 in case of histogram equalized image.

$$b_{x,y} = \begin{cases} 0 & if\ G_{x,y} < Th \\ 1 & if\ G_{x,y} > Th \end{cases} \qquad (2)$$

where $b_{x,y}$ is binary image, optic disc boundary is smoothen and unwanted pixels are erased using morphological operations like erosion. After process of erosion some pixel in optic disc will also be erased, so dilation is used to reconstruct the image. Figure 1 shows results obtained using threshold method on images taken from DRIONS-DB database.

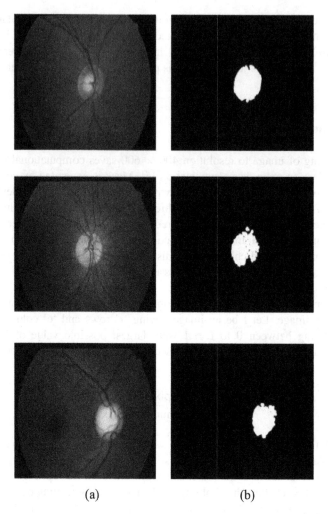

(a)   (b)

Fig. 1. Threshold method result, (a) Input image, (b) Segmented optic disc

3   K-Means Clustering

Clustering is unsupervised learning method in which pixel with similar features is separated into groups in an image. Clustering can be thought as an optimization problem where attempt is made to minimize dissimilarity between clusters with constraints like clusters must have minimum distance between them.

$$Variability(c) = \sum_{e \in C} distance(mean(c), e)^2 \qquad (3)$$

where c is single cluster and square of Euclidean distance between mean of the cluster is calculated. Dissimilarity is sum of all variability in a group of clusters.

$$Dissimilarity(C) = \sum_{c \in C} variability(c) \qquad (4)$$

where C = group of clusters, and without constraints minimization of dissimilarity will lead to as many clusters as there is point because variability and dissimilarity will be zero.

Out of many clustering technique available like hierarchical, fuzzy C-mean and K-means: K-means is used in majority of applications. K-means is an efficient clustering technique where data is divided into k groups or clusters user wants. To each cluster a centroid is assigned and distance between a point and cluster centroid is calculated. Point is assigned to a cluster having least distance between them; again update the centroids of respective clusters and this process continues until there is no change in centroid position.

K-means clustering requires less computation time as compared to hierarchical clustering. Hierarchical clustering has time complexity of N^3, while in case of K-means a data having k centroids, n points and takes d time for each clusters.

$$Time \ required(T) = k \times n \times d \qquad (5)$$

which is quite less as compared to time complexity of N^2.

The main disadvantage of K-means clustering algorithm is a-priori knowledge of number of clusters (k) and high dependence on initial centroid selection. One way to overcome the problem is to apply hierarchical clustering on subset of data and estimate k. Another method is to select multiple set of randomly chosen initial centroids, apply K-means and compute dissimilarity between set of centroids, a set whose dissimilarity comes out to be minimum is ideal centroid. Unlike hierarchical clustering, K-means clustering is non-deterministic in initial phase prior to centroid selection and it is unable to identify clusters with arbitrary shapes, thereby imposing hyper-spherical cluster on data.

3.1   Step by Step Procedure for Obtaining K Clusters Using K-Means Algorithm Is Given Below

Input: Data to be clustered and Number of clusters (k)
   Output: Clustered data
   Method:

   i. Create k clusters and assign them a centroid
  ii. Compute distance between a point and k centroids
 iii. Distance to a cluster centroid which comes out to be least is cluster to which point belongs
  iv. Repeat this procedure for each point in data
   v. Update centroid and again assign a point to a cluster depending upon distance
  vi. Repeat whole process until there is no change in centroid position in successive iterations.

Figure 2 shows result obtained using K-means clustering, left column contains input image from DRIONS-DB database, right column contains zoom in view of optic disc with optic disc, cup and Neuroretinal Rim depicted with different colour.

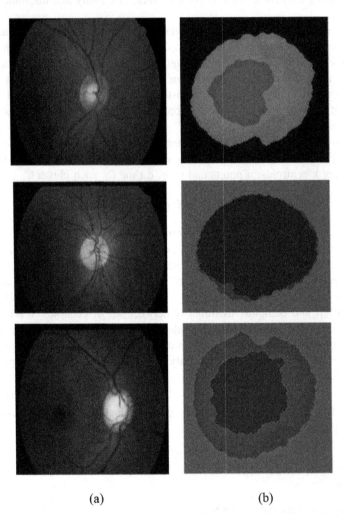

(a)   (b)

Fig. 2. K-means clustering results, (a) Input image, (b) segmented optic disk and cup. (Color figure online)

4 Active Contour

Thresholding and K-means method perform segmentation pixel by pixel but human being segment objects in an image depending upon geometry or curve. Active contour method tries to exploit this idea using image features like shape of object and intensity of pixels inside object.

Active contour model is also known as snakes, snake is energy minimizing, deformable spline controlled by constraints and an image feature that pulls snake towards object boundary and internal forces resists deformation. Energy function of snakes is composed of internal and external energy.

$$E(c) = E_{internal}(c) + E_{external}(c) \qquad (6)$$

where internal energy depends only on shape of curve i.e. continuity and smoothness of contour, while external energy depends on image intensity.

$$E_{int}(c) = \int_0^1 \propto \|c'(s)\|^2 + \beta \|c''(s)\|^2 ds \qquad (7)$$

c'(s) represents how stretched the curve is and it tries to keep point on curve while c''(s) prevents point on curve from oscillating.

$$E_{ext}(c) = \int_0^1 -\|\nabla I(C(S))\|^2 ds \qquad (8)$$

For minimizing energy, curve approximation method is used; objects boundary is divided into k discrete points and curve inch along points until points around boundary stops changing.

4.1 Method

Optic disc segmentation using Active contour method requires following steps. (a) Red channel extraction, (b) Gaussian blurring, (c) morphological operation, (d) selecting Region of Interest (RoI) or mask generation, (e) implement active contour method. In this work Chan-Vese model [26] has been used. In absence of strong edges snakes does not contract, this problem occurs when optic disc boundary is blurred. Noise is to be filtered because noise will generate small gradient and contour gets hung up on them. Figure 3 shows result obtained using active contour method, left column contains input image from DRIONS-DB database. Right column contains segmented optic disc; different anatomical structure of optic disc is represented with different colours.

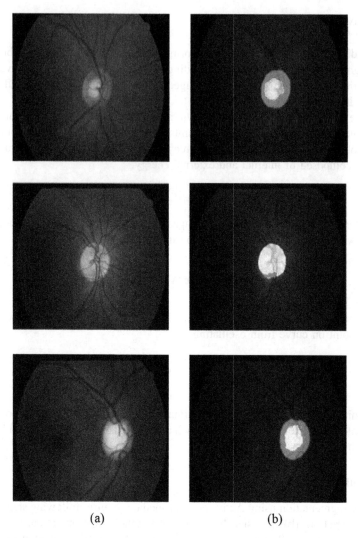

(a)   (b)

Fig. 3. Active contour method results, (a) Input image, (b) segmented optic disk and cup. (Color figure online)

5   Results

Out of three methods compared, threshold method requires least computation time and can be used for real time implementation but with little more time clustering method like K-means provide better results. Active contour has better maneuverability along edges but it takes more time as compared to other two methods. Computation time presented in this paper is sum of time consumed by morphological operation and time consumed by respective method.

Quantitative analysis is used to analyze overall performance of optic disc segmentation. For testing performance of methods, images from test section of DRISHTI-GS dataset were used. DRISHTI-GS method consists of total 101 images divided into two sections i.e. test and train each consisting of 51 and 50 images respectively. Pixel wise value of Sensitivity, Specificity, Accuracy, Dice coefficient, and Jaccard index is calculated. These parameters are defined as

$$\text{Sensitivity} = \frac{tp}{tp + fn} \tag{9}$$

$$\text{Specificity} = \frac{tn}{tn + fp} \tag{10}$$

$$\text{Accuracy} = \frac{tp + tn}{tp + tn + fp + fn} \tag{11}$$

$$\text{Dice} = \frac{2tp}{2tp + fp + fn} \tag{12}$$

where tp is number of correctly identified foreground pixels, tn is number of correctly identified background pixels, fp is number of background pixel identified as foreground pixel, and fn is number of foreground pixels identified as background pixels. Sensitivity can be understood as ratio of number of correctly identified foreground pixels (tp) to the total number of foreground pixels (tp + fn) i.e. Sensitivity is measure of how precisely algorithm is able to identify foreground pixels or optic disk. Specificity is measure of how precisely algorithm is able to identify background pixels. Accuracy is measure of how precisely algorithm has detected foreground and background pixels. Table 1 represents assessment of disc segmentation results using sensitivity, specificity, accuracy, Dice, and Jaccard.

Table 1. Quantitative assessment of optic disc segmentation using different methods

Parameters	Methods		
	Threshold	K-means	Active contour
Sensitivity	0.7644	0.9454	0.9629
Specificity	0.9970	0.9991	0.9966
Accuracy	0.9881	0.9973	0.9954
Dice	0.8129	0.8692	0.9331
Jaccard	0.7265	0.7753	0.8999
Computation time (sec)	0.59	0.96	1.15

6 Conclusion

Threshold method doesn't require a-priori knowledge of image; it is computationally inexpensive and can be used in real time application. This method neglects spatial information; detected optic disc boundary consists of discrete pixels and can be discontinuous.

K-means clustering approach requires more computation time then threshold method but produces more homogeneous regions with continuous boundary. Difficulty with K-means is segmented boundary is not smooth or K-means method is not able to trace boundary of optic disc with greater precision as active contour does.

Active contour method performs best; it has high maneuverability on boundary of optic disc. In some fundus image having blurred optic disc boundary due to lack of strong image gradient method fails to precisely envelope boundary of optic disc.

A combination of these methods can be used to automate and segment optic disk with higher accuracy as compared to individual methods.

References

1. Murthy, G.V., Gupta, S.K., Bachani, D., Jose, R., John, N.: Current estimates of blindness in India. Br. J. Ophthalmol. **89**, 257–260 (2005)
2. Chrástek, R., Wolf, M., Donath, K., Michelson, G., Niemann, H.: Optic disc segmentation in retinal images. In: Meiler, M., Saupe, D., Kruggel, F., Handels, H., Lehmann, T.M. (eds.) BVM 2002. INFORMAT, pp. 263–266. Springer, Heidelberg (2002). https://doi.org/10.1007/978-3-642-55983-9_60
3. Abdel-Ghafar, R.A., Morris, T.: Progress towards automated detection and characterization of the optic disc in glaucoma and diabetic retinopathy. Inform. Health Soc. Care **32**(1), 19–25 (2007)
4. Pallawala, P.M.D.S., Hsu, W., Lee, M.L., Eong, K.-G.A.: Automated optic disc localization and contour detection using ellipse fitting and wavelet transform. In: Pajdla, T., Matas, J. (eds.) ECCV 2004. LNCS, vol. 3022, pp. 139–151. Springer, Heidelberg (2004). https://doi.org/10.1007/978-3-540-24671-8_11
5. Lu, S.: Accurate and efficient optic disc detection and segmentation by a circular transformation. IEEE Trans. Med. Imaging **30**, 2126–2133 (2011). https://doi.org/10.1109/TMI.2011.216426
6. GeethaRamani, R., Dhanapackiam, C.: Automatic localization and segmentation of Optic Disc in retinal fundus images through image processing techniques. In: International Conference on Recent Trends in Information Technology, Chennai, pp. 1–5 (2014). https://doi.org/10.1109/ICRTIT.2014.6996090
7. Nugroho, H.A., Listyalina, L., Setiawan, N.A., Wibirama, S., Dharmawan, D.A.: Automated segmentation of optic disc area using mathematical morphology and active contour. In: International Conference on Computer, Control, Informatics and its Applications (IC3INA), Bandung, pp. 18–22 (2015). https://doi.org/10.1109/IC3INA.2015.7377739
8. Kass, A., Witkin, A., Terzopoulos, D.: Snakes: active contour models. Int. J. Comput. Vis. **1**, 321–331 (1987)

9. Omid, S., Shanbehzadeh, J., Ghassabi, Z., Ostadzadeh, S.S.: Optic disc detection in high-resolution retinal fundus images by region growing. In: 8th International Conference on Biomedical Engineering and Informatics (BMEI), Shenyang, pp. 101–105 (2015). https://doi.org/10.1109/BMEI.2015.7401481

10. Duanggate, C., Uyyanonvara, B., Makhanov, S.S., Barman, S., Williamson, T.H.: Parameter-free optic disc detection. Comput. Med. Imag. Graph. **35**, 51–63 (2011)

11. Aquino, A., Gegundez-Arias, M.E., Marin, D.: Detecting the optic disc boundary in digital fundus images using morphological, edge detection, and feature extraction techniques. IEEE Trans. Med. Imaging **29**, 1860–1869 (2010). https://doi.org/10.1109/TMI.2010.2053042

12. Mahfouz, A.E., Fahmy, A.S.: Fast localization of the optic disc using projection of image features. IEEE Trans. Image Process. **19**, 3285–3289 (2010)

13. Sudhan, G.H.H., Aravind, R.G., Gowri, K., Rajinikanth, V.: Optic disc segmentation based on Otsu's thresholding and level set. In: International Conference on Computer Communication and Informatics (ICCCI), pp. 1–5. IEEE (2017). https://doi.org/10.1109/ICCCI.2017.8117688

14. Choukikar, P., Patel, A., Mishra, R.: Segmenting the optic disc in retinal images using thresholding. Int. J. Comput. Appl. **94**(11), 6–10 (2014)

15. Kowsalya, N., Kalyani, A., Chalcedony, C.J., Sivakumar, R., Janani, M., Rajinikanth, V.: An approach to extract optic-disc from retinal image using K-means Clustering. In: 4th International conference on Biosignals, Images and Instrumentation (ICBSII) (2018)

16. Sharma, N., Verma, A.: Segmentation and detection of optic disc using K-means clustering. Int. J. Sci. Eng. Res. **6**, 237–240 (2015)

17. Nugroho, H.A., Ilcham, Jalil, A., Ardiyanto, I.: Segmentation of optic disc on retinal fundus images using morphological reconstruction enhancement and active contour. In: 2nd International Conference on Science in Information Technology (2016)

18. Joshi, G.D., Sivaswamy, J., Krishnadas, S.R.: Optic disc and cup segmentation from monocular color retinal images for glaucoma assessment. IEEE Trans. Med. Imaging **30**, 1192–1205 (2011)

19. Singh, A., Dutta, M.K., Parthasarathi, M., Burget, R., Riha, K.: An efficient automatic method of optic disc segmentation using region growing technique in retinal images. In: International Conference on Contemporary Computing and Informatics (IC3I), pp. 480–484 (2014)

20. Sedai, S., Roy, P.K., Mahapatra, D., Garnavi, R.: Segmentation of optic disc and optic cup in retinal fundus images using shape regression. In: 38th Annual International Conference of the IEEE Engineering in Medicine and Biology Society (EMBC), pp. 3260–3264 (2016). https://doi.org/10.1109/EMBC.2016.7591424

21. Kavya, N., Padmaja, K.V.: Glaucoma detection using texture features extraction. In: 51st Asilomar Conference on Signals, Systems, and Computers, pp. 1471–1475 (2017). https://doi.org/10.1109/ACSSC.2017.8335600

22. Khunger, M., Choudhury, T., Satapathy, S.C., Ting, K.C.: Automated detection of glaucoma using image processing techniques. In: Abraham, A., Dutta, P., Mandal, J., Bhattacharya, A., Dutta, S. (eds.) Emerging Technologies in Data Mining and Information Security. AISC, vol. 814, pp. 323–335. Springer, Singapore (2019). https://doi.org/10.1007/978-981-13-1501-5_28

23. Devasia, T., Jacob, K.P., Thomas, T.: Automatic early stage glaucoma detection using cascade correlation neural network. In: Satapathy, S.C., Bhateja, V., Das, S. (eds.) Smart Intelligent Computing and Applications. SIST, vol. 104, pp. 659–669. Springer, Singapore (2019). https://doi.org/10.1007/978-981-13-1921-1_64

24. Hashim, F.A., Salem, N.M., Seddik, A.F.: Preprocessing of color retinal fundus images. In: Second International Japan-Egypt Conference on Electronics, Communications and Computers, pp. 190–193 (2013)
25. Otsu, N.: A Threshold selection method from gray-level histograms. IEEE Trans. Syst. Man Cybern. **9**, 62–66 (1979)
26. Chan, T., Vese, L.: Active contours without edges. IEEE Trans. Image Process. **10**, 266–277 (2001)

Next Generation Noise and Affine Invariant Video Watermarking Scheme Using Harris Feature Extraction

Himanshu Agarwal[1](✉), Farooq Husain[2], and Praveen Saini[1]

[1] Department of Computer Science and Engineering,
Moradabad Institute of Technology, Moradabad, India
himanshu.agg2000@gmail.com, praveensaini5@gmail.com
[2] Department of Electronics and Communication Engineering,
Moradabad Institute of Technology, Moradabad, India
farooqhusain100@gmail.com

Abstract. Digital watermarking always attracts the attention of researchers from early nineties to present scenario, in the ever changing world of digital creation, transmission and modification of information. In this paper we draw our attention towards a next generation of digital watermarking based on specific features of digital information using Harris corner detection (strongest) method. In this scheme first twenty strongest corner points obtained using Harris method are used as a reference for embedding watermark information and to retain the synchronization information after distortions. The scheme is time efficient as only twenty strongest corner points per frame are computed. Hence the proposed scheme is useful for time constrained applications. The experimental results confirms that the suggested scheme show a adequate level of resilience against the majority of image processing attacks together with affine transformations.

Keywords: Perceptually significant features · Intentional attacks ·
Next generation watermarking · Autocorrelation function

1 Introduction

Due to the exponential growth of multimedia technology and ubiquitous networks the easy access, modification, broadcasting and reproduction to digital information may cause considerable financial loss to the owner. There are a numerous ways aiming to solve these problems including legal protection, digital rights management and copyright protection.

Digital watermarking gives the creator of information a safeguard against these losses by embedding the watermark into digital host data and when required extract the watermark to prove his/her the ownership to a court against unauthorized processing and broadcasting of digital information. Other prominent areas of digital watermarking include authentication [1], copy control [2], temper detection [3] and fingerprinting [4]. For multimedia objects, like images, videos and sound the problem of the protection of copyright against piracy, or false ownership claims take a lot of attention of the

© Springer Nature Singapore Pte Ltd. 2019
M. Singh et al. (Eds.): ICACDS 2019, CCIS 1046, pp. 655–665, 2019.
https://doi.org/10.1007/978-981-13-9942-8_61

researchers these days. Even though watermarking is one of promising solution against the losses of owner but embedding additional information in the host data can cause damage of vital information of the host data. Considering this parameter is it important to design an effective scheme which embed the watermarking information and at the same time preserve the vital information of the host data.

The first record of visible watermarking was applied on paper in Italy in 1282 B.C. [5]. This method was introduced by papermakers in order to mark and identify their products. Back to 1983 [6], the initial work on hiding digital data in to the host signal named as "Writing on dirty paper", was carried out from the viewpoint of communication theory, while the first meticulous work on digital watermarking was presented in 1997 [7]. Till than a lot of improvement has been carried out in digital signal processing techniques by many researchers to efficiently utilize this field of engineering and technology.

According to the data embedding techniques we classify the watermarking methods into two broad categories: Spatial domain [8] and transform domain [9]. Many researcher [8, 10, 11] develop attractive solutions to encounter unauthorized processing of digital information using spatial pixels directly. These pixel values are modified by change the least significant bits of the pixel because this resulted very less or no visible change in the digital data. Methods in this domain have low data processing complexity but they can be easily wrecked out by simple signal processing attacks like rotating, filtering, JPEG compression and even watermark becomes unreadable by most of the noise attacks [11]. To overcome the problems encountered in the spatial domain the method of frequency domains transforms was proposed by [12]. Frequency domain methods first decompose the digital information in various frequency components and than use the transformed frequency coefficients to embed the watermarking information. Discrete cosine transform (DCT) and discrete wavelet transform (DWT) [13] are much popular decomposition techniques used by the researcher. Transform domain methods are considered by many researchers to have better properties than those operating in the spatial domain.

But now a days, more sophisticated attacks against watermarking systems works and the schemes designed by the earlier researchers [13–15] does not provide a safeguard against specialized intentional attacks. In general, attacks against watermarking schemes can be categorized into simple signal processing attacks [15] such as translation, rotation, sub sampling, histogram stretching, compression and specialized intentional attacks like swapping, averaging, deletion and insertion of frames including various types of noise [15, 16]. Most of these attacks reduce watermark energy between the original and the extracted watermark due to the poor location selection procedure for watermark embedding. The drawback of all most all the schemes described so far is that there is no proper relationship between the watermark and the significant features of the data and hence such schemes are likely to suffer by the attacks that destroying the commercial importance of the host data. The techniques discussed above are often motioned to as first generation digital watermarking schemes. As first generation techniques have been mainly focused on embedding the watermark on the complete image/video domain so these schemes are not compatible newer approaches (JPEG 2000, MPEG4/7 or likewise schemes) of image and video compression.

A lot of modern computer practices such as computer vision, machine learning, video tracking, motion detection and pattern recognition use features as their backbone. We can really extract a lot of information from features depending on the problem or the nature of the application. Next generation watermarking is based on the perceptually significant features of the data. Because all the features are not significantly useful, so careful selection of semantically meaningful data features are so much important in next generation watermarking schemes. If we take the example of images, significant features are the edges, textured areas or corners. Selected data features appropriate for watermarking purpose must have the following basic properties:

1. The features should not vary if noise is added or compression is performed in the host data. It is called invariance property of the data against noise and compression. Noise signal may be of any type such as additive, multiplicative or Gaussian noise. Compression can vary from novel to modern techniques of image and video compression. The invariance property ensures that noise/compression do not alter the features of the data and hence retains the commercial value of the data.
2. If some of the data should be altered than it should not effect on the remaining part of the data. It is called localized property of the data. Localized property is perhaps the most difficult property to achieve [16]. For example, if we crop some part of the data than remaining features of the data should not change and show resilience against cropping and likewise attacks.
3. Data should retain its form when the data is linearly transformed by some degree of geometrical transformations such as translation, rotation, scaling, sub-sampling, mirroring or in change of aspect ratio. It is called covariance property of data. To achieve this property we choose the data features in a manner that a reasonable amount of geometrical changes should not modify the data features significantly.

We can use the perceptually significant features in the watermarking process by two different ways [17, 18]:

1. The significant features itself serves as reference, i.e. we can use the features to provide a reference orientation for the watermarking techniques.
2. The significant features are directly altered for embedding the watermark in the data.

Kutter et al. [16] have first discussed the perceptually significant portion of data where watermark can be embedded. They first introduce the watermarking procedure by employ the notion of data features or object features to embed the watermark using scale interaction technique based in 2d wavelet transform. Their scheme gives fair quality of results against simple translation and cropping attack but not efficient against the attacks that changes the locations of some pixels. A high degree of robustness can be achieved if the selected data features are used as a reference location for inserting the watermark.

In the following sections we describing a watermarking scheme that uses features of the data as reference points rather than fixed coordinates to embed the watermark and to solve all the issues and challenges mentioned above. The rest of the paper is designed as follows. For better understanding the scheme, in section two, we briefly introduce the mathematical aspects of Harris corner detection method. In section three, we explain implementation scheme for watermarking of video. In section four, the experimental setup was discussed and we present the results of our study in section five. The conclusions of study are discussed in section six. Finally, the proposed future works and suggestion for future research are discussed in section seven.

2 Preliminary

Corner detection methods are popularly used in computer vision to detect the features in an image. We can simply define a corner as the intersection of two edges i.e. it is a location in image space for which two dominant and different edge directions in a local neighborhood of the point. A corner is awesome feature for watermarking purpose because it shows significant variations in all directions, unlike the edges where the variation is in only one direction. In this paper we use Harris corner detector method because detect the corner irrespective of different sampling, small changes in scales and affine transformations.

2.1 Harris Corner Detector

Harris corner detector is a popular method and is based on autocorrelation function which is used to find out the differential of the corner score unit with respect to direction directly [18]. Through an autocorrelation function, a small square window is placed around each pixel and window is shifted in all eight directions. If autocorrelation function produces a large variation in the pixels intensity then the pixel is marked as a corner point. Since the details of the Harris corner detector found in [18], so we present only the mathematical aspects of this method.

Let a window 'w' (the center) be located at position (x, y). Let the intensity of the pixel at this location be G(x, y). If this window slightly shifts to a new location with displacement (Δx, Δy), the intensity of the pixel at this location will be G(x + Δx, y + Δy). Hence [G(x + Δx, y + Δy) − G(x, y)] will be the difference in intensities of the window shift. For a corner, this difference will be very high. The autocorrelation function or corner score can be defined in Eq. (1) as:

$$cs(x, y) = \sum_{w} [G(x_i + \Delta x, y_i + \Delta y) - G(x_i, y_i)]^2 \tag{1}$$

As we know that if the function at any point is known, continuous and differentiable at that point then its value at neighboring points can be found using Taylor's expansion, so using the Taylor's expansion we can approximate the shifted image as,

$$G(x_i + \Delta x, y_i + \Delta y) \cong \left[G(x_i, y_i) + \Delta x \frac{\partial}{\partial x} G(x_i, y_i) + \Delta y \frac{\partial}{\partial y} G(x_i, y_i) \right] \tag{2}$$

Now, for computing cs(x, y) we simply put the value of Eq. (2) in Eq. (1) and for speedy calculation we neglect the higher order terms,

$$cs(x,y) = \sum_w \left[\begin{array}{l} \left(\Delta x \frac{\partial}{\partial x} G(x_i, y_i)\right)^2 + 2\Delta x.\Delta y.\frac{\partial}{\partial x} G(x_i, y_i). \\ \frac{\partial}{\partial y} G(x_i, y_i) + \left(\Delta y \frac{\partial}{\partial y} G(x_i, y_i)\right)^2 \end{array} \right] \tag{3}$$

Equation (3) is a quadratic equation in Δx and Δy, so we can write it in the form uMu^T, where u is row matrix and

$M = \begin{bmatrix} A & H \\ H & B \end{bmatrix}$. Accordingly corner score cs(x, y) is given as, $cs(x,y) =$

$\begin{bmatrix} \Delta x & \Delta y \end{bmatrix} \begin{bmatrix} A & H \\ H & B \end{bmatrix} \begin{bmatrix} \Delta x \\ \Delta y \end{bmatrix}$ where, $A = \sum_w \left[\frac{\partial}{\partial x} G(x_i, y_i)\right]^2$, $B = \sum_w \left[\frac{\partial}{\partial y} G(x_i, y_i)\right]^2$ and

$H = \sum_w \left[\frac{\partial}{\partial x} G(x_i, y_i).\frac{\partial}{\partial y} G(x_i, y_i)\right]$.

The intensity structure captured by the autocorrelation function is smoothed by linear Gaussian filter. The Gaussian-smoothed matrix M is used to find windows with large variations. In general corner score associated with each such window is calculated as given in Eq. (4),

$$R = \det(M) - \gamma(\text{trace}(M))^2 \tag{4}$$

where γ is an empirical constant with a range of 0.04–0.06. Assume that $\lambda 1$ and $\lambda 2$ be the Eigen values of the matrix M, then det(M) can be calculated as multiplication of Eigen values and trace(M) as sum of the Eigen values. Depending on the value of 'R', the window is classified as consisting of flat, edge, or a corner. A large value of 'R' indicates a corner; a negative value indicates an edge. Also, to pick up the optimal corners, we can use non-maximum suppression.

3   Implementation Scheme

In this section we explain the strategy used for watermark embedding and extraction. To preserve the contextual relationship among the contents of the image we take the gray-scale image logo.tiff of size 75×75 pixels as watermark instead of considering binary image. The perceptually significant features of the each video frame are detected by using Harris corner detection (strongest) method. The first twenty strongest corner points serves as reference points for embedding and extraction.

3.1   Watermark Embedding Process

1. Convert each RGB video frame into YCbCr frame by using the standard conversion equations.

2. Consider the luminance Component (Y) of the video frame.
3. A set of key points in the data frame are selected in such a way that they should be linked at the semantic content of the data frame. In our case they may corresponds to the corners points. We use Harris corner detection (strongest) method the find the selected points.

$$\text{Coners\_Points} = \text{Harris Corners}(Yi)$$

where 'i' represents the ith frame of the video sequence. Chooses a significant number of strongest corner points from the key set of points. Having too much corner points may result in a high false detection rate and if we choose too less than very less number of the key points making it almost impossible to watermark the frame. In our case we use twenty strongest corner points to work as a reference points for embedding and extraction. For time constrained applications, choosing strongest twenty points is also considered as time effective solution as number of points have a direct impact on the time an embedding process takes and the same time it increases the robustness.

$$\text{Strongest\_Coners\_Points} = \text{Strongest}(\text{Coners\_Points}, 20)$$

4. Scale the each value of the watermark by a factor of α, which is used, to maintain the balance between the robustness and imperceptibility. The value of α is taken as 0.1 in our scheme.
5. The whole video is watermarked by calculating the circular neighborhoods of strongest corner point with a radius of five points and determines the local maxima of calculated neighborhoods. Watermark is perceptually shaped by adding its value on the local maxima. Same procedure is repeated for all twenty strongest corner points.
6. Reconstruct the watermarked frame from the modified luminance part and chrominance parts of the original frame by convert the YCbCr into RGB color space.

3.2 Watermark Extraction Process

1. Convert each RGB video frame into YCbCr frame by using the standard conversion equations.
2. Consider the luminance Component (Y) of the video frame.
3. Extract the watermark values by first find the location of twenty strongest corners using Harris corner detection and than finding the modified pixel values by calculating local maxima of the circular neighborhoods of strongest corner point formed by considering each detected strongest point as a center with a radius of five points.

4. Divide the extracted watermarked values by scaling factor α to get the original intensity of the watermark values.

4 Experimental Setup

The adjustment between imperceptibility and robustness of our watermarking scheme is established using MATLAB software and standard color video akiyo.avi in 252×388 pixels with the frame rate of 30 fps and a length of 295 frames is taken into consideration. Gray-scale image logo.tiff of size 75×75 pixels is selected as watermark. Eleven different types of intentional and unintentional attacks are applied to the watermarked video for judging the imperceptibility and robustness of the our scheme. Imperceptibility is an estimation of peak signal to noise ratio (PSNR). High PSNR means less distorted frame obtained. Its value is measured in decibels (dB) as:

$$PSNR = 10 \log_{10} \frac{f_{Peak}^2}{Mean\ Square\ Error}$$

where, mean square error is the error between the watermarked frame, fr_w and the original one, fr_0. Mean Square Error is calculated as,

$$Mean\ Square\ Error = \frac{\sum_{i=1}^{N_1} \sum_{j=1}^{N_2} [fr_o(i,j) - fr_w(i,j)]^2}{N_1 \times N_2}$$

Twelfth frame of the original video together with watermarked and attacked frames is shown in Fig. 1. Through Human Visual System (HSV) can not differentiate between the frames shown in figure.

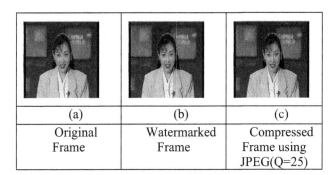

(a)	(b)	(c)
Original Frame	Watermarked Frame	Compressed Frame using JPEG(Q=25)

Fig. 1. Original, watermarked and extracted frame

Robustness which is the ability of system to cope up with errors generated due to the signal modifications and is calculated by the correlation coefficient (CC). CC between gray-scale watermark frame (*WF*) and extracted watermark frame (*WF'*) is given as,

$$CC = \frac{\sum_m \sum_n (WF_{mn} - \bar{W}F)(WF'_{mn} - \bar{W}')}{\sqrt{\left(\sum_m \sum_n (WF_{mn} - \bar{W})^2\right)\left(\sum_m \sum_n (WF'_{mn} - \bar{W}')^2\right)}}$$

where, *WF* and *WF'* are the matrices of the same size and $\bar{W}$ and $\bar{W}'$ are the mean value of embedded and extracted watermark images.

Figure 2(a) shows the original watermarks embed in the original video while Fig. 2 (b) shows the extracted watermark after applying the JPEG compression with quality factor 25. The extracted watermark on such high compression shows that watermark is highly robust and imperceptibility of watermark video is maintained by the proposed scheme.

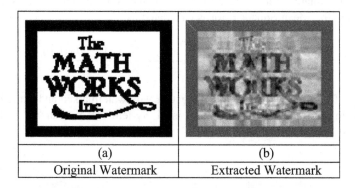

(a)	(b)
Original Watermark	Extracted Watermark

Fig. 2. Original and extracted watermark

5   Summarized Results

Table 1 summarized the result of the tests obtained using the video akiyo.avi under diverse types of attacks.

Table 1. PSNR for the cover video and obtained correlation between original and extracted watermark (logo.tiff) under diverse attacks

Attack Type	PSNR Value	Correlation Coefficient (CC)	Extracted Watermark
Cropping (40 Columns)	30.2870	0.9617	
Rotation (0.5° Degree)	39.5982	0.9512	
Salt and Peeper (Density = 0.01)	35.8433	0.7948	
Speckle Noise (Variance = 0.001)	37.5899	0.8989	
Poisson Noise	39.1638	0.8993	
Compression using JPEG (With Quality Factor of 25)	38.9343	0.8981	
Compression using Indeo5 (With Quality Factor of 25)	38.5594	0.8899	
Swapping of Six Frames	39.8610	0.8730	
Averaging of Two Frames	38.9146	0.8979	
Insertion of Ten Frames	34.1094	0.9193	

Adjustment of Intensity Between [.2 .3 .1] to [.6 .7 1]	31.1467	0.9655	

6 Conclusions

In this paper we proposed a next generation noise and affine invariant video watermarking scheme using Harris feature Extraction. Eleven different types of geometric and video processing attacks were applied on the watermarked video in the proposed scheme. Experimental results show that the retrieval method of our scheme has shown a fair degree of resilience against considered attacks.

According to the results summarized in the Table 1 the proposed next generation watermarking scheme can be concluded as follows:

(1) In the proposed next generation watermarking scheme, we embed the watermark, by considering only the twenty strongest corner points, so the scheme becomes time effective for time constrained applications and also robust at the same time.
(2) Scale the each value of the watermark by a factor of α, which is used, to maintain the balance between the robustness and imperceptibility. The value of α is taken as 0.1 in our scheme.
(3) Because the proposed scheme perceptually shaped the watermark considering significant features as reference points, it shows notable resistance against the different types of noise and affine transformations.

7 Future Work

The proposed method solves problems that typically exist in protecting the ownership of a video. But some work is still possible as the propose scheme does not emphasize much more on the newer type of attacks such as frame rate change, format conversion and adding of another watermark by the opponent. So in future we can extend the work for newer types of attack that comes due to rapid growth of information and communication technology. In future we can design such a scheme which can solve the problem when set of malicious users merge their knowledge to produce illegal contents, such an attack is known as collusion and it is another big challenge that exist in the field of watermarking. The problem of change in frame rate of the video is not pointed out in the present work, so we can extend our work in the direction to solve such attacks.

References

1. Sk, A., Masilamani, V.: A novel digital watermarking scheme for data authentication and copyright protection in 5G networks. Comput. Electr. Eng. **72**, 589–605 (2018)
2. Chung, T.-Y., et al.: Digital watermarking for copyright protection of MPEG2 compressed video. IEEE Trans. Consum. Electron. **44**(3), 895–901 (1998)
3. Iwata, M., et al.: Digital watermarking method for tamper detection and recovery of JPEG images. In: 2010 International Symposium on Information Theory and its Applications (ISITA). IEEE (2010)
4. Hsieh, S.-L., Chen, C.-C., Shen, W.-S.: Combining digital watermarking and fingerprinting techniques to identify copyrights for color images. Sci. World J. **2014** (2014)
5. Fotopoulos, V.: Digital image watermarking. Ph.D. thesis. University of Patras (2003)
6. Costa, M.: Writing on dirty paper (corresp.). IEEE Trans. Inf. Theory **29**(3), 439–441 (1983)
7. Cox, I.J., Miller, M.L.: Review of watermarking and the importance of perceptual modeling. In: Human Vision and Electronic Imaging II, vol. 3016. International Society for Optics and Photonics (1997)
8. Nikolaidis, N., Pitas, I.: Robust image watermarking in the spatial domain. Signal Process. **66**(3), 385–403 (1998)
9. Zhang, Z., Wang, C.Y., Zhou, X.: Image watermarking scheme based on DWT-DCT and SSVD. Int. J. Secur. Appl. **10**, 191–206 (2016)
10. Abraham, J., Paul, V.: An imperceptible spatial domain color image watermarking scheme. J. King Saud Univ.-Comput. Inf. Sci. **31**(1), 125–133 (2019)
11. Singh, A.K., et al.: A novel technique for digital image watermarking in spatial domain. In: 2012 2nd IEEE International Conference on Parallel Distributed and Grid Computing (PDGC). IEEE (2012)
12. Pardhu, T., Perli, B.R.: Digital image watermarking in frequency domain. In: 2016 International Conference on Communication and Signal Processing (ICCSP). IEEE (2016)
13. Abdulrahman, A.K., Ozturk, S.: A novel hybrid DCT and DWT based robust watermarking algorithm for color images. Multimed. Tools Appl. **78**(12), 17027–17049 (2019)
14. Fzali, S., Moeini, M.: A robust image watermarking method based on DWT, DCT, and SVD using a new technique for correction of main geometric attacks. Optik **127**, 964–972 (2016)
15. Agarwal, H., Ahuja, R., Bedi, S.S.: Highly robust and imperceptible luminance based hybrid digital video watermarking scheme for ownership protection. Int. J. Image Graph. Signal Process. **4**(11), 47 (2012)
16. Kutter, M., Bhattacharjee, S.K., Ebrahimi, T.: Towards second generation watermarking scheme. In: Proceedings of IEEE ICIP 1999, vol. 1 (1999)
17. Seo, J.S., Yoo, C.D.: Localized image watermarking based on feature points of scale-space representation. Pattern Recogn. **37**(7), 1365–1375 (2004)
18. Qi, X., Qi, J.: A robust content-based digital image watermarking scheme. Signal Process. **87**(6), 1264–1280 (2007)

Presentation Abstraction Control Architecture Pattern in Business Intelligence

Aksha Iyer, Sara Bali, Ishita Kumar$^{(\boxtimes)}$, Prathamesh Churi,
and Kamal Mistry

Computer Engineering Department, Mukesh Patel School of Technology
and Management Engineering, Mumbai, Maharashtra, India
kumar.ishita@gmail.com, prathamesh.churi@nmims.edu

Abstract. This paper presents a new approach to study the use of the Presentation Architecture Control model in Business Intelligence. BI Tools are in heavy demand as they are used to extract data components and reports. The model view controller architecture while being most commonly used interactive system is still not a universal solution and fails in certain scenarios. The presentation abstraction controller architecture has several agents with different responsibilities in a software system has layers with completely different functionalities. It also solves the issue of separability in Business Intelligence We describe the object-oriented models and define their characteristics. While stating the limitations of the MVC model, The PAC model is explained with the help of scenarios and its limitations are also highlighted.

Keywords: Model · View · Presentation · Abstraction · Controller ·
Business intelligence · PVC · BI · Agents · Software architecture

1 Introduction

Business Intelligence is a tool driven process for analyzing a heterogeneous amount of data that enables organizations to collect data from internal and external sources, develop and run queries against that data. It allows creating data visualization in a smart form of reports and graphical diagrams which is easier to understand the business actions and allows to make essential business decisions [1]. The Organization is most competitive and strategic in nature as they always want to remain top in the market. The most potential benefits of BI tools are to accelerate and improve the decision-making business process. Using the tool can not only help in the company's market trends but also spot business issues that need to be addressed.

The fundamental BI component contains raw data, log files, and other varied data that must be integrated and cleaned using ETL tools that ensure users are analyzing accurate and consistent information. BI software offers flexible back ends to connect to a range of data sources whereas front end interfaces are used for big data systems. Using BI tool can make employees do multiple tasks and operations like creating reports, preparation of plans and budgets [2]. The problems associated with business intelligence are maintaining a large amount of historical data and the cost of storing those data at some place. Another problem of BI architecture is to present the data in

M. Singh et al. (Eds.): ICACDS 2019, CCIS 1046, pp. 666–679, 2019.
https://doi.org/10.1007/978-981-13-9942-8_62

synchronized formats for multiple views with the same architecture. This could be achieved using the architectural pattern of the present abstraction controller where the flow of data and efficiency of data can be controlled [3].

For any software system, the user interface comes as a priority where interactive pattern focuses on the interaction of users. So, the main objective of BI is to provide real-time reports and data components.

To solve the problem of business intelligence architecture we can use the Presentation-Abstraction-Controller pattern as separability of components is the important characteristic of it. The whole hierarchal is a transitive connection between the agents. Abstraction plays like a model where it stores a large amount of raw data which can be manipulated using the ETL process and maintains the database. The presentation is a major part which plays a vital role in this problem as it visualizes the graphical reports and displays the information that is stored in data mart and Data warehouse. The controller will handle user input which is restricted to a read-only mode where all the events are fired and make the decision for presentation and abstraction. It performs business logic and communicates using an agent where the user can just view the information in Data warehouse. So, PAC pattern consists of three agents i.e.: a top-level agent which provides the functional core of the system and controls the hierarchy. The bottom level agent represents a group of functionalities that are associated with human interactions. Finally, intermediate level agent plays a vital role in solving the issue of BI architecture as it coordinates with a bottom level agent and top-level agent and can create multiple views for the same data [4].

1.1 The MVC Architecture

Model – View – Controller is an application framework of Asp.Net, developed by Microsoft which is used for implementing model-view-controller (MVC) patterns.

1. Model – it is the data layer which stands for the state of the application that shows the structure of a database in hierarchical form.
2. View – It is the display layer that accepts necessary information from the controller and manifests a user input interface to display information.
3. Controller – It is a business layer where it handles the business logic between view and model.

Let's take an example of the Client application that holds Client ID, Client Name, and Company Name. We can create this application using the same framework (Fig. 1).

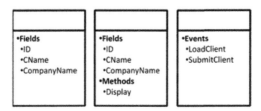

Fig. 1. MVC model

In the model, the Client object will retrieve the client information from the database, and performs the application-specific operation, manipulates the data, or use to render the data. In View, designing of the page is implemented using UI logic. The application is used on the client side. Whatever action the client performs, the event is fired using a controller and displays information. Client view includes all UI components like text box, dropdown and submits button. In Controller, all the data manipulation and events are fired and make the decision for view and model. It performs all the business logic between model and view. In our example, the client controller will manage all the interaction, takes input from Client View, and updates the database using the Client Model. It also waits for someone to call the application URL and send the request to view the Client data. Now the same application can be built using PAC Architecture. MVC Architecture can be applied in various business scenarios. Romsaiyud et al. uses Hadoop framework to build a business scenario. The model is the domain around which they build their software whereas view gives the visual representation of the model [5].

1.2   Business Intelligence

In today's data-driven age, Business Intelligence emerges as a medium from bridging the information gap many marketers and technicians face. Business intelligence thus proposes a new methodology in presenting business Information. Internally structured heterogeneous data can be efficiently handled with Business Intelligence. Aruldoss et al. defines business intelligence with seven underlying parameters such as purpose, domain, benefit and outcome [6].

Business Intelligence Architecture contains Information Management and Technology Components. Data can be handled more efficiently using business intelligence.

Business Intelligence offers an in-depth analysis of data at hand including application frameworks and database. Talati et al. proposes a methodology wherein business intelligence can intelligently be used to deliver to small and medium sized enterprises using application programming interface and mobile technologies [7].

These are tools that aid in the management of knowledge.

Most cycle stages differ and are related to the application at hand, we can define necessary and sufficient layers that Business intelligence envelopes.

The different layers that Business Intelligence Architecture defines:

1. Data Source Layer: An amalgamation of various data sources; be it operational, historical or information currently in the data warehouse environment. It can also be structured or unstructured as data can be displayed in plaintext files or with pictures or other multimedia.
2. ETL: A three-stage process.

ETL provides the flexibility of adding constraints and triggers to a classical dataset to match customers' requirements. ET requires a high-performance system with multiple terabytes requirement. It can also exhibit parallelism in terms of Data, Pipes, and components [8].

Data Extraction
Data extraction is carried out as data originates from multiple archived sources, and it becomes challenging to consolidate it. Relational and non-relational databases must be extracted from outside sources. Data parsing is also an important part of Data extraction, as it must abide by the structure of data followed.

Data Transformation
During the transformation of Data, its characteristic attributes must be altered well to fit into the database. Values may need to be manipulated as they are from foreign data sources and may be required to fit more a more general category. Freeform values can be encoded, and Data might have to be sorted, new derived Values are added into the database. Surrogate Key values might be added. Other actions can be Aggregation or disaggregation: such as Slicing and dicing of data into multiple views, Transposing Data, Pivoting Data and Validation of Data to ensure it matches the rules that are obligatory to the performance of the model.

Data Loading
Loading stage simply loads data into the data warehouse. Updating of data varies in models. The period of overwriting can vary for different models as well.

Data Warehouse Layer
Data warehousing enables unified storage of data. A key tool when it comes to Decision making. This helps perform in-depth and advanced analysis and addresses the need for interacting with historical data. Usually, a star schema is used in data warehouses having a central fact table with surrounding multiple table dimensions [9].

Metadata Layer
Metadata is the data about the data. It gives supporting information and maintains a log of data storage. It supports the surrounding Business rules that the model is based on

End User Layer
A simple view of how information is displayed to the user through the database. The heterogeneous data is made readable and readily accessible by the user. The end user layer can further enhance the user's capability of improving the model with respect to the attributes of the dataset.

Objectives of Business Intelligence
As defined by Ranjan in [10], the main objectives of implementing business intelligence are:

1. The position of the model with respect to its competitors
2. Predicting future market trends
3. Gathering the demographic and economic information of subjects
4. Analytic tools to help understand market needs
5. Improvement of Performance by predicting failure and downtime.

Tools of Business Intelligence

1. Text mining
2. Mining text

3. Data mining
4. Data farming
5. Query Processing
6. Report Generation
7. Knowledge Management
8. Customer Relationship Management
9. Decision Support
10. Business planning
11. Data Warehouse
12. Reengineering of business process
13. Score carding
14. Online Analytical Processing tools n
15. Real-time business intelligence
16. Analysis of market trends
17. Geographical Information Systems.

Due to the tremendous growth in the amount of available data, business intelligence trends have been largely reformed. In Larson et al. discusses how business Intelligence has been impacted with the growing industry trends and exponential supply of big data and its evolution with agile principles [11]. BI investments, assets and impacts improved organizational performance, have been subjected to a great amount if study however researchers have not sufficiently studied the probabilistic processes and the link between them. Trieu et al. proposes to study which parts of business intelligence need more research with the aim of performing specific research questions' in the future [12].

2 Related Work

2.1 MVC in BI

Business intelligence applications require a Multiview, synchronized environment. Also, the human-computer interface must be efficient enough that a commercial user is able to view the interactive applications. Business Intelligence architecture with its abundance of data is always in need of a more efficient way to manage its data while also keeping it transparent and flexible.

Model view architecture disseminates the input-output and the overall processing.

The model phase contains core data and functionality while View is responsible for the output of data warehouse to the corresponding user. The controller is responsible for users input and imitates event handling techniques.

The Dynamic Behavior of MVC in BI
Since there exist multiple views and controllers, the presence of a single copy of Model is insufficient to handle the input requests. Thus we make use of multiple models which also helps intakes of network and hardware failures.

To explain the dynamic behavior of MVC, Prathamesh et al. have illicit the challenges in MVC using the dashboard as a study. Isolation of user groups is also imperative when it comes to the MVC architecture as it will benefit more than an all-purpose solution [13]. Hence, multiple user groups and their needs must be identified in the planning phase.

Another challenge faces is accommodating a plethora of users needing different levels of access. MVC solves this issue more effectively by providing the same or a different dashboard with varying comfort levels.

MVC also provides content prioritization in order to display the most important information d support and prop action within the dashboards with sharing sending order to drive the needed resultant action.

Benefits of MVC in BI

1. Multiple views for the same Model
2. Pluggable views and controllers
3. Look and feel methodology in UI
4. Simplified Overhead view.

PAC is like MVC architecture which separates an interactive software system between agents and components in the hierarchal form. Every agent is responsible for the applications functionality and its components – presentation, abstraction, and architecture. Before moving ahead let's have a basic understanding of these components.

2.2   PAC

Fig. 2. The PAC internal alignment

1. Presentation – This is like View in MVC where we can display the information that is built using UI logic. It supplies visible behavior of PAC agent (Fig. 2).
2. Abstraction – This is like Model in MVC shows the structure of the database and agent performs the application-specific operation, manipulates the data, or use to render the data.
3. Controller – It plays the same role as Controller in MVC. all the events are fired and make the decision for Presentation and abstraction. It performs the business logic between abstraction and presentation. Also allows the agents to communicate with each other.

3 Methodology

3.1 Function of PAC

Any interactive system made for commercial use to a wide number of clients would require several cooperating agents. These agents are assigned various tasks such as interpreting user data or providing maintenance, operations on this data, error handling and communication. Thus, these agents, each exhibit a unique function, sustain a cooperative behavior.

The internal design of an integrated system is a tree-like structure with a top-level agent and several bottom level agents. All these agents contain the presentation, abstraction, and control modality. The agents have transitive dependencies between them and the higher level agents. One may define several layers of agents. The most common being the Top level, intermediate level, and bottom level agents (Table 1).

Table 1. Structure of different PAC agents

Agents	Type	Function
Top Level		Functional core of the system
	Presentation	Maintains components common to UI
	Abstraction	Provides Global Data Model of s/w
	Controller	Accessibility to services by lower-level agents
		Coordinates hierarchy of PAC agents
		Maintains a history of user interaction
Intermediate Level		Combinations/Views of Lower level Agents
	Presentation	Implements U/I
	Abstraction	Maintains specific Data
	Control	Similar to top and bottom agents
Bottom Level		Presents semantic concepts at the user's disposal
	Presentation	A specific view of the semantic concept
	Abstraction	Similar to top-level agent
	Control	Maintains consistency

The top-level agent provides functional core in which all other agents depend upon. Parts of the user interfaces cannot be assigned to lower level subtasks, i.e. Menu bar or dialogue box/pop-up. They are the Global Data Model of the software maintained by the Abstraction component. Representation of data is media independent in the abstraction component. This data can be represented in different environments by manipulating it. The presentation level model has a menial role in maintaining User interface elements common to the whole application and may not be present in every model. The control agent of the top-level agent has responsibilities

1. Lower level agents can enjoy the use of top-level agents
2. Relationship Manager/Coordinator of the hierarchy of all PAC agents and how they are connected
3. Log of User Interaction with the system.

Bottom level PAC Agents represent specific task concepts needed for the respective applications of varying complexities.

Presentation Component gives a specific view of the concept and all underlying functions needed by the user. The abstraction component of bottom level agents have aspects similar to that of top-level agents however no other PAC agents depend on the data. The control components of bottom level PAC maintain the consistency between the other two components. The control component of bottom-level PAC agents communicates with agents at a higher level for the exchange of events and data. Agents at the bottom level PAC are atomic. These are indivisible units that users may manipulate.

Intermediate Agents carry out two major tasks: Composition and Co-ordination.

It groups object to form a composite graphical object and maintain consistency between lower level agents. Abstraction component maintains specific data while the presentation level is responsible for the user interface. Control component carries out the same responsibilities as the bottom and top level agents.

3.2 Internal Structure of PAC

The whole hierarchal is a transitive connection between the agents. Each agent is depended on top level agents. The structure of an application with PAC agent is described below (Fig. 3).

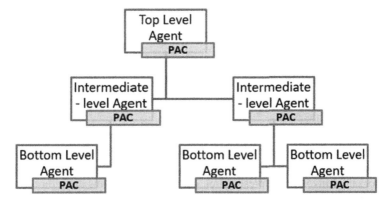

Fig. 3. Collaboration between different PAC agents

Let's take the example of displaying client information where we can download it in a spreadsheet and have a graphical representation of it. Client invoice includes Client Id, Client Name, and Company Name and shows details of the monthly invoice in graph format and at the same time we can download the information in excel spreadsheet.

Top level Agent – It supplies the functional core of the system. Most of the external agents linked on this core. It includes only those UI part that is not assigned to subtasks such as menu bars or a pop-up displaying information about the application. The main concern is to provide a universal data model of the software. In our example displaying the information for client invoice, the abstraction component of the top-level PAC agent provides an application specific interface to the data repository. It implements functions for reading and writing client data. It also implements backend operations on the client data, such as algorithms for generation client invoice using Client ID and Client Name, downloading the spreadsheet. It further includes functions for maintaining data, such as those for updating and inserting new client details. The control component organizes communication and flows with lower-level agents (Table 2).

Table 2. Class responsibility collaborator for top level agent

Class Intermediate level agent	Collaborators
Responsibilities Provides functional core of the system Controls the PAC hierarchy	Intermediate – level agent Bottom – level – agent

Intermediate Level Agent – It is the middle layer of the agent which connects the top-level agents to bottom-level agents. There can be few intermediate level agents connected to top-level agents. In our example displaying the information for client invoice, Its presentation component provides a canvas that allows users to create views of the client data, displaying it in line graphs or pie charts. The abstraction component upholds data about the invoice generated by the client, each of which is realized by its own bottom-level agent. The main concern of the control component is to coordinate all subordinate agents. Using this agent we can create multiple views for the same data (Table 3).

Table 3. Class responsibility collaborator for intermediate level agent

Class Top level agent	Collaborators
Responsibilities Co-ordinates with a bottom level agent and top-level agent Can create multiple views for the same data	Top level agent Intermediate – level agent Bottom – level – agent

Bottom Level Agent – It is the last layer of the PAC Agent or may be called as a low-level agent which represents a group of functionality that the user performs. There can be several Bottom level agents in PAC architecture. In our example displaying the information for client invoice, the presentation component maintains the information about the view such as alignment of the screen, textbox, and other features. Bottom-level agent handles summarizing of the data and presents in graphical form. The control component of a bottom-level PAC agent maintains a balance between the abstraction and presentation components, by avoiding direct dependencies between them [8] (Table 4).

Table 4. Class responsibility collaborator for bottom level agent

Class	Collaborators
Bottom level agent	
Responsibilities	Top – level agent
It represents a group of functionalities that are associated with human	Intermediate – level
interactions	agent

Every task has its own PAC agent and so graph has its own, which is responsible for the applications functionality and its components – presentation, abstraction, and controller. Let us define graph agent from the example. The abstraction component keeps a copy of the client data displayed in the line and pie chart using setter and getter of chart data. The presentation component is pictured into components that provide the

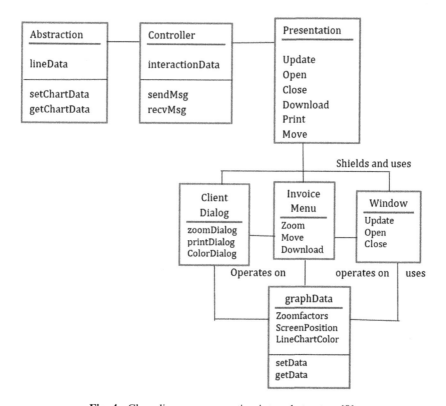

Fig. 4. Class diagram representing internal structure [8]

functionality of user interface like, menus, dialogs, and maintains the presentation-specific data. The control component of the pie chart PAC agent is simple. It just forwards data read requests from the presentation component to the abstraction component (Fig. 4).

3.3   Sequence Diagram of Agents

To understand the coordination and communication between the different PAC agents let's consider a scenario where a histogram agent is needed to study the distribution of exam scores of various students.

Here the histogram agent's main responsibility is to study the complex data and provide different functionalities to the user that he can manipulate.

The internal behavior of this agent is highlighted with the Sequence Diagram.

The cycle goes as follows:

1. End User requests Histogram Rights to the View coordinator Agent through its presentation component
2. Message Request is instantiated to Histogram agent is instantiated by the Control of View coordinator
3. Control Component of Histogram Agent retrieves repository data from Top level PAC agent
4. Data retrieved is stored in the abstraction component and the control component then calls the presentation component for its display (Fig. 5).

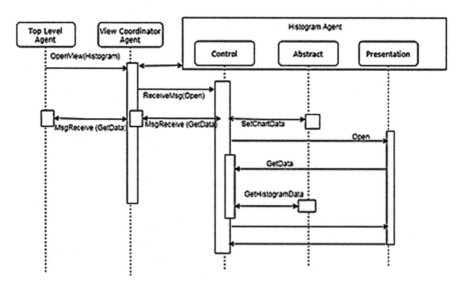

Fig. 5. PAC agent scenario

3.4   Benefits

Presentation - Abstraction - Control provides us with some new ways and ideas for designing any software or application. While the Presentation - Abstraction - Control is a very well-known design technique, it has always been compared to the model - view - controller design technique. While the model - view controller technique the controller system interacts with the view for the output, in PAC the Controller takes input, not the display component. The Controller has all the business logic and routing information which gives keeps the output separate and does not let the GUI/Presentation issues mix with the business logic.

Some of the basic advantages of the Presentation - Abstraction - Control model over model - view - controller design technique is that in PAC the complexity is lesser as compared to MVC. Presentation - Abstraction - Control also decreases the difficulty ratio of user interface design when compared to MVC. In Presentation - Abstraction - Control, the need for multiple programmers is not eliminated completely but decreased as compared to the MVC design technique. Hence Presentation - Abstraction - Control tries to eliminate a lot of the disadvantages of the MVC model.

PAC also uses separate agents to represent different semantic concepts and each agent maintains its own data and its own state so this helps the PAC agents to stay independent. Individual agents provide an individual user interface to the development of dedicated data models within the application, this intern provides support for the extension of the application or changes in the application. PAC also supports multitasking.

3.5   Liabilities

Presentation - Abstraction - Control tries have a lot of benefits but it has liabilities too like even though there are separate agents and layers there is still some inefficiency of data access across the layers. The developer must also know multiple programming languages.

PAC also makes it difficult to determine the correct amount of agents because of high independence and loose coupling among the multiple agents. In PAC there is a large amount of overhead due to the control bridge between abstraction and presentation and the communication of the controls present amongst these agents. PAC also is a little time consuming as compared to MV because it hosts separate agents for separate tasks which further increases the overhead making the application a little slower and time-consuming. The complete separation of presentation and abstraction by the control in each agent generate development complexity since communications between agents only take place between the controls of agents.

3.6   OMT Factors

OMT factors or Object Modelling Modeling Technique is a widely used object-oriented analysis and object design method. It consists of the object, functional and the dynamic model.

It depicts objects relationship with each other, their functionality, their attributes, and their methods. They follow the object model notation as the other UML diagrams. The following is the OMT diagram for MVC and PAC pattern (for multiple PAC's).

The attributes mentioned in the boxes are the OMT factors. OMT factors are the factors affecting an OMT diagram, for example, the relationship between 2 objects, attributes of classes, number of subclasses, etc.

Based on the user/client's requirement, different OMT diagrams are created based on different factors because every scenario has a different set of variables that affect it. Hence a generic diagram for both models is given below (Fig. 6).

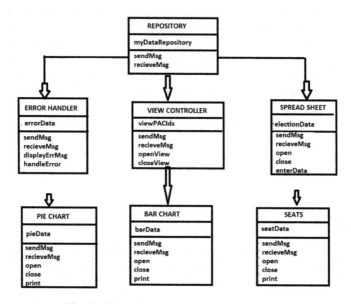

Fig. 6. Class diagram representing the behavior

4   Conclusion

With so many businesses emerging in the market, business intelligence is now at its peak, more than ever. Due to this, all these businesses need a new layout or blueprint fitting all the requirements, constraints and obstacles. Keeping this in mind, we have evaluated well-reputed techniques in the design layout category (MVC and PAC), and have observed that after considering all factors, advantages, disadvantages, varieties etc. PAC comes out to be the easier, user-friendly and simpler way to plan out the business applications or various subtasks to be done day to day in the majority. PAC also offers more different approaches, independent agents and separability than MVC, which in turn makes PAC a better choice while using business intelligence.

References

1. https://searchbusinessanalytics.techtarget.com/definition/business-intelligence-BI. Accessed 22 Feb 2019
2. Andreas, D.: http://www.dossier-andreas.net/software_architecture/pac.html. Accessed 04 Nov 2018
3. Churi, P.P., Wagh, S., Kalelkar, D., Kalelkar, M.: Model-view-controller pattern in BI dashboards: designing best practices. In: 2016 3rd International Conference on Computing for Sustainable Global Development (INDIACom), New Delhi, pp. 2082–2086 (2016)
4. Buschmann, F., Henney, K., Schmidt, D.C.: Pattern-Oriented Software Architecture, on Patterns and Pattern Languages, vol. 5. Wiley, Hoboken (2007)
5. Romsaiyud, W.: Applying MVC data model on Hadoop for delivering the business intelligence. In: 2014 Twelfth International Conference on ICT and Knowledge Engineering, pp. 78–82. IEEE, November 2014
6. Aruldoss, M., Lakshmi Travis, M., Prasanna Venkatesan, V.: A survey on recent research in business intelligence. J. Enterp. Inf. Manag. 27(6), 831–866 (2014)
7. Talati, S., McRobbie, G., Watt, K.: Developing business intelligence for Small and Medium Sized Enterprises using mobile technology. In: International Conference on Information Society (i-Society 2012), pp. 164–167. IEEE, June 2012
8. Golfarelli, M., Rizzi, S.: Data Warehouse Design: Modern Principles and Methodologies, vol. 5, pp. 12–19. McGraw-Hill, New York (2009)
9. Gatziu, S.: Data warehousing: concepts and mechanisms. In: Wirtschaftsinformatik als Mittler zwischen Technik, Ökonomie und Gesellschaft, pp. 61–69. Vieweg+Teubner Verlag (1999)
10. Babu, K.V.S.N.: Business intelligence: concepts, components, techniques and benefits. In: Components, Techniques and Benefits, 22 September 2012 (2012)
11. Larson, D., Chang, V.: A review and future direction of agile, business intelligence, analytics and data science. Int. J. Inf. Manag. 36(5), 700–710 (2016)
12. Trieu, V.H.: Getting value from Business Intelligence systems: a review and research agenda. Decis. Support Syst. 93, 111–124 (2017)
13. Kalelkar, M., Churi, P., Kalelkar, D.: Implementation of model-view-controller architecture pattern for business intelligence architecture. Int. J. Comput. Appl. 102(12) (2014)

Discriminative Gait Features Based on Signal Properties of Silhouette Centroids

K. Sugandhi[1(✉)] and G. Raju[2]

[1] Department of Information Technology, Kannur University,
Kannur 670567, Kerala, India
sugandhikgs@gmail.com
[2] Department of CSE, Faculty of Engineering, Christ (Deemed to be University),
Bengaluru 560764, Karnataka, India
kurupgraju@gmail.com

Abstract. Among the biometric recognition systems, gait recognition plays an important role due to its attractive advantages over other biometric systems. One of the crucial tasks in gait recognition research is the extraction of discriminative features. In this paper, a novel and efficient discriminative feature vector using the signal characteristics of motion of centroids across video frames is proposed. These centroid based features are obtained from the upper and lower regions of the gait silhouette frames in a gait cycle. Since gait cycle contains the sequence of motion pattern and this pattern possesses uniqueness over individuals, extracting the centroid features can better represent the dynamic variations. These variations can be viewed as a signal and therefore the signal properties obtained from the centroid features contains more discriminant information of an individual. Experiments are carried out with CASIA gait dataset B and the proposed feature achieves 97.3% of accuracy using SVM classifier.

Keywords: Gait · Gait cycle · Centroid · Gait silhouette · Signal properties

1 Introduction

Human recognition via gait analysis is a topic of interest in the current scenario. Gait is one of the most important behavioral traits. It has many advantages compared to other biometric traits. Gait is defined as the walking manner of a person [1]. Hence it can be captured at anywhere without the need of prior knowledge of the person. Low resolution camera is enough to collect gait data and it is perceivable at a distance [2]. Even though gait recognition systems gained much attention due to its remarkable advantages, it faces many challenges due to external as well as internal factors. As gait is captured in a natural way, several external factors like "walking surface conditions, viewing angles, lightning conditions, different shoe types, carrying things and time of walk" influence the efficiency of the gait recognition systems [3]. Similarly, gait might vary in different emotional situations, during pregnancy, intoxicated state due to alcohol or drugs are some of the internal factors influencing the performance of human recognition systems [3].

© Springer Nature Singapore Pte Ltd. 2019
M. Singh et al. (Eds.): ICACDS 2019, CCIS 1046, pp. 680–688, 2019.
https://doi.org/10.1007/978-981-13-9942-8_63

The major applications of the gait recognition systems lie in the fields of security, medical and sports. In security, these systems mainly concentrated on the crowded areas such as airports, embassies, shopping malls, etc. to alert the authorities to unauthorized entry. In medical field, patients gait may give early diagnostic clues for the diseases like cerebral palsy, Parkinson's disease etc. In sports, gait analysis helps the athletes to achieve better success in their game activity by overcoming the gait abnormalities [4].

In the research community, model based as well as model free approaches are used for human recognition using gait. Model based approaches [5–7] are based on a prior model of the human body and it mainly concentrated on the physical measurements such as angle between joints, distance between legs, left thigh length, right thigh length, etc. But, model free approaches [8–11] follows an appearance based recognition criteria. The unique gait characteristics are extracted from both the spatial as well as temporal domain via individual or combination of frames in a gait video sequence.

In this work, a novel and discriminative gait feature, extracted from the signal properties of the silhouette centroid is proposed. The basic idea is that at each temporal point, human body undergoes forward propulsion which leads to the oscillation of silhouette centroid points. These oscillating centroid points can be considered as a signal. Properties of these centroid signals possess unique characteristics, with which identification of an individual from the gait become more feasible.

The paper is organized as follows: Sect. 2 gives an overview of the state of the art methods and followed by proposed methodology in Sect. 3. Experimental results are discussed in Sect. 4. Section 5 concludes the paper.

2 Related Works

A selected set of existing works on human gait recognition system is summarized below:

In [12], Htun et al. proposed a feature extraction method using Gray Level Co-occurrence Matrix (GLCM) statistical features calculated from the result of Speed Up Robust Features (SURF). Meta-sample based sparse representation method is used for classification and the authors claimed that their approach significantly improved gait recognition accuracy and decreased computation time. Chaurasia et al. in [13] proposed a novel feature extraction strategy for extracting gait information from dynamic part via discrete Fourier transform (DFT)-based frequency component of the gait. Also, proposed a feature vector by fusing both the dynamic part and the static part gait information via random walk (RW) method. The authors provided a statement that the proposed method systematically retains the discriminative static gait information along with the frequency attribute embedded as the dynamic gait information. Li et al., in [14], gave a dynamic approach to Long Short-Term Memory (LSTM) network for gait recognition from skeleton data. They claimed that the skeleton data has discriminative information and without extracting any hand-crafted features in advance. In [15], authors proposed two multi-scale feature descriptors based on Multi-scale Local Binary Pattern (MLBP) and Gabor filter bank through Spectra Regression Kernel Discriminant Analysis (SRKDA) reduction algorithm. These features are extracted from Region of

Interest (ROIs) in Gait Energy Image (GEI) representation. Experiments were conducted on CASIA as well as USF databases and they achieved better recognition performance up to 92% in terms of identification rate at rank 1. Without extracting the human silhouette, in [16], individual identification was accomplished based on the spatial and temporal motion characteristics. Fisher vector encoding and Gaussian mixture model-based codebook were used for encoding the proposed feature. Classification is carried out using the support vector machine. Indoor and Outdoor experiments were conducted using CMU MoBo, CASIA B, NLPR, CASIA C, TUM GAID databases and the authors claimed that the results showed excellent performance on all the five databases and outperforms the state-of-the-art methods. In [17], Sharma et al. proposed a novel gait feature based on the information set theory. They developed a gait representation image, namely Gait Information Image (GII) based on an entropy function in account of uncertainty in the information source values. Then, GII based bipolar sigmoid feature (GII-BPSF) is extracted and efficiency of their proposed feature were tested on CASIA gait dataset B. The authors claimed that they achieved better recognition performance compared with previously established gait recognition approaches. A generalized LDA based on Euclidean norm (ELDA) for gait recognition was proposed in [18]. Firstly, the contour is unwrapped counterclockwise and ELDA is applied to obtain more discriminative feature space. Finally, multi-class Support Vector Machine (SVM) is used for classification. The authors claimed that their algorithm achieved better results in terms of accuracy and efficiency than the state-of-the-art methods.

3   Proposed Methodology

In this section, firstly the basic background information needed for the centroid feature extraction is introduced. Then a detailed explanation of the proposed feature extraction method is given. Finally, the fusion strategy of the proposed signal features is described. The block diagram of the proposed work is depicted in Fig. 1.

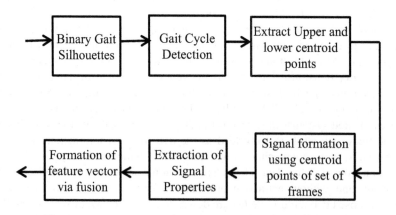

Fig. 1. Block diagram of the proposed feature extraction method.

3.1   Gait Cycle Detection

In this work, we use an overlap based gait cycle detection strategy proposed in [19] as the preliminary step. Consider a sequence of n skeletonized silhouette frames $f_1, f_2, f_3, \ldots, f_n$. For a given frame f_i, the first task is to determine the zero-crossing counts in order to obtain the overlapping condition.

For each row j in frame f_i, the zero crossing count is calculated as follows:

$$zcc(j) = \sum_{k=1}^{c-1} zc(k, k+1) \tag{1}$$

where

$$zc(k, k+1) = \begin{cases} 1, & \text{if } f_i(j, k) = 0 \text{ and } f_i(j, k+1) = 1 \\ 0, & \text{otherwise} \end{cases} \tag{2}$$

Also, c is the number of columns in f_i and finally an overlap is defined as a frame in a sequence of frames where zcc is minimum. From the obtained overlaps, gait cycles are determined from the gait sequences as explained in [15]. Since gait cycle detection is a difficult task, the major benefit of overlaps based method adopted in this work is its simplicity as well as the efficiency.

3.2   Centroid Feature Extraction from Upper and Lower Silhouette Regions

Gait period extraction step is followed by the division process of gait silhouette into upper and lower body parts. In the normal walking condition, the upper body part is motionless compared to lower body part. The centroid point from both the regions has its own significance for each individual gait.

In this work, each frame f_i, is converted to a minimum rectangle region and the frame is divided into two portions- upper and lower silhouette regions. Figure 2 depicts the partition of gait silhouette into upper and lower regions and the corresponding centroid points.

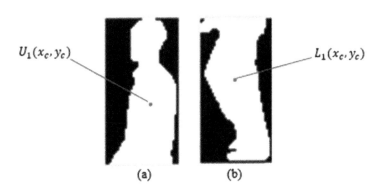

Fig. 2. Depicts the upper and lower centroid points of subject *001* in CASIA dataset B.

Let m and n be the row and column size of the frame f_i, then

$$U_i = f_i\left(1 : \left(\frac{m}{2}\right), 1 : n\right) \tag{3}$$

$$L_i = f_i\left(\left(\frac{m}{2}\right) + 1 : m,\ 1 : n\right) \tag{4}$$

where U_i and L_i are respectively the upper and lower regions of f_i. Once the upper and lower regions of f_i in the gait cycle GC_i are obtained, centroid points are given as $U_i(x_c, y_c)$ and $L_i(x_c, y_c)$ respectively for the regions U_i and L_i of f_i. The 2D centroid coordinate positions x_c and y_c is computed as

$$x_c = \frac{1}{N}\sum_{t=1}^{N} x_t \tag{5}$$

$$y_c = \frac{1}{N}\sum_{t=1}^{N} y_t \tag{6}$$

where N is the size of the respective region.

Hence, the centroid features, U_c and L_c, the upper and lower centroid points of all the frames $f_1, f_2, f_3, \ldots, f_n$ within a gait cycle GC_i of a subject S_i can be represented as in Eqs. 7 and 8 respectively.

$$U_c = [U_1(x_c, y_c), U_2(x_c, y_c), U_3(x_c, y_c), \ldots, U_n(x_c, y_c)] \tag{7}$$

$$L_c = [L_1(x_c, y_c), L_2(x_c, y_c), L_3(x_c, y_c), \ldots, L_n(x_c, y_c)] \tag{8}$$

3.3   Extraction of Signal Properties from Centroid Features

The centroid feature vectors U_c and L_c possesses signal characteristics due to the forward body propulsion during walking. Therefore, it is relevant to extract signal properties from the centroid features. We extract simple and effective signal properties such as mean frequency, max-min difference of signal, period of a sequence in a signal and maximum and minimum of peaks in a signal from U_c and L_c. Figure 3 depicts the signal wave forms of centroid points in upper and lower regions of a silhouette frame.

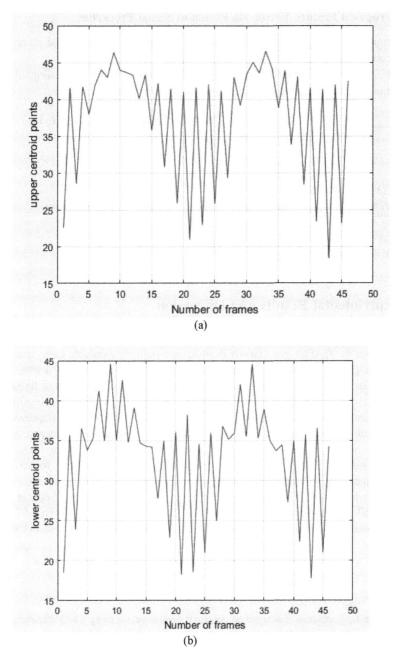

Fig. 3. Represents the centroid features with signal characteristics of *subject 001* of the CASIA dataset B. (a) Signal form of centroid points in upper region (b) Signal form of centroid points in lower region.

3.4   Proposed Feature Vector via Fusion of Signal Properties

The extracted signal properties from the centroid feature vector U_c and L_c are fused using concatenation to obtain final feature vector.

Let S_i be the ith subject, then the proposed feature vector via fusion of signal properties from the centroid features, $spcfs_i$ is given as,

$$spcfs_i = [MF(U_c), MF(L_c), MMD(U_c), MMD(L_c), P(U_c), P(L_c), \\ MaxP(U_c), MinP(U_c), MaxP(L_c), MinP(L_c)] \qquad (9)$$

where

$MF(x)$ – Mean Frequency of signal x.
$MMD(x)$ – Difference between Maximum and Minimum Value in x.
$P(x)$ – Period of sequence in x.
$MaxP(x)$ – Maximum of peaks of signal x.
$MinP(x)$ – Minimum of peaks of signal x.

4   Experimental Results and Discussion

To evaluate the efficacy of the proposed feature extraction method, experiments are conducted on the CASIA gait Dataset B which is a publicly available large, multi-view gait dataset [20]. This dataset contains 93 males and 31 females and a total of 124 subjects. Gait videos of these subjects are captured using 11 cameras fixed at 11 different viewing directions starting from 0° to 180° with 18° interval. Each subject has 10 sequences of 3 covariate conditions including six normal walking sequences, two sequences of wearing coats and two of carrying bags. For our experiments, we have selected six normal walking sequences of 100 subjects with 90° viewing angle. As the preprocessing step, basic morphological operations are applied in order to remove the holes and unwanted points on the binary gait silhouettes.

In order to evaluate the efficiency of our proposed feature vector, Support Vector Machine (SVM) classifiers are adopted. The cubic SVM classifier gives 97.3% of accuracy while all other SVM variants provide better results. Table 1 shows the performance of the proposed feature vector based on SVM classifiers. Also, comparison of the recognition accuracies obtained for different classifiers are listed in Table 2.

Table 1. Performance analysis of proposed feature vector using SVM classifiers.

Sl. no	SVM classifiers	Accuracy in %
1	Linear SVM	87.0
2	Quadratic SVM	96.7
3	Fine Gaussian SVM	94.0
4	Median Gaussian SVM	96.7
5	Cubic SVM	**97.3**

Table 2. Comparison of the best recognition accuracies obtained for different classifiers.

Sl. no	Classifiers	Accuracy in %
1	KNN	96.0
2	Discriminant Analysis	70.8
3	Ensemble Classifier	96.0
4	SVM	**97.3**

From Tables 1 and 2, it is evident that the proposed feature vector based on signal properties from centroid features gives superior performance for gait recognition. Table 2 reveals that SVM classifier outperforms other classifiers in terms of recognition accuracy. Among the SVM classifiers, cubic SVM provides the best results as shown in Table 1.

5 Conclusion

In this paper, a novel feature vector based on the signal properties of centroid features for human gait recognition is proposed. The silhouette frames are partitioned into two equal body parts - upper and lower regions. In order to determine the variation during forward motion, centroid features are extracted for each regions of the frame within a gait cycle. Since the forward motion possesses signal characteristics, centroid features are considered as fluctuating signal and the signal properties such as mean frequency, difference of maximum and minimum value, period of the sequence and the maximum and minimum of the peaks are extracted. The experiments carried out using CASIA gait dataset B shows that these signal properties from the upper and lower body centroids has better capability to discriminate the individual gait characteristics. Multiple classifiers are used to evaluate the efficiency of the proposed feature vector and it is found that SVM classifier outperforms other classifiers in terms of recognition accuracy. Also, among SVM classifier family, cubic SVM gives high performance efficiency for human gait recognition using the proposed feature vector.

Acknowledgement. The authors would like to acknowledge Department of Science and Technology (DST), New Delhi, India for the financial support extended under INSPIRE fellowship scheme.

References

1. Lee, T., Belkhatir, M., Sanei, S.: A comprehensive review of past and present vision-based techniques for gait recognition. Multimed. Tools Appl. **72**, 2833–2869 (2013)
2. Liu, Y., Wang, X.: Human gait recognition for multiple views. Proc. Eng. **15**, 1832–1836 (2011)

3. K., S., Wahid, F.F., Raju, G.: Feature extraction methods for human gait recognition – a survey. In: Singh, M., Gupta, P.K., Tyagi, V., Sharma, A., Ören, T., Grosky, W. (eds.) ICACDS 2016. CCIS, vol. 721, pp. 377–385. Springer, Singapore (2017). https://doi.org/10. 1007/978-981-10-5427-3_40

4. Whittle, M.: Applications of Gait Analysis in Gait Analysis. Butterworth-Heinemann, Edinburgh (2011)

5. Preis, J., Kessel, M., Werner, M., Linnhoff-Popien, C.: Gait recognition with Kinect. In: First Workshop on Kinect in Pervasive Computing (2012)

6. Gabel, M., Gilad-Bachrach, R., Renshaw, E., Schuster, A.: Full body gait analysis with kinect. In: 2012 Annual International Conference of the IEEE Engineering in Medicine and Biology Society (2012)

7. Araujo, R., Graña, G., Andersson, V.: Towards skeleton biometric identification using the microsoft kinect sensor. In: Proceedings of the 28th Annual ACM Symposium on Applied Computing, SAC 2013 (2013)

8. BenAbdelkader, C., Cutler, R., Davis, L.: Gait recognition using image self-similarity. EURASIP J. Adv. Signal Process. **2004**, 721765 (2004)

9. Das Choudhury, S., Tjahjadi, T.: Gait recognition based on shape and motion analysis of silhouette contours. Comput. Vis. Image Underst. **117**, 1770–1785 (2013)

10. Wang, L., Tan, T., Weiming, H., Ning, H.: Automatic gait recognition based on statistical shape analysis. IEEE Trans. Image Process. **12**, 1120–1131 (2003)

11. Wang, C., Zhang, J., Wang, L., Jian, P., Yuan, X.: Human identification using temporal information preserving gait template. IEEE Trans. Pattern Anal. Mach. Intell. **34**, 2164–2176 (2012)

12. Htun, K., Zaw, S.M.M.: Human identification system based on statistical gait features. In: 2018 IEEE/ACIS 17th International Conference on Computer and Information Science (ICIS) (2018)

13. Chaurasia, P., Yogarajah, P., Condell, J., Prasad, G.: Fusion of random walk and discrete fourier spectrum methods for gait recognition. IEEE Trans. Hum.-Mach. Syst. **47**, 751–762 (2017)

14. Li, J., Qi, L., Zhao, A., Chen, X., Dong, J.: Dynamic long short-term memory network for skeleton-based gait recognition. In: 2017 IEEE SmartWorld, Ubiquitous Intelligence & Computing, Advanced & Trusted Computed, Scalable Computing & Communications, Cloud & Big Data Computing, Internet of People and Smart City Innovation (SmartWorld/SCALCOM/UIC/ATC/CBDCom/IOP/SCI) (2017)

15. Lishani, A., Boubchir, L., Khalifa, E., Bouridane, A.: Human gait recognition using GEI-based local multi-scale feature descriptors. Multimed. Tools Appl. **78**(5), 5715–5730 (2018)

16. Khan, M., Farid, M., Grzegorzek, M.: Spatiotemporal features of human motion for gait recognition. Signal Image Video Process. **13**, 369–377 (2018)

17. Sharma, H., Grover, J.: Human identification based on gait recognition for multiple view angles. Int. J. Intell. Robot. Appl. **2**, 372–380 (2018)

18. Wang, H., Fan, Y., Fang, B., Dai, S.: Generalized linear discriminant analysis based on euclidean norm for gait recognition. Int. J. Mach. Learn. Cybern. **9**, 569–576 (2016)

19. Sugandhi, K., Wahid, F., Nikesh, P., Raju, G.: An overlap-based human gait cycle detection. Int. J. Biometrics. **11**, 148 (2019)

20. Zheng, S., Zhang, J., Huang, K., He, R., Tan, T.: Robust view transformation model for gait recognition. In: 2011 18th IEEE International Conference on Image Processing (2011)

An Algorithm for Prediction of Web User Navigation Pattern and Restructuring of Web Structure Based on Visitor's Web Access Pattern

Deepak Mangal$^{(\boxtimes)}$, Saurabh Singhal$^{(\boxtimes)}$, and Dilip Sharma$^{(\boxtimes)}$

Department of CEA, GLA University, Mathura, U.P., India
{deepak.magal,saurabh.singhal,dilip.sharma}@gla.ac.in

Abstract. The automatic discovery of user navigation pattern can be done by web usage mining. The web logs which are created on daily basis at the time web pages access by various user. The paper presents restructuring of web contents according to the user preference and pattern. The proposed algorithm suggests optimal path for users by considering eye tracking and mouse movement. The path suggests by the proposed algorithm considers only the true users those who are physically present and suggests a optimal path as per the logs recorded.

Keywords: Time to first fixation (TTFF) · Eye fixation

1 Introduction

The internet with web structure serves as the powerful tool for searching and communicating information to a widely distributed environment. It consists a database that has a dynamic collection of hyperlinks and information of dynamic data on web corpus. The data on Web classified in four main categories [1]: Usage data, Content data, Structure data and User profile. Content data is related with text data, pictures, or systematic data. The HTML tags XML tags are example of structured data. Hyperlinks on web page is also important. IP address of user's machine, the day and time of access and directories path forms web usage data while the user profile consists of profile with information. The mining of data on web is done through web mining [7, 9–12]. The large amount of log data has been stored to improve web services and web logics. Applying web usage mining on web logs, information about web access pattern and web personalization can be extracted.

Therefore, patterns of frequently co-occurred path can be discovered by using web mining. These patterns are beneficial to improve the website design by providing proficient access among highly correlated websites, suggesting navigation path for users. These patterns also help in providing useful information for developers and decision makers to provide optimal web path traversal pattern (WPTP) to all users and decision regarding advertisement policies and customer classification.

© Springer Nature Singapore Pte Ltd. 2019
M. Singh et al. (Eds.): ICACDS 2019, CCIS 1046, pp. 689–700, 2019.
https://doi.org/10.1007/978-981-13-9942-8_64

Various approaches are present in literature for finding optimal WPTP that uses log data mining, way of access the path mining, utility mining [2, 3, 8] etc. Approaches that have been considered in [2–4, 13] spent more time as proficient parameter to calculate the weight of web pages. Similarly, number of visits on web page is also used as parameter weight for web pages. However, both are important parameter but individually cannot work for best optimal WPTP.

In this paper, in order to achieve optimize web environment and better customer satisfaction, we are considering a combination of various utility weight parameters that include number of visits on web page, spent time, mouse movement [5] and eye tracking [6]. However, to know the actual presence of the user is difficult. Therefore, we are putting a threshold value on the mouse movement in order to discard too much and too less mouse movement on a web page. This is done as too much or too less movement affects the overall result and gives a false navigation path.

In this paper the Sect. 2, will describe the previous research work. Section 3, describe the used parameters in proposed algorithm and architectural block diagram for optimal WPTP. In Sect. 4 the mathematical formula for calculating the weights of parameters and proposed algorithm. Section 5 experimental results in the form of graph and table and compares our algorithm with exiting RFTCM approach. Finally, summary of paper and future work will be written in Sect. 6.

2 Related Work

To obtain optimize web path traversal pattern, a number of researchers have proposed different algorithms and models. Web log data and web pages are excellent source of providing meaningful information. The web server logs have also provided valuable information to the researchers. The section below provides the summary of the literature reviewed.

A research paper [8] has been presented by Mangal et al. to find user navigation pattern. In this paper the researcher used mouse movement to store the physical presence of user. They have combined weights of all attributes of web pages with respect to time and provide user such environment of web pages so user could access required information in minimum time. The limited attributes are used to identify user physical presence.

Hasegawa et al. [14] has been provide a process for web path navigation planning by self-directed learning. They have introduced adaptive previewing to get navigation plan. The hyperspace is not directly access before that background system allow user to manage sequence of web pages accordingly. The research paper is not describing adaptive learning in detail with system and user perspective.

To prepare base data in web mining two algorithms (GSMaxFRS and ISMaxFRS) were designed by Chen et al. to find maximal forward references with respect to gap session in the paper [14]. The gap session and interval session of user is not completely recognized by both algorithms.

The Raju et al. [15] has been discussed method to clean and reduce size of web log data with increasing quality. The method extracts user identification, session and their visits. The relational data base used to store the structure of website and user information.

As compare to traditional algorithm a two phase utility algorithm has been suggested to find web path with user interest in [12]. The aim of Zhou et al. finding such sequence whose weight of transaction utility is higher than user specified minimum value. The algorithm proposed to refined set of high transaction level utility by removing low transaction level utility from the set in phase II. The limitation of this paper is accuracy, effectiveness of algorithm is applied on limited utility.

Agrawal et al. proposed a framework with number of attribute to identified user preference in [16]. They have used frequency (visit of user), Spent Time event on web page to get user preference. At the end the framework arranged all web pages for individual user according his/her higher preference to lower preference. The user physical presence is not identified at the time visiting the web site.

Modified Span algorithm and User Personalization algorithm has been proposed by Prakash et al. [17] as a state of art algorithm. They classified web logs data to analyze user interest. They have not considered fairness of user in their research work.

3 Proposed Architecture for Optimal WPTP

The architecture considered for the web path traversal is shown in Fig. 1, comprising of three modules. Based on the URL request, the first modules store the navigation pattern of the user. Classification of data and calculation of weight of web page as per different parameter is the job of second module. The third module uses the calculation done by second module to suggest the best navigation plan to the user.

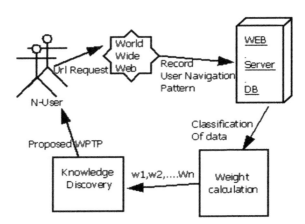

Fig. 1. Architecture of proposed model

3.1   Preliminaries

A mathematical model is proposed for predicting optimal WPTP and compare the performance of traditional approach RFTCM and proposed approach. The following section discuss the preliminaries used in calculating the weight of the web page.

a. $U = \{u_1, u_2, u_3........u_n\}$ is the set of users navigating web pages.
b. $S_i = <P_{i1}, P_{i2}.........P_{ix}>$ is the way of access the web pages. The ith user u_i access the j_{th} webpage then P_{ij} represent it in sequence S_i.

3.2   Page Rank

Page rank helps in determining the sequence of web page during search. Page rank has a significant impact on sequences of web pages. It depends on the link model of web graph. Page Rank can be expressed as probability distribution of random actions of a user accessing web pages without having the past knowledge and reach of a web page.

Link structures are often use to determine the Page Rank. Generally, page rank is evenly divided in all web pages in the link structure. The residual probability d = 0.85, given by the probability distribution, is calculated from the frequency of web pages.

Let p_1, $p_2...p_n$ are web pages in any link structure having N number of web pages. A set of, web pages M (p_i) is considered that link to p_i.

Thus, the page rank (PR) for any web page can be calculated as:

$$PR(p_i) = \frac{1-d}{N} + d \sum_{p_j \in M(p_i)} \frac{PR(P_j)}{L(P_j)} \qquad (1)$$

3.3   Number of Visits

Number of visits can be defined as the number of times a particular web page is accessed by a user. Since, a user may visit a web page multiple times in a day; it may show the strong preference of the user for that web page. However, to determine the preference a minimum time period 't' is considered. If the web page is not opened for the time period, it will not be considered in determining the preference of the web page.

$uf_1, uf_2............uf_n$ is a set a access frequency and ufj represents the number of visits for j_{th} webpage by a user.

$vf_1, vf_2...vf_n$ is the set of web pages which were closed before t time. Average number of visits of i_{th} visitor is represented by F_{avg}, is calculated as

$$F_{avg} = \frac{(\sum_{i=1}^{n} uf_i - \sum_{i=1}^{m} vf_i)}{n} \qquad (2)$$

Where n is number of web page visited by a user and m is the number of web pages closed by the user in less than t time.

3.4   Mouse Tracking

Mouse movement on any website can help the developer to know the interest of user for a given page. For this, mouse tracking can be considered which can measure the behavior and attention of user in real time. Web developers track mouse movement over a web page to determine the level of interest and activeness of user in a particular webpage or particular segment of web page. Mouse tracking is online mechanism that helps in measuring the movement of mouse as scroll up or down, mouse click and mouse movement on a web page.

T_i is the time period for which the ith webpage was opened.

$Mm = \{Mm_1, Mm_2, Mm_3, \ldots, Mm_n\}$ is set of Mouse movement and Mm_i shows mouse movement on i^{th} web page which can calculated as

$$Mm_i = \frac{\sum |Start\ point - Last\ point|}{T_i} \tag{3}$$

$$Mm_i = \sum |Start\ Point - Last\ Point| \tag{4}$$

Relative time spend with mouse movement is also consider to learn the interest of the user.

3.5   Eye Tracking

Eye tracking is a process of measuring the point of staring of the user on the system. It is intended to find the physical presence of the user along with its interest on the particular page. Eye trackers are used to measuring the eye position and eye movement of the user. The eye tracking helps in knowing the usability and effectiveness of the web page that the user has currently open. Web developers are using this knowledge to better understand how the user sees a particular web page and are gaining more informed design decisions form them. The output measures for eye tracking are fixations and gaze points. The Area of Interest (AOI) is a tool to select an interested region by a user to find measures. For example, a user is interested in a picture and want to access that link, how much time your respondents spent in the region, how many fixations were counted, how many people looked away and back. it shows user preference. So, eye tracking is measure component to find the user behavior to access web pages. The weight of eye tracking must be calculated. It can be measured in terms of time spent, fixation, count of re-visitors and ratio with re-visitors with a total visitor.

3.6   Weight of Eye Tracking(W)

A survey has been contacted by designing a web site on asp.net for hundred users to collect the eye-tracking measures. All system consists webcams to track the eye movement to find the measures. All measurement has been stored in a Table 1. Table 1 shows the statistical data of eye tracking on the web pages. This table shows various metrics which involve in eye tracking. To calculate the weight of eye tracking the mean values (M) and standard deviation (SD) of metric will be calculated, several multivariate analyses of variance (MANOVA) were performed to identify AOI, whether looking to the web page or not. AOI can help the users' which link can have better move. The dependent variables for eye tracking on interested web page were time to first fixation (TTFF) and fixation duration.

Table 1. Parameter values for eye tracking

Web page	TTFF (in seconds)	Time spent (in seconds)	Re-visitors	Revisits	Fixation
A	4.9	0.1	2/11	2	15
B	3.6	0.2	6/16	2.2	26
C	2.9	0.3	10/18	2.3	34
D	2.7	0.3	14/27	2.1	40

Weight of eye tracking = Average Fixation time of n users for access the web page T_i is the time period for which the ith webpage was opened.

$Em = \{Em_1, Em_2, Em_3, \ldots, Em_n)$ is set of eye movement and Em_i shows eye movement on i^{th} web page which can calculated as

$$Em_i = \frac{\sum |Fixation - TTFF * Revisitors|}{Time\ Spent} \qquad (5)$$

4   Proposed Algorithm for Optimal WPTP

The proposed architectural model will use data mining association approach to get optimal WPTP. The new approach adds calculated weights of parameters with threshold value such as number of visits, spent time on page, mouse movement and eye tracking movement. It describes valid user's preference to access the web pages. The tracking of eye movement is very much useful for identification of valid user. The calculation of weight to find the accessing pattern of users.

4.1   Weight of Web Page Based on Visits (VW)

Visits weight (VW) of web page (P_{ij}) can calculate as

$$VW(Pij) = \frac{Access\ frequency\ of\ web\ page}{F_{avg}} * PR(v) \qquad (6)$$

where F_{avg} can be calculated from above Eq. 1.

4.2 Weight of Average Time Spent on Page (ATPW)

The spent time that the user spent on a web page also help in determining the user's access desire for the page. Dtime is considered as download time of web page so time spent on web page (TSWP) will be use. The weight ATPW can be formulized as

$$ATPW = \frac{\sum_{i=1}^{Vfi} Ti(P) - (Dtime * Afrequency(P))}{\sum_{j=1}^{n} \sum_{i=1}^{Vfi} Ti(Pj)} * PR(v) \qquad (7)$$

Where Afrequency is number of page visit.

$$Dtime = TSWP/Pagesize \qquad (8)$$

4.3 Mouse Movement Page Weight (MMWP)

From Eq. 2

$$MMPW = \frac{Mm_i}{\sum Mm_{ij}/n} \qquad (9)$$

Where Mm_i is sum of all movement of mouse used by visitor on i^{th} page. Mm_{ij} mean of sum of all movement of mouse used by visitor on P_1 to P_n pages.

4.4 Eye Movement Page Weight (EMWP)

$$EMPW = \frac{Em_i}{\sum Em_{ij}/n} \qquad (10)$$

Where Em_i is sum of all eye movement used by visitor on i^{th} page. $\sum Em_{ij}$ is mean of sum of all eye movement used by visitor on P_1 to P_n pages.

So, page weight P_{ij} with parameters i.e. number of visits, mouse movement, time spent and eye movement will be measure as

$$W(Pij) = VW(Pij) + ATWP + MMPW + EMPW \qquad (11)$$

Only those value will be considered which are higher than threshold value (Table 2).

5 Performance Evaluation

The performance can be evaluated of the proposed algorithms for finding best optimal web path traversal pattern, the following evaluation metrics have been used.

Table 2. Proposed ETMMC algorithm

Eye tracking Mouse Movement based classification Algorithm (ETMMC)
Algorithm: ETMMC
Input: Web traversal path logs.
Output: Predicted optimal Web traversal path
1.   **For** each user u_i **do**
2.   Calculate web page Rank (PR_i)
using Equation (1)
3.   calculate VW using Equation (2) &(4)
4.   calculate ATW using Equation (5)
5.   calculate MMWP using Equation (3) &(7)
6.   calculate EMWP using Equation (6)
7.   if value > threshold value then
8.   SET W(Pi) = VW + ATW + MMPW+ EMPW
(W(Pi): weight of ith web page)
9.   **For** each user **do**
10.   **if** user is new **then**
11.   Input user preferences
12.   return Predicted optimal Web traversal path
13. **End if**
14.   **else**
15.   Return Stored web path traversal pattern with their page weight
16. **End for**
17. **For** each user **do**
18.   For each web page do
19.   WPi = WPi + W(Pi) where WPi is collective weight of ith webpage
20. Return collective weight of web pages in decreasing order to web administrator for restricting the web structure

Based on proposed architecture as described in Fig. 2 a .Net framework using C# based simulator has been developed for evaluating the performance of the proposed algorithm. All request of new user or old user are considered. Accordingly, visiting preference has been asked from the new user. As per the desire of the user a most predictable path has been provided to him. So, he/she can access maximum information in minimum time. For old user the calculated weight-based path has been already stored as per their previous visit and similar users WPTP. For this a web structure has been formed it consist of four pages A, B, C and D as shown in Fig. 2. The web page A have sports related information. The web page B have business news. The web page C have local information. The web page D have world level related information. All web pages are linked with each web page directly with page reference. So visitor can switch anywhere as he/she is interested to get. The behavior of various users randomly picked was observed and recorded on the proposed web structure. According to the recorded observation, the estimation of experimental result is discussed in next section.

5.1   Experimental Results

The access pattern of different users based on the considered parameters evaluated in the proposed algorithm and RFTCM are shown in Figs. 3 and 4 respectively. The

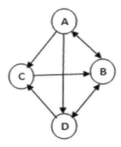

Fig. 2. Web structure used for calculating performance

comparison between proposed algorithm ETMMC and existing RFTCM algorithm for WPTP prediction has been shown in Fig. 5. Addition of eye movement in ETMMC makes the proposed algorithm fairer as compare to RFTCM for the predicted WPTP. So, the predicted path by ETMMC is much desirable and provide maximum information to user in minimum time. The eye movement tracking shows that user was always present at the time of access the web page. So, the time spent is actual spent time of user on web page. The figure shows that in ETMMC algorithm provide optimal WPTP. So, any user can access web pages data in less time. The eye movement tracking shows the fairness of user presence.

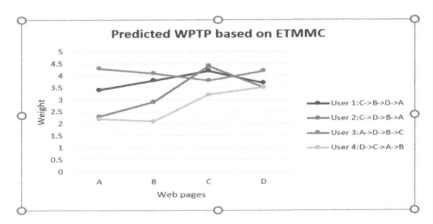

Fig. 3. Comparison of predicted WPTP based on ETMMC

The Table 3 shows the comparison between RFTCM algorithm with ETMMC algorithm. The parameters used in table shows that ETMMC is more powerful recommendation algorithm as compare to RFTCM. So more valuable parameters show that proposed algorithm efficiency may increase with fairness of user.

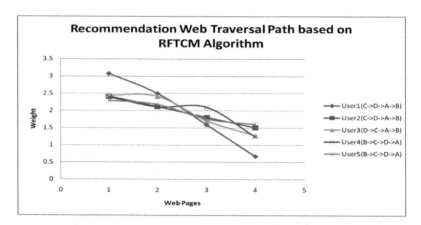

Fig. 4. Recommended web traversal path based on RFTCM

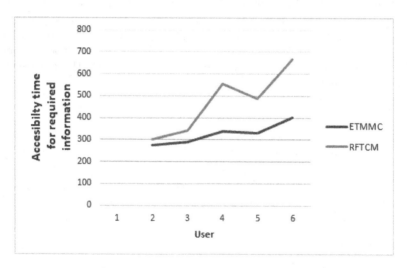

Fig. 5. Comparison of RFTCM and ETMMC

Table 3. Comparison between RFTCM and ETMMC algorithm

Parameters	RFTCM	ETMMC
User preference	√	√
Visited frequency	√	√
Page rank	√	√
Time spent	√	√
Page size	√	√
Webpage navigation	√	√
Mouse movement	√	√
Eye movement	√	√
Fairness of user	X	√
Information accessibility in less time	X	√
Restructuring of web structure	X	√

6 Conclusion and Future Work

The suggested algorithm ETMMC provides prediction of the web page traversal path for all users. The suggest algorithm uses eye movement parameter for maximum fairness of user at the time of access the web page. The experimental result figure clearly shows that ETMMC provide maximum access of web data in minimum time of the all users in comparison to the traditional algorithm. In conclusion, the behavior and preference of user is very important to increase the popularity of web pages. So, The Web Usage Mining will continuously play a vital role in the learning of user preference and behavior. There is a limitation of hardware if camera is not available then it is not easy to track the eye movement. So, In the future, researcher can improve the algorithm which can also work without camera module. Algorithm can also improve in terms of new technologies like deep learning approaches. The researches can also think for such a new parameter which also improve the fairness of visitor.

References

1. Hasegawa, S., Kashihara, A., Toyoca, J.I.:. A support for navigation path planning with adaptive previewing for web-based learning. In: International Conference on Computers in Education, pp. 1250–1251 (2002)
2. Velásquez, J. D., Yasuda, H., Aoki, T., Weber, R.: Acquiring knowledge about user's preferences in a web site. In: International Conference on Information Technology: Research and Education, pp. 375–379 (2003)
3. Mobasher, B., Jain, N., Han, E.H., Srivastava, J.: Web mining: pattern discovery from world wide web transactions, pp. 558–567. Technical report TR96-050. Department of Computer Science, University of Minnesota (1996)
4. Borges, J., Levene, M.: A fine grained heuristic to capture web navigation patterns. SIGKDD Explor. **2**(1), 40–50 (2000)
5. Caruccio, L., Deufemia, V., Polese, G.: Understanding user intent on the web through interaction mining. J. Vis. Lang. Comput. **31**, 230–236 (2015)
6. Slanzi, G., Pizarro, G., Velasquez, J.D.: Biometric information fusion for web user navigation and preferences analysis: an overview. Inf. Fusion **38**, 12–21 (2017)
7. Chen, M.S., Park, J.S., Yu, P.S.: Efficient data mining for path traversal patterns. IEEE Trans. Knowl. Data Eng. **10**(2), 209–221 (1998)
8. Mangal, D., Arya, K.V.: An efficient approach for web path traversal pattern based on visitor preferences and navigation behavior. In: 2014 9th International Conference on Industrial and Information Systems (ICIIS), pp. 1–5 (2014)
9. Spiliopoulou, M., Faulstich, L.C.: WUM: a web utilization miner. In: International Workshop on the Web and Databases, Valencia, Spain (1998)
10. Srivastava, J., Cooley, R., Deshpande, M., Tan, P.N.: Web usage mining: discovery and applications of usage patterns from web data. ACM SIGKDD Explor. Newsl. **1**(2), 12–23 (2000)
11. Mobasher, B., Jain, N., Han, E.H., Srivastava, J.: Web mining: pattern discovery from world wide web transactions, pp. 558–567 (1996)
12. Zhou, L., Liu, Y., Wang, J., Shi, Y.: Utility-based web path traversal pattern mining. In: Seventh IEEE International Conference on Data Mining Workshops, pp. 373–380 (2007)

13. Xu, G., Zhang, Y., Yi, X.: Modelling user behavior for web recommendation using LDA model. In: 2008 IEEE/WIC/ACM International Conference on Web Intelligence and Intelligent Agent Technology, vol. 3, pp. 529–532 (2008)
14. Chen, Z., Fowler, R.H., Fu, A.C.: Linear time algorithms for finding maximal forward references. In: Proceedings ITCC 2003. International Conference on Information Technology: Coding and Computing, pp. 160–164 (2003)
15. Raju, G.T., Satyanarayana, P.S.: Knowledge discovery from web usage data: complete preprocessing methodology. Int. J. Comput. Sci. Netw. Secur. 8(1), 179–186 (2008)
16. Agarwal, R., Arya, K., Shekhar, S.: An architectural framework for web information retrieval based on user's navigational pattern. In: 2010 5th International Conference on Industrial and Information Systems, pp. 195–200. IEEE, July 2010
17. Om Prakash, P.G., Jaya, A.: Analyzing and predicting user navigation pattern from weblogs using modified classification algorithm. Indonesian J. Electr. Eng. Comput. Sci. 11(1), 333–340 (2018)

Computational Representation of Paninian Rules of Sanskrit Grammar for Dictionary-Independent Machine Translation

Vishvajit Bakarola$^{(\boxtimes)}$ and Jitendra Nasriwala

Uka Tarsadia University, Bardoli, India
vishvajitbakrola@gmail.com, jvnasriwala@utu.ac.in

Abstract. Since the beginning of computational linguistics machine translation is being one of the holy grail of natural language processing. With the advancement of world wide web and emergence of data driven methods the machine translation has received a jolt of new activity and more visibility. Still the visible lack of accuracy in machine translation shows that the much work remains to be done in concern of human identical translation. The approaches of machine translation uses the dictionary meaning of the target language as a heart of translation process. Dictionary based machine translation system continuously requires the intervention from the human expert. Unlike other languages Sanskrit is having a standalone procedure for developing new words and defining its meaning as well. Maharshi Panini developed a complete set of grammatical rules that defines the whole procedure to process the input language. The paper presents the computer simulation of Paninian rules of Sanskrit grammar focuses on the generation of meaning of unknown word using most elementary component of a language - dhAtu. We have used the direct machine translation approach for achieving dictionary-independent machine translation.

Keywords: Dictionary-independent machine translation ·
Natural language processing · Computational linguistics · Astadhyayi ·
Paninian grammar · Sanskrit grammar · Direct machine translation

1 Introduction

Since 1940s, scientists are trying to impute artificial intelligence into the computer system for the purpose of exchanging knowledge. Efforts have been on to develop a complete system of machine translation for the purpose of functional, literacy and technological communications. Perfect AI system is by itself capable in automatic translation of natural language with generation of language's grammatical structure to communicate directly with the human user. The efforts to develop a fully automatic and human identical machine translation system are

© Springer Nature Singapore Pte Ltd. 2019
M. Singh et al. (Eds.): ICACDS 2019, CCIS 1046, pp. 701–710, 2019.
https://doi.org/10.1007/978-981-13-9942-8_65

in their infant stages. However, numerous amount of efforts are already delivered to address the issue, but still machine translation is challenging and fascinating task.

Sanskrit is recognized as the mother of almost all Indo-European languages. The tradition of Sanskrit is so reach and since long back to more than 5000 years. The grammar of Sanskrit is in routine use from Vedic period. In ancient time Sanskrit was a primary language and four Vedas as well as all the six core fields of study to learn the Vedas are written in Sanskrit. In modern age, nearly 2300 B.C. Maharshi Panini laid universal foundation of Sanskrit grammar in his book - *Astadhyayi*. It is the central part of Panini's grammar. *Astadhyayi* is most precise classical work ever written on descriptive linguistics. In acknowledgement of Maharshi Panini, One of the renowned linguists Max Muller stated in his book that *Every grammarian will readily admit that there is no grammar in any language that could vie with the wonderful mechanism of Paninian grammatical rules.*

In processing of natural language the grammatical structure and the a set of collection of words associated in that language plays a very important role. Any of the machine translation system is dependent of both of these aspects. Almost all human natural languages introduce a word that symbolize an object and we as human require dictionary meaning of that word for understanding it. The grammar of Sanskrit allows the flexibility for generating new words and hence the meaning of the word. Unlike other natural language grammars, Sanskrit has its full-fledged procedure for generating new words.

Our work covers the fundamental idea of machine translation and the use of direct machine translation approach in translation of Sanskrit-English language pair. The presented work mainly unfold the implementation of Paninian structure of Sanskrit grammar to achieve dictionary independent machine translation. Paper presents an approach of generating meaning of unknown word in a source language sentence.

In Sect. 2, we have presented the machine translation with its significant need and the working idea of direct machine translation approach. Section 3 focus of the grammatical tradition of Sanskrit with the preliminary knowledge of Sanskrit *dhAturoop*. Section 4 describe the proposed approach. Section 5 presents implementation and results. We have concluded with future scope in Sect. 6.

2   Machine Translation

Machine translation is technically a task of converting one language into another preserving the meaning and considering the grammatical structure of the source language. The first faltering steps in machine translation were taken in 1950s [1,2]. Since then the efforts are focused on the development of system that can mimic the human accuracy and fluency of natural language translation. Machine translation is inexpensive, immediate and simultaneous task. The research in the area is with an objective to melt away the barrier of languages and open up the literature to everyone and so to connect the world intellectually and culturally united into one [3,4]. The machine translation system can be designed either for a pair of two particular languages - known as *Bilingual machine translation* system or for more than a single pair - known as *Multilingual machine translation* system. The 1990s was remarked as the breakthrough of a fairly new approaches to challenge and eventually improve the already established methodologies.

2.1   A Direct Machine Translation Approach

The direct machine translation is one of the initial approaches of machine translation [5]. As the name suggests this approach provides the direct translation without any intermediate representation of source language. A direct translation system is done on a word by word translation using a bilingual dictionary usually followed by some syntactic rearrangement [5]. These systems take a monolithic approach towards development. They involve little analysis of the source text, no parsing, and rely mainly on a large bilingual dictionary. Besides dictionary translation, the analysis includes morphological analysis, preposition handling, syntactic arrangement and morphological generation. The steps followed by direct machine translation and the systematic flow of process is as mentioned in Fig. 1.

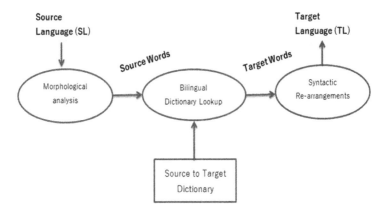

Fig. 1. The process of direct machine translation.

1. *Morphology analysis in order to identify the base forms of words of Source Language by removing inflections and resolve ambiguities.*
2. *Look up the bilingual dictionary to get the target language words corresponding to the source language words.*
3. *The use of grammatical rules for reordering of the translated word in order to align with the word structure of the target language. For example, the English uses the subject-verb-object (SVO) word structure, where most of the Indic language use subject-object-verb (SOV) word structure.*
4. *The last stage of the direct machine translation system produces the necessary target language as an outcome.*

3   Sanskrit Grammatical Tradition

Sanskrit is having a very long grammatical tradition. The grammar is designed for a purest utterances and a precise understanding of the language. Grammarian Maharshi Patanjali defined grammar as - *Laksya laksane vyakaranam* meaning - *Instances and rules together constitutes vyakarana.*

The Sanskrit is being natural language for routine human communication since the Vedic times. In modern age Maharshi Panini restructure the grammar and presented in the most precise but in depth form in *Astadhyayi*. Panini himself stated the earlier work done on the grammar by *Apishil, Gargya, Gaalav, etc.* Later *Kaatyayan* wrote his writings and *Patanjali* gave his detailed commentary on the *Astadhyayi*.

In today's age, the *Astadhyayi* is an excellent material to work with a Sanskrit grammar in any aspect. Many of the linguistics across the world admired the *Astadhyayi* as the most perceptive analysis of Sanskrit written in style very near to a computer program [6]. Unlike other languages, Sanskrit is having such a beautiful grammatical structure that carries a complete process for generating a new words from their verbal roots. Panini penned set of rules focuses on formation of words. The process of generating new word is based on the most elementary part of the language known as dhAtu or verbal root. Panini has presented 2012 *dhAturoop* in one of the components of Sanskrit grammar - *dhatupath*.

3.1   dhAtu Roop

Maharshi Panini's Sanskrit grammar is universally praised for its intuitive analysis of Sanskrit [7]. The grammar is based on the human spoken language or bhAsa. It is entirely synchronic, where variants are simply considered as alternate forms, indeed the very concept of linguistic change is foreign to the tradition. The grammar consists of four components [7] as -

1. *Astadhyayi - contains nearly 4000 phrases or grammatical rules of a Sanskrit languages.*
2. *Sivasutras - are morphological segments is the inventory of phonological segments.*
3. *Dhatupatha - is a collection of nearly 2012 verbal roots or dhAtu, which are most elementary components of Sanskrit grammar.*
4. *Ganapatha - is a collection of 261 lexical components which are idiosyncratically, subject to several rules.*

The rules of the *Astadhyayi* fall into three broad classes, each of which effects a mapping between what we could see as different levels of representation. The Sanskrit grammar analyze given input corpus in a hierarchy of four levels, which traverse in the direction from semantics to phonology [7].

4   Proposed Approach

Every machine translation system requires the processing of source language (SL) and target language (TL) in context to derive the grammatical structure of target language. The translation of words in the language pair is also very essential. There are 100s of million words of translated text exists. Feasibly it is not a practical solution to design full-fledged machine translation system that works without any human intervention.

Our proposed approach is to develop a full-fledged machine translation system that can able to work on bilingual Sanskrit-English language pair without depending on the dictionary meaning of source word for target language generation. dhAtu representation of Sanskrit word in source sentence can deliver the meaning of inflected unknown words. The existing approach LR parsing [8,9] is used to parse the input Sanskrit sentence in order to get the word which is not known to the machine translation system.

5   Implementation

5.1   System Environment

We have used Python 3.6 with NLTK library. The morphological class analysis has been implemented to associate individual word with its languages related tags like NN - Noun, NNP - Proper Noun and VB - Verb. The direct machine translation system is implemented to perform translation.

5.2   Morphological Class Analysis

Morphological classes or POS tagging are important study for processing a language as they give large amount of information about word and its neighbors [10]. It is a fundamental task in natural language processing. Morphological analysis gives the relevant language tags to the input word. It is a method of splitting the given input corpus into sentences and then sentences into words. Here each word is assign with a proper tag such as verb, noun, adjective, adverb, etc. We have implemented POS tagging in order to understand the grammatical quantities associated with the source sentence as well as with the translated target sentence. The input sentence we have taken is - *Ram Gruhe Pankajaa Aasti.*

<big>राम ग्रुहे पन्कजा अस्ति।</big>

Fig. 2. Input Sanskrit sentence

However the input is given to the tagger in Sanskrit language as shown in Fig. 2 with appropriate tag. For achieving morphological class analysis on the Sanskrit sentence we have designed a POS tagger that can be trained with the new tag set. Figure 3 shows the output of the POS tagger. As shown in the Fig. 3 the tagger has successfully assigned appropriate tags to each of the Sanskrit word.

Morphological Class Analysis on – राम गृहे पन्कजा आस्ते

[('राम', 'NP'), ('गृहे', 'NNP'), ('पन्कजा', 'NN'), ('आस्ते', 'VB')]

Accuracy: 1.0

Fig. 3. Morphological analysis on source Sanskrit sentence.

5.3   Dictionary-Independent Machine Translation Algorithm

For achieving the Sanskrit to English dictionary independent machine translation, direct machine translation approach has been used. As stated earlier in the discussion under Sect. 2, the direct machine translation approach not generates any intermediate representation of source language and directly translate each word into correspondent target language using dictionary. The following procedure demonstrate the dictionary-independent machine translation:

Algorithm 1. Dictionary-Independent Machine Translation

1: **procedure** GETINPUT(*sourcesentence*)
2:    Remove inflection associated in *sourcesentence*
3:    Let *list* be the collection of words from *Sanskrit_Corpus*
4:    *tags* = POS_TAGGING[*list*]
5:    *verb_list* = EXTRACT_VERB[*tags*]
6:    N ← length(*verb_list*)
7:    **for** each *verb* in *verb_list* **do**
8:        **if** *verb* ϵ *dictionary_table* **then**
9:            **return** meaning
10:       **else**
11:           U_w = *verb*
12:           Apply parsing to get associated *dhAtu* in U_w and derive the meaning from *dhAtu_table* by removing inflection in *verb* to generate target U_w.
13:           *newverbSet* ← meaning of U_w
14:           **return** *newverbSet*
15:    Analyze the syntactic arrangements of generate *targetsentence* and re-arrange in *SVO* form, if not.

5.4   Results

The stage wise implementation of above stated Algorithm 1 is presented as below:

Stage-1: Take Sanskrit sentence as shown in Fig. 4 or corpus as an input to the machine translation system.

राम ग्रुहे पन्कजा अस्ति।

Fig. 4. Input Sanskrit sentence

Stage-2: Execute the procedure of POS tagging for the morphological class analysis of the source Sanskrit sentence and perform the bilingual dictionary look up from the source to target *dictionary table* as shown in Fig. 9.

Morphological Class Analysis on - राम ग्रुहे पन्कजा अस्ते

[('राम', 'NP'), ('ग्रुहे', 'NNP'), ('पन्कजा', 'NN'), ('अस्ते', 'VB')]

Accuracy: 1.0

Fig. 5. Morphological class analysis of source Sanskrit sentence.

Stage-3: Get the meaning of each tagged word from the *dictionary table* and identify unknown word(s) U_w.

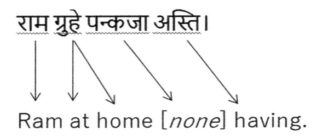

Fig. 6. Output of dictionary lookup

Here from Fig. 6, we can observe that the meaning of the Sanskrit word *Pankajaa* is not available in the dictionary table.

Stage-4: Parse the unknown word(s) U_w by removing associated inflections. With the help of dhAtu table generate the meaning of U_w.

We have encountered $U_{w_i} = Pankajaa$. After removing the inflections and *SandhiSplitting*, we get the *Panka* and *Jaa* separately as shown in Fig. 7.

पन्कजा = पन्क + जा

Fig. 7. Sandhi splitting of unknown input word U_W

The words we derived as an output of *SandhiSplitting* are the *dhAturoop* - the indivisible language components or verbal roots. The meaning of each of 2012 *dhAturoop* are supposed to available in the *root_table*. Here, we have taken use of few *dhAturoop* as shown in Fig. 8.

S_wordname	S_wordmeaning
गच्छ	going
जल	water
जा	born of
ति	is
नीर	water
पङ्क	mud
वारि	water

Fig. 8. Root table

As an outcome of the parsing we will get the meaning of each unknown verbal roots from the *root_table*. And the meaning is updated in the *dictionary_table* as shown in Fig. 9 for the further use.

S_word_Name	S_word_Meaning
बालक	a boy
गृहे	at home
पङ्कजा	born of mud
अस्ति	having
मम्	I am
रोचते	like
न	not
राम	Ram
शिवा	Shivah
क	why
त्वम्	Your

Fig. 9. Dictionary table

Stage-5: Use the meaning of unknown word generated in **Stage-4** and with the help of associated knowledge we will get the exact translation for the unknown Sanskrit word. Perform the syntactic rearrangement to produce a final target sentence in to *subject-verb-object (SVO)* format from *subject-object-verb (SOV)* as shown in Fig. 10.

As the initial output generated from the machine translation is in the form identical to grammatical structure of source language, it is necessary to rearrange it in the grammatical structure of target language.

Ram at home **lotus** having. (SOV Structure)

Ram having lotus at home. (SVO Structure)

Fig. 10. Output of syntactic arrangements of target sentence

6   Conclusion and Future Work Plan

With the fundamental study of Sanskrit grammar and Paninian rules for word formation the grammar is found most appropriate for processing the natural languages. The Paninian rules for generating the meaning of unknown word U_w are successfully implemented in form of parser. The developed morphological class analyzer is trained with the grammatical tags associated with the source Sanskrit sentences. It is observed that the Sanskrit is word order free language i.e. the grammatical structures like SOV, SVO, etc. deliver the same syntactic and semantic meaning. We have presented the dictionary-independent machine translation algorithm. Algorithm is successfully implemented to achieve the translation of SL to TL without any type of human intervention, that is even in the case when the algorithm is not having the dictionary meaning of few or more words.

The work implemented and presented in the paper is limited with the use of *dhAturoop*, as we have used very few from available 2012. The future plan is to understand and model large set of known verbal roots in order to develop machine translation model more effective and accurate. Earlier some work has been carried out in modeling of Indic languages using neural models [11]. In the present work the modified direct machine translation approach has been used, in future there is a scope to use the neural model for Sanskrit language processing, which is capable to model the SL-TL language pair more easily and accurately.

References

1. Bikel, D., Zitouni, I.: Multilingual Natural Language Processing Applications. Pearson, London (2013)
2. Rathod, S.G.: Machine translation of natural language using different approaches: ETSTS. Int. J. Comput. Appl. (0975 – 8887)
3. Bharati, A., Chaitanya, V., Sangal, R.: Natural Language Processing - A Paninian Perspective (2016)
4. Upadhyay, P., Jaiswal, U.C., Ashish, K.: TranSish: Translator from Sanskrit to English-a rule based machine translation (2347–5161)
5. Siddiqui, T., Tiwary, U.S.: Natural Language Processing and Information Retrieval. Oxford Higher Education, Oxford (2015)
6. Briggs, R.: Knowledge representation in Sanskrit and artificial intelligence. AI Mag. **6**, 32 (1985)
7. Kiparsky, P.: On the architecture of Panini's grammar, January 2002
8. Panchal, B., Bakrola, V., Dabhi, D.: An efficient approach of knowledge representation using paninian rules of Sanskrit grammar. In: Sa, P.K., Bakshi, S., Hatzilygeroudis, I.K., Sahoo, M.N. (eds.) Recent Findings in Intelligent Computing Techniques. AISC, vol. 709, pp. 199–206. Springer, Singapore (2018). https://doi.org/10.1007/978-981-10-8633-5_21
9. Satyam, S., Bakarola, V., Sutaria, V.: Simulating the Paninian system of word formation in Sanskrit with computational linguistics for effective machine translation, August 2016
10. Jurafsky, D., Martin, J.H.: Speech and Language Processing. Pearson, London (2008)
11. Shah, P., Bakarola, V., Pati, S.: Neural machine translation system for Indic languages using deep neural architecture. In: Bhattacharyya, P., Sastry, H.G., Marriboyina, V., Sharma, R. (eds.) Smart and Innovative Trends in Next Generation Computing Technologies. CCIS, vol. 827, pp. 788–795. Springer, Singapore (2018). https://doi.org/10.1007/978-981-10-8657-1_62

QoS Based Resource Provisioning in Cloud Computing Environment: A Technical Survey

Shefali Varshney⑩, Rajinder Sandhu⑩, and P. K. Gupta⁽✉⁾⑩

Department of Computer Science and Engineering,
Jaypee University of Information Technology, Solan 173234, HP, India
shefali1926@gmail.com, rajsandhu1989@gmail.com, pkgupta@ieee.org

Abstract. Cloud computing is one of the computing methodology that can address the on demand requirement of most of the applications in efficient manner. This system also permits the pay-per usage rating model for the purpose of computing services which are delivered to the end users throughout the globe using Internet. Because of reduced resources it becomes very difficult for the cloud purveyors to offer all the end users their required services. One such challenge raised by the cloud application is management of Quality of Service (QoS) that is the matter of allocating resources to provide assured service on the basis of availability, performance and reliability. From the cloud vendors impression of cloud resources can be assigned in a reasonable manner. Thus it is at most importance to meet the QoS requirement and satisfaction level of cloud users. This paper aims at the study of various researchers in the field of Resource allocation and resource availability in cloud computing environment based on QoS requirements.

Keywords: QoS · QoE · Cloud computing · Resource availability · Resource allocation · Scheduling

1 Introduction

With the recent advancement in various technologies, cloud computing has emerged as a new paradigm providing various services to the end user. It has various characteristics which include multitenancy, scalability, productivity and performance [1]. Cloud computing refers to operations such as distribution of services over the web, hardware, and system software that grants the various required services in the data centres. At the same time cloud computing also faces some challenges like limited control to the end user, security, privacy and many quality issues [2]. Some of the quality issues are like Quality of Service (QoS) and Quality of experience (QoE) have a huge impact on cloud computing environment. Basically QoE is a subset of QoS that also endeavors the amount of service parameters. Services like cloud computing storage or computer network

© Springer Nature Singapore Pte Ltd. 2019
M. Singh et al. (Eds.): ICACDS 2019, CCIS 1046, pp. 711–723, 2019.
https://doi.org/10.1007/978-981-13-9942-8_66

falls under QoS which is defined as the amount of overall performance of the service. Further emergence of IoT has made this challenge more critical to tackle due to continuous interaction of user with the system.

IoT and cloud have developed into two very closely related internet technologies providing support to one another. Some previous studies have provided the evaluation model for QoS but to our knowledge no evaluation models have been proposed for IoT based applications based on QoE [3,4]. IoT based application are devices on web that collect data on real time basis which some time can result in late delivery of data. This late delivery of data affects QoE in many ways as it is not efficient enough for the end user to use IoT application devices [5]. To overcome from this issue one can do computations near to data generating devices which improves QoE in turn.

QoS is defined as the estimation on the whole performance of a service whereas QoE is defined as the level of user satisfaction over a service or product. QoS is basically a set of procedures that helps to manage the network resources based on some attributes. There are various attributes in QoS which are helpful in making the quality of services or applications better than their previous results. QoS and QoE are two quality issues which are interlinked with each other as they both helps in improving the quality of services and applications used in cloud [5]. Figure 1 shows the relation between various qualities aspects related to one single quality issue that is quality of service (QoS). All these quality aspects such as quality of data (QoD), quality of information (QoI) and quality of performance (QoP) share some indistinguishable attributes. As we know that QoE is directly related to QoS which results in mapping of the QoS into the users perceived QoE. Also, QoS is affected by various aspects of QoS which can be technical or non-technical. Technical aspects include the end to end network delay, coverage area and equipment flexibility whereas non-technical includes the support to customers, price decision based on service and providing services to the end user. QoS and QoE are equally important in providing good quality services to the applications.

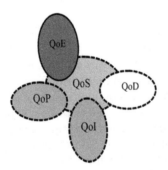

Fig. 1. Relationship of various quality metrics with QoS.

2   QoS Models

For delivering good quality characteristic, QoS is useful for cloud consumers who expect this and for the cloud purveyors, whoever requires the trade-off between the QoS levels and the operational cost. Various QoS based models have been proposed in the field of cloud computing to handle the challenges like security and privacy, latency, resource scheduling, fast internet speed, energy consumption, load balancing, service composition and performance, as represented in Fig. 2 [6]. The major issue in cloud is of security and privacy, as there is no control on data which is being transferred or received. Performance is another issue in cloud computing that consider the capability of cloud organisation. Resource scheduling in cloud is considered at various levels namely hardware, software, security and privacy and further other features are dependent on management and resources. The QoS here means the availability, reliability and level of concert on hand with the help of a platform. QoS is basic for cloud users and expect from the purveyors to deliver the declared features. In this technical survey we have discussed the issues related to resource allocation based on QoS in cloud computing environment. QoS can be improved by balancing the load on various machines by consecutively reducing the delay. Further using these system models the values of QoS such as availability, reliability and response time are evaluated. There are various QoS methods like resource management, admission control mechanism, scheduling mechanisms, performance models and monitoring mechanisms [8]. All these mechanisms provide a closer view about the current methods, techniques and the applications to cloud computing problems.

Fig. 2. Relationship of various quality metrics with QoS.

2.1   Cloud Based Model

The term cloud computing can be portrayed as the organised device mechanism in which the users would be able to utilize the computing applications [9–12]. The main objective is to make the storage infrastructure and computing available for the end users regardless of their location and time. However, various cloud based models have been proposed in the field of the trust management, load balancing and queuing model but still a lot of improvement is required to obtain better QoS [13]. Here, Table 1 summarizes various cloud based models proposed over the period of time.

2.2   Cloud Computing Challenges

There are various challenges [30] which have serious risk to the end user satiability factor. All these challenges are listed as follows:

- **Resource Scheduling** [6]: It is a challenging job and scheduling particular resources to cloud efforts relies on the QoS demands of cloud appliances. In cloud computing environment issue such as uncertainty, heterogeneity and dispersion of resources discovered the resource allocation problem which cannot be considered with available resource allocation strategies.
- **Security** [6]: It is one of the main issue which leads to causing risk for a huge amount of data stored on cloud in different locations even in all over globe. Through many approaches on the subject in cloud computing, data privacy and security are more significant for the forthcoming growth of cloud computing technology in industry and government.
- **Performance** [6]: It is also one of the important issue which measured the power of cloud organisation. The results might not come out to be good enough with respect of some parameters such as memory, CPU speed and bandwidth.
- **Load balancing** [6]: With the help of this technique in cloud computing workload has been scattered among all the nodes. Basically it is used to get in touch with great consumers and evaluate the proportion of resources to make sure none of the nodes are overloaded.
- **Service Composition** [13]: Due to ebullient development of the services which are offered cloud service agents faces some difficulties in delivering the quality of service advancements.
- **Fast internet speed** [6]: With the support of cloud systems, business gets the ability to keep money on hardware and software however requires overspending on bandwidth. This is not feasible to fully utilize the services of cloud with low speed communication channels.
- **Latency** [6]: One of the major issues in cloud computing environment which causes difficulties in the enjoyable and usable devices. Latency in the data exchanges over the Internet can be much higher. This delay can cause increase in the costs to users of several cloud services.
- **Energy Consumption** [16]: Amazon conducted a survey which conveys the cost depletion of its data centres to be 53% and the entire cost is used by the servers. The CPU, memory, disk storage and network are important consumers of energy in a server.

Table 1. Cloud based models

S.No.	Category	Authors	Proposed model	Description/advantage	Challenges
1.	Trust model	Manuel [9]	Trust Management system	Considers only four parameters like turnaround time, availability, reliability and data integrity	No information about parameters like Honesty, utilization of resources, and return on investments
		Chandrasekar [14]	To monitor QoS and trust using Markov chain model	Proposed model is used to establish the trust and compression technique	Issue of trust on service provider need to be considered
		Abbadi and Alawneh [15]	Proposed a framework for developing trust in cloud	Framework helps in addressing the identified challenges	Issues related to scheduling need to be improved
2.	Load balancing	Zhao and Huang [13]	Developed a load balancing model COMPARE AND BALANCE	The problem of intra cloud load balancing is resolved using proposed model through the adaptive live migration of virtual machines	This model does not support affinity and anti-affinity
		Maguluri et al. [6]	Proposed a stochastic model for cloud computing cluster	This model discusses resource allocation problem for scheduling and load balancing in cloud computing	Proposed model disscusse only about resource allocation and consider the parameters like throughput and delay for performance improvement

(continued)

Table 1. (*continued*)

S.No.	Category	Authors	Proposed model	Description/advantage	Challenges
		Peng et al. [7]	Proposed a bee colony load balancing algorithm based mathematical model	Discusses about the cloud task scheduling process	Discussed load balancing issue in cloud using bee colony algorithm only
		Bhandari and Kaur [16]	Proposed an algorithmic model based on the availability of Virtual machine (VM)	Availability index value is calculated for each and every VM over a to load in real time	They have not evaluated appropriate assign tasks
3.	Security and privacy	Choi et al. [17]	Proposed an ontology based access semantic model	This model help in identifying the variation between service provider and user in permitted access control	This model can address the limitation of cloud computing only for dynamic access control
		Wei et al. [18]	Proposed a secure computation auditing and privacy cheating discouragement protocol is proposed	This protocol provides data security in cloud	They have not formalized the security model in cloud
		Kavin and Ganapathi [19]	Chinese Remainder theorem (CRT) based data storage model	This model helps in storing data more securely using cloud database	Implements traditional encryption and decryption techniques only
		Al-Sharhan et al. [20]	Proposed a security framework for cloud computing environment	This model helps in providing various security mechanisms such that the benefits of cloud computing are realised	Issue of access control, identity, and authentication management need to addressed

Table 2. Resource provisioning in cloud computing

Category	Author	Proposed technique	Advantages	Challenges
Resource availability	Samimi et al. [21]	Combinatorial Double Auction Resource Allocation (CDARA)	This model helps in evaluating the efficiency from an economic perspective	The model evaluate on only two criteria's
	Goiri et al. [22]	Proposed a resource level metric	This model helps resource suppliers to allocate their resources dynamically	Need to consider resource utilization of the services in real-time
	Calheiros et al. [5]	Proposed a technique for distributing resources to software as a service (SaaS) applications	This technique adapts to the workload variations associated to applications	Need to address changes in VM's and their capacity
	Calheiros et al. [5]	Proposed a technique to extend the capacity of desktop grids	Discusses features and key concepts that maintains this integration	Requires some new policies for scheduling service
Resource allocation	Zhou et al. [23]	Resource evaluation and selection algorithm (RESA)	This method helps in providing multi QoS Constraints	Focuses only on scheduling method and combined preference matrix
	Wang et al. [24]	An adaptive scheduling with QoS satisfaction Algorithm (AsQ)	Designed fast scheduling strategies	Need to discuss various factors like energy efficiency and operation cost

Table 3. Various algorithms for resource provisioning in cloud computing

Algorithms	Author	Technique used	Challenges
Offloading algorithms	Xiao et al. [8]	Proposed an offloading forwarding approach	Need to include the wireless network supported system
	Wang et al. [24]	Proposed a technique to minimize average response timefor events reported by vehicles	The utilisation of vehicles outside the communication range is not considered
	Wang et al. [25]	Proposed an optimal allocation techinique	Doesn't discusses any online mechanism to allocate the computing service
Cloud computing algorithms	Ye et al. [26]	Proposed an approach based on genetic algorithm for composition of services	QoS values are already known needs to be eliminated
	Xu et al. [27]	Proposed a Berger model based algorithm	Based on the mapping relation between QoS and resource
	Li et al. [28]	Proposed an optimizing chord algorithm	Need to consider interaction with storage resources
	Dutta et al. [29]	Some popular genetic cross over operators like PMX, CX and mutation operators are used	Need to consider more real time job allocation restriction like machine failure and political concern

3   Resource Provisioning in Cloud Computing

Resource provisioning in cloud computing as presented in Table 2, is supported with two major factors known as resource availability and resource allocation. Resource availability is the vision to make available the resources anywhere and anytime. If the allotment to the resources is not organized accurately then the services gets starve for allocation of their required resources. Thus by analyzing a single cloud service resource and therefore on the basis of some models the availability of cloud computing services gets evaluated [31]. Samimi et al. [21] have proposed a new technique for allocating resources in cloud computing environment known as Combinatorial Double Auction Resource Allocation (CDARA) technique. This model is helpful in evaluating its efficiency with an economic perspective. Later new approaches have been proposed for allocating resource with less amount of wastage and more profit. These approaches consider various parameters like time, number of processor requests, cost, resource assigned, resource availability, resource selection etc. In [22], Goiri et al. have presented a resource level metric that enables the users to allocate their resources dynamically between the running services with respect to their demands. This metric helps in performance of CPU by managing and specifying fine grain guarantees. So with the help of this metric resources can be allocated dynamically. In [5], Calheiros et al. have proposed a technique for distributing resources to software as a service (SaaS) applications. The main aim of this model is to fulfill the QoS targets related to service time and usage of available resources. They have used Aneka platform for developing scalable applications and for integration between the Desktop Grids and cloud [5]. In [23] an algorithm for resource evaluation and selection is presented with an extensible QoS model. In private cloud to increase the rate of resource utilization an algorithm is proposed to reduce task response time in [24].

3.1 Resource Provisioning Algorithms

To improve the QoS and QoE various types of algorithms such as offloading algorithm, cloud computing based algorithms [32,33] and scheduling algorithms [34] are being used as presented in Table 3. The development in cloud computing technologies has led to provide distinct cloud services to its service subscribers. These services can be classified into two groups: Application services and Utility computing services. These services are measured with the help of some QoS parameters and QoS model [26]. Further, considering the characteristics of the cloud computing a job scheduling algorithm based on Berger model has been proposed. This algorithm can execute the user tasks [27]. The main aim of the cloud provider is to achieve greater benefit and, satisfy the various QoS for user's jobs. A genetic algorithm has been proposed for a much better scheduling in the cloud environment in. Proposed technique is helpful in maximizing the profit of cloud providers which is supported by a number of evaluations and results [29]. In a system, resources also need to be scheduled such as they are not creating problems for the user in future works. Thus QoS differentiate system model has been presented in [28] for allocating resources in cloud computing system among various QoS - constrained users. To model the problem of cloud service composition an approach based on Genetic Algorithm is proposed in [35].

4 Challenges and Discussions

QoS main objective is to enhance the QoS by maintaining the delay to a smaller quantity by weighing the load in cloud computing environment. Audio, multimedia video conferencing etc. are planned to be the primary applications of this area where some improvement in delay might be useless. This section describes some challenges such as security and privacy, latency, resource scheduling, fast Internet speed, energy consumption, load balancing, service composition and performance which are described as follows:

- Strictly providing the required resources to the cloud and by proper scheduling of the resources would make the resources more organised.
- Exponential increase in the links which are harmful and can be utilised by the invaders for malicious activities. Also increasing usage of data can led to sensor based connectivity and these nodes can further misuse the data collected from the users.
- By fulfilling the user demands and services of the end users from the cloud, the performance can be improved.
- Data in the cloud is dynamically stored among all the nodes resulting in reduce in load balancing problem in cloud computing.
- Difficulties as faced by the cloud service purveyors for delivering an extensive range of composite cloud services, the purveyors requires to setup a shared understanding on large scale cloud scheme leading to a proper service composition.
- To make the network speed work faster for the cloud the computer, servers and routers must be able to communicate continuously sharing information.
- In resource allocation there are two types of workloads in cloud known as homogeneous and heterogeneous. Thus the cloud systems should be prepared such that both of these types of workloads can be allocated.
- Latency is the main issue which can be improved by using a wired connection and thus resulting in reduce costs which improves the satisfaction level of the customers.
- A server is built consisting of various components such as CPU, power supply, fans, memory and disks whose power intake can be enhanced by using hardware optimization leading to less energy consumption.

5   Conclusion

Cloud has extremely eased the provisioning of capacity method, at the same time it also produces various issues in the administration of the QoS. QoS includes availability, the levels of performance and reliability provided by the application or platform or the infrastructure that serves it. Research in modeling of workload and their applications in QoS supervision in cloud computing. Various QoS related parameters have been addressed in this work in which throughput, availability, and response time are some of the essential factors considered for cloud computing. QoS attributes consumer class supplies a structure for the choice of the better matched service according to the end user. The security class is helpful in the assessment of security and privacy issue in service associates. Eventually, the network architecture and service execution time groups provisions a structure for evaluating hardware functioning and sketching an understanding of the network architecture. This paper also discusses the various research actions that are being considered in the system and workload modeling, their distinct applications in managing QoS in cloud computing environment. In this paper, we have provided the technical measures for provisioning of resource allocation and resource availability in cloud computing environment. Further, we have discussed the various challenges in cloud computing environment and how these challenges could be important in proposing future designs and algorithms. Also, a detailed discussion related to various cloud based QoS models for developing trust in cloud, designing load balancing algorithms and most importantly for security and privacy preparing such algorithms which help in detecting the difference between the service suppliers and the authorised access control users.

References

1. Akpan, H.A., Vadhanam, B.R.: A survey on quality of service in cloud computing. Int. J. Comput. Trends Technol. **27**(1), 58–63 (2015)
2. Floris, A., Atzori, L.: Quality of experience in the multimedia Internet of Things: definition and practical use-cases. In: Proceedings of IEEE International Conference on Communication Workshop (ICCW), pp. 1747–1752. IEEE (2015)
3. Dey, S., Sen, S.K.: Trust evaluation model in cloud using reputation, recommendation and QOS based approach. In: Procedings of 2018 International Conference on Research in Intelligent and Computing in Engineering (RICE), pp. 1–5. IEEE (2018)
4. Gupta, P.K., Maharaj, B.T., Malekian, R.: A novel and secure IoT based cloud centric architecture to perform predictive analysis of users activities in sustainable health centres. Multimed. Tools Appl. **76**(18), 18489–18512 (2017). https://doi.org/10.1007/s11042-016-4050-6
5. Calheiros, R.N., Ranjan, R., Buyya, R.: Virtual machine provisioning based on analytical performance and QoS in cloud computing environments. In: Proceedings of International Conference on Parallel Processing, pp. 295–304. IEEE (2011)
6. Maguluri, S.T., Srikant, R., Ying, L.: Stochastic models of load balancing and scheduling in cloud computing clusters. In: Proceedings of Infocom, pp. 702–710. IEEE (2012)
7. Peng, H., Han, W., Yao, J., Fu, C.: The realization of load balancing algorithm in cloud computing. In: Proceedings of the 2nd International Conference on Computer Science and Application Engineering, p. 140. ACM (2018)
8. Xiao, Y., Krunz, M.: QoE and power efficiency tradeoff for fog computing networks with fog node cooperation. In: Proceedings of INFOCOM 2017-IEEE Conference on Computer Communications, pp. 1–9. IEEE (2017)
9. Manuel, P.: A trust model of cloud computing based on Quality of Service. Ann. Oper. Res. **233**(1), 281–292 (2015)
10. Gupta, P.K., Tyagi, V., Singh, S.K.: Predictive Computing and Information Security. Springer, Singapore (2017). https://doi.org/10.1007/978-981-10-5107-4
11. Thakur, A.S., Gupta, P.K.: Framework to improve data integrity in multi cloud environment. Int. J. Comput. Appl. **87**(10), 28–32 (2014)
12. Gupta, P.K., Maharaj, B.T., Malekian, R.: A novel and secure IoT based cloud centric architecture to perform predictive analysis of users activities in sustainable health centres. Multimed. Tools Appl. **76**(18), 18489–18512 (2017)
13. Zhao, Y., Huang, W.: Adaptive distributed load balancing algorithm based on live migration of virtual machines in cloud. In: Proceedings of Fifth International Joint Conference on INC, IMS and IDC, pp. 170–175. IEEE (2009)
14. Chandrasekar, A., Chandrasekar, K., Mahadevan, M., Varalakshmi, P.: QoS monitoring and dynamic trust establishment in the cloud. In: Li, R., Cao, J., Bourgeois, J. (eds.) GPC 2012. LNCS, vol. 7296, pp. 289–301. Springer, Heidelberg (2012). https://doi.org/10.1007/978-3-642-30767-6_25

15. Abbadi, I.M., Alawneh, M.: A framework for establishing trust in the cloud. Comput. Electr. Eng. **38**(5), 1073–1087 (2012)
16. Bhandari, A., Kaur, K.: An enhanced post-migration algorithm for dynamic load balancing in cloud computing environment. In: Chakraborty, M., Chakrabarti, S., Balas, V.E., Mandal, J.K. (eds.) Proceedings of International Ethical Hacking Conference 2018. AISC, vol. 811, pp. 59–73. Springer, Singapore (2019). https://doi.org/10.1007/978-981-13-1544-2_6
17. Choi, C., Choi, J., Kim, P.: Ontology-based access control model for security policy reasoning in cloud computing. J. Supercomput. **67**(3), 711–722 (2014)
18. Wei, L., et al.: Security and privacy for storage and computation in cloud computing. Inf. Sci. **258**, 371–386 (2014)
19. Kavin, B.P., Ganapathy, S.: A secured storage and privacy-preserving model using CRT for providing security on cloud and IoT-based applications. Comput. Netw. **151**, 181–190 (2019)
20. Al-Sharhan, S., Omran, E., Lari, K.: An integrated holistic model for an eHealth system: a national implementation approach and a new cloud-based security model. Int. J. Inf. Manag. **47**, 121–130 (2019)
21. Samimi, P., Teimouri, Y., Mukhtar, M.: A combinatorial double auction resource allocation model in cloud computing. Inf. Sci. **357**, 201–216 (2016)
22. Goiri, Í., Julià, F., Fitó, J.O., Macías, M., Guitart, J.: Resource-level QoS metric for CPU-based guarantees in cloud providers. In: Altmann, J., Rana, O.F. (eds.) GECON 2010. LNCS, vol. 6296, pp. 34–47. Springer, Heidelberg (2010). https://doi.org/10.1007/978-3-642-15681-6_3
23. Zhou, J., Yan, M., Ye, X., Lu, H.: An algorithm of resource evaluation and selection based on multi-QoS constraints. In: Proceedings of Seventh Conference on Web Information Systems and Applications, pp. 49–52. IEEE (2010)
24. Wang, W.-J., Chang, Y.-S., Lo, W.-T., Lee, Y.-K.: Adaptive scheduling for parallel tasks with QoS satisfaction for hybrid cloud environments. J. Supercomput. **66**(2), 783–811 (2013)
25. Wang, X., Ning, Z., Wang, L.: Offloading in Internet of vehicles: a fog-enabled real-time traffic management system. IEEE Trans. Ind. Inf. **14**(10), 4568–4578 (2018)
26. Ye, Z., Zhou, X., Bouguettaya, A.: Genetic algorithm based QoS-aware service compositions in cloud computing. In: Yu, J.X., Kim, M.H., Unland, R. (eds.) DASFAA 2011. LNCS, vol. 6588, pp. 321–334. Springer, Heidelberg (2011). https://doi.org/10.1007/978-3-642-20152-3_24
27. Xu, B., Zhao, C., Hu, E., Hu, B.: Job scheduling algorithm based on berger model in cloud environment. Adv. Eng. Softw. **42**(7), 419–425 (2011)
28. Li, B., Song, A.M., Song, J.: A distributed QoS-constraint task scheduling scheme in cloud computing environment: model and algorithm. Adv. Inf. Sci. Ser. Sci. **4**(5), 283–291 (2012)
29. Dutta, D., Joshi, R.C.: A genetic: algorithm approach to cost-based multi-QoS job scheduling in cloud computing environment. In: Proceedings of the International Conference & Workshop on Emerging Trends in Technology, pp. 422–427. ACM(2011)
30. Singh, M., Gupta, P.K. Srivastava, V.M.: Key challenges in implementing cloud computing in Indian healthcare industry. In: Pattern Recognition Association of South Africa and Robotics and Mechatronics (PRASA-RobMech), pp. 162–167. IEEE (2017)
31. Shen, J., Zou, D., Jin, H., Yuan, B., Dai, W.: A domain-divided configurable security model for cloud computing-based telecommunication services. J. Supercomput. **75**(1), 109–122 (2019)

32. Gugnani, G., Ghrera, S.P., Gupta, P.K., Malekian, R., Maharaj, B.T.J.: Implementing DNA encryption technique in web services to embed confidentiality in cloud. In: Satapathy, S.C., Raju, K.S., Mandal, J.K., Bhateja, V. (eds.) Proceedings of the Second International Conference on Computer and Communication Technologies. AISC, vol. 381, pp. 407–415. Springer, New Delhi (2016). https://doi.org/10.1007/978-81-322-2526-3_42

33. Gupta, P.K., Singh, G.: A novel human computer interaction aware algorithm to minimize energy consumption. Wirel. Pers. Commun. **81**(2), 661–683 (2015)

34. Malekian, R., Kavishe, A.F., Maharaj, B.T., et al.: Smart vehicle navigation system using Hidden Markov Model and RFID technology. Wirel. Pers. Commun. **90**(4), 1717–1742 (2016). https://doi.org/10.1007/s11277-016-3419-1

35. Kholidy, H.A., Hassan, H., Sarhan, A.M., Erradi, A., Abdelwahed, S.: QoS optimization for cloud service composition based on economic model. In: Giaffreda, R., et al. (eds.) IoT360 2014 LNICST, vol. 150, pp. 355–366. Springer, Cham (2015). https://doi.org/10.1007/978-3-319-19656-5_48

Optimizing Smart Parking System by Using Fog Computing

Righa Tandon and P. K. Gupta[✉]

Department of Computer Science and Engineering,
Jaypee University of Information Technology, Solan 173 234, HP, India
righatandon@gmail.com, pkgupta@ieee.org

Abstract. Finding the vacant space for parking a vehicle during peak hours is becoming a difficult task at ones end. Parking process whether in shopping malls, restaurants, or offices etc. is a long process and also leads to waste of gasoline. Smart car parking helps in finding the parking slot through Vehicular Ad Hoc Networks (VANET's). For vehicle communication, some devices such as roadside units and on-board units are present that provides parking slot information. In the proposed work, we have introduced an online reservation facility for parking slot. People can reserve their parking space in advance before reaching to their venues in advance. This will help in reducing the waiting time for the parking allocation to the particular vehicle. This will also help to enhance the parking capabilities and will increase the efficiency when compared to other parking strategies. Our proposed approach can minimize the cost of parking on per person basis, exhaust of vehicle, and indirectly it will impact on save of wastage of gasoline and will keep the environment green.

Keywords: VANET · Fog computing · Cost · Vehicles

1 Introduction

Recently with the growth of technology in every possible dimensions of human life, the quality of life has been improved a lot and one can not deny the contribution of various smart applications in this improvement. Several studies have already been performed on these smart applications designed for vehicle parking allocation and management. Finding the best location for vehicle parking in the parking area is one of the time consuming process and also becoming one of the major problem in almost every countries. There are two major problems faced by most of the vehicle owner (1) wastage of time (2) wastage of gasoline [1]. One has to keep on waiting or roaming near parking area unless and until they find any space for parking their vehicle. This scenario leads to vehicles keep on waiting outside the parking space for getting their turn but they have no way to get the information that when their turn will come for parking their vehicle or when an already parked vehicle will leave the parking premises. This results

M. Singh et al. (Eds.): ICACDS 2019, CCIS 1046, pp. 724–737, 2019.
https://doi.org/10.1007/978-981-13-9942-8_67

into traffic jams outside of most of the parking area. So to overcome from this worst scenario, there is a requirement of an effective and efficient vehicle parking system.

In the proposed smart vehicle parking system and ad-hoc networks and road-side units have been used. Communication devices such as on-board units have also been used for collecting the information regarding availability of parking space and the same has been shared with other vehicles. Number of sensor based devices have been used to implement this smart parking system. Still there are few challenges for VANET based parking system like collection of information and sharing it with other vehicles by using ad hoc network may not support timely updation of information, which can be a critical issue. Thus for real time smart parking systems, VANET based parking system provide a perfect solution for many types of parking related problems [2]. In order to overcome from the above-mentioned problems of allocation of parking space using VANET, fog computing archetype has been introduced in this paper for designing smart parking system.

Fog computing model provides all the resources at the edge of the network. Various fog nodes will be available near each parking premises that will provide the information related to availability of parking area to the vehicles and help them to take parking decision. Also in addition to that, an online facility has also been provided for the reservation of the parking space in advance. Users can reserve their parking before reaching to any parking premises. User has to register himself first if he is using online reservation for parking. Once he is registered for that online facility, then he can simply login to reserve his parking area before reaching to that place. User can also cancel the reserved parking area and in that case that parking area will be allocated to another vehicle from the waith list. Parking cost will be lesser for the online reservation parking as waiting time is lesser. The information regarding online reservation parking gets updated using fog nodes and also the availability of parking space is checked by considering both the information about online and on spot parking reservation. All the information regarding parking gets up-to-date using fog nodes. Parking requests are processed for both online and on spot parking area by using fog nodes. Requests that are in waiting list gets uploaded to the cloud for their further later processing as per the availability of the parking space. Allocation of parking area is provided by applying fog computing to VANET based real time parking systems.

2   Related Work

For finding parking area, smart parking makes use of information and communication technologies, fog computing, and cloud computing. Previously, a number of studies have been done to resolve the issue of allocation of parking space by number of researchers [3–8]. However, smart transportation is getting more attention nowadays. In [9–14], for smart parking, fog computing was applied that support various computations and also reduces the response time. Fog computing provides various resources at the edge of the network that is closer to the sensors and IoT devices.

2.1 Smart Parking Models

In [15], Zhu et al. have introduced five sensor cloud pricing models. Each model of sensor cloud pricing examines the following aspects: contract span of each sensor cloud user, running schedule of sensor cloud, resources utilization of sensor cloud by each sensor cloud user, sensitive data volume and the path that sensor cloud follows to communicate sensitive data to sensor cloud user through wireless sensor network. In [9], Balzano and Vitale have presented a model in which vehicle to vehicle, distance geometry problem and wireless positioning have been considered. Proposed model was aligned for the indoor navigation in the parking areas. This model also provides facility of anti-theft and anti-collision protection and helps in finding the area and location for the parking of a vehicle. In [16], Hou et al. have discussed a novel system model for computation and communication of available resources. They have introduced the vehicular fog computing model for the direct communication between vehicles. In [17], Huang and Xu have used adaptive content reservation scheme model for the reservation of data in vehicular cloud-fog network. The proposed scheme is used for the quality of service in real time streaming. Tokens are used for preallocating the content in the real time streaming in the proposed model. In [18], Kim et al. have introduced a shared parking model based on roadside cloud and fog computing parking slot repository (RFPARK) in which vehicles will directly communicate with the fog servers. User can make request for parking anytime that will be processed using fog server. In [19], Mukherjee et al. have introduced a framework model for reducing the traffic overhead in industrial applications. This framework helps in preventing the uploading of irrelevant data to the cloud data centres. In [20], Zhang et al. have proposed hierarchical resource management model for optimizing the performance of cooperative fog-computing based intelligent vehicular network. Distributed computation and storage is possible using this model. Inter-fog and quality of service resource management has also been included in this proposed model. In [21], Park and Yoo have used fog computing, Software Defined Networks (SDN), and Fifth-Generation (5G) networks based model for managing the network state information, connection recovery and server failure recovery process. In [22], Rajabioun and Ioannou have used multivariate spatiotemporal models for predicting the available space in the parking lot. The proposed model is also used for recommending the location for the parking of the vehicles. The availability for the parking location is checked in both context i.e. on-street and off-street. In [23], Mei and Tian have introduced a parking choice behavior model for analyzing the parking choices of the users. Parking guidance model is also used for the prediction of parking guidance and information.

2.2   Smart Parking Algorithms

In [10], Wang et al. have discussed the distance geometry problem (DGP) algorithm for determining the graph that will represent best network for the parking. This algorithm also helps in finding the location of the vehicles in the parking area. Availability of parking area will be easily shown to the user by using DGP algorithm. In [18], Kim et al. have used the parking slots association (PSA) algorithm for finding available area for parking. This algorithm helps in allocating the parking area to the vehicles in the fair manner. Also fair tradeoff is also discussed between vehicles and parking areas by the discussed PSA algorithm. In [20], Zhang et al. have used the inter-fog quality of service aware resource management algorithm for enhancing the load balancing and stability of fog network. Resource management behavior is managed by the coordinator through balancing data flow of local fog servers. In [23], Mei and Tian have discussed the standard genetic algorithm for finding any illegal parking in the parking space. Proposed algorithm is responsible for finding the available space and location of the parking space in the parking area for the vehicles. In [24], Zoeter et al. have used an algorithm for calculating the parking charges of the parked vehicles in the parking area. Parking rates will be high if there is any congestion otherwise reduced rates will be applied accordingly.

3   Methodology

To overcome from the various issues related to allocation of parking area as discussed in the previous section, we have proposed a fog computing based system model for smart vehicle parking as shown in Fig. 1. Fog servers have been used whether the space is vacant or filled will be informed to each fog node and similar information is updated throughout all the fog servers. The information for available space is delivered to all the roadside units (RSUs) by fog servers which is independent of geographical location of parking area. proposed system model consist of following layers:

- *Parking area* - represents both public and private area for vehicle parking. Here, parking of vehicles is under the surveillance of CCTV cameras and sensors and are also embedded for the monitoring purpose. With the help of sensors available spaces for the parking can be detected. Benefits of smart parking can be for both owner of the vehicle and the parking in-charge.
- *Fog Nodes* - In the proposed system model, we have used fog computing for the smart vehicle parking system. Fog computing is an extension of cloud computing that can easily process the user requests as it provides resources at the edge of the network. In the proposed model, fog nodes consist of sensors and fog servers. Information regarding available and occupied spaces in the parking area is further updated with all the fog servers.
- *Roadside units* - It help the vehicles to communicate with each other. Roadside units find the parking related information on availability basis and send

it to the requesting vehicles. Vehicle owner can also make requests accordingly. Request is further processed by the fog nodes and information regarding request gets stored in the cloud for future purpose.

– *Cloud* - All the information related to the vacant spaces and occupied spaces in parking area gets collected on timely basis and sent to cloud via fog-nodes, for information storage. Requests of all vehicles gets processed according to the updated information present in the cloud.

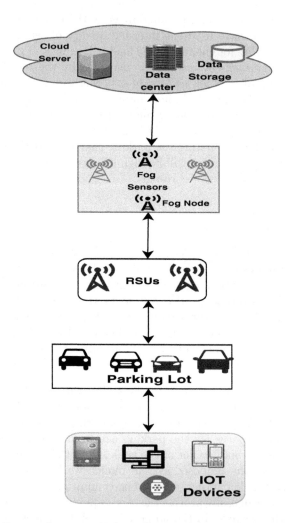

Fig. 1. Proposed smart vehicle parking model using fog environment.

3.1 On-Line Vehicle Reservation Parking

On-line reservation for vehicle parking facility has been provided in the proposed model. User can register for reserving the vehicle parking on-line. Once vehicle owner completes the one time on-line registration process, they can reserve the parking area before reaching to that place. One can also cancel the reservation for parking if there is any previous reservation done for parking area. In this case, user who is in waiting list gets allocated the space in the parking area. The information regarding on-line reservation also gets updated to the cloud so that other vehicle owner who have requested for the parking area can be allocated the space in the reserved parking area. This parking information has to be synced with the parking model of fog environment for smart parking purpose. The on-line process for the parking reservation of the vehicles gets tracked using fog nodes. Fog nodes frequently updates the availability of parking space on the clouds. Vehicle owner whose parking space is reserved before hand, must reach timely to the parking area otherwise that parking area gets allocated to other from the wait list. On-line vehicle reservation parking system is more beneficial as compared to on-spot parking system which is still in use in most of the countries. In on-line reservation parking, one can reserve the parking area for any particular day. Once the parking space is reserved and confirmed, then one need not to wait in the long waiting queues for parking a vehicle and will obtain the location for parking his vehicle (Fig. 2).

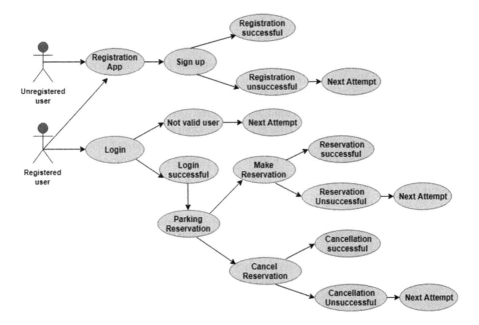

Fig. 2. A use case diagram for on-line vehicle reservation parking.

3.2   Proposed System Design

In this section, we have considered reservation parameters for parking so that the waiting time of vehicles could be minimized. In this paper, we have mentioned how the parking requests are further processed. Fog nodes have been used for storing and managing the below parameters and status of parking lot. For the proposed work we have considered the following parameters:

- **Parking ID (PID)**: Smart parking premises in the cities are assigned with unique identification that differentiates one parking area from other.
- **Parking area status (PS)**: Status of the parking area gets checked whether the requested space is occupied or not. If space is occupied during the requested period then set $PS = 1$ otherwise set $PS = 0$.
- **Vehicle ID (VID)**: Each vehicle is represented by unique identification number via its number plate. This identification can also be used to find which vehicle is parked at particular parking slot. On board units present in the vehicles can also be used as unique identification for the vehicles.
- **Time Stamp (TS)**: At parking place when vehicle owner starts to park their vehicles, the time taken is recorded in this time stamp field. If PS is zero, this field will be kept empty.
- **Time duration (TD)**: When fog-nodes interact with vehicles, they can find out the parking slot status. So time duration can also be used to find the approximate parking time.
- **Special quota (SPL)**: Some parking space in the parking area is reserved for special purpose. So that parking comes under special quota for granted people.

Vehicles that want to send parking request first has to initialize the connection with roadside units and fog-nodes. Once the connection has been established, request for parking could be sent by vehicle to fog-nodes. Fog-nodes further send that request to cloud for checking the status of parking area for the mentioned period. If the space is available then this information is delivered to the requesting entity through the fog-nodes. If the space is fully occupied for the mentioned period then the request for parking will be processed later and updated information is provided to the requested vehicle once the wait list gets cleared (Fig. 3).

- **Parking allocation cost**: Here, many factors affect the decision making for assigning parking space to the vehicles like parking priorities, parking fees, wait time and number of requests for parking space. Parking requests are processed according to the availability of the parking area. The total cost for allocation of parking area can be calculated as follows:

$$Total cost = cost_{waiting} + cost_{timeduration}$$

Sensors like surveillance cameras will monitor the vehicles and fog-nodes will keep the track of vehicles that are waiting at the parking entrance. The parking request will be processed based on the confirmed information sent by the vehicle.

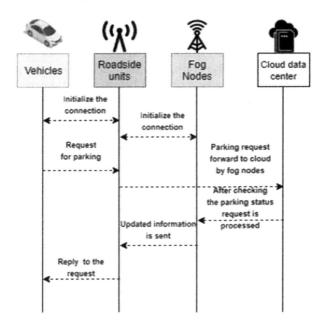

Fig. 3. Vehicles request for parking.

Waiting queue can also be monitored. Estimation time for each vehicle as it arrives can be calculated by fog-node based on the parking request of vehicles. Parking space information is further upgraded after every fixed time interval and is denoted by T_{inv}. The count of number of vehicles that are waiting at the parking entrance is denoted by Num_{Vi}. Total waiting time is expressed as T_{Wi}. We have calculated the minimum number of updates for parking space:

$$M_{min} = mi\left\{M|\sum_{n=1}^{M}VCSL[j] \geq Num_{vi}\right\} \tag{1}$$

where $VCSL[j] =$ Number of vacant slots for parking

Waiting time can now be expressed as follows:

$$T_{wi} = M_{min} \times T_{inv} + T_{dur}$$

where T_{dur} is the time duration that starts when vehicle begins to park till whole parking procedure is finished. Waiting cost for vehicle i can be expressed as $Cost_{waiting}$ and is calculated as follows:

$$Cost_{waiting} = L \times T_{Wi} \tag{2}$$

where L is the waiting cost per time unit.

3.3 Proposed Algorithm for Parking Area Allocation

In this section, we have used modified greedy algorithm for the allocation of parking area to the vehicles. Fog-nodes keep the track of all the requests made by vehicle owners. Parking status gets checked before allocating the parking space to the vehicles. Here parking request is received by the fog-nodes. After receiving the request for the parking space, availability will be checked for the available parking area. If the space is available for the parking, then the particular request for the parking gets processed and location is assigned to the vehicle accordingly. If the parking space is not available at that particular time, then that request for parking will be uploaded to the cloud data center and processed later-on. After assigning the location to a vehicle, the total cost gets calculated for the vehicle by considering the waiting time and time duration.

Algorithm 1. Modified Greedy Algorithm

Input: Fog Nodes (FN), parking status, parking requests by vehicles PReq.
Output: Decision of parking slot allocation.
Procedure: 1. IF Parking request is received by fog node DO
2. Check for available space.
3. IF AVLS[i] > 0 THEN
4. Parking request is processed by assigning LOC[i].
5. ELSE
6. Parking request will be uploaded to cloud data center.
7. FOR k=0:N DO
8. IF vehicle is parked at parking location DO
9. Calculate the total cost (by considering waiting time and time duration)
10. END
end Procedure

---

4 Experimental Results

The initial experimental setup starts by considering the intake capacity of parking lot for parking. Once parking space capacity is mentioned, proposed system can allocate parking area to the each requesting vehicles. Proposed system also consider the time duration of parking as one of the input. This ensures in calculating the waiting time for the vehicles. A vehicle for which online reservation for the parking is done need not to wait for the allocation of the parking space. Fog-nodes helps to share the parking information among other requesting vehicles. Fog-nodes tries to process the parking requests in the order they are received by the servers. This also keeps the track of online parking requests and processes them according to the vacant space available. Total cost is calculated by considering the waiting time and time duration.

In the experimental results we have used modified greedy algorithm for parking space allocation in which cost calculation is modified by considering the different parameters. Figure 4 represents the average cost for on-spot parking for the various number of parked vehicles. Whereas, Fig. 5. represents the average cost for on-line reservation parking for the various number of parked vehicles. We have evaluated our results by calculating the total cost. The comparison of total cost for on-spot parking and on-line parking reservation is also shown in Fig. 6. Obtained results shows that the total cost of using on-line reservation for parking is less as compared to the total cost for on spot parking by using fog nodes.

From Table 1, it is clear that the average cost for the on-line reservation parking is less as compared to on-spot parking average cost. The number of

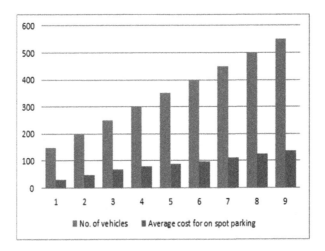

Fig. 4. Number of vehicles versus average cost for on spot parking using fog nodes.

Table 1. Average cost for on spot and online reservation parking

Number of vehicles	Average cost for on spot parking (cost per minute)	Average cost for online reservation parking (cost per minute)
150	30	14
200	48	32
250	67	51
300	79	63
350	87	71
400	98	81
450	110	93
500	125	106
550	138	118

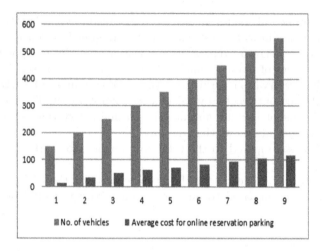

Fig. 5. Number of vehicles versus average cost for online reservation parking using fog nodes.

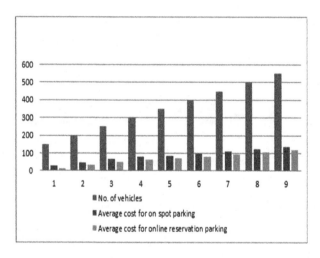

Fig. 6. Comparison between average cost for on spot parking and online reservation parking using fog nodes.

vehicles whose parking request has been processed by the fog-nodes according to the availability of the parking space, proposed algorithm will calculate the total cost for that particular vehicle. In case of on-spot parking, the parking request will be processed in the order as the vehicle arrives in the parking area. In on-line reservation of parking, the parking request of user will be processed on-line and the information regarding availability of the parking space in the parking area gets updated on-line. One need not to wait in the parking queue to know the parking status of the vehicles in case of on-line reservation parking is done successfully. Therefore, there is difference between total cost of parking a vehicle using on-line reservation as compared to on-spot reservation. Proposed algorithm calculate the cost for different vehicles and the results for both the on-spot and on-line reservation parking is displayed in the Table 1. Also the comparison between average cost for on spot and on-line reservation parking is shown in Fig. 6 which clearly indicates that the average cost for on-line reservation parking is less as compared to the on spot parking.

5 Conclusion

Nowadays, parking problem is becoming an important research issue due to the increase in the number of vehicles. In this work, we have proposed an online reservation facility for parking area that helps to reduce the waiting time and cost of parking on per vehicle basis. We have proposed a modified greedy algorithm to calculate the total cost of the vehicles. The results have shown that the total cost for parking using online reservation is less as compared to on-spot parking by using fog nodes. Online reservation for parking is more efficient and reliable. Obtained results also shows the significant improvement to resolve the parking problems in more efficient manner by allocating the parking space to more number of vehicles. In future work, we will try to use enhanced algorithms for parking strategies.

References

1. Aydin, I., Karakose, M., Karakose, E.: A navigation and reservation based smart parking platform using genetic optimization for smart cities. In: Proceedings of 5th International Istanbul Smart Grid and Cities Congress and Fair (ICSG), pp. 120–124. IEEE (2017)
2. Tang, C., Wei, X., Zhu, C., Chen, W., Rodrigues, J.J.P.C.: Towards smart parking based on fog computing. IEEE Access **6**, 70172–70185 (2018)
3. Lin, T., Rivano, H., Le Mouël, F.: A survey of smart parking solutions. IEEE Trans. Intell. Transp. Syst. **18**(12), 3229–3253 (2017). https://doi.org/10.1109/TITS.2017.2685143
4. Hassoune, K., Dachry, W., Moutaouakkil, F., Medromi, H.: Smart parking systems: a survey. In: Proceedings of 11th International Conference on Intelligent Systems: Theories and Applications (SITA), Mohammedia, pp. 1–6, (2016). https://doi.org/10.1109/SITA.2016.7772297
5. Idris, M.Y.I., Leng, Y.Y., Tamil, E.M., Noor, N.M.: Car park system: a review of smart parking system and its technology. Inf. Technol. J. **8**(2), 101–103 (2009). https://doi.org/10.3923/itj.2009.101.113
6. Polycarpou, E., Lambrinos, L., Protopapadakis, E.: Smart parking solutions for urban areas. In: Proceedings of 14th International Symposium on A World of Wireless, Mobile and Multimedia Networks (WoWMoM), Madrid, pp. 1–6 (2013). https://doi.org/10.1109/WoWMoM.2013.6583499
7. Delot, T., llarri, S., Lecomte, S., Ceneratio, N.: Sharing with caution: managing parking spaces in vehicular networks. Mob. Inf. Syst. **9**(1), 69–98 (2013). https://doi.org/10.3233/MIS-2012-0149

8. Mahmud, S.A., Khan, G.M., Rahman, M., Zafar, H.: A survey of intelligent car parking system. J. Appl. Res. Technol. **11**(5), 714–726 (2013). https://doi.org/10.1016/S1665-6423(13)71580-3

9. Balzano, W., Vitale, F.: DiG-Park: a smart parking availability searching method using V2V/V2I and DGP-class problem. In: Proceedings of 31st International Conference on Advanced Information Networking and Applications Workshops (WAINA), Taipei, pp. 698–703 (2017). https://doi.org/10.1109/WAINA.2017.104

10. Wang, T., et al.: Data collection from WSNs to the cloud based on mobile Fog elements. Future Gener. Comput. Syst. (2017). https://doi.org/10.1016/j.future.2017.07.031

11. Wang, T., et al.: Fog-based storage technology to fight with cyber threat. Future Gener. Comput. Syst. **83**, 208–218 (2018). https://doi.org/10.1016/j.future.2017.12.036

12. Gupta, P.K., Maharaj, B.T., Malekian, R.: A novel and secure IoT based cloud centric architecture to perform predictive analysis of users activities in sustainable health centres. Multimed. Tools Appl. **76**(18), 18489–18512 (2017). https://doi.org/10.1007/s11042-016-4050-6

13. Malekian, R., Kavishe, A.F., Maharaj, B.T., et al.: Smart vehicle navigation system using hidden Markov model and RFID technology. Wirel. Pers. Commun. **90**(4), 1717–1742 (2016). https://doi.org/10.1007/s11277-016-3419-1

14. Gupta, P.K., Tyagi, V., Singh, S.K.: Predictive Computing and Information Security. Springer, Singapore (2017). https://doi.org/10.1007/978-981-10-5107-4

15. Zhu, C., Li, X., Leung, V.C.M., Yang, L.T., Ngai, E.C., Shu, L.: Towards pricing for sensor-cloud. IEEE Trans. Cloud Comput. (2017). https://doi.org/10.1109/TCC.2017.264952C

16. Hou, X., Li, Y., Chen, M., Wu, D., Jin, D., Chen, S.: Vehicular fog computing: a viewpoint of vehicles as the infrastructures. IEEE Trans. Veh. Technol. **65**(6), 3860–3873 (2016). https://doi.org/10.1109/TVT.2016.2532863

17. Huang, C., Xu, K.: Reliable realtime streaming in vehicular cloud-fog computing networks. In: International Conference on Communications in China (ICCC), Chengdu, pp. 1–6 (2016). https://doi.org/10.1109/ICCChina.2016.7636838

18. Kim, O.T.T., Tri, N.D., Nguyen, V.D., Tran, N.H., Hong, C.S.: A shared parking model in vehicular network using fog and cloud environment. In: Proceedings of 17th Asia-Pacific Network Operations and Management Symposium (APNOMS), pp. 321–326. IEEE, Busan (2015). https://doi.org/10.1109/APNOMS.2015.7275447

19. Mukherjee, M., Shu, L., Wang, D., Li, K., Chen, Y.: A fog computing-based framework to reduce traffic overhead in large-scale industrial applications. In: Proceedings of Conference on Computer Communications Workshops (INFOCOM WKSHPS), Atlanta, pp. 1008–1009. IEEE (2017). https://doi.org/10.1109/INFCOMW.2017.8116534

20. Zhang, W., Zhang, Z., Chao, H.: Cooperative fog computing for dealing with big data in the internet of vehicles: architecture and hierarchical resource management. IEEE Commun. Mag. **55**(12), 60–67 (2017). https://doi.org/10.1109/MCOM

21. Park, S., Yoo, Y.: Network intelligence based on network state information for connected vehicles utilizing fog computing. Mob. Inf. Syst. 1–9 (2017). https://doi.org/10.1155/2017/7479267

22. Rajabioun, T., Ioannou, P.A.: On-street and off-street parking availability prediction using multivariate spatiotemporal models. IEEE Trans. Intell. Transp. Syst. **16**(5), 2913–2924 (2015)

23. Mei, Z., Tian, Y.: Optimized combination model and algorithm of parking guidance information configuration. EURASIP J. Wirel. Commun. Netw. (1), 101 (2011)
24. Zoeter, O., Dance, C., Clinchant, S., Andreoli, J.: New algorithms for parking demand management and a city-scale deployment. In: Proceedings of International Conference on Knowledge Discovery and Data Mining, pp. 1819–1828. ACM (2014)

Formal-Verification of Smart-Contract Languages: A Survey

Vimal Dwivedi$^{(\boxtimes)}$, Vipin Deval, Abhishek Dixit, and Alex Norta

Department of Software Science, Tallinn University of Technology,
Akadeemia tee 15A, 12816 Tallinn, Estonia
vimal.dwivedi@ttu.ee

Abstract. A blockchain is a peer-to-peer electronic ledger of transactions that may be publicly or privately distributed to all users. Apart from unique consensus mechanisms, their success is also obliged to smart contracts. Also, These programs let on distrusting parties to enter reconciliation that are executed autonomously. Although a number of studies focus on security of introducing new programming languages., However, there is no comprehensive survey on the smart-contract language in suitability and expressiveness concepts and properties that recognize the interaction between people in organizations and technology in workplaces. To fill this gap, we conduct a systematic analysis about smart-contract language properties that focus on e-contractual and pattern-based exploration. In particular, this paper gives smart-contract language taxonomy, introducing technical challenges of languages as well as recent solutions in tackling the challenges. Moreover, this paper also represents the future research direction in the introducing new smart-contract language.

Keywords: Ontological completeness · eSML · Socio-technical ·
Legal relevance · ANTLR · Block-chain · Smart contracts

1 Introduction

With traditional contract system, contract [14] refers to a liability that specifies legal action or liability that is required at the time of business collaboration as per the layout of terms and agreements, the obligation is formed. The contract includes agreements for binding parties together in terms and conditions so that they can collaborate businesses under a set of rules without any discrepancies. In traditional contract, every terms and condition which is written in the contract must be fulfilled in order to protect everyone's legal rights as communicated by an expert or lawyers. It overcomes the chances of risk, provides clarity of party expectation that is specified in contracts, enhances enforcement, limits flexibility. The conventional contract is a trust-based centralized system which requires intermediaries that leads to alleviated cost and is usually time-consuming.

With the emergence of blockchain technology, Smart contract [17] has become a necessity. It refers to a self-executing computer code, supervised by nodes. It

© Springer Nature Singapore Pte Ltd. 2019
M. Singh et al. (Eds.): ICACDS 2019, CCIS 1046, pp. 738–747, 2019.
https://doi.org/10.1007/978-981-13-9942-8_68

runs on a distributed Ledger which thrives to achieve a trustless based system without the involvement of any intermediaries. It further accelerates the processing of the business processes and helps in attaining a higher accuracy rate. Another way to understand the smart contract is to compare the technology to a vending machine. Ordinarily, when you need water, you just need to drop a coin into the vending machine like a Ledger or escrow in another form and get water from the machine. Traditional contract system [14] works on every obligation in the exact same way but lacks the ability of self-execution as in the case of smart contract. The smart contract can applicable in numerous domains such as vehicle self-parking, real estate, healthcare, electronic voting because of its ability of self-execution and independence from the involvement of intermediaries.

With respect to current smart contract languages such as ethereum solidity language [6], Bitcoin scripting language and other existing procedural languages are facing vivid challenges such as adoption of issues relating to social meaning and legal relevance caused by incorrect arrangement between semantics and programmer intuition. It leads towards development of a new smart contract language that contains construct to deal with domain-specific aspects having social control [16] and artifact of law [7].

With smart contract ontology [11], we explore the eSourcing markup language (eSML) that specifies various aspects arising among collaborative business organizations due to the existence of process views for creating an agreement among the participating parties. In this study, we explore the socio-technical suitability and expressiveness for guiding business collaborations in a legally relevant way. Suitability means smart contract language encapsulates concept and properties and adoption in the construct of semantic which formulate into guiding business collaboration into the legally relevant way. With reference to smart contract language, we take into account solidity language of ethereum which is a key element in irreversibly changing the nature of the smart contracts. On the basis of smart contract ontology, we are focusing on the diversity of suitability and expressiveness among solidity, Rholang which is based on the property of syntactic language specification and ANTLR based language development. Solidity has played an essential role in the evolution of ontology for the smart contract. It has resulted in the efficient and effective management of concepts and properties that eSourcing Markup language embodies. However, Solidity does not support the pattern-based design, process awareness, and process matching. Inversely, these concepts are specified in smart contract ontology. The next generation language Rholang [13] captures these limitations. The utility required for handling business processes is one of the major aspects relating to collaborative business processes, but it is not handled properly with solidity as for Rholang. Unfortunately, the matching of processes, the process verification, and conclusion is not documented properly. ANTLR based language provides a powerful mechanism required to read, process, execute or translate the process according to its legal relevance. So in this study, we explore various suitability and expressiveness based languages that fulfil the limitations corresponding to the use of smart contracts i.e. of process awareness and verification requirement for establishing an automated business collaboration.

The hypothesis of the thesis states that the development of smart contract language must not be domain specific. It should adhere to socio-technical and legally relevance. This paper addresses the existing challenges in terms of socio-technical and legal relevance. In our thesis work, we will try to bridge the gap between the ideal situation and reality environment for the development of smart contract language.

2   State of the Art

Research in [14], gives an insight into the existence of a business contract. It provides knowledge regarding the use of contracts for facilitating communication between the participating entities. It further explains factors that lead to differences between the two most widely used types of contracts i.e. transactional and relational contracts and that the latter aids in its implementation without litigation or conflicts. The study emphasizes that contracts are focused more on strengthening business relationships rather than enforcing laws of the agreement.

A solution to the most fundamental problem in the implementation of Blockchain technology is provided in [18]. This naive technique addresses the issues related to trust in collaborative process enforcement using block-chain technology and its smart contracts to surpass the need of a centralized party. The proposed methodology comprises a three-step process with translator, block-chain infrastructure and triggers being major components.

A detailed introduction on bitcoin and its usage is illustrated in [10]. The subject deals with the evolution of bitcoin as a virtual currency, or decentralised digital currency coined by Satoshi Nakamoto in 2008 and its usage in public domain since early 2009. Bitcoin is used in an electronic payment business system which is based on cryptographic proof in lieu of trust and not managed by any financial authority (institution). Bitcoins are based on the pillars of transactions, proof of work, mining and digital wallet. It further provides a detailed expression on the working of bitcoin transactions, collection of transactional data into blocks, its peer to peer status, anonymity of users among others and formation of block-chain. The work further gives insight into the security issues and legal considerations in the use of bitcoins.

This paper [11] presents an esourcing ontology which is used as input for developing eSourcing markup language. Esourcing ontology comprises essentially concepts for the decentralized autonomous organization. Automating socio-technical business collaboration promises several benefits, including increases in efficiency, effectiveness, and quality, for developing a new generation of the so-called decentralized autonomous organization.

Norta et al. [11] presented the utility such as suitability and expressiveness as a gap in the cross-organizational business organization. In addition, Norta [12] presents esourcing markup language (eSML) which worked as choreography language for the automated cross-organization business process. Norta focuses on basis contractual elements for making the smart contract as a legal. Furthermore, a reduction of contractual elements that helps for improving difficulty level for legal issues such as obligation, artifacts of law. This is crucial when you are focusing on the cross-organizational business process in which less trusted participant involved [18].

Norta developed an esourcing ontology as a framework for building automated smart contract in a business collaboration [18] which would provide immutability and auditability. At a moment of writing contract in the collaborative business process, no mechanism exists for mapping high-level choreography language to smart contract language while maintaining legal recognisability.

Solidity [6] is a more popular language for smart contract development that runs on ethereum virtual machine. Butrin presents intention behind combining ethereum and EVM [3] for improving the concept of scripting, altcoins and on chain protocol that achieves consensus-based application that has scalability, feature completeness, interoperability and ease of development. The code is written in a low-level stack-based language and compiled into ethereum virtual machine in the byte code.

Despite the popularity, There are several reasons which make the implementation of smart contracts particularly prone to [security] errors in Ethereum [1]. The main reason is misalignment between semantics and intuition of the programmer. Solidity has various vulnerability such as the execution runs out of gas, call stack reaches its limit, the command throw is executed.

This paper [16] presents socio-technical utility for an autonomous business organization that enables flexible governance by providing organized structure in a way that has social meaning control of participants and high level of trust between parties. Additionally, highlights the compact contrast vision with existing approaches.

With the evolution of blockchain technology, computerized transaction protocol offering high reliable of trust, less transactional cost in which terms and condition are executed autonomously. This paper [7] expose the gap by considering potential issues for that smart contract considerable difficulty for adopting the current legal framework.

3   Problem Statement and Contributions

A study of the existing development scenario of smart contract language revealed that it has overlooked socio-technical perspectives during development. It means that it does not specify social control, social meaning, and utility for legal relevance. This paper exploits the address gap by investigating ideal and real world situation of existing business collaborations. Due to lack of semantics smart contract languages does not support cross-organizational business processes such as pattern-based design, process awareness, matching of the processes etc. Further, we examine transparency control in block-chain system in case of disputes among stakeholders due to lack of interdependence for the action. It exploits the address gap in existing smart contract programming language. Another major limitation is the difficulty to recover the losses that may arise if a faulty contract is embedded in the blockchain which may be due to misalignment between language library and intuition of the programmer [1].

Contract law for automated business collaboration is another research challenge that specifies assurance of terms and conditions. Therefore, we examine the address gap for legal relevance such as establishing capacity, contracting under a mistake, formation via technology and determine the conditions for the offer and acceptance of the contract. The essential part is establishing legal intent in 'follow-on contracting', the certainty of terms imbibed in the smart contract [7].

Generally, the smart contract does not include obligation duty which is a major issue pertaining to its legal relevance. To every mutually agreed upon the law in the smart contract, there must be an obligation duty so that we can overcome this above said issue. Along with that, we must have some screening procedure so that we can determine the age of the participating individual prior to his entry in block-chain transaction system so that we can establish legal intent for establishing capacity.

Our planned contribution includes the development of a language that has suitability and expressiveness for automated business collaborations in order to achieve higher efficiency, transparency among participants and automatic verification. This will help in fixing the address gap for the socio-technical relevance of the smart contract. We planned to enable contract for business collaborations by fixing the certainty of terms and condition and remedial issues which are revetment in smart contract block-chain.

This paper fills the gap by posing the research question how to develop a smart contract language that has the utility for guiding business collaboration in a legally relevant way? By posing this question, We examine the utilities for socio-technical such as appropriate semantics, participants control, process awareness, process matching that has legal relevance. After that, we deduce the main sub question into several sub question by fixing the sequence of order that specifies the proper layout to handle the address gap. To answer this question, a number of challenges (sub-question) need to be addressed.

The first sub-question pertains to establish legal relevance for a smart contract that has socio-technical utility. To justify this question, we focus on various grammar available for development and the requirements for business collaboration in a legally relevant way. Another subtask is the development of the ontology for autonomous legal business collaboration. And also, the targeted business process in autonomous business collaboration.

One of the key elements of legal relevance is an obligation. Obligation means, rights i.e. lawfully enforced rules that must have correlative duty between two parties. Therefore, the second sub-question highlights a process to design a language that combines the strengths of established languages of various generations while overcoming their limitations. To provide a solution to this question, we focus on strength of libraries of various generations of languages that make the language suitable and expressive.

As the abstract grammar pattern is a key element for the language development, the third research questions adhere to identification and implementation of abstract grammar patterns for a smart contract language that has the expected application utility and verifiability.

4   Research Methodology and Approach

Methodology is a sequence of methods that are used in the particular area of study that specifies how to do a task in a systematic manner. We study various methodology such as action design science [15], case study research [15], experimental research method [4]. We examine design science research [9] which is most suitable for information system design that evaluates sociotechnical artifacts. We use an ANTLR tool in this research for designing and evaluation smart contract language. A potential solution to the identified research goal would be to use the eSML schema previously defined by Norta, in order to develop a context-free grammar. The next step would be the use of existing tools such as ANTLR to help reach closer to the solution of our research goal. Use of ANTLR to develop such grammar comes with certain constraints such as the grammar produced using the tool has to be in an explicit format, as ANTLR notation.

In subsequent phases, ANTLR can then translate "recursive descent parsers from grammar rules .. which are exceptionally identical to the hand build rules by an adept programmer." By definition "recursive descent parsers are actually a collection of recursive methods, one method per rule derived. The term descent relates to the fact the starting point of parsing is the root i.e. the topmost node of a parse tree and it gradually proceeds towards the lowermost nodes i.e. the leaves as the rule gets more refined." as explained by Parr. The data structure used by ANTLR parsers are parse trees and this data structure is used to record "the way the parser perceives the complete structure of the input i.e. sentence and its constituent phrases." The next step is the implementation of a custom parse tree walker by applying the parsers generated using ANTLR tool. The parse tree walker so developed is aimed towards triggering callbacks on the identification of distinct tokens. The tokens so identified would then be transcribed into the solidity code parts with the aid of already acknowledged callbacks. The final phase would eventually be the development of smart contract after the parsing is exhaustively over.

The results so obtained can be validated from the fact that in our work we are using context-free grammar to define and explain the schema of the languages [8], which is the most widely used and accepted method of describing languages. Further, to verify and validate the working of obtained smart contracts, already-in-use tools from Truffle, will be referred to imitate calls to the blockchain, i.e. the smart contracts deployment site. Also, automated tests will be used to assure that the deviation between the actual and expected working on smart contracts is void. "Truffle is a development environment, testing framework and asset pipeline for Ethereum, aiming to make life of an Ethereum developer easier" [5] The research area, in general, is a prevailing research trend, as the underlying architecture i.e. blockchain and also, smart contract development technology is a naive concept and have been attracting smart programmers for evolution. Quoting Bartoletti et al. [2]: "In particular, the public and append-only ledger of transaction (the blockchain) and the decentralized consensus protocol that Bitcoin nodes use to extend it, have revived Nick Szabo's idea of smart contracts i.e. programs whose correct execution is automatically enforced without relying on a trusted authority [17]".

5   Preliminary or Intermediate Results

The research problem addressed by us can be considered as an intermediate result for examining sociotechnical utility [16] and legal relevance [7]associated with smart contracts. Ideally, the start contract must possess process awareness to avoid situation of security breach and transparency to all the participating parties for smooth execution in case a conflict arises. Along with this, verification of the correctness of the smart contract being developed is provided to improve its effectiveness at execution time and efficiency of cross organisational business.

The address gap extracted focuses on socio technical and legal relevance elements for the development of a smart contract language. It also includes issues relating to lack of control for participants, dearth of social meaning and understanding of business process in cross organisational infrastructure. Also, we examined and identified various impediments for adopting existing legal framework of the contract.

These findings set the vision of our research work, to improve the language development that combines the social element of business collaboration in a legal framework.

6   Discussion

This section discusses the study results and answers the research questions that we defined in Sect. 3.

Ethereum is one of the most suitable platforms to propose the conception of smart contracts in the blockchain. It boasts the turing completeness of its smart contract platform. The language used i.e. Solidity is good enough to make it Turing complete but it does lack in the flexibility which is provided by the languages used today. Wanchain's distributed ledger relies on the strengths of Ethereum, and any Ethereum DApp will run on Wanchain without any code alteration. To enhance these applications, Wanchain uses solidity that offers a number of APIs designed to expand cross-chain capabilities and improve privacy protection.

The overreaching functional goal of Æternity blockchain smart contracts is to be able to runs code on the chain. That is, code execution that is verifiable by a miner and which can alter the state of the chain. For efficient contract execution Æternity provides a very high level language for blindingly fast execution of simple contracts. For more advanced contracts the Sophia language is used and that is compiled to a virtual machine tailored for execution of the contracts. This machine is a high level machine with instructions for operating on the chain and on Sophia data structures without any need to do explicit stack and memory management.

Zen blockchain uses a Total language to express smart contracts rather than depending on evaluation model which tracks gas in order to ensure the totality. Total languages are capable of expressing arbitrary logic like recursion and loops, and this is also the case for Zen Protocol. Zen's smart contracting language is 'Dependently Typed', i.e every expression has a type that depends on both the expressions and the types. Dependent type systems are expressive to use them for the purpose of the formal Verification. Such types can express arbitrary properties of expressions. Zen Protocol's smart contract takes dependently typed source code, that must express the resource consumption. Zen Protocol is very limited by the time taken to run the smart contracts, and therefore, must be able to process transactions involving smart contracts faster—smart contracts in Zen are not only faster to run, but can be executed most of the time in parallel.

Counterparty blockchain relies on Bitcoin for its consensus. But it also supports ethereum smart contracts. It uses solidity or serpent to write smart contract code and compile it to a more compact form (bytecode). Serpent is a language for smart contract development based on Python language. Python is arguably one of the best language for novice programmers, and a very productive language for experienced developers. Serpent, originally developed for Ethereum, is currently being used in complex enterprise projects.

RChain is a project that focuses on scalability by using a multi-threaded blockchain with its own smart contract language. Smart contracts employ a number of industry-leading functions such as meta-programming, reactive data streams, pattern matching. As a result, RChain contracts have programmability that can be used on RChain nodes. Rholang is a "process-oriented" i.e. computations being done by message passing. Messages are passed via "channels", that are like message queues.

Qtum is an Ethereum-based smart contracts system that run on top of a Bitcoin-based blockchain. It uses a modified version Blackcoin's Proof of Stake (PoS) implementation for consensus. Qtum has added the custom adaptation layer that maps the Ethereum account balances to sets of Bitcoin Unspent Transaction Outputs (UTXOs). Qtum is planning to extend their smart contracts offering to include a x86 virtual machine that will enable the smart contracts development in languages such as Java, C++, and Haskell. However, leverage with existing tooling, it doesn't specifically address the security issues inherent to Solidity's design.

7 Conclusions

Presently solidity language is being used to develop smart contracts in blockchain systems. It has some limitations associated with it such as pattern-based design, process awareness, matching of the process. In this study, we develop artifacts that incorporate socio-technical utility which enables to automate cross organizational business collaboration adhering to the legal relevance. Further, we develop a language for smart contracts that can preserve autonomy and transparency among participants in peer to peer decentralized infrastructure.

In our work, we will provide a language incorporating the strength of existing languages while overcoming their limitation. Future, we will refine the language features along with its testing in a realistic environment.

Acknowledgement. This Ph.D. research is partially supported by Quantum Foundation, Singapore under the supervision of Prof. Alex Norta, Associate Professor, Department of Software Science, Tallinn University of Technology, Tallinn, Estonia. Email: `alex.norta.phd@ieee.org` We thank our Prof. Alex Norta who provided insight and expertise that greatly assisted the research.

References

1. Atzei, N., Bartoletti, M., Cimoli, T.: A survey of attacks on ethereum smart contracts (SoK). In: Maffei, M., Ryan, M. (eds.) POST 2017. LNCS, vol. 10204, pp. 164–186. Springer, Heidelberg (2017). https://doi.org/10.1007/978-3-662-54455-6_8

2. Bartoletti, M., Pompianu, L.: An empirical analysis of smart contracts: platforms, applications, and design patterns. In: Brenner, M., et al. (eds.) FC 2017. LNCS, vol. 10323, pp. 494–509. Springer, Cham (2017). https://doi.org/10.1007/978-3-319-70278-0_31

3. Buterin, V., et al.: A next-generation smart contract and decentralized application platform. White paper (2014)

4. Christensen, L.B.: Experimental Methodology. Allyn & Bacon, Boston (2004)

5. ConsenSys: trufflesuite/truffle (2015). https://github.com/trufflesuite/truffle. Accessed 3 Mar 2018

6. Ethereum: ethereum/solidity (2015). https://github.com/ethereum/solidity. Accessed 3 Mar 2018

7. Giancaspro, M.: Is a 'smart contract' really a smart idea? Insights from a legal perspective. Comput. Law Secur. Rev. **33**(6), 825–835 (2017)

8. Knuth, D.E.: Semantics of context-free languages. Math. Syst. Theory **2**(2), 127–145 (1968)

9. March, S.T., Storey, V.C.: Design science in the information systems discipline: an introduction to the special issue on design science research. MIS Q. **32**, 725–730 (2008)

10. Nakamoto, S.: Bitcoin: a peer-to-peer electronic cash system (2008)

11. Norta, A., Ma, L., Duan, Y., Rull, A., Kõlvart, M., Taveter, K.: eContractual choreography-language properties towards cross-organizational business collaboration. J. Internet Serv. Appl. **6**(1), 8 (2015)

12. Norta, A.H.: Exploring dynamic inter-organizational business process collaboration. Dissertation Abstracts International, 68(04) (2007)

13. RChain: RChain/rholang. https://steemit.com/smart/@alexbafana/smart-contract-languages-comparison

14. Roxenhall, T., Ghauri, P.: Use of the written contract in long-lasting business relationships. Ind. Mark. Manag. **33**(3), 261–268 (2004)

15. Sein, M.K., Henfridsson, O., Purao, S., Rossi, M., Lindgren, R.: Action design research. MIS Q. **35**, 37–56 (2011)

16. Singh, M.P., Chopra, A.K.: Violable contracts and governance for blockchain applications. arXiv preprint arXiv:1801.02672 (2018)

17. Szabo, N.: Formalizing and securing relationships on public networks. First Monday **2**(9) (1997)
18. Weber, I., Xu, X., Riveret, R., Governatori, G., Ponomarev, A., Mendling, J.: Untrusted business process monitoring and execution using blockchain. In: La Rosa, M., Loos, P., Pastor, O. (eds.) BPM 2016. LNCS, vol. 9850, pp. 329–347. Springer, Cham (2016). https://doi.org/10.1007/978-3-319-45348-4_19

Author Index

Printed in the United States
By Bookmasters